Shared Memory Multiprocessing

Shared Memory Multiprocessing

edited by
Norihisa Suzuki

The MIT Press
Cambridge, Massachusetts
London, England

This book was printed and bound in the United States of America.

Library of Congress Cataloging-in-Publication Data

Shared memory multiprocessing / edited by Norihisa Suzuki.
p. cm.
Includes bibliographical references.
ISBN 0-262-19322-1
1. Multiprocessors. 2. Memory management (Computer science) I. Suzuki, Norihisa, 1946–
QA76.5.S4445 1992
004'.35—dc20 92-23489
CIP

Contents

Preface

The papers included in this book are selected from those presented at the International Symposium on Shared Memory Multiprocessing, which was held in Tokyo from April 2 to April 4 in 1991 under the sponsorship of the Information Processing Society of Japan. It was the first meeting to focus on shared memory multiprocessing, and I am happy to report that it was very successful, with excellent papers and an enthusiastic audience.

Shared memory multiprocessors have been in existence for quite some time. However, the invention of snoop cache in the early 1980's and the subsequent explosion in the computational power of microprocessors and in the density of ASIC chips made it possible to build shared memory multiprocessors economically and reliably. Since then, not only have research prototypes flourished, but many commercial products have also been introduced. Now the first decade is drawing to a close, and it was thus a very appropriate time to hold the conference.

If we look at the commercial market place, not only have many commercial products been introduced with considerable economic success, but also many of the commercial microprocessors and peripheral chips now contain mechanisms to support shared memory multiprocessors.

Mechanisms for supporting shared memory multiprocessing at the operating system level have been studied well, and they have been introduced into proprietary operating systems. Now, they are being incorporated into widely available operating systems. Compiling techniques are also progressing, and parallelizing FORTRAN and C compilers are now available on most systems.

On the research side, so-called scalable architecture is being hotly pursued and is the major theme of this book. Investigations are being made to see whether we can construct distributed memory multiprocessors with hardware support to realize a shared memory model. This architecture is considered to be able to support hundreds of microprocessors without performance degradation. The speed of microprocessors is also increasing very rapidly, so it is a big challenge to connect them efficiently and package them economically.

I believe that this book gives a clear perspective on the state of the art in shared memory multiprocessors.

I would like to thank the organizations that supported this conference financially: the International Information Science Foundation, IBM Japan, and NEC.

Finally, I would like to thank the following people who worked on organizing the symposium:

General Chair:	Takashi Masuda
Treasurer:	Kazuya Tago
Local arrangement:	Yoshikatsu Tada
Program committee:	Tilak Agerwala
	Forest Baskett
	Ed Clarkc
	David Gifford
	Jim Goodman
	John Hennesy
	Paul Hilfinger
	Nobuhiko Koike
	Norihisa Suzuki (Chairman)
	Chuck Thacker
	Shinji Tomita
	Akinori Yonezawa

Tokyo, Japan
October 1991

Norihisa Suzuki

I EXPERIENCE

1 Experience with the Firefly Multiprocessor Workstation

Susan Owicki

Commercial multiprocessors are used successfully for a range of applications, including intensive numeric computations, time-sharing, and shared servers. The value of multiprocessing in a single-user workstation is not so obvious, especially in an environment where numeric problems do not dominate. The Digital Equipment Corporation, Systems Research Center has had several years of experience using the five-processor Firefly workstation in such an environment. This report is an initial assessment of how much is gained from multiprocessing on the Firefly.
Reported here are measurements of speedup and utilization for a variety of programs. They illustrate four sources of concurrency: between independent tasks, within a server, between client and server, and within an application. The nature of the parallelism in each example is explored, as well as the factors, if any, that constrain multiprocessing. The examples cover a wide range of multiprocessing, with speedups on a five-processor machine varying from slightly over 1 to nearly 6. Most uses derive most of their speedup from two or three processors, but there are important applications that can effectively use five or more.

1.1 Introduction

Commercial multiprocessors are used successfully for a range of applications, including intensive numeric computations, time-sharing, and shared servers. In these uses, there is abundant scope for multiprocessing in handling simultaneous requests from separate users or in single-user computations where there is substantial concurrency in the structure of the problems.

The value of multiprocessing in a single-user workstation is not so obvious, especially in an environment where numeric problems do not dominate. Can other applications besides scientific computation exploit multiple processors? Are multiple users essential to generate a reasonable workload for the system?

For several years, the Firefly multiprocessor workstation [9] has been the primary source of computing at the Digital Equipment Corporation, Systems Research Center (SRC). Software for the Firefly spans a wide range of systems and applications programs. Most Firefly programs are written in an extension of Modula 2 [12] called Modula 2+ [7], which provides threads and synchronization primitives for concurrent programming. The Firefly workload does not include the sort of lengthy numeric calculations that have traditionally benefited from concurrency. Nevertheless, much of the software has been designed to take advantage of multiprocessing. Thus there has been substantial experience at SRC with using multiprocessor workstations for non-numeric computation, and it seems appropriate now to assess their value. To do so, a number of instances of multiprocessing on the Firefly were examined. This report gives measures of concurrency for these examples, and describes the sources and limits of their parallelism.

The Firefly used for these measurements has five 1-MIP MicroVAX processors, so it is called a 5-MIP machine. In actual use, though, the Firefly has less computational power than a 5-MIP uniprocessor. This is partly because some of the software was originally written for a uniprocessor. But even code written for the Firefly seldom exploits all the concurrency that the processors provide. There are many reasons: some problems have limited parallelism, sometimes the overhead of concurrency is too high, sometimes another part of the machine is a bottleneck, and sometimes the implementor chose to avoid the complexity of concurrent programming.

However, the Firefly doesn't have to provide a full 5 MIPS of computing power to be cost-effective, since it is generally cheaper to build a multiprocessor than a uniprocessor with the same MIPS rating. Building a multiprocessor with, say, three to thirty processors may not cost a great deal more than building a uniprocessor with the same CPU. Thus the multiprocessor may be economically attractive even if its processors are not always fully utilized. The benefit gained from greater computing power must be weighed against the increased cost of the multiprocessor.

This report is concerned with assessing the benefit side of the cost-benefit equation. Benefit is estimated using the standard metrics speed-up and processor utilization. These metrics, which are discussed in Section 2, are less than ideal, but they do give some feeling for the degree of success in exploiting multiprocessing.

Four sources of concurrency were identified in day-to-day workstation activities:

- single-user time-sharing: concurrency between independent tasks. A user may undertake several tasks in parallel, such as editing or reading mail while a compilation is in progress.

- concurrency within a server. The window system, the file system, and other basic services are implemented with algorithms that use multiprocessing.
- concurrency between client and server. Sometimes a server can return an immediate answer to a request, then compute in parallel with its client to complete processing the request.
- concurrency within an application: some application programs are coded with multiple threads for performance.

Note that the first three sources of concurrency are available in all uses of the workstation, without requiring an application programmer to write multi-threaded code. So multiprocessors in a workstation can be useful even when running applications that do not attempt to exploit concurrency.

Sections 3 to 6 contain speedup and utilization data for a number of examples from each of the areas above. All the measurements were taken on a 5-processor, 16 Megabyte Firefly, unless otherwise noted.

1.2 Metrics

Parallel sorting will be used as an example to illustrate speedup and processor utilization. Figure 1.1 gives graphs of speedup and utilization for a quicksort program [11] working on an array of 10000 integers. The algorithm sequentially partitions the array and then recursively applies quicksort in parallel to the two subarrays.

The speedup reported in Figure 1.1a is defined in the conventional way: speedup for n processors is

$$S(n) = T(1)/T(n), \tag{1.1}$$

where $T(k)$ is the execution time when the program is run using k processors. Speedup is determined using an option of Taos, the Firefly operating system, that restricts the set of processors available to the scheduler. Thus $T(k)$ is measured by disabling all but k processors and noting the elapsed time to execute the program. Since elapsed time can fluctuate due to other activities in the system, $T(k)$ was taken as the median elapsed timc of three to five runs.

The dotted line in Figure 1.1a represents the theoretical "perfect" speedup. For two and three processors, Quicksort has a nearly optimal

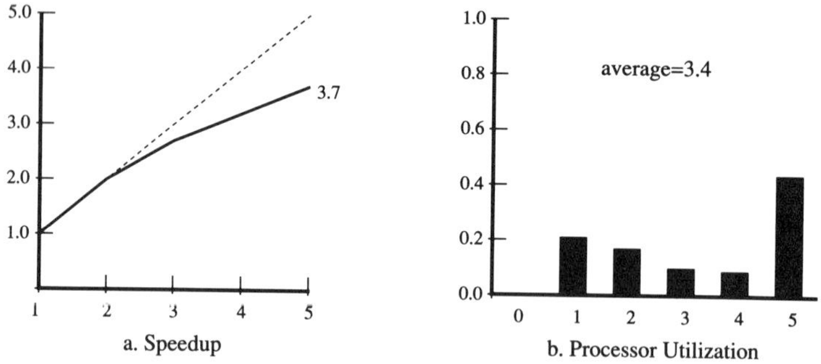

Figure 1.1
Quicksort of 10000 integers.

speedup. There is some additional benefit from the fourth and fifth processors, but it is less significant. The amount of parallel computation is limited by the structure of the algorithm: during the initial partitioning, for example, only one thread is active.

Processor utilization for a five-processor run of Quicksort is shown in Figure 1.1b. The height of the kth bar represents the fraction of the time when exactly k processors were busy. There was essentially no time when all processors were idle, which is to be expected in a compute-bound task like sorting an array. All five processors were busy for more than 40% of the time. This is somewhat surprising, given that the speedup figures for four to five processors were not impressive. With five processors, the highly parallel parts of the run keep all the processors busy, leaving a substantial amount of time when only one processor is busy. With fewer processors, sequential segments in one partition are more likely to overlap parallel segments of another, and each processor is busy a larger fraction of the time. The average processor utilization on a five-processor Firefly was 3.4.

Processor utilization was measured by instrumenting the operating system to record the amount of time spent with k processors busy. Once this instrumentation has been done, measuring utilization is much easier than measuring speedup, because speedup requires multiple runs for each value of n.

There is a correspondence between speedup and average processor utilization. If a program does the same amount of work when run with 1 processor or with n processors, its speedup and average utilization should be equal. When they are different, utilization is usually higher, due to overhead in the parallel version. For Quicksort, however, speedup is higher than utilization. This is because of background activity in the operating system, which averages about 20% of a processor, regardless of workload or number of available processors. Background work directly contributes to processor utilization. It also increases speedup, because the 0.2 CPU lost to background activity slows a one-processor computation more than a five-processor computation. For Quicksort, background activity increases speedup more than utilization.

Neither of the metrics discussed so far is ideal. The problem with utilization is that it measures consumption of processor cycles, but not the benefit obtained. A program that uses extra processors inefficiently may show large processor utilization but very little speedup. Even though speedup is more relevant in assessing the benefits of multiple processors, sometimes only utilization is reported here. This is because speedup is harder to measure. For some programs, interactive ones in particular, speedup cannot be measured at all because the timing of runs is not reproducible.

Unfortunately, high speedup numbers can be misleading as well. The problem is that a parallel program may perform badly when run on one processor. Introducing parallelism entails overhead: creating threads, dividing the workload, synchronization operations, and so on. When a parallel program is run on a single processor, it is likely to be slower than a good sequential algorithm. Overhead leads to a large value for $T(1)$, and this inflates the speedup figures. Ideally, speedup would be measured against a good single-processor solution to the problem. For most of the examples in this report, no such solution was available, so the speedup reported is based on the formula in equation 1. Speedup over a good sequential program is reported whenever possible; usually this is because the concurrent program was derived from an earlier sequential version.

One other speedup measure is used in this report. Some of the programs studied have a variable number of threads, and speedup can be measured by comparing the elapsed time for n threads with the time for 1 thread, with the number of processors kept constant. Computing speedup in this way measures the advantage obtained from program structure rather than from multiprocessors. Thread-based speedup may be higher or lower than processor-based speedup. It may be higher because a program can benefit from overlapping computation with some other activity, such as I/O. This requires multiple threads, but not multiple processors. It may be lower because there can be concurrent processing in the system (within the file server, for example) while even a single-threaded program is executed. Processor-based speedup is more relevant to evaluating multiprocessor workstations, but in some cases thread-based speedup is reported because it is the only data available.

1.3 Single-user Timesharing

A workstation often operates like a single-user time-sharing system. A user can pursue several activities at once – perhaps compiling a program, running a simulation, and reading mail at the same time. Having a multiprocessor workstation makes it possible to do this without suffering degraded performance.

The primary constraint on this sort of concurrency is the user's ability to juggle multiple active tasks. Doing two things at once is common, and doing three is not unusual. While a module is compiling, for example, a user typically does something else, such as edit another module, read mail, or examine an online calendar. A long-running computation may provide a third activity. One researcher regularly commits one processor on his Firefly to a symbolic computation which can take days to complete a single problem. This CPU-intensive background program does not significantly degrade the performance of his workstation for day-to-day activities. However, he is using a Firefly with 32 Megabytes of memory. The symbolic computation requires a good deal of memory, and running it in the background with a 16 Megabyte Firefly led to unacceptable thrashing.

The Firefly operating system also takes advantage of the UNIX[1] pipe construction to obtain command-level parallelism. A pipe is a way to direct the output of one program to the input of another. For example, the command

$$ls \mid wc - l$$

directs the output of ls, a list of files in the current directory, to the program wc, which counts the number of lines in its input. Thus the result is a count of the number of files in the current directory. On a

[1] UNIX is a trademark of AT&T Bell Laboratories.

Firefly, the stages in such a pipeline are executed in parallel whenever possible.

To get a feeling for the level of multiprocessing arising from independent tasks, CPU utilization was monitored on one Firefly during several days of ordinary use. Speedup was not measured because much of the activity was interactive, and the timing of mouse motions and key strokes is too hard to reproduce. The most common parallel activity was editing while compiling. Editing is not a CPU-intensive activity, and editing while compiling used scarcely more processor-power than compiling alone. However, other parallel activity led to significant multiprocessing. In one fairly typical sequence, the user began a remote login to a time-sharing machine. Since remote login is annoyingly slow, the user filled in the time by checking for new mail. This also required communication with a remote server. While waiting, the user requested a new typescript window. Figure 1.2 shows the processor utilization graph for this set of operations. Average processor utilization was over 2, and at least 10% of the time there were 5 processors busy.

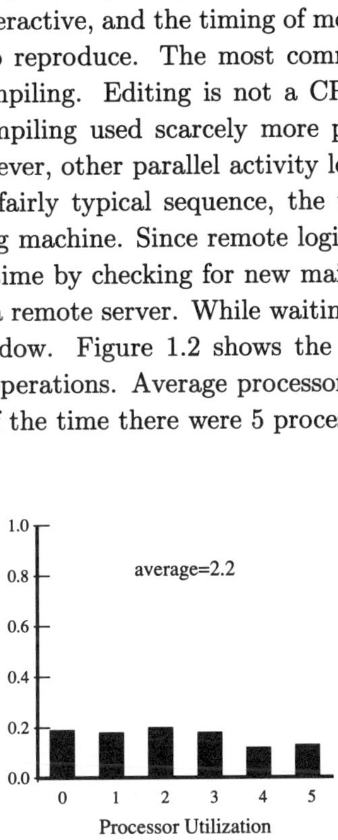

Figure 1.2
Set of Independent Tasks.

Another example arose very naturally when logging in to the Firefly. At login, this Firefly was configured to start two programs, the text editor Ivy and the mail system Postcard. Both require a fair amount of file access and computation at startup. Ivy recovers the state of all files that were being edited when the server was last running. Postcard checks the status of a number of mail folders and scans one of them to build a list of its current messages. Running both initializations in parallel led to an average processor utilization of 2.0.

A more systematic exploitation of single-user time-sharing is illustrated by the program parmake [6]. Parmake is a variant of the UNIX utility make [4], which builds a software object, such as a load module, following instructions found in a file. The difference is that, wherever possible, parmake builds components in parallel. (Parmake can enlist idle workstations in this task, as well as using multiple processors on the Firefly where it is invoked. For this report, only the single-machine behavior is important.) Parmake was measured on a large-scale recompilation consisting of 238 Modula-2+ files (65,000 source lines) drawn from various library packages at SRC. Speedup was measured by varying the number of threads, that is, the number of parallel compilations, rather than the number of processors. The maximum speedup in this benchmark was 2.2, attained by running three compilations in parallel. Running more compilations in parallel led to a severe degradation in performance, because of memory thrashing. Subsequently, the measurements were repeated on a Firefly with twice as much memory, (and faster processors, as well). The speedup was only slightly better: 2.3 for three threads, and 2.4 for four threads. It appears that the bottleneck for parmake on the larger machine is file I/O to the single local disk. A large part of the demand comes from loading the 4 Megabyte compiler once for each source file.

It should be noted that there were almost no dependencies among the modules compiled in this test. Thus most compilations could logically proceed in parallel, and speedup was limited by the resources of the machine. Bubenik and Zwaenepoel [2] found that when make is used for program development, dependencies substantially constrained the available parallelism.

A final example concerns a theorem-prover called Reve. As an experiment, up to five copies of Reve were run in parallel on the same test case. (This gives an indication of how much might be gained by splitting a large proof into independent components and running them concurrently.) The test case was very compute-intensive. Two copies of Reve were able to run in nearly the same time as one, giving a speedup of 1.91. Improvement was less than linear as the number of copies increased: still, the speedup with 5 copies was 4.05.

1.4 Concurrency within a server

Software at SRC makes frequent use of the client/server program structure. Typically, servers and clients run in different address spaces or even on different machines, with communication by remote procedure call. There are also some servers that operate in the same address space as their clients, with communication by ordinary procedure call.

The Taos operating system is the most important server. Taos runs in its own address space. It provides a number of operating system facilities: display management, file system, and so on. Taos itself is multi-threaded, and its interface allows multi-threaded programs to make parallel requests to the operating system [5].

There are also other servers in the Taos address space. The Trestle window system provides a powerful set of operations for managing windows on the Firefly displays. The File Server allows files on one Firefly to be accessed from another. Other servers run in their own address space: most Fireflies run the monarch server, for remote login, and the dp server, which allows an idle Firefly to be used by distributed computations. The Ivy text editor also runs as a server in its own address space.

When a server is multi-threaded, as many are, its client programs can get improved performance on a multiprocessor, even if the clients are single-threaded. This effect can be observed in copying a set of files in the Firefly's local file system. The concurrency of copy was measured by invoking the operation from the command line, on a directory containing 9.5 megabytes in 89 files. This led to one call on the Taos Copy command for each file in the directory. Figure 1.3 shows the processor utilization and speedup for this operation. Even though copying files is an I/O intensive activity, there is about 50% speedup in going from one to two processors, and a slight increase in going from two to three. The utilization graph shows that two processors are in use about 30% of the time. The dip in speedup at 4 processors is a measurement artifact.

The concurrency in the Copy operation comes from the activity of five threads. Two are created by the Copy procedure: one to read the input file to a buffer and the other to write the output file from the buffer. At a lower level, the file system maintains a read cache filled by two read-ahead threads, and a write buffer emptied by one writer thread. In spite of these five threads, however, average processor utilization is only

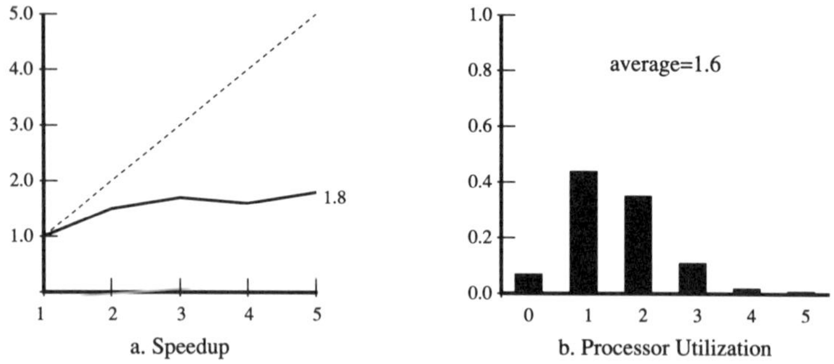

Figure 1.3
Concurrency within a server: copying files.

1.6. The low-level threads spend most of their time waiting for the disk: multiple threads are used to keep the disk busy, not the processors.

Trestle, the primary Firefly window system, is more able to exploit multi-processing. Trestle uses parallelism in two ways. The first is a 4-stage pipeline that handles paint requests. The first stage combines client paint requests into batches; it operates in the client address space. The second stage is the remote procedure call to send a batch of requests to the Trestle server, usually on the same Firefly. The third stage's main task is clipping, and the fourth stage translates the batch into display-controller commands. A benchmark program that blackens a large number of rectangles on the screen showed that the pipeline gave a speedup of 4.0, according to the naive speedup definition of equation 1. To obtain a more realistic measure, Trestle was reconfigured for a uniprocessor by removing all pipeline code. This resulted in a speedup measure of 3.1.

The second source of concurrency in Trestle can be seen when a window is re-configured. A window may contain subwindows, which may have subwindows of their own, and so on. When a window is reconfigured, its subwindows are processed in parallel. A benchmark program called the Tiling Monster builds and then reconfigures a window with many nested subwindows. Measurements of the Tiling Monster showed a speedup of 4.7, or nearly the entire processing power of the Firefly. Once again, it was possible to measure the performance of a good sequential algorithm; using the sequential algorithm as a basis, the speedup was 3.7.

Of course, both of the Trestle benchmarks were designed to take full advantage of the potential concurrency in Trestle's algorithms. A workstation user typically does not drive the window system so hard. But the power is available to graphics-oriented applications.

Another server, Facades, is a windowing package that incorporates a desktop paradigm for display management. It provides some of the functionality of Trestle, but has better performance when bound into the same address space as the client. The goal of Facades is to make it easier to write applications that use windows for an interactive user-interface. Like Trestle, Facades uses a pipeline to handle paint requests. It has three stages. The first stage accepts a request and checks whether the window to which it applies is on-screen. If it is, the request is passed to the second stage. The second stage relocates the request to the screen and clips it to the visible portions of the window. The third stage transforms the relocated and clipped paint actions into commands to the screen controller. For a long sequence of easy requests, these pipeline stages took 100, 100, and 60 microseconds respectively. This suggests a CPU utilization of about 2.6 by the pipeline. To evaluate speedup, Facades can be compared to a good sequential program, which would not contain code to buffer requests between pipeline stages. Based on experimentation and instruction counting, it was estimated that the speedup over such an implementation would be less than two.

Zeus, a system for algorithm-animation, provides yet another example of concurrency within a server. Zeus allows a user to observe multiple views of a program's execution. All views are updated in parallel as the program runs. It is also possible to have multiple threads in the program being animated. For a single-threaded algorithm, the concurrency in a Zeus run comes from Zeus's updating multiple views in parallel, and from the concurrency provided by the Trestle server.

In an animation of insertion sort for 500 random integers, CPU utilization was 2.4 when only one view was displayed. The sort algorithm itself is sequential, so the concurrency here must be due to Trestle. With two views, CPU utilization increased to 3.3, while with four views it rose to 4.1. Further increasing the number of views led to slower execution rather than greater CPU utilization.

The final example in this section shows that multiprocessing can sometimes speed up a computation by reducing overhead. Benchmark measurements of a single thread making inter-machine remote procedure calls show a speedup of 1.33 when the calling machine uses 2 processors [8]. (Adding more processors gives a very small additional speedup.) This is surprising, given that the calls are made sequentially and there is no concurrency in the RPC implementation. The explanation involves the background activity mentioned in section 2. Part of the speedup comes from processing RPC's in parallel with background tasks. But that is not enough to account for the whole change. It appears that additional speedup comes from reducing the number of context switches. The Firefly scheduler allows a waiting thread to remain in an idle loop as long as its processor is not needed by another thread. In RPC, the calling thread must wait to receive a response from the server machine. With one processor, the odds are good that the waiting thread will lose its processor to a background thread. Then, when the response arrives, the RPC thread will have to be rescheduled. Having two processors makes it more likely that the RPC thread will still be scheduled on a processor when the response is received.

1.5 Concurrency between Client and Server

The procedure-call interface between client and server is synchronous, that is, the client is delayed until the call returns. But sometimes the semantics of an operation allow a server to return control to the client before the work is completed. The client can continue while one or more threads in the server complete the work.

Trestle provides an example of this sort of concurrency. The Trestle pipeline operates in such a way that requests to paint the screen return control to the client early on, while the paint request is moving its way through the pipeline. This effect can be seen in the execution of the program Forest. Forest recursively draws a picture of an attractive tree whose shape is determined randomly. It is typical of graphics applications that perform some computation and call on Trestle to display the results on the screen. Forest is completely compute-bound, and its single-threaded computation is the limiting factor in the performance of the program.

Figure 1.4 shows the speedup and utilization measurements for Forest. Forest itself keeps one processor busy at all times, so utilization never falls below 1. When two or more processors are busy, it is because of concurrency between Forest and Trestle. When three or more processors are busy, it is because of additional concurrency within Trestle. The speedup graph shows that using more than three processors does not improve performance, and most of the benefit is achieved with two.

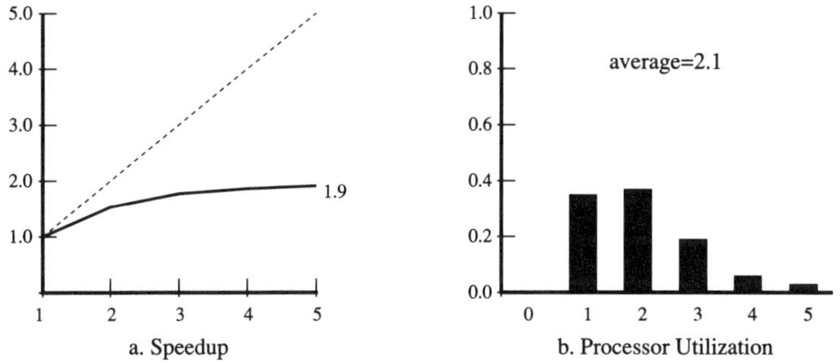

Figure 1.4
Concurrency between client and server: Forest.

Another example of client/server concurrency occurs in Zeus, when the algorithm to be animated continues to run one or more threads while Zeus is updating the display. This possibility is exploited in the animation of a multi-level hashing scheme [1]. The animation shows the filling of hash tables as a series of keys are entered. The algorithm's behavior is most interesting when there are many collisions. In order to illustrate this case, keys are selected in a way that gives a high probability of collision. Finding such keys requires more computation than the hashing algorithm itself. From one to three producer threads find the keys, while a single consumer thread uses them to drive the animation. CPU utilization averages about 3.8 when presenting a single view of the algorithm, compared with an average utilization of 2.4 for animating a single view of insertion sort.

A final example of concurrency between client and server is concurrent garbage collection. A garbage collector is not a typical server, because it is part of the runtime system, and because its actions are not explicitly invoked by the program. Nevertheless, it provides a service to the application program which can be a source of concurrency, so it is included in this section.

Modula2+ uses a reference-counting garbage collector which runs in a thread of its own, in parallel with the application program, or mutator.

Each mutator assignment that changes a reference count causes an entry to be enqueued for the collector. When a collection is initiated, the collector processes the queue and updates reference counts. This updating, plus the detection and reclaiming of garbage, take place in parallel with mutator operations. Measurements on several single-threaded applications showed that the collector thread ran about 40-70% of the time. The mutator thread ran most of the time, though it incurred a few percent overhead in synchronization operations. If these figures are typical for Modula2+ programs, the collector thread must use about 55% of a CPU to keep up with one compute-bound mutator thread. This suggests that, on a five-processor Firefly, a multi-threaded mutator could have an average CPU utilization of over 3 and still leave adequate CPU available to the collector.

An experimental copying collector for the programming language ML has also been implemented on the Firefly [3]. On one benchmark, a program using the concurrent version of this collector ran 18% faster than one using a sequential version. The collector thread was active about 40% of the time.

1.6 Concurrency within an Application

Quite a number of the applications written for the Firefly are multi-threaded. In fact, about 40% of the software packages at SRC fork one or more threads. (Packages vary in size, but typically contain code for a single application program or a library of related procedures.) Often the threads are created for program structure rather than performance; a rough estimate is that 20% of the packages use threads to gain performance through multiprocessing.

Simulation is an application area that seems especially suited to concurrency, although sometimes speedup may be harder to achieve than it first appears. Regsim, a register-level simulator for synchronous digital logic, is able to successfully exploit the parallelism in its input. The circuits input to Regsim are composed of connected objects. In each simulation phase, some fraction of the objects are evaluated. Certain objects must be evaluated every phase; others are evaluated on demand. When more than one thread is used for evaluation, the synchronization is such that some objects may be evaluated more than once.

Figure 1.5 shows the processor utilization and speedup for the simulation phase of Regsim on a circuit consisting of about 5000 objects. (The simulation phase, which took 1693 seconds with five processors, was preceded by a largely sequential initialization phase that took 99 seconds.) In this case, the number of threads was a parameter. For the speedup measurements it was set to give the best performance; this meant n threads when running on n processors, except that with five processors, four threads was optimal. In the utilization graph, note that 90% of the time there are four or five processors busy. Clearly Regsim contains enough parallelism to keep the Firefly processors busy. Moreover, they are being used productively, as illustrated by the speedup diagram. In fact, the speedup is better than linear.

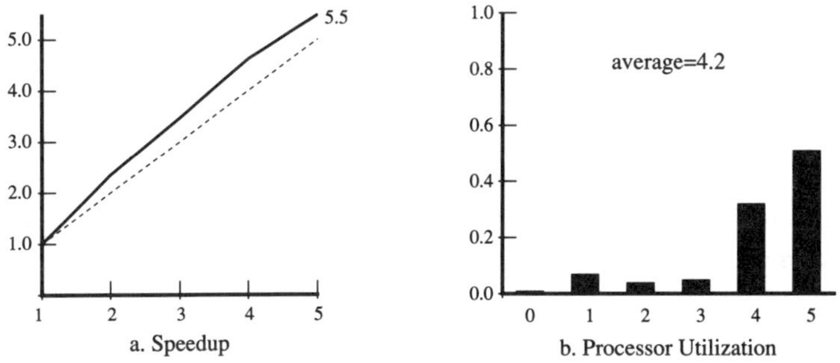

Figure 1.5
Concurrency within an application: Regsim.

Of course, no theoretical limit is really being exceeded. The anomaly occurs because of background activity on the Firefly, as mentioned in Section 2. Even when no user task is being executed, about 20% of a processor, on average, is consumed with ethernet activity, operating system timers, and so on. The level of background activity is essentially independent of the amount of work being done on the Firefly. Thus, when one processor is available for computation, only about 0.8 processor can be used by an application program. When 5 processors are available, 4.8 can be used by the application. This allows the application to speed up by a factor of 6 rather than 5.

Prf is another design automation tool that gains considerably from multiprocessing. Prf is a post-processor for routed printed-circuit boards.

Its input is produced by a router with an abstract model of routing; prf adjusts the routing to conform to a more physically accurate model. For example, it introduces jogs to route traces around holes and rounds off sharp corners. Prf can process traces in parallel because the modifications it makes are strictly local to a trace. A typical run may have about 900 traces, so there is ample scope for concurrency. In fact, the average utilization for the processing phases of prf is 4.6, so nearly the full processing power of the Firefly is exploited. The final output phase is also parallel; here the parallelism comes from independent processing of the ten layers of the circuit board. In this phase, processor utilization averages 4.4. Unfortunately, the overall performance of prf is not as good as these figures suggest. First, about 40% of execution time is consumed by a sequential phase in which lex and yacc are used to parse an input file. In this phase, utilization is 1.6 because of concurrency in the file system. It would probably be possible to parse the input file in parallel, but this optimization has not been pursued. Second, some of the processing phases do not achieve as much speedup as the utilization figures suggest, for reasons that are not yet known. For example, the longest processing phase has a utilization of 4.7 and a speedup of 3.2. The result is that average utilization for the entire program is reduced to 3.1, and speedup is 2.3.

Several multi-threaded compilers have been developed for the Firefly. The current Modula 2+ compiler exploits a limited amount of concurrency, by running the lexical analyzer as a separate thread. The lexical analyzer thread is able to produce tokens faster than they can be used, so the main compiler thread never has to wait for a token. Thus lexical analysis is essentially free so far as elapsed time is concerned.

Michael Junkin and David Wortman, at the University of Toronto, have made considerable progress in parallelizing the Modula 2+ compiler. The Toronto compiler gets parallelism from two sources. First, scopes (procedures, main modules, and definition modules) are compiled in parallel. The primary limits on this easy parallelism are fast recognition of scopes, and data-dependencies between scopes. Second, some parallelism is exploited in compiling a single scope. This involves pipelining lexical analysis and analyzing declarations in parallel with parsing statements. Preliminary measurements comparing the Toronto compiler with a traditional single-threaded compiler show that, with one processor, the Toronto compiler is 1.3 times faster. The speedup is 3.1

for five processors, and 3.3 for a specially configured Firefly with seven processors.

Figure 1.6 is a graphical illustration of the performance of the Toronto compiler. The figure is a second-by-second display of the number of active processors during a sequence of compilations on a seven-processor Firefly. The graph was obtained by repeatedly compiling the same module, first with one processor, then with two, and so on. A 10 second idle period separates compilations. The image illustrates both the use of multiple processors (the height of the bars) and the elapsed time for each compilation (the width of the active periods).

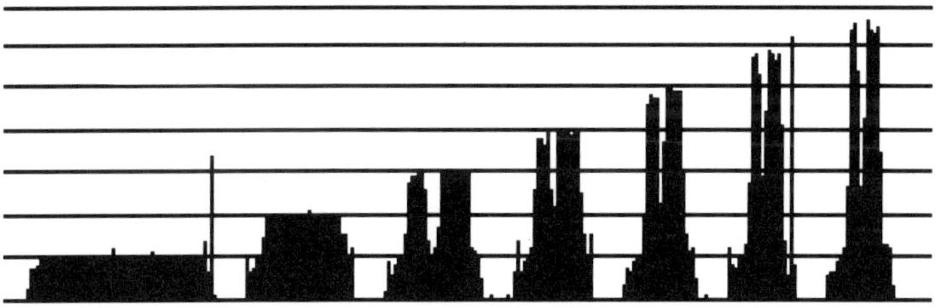

Figure 1.6
Parallelism in the Toronto Modula 2+ Compiler.

There is also a parallel C compiler for the Firefly [10]. This compiler consists of a two-stage pipeline. The first stage performs extended lexical analysis for the second stage, much like the current SRC Modula 2+ compiler. The second stage does the parsing and assembly code generation. It processes units of the source program concurrently; the unit granularity can vary from a single statement to a procedure.

Experiments compared the concurrent compiler, with various granularities of concurrency, to a sequential compiler on nine large source files (more than 1200 lines). Pipelined scanning, with a sequential second phase, gave a speedup of 1.07 to 1.18. With a concurrent second phase and the finest unit of granularity, the compiler achieved a speedup of 2.5 to 3.3. Compiling with the finest granularity never hurt performance. For six of the source files, most of the concurrency came from processing procedures in parallel. For the remaining three, a finer granularity, at the statement level, gave a significant increase over the procedure level.

An important tool for insuring that Modula2+ programs do not contain inconsistent versions of component modules is the inter-module checker, or imc. It takes a list of separately compiled object modules and libraries and checks that all the compilations used consistent versions of definitions files. It is organized as a 4-stage pipeline. The first stage opens the files listed on the command line. The second stage separates libraries into individual object modules. The third stage builds a list of module version numbers, and the fourth stage merges the lists and checks them for consistency. After all stages have completed, a summary report is printed. Running on a set of 20 modules and 10 libraries, the concurrent version of the program exhibited a speedup of 1.3 over an earlier, sequential version.

The program Proof allows a user to preview a typeset document on the Firefly display. A substantial amount of processing is required to transform the typesetter instructions into commands to the Trestle window system. Proof is composed of three parallel tasks: building a display list of characters and boxes (one thread), painting the display list (up to three threads, one for each page visible on the screen), and processing font descriptions (six threads). In addition, a background thread converts the representation of frequently used fonts to speed up Trestle's processing of characters. Because Proof is used interactively, it is important to display the first page as soon as possible. To achieve this, a painter thread can inform a font-loading thread that a certain character is needed immediately. The font-loader will interrupt its current activity in order to load the requested character. Processor utilization for Proof averages 3.9 while preparing to display the first page of a document.

The program treeupdate is used to update a Firefly's local file system so that it has current copies of the files stored in a shared file system. Treeupdate recursively descends the tree of directories and files in the shared system, comparing with the local tree and doing any necessary updates. The parallel version maintains a work queue of tree nodes to be updated, with a crew of N threads serving the queue. Treeupdate is an example of "embarrassing parallelism" – except for the queue, there is no synchronization necessary. (Here "embarrassing" means "overabundant," as in "an embarrassment of riches.") Comparing this parallel version with the previous sequential one, a speedup of 3.7 was observed when running over an already consistent file system. Presumably the speedup is due to the overlapping of the overheads associated with getting the status of files in the local and remote file systems, and with sorting of directory entries.

One further parallel application must be mentioned even though it derives much of its parallelism from using multiple workstations. Factor is a program for factoring large numbers that runs continuously at SRC. It is controlled by a single program that watches for Fireflies that have been idle for some threshold period. When an idle machine is found, the control program adds it to the pool of factoring machines and starts one factor program for each of its processors. Factor is able to use virtually all of the available CPU cycles on a machine, because there is almost no synchronization between the separate programs, and the CPU is almost the only resource required. The number of Fireflies in the Factor pool fluctuates over the course of a day, with an average of about 40 machines at any time. On a typical day in January, 1989, Factor executed approximately 10^{13} VAX instructions at SRC. Compared to tuned code for factoring on Cray X-MP's and NEC SX-2's, the "idle" Fireflies are factoring numbers slightly faster than one dedicated supercomputer.

1.7 Conclusion

The examples presented in the preceding sections should give a feel for the variety of ways in which concurrency is exploited on the Firefly. A substantial part of SRC's computing now is faster because of multiprocessing.

Even when running a single sequential application, a Firefly user benefits from having two processors, because of concurrency associated with servers. Submitting independent tasks in parallel is a common activity; here two to three processors are of value. Thus the benefits of having at least three processors are very real, even for a user who runs no concurrent applications. A number of applications exist that effectively use four to five processors, and could probably take advantage of more. For those who frequently use such applications, having five or more processors gives a substantial increase in productivity. Other users would probably find that, most of the time, their work was adequately supported by three processors.

Many of the application programs run on the Firefly are nearly sequential. Some were developed for a uniprocessor and later ported to the Firefly. But even among programs designed for the Firefly, there are a number that take little advantage of multiprocessors. Some tasks are simply not well suited to concurrency. In other cases, designers are primarily interested in exploring new functionality, and do not want to spend their time on performance.

Still, as more applications are programmed for the Firefly, more of SRC's computing will benefit from concurrency. For example, Fireflies are often used for program development, so compiling is a common activity. The current compiler has limited concurrency, but a more parallel compiler will soon be available. In addition, a project to facilitate the development of large software systems will provide facilities that resemble parmake but avoid some of the problems that currently limit its use.

Experience at SRC makes it clear that multiple processors can be used effectively in workstations. Although current measurements suggest that most users derive most of their benefit from the first three processors, this should be considered a preliminary estimate. The use of concurrency for speedup is increasing at SRC, and it will be some time before its limits can be determined.

1.8 Acknowledgements

The programs described in this report are the work of a number of people at SRC. In addition to those cited in the references, they include Bob Ayers, Andrew Birrell, Marc H. Brown, Mark R. Brown, Patrick Chan, Anthony Discolo, Hans Eberle, John Ellis, Jim Horning, Bill Kalsow, Mark Manasse, Greg Nelson, Lyle Ramshaw, and Jorge Stolfi. John DeTreville worked jointly with the author to survey concurrency in SRC software; some conclusions from that survey are included here. Marc H. Brown, Mark R. Brown, Sheng-Yang Chiu, Jim Horning, Bill Kalsow, Ed Lazowska, Roy Levin, Michael Schroeder, Jorge Stolfi, and David Wortman made useful comments that improved the presentation of the paper.

References

[1] Andrei Broder and Anna Karlin. Multilevel adaptive hashing. In *First Annual ACM-SIAM Symposium on Discrete Algorithms (SODA)*, January 1990.

[2] Rick Bubenik and Willy Zwaenepoel. Performance of optimistic make. In *1989 ACM SIGMETRICS and PERFORMANCE '89 International Conference on Measurement and Modeling of Computer Systems*, May 1989.

[3] John Ellis, Kai Li, and Andrew Appel. Real-time concurrent collection on stock multiprocessors. Research Report 25, Digital Equipment Corporation Systems Research Center, February 1988.

[4] S. Feldman. Make–a computer program for maintaining computer programs. *Software Practice and Experience*, 9(4), April 1979.

[5] Paul McJones and Garret Swart. Evolving the unix system interface to support multithreaded programs. Research Report 21, Digital Equipment Corporation Systems Research Center, September 1987.

[6] Eric Roberts and John Ellis. parmake and dp: Experience with a distributed, parallel implementation of make. In *Second Workshop on Large-Grained Parallelism*. Software Engineering Institute, Carnegie-Mellon University, November 1987. Report CMU/SEI-87-SR-5.

[7] Paul Rovner. Extending modula-2 to build large, integrated systems. *IEEE Software*, 3(6), November 1986.

[8] Michael Schroeder and Michael Burrows. Performance of firefly rpc. In *12th ACM Symposium on Operating Systems Principles*, December 1989.

[9] Charles P. Thacker, Lawrence C Stewart, and Edwin H. Satterthwaite, Jr. Firefly: a multiprocessor workstation. *IEEE Transactions on Computers*, 37(8), August 1988.

[10] Mark Vandevoorde. Parallel compilation on a tightly coupled multiprocessor. Research Report 26, Digital Equipment Corporation Systems Research Center, March 1988.

[11] Mark Vandevoorde and Eric Roberts. Workcrews: An abstraction for controlling parallelism. Research Report 42, Digital Equipment Corporation Systems Research Center, April 1989.

[12] Niklaus Wirth. *Programming in MODULA-2*. Springer-Verlag, third edition, 1985.

2 Design and Evaluation of Snoop-Cache-Based Multiprocessor, TOP-1

Shigenori Shimizu, Nobuyuki Oba, Atsushi Moriwaki, and Takeo Nakada

TOP-1 is a snoop-cache-based multiprocessor workstation that was developed to evaluate multiprocessor architecture design choices as well as to conduct research on operating systems, compilers, and applications for multiprocessor workstations. It is a ten-way multiprocessor using the Intel 80386 and Weitek 1167, and is currently running with a multiprocessor version of AIX, which was also developed at IBM's Tokyo Research Laboratory. The research interest was focused on the design of an effective snoop cache system and quantitative evaluation of its performance. One of the unique aspects of TOP-1's design is that the cache supports four different original snoop protocols, which may coexist in the system. To evaluate the actual performance, we implemented a hardware statistics monitor, which gathers statistical data on the hardware. This paper focuses mainly on a description of the TOP-1 memory system design with regard to the cache protocols, and its evaluation by means of the hardware statistics monitor mentioned above. Besides its cache design, the TOP-1 memory system has three other unique architectural features: a high-speed bus-locking mechanism, two-way interleaved 64-bit buses supported by two snoop cache controllers per processor, and an effective arbitration mechanism to allow a prioritized quasi-round-robin service with distributed control. These features are also described in detail.

2.1 Introduction

Multiprocessor workstations are a very promising solution to the continuously increasing need for personal computing power. In the past several years, shared-memory shared-bus multiprocessors have been extensively analyzed and developed, because of the simplicity of the hardware and its flexibility with respect to various parallel programming models. Most such multiprocessors use a snoop cache mechanism to reduce bus traffic and to maintain multi-cache coherency [2, 5, 6, 10].

IBM's Tokyo Research Laboratory has been working on a multiprocessor workstation since 1986. As a research vehicle, we developed a snoop-based multiprocessor workstation, TOP-1 to evaluate the multiprocessor architecture design as well as to do research on operating systems, compilers, and applications for multiprocessor workstations. Overview of the project is given in [9].

Because of the ease of developing and porting software, we decided to build a tightly coupled shared-memory multiprocessor workstation. The result, TOP-1, is currently running with a multi-threaded multiprocessor version of AIX. TOP-1 is a ten-way multiprocessor using the Intel 80386 and Weitek 1167. Each processor has 128K bytes of snoop cache (see Figure 2.1).

This paper focuses on a description and evaluation of TOP-1's memory system design. The unique architectural features of the memory system are a mechanism that allows several different snoop coherency protocols to coexist in the system and also to be changed by software for each memory operation; a high-speed bus locking mechanism, which allows in-cache semaphore on any address boundary; a two-way interleaved dual 64-bit buses supported by two snoop cache controllers per processor card; and an efficient arbitration mechanism that allows prioritized quasi-round-robin service with distributed control. Moreover, TOP-1 has a statistics unit that makes it possible to obtain various statistics on the memory system's behavior for various operating systems and applications.

Section 2 gives an overview of TOP-1's hardware architecture. Section 3 discusses considerations in the design of the TOP-1 memory system. Section 4 evaluates the memory system design, especially the cache design, on the basis of the performance results that were measured by using a special assist hardware unit embedded in the cache and bus subsystem of the TOP-1 processors.

2.2 Hardware Architecture Overview

One principal objective of the project is to study the trade-off between hardware and software. Very little is known about the behavior and characteristics of software on a shared-memory multiprocessor. We therefore wanted to analyze run-time statistics, and to reflect them in the design of future multiprocessors. For this purpose, we built a hardware statistics unit that gathers various statistics from the actual machine without incurring any run-time overhead. We also wanted to use the statistics to change the hardware algorithms used by the compiler and operating system. For this reason, we implemented multiple snoop cache protocols and variable priority arbitration mechanisms.

As shown in Figure 2.1, TOP-1 is organized around a shared common bus. Attached to the bus are up to 128M bytes of system memory and up to 11 identical processing units, each of which consists of an Intel 80386

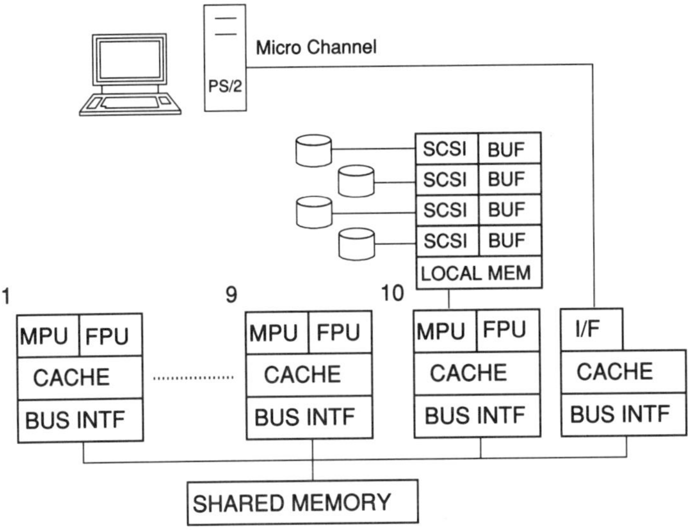

Figure 2.1
TOP-1 Hardware Block Diagram

and a Weitek 1167 floating-point coprocessor, a 128K-byte snoop cache, and the system bus interface. Also on this bus is the Micro Channel Interface adapter, for connecting TOP-1 to the PS/2 Model 80 through the Micro Channel standard. It has a 128K-byte snoop cache as with other processors, and enables the PS/2 Model 80 to access the TOP-1 shared bus directly, and thus also the shared memory. This allows the use of various standard PS/2 I/O adapters as I/O devices of TOP-1. We built a special hard disk adapter on the TOP-1 bus to give the hard disk subsystem high performance and large capacity. All 11 processors are completely identical, but one processor is dedicated to hard disk management, being connected to the hard disk control adapter via the local bus extension.

2.3 Memory System Design

The memory system uses a so-called snoop cache mechanism like those in other small-scale, tightly coupled multiprocessors, to reduce the bus traffic and to maintain multicache coherency. Its unique feature is that it supports four different protocols.

2.3.1 Cache Organization

The main specifications of the TOP-1 cache are summarized in Table 2.1, and can be described as follows:

• 128K-byte cache size: In general, a larger cache size gives a higher hit ratio, and hence better performance and lower bus traffic. On the other hand, in practice, the cache size should not be so large that it represents an expense out of proportion to the added performance, nor should it occupy an unreasonable fraction of the physical space within the processor part. Moreover, in a multiprocessor system with an update-type snoop cache, a very large cache may also increase the number of shared blocks, and hence require unnecessary updating of the blocks. In view of these trade-offs, TOP-1 adopts a fairly large cache size of 128K bytes to get a higher hit ratio, and thus a better performance, by using IBM's fast SRAM with 30-ns access time and an 8K x 18-bit configuration

• 64-bit line size: There are a number of trade-offs between small and large line size. In general, a larger line size gives a higher hit ratio and hence a better performance, since the load of a large cache line has in some degree a prefetch effect, although the improvement in the hit ratio achieved by using a larger cache line is thought to be very slight when the cache size is large enough. A larger cache line requires a longer latency delay for the transfer to be completed because of a so-called burst transfer. If we assume extra latency delay for transferring a larger cache line (this extra latency delay can be eliminated by using a fetch bypass or load-through mechanism), the average memory access time is not necessarily decreased, even if the cache hit ratio is improved by only a few tenths of a percent. At least, with regard to the bus traffic, the extra bus cycles needed to transfer a longer cache line may cancel out the very small improvement in the hit ratio, even if the fetch bypass mechanism can be used. Moreover, in a snoop-based multiprocessor, a larger line size may increase the number of shared blocks in the cache, since an entire cache line has to be in the SHARED state even if only one byte in the long cache line is actually shared. In fact, our experimental simulation results show that the shared ratio for the 128-bit line size is about 1.5 times that for the 64-bit line size, if we do not assume any software technique for gathering actually shared data within a restricted memory area. In view of these criteria, TOP-1 adopts a 64-bit line size, which is the same as the data width of the system bus.

• Direct mapping: There are also various trade-offs between larger and smaller set associativity or a direct mapping as the cache placement algorithm. In general, larger set associativity gives a higher hit ratio and hence a better performance, since it can easily handle several access streams each with its access locality (such as code fetch and data access, source data access and destination data access, and multiple concurrent processes). For a large cache size, however, the improvement in the hit ratio achieved by using larger associativity is thought to be very slight, since the possibility of conflicts on the same cache line is drastically decreased if the cache size is large enough. Moreover, in practice, larger set associativity requires a larger circuit delay for the tag comparator, since more address tags have to be compared with the requested address. In addition, for a read hit, since the output from the cache data memory array of the set associative cache must be selected after the comparison of the tag fields has been completed, an extra latency delay will be incurred before the data become available to the processor. For these reasons, TOP-1 uses a direct mapping cache.

• Duplicated tag memory: The cache tag memory is duplicated so that the MPU can access the cache tag memory in parallel with the snooping hardware. Cache access conflicts will occur only when either the MPU or the snooping hardware requires the tag memory to be updated in the same cycle, or when both the MPU and the snooping hardware request the cache data memory to be accessed in the same cycle. A read access to the tag memory for a snoop address comparison does not interfere at all with the cache access induced by the MPU as long as the MPU cache access does not require the tag memory to be updated with a new value. When cache access conflicts between the MPU and the snooping hardware occur, the snooping hardware always has a higher priority than the MPU. Therefore, the MPU access will be delayed more than one cycle until the conflict condition is broken off. This arbitration policy ensures that the snoop access will be completed in a fixed period, and hence simplifies the system bus protocol.

Item	Description
Protocol	TOP-1 Protocol 2 Protocols (Update & Invalidate) 2 Modes (Standard & I/O)
Cache Size	128K Bytes
Line Size	64 bit
Placement	Direct Mapping
Memory Update	Copy Back
Tag	32K Bytes x 2 (Duplicated Tag)

Table 2.1
TOP-1 Cache Summary

2.3.2 Snoop Protocol

The cache controller is implemented by using an IBM CMOS gate array with 16,000 gates. Both the cache tag and data memory are implemented by using IBM's fast SRAM with 30-ns access time and an 8K x 18-bit configuration. The controller handles the TOP-1 snoop cache as well as the shared bus interface, including the arbitration logic. It also includes a hardware unit for collecting statistics such as program characteristics, snoop cache performance, and bus performance.

A number of snoop cache protocols have been proposed, but none of them is considered to be ideal in all situations [1]. Coherency protocols can be generally classified into two types, update and invalidate protocols, each of which is suitable for different situations.

A novel aspect of TOP-1 is that it supports both update and invalidate protocols. Furthermore, each type of protocol can have two protocol modes: standard and block I/O. In total, there are thus four kinds of protocol combination, all of which can coexist in the system, and on each processor the protocol can be dynamically changed by programs for each memory operation.

Figure 2.2 shows a state transition diagram of TOP-1's protocol, combining both update and invalidate protocols. For simplicity of discussion, only the standard mode is depicted in the figure. We will discuss the block I/O mode later in this section.

In TOP-1's protocol, each cache block is in one of five states: INVALID, CLEAN-PRIVATE (not modified, only copy in caches), DIRTY-PRIVATE (modified, only copy in caches), CLEAN-SHARED (possibly

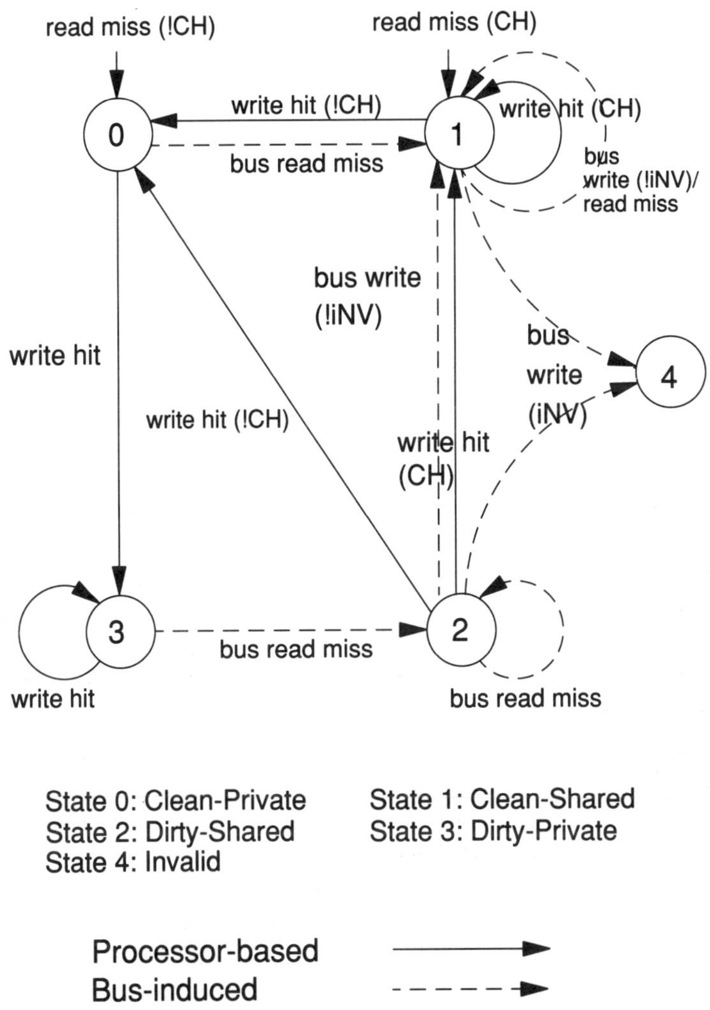

Figure 2.2
TOP-1 Snoop Protocol

other caches with a copy, may or may not be a modified copy but write-back is not needed at replacement), or DIRTY-SHARED (write-back required at replacement, possibly other caches with a copy). There is a special bus line used to detect sharing, which is referred to as the CH (Cache Hit) line in this paper. The CH line is an open-collector wired-or line that is activated by two or more snooping cache controllers when they have a copy of the memory address driven by the requesting cache. The requesting cache controller can recognize whether other caches have a copy of the requested memory line by examining the CH line at the end of a bus cycle.

Each cache controller has a "cache mode register" that uses two bits to specify the snoop protocol type of update or invalidate and the protocol mode of standard or block I/O. The first bit specifies "iNV (invalidate protocol)" if it is set to "1", which is shown in Figure 2.3 to specify the condition of state transition. The second bit specifies "I/O (block I/O mode)" if it is set to "1". The TOP-1 protocol can be described as follows:

1. Read miss: If another cache has a DIRTY-PRIVATE or DIRTY-SHARED copy, that cache supplies the data, raises the CH line and sets its block state to DIRTY-SHARED, because main memory is not updated with the data. Otherwise, the block comes from main memory. Any cache with a CLEAN-PRIVATE or CLEAN-SHARED copy raises the CH line and sets its local block state to CLEAN-SHARED. The requesting cache loads the block in the CLEAN-SHARED state when the CH line is active. Otherwise, it loads the block in the CLEAN-PRIVATE state.
2. Write hit: If the block is DIRTY-PRIVATE, the write can be locally completed without using the shared bus, and no state change occurs. If the block is CLEAN-PRIVATE, the write can also be completed without using the shared bus, but the state is changed to DIRTY-PRIVATE. If the block is in either the CLEAN-SHARED or DIRTY-SHARED state, the write requires the shared bus, and the entire cache line is broadcasted via the shared bus. Other caches with a copy observe the bus, update their own copies with the new data on the bus, and activate the CH line if the snoop protocol bit in the cache mode register specifies the update protocol (not iNV). On the other hand, if the snoop protocol bit specifies the invalidate protocol (iNV), those snooping caches invalidate

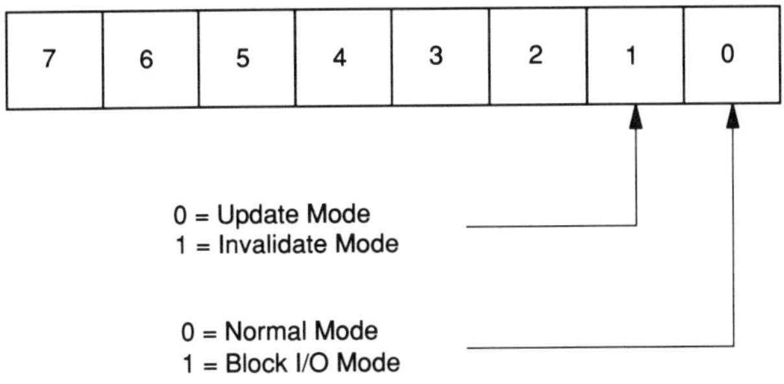

Figure 2.3
Cache Mode Register

their own copies and do not activate the CH line. The requesting cache can determine whether the sharing is still continued on that cache line by examining the CH line. If the CH line is not activated, the requesting cache changes the block state to CLEAN-PRIVATE, since no other cache has a copy and successive writes no longer need be broadcasted. If the CH line is activated, the block state remains in the CLEAN-SHARED state, since sharing continues.
3. Write miss: In TOP-1's protocol, a write miss is performed as a combination of read miss and write hit. The requesting cache controller generates a read miss access on the bus, and then immediately generates a write access if the CH line is raised in the first read miss access. Otherwise, the write is locally performed without using the bus, because there is no sharing.

TOP-1's protocol is designed to optimize the cache performance by taking account of the difference between the cycle times of the cache memory and the main memory.

• In TOP-1's protocol, the clean data comes from the main memory rather than another cache that also has a clean copy. Since the memory can return data in three clock cycles of 16 MHz, as with the data response from a snooping cache, there is no difference in access latency between main memory and a snooping cache. Furthermore, this data reply policy can reduce the interference between the MPU-induced access and the bus-induced access on a snooping cache (if the other cache returns a clean copy, that cache must delay a cache access induced by the MPU until the completion of the snoop data reply cycle).

- When a write access occurs on the bus, the main memory is always updated with the new data, since the main memory can be written in three clock cycles of 16 MHz, as with the snooping cache update time. This policy reduces the number of DIRTY lines in the cache that have to be written back to the main memory at the time of replacement, and hence reduces the bus traffic induced by write-back activities.
- When a dirty copy is returned from the owing cache to the requesting cache, the main memory is not updated with the new data. This policy simplifies the memory and cache control logic, since every bus activity can be completed within a regular number of clock cycles (on the other hand, if the owing cache of the DIRTY block updates the main memory as well as the requesting cache, as in the Firefly protocol, extra cycles are needed to update the main memory). Although this policy may increase the bus traffic caused by write-back activities, the effect can be predicted to be very small, since in TOP-1's protocol every bus write updates the main memory and changes the block state from DIRTY to CLEAN, as described above.

The above description of the protocol shows that the requesting cache need not know which snoop protocol (update or invalidate) other caches use. In other words, the snoop protocol bit in the cache mode register does not have any influence on an operation of the cache controller when it is a requesting cache, but acts on the operation when it is a snooping cache. The requesting cache has only an indirect influence through the response on the CH line from other caches. Therefore, it should be noted that each controller can arbitrarily take either an update or invalidate protocol at any time. Figure 2.4 shows a situation in which two protocols coexist in the system. In the figure, processors 2 and 4 are set in the update protocol, and processor 3 is set in the invalidate protocol. The protocol type of processor 1 is irrelevant in this case, since it is a requesting processor. When a write access occurs on the bus, the corresponding cache lines in processors 2 and 4 are simultaneously updated with the new data on the bus, while the cache line in processor 3 is invalidated. The cache controllers of processors 2 and 4 activate the CH line, but that of processor 3 does not. In this case, the block state in processor 1's cache remains SHARED because the CH line is activated.

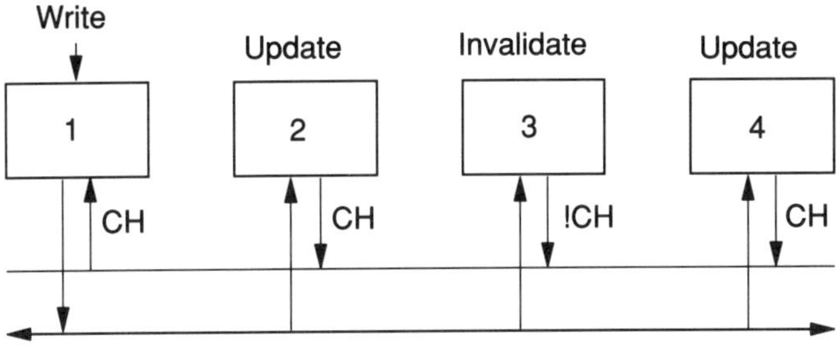

Figure 2.4
Two Coexisting Modes

When the cache mode registers of all cache controllers have been set in the update protocol, TOP-1 updates all shared cache lines in other caches if a write is performed. In this respect it is similar to the protocols of Xerox's Dragon [2] and DEC's Firefly [10].

When the cache mode register of all cache controllers in the system have been set in invalidate protocol type, TOP-1's protocol invalidates all the shared lines in other caches when write occurs, as in Berkley's SPUR [6].

The block I/O mode is prepared for consecutive block data transfer to and from external devices so as not to leave blocks that are no longer needed in the cache. Data transfer from/to input and output devices must be carefully designed, so as to maintain data consistency in the multicache system. In TOP-1, we solved the problem by using snoop cache for input and output subsystems as with the processors. However, this method involves a new problem in that the number of shared data in the system after data transfer increases. The sharing will increase particularly after paging from a hard disk. The data read into the shared memory also resides in the I/O controller's cache, even after the line has been actually used by a requesting processor. The writing overhead for shared blocks adds extra bus traffic and degrades the system performance. The block I/O mode of cache protocol forces the cache line of the transmitting processor to be written back to the memory and to be invalidated when the last word of the cache line is written from the I/O.

The second bit (mode modification bit) of the cache mode register of each cache controller specifies "I/O (block I/O mode)" if it is set to "1". This bit does not have any influence on the operation of the cache controller when it is a snooping cache, but acts on the operation when it is a requesting cache. This control mechanism is orthogonal to the protocol type control. Hence, it should be noted that each cache controller can arbitrarily take either standard or block I/O mode without regard to the protocol type. In other words, either protocol type, update or invalidate, can be modified with either protocol mode, standard or block I/O.

2.3.3 System Bus

Our goals in system bus design are to increase the bus bandwidth and to decrease the access latency delay with a reasonable cost and complexity of hardware, even if the private cache can drastically reduce the bus traffic.

To maximize the bus bandwidth, there are various design choices for the bus transfer mechanism, such as an ECL high-speed bus, a block-transferred bus, and a packet-controlled bus. The block-transferred bus can provide a higher bus bandwidth if the memory cycle time is much larger than the bus cycle pitch, because one memory cycle is required for the first word and only one bus cycle for each consecutive word. In case of TOP-1's technology, however, the memory cycle time is only a few times larger than the bus cycle (62.5 ns for the bus and 187.5 ns for the memory in the case of TOP-1), because the bus cycle time is a technically limited by buffer delays and clock skews. This being so, the data width of the bus and shared memory should usually be the same as the line size, since it is desirable to transmit an entire line in one transfer cycle time. A packet-controlled bus complicates the snoop mechanism and increases the latency delay time for a bus access.

Instead of using a block-transferred bus or a packet-controlled bus, TOP-1 uses two-way interleaved buses, each with a 64-bit data width. The bus, the shared memory, and the cache are all two-way interleaved with an 8-byte boundary. Each bus is independently arbitrated. Consequently, the shared bus can provide an 85M-byte/sec effective data transfer rate for both read and write operations.

Another novel aspect of the shared bus design is the high-speed and fair-service arbitration mechanism. Using a unique high-speed arbitration mechanism, which we named a "modified back-off arbitration mechanism," the shared bus is arbitrated in one bus cycle, or 62.5 ns at

16-MHz operation, in a distributed manner. Instead of an encoded arbitration code, as used in a so-called back-off mechanism, each requester issues a decoded code on the bus according to the current request priority. This mechanism allows high-speed arbitration, because no feed-back loop is required for settling the arbitration bus. After a requester has obtained right of access to the bus as a result of the arbitration, each arbiter counts up its arbitration code, so that a quasi-round-robin service is realized. Moreover, each arbiter can set its priority range so that the arbitration code ID rotates within the range specified. Since this mechanism allows processors to be classified into several groups with regard to the arbitration priority range, it is useful for process scheduling. For instance, some processors on which high-priority processes are allocated can run faster if a high-priority range is assigned.

2.3.4 Atomic Memory Operation

We adjusted 80386 locked-instructions, which correspond to "test-and-set," so that they worked correctly. When an 80386 issues a locked-instruction such as XCHG, the bus is locked regardless of whether a cache hit or miss occurs, and the effects of the memory modification are broadcasted instantaneously. Moreover, both even and odd buses are locked simultaneously, without regard which bus is actually used, because an atomic operand may extend over multiple buses. TOP-1's unique bus-locking mechanism can lock the bus in only two additional bus cycles, with no possibility of deadlock. This makes it possible to implement spin lock on any address boundary. A process that enters a critical region makes a spin lock on a semaphore by using a read loop. When the process changes the semaphore, it issues a locked-instruction to make sure that nobody goes in the critical region.

Lock and Unlock instructions are also provided to lock and unlock the bus, respectively. Higher-level synchronization operations such as enqueue and dequeue can be easily implemented by a sequence of few instructions, if the sequence can be treated as an atomic operation. To assure atomicity, the bus must be locked while such an instruction sequence is being executed.

2.4 Performance Evaluation of Memory System

2.4.1 Evaluation Environment

2.4.1.1 Statistics Unit The cache behavior of uniprocessors has been extensively analyzed in the literature, and the cache performance of tightly coupled multirpcessors have been reported by some papers also [1, 3, 18, 7]. However, most such reports have been based on tests using software simulators driven by statistical parameters or traces, as in our preliminary performance evaluation.

In contrast, we used the hardware statistics unit built into the TOP-1 cache/bus controller to evaluate the actual cache and bus performance of TOP-1. This statistics unit makes it possible to gather statistical data from the real machine without any overheads. Furthermore, it allows an accurate count of the number of fetches, including instructions that are prefetched but are not actually executed owing to the prefetch queue flush. When a program has a tight loop that is intensively executed, normal software simulations should give an incorrect result, because the effect of the prefetch queue cannot be taken into account. The statistical events captured by this unit are as follows:

1. Number of memory accesses (instruction fetch, data read, and data write, separately),
2. Cache hit ratio for each type of memory access,
3. Number of write accesses to private data and shared data,
4. Number of write-backs for dirty lines,
5. Number of cache updates/invalidations by snoop,
6. Number of dirty data returned to the requester, and
7. Number of bus cycles that a processor waits for the bus

In addition, we can dynamically specify the address range (page base) in which the statistics unit counts the numbers shown above. Thus, if the program mapping is previously known or can be controlled by the operating system, we can selectively gather the various statistics corresponding to the high-level language source code. For example, we can get the cache hit ratio only for the OS kernel, only for the synchronization variables, or only for the processing data.

2.4.1.2 OS Structure and Applications To obtain the statistical data on TOP-1 we used four standard benchmark programs, two from SPEC and two from Livermore loops. Although these four programs are well-known standard, each program is briefly explained here to clarify the measurement environments.

Gcc and espresso are selected from SPEC benchmark programs as two representatives. Gcc is an integer benchmark. The gcc compiler compiles C description of gcc compiler itself and some large C program. Espresso is also an integer benchmark, which performs set operations such as union, intersect and difference. For the input functions used, the memory working set is less than 1M bytes and the program text is less than 100K bytes.

Livermore loop kernels 7 and 11 are selected from the Livermore loops coded in C as two representatives. The kernel 7, called "Equation of State Fragment," doesn't include any data dependency among repetitions of DO loop. Each repetition of DO loop can be easily parallelized by multiple processors. The processors compete for the execution of a loop with each other through a shared memory semaphore. The kernel 11, called "First Sum," is a representative that doesn't include any concurrency because of complete data dependency. Although each repetition of DO loop is parallelized to multiple processors, a new repetition of DO loop can not be started until the previous repetition completes. The processors compete for the execution of a loop with each other through a semaphore as with the kernel 7, but synchronize the completion of the previous loop with "Wait and Advance" synchronization model.

Before discussing the evaluation results, we must describe the structure of TOP-1 OS, since the above-mentioned evaluation programs executed on the TOP-1 OS and their statistical data are greatly affected by the OS structure. TOP-1 OS, implemented at Tokyo Research Laboratory, is a multiprocessor extension of the AIX PS/2 operating system. In TOP-1 OS, a modified AIX kernel runs on a dedicated processor attached to the hard disk controller. The other processors run user programs. In the following context, we use shorthand notations, KP and UP, to specify the processor dedicated to the kernel execution and those for user-mode execution, respectively. A user-mode process running on a UP is migrated to the KP when it asserts a kernel call, and then is dispatched to one of UPs after the completion of the kernel call. This scenario suggests that some amount of data sharing between UPs and between KP and UP is induced solely by process migration.

2.4.1.3 Measurement Conditions We measured various hardware statistics for the entire execution of gcc and espresso both of which take several thousand seconds to execute on TOP-1. The hardware statistics for the entire duration are simply summed and averaged. Only one UP is dedicated for the execution of the benchmark. Other UPs execute dummy tight loops which never generate any bus traffic, not to incur unnecessary process migration.

For the Livermore kernel 7 and 11, we used long-word data array of 1000 elements. Outer loop repetition is 10000 for both kernels, and intentional cache flush between each outer loop repetition is not performed. Owing to a practical reason, we used 8 UPs for this measurement.

As described earlier, the TOP-1 cache system provides four different types of cache protocol: the update-standard, invalidate-standard, update-BIO, and invalidate-BIO modes. BIO stands for Block I/O mode. Each processor can use each convenient cache protocol independently each other. It is interesting to see how the cache behaves under these protocols [8, 11]. Therefore, we measured statistics in four cases with regard to the cache protocol. In Case A, both UPs and KP are set to update mode. In Case B, on the other hand, all processors are set to invalidate mode. In Case C, the UPs are set to update mode, while the KP is set to invalidate mode. In this context, the standard mode is default, unless the BIO (block I/O mode) is specified. In Case D, the UPs are set to update mode, while the KP is set to invalidate-BIO mode. The measurements in Cases C and D imply that we would like to evaluate the effect of unnecessary data sharing between the KP and UPs due to the hardware affinity and the OS structure. Also, we would like to distinguish this extra KP-UP data sharing from the real data sharing of the application processes. Although it would be effective to change the cache mode of the KP from **standard** to **BIO** before starting page-in or file-read and then change it again from **BIO** to **standard** after finishing, we have not implemented such a sophisticated cache control in the TOP-1 OS. In the BIO mode, the KP always runs in the BIO mode.

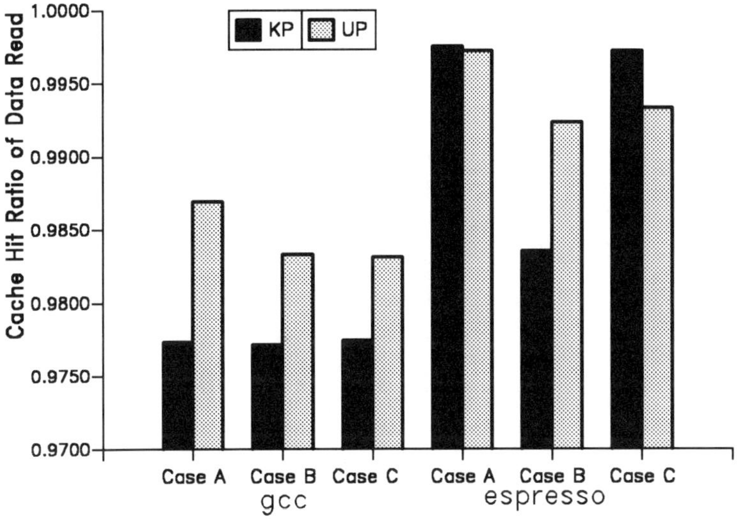

Figure 2.5
Cache Hit Ratio of Data Read (gcc and espresso)

2.4.2 Measurement Results and Considerations

2.4.2.1 Hit Ratio The first criteria of the cache evaluation is the cache hit ratio. Figure 2.5 and Figure 2.6 show the data hit ratio for the four benchmark programs in cases A, B and C of cache protocol combination (since the instruction hit ratio is much higher than the data hit ratio for all situations, we don't show it). The first remark is that the 128KB direct-mapping cache can provide considerably high data hit ratio even for applications with fairly large working set. Since 128KB cache can store 32 4KB physical pages and virtual memory scheme scatters the physical pages even if they have contiguous virtual addresses, the direct mapping cache can be still expected to provide considerably high data hit ratio even though the working set size is much larger than the cache size.

The second remark is that the invalidate mode always degrade the hit ratio but the degradation ratio is not so large, around 1%. An exception is the Livermore kernel 11 where the data hit ratio in Case B is degraded about 5% comparing with that in Case A, as you can see in Figure 2.6. Since, in Livermore kernel 11, the UPs synchronize the com-

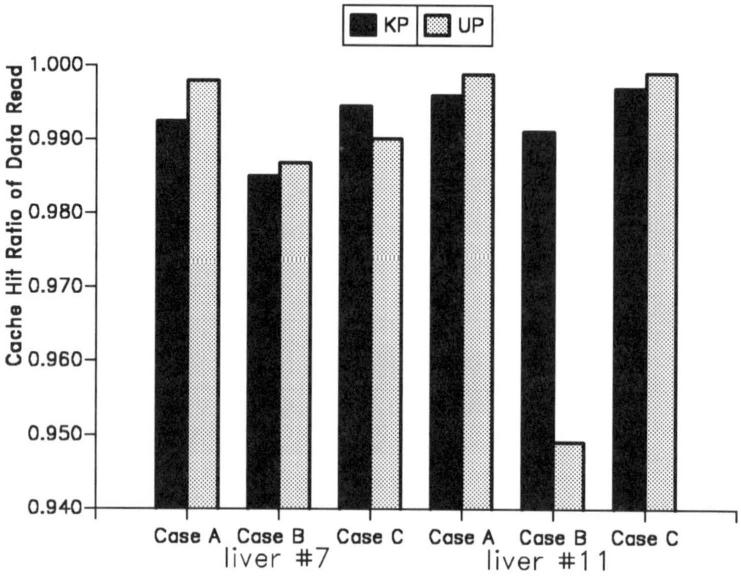

Figure 2.6
Cache Hit Ratio of Data Read (Livermore Loop #7 and #11)

pletion of the previous loop with 'Wait and Advance' synchronization model on a common semaphore, one execution of 'Advance' command by a UP incurs 7 times read misses by other 7 UPs. Therefore, this is apparently an example to show that the update type snoop protocol can achieve better performance than the invalidate type protocol when the processors tightly share a data block with frequent accesses.

2.4.2.2 Data Sharing To evaluate the cache behavior in terms of data sharing, we focus on the write-to-shared-data ratio and the snoop-write hit ratio. The write-to-shared-data ratio (WSDR) is a ratio of the number of processor writes to the shared data against the total number of processor writes. The snoop-write hit ratio (SWHR) specifies the ratio of the number of bus writes that hit the snooping cache against the total number of snoop transactions including both reads and writes.

Figure 2.7 and Figure 2.8 show the write-to-shared-data ratio (WSDR) for the four benchmark programs in cases A, B and C of cache protocol combination. The WSDR of UPs in Case A is much higher than that in Case C for all benchmarks (e.g., 14.6% vs 2.4% for gcc) even though

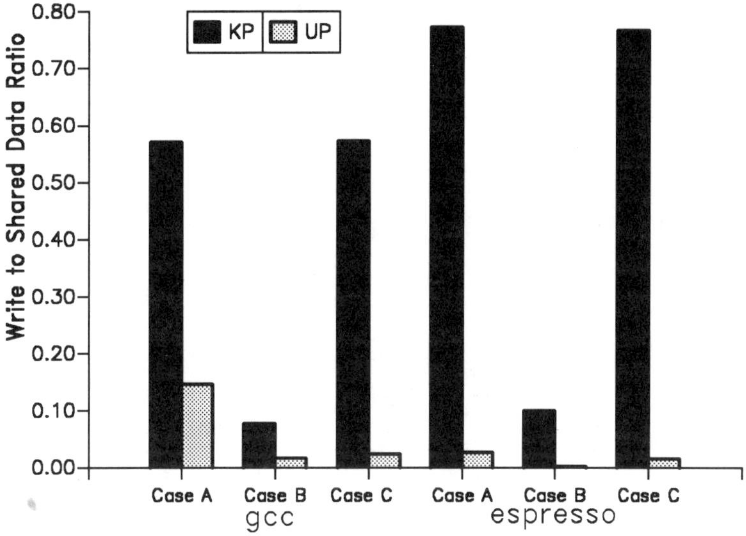

Figure 2.7
Write to Shared Data Ratio (gcc and espresso)

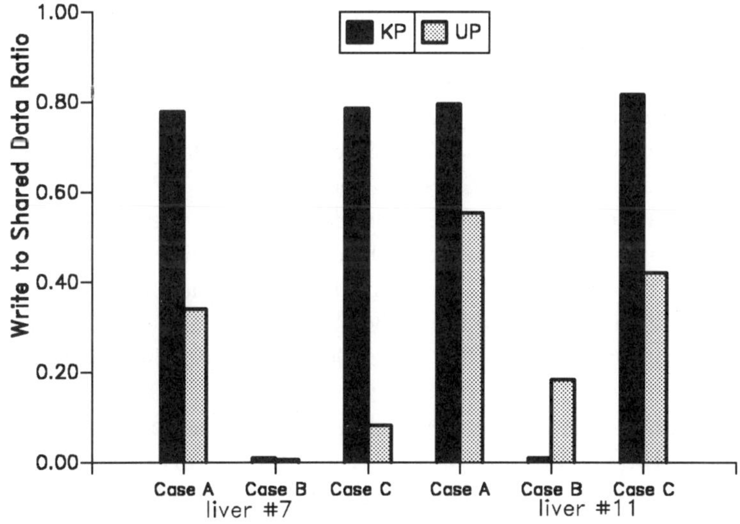

Figure 2.8
Write to Shared Data Ratio (livermore loop #7 and #11)

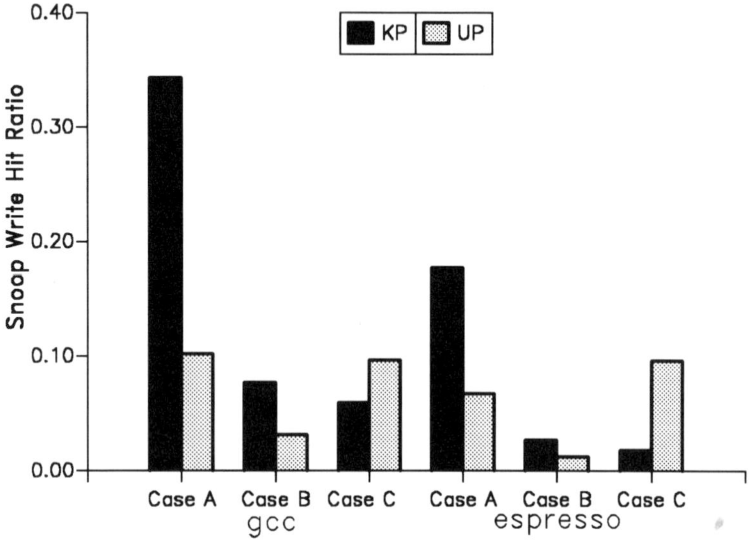

Figure 2.9
Snoop Write Hit Ratio (gcc and espresso)

the UPs are set to the update mode in both cases. This indicates that considerably large amount of data sharing occurs between KP and UPs.

When the KP is set to the invalidate mode (Case C), the first write by the UP invalidates the unnecessary shared data in the KP's cache, and hence the the succeeding write accesses by the UP can be write hits to the private data. When the KP is set in the update mode (Case A), on the other hand, the unnecessary shared data in KP's cache survive until they are evicted from the cache due to replacement. The SWHR shown in Figure 2.9 and Figure 2.10 can back up this assertion.

The SWHR of KP in Case C is much lower than that in Case A for all benchmarks (e.g., 5.9% vs 34.3% for gcc), since in Case C the unnecessary shared data in KP's cache are invalidated by a write access of a UP.

The WSDR of the KP is very high for all benchmarks when the UPs are set to the update mode (Cases A and C). In this benchmark execution, an implementation dependent feature of the OS probably incurs large amount of write accesses to shared data on the KP. Since the KP periodically executes a polling to examine UPs' status, the UP status data block is shared between the KP and the UP. Locked-accesses in a

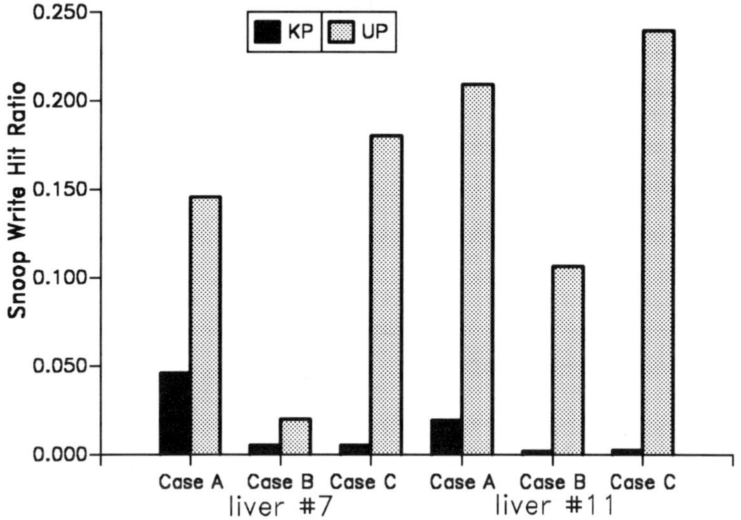

Figure 2.10
Snoop Write Hit Ratio (livermore loop #7 and #11)

polling loop generate write-to-shared-data accesses, unless the UP status data block is evicted or invalidated from the UP's cache. When the UPs are set to invalidate mode (in Case B), we can see that the WSDR of the KP is drastically reduced, since the UP status data block is invalidated from the UP's cache by the KP's first write access to the block.

The other remark in terms of data sharing, as we can see in Figure 2.8, is that the WSDR of UPs is considerably high when the programs really present data sharing such as Livermore kernels 7 and 11. Most of data sharing among UPs, however, can be eliminated when the invalidate mode is used for UPs, as shown in Case B of Figure 2.8. As we discussed in the previous section, it should be noted that the data hit ratio of the invalidate type protocol is largely degraded comparing to that of update type protocol when the processors tightly share a data block with frequent accesses as shown in Livermore kernel 11 of Figure 2.6.

To evaluate the effect of unnecessary data sharing between the KP and UPs due to the hardware affinity and the OS structure, we also measured the statistics data in the cache mode combination of Case D where the UPs are set to update mode, while the KP is set to invalidate-BIO mode. Figure 2.11 shows the WSDR of the UP and the SWHR of

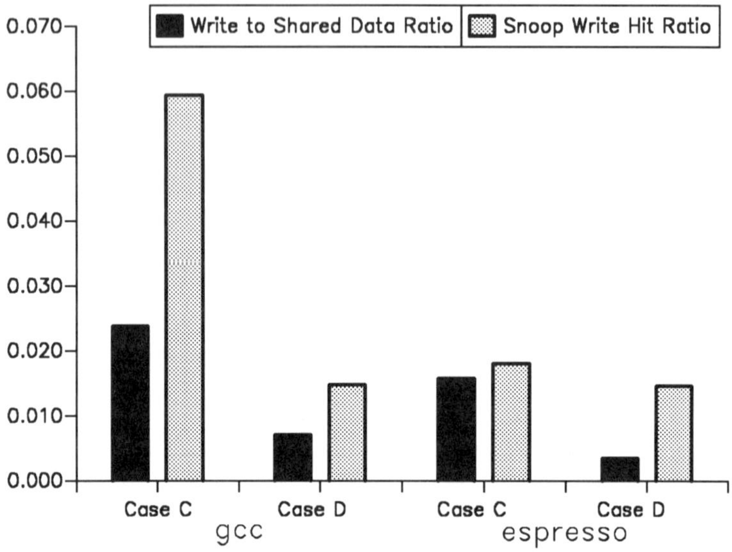

Figure 2.11
Write to Shared Data Ratio of User Processor and Snoop Write Hit Ratio of Kernel Processor

the KP for gcc and espresso benchmarks, since both of these statistics represent the effect of the shared data residing in the KP's cache. This result shows that the BIO mode effectively reduces the extra data sharing between KP and UP due to process migrations induced by system calls such as page-fault and file-read. However, it should be noted that the BIO mode makes the cache hit ratio of the KP lower, because the cache line is immediately flushed out from the cache whenever the processor writes the last word of the cache line. Since the KP always runs in BIO mode in case of TOP-1 OS implementation, the KP's cache hit ratio is probably degraded especially for stack operations. Thus, we should turn the BIO mode on and off before and after the block I/O operation in the OS.

2.4.2.3 Snoop Interference As previously described, the TOP-1 cache employs a duplicated tag memory so that the MPU can access the cache tag memory in parallel with the snooping hardware. Cache access conflicts will occur only when either the MPU or the snooping hardware updates the tag memory in the same cycle, or when both the MPU and

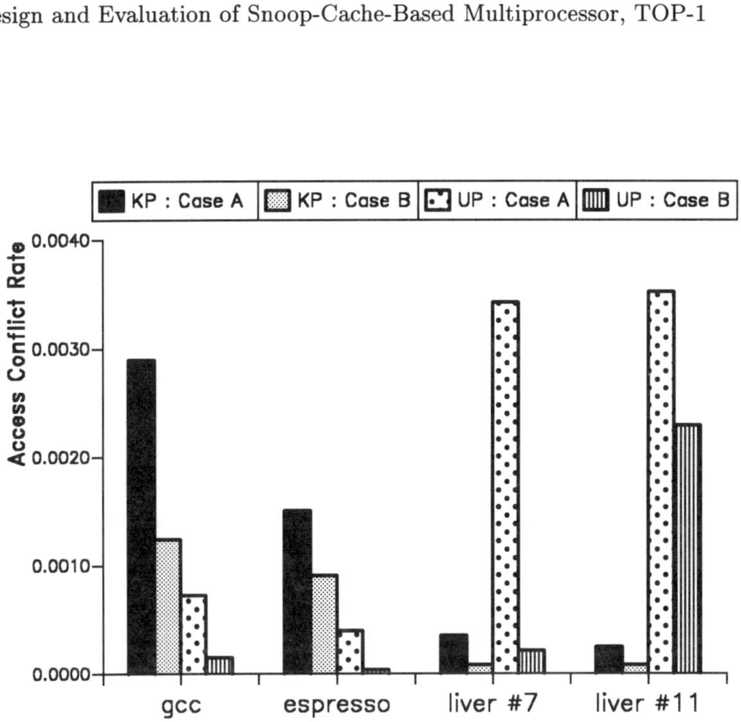

Figure 2.12
Access Conflict Rate between Snooping and Processor Accesses

the snooping hardware access the cache data memory in the same cycle. Figure 2.12 shows the cache access conflict rate for the four benchmark programs in Cases A and B cache mode combination. Here, 0.010 means that one of a hundred processor accesses is blocked by snooping and is delayed by one cycle. As shown in Figure 2.12, the conflict rates are so small that the snoop interference overhead is negligible. Major reason is due to the TOP-1 bus protocol design.

In the TOP-1 design, each bus transfer such as a miss-read access, a copy-back transfer and a write access to the shared data occupies around 7 bus clock duration, and requires one cycle for snoop tag read and one additional cycle for tag memory update and/or data cache array access. This indicates that the snoop interference ratio is one 7th at most even if the bus is 100% used and the MPU accesses the cache every cycle.

In practical, the average bus utilization is around 10% as shown in Table 2.2 and Table 2.3. The MPU memory access ratio is about 50%. These facts indicate that the access conflict rate is impossibly so high without regard to the cache protocol used. This is an implementation specific fact, but not a general fact. If the bus is designed to be heavily used, each bus transfer occupies the snooping cache for a long duration, and the MPU generates very frequent memory accesses as in case of RISC processors, the snoop interference overhead should be a serious performance degradation factor. Thus, we would like to know the effect of the snoop protocol to the snoop interference overhead. The update mode always has a slightly higher conflict rate for all four benchmarks, because the cache controller must update the cache data memory and occasionally the tag memory when snoop write hits take place. The invalidate mode, on the other hand, updates (invalidates) only the tag memory, and consecutive invalidations to the same cache line never occur as long as the invalidated processor accesses the data again.

2.4.2.4 Processor Performance and Bus Traffic Needless to say, the processor has optimal performance when it runs with **no wait memory access**. TOP-1's cache system allows no wait memory accesses as long as processor accesses are read hits or write hits to private data. However, it needs some wait cycles when a cache miss or a write access to the shared cache line occurs. Copy back transfer of a dirty cache line adds extra wait cycles when a cache miss occurs. Furthermore, the snoop interference overhead discussed in the previous section also increases the wait cycles and hence degrades the processor performance. We believe that looking at the average memory access cycle is a good way to evaluate the system performance. Figure 2.13 shows the average wait cycle for the four benchmark programs in the same presentation style with Figure 2.12. Here 0.10 of the average wait cycle, for instance, means that a memory access which consists of two clock cycles in case of i386 needs 0.1 additional clock cycles due to the wait on average. Hence, 0.1 wait cycle means 5% degradation of memory access performance comparing to an ideal memory system of no-wait. Since the MPU memory access ratio is about 50% as mentioned previously, 5% degradation of memory access probably corresponds to 2.5% degradation of the processor performance. These results shown in Figure 2.13 indicate that the UPs run with an overhead of only a few percent for all benchmarks without regard to its protocol type used. Roughly speaking, Figure 2.13 indicates that the invalidation protocol gives slightly better performance for almost all situations, since it can naturally eliminate unnecessary data sharing, although the fact is possibly dependent on the OS implementation. In fact, we can see that the update proto-

	gcc				espresso			
	Case A		Case B		Case A		Case B	
	KP	UP	KP	UP	KP	UP	KP	UP
Cache Miss	0.0154	0.0173	0.0112	0.0204	0.0036	0.0022	0.0014	0.0047
Write to Shared Data	0.0391	0.0228	0.0054	0.0028	0.0394	0.0040	0.0052	0.0002
Replace	0.0041	0.0050	0.0043	0.0073	0.0005	0.0007	0.0005	0.0009
Subtotal	0.0586	0.0451	0.0208	0.0306	0.0435	0.0070	0.0071	0.0059
Total	0.1037		0.0515		0.0506		0.0131	

Table 2.2
Bus Utilization (gcc and espresso)

	Livermore #7				Livermore #11			
	Case A		Case B		Case A		Case B	
	KP	UP	KP	UP	KP	UP	KP	UP
Cache Miss	0.0039	0.0083	0.0041	0.0401	0.0008	0.0003	0.0027	0.0985
Write to Shared Data	0.0389	0.1401	0.0004	0.0031	0.0391	0.0950	0.0004	0.0287
Replace	0.0002	0.0009	0.0003	0.0015	0.0002	0.0004	0.0003	0.0010
Subtotal	0.0431	0.1493	0.0049	0.0447	0.0401	0.0958	0.0035	0.1282
Total	0.1924		0.0496		0.1359		0.1317	

Table 2.3
Bus Utilization (livermore loop #7 and #11)

col gives better performance for the Livermore 11 benchmark where the processors tightly share a data block with frequent accesses.

The average wait cycle should be in proportion to the bus traffic generated by each processor except an effect of the snoop interference overhead. Thus, we would like to know the bus traffic details separately in cache-miss traffic, shared-write traffic, and copy-back traffic. Table 2.2 and Table 2.3 show the results. Here, 0.1 means 10% bus usage to the total bus bandwidth. In Case A for all benchmarks, shared-write traffic is majority, while the miss-read traffic is majority in Case B where both KP and UPs are set to invalidate mode. This trend is more apparently observed for the parallel programs such as Livermore kernels. This can be derived from the previous discussion on the data sharing and the cache hit.

2.5 Summary

We have described the unique hardware features of the TOP-1 memory system, explaining and evaluating the design choices we made. The unique architectural features are the mechanism that allows several different snoop protocols to coexist, the high-speed bus-locking mechanism to allow in-cache semaphore on any address boundary, the two-way interleaved dual 64-bit buses, and the efficient and fair arbitration mechanism. The statistics unit is especially useful for evaluating the design

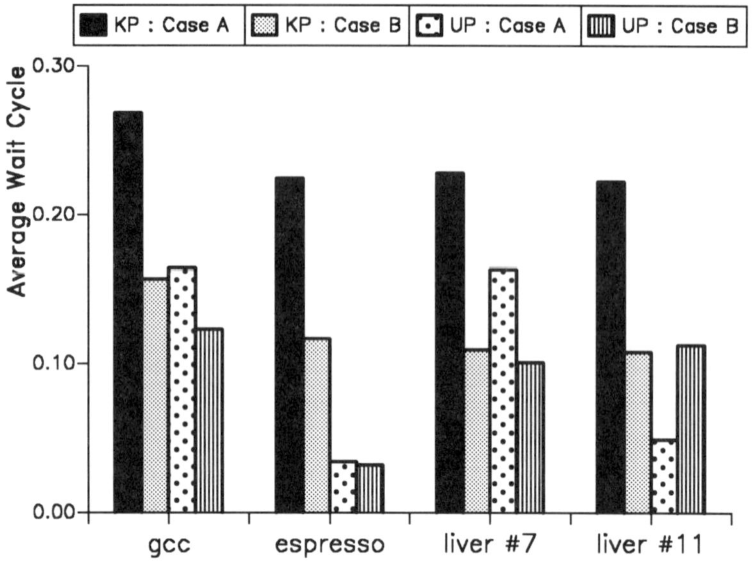

Figure 2.13
Access Wait Cycle

precisely and for controlling various aspects of the hardware mechanism dynamically to give a better performance. It will also be valuable for developing highly parallel software. The TOP-1 hardware is now fully operational and several machines have been built.

The update mode provides high cache-hit ratios but has a high data-sharing rate. When the update mode protocol is used, it is necessary to take account of unnecessary data sharing. In other words, a mechanism to invalidate unnecessary data sharing is needed. The block I/O mode also reduces the write-to-shared-data ratio, but it must be controlled according to OS operations.

Acknowledgments

The authors would like to thank Dr. Norihisa Suzuki and Toshiaki Kurokawa who initiated and managed TOP-1 research project, respectively. We want to thank the members of the Workstation Systems and Parallel System groups in Tokyo Research Laboratory, IBM Japan Ltd.

for technical discussions. Especially, we thank Mr. Munehiro Fukuda who gave us the measurement data for the Livermore kernels.

References

[1] J. Archibald and J. L. Baer *Cache Coherence Protocols: Evaluation Using a Multiprocessor Simulation Model* ACM Trans. on Computer Systems, Vol. 4, No. 4, pp. 273 - 298, 1986.

[2] R. R. Atkinson and E. M. McCreight *The Dragon Processor* Proceedings of the Second International Conference on ASPLOS, pp. 65 - 69, 1987.

[3] S. J. Eggers and R.H. Katz *A Characterization of Sharing in Parallel Programs and Its Application to Coherency Protocol Evaluation* Proceedings of the 15th Annual International Symposium on Computer Architecture, pp. 373 - 382, 1988.

[4] S. J. Eggers and R.H. Katz *Evaluating the Performance of Four Snooping Cache Coherence Protocols* Proceedings of the 16th Annual International Symposium on Computer Architecture, pp. 2 - 15, 1989.

[5] J. R. Goodman *Using Cache Memory to Reduce Processor-Memory Traffic* Proceedings of the 10th International Symposium on Computer Architecture, pp. 124 - 131, 1983.

[6] R. Katz et al. *Implementing a Cache Consistency Protocol* Proceedings of the 12th International Symposium on Computer Architecture, pp. 276 - 283, 1985.

[7] R. L. Lee et al. *Multiprocessor Cache Design Considerations* Proceedings of the 14th International Symposium on Computer Architecture, pp. 253 - 262, 1987.

[8] N. Oba, A. Moriwaki, and S. Shimizu *TOP-1: A Snoop-Cache-Based Multiprocessor* Proceedings of the 9th IEEE International Phoenix Conference on Computers and Communications, pp. 101 - 108, 1990.

[9] N. Suzuki *Parallel Lisp: Languages and Systems* Lecture Notes in Computer Science 441, Springer-Verlag, pp. 353 - 363, 1990.

[10] C. P. Thacker and L. C. Stewart *Firefly: a Multiprocessor Workstation* Proceedings of the Second International Conference on ASPLOS, pp. 164 - 172, 1987.

[11] N. Yamanouchi *Performance Effects of Program Structures on a Snoop-Cached Multiprocessor System* Proceedings of the International Conference on InfoJapan '90, pp. 339 - 346, 1990.

3 Symbolic Computation Algorithms on Shared Memory Multiprocessors

E. M. Clarke, S. Kimura, D. E. Long, S. Michaylov, S. A. Schwab, and J. P. Vidal

We describe the implementation of three symbolic computation algorithms on shared memory multiprocessors. We also evaluate the performance of the implementations, point out some of their common characteristics, and describe why these algorithms should be able to take advantage of the large scale heterogeneous shared memory machines currently being developed.

3.1 Introduction

Symbolic computation algorithms have proven useful in a wide range of applications from formal verification to computer algebra. However, the time required by these algorithms restricts the size of the problems which can be solved. In light of this, it is somewhat surprising that there have been few parallel implementations of these algorithms. One possible reason is the inherent complexity of these algorithms; obtaining a good sequential implementation can require deep knowledge of the problem domain and extensive programming skills. In this paper, we consider typical symbolic algorithms from three different areas: theorem proving, computer aided design, and computer algebra. We show that on a shared memory multiprocessor each of the algorithms has a natural decomposition into parallel processes. We evaluate the performance of each algorithm on several different multiprocessors in order to gain an understanding of what architectural features facilitate the construction of such a program.

There are two obvious ways of obtaining faster symbolic algorithms. The first is to use new insight into the problem domain to improve the algorithm. This is certainly the most natural way of obtaining a faster algorithm, but it may be quite difficult in practice to gain such insight. Building a parallel implementation of the algorithm also has some drawbacks. One of the most serious is that a parallel implementation may not be able to take advantage of all the optimizations possible in a sequential algorithm. Nevertheless, in many cases it is possible to obtain near linear speedup using parallelism. This can have a dramatic effect on the usefulness of the algorithm. In this paper, we consider three implementations of symbolic algorithms. Each required a considerable amount of programming effort as well as study of the problem domain. We believe that our results are realistic and demonstrate what can be achieved by using parallelism. We briefly describe each of the three problems below.

Resolution theorem proving forms the basis for logic programming and is used in many automated reasoning systems. The OTTER [20] theorem proving system has been used to discover new results in combinatory logic. Stickel's Prolog Technology Theorem Prover [24] demonstrated that resolution systems could achieve high inference rates. Parallel logic programming languages are currently the focus of intense research [26]. We discuss a parallel resolution theorem prover called Parthenon [3] which uses or-parallel Prolog technology to achieve good performance.

Boolean decision diagrams are an efficient symbolic representation for boolean functions [6]. They are rapidly becoming widely used in circuit verification [10, 15] and simulation [5]. There have been a number of highly optimized sequential implementations [4]. Nevertheless, the enormous complexity of modern VLSI designs can strain the capabilities of these systems. We describe a parallel implementation of the boolean decision diagram manipulation routines [18].

The last example is a parallel implementation of the Gröbner basis algorithm. This algorithm has a large number of applications. In particular, it can be used to find exact solutions of systems of polynomial equations. The algorithm is a key component of most symbolic mathematics systems such as Mathematica, Scratchpad, and Maple. There have been several good sequential implementations such as that in the Macaulay system. An implementation on a Cray X-MP using a vectorized big number package is described by Neun and Melenk [22]. Vidal [25] was apparently the first to develop a parallel implementation of the algorithm for a shared memory multiprocessor. Schwab [23] has demonstrated additional performance benefits by utilizing two levels of parallelism.

We evaluated our implementations on three different architectures. We were primarily concerned with three issues: speedup, memory access patterns, and difficulty in programming and debugging. In the next four sections, we describe the machine architectures and the three parallel implementations in more detail. We sketch how each algorithm works and give performance statistics for the various machines. In the conclusion, we propose some general principles about symbolic computation on shared memory multiprocessors that we have learned from the examples we have considered.

3.2 Shared memory architectures

A wide variety of multiprocessor architectures have been described in the literature over the past few years. The characteristics of these architectures vary widely and are determined by the available technology, the class of applications addressed, the trade-offs between processor speed, memory system complexity and communication costs, and other design decisions. In this paper, we describe algorithms implemented on three shared memory architectures.

The Encore Multimax is a classic shared memory multiprocessor using a central bus for communication between processors and main memory. Each processor has a local cache and uses a snooping protocol to maintain cache coherency. The Multimax is suitable for medium and coarse grained parallel applications [13]. The particular machine used in these experiments had 16 National Semiconductor 32332 processors, each rated at roughly 2 MIPS, and 32 megabytes of shared memory. The local cache size is 64K bytes.

The RP3 is a large-scale research parallel processor developed at the T. J. Watson Research Center. The machine consists of a number of processor-memory elements connected by an Omega-interconnection network. Local memory references are handled immediately, while remote memory references must be resolved over the network. The architecture provides three types of memory pages: local pages, global pages, and replicated pages. The machine does not support automatic cache coherency; instead, cache management is the responsibility of the programmer or compiler [17]. The virtual memory interface allows each page to be marked as cacheable or non-cacheable, as well as allowing the cache to be flushed under user level control. The current version of the system has 64 ROMP processors. Each processor has 8 megabytes of storage, and a 64K byte local cache.

The Plus architecture [2] is a mesh of processor-memory elements connected by a deterministic routing network. Remote memory references are transparently routed to the appropriate destination. In addition several special features enhance this basic design. Local computation proceeds while remote writes are being completed, increasing overall throughput. When needed, a fence operation is used to stall the local processor until all remote writes have completed. Also, any page in memory may be replicated to other processing nodes. Reads from these replicated pages are handled locally, while writes are directed to the master copy of the page and transparently propagated to all replicated copies. Tuning an application to run on this architecture involves studying reference patterns of the algorithm and selecting a memory replication scheme that minimizes remote read references, while limiting remote writes and overall network traffic. This type of architecture is expected to perform better than a pure message-passing architecture because additional hardware supports the remote memory references, as opposed to a software layer processing these memory requests. The experiments described in the paper were run on the Plus simulator. A machine with 40 nodes is currently under construction.

These implementations were all written in C and use the C-Threads package [12], which allows parallel programming under the MACH operating system [8]. The programming model provided by C-Threads is one of many executing processes sharing a common global address space. Synchronization is provided through locks for mutual exclusion and conditions for waiting and signaling of events. The model is augmented on the non-uniform memory access machines to provide for the assignment of specific threads to specific processors, and for controlling the placement and replication policy of memory pages.

3.3 Parthenon: a resolution theorem prover

An area of symbolic computation where parallelism is just beginning to be applied is automated theorem proving. Most procedures for theorem proving are highly nondeterministic, since at each step of the procedure there are typically a number of inference rules which may be applied, and each inference rule can usually be applied to a large number of axioms. This leads to a combinatorial explosion in the search for a proof, and while attempts to limit this explosion have been partially successful, large search spaces still result.

Parthenon is a parallel theorem prover which uses Loveland's model elimination procedure [19]. Stickel recognized that model elimination is in fact very similar to Prolog's SLD resolution and used this observation in his Prolog Technology Theorem Prover (PTTP) [24]. By using sequential Prolog implementation techniques, he was able to obtain a very fast system. We have taken these ideas further by applying or-parallel

Prolog implementation technology to achieve a fast parallel model elimination implementation.

3.3.1 Model elimination

The model elimination procedure is a variant of resolution with two inference rules. Given a set of input clauses, it can be used to prove that the clauses are unsatisfiable. Each inference rule operates on a chain, which is essentially a clause with certain literals regarded as special. We will refer to the special literals as framed literals and indicate them by placing them in a box. The inference rules are:

Extension To perform an extension operation on a chain, we must find an input clause which contains a literal that unifies with the rightmost literal in the chain. We then turn the rightmost literal of the chain into a framed literal and add the other literals of the input clause to the right of the chain, applying the unifying substitution.

Reduction If the rightmost literal of a chain unifies with a framed literal in the chain, we may delete the rightmost literal. Again we must apply the unifying substitution.

Framed literals at the right of a chain are always deleted. The procedure starts from one of the input clauses (which is regarded as a chain with no framed literals.)

As an example, we prove that $\exists x\, p(x)$ follows from the single assumption $\exists a\, \forall y\, (\neg p(a) \rightarrow p(y))$. Negating the desired conclusion and putting the statements into clause form gives the two clauses $\neg p(x)$ and $p(a) \vee p(y)$. We start the model elimination procedure from the chain $\neg p(x)$.

1.	$\neg p(x)$	initial chain
2.	$\boxed{\neg p(a)} \vee p(y)$	extension, $x = a$
3.	$\square$ (the empty clause)	reduction, $y = a$

3.3.2 Searching for a proof

In an or-parallel search, multiple processes can attempt to apply different inference steps in parallel with the restriction that if a conjunction must be proved, the individual conjuncts must be proved sequentially. In the context of the model elimination procedure, or-parallel search corresponds to trying the different extension and reduction possibilities for a chain in parallel. Since it is possible to have infinite chains of inferences which do not lead to a proof, it must be possible to guarantee that no inference is postponed indefinitely. One possible way to insure this would be to perform a breadth first search of all possible proofs, but the space required for this quickly becomes prohibitive. A better alternative is to perform a depth first search to a specific depth bound, and if no proof is found, to increase the bound and try again. This technique is called depth first iterative deepening. It would seem that this technique is very wasteful, since some parts of the tree are searched many times, but it is possible to show that it is within a constant factor of optimal. Furthermore, this constant factor is the average branching factor of the search. Hence, we can expect the speedup from parallelism to dominate this cost.

Each process in Parthenon performs a bounded depth first backtracking search of a different part of the search space. When a process exhausts its part of the space, it can obtain a new subtree from one of the other processes and continue searching there. A distributed scheduling algorithm handles the distribution of work to processes. In the remainder of this section, we give details on the or-parallel search, details of the scheduling algorithm, and some performance figures for Parthenon.

3.3.3 Representing the search space

The goal of Parthenon's inference mechanism is to make each individual resolution step as fast as possible. Like Stickel's PTTP, it exploits the similarity between model elimination and Prolog's SLD resolution to make model elimination efficient. In a Prolog system, each derived clause is represented by the inferences used to derive the clause. The individual inference steps are activation records on a stack, each describing which input clause was used in the inference step and what variable bindings were made in the input clause. To perform an inference step, a new activation record is added to the current stack of activation records, and variables are bound during unification. This process will often involve making new variable bindings in the original activation record chain, i.e., specializing some of the variables in the original clause. If the search fails at some point, other input clauses must be tried, and hence we must be able to undo this specialization. In order to accomplish this, another stack called the trail is used. Whenever a variable is bound, we record this fact in the trail and record the height of the trail in the activation record we are building. When backtracking, we pop activation records from the stack and unbind any variables indicated by the trail.

The model elimination extension step is almost exactly the same as Prolog's resolution step, and can be implemented in the above manner quite easily. The reduction operation is only slightly more expensive; it requires searching back through the stack of activation records to find the framed literals in the current chain.

When multiple processes can search in parallel, it is necessary to represent several chains simultaneously. We do this by having multiple stacks of activation records. In addition, if two chains were derived from a common ancestor chain, they will also share the activation records corresponding to that ancestor. This is done for two reasons.

1. There is never any need to copy an entire chain from some other process when performing an inference.
2. In order to ensure that inferences are not duplicated or omitted, it is necessary to have information about the possible inferences stored in a central location. Since this information is associated with each chain, it is natural to store it in the activation records and use locks in the activation records to coordinate access.

Because of this sharing of activation records, it may be the case that two chains with a common ancestor have incompatible bindings for some variables. Therefore, each process must be able to have its own set of bindings. This is accomplished by giving each process a semi-private binding array. This binding array corresponds directly to the variable stack in a Prolog implementation. When a process moves to a different part of the search tree, it must update this binding array in some manner. This is done by augmenting the trail to record the bindings of variables as well as which variables were bound. When a process wants to start working at an activation record, it uses the portion of the trail indicated by that record to fill in its binding array.

One key point is that almost all references made by a process can be considered local. Each binding array is associated with a single process, and the activation records and trail are stored in a distributed fashion as well. In particular, activation records and trail entries which are created by a process are created locally. The only time a process references nonlocal memory is when moving to a part of the search tree which was created by a different process. Measurements show that because of the large amount of work available in theorem proving contexts, this is very rare. Thus, we expect that Parthenon would run well on the heterogeneous shared memory machines currently being developed. We are currently experimenting with running Parthenon on the Plus simulator to verify this claim.

3.3.4 Coordinating the search

There are a number of desirable, but sometimes mutually exclusive, properties for a scheduling algorithm in a system like Parthenon.

1. It should have low overhead in terms of time and space.
2. It should be scalable to large numbers of processes.
3. It should keep all the processes busy.
4. It should assign large jobs to processes so as to minimize context switch overhead.

Fortunately, in a theorem proving context, there is a large amount of available parallelism due to the high branching factors (often considerably greater than 2) in many problems. Hence, simple distributed scheduling algorithms which have the first two properties may also satisfy the last two constraints. A more complicated distributed scheduling algorithm (such as those used in or-parallel Prolog systems [11]) or a global scheduling algorithm might be better able to assign processes to jobs when work is scarce. However, because of the nature of the problem, any advantage is likely to be slight. In addition, complicated distributed algorithms typically have more overhead than simple schemes, and global scheduling algorithms do not scale well.

In Parthenon, when a process searches for a job, it essentially performs a depth first, left to right traversal of the search tree. There are a few refinements to this basic strategy.

1. A process begins searching at its current node. Because long distance moves correlate with extensive updates to the binding array, it is best if a new job can be found close to the old one.
2. If a process finishes traversing the tree without having found a job, it repeats the search starting from the root of the tree.
3. A pure left to right traversal tends to result in situations where many processes are working in the left part of the tree and few are working in

the right part. In order to achieve a better distribution of work, subtrees where there are few other processes should be preferred to subtrees where there are many other processes. To implement this, each node in the tree contains a count of the number of processes working in the subtree rooted at that node. When a process moves deeper in the tree, it moves to the subtree with the smallest count. Ties are broken by favoring nodes to the left.

Some care must be taken during traversal and modification of the tree to ensure mutual exclusion at various points. For example, when a node is being removed from the tree, we must make sure that other processes do not try to enter the node. Another error which must be prevented is having two processes both take the same job. To avoid such problems, each node in the tree contains a lock. The rules for using these locks are as follows.

1. When checking for alternatives, creating a child node, etc., the current node must be locked.
2. When moving from the current node to one of its children or to its parent, both the current node and the destination node must be locked.

To avoid deadlocks, whenever a process must acquire two locks the node closest to the root of the tree is always locked first.

3.3.5 Implementation, performance and evaluation

We have tested Parthenon on a large number of examples used by Stickel. For the problems requiring more extensive searches, the inference rates show an almost linear speedup with the number of processes. This is probably because most theorem proving problems have relatively high branching factors. The data in this section represent single runs, but the measurements are repeatable.

Figure 3.1 gives speedup curves for the Multimax, and figure 3.2 gives speedup curves for the RP3. Each figure consists of two graphs, representing two different problems. Each graph has two curves which show the speedup in inferences per second (solid curve) and the speedup in execution times (dotted curve). For the RP3, the speedup values were calculated relative to the 10 or 20 process case, i.e., a factor of 2 speedup going from 10 to 20 or 20 to 40 processes was considered perfect. For the problem which was not run with 10 processes, we calculated the speedups by assuming that the 20 process case had a speedup of exactly 2. We should point out that the RP3 does not support cache coherency in hardware, and that Parthenon was originally written assuming that such support would be available. We modified Parthenon slightly for the RP3; for example, the variable stacks were made to reside in the local memory of the appropriate process. However, the RP3 implementation certainly does not take full advantage of the machine.

3.4 Boolean decision diagrams

An ordered boolean decision diagram [6] is an acyclic graph representation for boolean functions. Because this representation provides a canonical form (two functions are logically equivalent if and only if they have the same form) and is quite succinct in many cases, it has become widely used in CAD applications. However, the construction of boolean decision diagrams for certain large or particularly complex boolean functions can be very time consuming. In this section, we present a parallel algorithm for this task and describe its implementation.

3.4.1 Boolean decision diagrams and finite automata

Our approach to boolean decision diagrams uses some simple ideas from finite automata theory. If we fix an ordering of the variables, then an n-argument boolean function can be identified with the set of boolean vectors that make it true. For example, the function denoted by the boolean expression $x_1 \wedge x_2 + \neg x_2 \wedge x_3$ with the variable ordering $x_1 < x_2 < x_3$ is uniquely represented by the set of vectors

$$\{(1,1,0),(1,1,1),(0,0,1),(1,0,1)\}.$$

The corresponding set of strings $\{110, 111, 001, 101\}$ is a finite language. Since all finite languages are regular, there is a minimal finite automaton that accepts this set. This automaton provides a canonical representation for the original boolean function. Since each node in the state-transition graph for a boolean function will have at most two successors (one for 0 and one for 1), we can view this graph as a boolean decision diagram for the function.

Logical operations on boolean functions can be implemented by set operations on the languages accepted by the finite automata: logical *and*

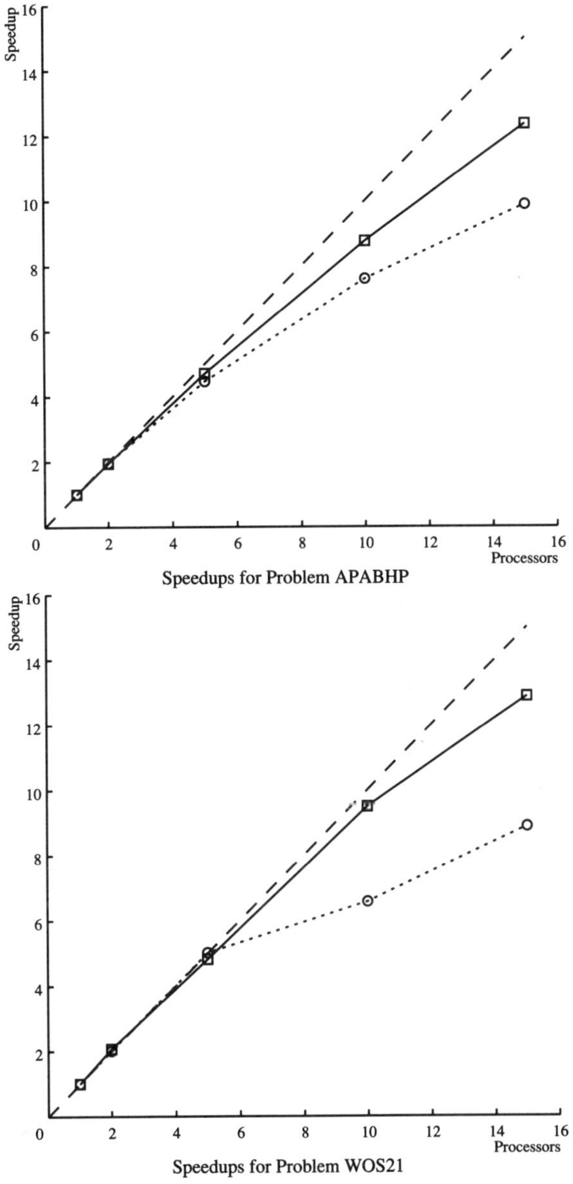

Figure 3.1
Multimax speedup curves for Parthenon

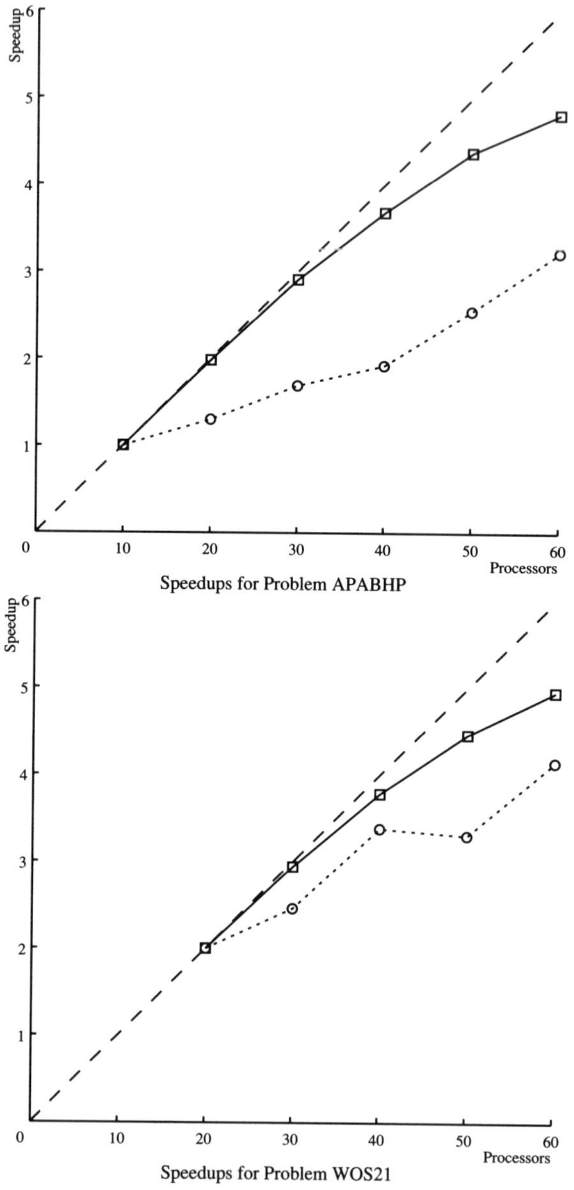

Figure 3.2
RP3 speedup curves for Parthenon

corresponds to set intersection, logical *or* corresponds to set union, and logical *not* corresponds to set complement (with respect to the set of all boolean strings of length n.) Standard constructions from elementary automata theory are used to perform these set operations. For example, let $M_1 = (Q_1, \{0, 1\}, \delta_1, q_0^1, F_1)$ and $M_2 = (Q_2, \{0, 1\}, \delta_2, q_0^2, F_2)$ be the boolean decision diagrams for two n-variable boolean functions f_1 and f_2. Then an automaton for $f_1 \wedge f_2$ is given by $M = ((Q_1 \times Q_2) \cup \{\perp\}, \{0, 1\}, \delta_\wedge, (q_0^1, q_0^2), F_1 \times F_2)$, where $\perp$ denotes the sink state ($\delta_\wedge(\perp, 0) = \delta_\wedge(\perp, 1) = \perp$) for the product automaton. $\delta_\wedge$ is defined as

$$\delta_\wedge((q_1, q_2), a) = \begin{cases} (\delta_1(q_1, a), \delta_2(q_2, a)) \\ \qquad \text{if } \delta_1(q_1, a) \neq \perp_1 \text{ and } \delta_2(q_2, a) \neq \perp_2 \\ \perp \quad \text{otherwise} \end{cases}$$

$\perp_1$ and $\perp_2$ are sink states of M_1 and M_2 respectively. An example of this procedure is shown in figure 3.3. In this figure, M_1 corresponds to $(\neg x_1 \wedge \neg x_3 \vee x_1)$, and M_2 corresponds to $(\neg x_1 \wedge x_2 \wedge x_3) \vee (\neg x_1 \wedge \neg x_2) \vee (x_1 \wedge x_2) \vee (x_1 \wedge \neg x_2 \wedge \neg x_3)$. The result of the logical *and* operation is $(\neg x_1 \wedge \neg x_2 \wedge \neg x_3) \vee (x_1 \wedge \neg x_2 \wedge \neg x_3) \vee (x_1 \wedge x_2)$.

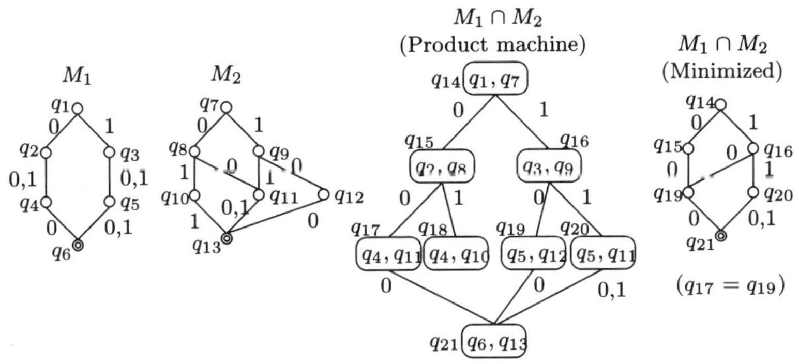

Figure 3.3
Product automaton generation for boolean decision diagrams

Automata for the other logical operations can be constructed in a similar manner. In general, determining the state set of the finite automaton for each of these operator involves a product construction. Also, in each case the resulting automaton may not be minimal. For this reason, a final minimization stage is needed after the product construction.

3.4.2 Implementation

We first describe the implementation of a single operation. Each operation consists of a product construction phase followed by a minimization phase. The construction of a product automaton begins with its initial state, i.e., the pair consisting of the initial states of the two argument automata. The successors of this state are determined for the inputs 0 and 1. As each pair of states is generated, it is entered into a queue of states to expand and into a hash table of generated pairs. When a pair is about to be produced, we check the hash table to see if it already exists. Pairs are removed from the queue and expanded in this manner until the queue becomes empty. In the minimization phase, states are processed starting at the lowest level and working upward. For each state, we hash its two successors and check a global hash table to determine if a state with those successors already exists. If not, the pair of successors is entered into the hash table along with a pointer to the state, and the state is returned. If such a state does exist, that state is returned. This procedure guarantees both that the result of an operation is a minimal automaton and that there are no equivalent states generated by operations which proceed in parallel. This last property is essential to control the storage requirements of the algorithm.

The above process of machine composition and state minimization is repeated once for each operation in the boolean formula. Some of these operations will be independent and may be performed in parallel. For example, to construct the boolean decision diagram for $f_1 \wedge f_2$, we may construct the decision diagrams for f_1 and f_2 in parallel before performing the final conjunction. More precisely, given a formula for which we wish to build the boolean decision diagram, the first step is to determine the level of each node in the parse tree for the formula. The leaf nodes of the tree are input variables; the non-leaf nodes correspond to the boolean operators that occur in the formula. The level of each node is determined by the rule:

1. The level of an input variable is 0.
2. The level of a non-leaf node is $max(l_1, l_2) + 1$, where l_1 and l_2 are levels of its operands.

The construction of the boolean decision diagram begins with level 0 nodes, which can be constructed immediately. In general, we can process a level i node as soon as all the level 1, 2, ..., $i-1$ nodes beneath it have been processed. Operations at the same level in the tree can be performed in parallel, since they do not conflict.

The levels at the top of the parse tree have only a few operations that can be performed in parallel. In order to extract more parallelism, we divide operations on such levels into several sub-operations. This can be done using Shannon's expansion:

$$f(x_1,\ldots,x_n) = \neg x_1 \wedge f(0,x_2,\ldots,x_n) \vee x_1 \wedge f(1,x_2,\ldots,x_n).$$

In the product and minimization phases, the 0 and 1 successors of the initial pair are generated. This corresponds to producing the initial states for $f(0,x_2,\ldots,x_n)$ and $f(1,x_2,\ldots,x_n)$. Then the product and minimization phases are performed (in parallel) for these two functions. We need one last merge step for the root state to complete the operation. Note that an operation can be decomposed further if needed using the above expansion.

An example of this procedure is shown in figure 3.4. This example is the same as that depicted in figure 3.3. To perform the operation, processor P_1 expands the 0 and 1 successors of the initial pair. Processor P_2 takes the 0 successor (q_2, q_8), generates the product automaton and minimizes it. Processor P_3 takes the 1 successor and does the same thing. After P_2 and P_3 have completed the minimization phase for their product automata, processor P_1 generates q_{14}.

3.4.3 Performance evaluation

We experimented with building the boolean decision diagrams for multipliers to evaluate the program. The decision diagrams for multipliers are known to grow quite rapidly (exponentially in the size of the operands, in fact.) Table 3.1 shows the execution time on the Multimax to construct decision diagrams for a multiplier with 10 bits (20 boolean variables). In the construction, there are 1726 operations (*and*: 527, *or*: 562, *not*: 0, *xor*: 307, *merge*: 330).

The execution time for a single processor is roughly the same as for the (sequential) program for constructing boolean decision diagrams described by Fisher and Bryant [14]. The graph in figure 3.5 shows the execution time speedup curve on the Multimax and Plus machines.

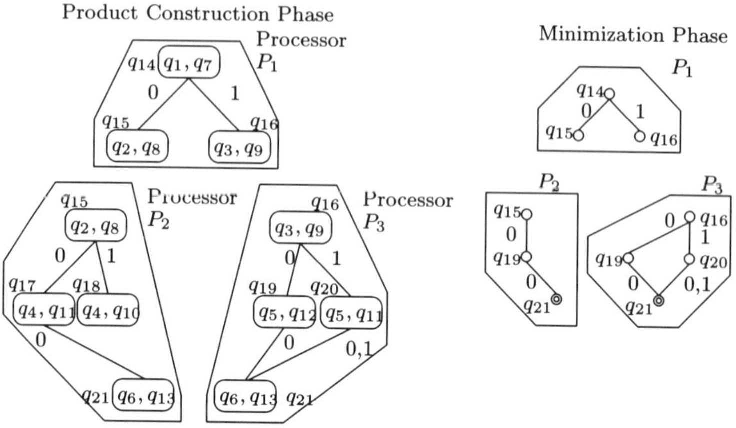

Figure 3.4
Decomposition of an operation for boolean decision diagrams

Processors	Seconds
1	1465.8
2	732.1
3	499.9
4	384.1
5	311.4
8	211.8
11	171.6
14	148.5
15	140.6

Table 3.1
BDD construction times for a 10 bit multiplier on the Multimax

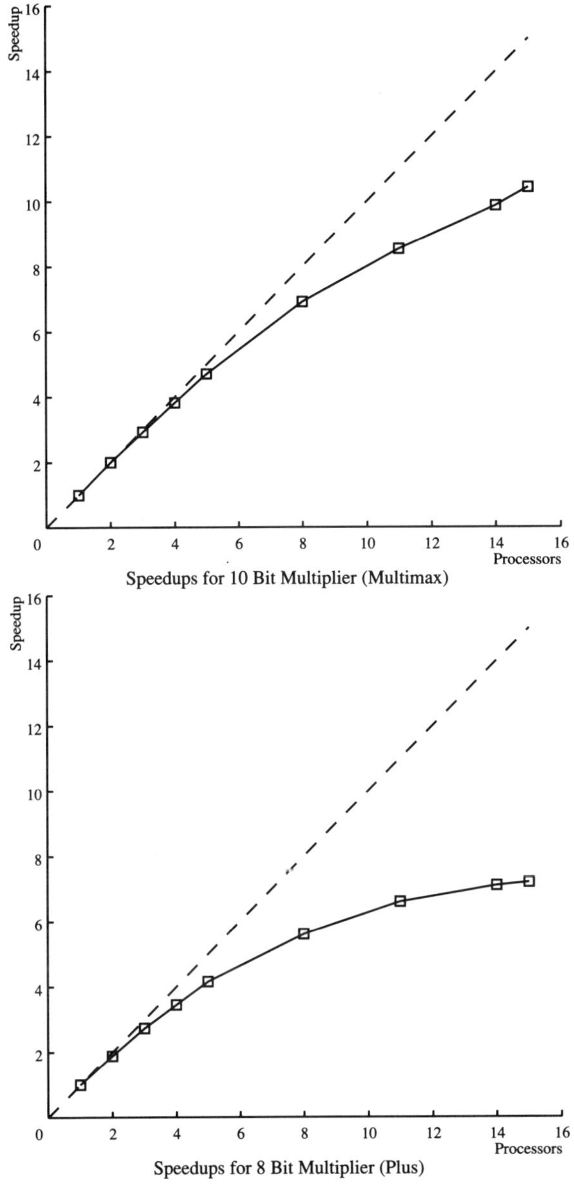

Figure 3.5
Speedup curve for 8-bit and 10-bit multiplier BDD construction

3.4.4 Manipulation of large decision diagrams

Even on a large machine, in some examples the number of states required is too large to fit in available memory. For example, we were originally unable to construct a boolean decision diagram for a 13-bit multiplier. To overcome this problem, we use the above decomposition to split the task into manageable pieces. Since the original parallel algorithm guarantees high-speed execution, each part of the boolean formula can be processed in reasonable time, and the total execution time is also reasonable. We were able to use this method to avoid running out of memory when it comparing the decision diagrams for two 16-bit multipliers. We divided the problem into 2048 parts. Each part required about 800,000 states for the decision diagrams took about 220 seconds to complete. The total execution time was about 100 hours.

3.5 Gröbner bases

Gröbner bases are one of the basic tools of computational algebraic geometry, the branch of mathematics which deals with the solution of sets of algebraic equations. Gröbner bases give a normal form to ideals in polynomials rings. Once a Gröbner basis is found for the corresponding ideals, it becomes easy to test if a polynomial belongs to an ideal, if two ideals are equal, if an ideal is contained in another, and so on. The interested reader is referred to Buchberger [7, 9], where one will find a complete introduction to Gröbner bases, a description of their computation, as well as a list of many applications. A review of the various attempts to parallelize the algorithm can be found in [25].

The algorithm transforms a set of polynomials into another set of polynomials, a Gröbner basis generating the same ideal. These polynomials are rational polynomials over some finite set of variables. While the theory behind the algorithm is quite complex, the actual computation is relatively simple to describe. This implementation is based on an algorithm given by Gebauer and Möller [16].

3.5.1 The basic algorithm

The primitive step of the computation, called reduction, involves deleting the first term of the current working polynomial, called the S-polynomial, by subtraction of an appropriate multiple of a polynomial already in the set. The result of this reduction is of lower order, but not necessarily smaller. A polynomial is totally reduced with respect to a set of polynomials when no further reduction is possible.

The S-polynomial of two polynomials already in the set is computed by finding the least common multiple of the leading terms, multiplying by appropriate monomials to make the two leading terms equal, and then finding the difference of these polynomials. Intuitively, each polynomial is scaled by the smallest factor such that the lead terms become equal; subtracting them cancels out the lead terms.

$$
\begin{aligned}
&\mathit{Spol}(P, Q) := \{ \\
&\quad G := \mathit{LCM}(\mathit{LeadingTerm}(P), \mathit{LeadingTerm}(Q)) \\
&\quad M_p := G/\mathit{LeadingTerm}(P) \\
&\quad M_q := G/\mathit{LeadingTerm}(Q) \\
&\quad \mathit{Spol} := M_p \cdot P - M_q \cdot Q \\
&\}
\end{aligned}
$$

$$
\begin{aligned}
&\mathit{Spol}(2x^2y + 3xy + 1, 3xy^2 + xy + 2y + 2) := \\
&\quad G = \mathit{LCM}(2x^2y, 3xy^2) = 6x^2y^2 \\
&\quad M_p = 6x^2y^2/2x^2y = 3y,\ M_q = 6x^2y^2/3xy^2 = 2x \\
&\quad \mathit{Spol} = 3y \cdot (2x^2y + 3xy + 1) - 2x \cdot (3xy^2 + xy + 2y + 2) \\
&\qquad\quad = -2x^2y + 9xy^2 - 4xy - 4x + 3y
\end{aligned}
$$

The simplest form of the algorithm can now be stated. Termination is guaranteed by restrictions on the ordering of terms in each polynomial. For our discussion, it is enough that such orderings exist.

The algorithm begins with the input set B, and constructs the set P of all pairs of distinct polynomials in B. Then, while pairs remain, the algorithm processes a pair from P. This processing consists of computing the S-polynomial of the pair, and then reducing it with the polynomials in B until no further reductions are possible. Sometimes, the S-polynomial reduces all the way to 0, in which case the algorithm proceeds to the next iteration of the loop with no additional work. However, if the S-polynomial reduces to a non-zero polynomial, then this new polynomial is added to the set B. In addition, the new polynomial is paired with each polynomial already in B, and these additional pairs are added to the set P. Eventually, the set of pairs is empty, and the algorithm terminates. It should be noted that while B is a Gröbner basis upon termination, a follow-up step to transform B into a reduced Gröbner basis is often needed. We have not addressed that step in this paper, although some of the techniques presented here can also be applied.

Of course, the order in which the pairs are selected is very important to the practical efficiency of the algorithm. One heuristic is to select the pair whose S-polynomial has the smallest leading term under the selected order. In addition, several tests have been developed to delete pairs whose S-polynomial will reduce to zero. These criteria can be found in [8, 16] and involve testing for certain constraints on the leading terms. The order in which reductions are performed is less well defined; in this implementation we use the order in which the polynomials first appear when searching for a reducing polynomial. Most of the computation time is spent in the S-polynomial and Reduction steps.

The typical computation described below consists of tens to hundreds of S-polynomial computations and hundreds to thousands of reduction steps. Because of the very rapid growth in the actual complexity of the problem, larger inputs will tend to produce polynomials with more terms and larger coefficients. In our sample executions, we observed that the total number of S-polynomials actually reduced does not grow as $|B|^2$, but at a somewhat greater than linear rate.

3.5.2 Coarse grain parallelism

The coarse grain parallelism in this algorithm consists of expanding and reducing several S-polynomials in parallel. A lock is used to ensure mutually exclusive access to the set of pairs P and the set of polynomials B. One potential bottleneck is access to these shared structures, which is minimal in the actual implementation. A greater problem, for small examples, is that processors may be left idle. This occurs because only a few pairs are produced at each stage in the algorithm. Also, in the parallel case, some pairs are expanded that would have been deleted in the sequential case. Typical data runs vary over a wide range, with small inputs taking milliseconds and modest ones hundreds or thousands of seconds on a sequential 2-MIPS processor. Other examples show greater than linear speedup, due to early reduction of pairs that prune part of the search space. As expected, larger inputs benefit the most from larger numbers of processors. However, inputs with very few large polynomials, or which produce only a limited number of pairs at any stage in the computation, benefit less from additional processors. Figure

3.6 presents the speedup versus number of processors for two examples from the research literature. (Box indicates Encore Multimax, Circle indicates IBM RP3, Triangle indicates Plus Simulator). On a single Multimax processor, the Rose example requires about 35 seconds, while the Trinks1 example requires only 10 seconds.

3.5.3 Fine grain parallelism

At the heart of the Gröbner basis computation is the operation of reduction, in which one polynomial is used to eliminate the most significant term from an initial polynomial. Speeding up this step is critical to improving the performance of the algorithm.

The source of fine-grain parallelism in the algorithm occurs in the reduction loop. The key observation of Melenk and Neun [21] is that the algorithm only branches based on the leading power product of the polynomials. This means that as soon as the first term of any polynomial is computed, the next step of the algorithm may begin concurrently with the computation of the remainder of the polynomial. We have implemented this approach explicitly in the program, as opposed to implicitly in a dataflow style as Melenk and Neun described.

The reduction loop consists of searching the list of polynomials for a reducing polynomial, then setting up the reduction, and finally performing it term by term. The critical observation here is that the next iteration of the loop will examine the terms in the same order as they are produced.

In order to exploit this parallelism, this implementation stores two synchronization fields with the polynomial. A size field keeps track of the number of terms and a done flag indicates that this polynomial is complete or still under construction. The reduction process begins as in the sequential case with an examination of the leading term and a search for a reducing polynomial. Then before actually computing the reduction, a second processor is assigned the task of performing the next loop iteration. The second processor busy waits, checking for either a new term or a done indication, while the first processor computes the polynomial term by term. When the first processor finishes, it will wait once more in a queue to be assigned additional work. The second processor, meanwhile, waits for a term to be produced. Once a term is produced, the polynomial is definitely known to be non-zero, and the second processor will search for another reducing polynomial. If the

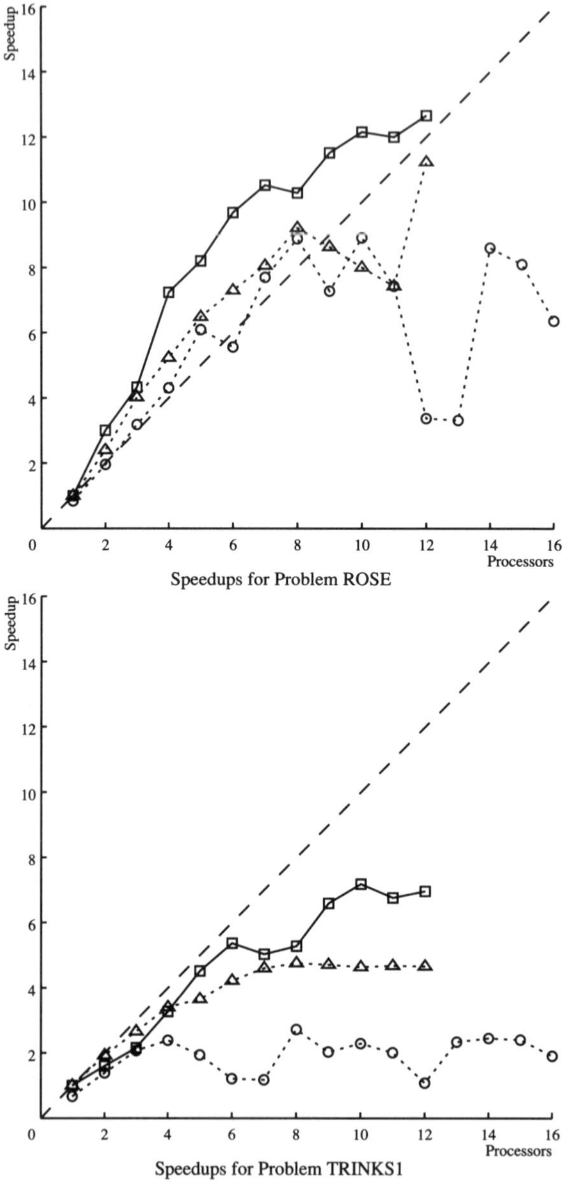

Figure 3.6
Gröbner Bases speedup curves

search is successful, the second processor will assign a third processor to consume the next intermediate result, and the process repeats. If no terms are produced, and the done flag is set, then the second processor has detected a zero polynomial. There is no need to update the pairs set, and a new pair may be expanded. If the search for another reduction fails the second processor begins the update-pairs routine, in which useless pairs are deleted and the new pairs are added. This overlaps with the previous computation. This processor then begins expansion of the next pair. The S-polynomial expansion may be forced to wait because one of the polynomials in the pair may still be incomplete. The code to compute the S-polynomials uses the same synchronization technique to consume terms as they are produced, overlapping additional computation and providing better speedup.

There are several issues to point out about this pipelined reduction process. (1) The busy waiting loops all spin on two cached variables. This means that the busy waiting does not saturate the bus and slow other processors down. (2) Once the reduction begins, each processor in the pipeline consumes terms at approximately the same speed as the previous processors produces them; therefore very little time is spent busy-waiting in the middle of a reduction pipeline. (3) Because the synchronization constraints flow in one direction only, no synchronization primitives are used beyond strong ordering of reads and writes. (4) There is no speculative parallelism in this part of the computation. Each reduction must be performed, and this approach simply overlaps the computation performed by the inner loop as much as possible.

3.5.4 Combining the two techniques

The two forms of parallelism described above combine in a complementary fashion. The coarse-grain method performs many reductions in parallel; the fine-grain method parallelizes the reduction chains. We experimented with a number of processor scheduling mechanisms before choosing the one used in the implementation. One version used a single work queue, another separate queues with locks, and the final version uses a fixed ordering among processors. We expect that the two forms of parallelism are independent, since performing the pair expansions in parallel, only faster, reduces the average time between pair expansion and updating the set of pairs. Because of this speedup, the fraction of time spent in the critical section updating the shared data increases. We believe that this will not become a bottleneck until hundreds of processors are used, but varying ratios of processor to synchronization speed across different architectures may make this an important consideration.

In figure 3.7 below, we present performance results for the full algorithm with both levels of parallelism. (Box indicates Encore Multimax, Triangle indicates Plus Simulator). The Rose example is large enough to benefit from the fine-grain parallelism, while the Trinks1 example is too small to speed up using this approach. The difference between these two problems is that the polynomials that appear in the first example tend to have 20 or more terms, while the second example has polynomials with 10 or fewer terms. The fine-grain parallelism only works when there are many terms to process in each polynomial. The Rose example seems to be more typical of the type of problems which arise in practice. A large multiprocessor will be able to operate on polynomials with hundreds of terms, allowing even better speed up from the fine-grain parallelism.

3.6 Conclusion

We observed essentially linear speedup for all three algorithms on many examples. There were also small examples where virtually no speedup was obtained regardless of the number of processors used. Furthermore, we occasionally observed superlinear speedup in Parthenon and the Gröbner bases algorithm. This is a well-known artifact of parallel tree searches.

There are two main difficulties which arise in parallel implementations of symbolic algorithms. The first is that it is essentially impossible to implement any type of static scheduling. Given an instance of the problem, there is no way to predict the number of steps that the algorithm will require, the types of steps that will be needed, or the amount of work which will be available at any point in time. In order to get good speedup, it is often necessary to resort to speculative parallelism; trying to interrupt processors which are found to be doing useless work can further increase the complexity of the scheduling problem.

The second problem is the difficulty of debugging a parallel implementation. The scheduling problem contributes greatly to this. In addition, symbolic algorithms often must deal with numerous cases. When many processors are operating in parallel, the number of combinations of cases which can be active at a given time, and hence the number of possible

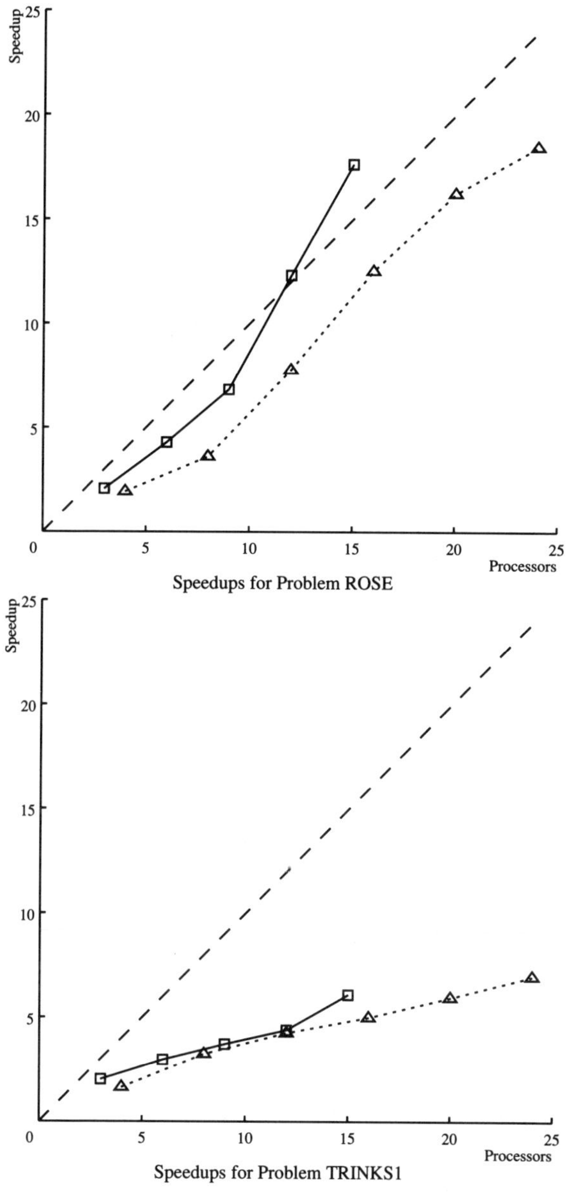

Figure 3.7
Gröbner Bases speedup curves

interactions, is large. Because of this and the nondeterminism associated with the scheduling, it is not unusual to encounter bugs which only occur once every hundred runs and only in large problems.

We feel shared memory machines have some advantages over message passing machines as platforms for implementing symbolic algorithms. First, the implementation on a shared memory machine should be easier. On a message passing machine, references to remote data must either be handled by a separate thread running at the remote node or by the application itself, typically at the beginning of a main loop. In the first case, the code for synchronization is likely to be just as complex as on a shared memory machine, and the message handling itself is usually nontrivial. In the second case, there is a loss of parallelism, and the application becomes more monolithic. In addition, having to check explicitly whether references are local or remote increases the complexity of the implementation.

Second, the software overhead of handling messages would probably make it difficult to obtain good performance. Typical symbolic algorithms access many small objects scattered throughout memory as they work, so there is little opportunity to use large block transfers; instead, it is message latency which is critical. Experiments with Parthenon and the Gröbner basis algorithm on the Plus simulator indicate that about one percent of references are remote. On the Plus, this would mean about twenty percent of the execution time would be spent waiting for the network. Another order of magnitude of overhead for remote references would seriously degrade the performance of these applications.

Our experiences lead us to believe that it is possible to develop useful parallel implementations of symbolic algorithms. We also feel that these implementations can usually be structured so that almost all their memory references can be considered local. Thus, they should map extremely well onto the non-uniform shared memory machines currently being developed. We hope to demonstrate this in the near future on the Plus machine which is currently being built.

3.7 Acknowledgments

D. E. Long was partially supported by an NSF graduate fellowship. S. Michaylov was partially supported by an IBM graduate fellowship. S. A. Schwab was partially supported by an NSF graduate fellowship.

References

[1] R. V. Baron, R. F. Rashid, E. Siegel, A. Tevanian, and M. W. Young. MACH-1: a multiprocessor oriented operating system and environment. In *New Computing Environments: Parallel, Vector and Symbolic.* SIAM, 1986.

[2] R. Bisiani and M. Ravishankar. PLUS: A distributed shared-memory system. In *Proceedings of the 17th Annual Symposium on Computer Architecture.* IEEE Computer Society Press, June 1990.

[3] S. Bose, E. M. Clarke, D. E. Long, and S. Michaylov. Parthenon: A parallel theorem prover for non-horn clauses. In *Fourth Annual Symposium on Logic in Computer Science.* IEEE Computer Society Press, 1989.

[4] K. S. Brace, R. L. Rudell, and R. E. Bryant. Efficient implementation of a BDD package. In *27th ACM/IEEE Design Automation Conference*, pages 40–45, 1990.

[5] R. E. Bryant, D. Beatty, K. Brace, K. Cho, and T. Sheffler. COSMOS: A compiled simulator for MOS circuits. In *24th Design Automation Conference*, 1987.

[6] Randal E. Bryant. Graph-based algorithms for boolean function manipulation. *IEEE Transactions on Computers*, C-35(8):677–691, August 1986.

[7] Bruno Buchberger. *An Algorithm for Finding a Basis for the Residue Class Ring of a Zero-Dimensional Polynomial Ideal (German).* PhD thesis, University of Innsbruck, 1965.

[8] Bruno Buchberger. A criterion for detecting unnecessary reductions in the construction of Gröbner bases. In *Proceedings of EUROSAM 79, Lectures Notes in Computer Science 72*, pages 3–21, 1979.

[9] Bruno Buchberger. Gröbner bases : An algorithmic method in polynomial ideal theory. In N.K.Bose, editor, *Recent Trends In Multidimensional Systems Theory*, pages 184–232. D.Reidel Publishing Company, 1985.

[10] J. R. Burch, E. M. Clarke, K. L. McMillan, D. L. Dill, and J. Hwang. Symbolic model checking: 10^{20} states and beyond. In *Proceedings of 5th Symposium on Logic in Computer Science*, 1990.

[11] R. Butler, T. Disz, R. Overbeek, and R. Stevens. Scheduling or-parallelism: An Argonne perspective. In R. A. Kowalski and K. A. Bowen, editors, *Proceedings of the Fifth International Conference on Logic Programming*, pages 1590–1605, Cambridge, 1988. MIT Press.

[12] E. C. Cooper. C threads. Technical Report CMU-CS-88-154, Carnegie Mellon University, Pittsburgh, PA 15213, June 1988.

[13] Encore Computer Corporation. *Multimax Technical Summary*, 1986.

[14] Allan L. Fisher and Randal E. Bryant. Performance of COSMOS on the IFIP workshop benchmarks. In *Proceedings of IMEC Conference*, 1989.

[15] M. Fujita, H. Fujisawa, and N. Kawato. Evaluation and improvement of boolean comparison method based on binary decision diagrams. In *1989 IEEE Conference on Computer-Aided Design.* IEEE Computer Society Press, 1989.

[16] Rüdiger Gebauer and Michael Möller. On an installation of Buchberger's algorithm. *Journal of Symbolic Computation*, 6(2 & 3):275–286, 1988.

[17] IBM. *Research Parallel Processor Prototype Principle of Operations.*

[18] S. Kimura and E. M. Clarke. A parallel algorithm for constructing binary decision diagrams. Submitted for Publication, February 1990.

[19] D. W. Loveland. A simplified format for the model elimination theorem-proving procedure. *Journal of the ACM*, 16:349–363, 1969.

[20] W. McCune. *OTTER: Other Techniques in Theorem Proving.* Argonne National Laboratory.

[21] Herbert Melenk and Winfried Neun. Parallel polynomial operations in the large Buchberger algorithm. In *Computer Algebra and Parallelism, Workshop at the TIM3 Laboratory, University of Grenoble, France.* Academic Press, London, June 1988.

[22] Winfried Neun and Herbert Melenk. Implementation of the LISP–arbitrary precision arithmetic for a vector processor. In *Computer Algebra and Parallelism, Workshop at the TIM3 Laboratory, University of Grenoble, France.* Academic Press, London, June 1988.

[23] S. A. Schwab. Extended parallelism in the Gröbner basis algorithm. Technical report, Carnegie Mellon University, 1991. In preparation.

[24] M. E. Stickel. A Prolog technology theorem prover. In *New Generation Computing 2, 4*, pages 371–383, 1984.

[25] Jean Philippe Vidal. The computation of Gröbner bases on a shared memory multiprocessor. Technical Report CMU-CS-90-163, Computer Science Department, Carnegie Mellon University, August 1990.

[26] D. H. D. Warren. Or-parallel execution models of Prolog. Technical report, Department of Computer Science, University of Manchester, 1987.

4 Experimental Evaluation of Algorithmic Performance on Two Shared Memory Multiprocessors

Anand Sivasubramaniam, Gautam Shah, Joonwon Lee, Umakishore Ramachandran, and H. Venkateswaran

The results of experimenting with three parallel algorithms on the Sequent Symmetry architecture and the BBN Butterfly architecture are reported. The main objective of this study is to understand the impediments to the efficient implementation of parallel algorithms, developed for theoretical models of parallel computation, on realistic parallel architectures. Scheduling, task granularity, and synchronization are the issues that are explored in implementing these algorithms on the two architectures. In the case of BBN Butterfly, which is a distributed shared memory architecture,data distribution in the distributed memories is also studied. The key findings are that synchronization is not a significant cost for the algorithms we studied on the two architectures; the bus is not a bottleneck for the configuration of the Sequent machine that we experimented with; and a fairly simple minded data distribution may be as good as any other on the BBN Butterfly.

4.1 Introduction

Parallel Computation provides some of the most challenging problems in computer science. The term parallel computation covers a broad spectrum of research ranging from purely theoretical models for complexity analysis of parallel algorithms, to detailed system performance issues of large problems that lend themselves to parallel implementations. Both ends of the spectrum have one thing in common, namely, to understand the performance potential of parallel computation. A computation is expressed as a task graph and the objective is to determine the speedup that is realizable for the computation. While the theoretical models are concerned with the asymptotic limits of computing in parallel, the system-oriented studies are concerned with determining the best heuristic mapping for a computation on a target architecture that would result in the best (average case) performance. Each study has its merits and de-merits. The asymptotic limits give a ceiling for maximum achievable performance for a given algorithm based on an abstract model of parallel architectures. The average case results are useful for determining what is achievable in reality.

Understanding the performance of parallel computation requires a knowledge of the capabilities of the underlying parallel architecture. Further, the performance limits depend on the mapping of the problem on to the parallel architecture. Theoretical models abstract away real life limits such as the number of processors, synchronization requirements, scheduling and data distribution to derive the asymptotic limits. On the other hand, system-oriented studies are so concerned with mapping the algorithm to real architectures that it is difficult to know from the results of such studies where the parallelism inherent in the algorithm has been lost. The aim of this study is to address some of the issues in the interface between theory and architecture, from the point of view of algorithmic performance.

Parallel algorithms for certain problems theoretically guarantee a certain amount of speedup. But when these algorithms are implemented on existing architectures, the results may not agree with the expected theoretical speedup. Some inherent features in the algorithm, its implementation, and the hardware capabilities of the machine together contribute to the slow-down. The parallel algorithms usually assume a certain minimum number of processors to be available with an underlying interconnection topology between them. To implement such algorithms, we may have to make do with a limited number of processors and simulate the assumed interconnection. The language run time and the operating system may further introduce synchronization costs not inherent in the algorithm but are necessary to implement them on the parallel machine. And lastly, the hardware capabilities like synchronization primitives, memory access times and caching strategies may introduce further slow-down.

One straightforward way to understand the architectural impact on parallel computation is to implement algorithms with intrinsic parallelism on parallel architectures and interpret the results with respect to the above factors. Therefore, we have chosen to perform our experiments on two parallel machines—the *Sequent Symmetry* and the *BBN Butterfly*—with entirely different architectures. The Sequent is a bus based shared memory multiprocessor machine. All processors are identical (in our system, there are 10 processors) each having a 64K cache memory and connected to a global shared memory through a single system bus. Sequent falls into the category of Uniform Memory Access (UMA) machines in that a user has no *a priori* knowledge of the access time for a given memory location. The Butterfly on the other hand is a collection of processors, each with its own local memory. However each processor can access non-local memories via a multistage interconnection network.

Such non-local accesses are more expensive than local ones. Thus Butterfly falls into the category of Non-Uniform Memory Access (NUMA) machines in that a user has *a priori* knowledge of access times to a given memory location based on whether it is local or non-local.

We have chosen three algorithms—*List Ranking*, *Parallel Prefix* and *Optimal Binary Search Tree*—each of which we feel identify a class of problems. List ranking is a fundamental operation on lists. The problem is: given a linked list, compute the distance of each cell from the end of the list. This algorithm is data dependent and thus the memory access patterns depend on the data placement. For such a problem, it is expected that data partitioning would play a vital role on performance, especially when implemented on a NUMA machine.

The parallel prefix on the other hand is a data oblivious algorithm implying that the running time of the algorithm is independent of the input data. The prefix problem takes as input n elements and gives an n element output, where the *i-th* output element is the product of the first i input elements. If the input data is partitioned appropriately for such an algorithm, then it is possible to reduce the amount of accesses to non-local data by a processor.

Optimal binary search tree is another data oblivious algorithm that takes a set of weights (leaf nodes) as input and constructs a tree of minimal weight. The interesting variation from the other two algorithms is the work imbalance that is inherent during different phases of the algorithm.

4.2 Programming Paradigms And Performance Metrics

There are several ways to implement the above algorithms on these machines. Both machines provide support for parallel programming such as the parallel programming library on the Sequent [7] and the Uniform System [8] on the Butterfly. In the description that follows, we use the term *task* to mean a unit of work and the term *process* to mean a virtual processor. The model of execution used is single-program-multiple-data wherein each process independently executes the same code on a different portion of the data (data partitioning). The parent process forks child processes that execute the parallel algorithm (works on the data partition assigned to it). During the course of execution of the child processes, they may need to synchronize. We use a barrier for this purpose.

4.2.1 Scheduling

For implementing these algorithms, we define a set of tasks and let processes work on these tasks. The assignment of a task to a process is called scheduling. This level of scheduling is from the point of view of algorithms as opposed to an operating system scheduler that does resource management[1]. Our experimental work considers two types of scheduling. *Static* scheduling pre-assigns tasks to processes at compile time. Even though static scheduling may be easy to program, it may not always be the most efficient in terms of processor utilization. *Dynamic* scheduling assigns the tasks to processes at run time and thus has the potential for better processor utilization. However dynamic scheduling may result in extra synchronization costs because it normally involves accesses to globally shared queues (critical sections).

For static scheduling, the data partition that each process works on is pre-determined. For dynamic scheduling on the other hand, the chunk of data that a process works on is determined at run time. The chunks of data that are ready for execution are in a global queue. When each process finishes with its chunk, it gets the next piece of work from this global queue. For the algorithms discussed in this paper, we simulate the global queue with an atomic counter.

4.2.2 Task Granularity and Synchronization

The processes need to synchronize between executions of successive tasks. If the tasks are too fine grain, then this synchronization overhead may affect performance. To study this effect, we decided to vary the task granularity and study its impact on performance. Task granularity has two dimensions: *computation granularity* and *data granularity*. The former deals with the amount of computation that a process needs to do for the particular task while the latter involves the size of the data partition in the task. These are important input parameters that need to be considered to determine the effect of task granularity and synchronization on performance. The data granularity is varied by changing the number of data elements in the chunk that is allotted to a process while the computation granularity is varied by introducing some artificial work in

[1] Recently, several researchers [1, 2, 3] investigate the relative merits of dynamic and static scheduling policies at the operating system and application level for multiprocessors.

the place where the process solves the problem for the chunk allotted to it. The artificial work is an idle loop and the loop count is used as a measure of the computation granularity.

4.2.3 Data Distribution

The above description has applicability to both the Sequent and the Butterfly. But on the Butterfly, there is an added dimension that is worth studying: *data distribution* (because of non-uniform memory access). The data distribution patterns that are included in this study are: *random distribution* (a processor may need to access any memory module for its data chunk), *skewed distribution* (in which successive data elements are allocated in successive virtual processors), and *local allocation* (where a processor's data chunk is locally allocated). Each of these data distributions generates differing network traffic. Such a study is expected to give us a feel for the effect of the switch contention and remote memory accesses on the performance. The corresponding effect for the Sequent is simulated by varying the computation granularity. If the computation granularity is made small, then there is more synchronization overhead which in turn generates more traffic on the bus.

In the discussions that follow, the completion time is used as a measure of the performance of parallel algorithms. In the Butterfly implementations, the times for process creation and termination are included in the completion time, whereas in the Sequent implementations, they are not. The results for the uniprocessor cases are obtained by running the multiprocessor parallel algorithm on a single processor. Hence the speedup using n processors refers to the ratio of the completion time of the parallel algorithm on *1* processor to that on n processors.

4.3 Related Work

To our knowledge, there are very few experimental studies that investigate the impact of architectural features on algorithmic performance. Anderson [4] reports results of an experimental and analytical study of parallel merge sort. In this study, implementation of this algorithm on the Sequent is used to verify the speedup with different number of processors with respect to the analytical model. Yew et al. [5], analyze specific parallel programs to identify the appropriate grain size of parallelism that exists in these programs. Further they present a simulation

```
For log n iterations repeat
   In parallel, for i := 1,...,n do
      list[i].rank ← list[i].rank +
               list[list[i].successor].rank;
      list[i].successor ←
               list[list[i].successor].successor;
```

Figure 4.1
List Ranking Algorithm

study to measure the impact of synchronization overhead on the execution of these programs. Lin and Snyder [15] compare message passing and shared memory paradigms for implementing specific parallel algorithms on shared memory multiprocessors. Our work is more general in that we experiment with algorithms that represent classes of problems and study synchronization, scheduling and task granularity issues in implementing these algorithms.

4.4 Observed Results

4.4.1 List Ranking

A parallel algorithm for the list ranking problem is discussed in [9, 10]. Figure 4.1 shows a pseudo-code for this algorithm.

The algorithm is data dependent. The randomness of access of the list elements does not favor data partitioning. Therefore, it is not known *a priori* the best way to partition the data and assign it to the processors. This feature of the algorithm makes it interesting to study its performance on architectures, with different organization and memory access capabilities, like the Sequent and the Butterfly. The input list (32K on the Sequent and 8K on the Butterfly) is generated using a standard random number generator.

4.4.1.1 Sequent Implementation The results for static scheduling is shown in Figure 4.4 which plots the completion time of the algorithm versus the number of processors. There is almost a linear improvement in performance as we increase the number of processors. This result shows that: (a) the processors are almost always allocated an equal amount of work, (b) there is negligible amount of overhead in synchronization (for instance, of a completion time of 1 second in the 8 processor case, the total amount of time spent in synchronization is around 10 milliseconds), and (c) the bus may not be a bottleneck for small number of processors. Increasing the computation granularity increases the completion time as can be expected but the shape of the speedup curve remains the same for a given computation granularity. This trend further supports our earlier remark that the bus may not be a bottleneck for static scheduling. Since the processors are almost always allocated an equal amount of work between any two successive synchronization points, there is negligible time spent waiting at the barrier.

Figure 4.5 shows the effect of data granularity on performance when dynamic scheduling is used on the Sequent. When it is extremely fine grain, the dynamic scheme performs very poorly compared to the static scheme. Extensive contention for the globally shared queue is the reason for this behavior. The bus does become a bottleneck in this case and hence this poor performance is quite understandable. This experimental result corroborates the simulation result reported in [11], wherein they show that lock contention leads to poor performance in bus-based shared memory multiprocessors. It is also the reason why the 8 processor performance is much poorer than the 4 or 2 processor case for extremely fine grain data granularity. As the data granularity increases, the performance improves until it becomes comparable to the static case. Increasing the data granularity further does not result in improved performance. In fact, when the data granularity is increased beyond that of the static case, the completion time increases which is quite understandable since one or more processors may be idle between any two barrier synchronization points. For a wide range of chunk sizes, dynamic scheduling seems to fare as well as static scheduling. Over these grains, the contention for the global queue is almost negligible. It is interesting to note that the dynamic scheme does not fare better than the static scheme at any point. Thus we may conclude that there is equal load balancing at all points of execution in the static case.

Figure 4.6 shows the effect of increasing the computation granularity. The results, as in the static case, are quite predictable for larger chunk sizes. The interesting observations are for smaller chunk sizes. It is reasonable to expect that increasing the computation granularity may result in poorer performance. However it is seen that as the computation granularity is increased, the performance of the 8 processor case improves. This improvement can be explained with reference to the contention for the queue (bus traffic). By increasing the computation granularity, the time between any two successive bus accesses increases, thus reducing the contention for the shared queue thereby improving the performance. As the computation granularity is increased further, the effect of contention becomes less significant which explains the observed result. The contention effect is quite similar to what is explained as quiesce[2] time in [12]. Note that this effect is less significant for 2 or 4 processors, which explains the better performance for 4 processors as compared to the 8 processor case for small data granularity.

4.4.1.2 Butterfly Implementation On the Sequent, there is no choice for data placement since it is a uniform memory access machine. On the other hand, the list could be allocated in any of the processors' memories on the Butterfly. Thus data partitioning is another dimension that makes an interesting study. Data partitioning is expected to affect performance because of the non-uniform memory access times. We study this problem with the three types of data distributions that we enumerated earlier (see Section 4.2.3).

Figure 4.7 shows the performance for static scheduling for each of these data partitioning schemes. Local allocation seems to have the best performance of the three. In the local allocation scheme, a processor writes only to the local memory even though it may read from non-local memory modules. In the other two schemes, the accesses (both reads and writes) are purely random. These results seem to indicate that the way in which we partition data has a significant effect on performance. Of the other two schemes, random allocation seems to show better performance than the skewed allocation. For both these schemes, the 2 processor performance seems to be worse than the 1 processor case. Increasing the number of processors results in an interplay of increased computation power, higher probability of non-local memory accesses (thus increasing network traffic) and the increased cost of synchronization. The first is a positive factor while the latter two have negative effects. Non-local memory access affects performance in two ways: increased latency and possible switch contention. Experiments performed with 1 processor with the data distributed among several memory modules results

[2] Quiesce time is the time it takes for spurious bus contention to settle down in a bus-based shared memory multiprocessor upon the release of a lock.

in much poorer performance compared to the case where the data is strictly in local memory. This result leads us to believe that increased latency is the more dominant factor affecting the performance. In the 2 processor case, the negative effects dominate. In general, the positive effect becomes more prominent for larger number of processors. But in the skewed allocation scheme, the performance worsens as we go from 8 to 16 processors. This is due to the increased likelihood of non-local memory accesses thus allowing the negative effects to dominate.

Figures 4.8 and 4.9 show the effect of increasing the computation granularity on the performance for random and skewed allocation schemes respectively. It can be seen that the poorer performance observed in going from 1 to 2 processors (see Figure 4.7) disappears as the computation granularity is increased. This result shows that increasing the computation granularity exploits the additional compute power available with increased number of processors, offsetting the negative effect due to the network traffic. The retarding factors that affect the performance in these two distributions do not have a significant role in the local allocation scheme (see Figure 4.7) even with no added computation granularity. As can be expected, increasing the computation granularity merely reinforces the positive effect.

The effect of varying the data granularity for dynamic scheduling is shown in Figure 4.10. Since in this scheduling strategy processors are assigned to tasks at run-time, the local allocation scheme may not have much meaning. Therefore only the random and skewed allocation schemes are considered. Since observed behavior for these two allocation schemes are similar, only the results for the random allocation scheme are presented in Figures 4.10 and 4.11. The performance at low chunk sizes is much worse than that observed in the static case (see Figure 4.10). As the chunk size is increased, the performance approaches that of static scheduling. This behavior is similar to the observed results for dynamic scheduling on the Sequent. An interesting observation that shows the effect of network traffic is the poorer performance for higher chunk sizes for 2 processors as compared to 1 processor. Further, the performance uniformly improves with increasing the number of processors showing no anomalous behavior as in static scheduling.

Figure 4.11 shows the effect of computation granularity on performance. We only present the results for low chunk sizes since at higher chunk sizes, the behavior is expected to be similar to static schedul-

```
Prefix(x,n,s)
        If n=1 then s_1 ← x_1
        else
                in parallel, for i:=1 to n/2 do
                        y_i ← x_{2i-1} * x_{2i}
                prefix(y,n/2,ss)
                ss_0 ← identity
                in parallel, for i:=1 to n do
                        if i even then s_i ← ss_{i/2}
                        else s_i ← ss_{(i-1)/2} * x_i
```

Figure 4.2
Parallel Prefix Algorithm

ing. Increasing computation granularity does not affect network traffic and thus the performance improves with the increase in the number of processors for a given computation granularity.

We noted that in dynamic scheduling, the processors have to access a global shared queue of tasks. The contention that results from this queue has a detrimental effect (at low chunk sizes) on the performance on the Sequent with larger number of processors (see Figure 4.5). On the other hand, this contention is not as pronounced on the Butterfly (see Figure 4.10). This observation reiterates the fact that the bus on the Sequent is a much more shared resource than the switch on the Butterfly.

4.4.2 Parallel Prefix

An algorithm for the parallel prefix problem is discussed in [13], and Figure 4.2 gives the pseudo code for this algorithm.

The algorithm is data oblivious. Each phase of the parallel part can be performed only after all processors in the previous phase have completed their task. The recognition of the end of a phase is by waiting on a barrier. In the static scheduling case, each processor knows the part of the data it has to work on, and all the work is equally distributed. In the dynamic scheduling case, each processor identifies the chunk of data it has to work on, by using a global counter (see Section 4.2.1). Experiments include data sizes of 4K, 16K and 32K elements in the array; and for the dynamic scheduling case, the data granularity ranges from 1 to 1K elements. In both cases, computation granularity is varied as in list ranking (see Section 4.4.1.1). Since the experimentation is over a range of data sizes, only an interesting selection of results is presented in the subsequent sections.

4.4.2.1 Sequent Implementation Figure 4.12 shows the completion time as a function of the number of processors for a data size of 32K on the sequent. It is observed that an almost linear speedup is achieved. In fact it is interesting to note that results for static scheduling are remarkably similar to the corresponding results for list ranking (see Figure 4.4). This confirms our earlier observation regarding the negligible effect of synchronization cost and bus overhead on the performance of these algorithms.

Figures 4.13 and 4.14 present the results for dynamic scheduling on the Sequent. Figure 4.14 shows the effect of increasing computation granularity on the completion time for fixed low data granularity (chunk size = 1). It is seen that at low computation granularity the performance with 8 processors is poorer than with lesser number of processors. This loss in performance may be attributed to the overhead of accessing the global counter, i.e., as the number of processors increase, the contention on the lock outweighs the added compute power. There is another interesting similarity between the observed results of list ranking and parallel prefix. With 8 processors, the completion time decreases with increase in computation granularity, a result that seems counter-intuitive at first glance. However, the reason for this phenomenon is exactly similar to the list ranking case (see Section 4.4.1.1). Figure 4.13 shows the effect of varying the data granularity on the completion time as a function of the number of processors. It is observed that the performance with 8 processors is poorer than lesser number of processors for data granularity less than 256. With reference to Figure 4.13, it is also observed that as the data granularity is increased the performance with dynamic scheduling tends to equal that with static scheduling, but it never does better.

4.4.2.2 Butterfly Implementation We experimented with three data distribution schemes in the case of the parallel prefix problem as in the list ranking case. The experiments included data sizes of 8K and 16K, and Figures 4.15 through 4.19 present the results for data size of 8K. The results for data size of 16K are similar. Figure 4.15 shows the completion time versus the number of processors for the three data distributions in the case of static scheduling. It is seen that local data distribution scheme performs the best. The performance is almost linear with the number of processors. This result is to be expected, since in this problem each processor works on its local data for the most part. However, note that we do not see a linear speedup with the number of processors for the other two distributions. This result is primarily due to the latency for non-local accesses. Further, there could be some contribution due to switch contention. The performance for random distribution is better than that for skewed distribution, since in the latter case, every local access is always followed by a non-local one. It is also noted that as in list ranking, the 2 processor performance is worse than the 1 processor case, for these two distributions. With reference to Figures 4.16 and 4.17, a behavior similar to list ranking (see Figures 4.8 and 4.9) is observed when computation granularity is varied for random and skewed distributions.

The results for dynamic scheduling on the Butterfly are shown in Figures 4.19 and 4.18. Figure 4.19 shows the effect of varying the data granularity on the performance. The observations are very similar to the corresponding results obtained for list ranking (see Figure 4.10). Since the measured times for parallel prefix are quite small, at larger chunk sizes the trend shown by the shape of the curves is more important than the absolute numbers.

It is observed that the 16 processor case is consistently worse than the 8 processor case. This behavior can be attributed to the detrimental factors (non-local memory access and contention for the shared queue) that start to dominate with increased number of processors. With respect to Figure 4.18, it is seen that as the computation granularity is increased, the positive factor (increased compute power) starts to overshadow the detrimental effects. For example, with a chunk size of 1 and for computation granularity beyond 40, our experiments indicate that the 16 processor performance is better than the 8 processor performance.

4.4.3 Optimal Binary Search Tree

A standard dynamic programming algorithm for this problem computes a 2-dimensional cost matrix as shown in Figure 4.3 [14].

This algorithm is data oblivious and traverses one diagonal after another (the values for the elements in the current diagonal depend on the values in the previous diagonal). The number of diagonal elements to be computed in each phase decreases by 1 as we step through the diagonals. Therefore, in the static scheduling case we divide the number of diagonal

```
For i := 1 to n do
    For j := i+1 to n do
```

$$C_{i,j} \leftarrow \min_{i \le k < j} (C_{i,k} + C_{k+1,j}) + \sum_{k=i}^{j} w_k$$

Figure 4.3
Optimal Binary Search Tree Algorithm

elements in each phase by the number of available processors and determine the elements that each processor has to work on. In the dynamic scheduling case, a global counter is used. Note that, for this algorithm, the unequal workload at each phase is an additional detrimental factor when compared to the other two algorithms.

4.4.3.1 Sequent Implementation Figure 4.20 shows the performance of this algorithm on the Sequent using static and dynamic scheduling. An almost linear speedup is observed for static scheduling showing that the unequal workload is not a significant detrimental factor.

Figure 4.21 shows the performance using dynamic scheduling with respect to chunk size. Unlike the other two algorithms, the performance worsens as the chunk size increases with multiple processors. This result can be explained as follows. In the dynamic scheduling case, the number of units of work depends on the chunk size and the number of diagonal elements to be completed. For example, there are 2 units of work when the chunk size is 16 and the number of diagonal elements is 31. Thus for the 4 processor case, 2 processors remain idle, creating work imbalance. However, with respect to Figure 4.20, it is observed that for a given chunk size, dynamic scheduling does result in speedup with increase in number of processors.

4.4.3.2 Butterfly Implementation Figure 4.22 shows the performance on the Butterfly using static and dynamic scheduling with skewed data allocation scheme. Since the data structure in this algorithm is 2-dimensional, only the skewed allocation scheme is used. It can be seen from the results for static scheduling that the speedup is not linear in the number of processors. The increase in the non-local memory references with the number of processors is the reason for this behavior.

Figure 4.23 shows the effect of chunk size on the performance for dynamic scheduling. For a given number of processors, increasing the chunk size results in poorer performance. This behavior is very similar to that observed on the sequent (see Figure 4.21), and is due to the work imbalance. However, there is a distinct difference between the two results as can be seen by comparing figures 4.21 and 4.23. In the case of the Butterfly, for a given chunk size, the performance worsens beyond a certain number of processors. This effect is more pronounced at higher chunk sizes (see the curve for chunk size = 16), since the added computing power with additional processors is offset by the detrimental factors.

4.5 Discussion

It is observed that there is almost a linear improvement in performance with the number of processors on the Sequent for all the three algorithms. Adding more processors while increasing the computing power also increases the synchronization overhead. But the results indicate that for the algorithms studied the overhead is not very significant on the Sequent. Further these results also show that the bus is not a bottleneck.

However a linear speedup is not always realized on the Butterfly for the three algorithms. Data distribution in the memories of the processors is another dimension on the Butterfly that seems to have a significant impact on the performance. For example, the speedup curve is almost linear for the parallel prefix algorithm with local data distribution. The reason for this result is twofold. The algorithm is data oblivious and the local data distribution provides a similar effect to having a private cache on the Sequent for this algorithm. For the other two data distributions considered, we do not observe a linear speedup for any of the three algorithms. Thus, we may conclude that even on the Butterfly synchronization overhead is not a dominant cost in limiting algorithmic performance; on the other hand network latency is a dominant factor. In comparing the data distribution schemes, local allocation seems to be the best followed by random allocation for both list ranking and parallel prefix algorithms.

It is intuitive that static scheduling should perform the best when the workload is known in advance. Our observations confirm this intuition. However, for data dependent algorithms such as list ranking the workload may be uneven. Furthermore, even for some data oblivious algorithms (such as optimal binary search tree) there could be uneven workload between phases, indicating that static scheduling may be inefficient. It is reasonable to expect dynamic scheduling to perform better under such circumstances. In fact our observations are contrary to this intuition, which can be explained by the fact that there is an inherent overhead in dynamic scheduling. This overhead is significant at low computation granularity. As the computation granularity is increased, the performance of dynamic scheduling tends towards static scheduling and may even become better when there is a significant imbalance in the workload.

An artifact of implementing dynamic scheduling is the choice of data granularity. When the data size is very small there is more overhead in dynamic scheduling. Our results show that this overhead can be overcome only by increasing the computation granularity. Note, that for a given data size, very large data granularity (chunk size) generates uneven workload, thus having a detrimental effect on the performance. For example, in an 8 processor system with 4K data size and 1K chunk size, 4 processors would remain idle.

4.6 Conclusions

There were several hypotheses regarding the effects of architectural features on algorithmic performance that motivated this research. One has to do with memory organization. For example, a multistage interconnection network can provide higher throughput, at the cost of increased latency for each individual request. On the other hand, bus-based systems offer lower latency for each individual request, but provide lower overall throughput. Our results show that while the bus is not a hindrance on the Sequent, the network latency on the Butterfly is a hindrance in achieving linear speedup.

The second hypothesis has to do with task granularity. While smaller granularity allows increased parallelism, it would also engender more synchronization overhead. A larger granularity while reducing the synchronization overhead limits the exploitation of the available parallelism especially when there are a large number of processors. Our results confirm this hypothesis.

The third hypothesis deals with the scheduling overhead. This overhead could be a limiting factor in exploiting the available parallelism in a computation. This factor is related to the granularity of tasks that we mentioned earlier. The specific strategy used could affect the performance of the algorithm. For example, with the dynamic scheduling scheme, there is high contention for the global queue especially if all the processors are looking for work after a barrier synchronization. This hypothesis is also borne out by our results since static scheduling outperforms dynamic scheduling for the most part.

The last hypothesis concerns synchronization primitives on the available parallel machines. It can be expected that synchronization would be crucial for both dynamic scheduling and algorithm implementation. Although the Sequent and the Butterfly provide different types of synchronization primitives, these differences do not significantly affect the algorithmic performance. This is due to the fact that the amount of synchronization required in these algorithms is not significant compared to the amount of computation involved. On the other hand, the absence of efficient high-level synchronization primitives such as queue manipulation primitives on both these architectures limits the performance of dynamic scheduling compared to static scheduling.

This study has generated several interesting research directions: a more realistic theoretical framework for analyzing algorithms and architectures, a classification of the architecture primitives that would allow the realization of the parallelism promised by the algorithms, an exploration of novel architectures suggested by the structure of the algorithms, and a set of metrics for evaluating the performance of parallel algorithms.

Acknowledgments

This work has been funded in part by NSF grants CCR-8711749, CCR-8619886, and MIPS-8809268.

References

[1] S.T.Leutenegger, M.K.Vernon. The Performance of Multiprogrammed Multiprocessor Scheduling Algorithms. *Conference on Measurement and Modeling of Computer Systems.* 1990.

[2] A.Tucker, A.Gupta. Process Control and Scheduling Issues for Multiprogrammed Shared Memory Multiprocessors. *12th ACM Symposium on Operating System Principles.* 1989.

[3] J.Zahorjan, C.McCann. Processor Scheduling in Shared Memory Multiprocessors. *Conference on Measurement and Modeling of Computer Systems.* 1990.

[4] R.J.Anderson. An Experimental Study of Parallel Merge Sort. *Preliminary Version, 0.1.* University of Washington. 1990.

[5] D.Chen, H.Su, P.Yew. The Impact of Synchronization and Granularity on Parallel Systems. *International Symposium on Computer Architecture.* 1990.

[6] C.Lin, L.Snyder. A Comparison of Programming Models for Shared Memory Multiprocessors. *International Conference on Parallel Processing.* 1990.

[7] Sequent Guide to Parallel Programming. Sequent Computer Systems Inc., Oregon. 1987.

[8] The Uniform System Approach to Programming the Butterfly Parallel Processor. BBN Advanced Computers Inc., Massachusetts. 1986.

[9] J.C.Wyllie. The Complexity of Parallel Computations. *PhD Dissertation.* Computer Science Dept., Cornell Univ., Ithaca, NY,1981.

[10] R.M.Karp, V.Ramachandran. A Survey of Parallel Algorithms for Shared-Memory Machines. *Technical Report UCB-CSD-88-408.* UC Berkeley. March 1988.

[11] J.Lee, U.Ramachandran. Synchronization with Multiprocessor Caches. *International Symposium on Computer Architecture.* 1990.

[12] T.E.Anderson. The Performance of Spin Lock Alternatives for Shared-Memory Multiprocessors. *IEEE Transactions On Parallel And Distributed Systems.* January, 1990.

[13] R.E.Ladner, M.J.Fischer. Parallel Prefix Computation. *Journal of Association of Computing Machinery.* Vol 27, No. 4, October 1980.

[14] A.V.Aho, J.E.Hopcroft, J.D.Ullman. The Design and Analysis of Algorithms. Addison-Wesley, 1974.

[15] H.T.Kung. The Structure of Parallel Algorithms. *Advances In Computers.* Vol. 19, 1980.

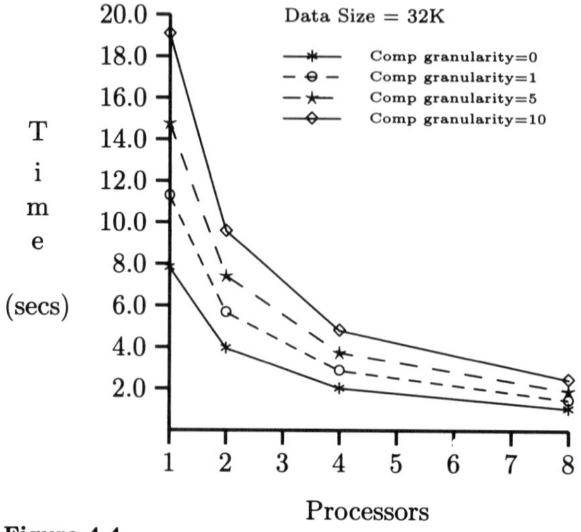

Figure 4.4
List Ranking – Static Scheduling On Sequent

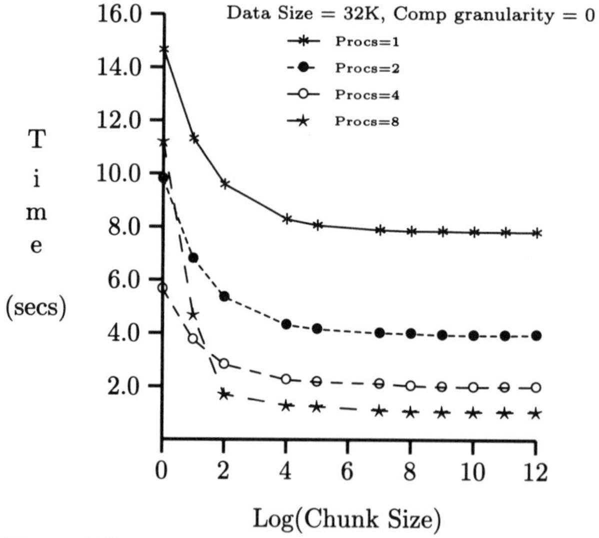

Figure 4.5
List Ranking – Dynamic Scheduling On Sequent (Data Granularity)

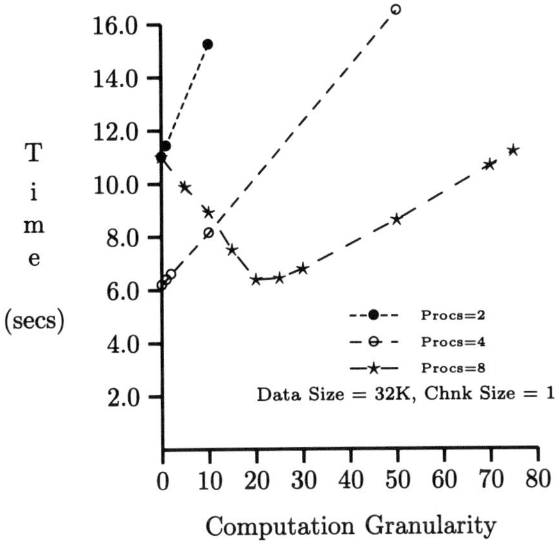

Figure 4.6
List Ranking – Dynamic Scheduling On Sequent (Computation Granularity)

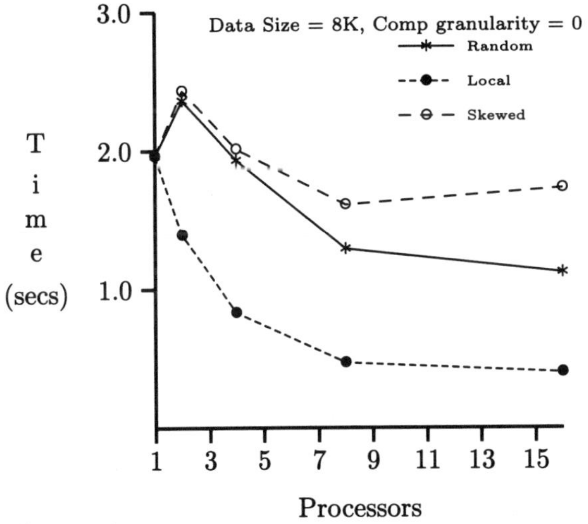

Figure 4.7
List Ranking – Static Scheduling On Butterfly (Data Distribution)

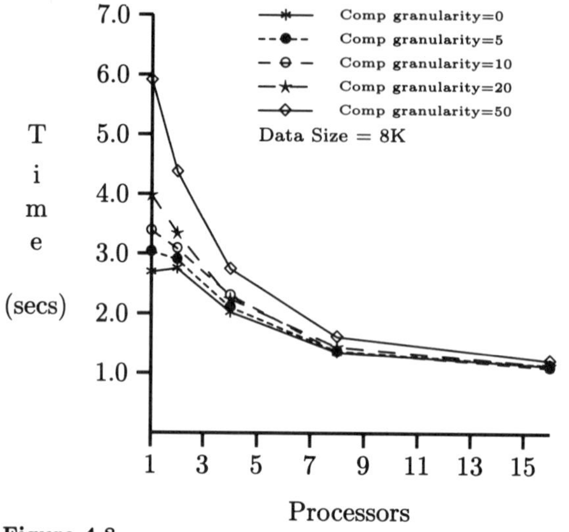

Figure 4.8
List Ranking – Static Scheduling On Butterfly (Random Distribution)

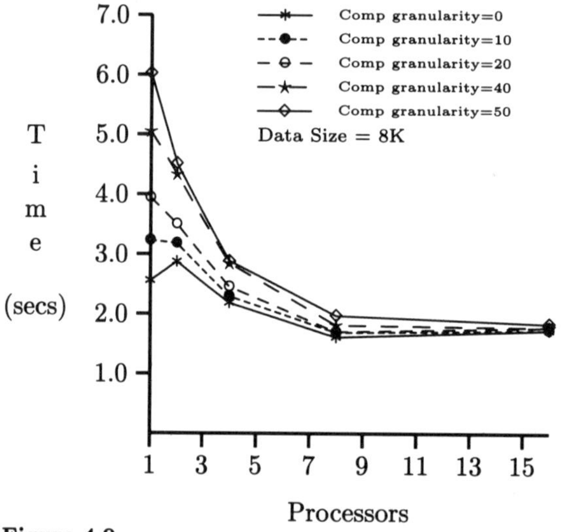

Figure 4.9
List Ranking – Static Scheduling On Butterfly (Skewed Distribution)

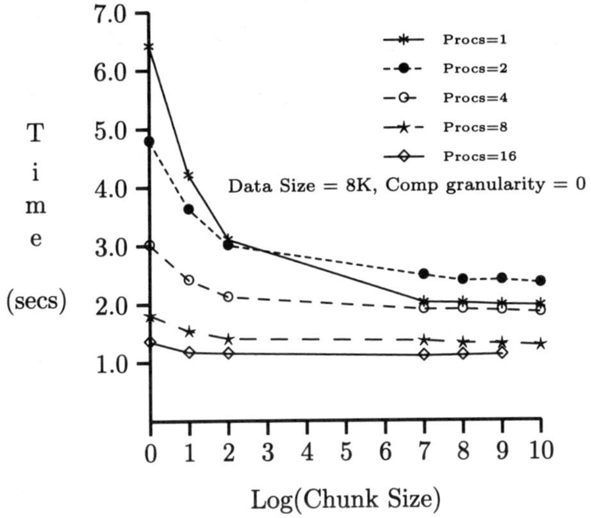

Figure 4.10
List Ranking – Dynamic Scheduling On Butterfly (Random Distribution, Data Granularity)

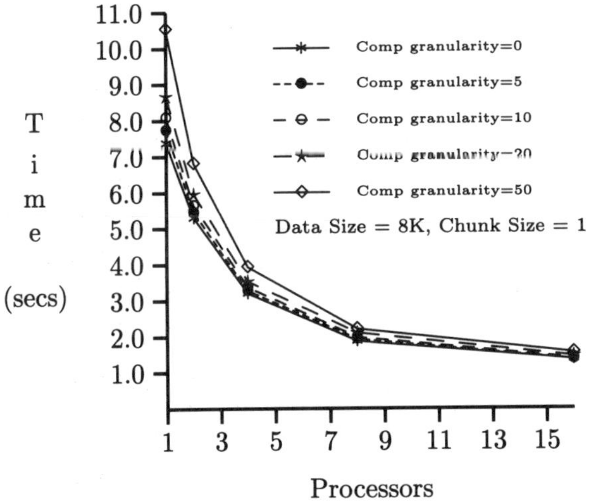

Figure 4.11
List Ranking – Dynamic Scheduling On Butterfly (Random Distribution, Computation Granularity)

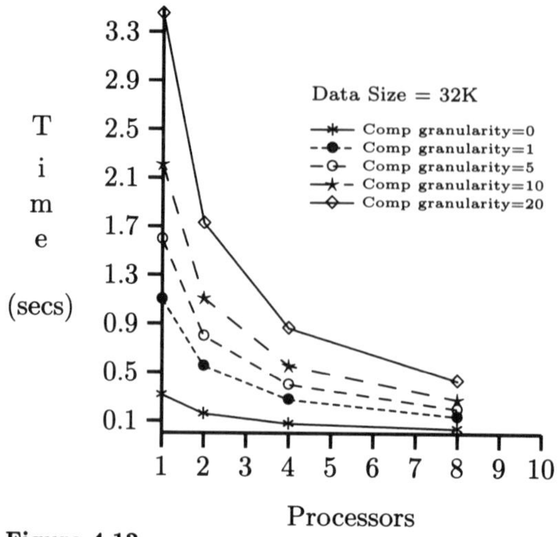

Figure 4.12
Parallel Prefix – Static Scheduling On Sequent

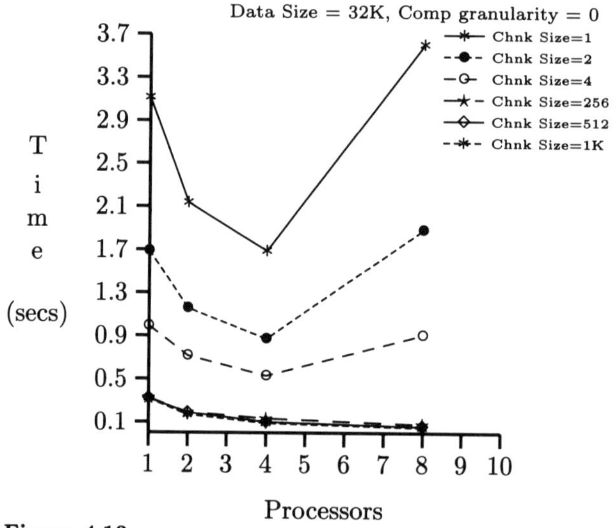

Figure 4.13
Parallel Prefix – Dynamic Scheduling On Sequent (Data Granularity)

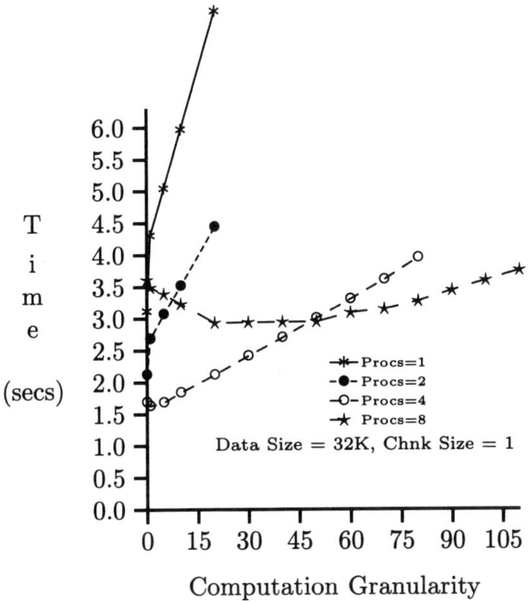

Figure 4.14
Parallel Prefix – Dynamic Scheduling On Sequent (Computation Granularity)

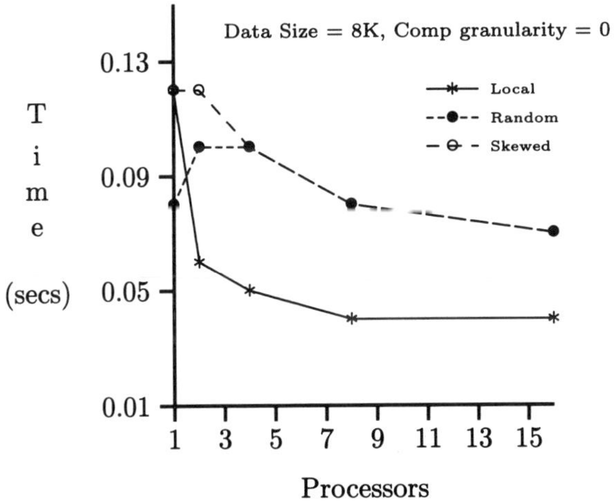

Figure 4.15
Parallel Prefix – Static Scheduling On Butterfly (Data Distribution)

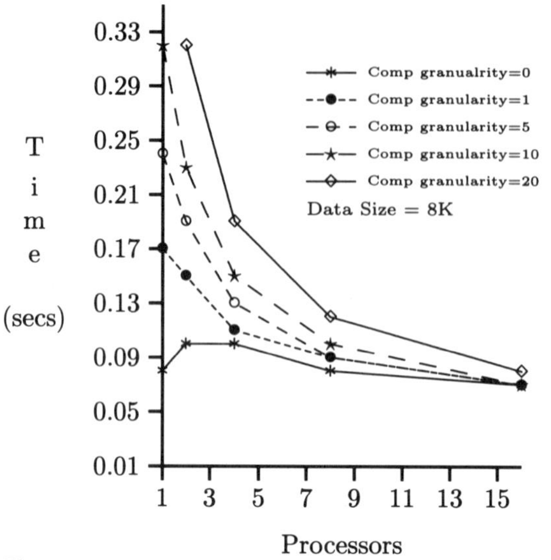

Figure 4.16
Parallel Prefix – Static Scheduling On Butterfly (Random Distribution)

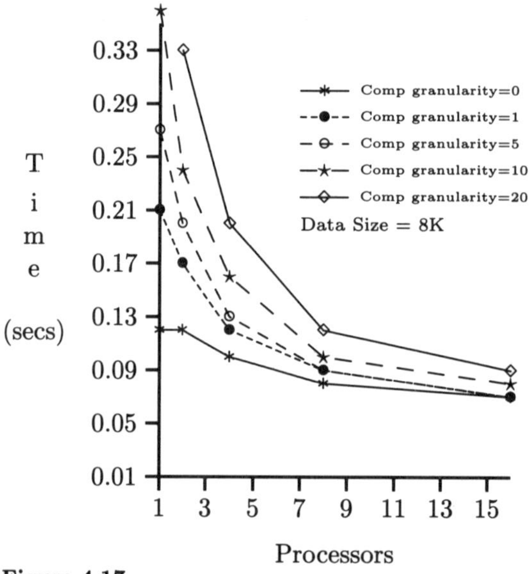

Figure 4.17
Parallel Prefix – Static Scheduling On Butterfly (Skewed Distribution)

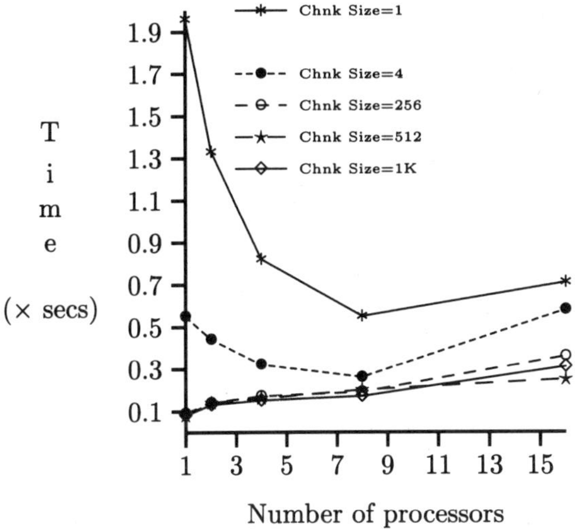

Figure 4.18
Dynamic Scheduling On Butterfly (Random Distribution, Data Size = 8K, No Artificial Work)

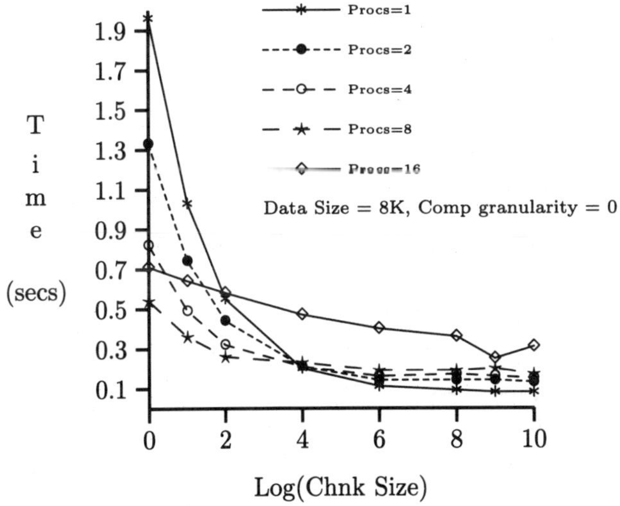

Figure 4.19
Parallel Prefix – Dynamic Scheduling On Butterfly (Random distribution, Data Granularity)

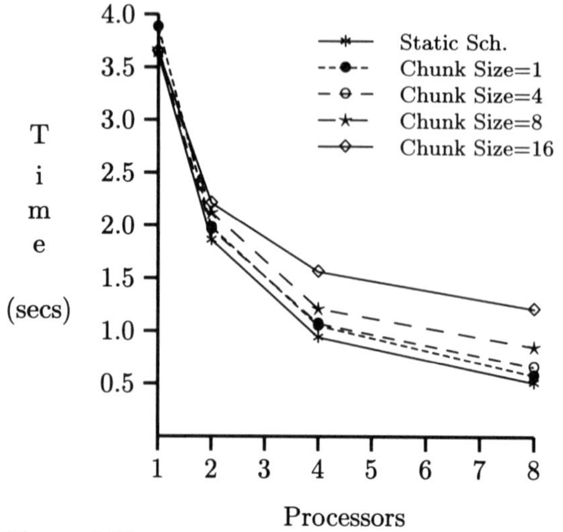

Figure 4.20
Optimal Binary Search Tree – Sequent Implementation

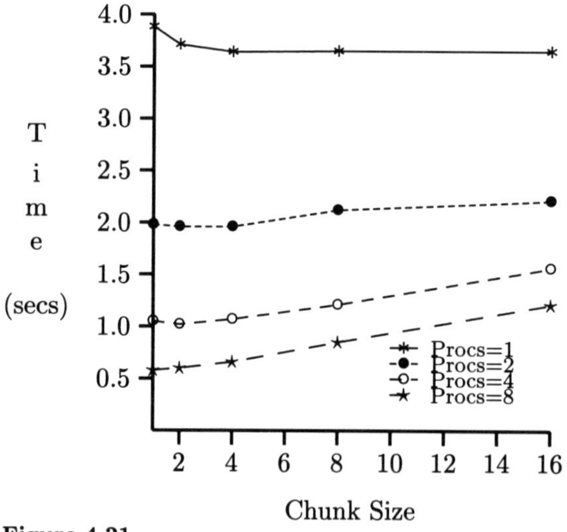

Figure 4.21
Optimal Binary Search Tree – Dynamic Scheduling On Sequent

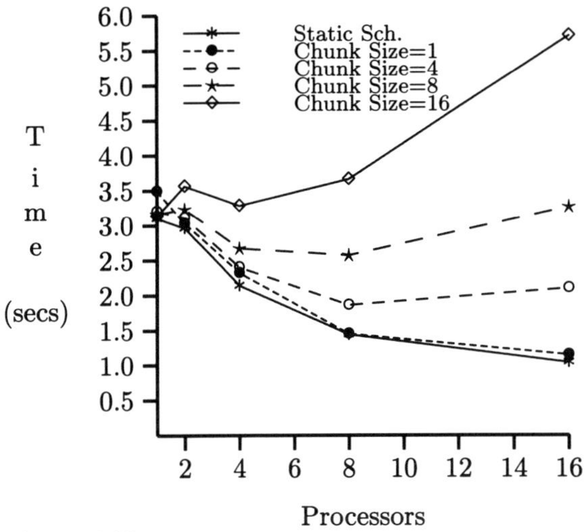

Figure 4.22
Optimal Binary Search Tree – Butterfly Implementation

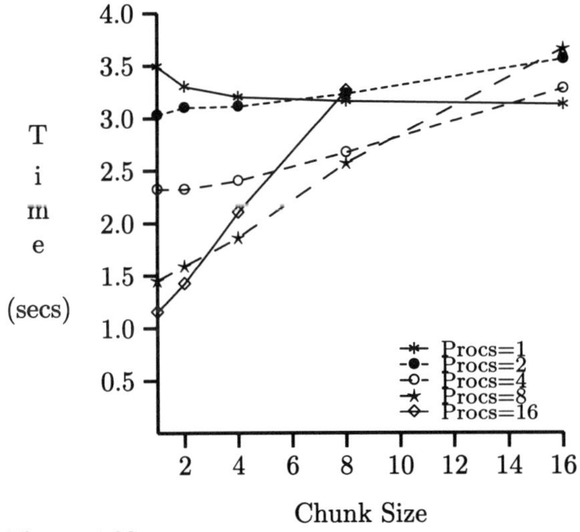

Figure 4.23
Optimal Binary Search Tree – Dynamic Scheduling On Butterfly

II CACHE COHERENCY

5 Formal Verification of the Gigamax Cache Consistency Protocol

Kenneth McMillan and James Schwalbe

One of the major recent innovations in automatic verification of concurrent finite state systems is the use of Boolean Decision Diagrams. This structure can be used to compactly represent Boolean functions, which can in turn represent state sets and graph relations which arise in a variety of algorithms used in automatic verification. This technique is known as *symbolic model checking*. It avoids the need to explicitly enumerate the state space of a finite state system, and hence can allow systems with extremely large numbers of states to be checked.

This chapter describes the application of symbolic model checking to a complex, real-life system – the memory hierarchy of the Gigamax multiprocessor, under development at Encore Computer Corporation. The complexity of this system, which uses both snooping cache methods and a message passing protocol to maintain consistency of distributed caches, led the designers to consider automatic verification, since it was clear that traditional simulation methods could not provide a sufficient degree of confidence in the system's correctness. After studying the system architecture, we constructed a formal model at a level of abstraction chosen to provide useful information about the design's correctness, without overwhelming detail. This model was then analyzed using a symbolic model checker based on Boolean Decision Diagrams. The symbolic model checker performed an exhaustive search of the model's state space without explicitly constructing the global state graph. This was important, since the number of states in the model varied from 10^9 to 10^{13}, depending on the level of detail and the configuration of the system being modeled. Checking the model for two important properties of a distributed memory system (consistency and absence of deadlock) exposed a number of design errors, including significant deadlocks which were not found by simulation. As the design evolved to correct these errors, the model was easily adapted, and was able to quickly provide an analysis of any new errors introduced by design changes.

The topics covered in this chapter include 1) an overview of the Gigamax memory architecture, 2) the construction of a finite state model of the system, 3) the formal specification in temporal logic, 4) the verification process and 5) some evaluation of the methods, and suggestions of areas for future research. Particular attention is given to relating the aspects of the model which result in efficient performance of the symbolic model checking procedure. These would seem to be fairly general and common to many computer system designs. A more detailed description of symbolic model checking can be found in [2, 3]. For techniques related to symbolic model checking, see [7, 9, 4, 5].

5.1 The Gigamax Memory Architecture

The Gigamax is a distributed, shared memory multiprocessor under development for DARPA at Encore Computer Corporation. The gross architecture of the Gigamax memory system is depicted in figure 5.1. The system is organized into a network of processor *clusters*. Each cluster is an Encore Multimax with a high speed, split transaction bus (called a *nanobus*), hosting a number of processor boards, some main memory, and a special interface card called a *UIC*. The UIC links the cluster into a star network. This network is centered around a global cluster, housing a collection of UIC's which link the global bus to each processor cluster. The processor boards within one cluster use a *snooping cache* protocol, similar to the protocols described in [1], but adapted for a split transaction bus. When a processor encounters a read (write) miss in its local cache, it issues a *read public* (*read private*) command on the nanobus, with a requester ID field indicating the source of the command. It then frees the bus for other transactions, while waiting for the memory, which is pipelined, to respond. The response to a read command contains the requester ID as a destination, and may be overlapped with any bus cycle which doesn't use the data part of the bus.

Each cache has a *bus watcher*, which keeps a copy of the cache tags. When the bus watcher detects an address on the bus which hits in the local cache, it may intervene by asserting the *memory bypass* signal on the bus and/or sending a command to the local cache to flush or invalidate the line. The specific response depends on the type of bus command and the *state* stored in the tag memory. Assertion of the memory bypass signal prevents the memory from responding to the command, and indicates that the asserting cache will respond to the command in the future with a *write response* command, which has the effect of simultaneously updating the contents of the main memory, and supplying the data to the original requester.

A simplified bus watcher state diagram is given in figure 5.2. The bus commands not mentioned previously are *write modified*, which occurs when a modified line is replaced in the cache (and must be written back to main memory) and *write invalidate*, which is used by non-caching devices and as an invalidation signal from remote clusters. Of particular interest are transitions to and from the *owned* state. A bus watcher enters the *owned* state when its cache issues a *read private* command.

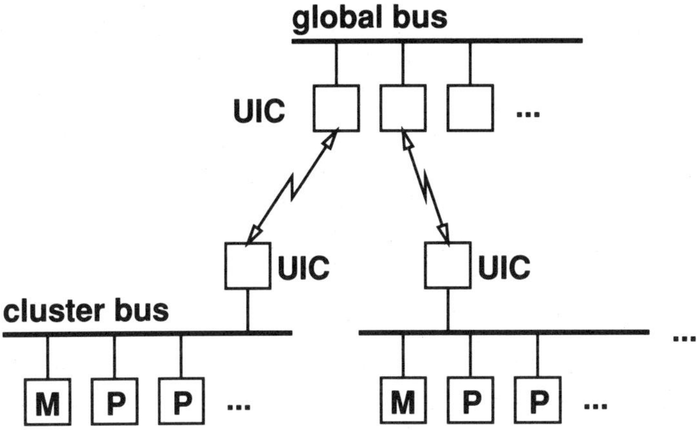

Figure 5.1
Gigamax memory architecture

If another bus watcher is in the owned state at this time, it asserts *memory bypass*, sends a *flush private* command to its local cache, and enters a special transitional state called *Xown*. Later, this cache will issue a *write response private* command on the bus, at which time the requester's cache goes valid, and the responder's bus watcher goes to the *invalid* state. In order to prevent any other requesters from interfering with this two phase ownership transfer process, an interlock is set in the requesting cache's bus watcher, which causes all future accesses to the observed address to be stalled until the ownership transfer is complete.

Each UIC also has a bus watcher which keeps track of addresses from the local main memory which are checked out in remote clusters. This allows the UIC to intervene on the bus on behalf of caches in remote clusters, eliminating the need for all processors to share the same bus. This system differs from a directory based cache system in that the UIC does not store the identities of all the other caches holding checked out copies. Instead, the tags stored in the global bus UIC's allow *invalidate*, *flush public* and *flush private* commands to be routed to all appropriate clusters. The UIC decides which command, if any, should be forwarded to the link based on its bus watcher state, the bus command type, whether or not the address is local, and the response of other bus watchers to the command. There are two parallel queues for storing messages in transit – one for read commands, and one for all other commands, with priority given to responses over requests. This allows responses to bypass requests in some cases, in order to avoid potential deadlock situations. The global bus UIC's are identical to the cluster UIC's, except in their address decoding.

As an example of Gigamax operation, consider the case where a miss occurs on a read in a local processor cache and where the address is located in a remote memory. This causes the local cache to issue a *read public* command on the bus. An interlock circuit is set to cancel any future access to that address while this command is pending. Now let's consider two cases:

- There is a cache in the local cluster in the *owned* state. The bus watcher of this cache intervenes in the transaction by asserting *memory bypass*. The requesting cache's bus watcher enters the *shared* state, while the intervening bus watcher enters the transitional state *Xown*, sending a *flush public* command to its local cache. Later, this cache issues a *write response public* command which causes its bus watcher to transition from the *Xown* state to the *shared* state, and the interlock to be canceled at the requesting cache. The UIC forwards this *write response public* command to the link with a null destination field, which causes the data to be written back to the remote main memory, since memory is now the implicit owner.
- No other local cache has a valid copy, but a cache in a different cluster is in the *owned* state. The local UIC forwards the *read public* command to the link (its default behavior for remote addresses). The command is issued on the global bus, setting an interlock on the global bus for this address. The global bus UIC connected to the cluster with the *owned* copy intervenes, forwarding the *read public* command to this cluster, and entering the *Xown* state. Eventually, a *write response public* returns from the remote cluster, its global UIC goes to the *shared* state, the *write response public* is returned to the local cluster, and the interlock is canceled on the global bus. Since main memory again becomes the implicit owner, the *write response public* is also forwarded to the main memory.

The complete set of rules governing the bus watchers, interlocks, and command forwarding is too complex to enumerate here. The interactions described above are fairly straightforward cases, but a number of

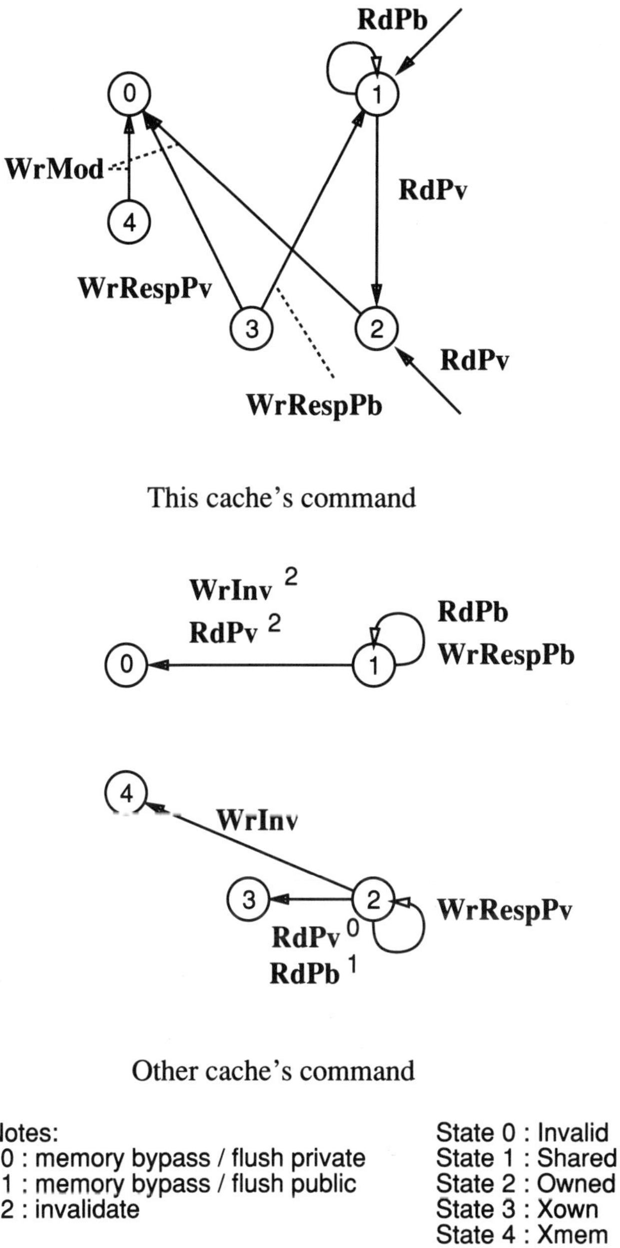

Figure 5.2
Bus watcher state diagram

unexpected things can happen when requests for the same location occur simultaneously on different clusters. When this happens, local state changes occur which are not immediately reflected in the state of remote UIC's, because of the latency in communication. This leads to complex interactions between clusters, and as we will see, can lead to deadlock.

5.2 Constructing the Formal Model

In order to apply model checking techniques to verify properties of the Gigamax cache protocol, we first need to model the system as a finite state machine, or more appropriately, a system of communicating finite state machines. A cache memory may be viewed as a finite state machine, whose state is an array of pairs, consisting of a tag and a data block. This amount of state information is prohibitively large, however, and is in any case largely redundant, since if one cache line remains consistent, then one can argue by symmetry that the others also remain consistent. To reduce the amount of state to a manageable size, we therefore choose to use abstraction – a process of discarding information about the state which is not relevant to the properties we are verifying. In this case, we choose to keep only the information that can be seen when a particular address is on the bus. Thus, if this address matches the tag of some line in the cache, then the state of the cache is considered to be the state associated with this tag, otherwise it is considered to be *invalid.* Likewise, in modeling the message buffers in the UIC's, the state is considered to be the set of messages who's address field matches the observed address. Whether or not the data part of a cache entry or message is kept in the abstraction, and how much of the data is kept, depends on the property which is being proved. In addition, a great many other details of the operation of the hardware are abstracted away – for example, the fact that certain subsystems, including the buses themselves, are pipelined. The external behavior of these systems is assumed to conform to an unpipelined view. The reason for this abstraction is that these details obscure the high level protocol issues which should be dealt with, ideally, before detailed design has even begun.[1]

[1] The models can later be refined at the component level, so that the effects of detailed design are confined to subsystems, making the overall complexity of the system manageable. See [13]

This kind of abstraction generally results in a degree of *non-determinism* in the model. This is because, in order to make the abstract model a sound basis for reasoning about the system, it must be constructed conservatively. If insufficient information exists in the abstract model to determine whether a transition is possible, one assumes that the transition might occur. A good example of this can be seen in the cache replacement policy. With no information about transactions on other memory locations, or their status in the cache, it is not possible to determine when the observed address is replaced, or when it will replace another address. It must therefore be assumed that replacement may occur at any time. While this may make it impossible to prove certain properties of the system, it has the advantage that properties we do prove hold independently of the cache replacement policy. Thus, by taking a bird's eye view, one can prove properties of a general class of systems rather than a particular implementation.

Another example of this non-determinism has to do with the latency of message delivery. Since the abstract model state contains information only about messages whose address field matches the observed address, the number of entries in a queue at any given time is not known. This introduces an arbitrary delay in the transmission of messages in the system.

Another technique for simplifying a model of a system is called an *unbalanced abstraction.* Such an abstraction of the Gigamax architecture is depicted in figure 5.3. The cluster model contains two processors, a local memory, and the UIC. The global bus model contains a UIC linking it to one cluster model, and a set of abstract UIC/cluster models, which represent the combination of a UIC card connected to a remote cluster. Thus, different components in the model are represented at different levels of detail. As we will see, some useful properties of the system can be proved by using these abstractions. In other cases, bugs in the design may be found automatically, even though not enough information exists in the model to prove that the system is correct.

5.2.1 Form of the model

The Gigamax model is written in a very simple description language based on Boolean logic. This language allows the description of finite state machines which are non-deterministic – a requisite in constructing abstract models. It also allows the description of a modular hier-

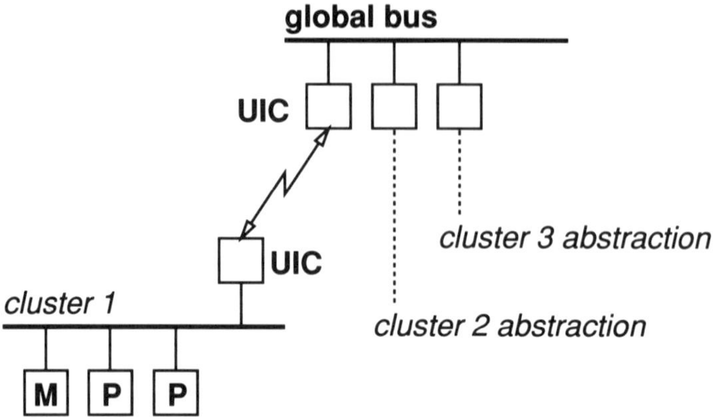

Figure 5.3
An unbalanced abstraction

archy. Most of the model is given as nested lists of condition/action rules, as illustrated in figure 5.4, making use of the "case" structure of the language. Variables in the language are divided into two sorts: state variables and auxiliary variables. Auxiliary variables are used to represent the value of communication signals and intermediate results. The transition relation is any relation which can be specified in Boolean logic, using the state variables, the auxiliary variables, and the "next" operator, which returns the next value of a given variable (much like the next or "new" operator in a data flow language, or in fact, the next time operator in a temporal logic). The case statement is actually syntactic sugar applied over Boolean logic. It is used to describe a list of rules to be used in priority order. This notation is translated into logic using implication and conjunction, but the case list form is much more readable. An additional feature of the language allows the description of systems which have components operating on separate clocks, such as the separate clusters in the Gigamax model. The transitions of these components are interleaved arbitrarily. This feature is used in the Gigamax model to account for the asynchrony between buses.

The text of the Gigamax model is about 500 lines of this code, and thus is a bit too complex to detail here.[2] It contains modules which

[2] The model text and the symbolic model checker software are available from the first author.

model the processor caches, the buses, the bus watchers associated with the UIC cards, and the buffers which hold messages in transit between cards, including the rules which govern the sending and blocking of messages. Overall, there are 10 different module types defined, about 70 rules related to bus watcher state changes, and about 25 dealing with message generation, as well as a small number dealing with interlocks and generation of bus cycles, and about 70 macro definitions.

5.2.2 Formal specifications in temporal logic

The memory system of the Gigamax is an example of a *reactive* system, in the sense that it responds to inputs from its environment continuously, rather than terminating after the computation of a result. To specify a reactive system, we need to describe an ongoing process in time rather than a function to be computed. Although there are a variety of formalisms for such specifications, the one we will use here is CTL, the temporal logic of branching time. CTL is a variant of propositional logic, with additional operators for expressing temporal relationships. For example, if g is a formula, then $\mathbf{F}g$ is true if and only if g holds at some state in the Future. The path quantified formula $\forall\mathbf{F}g$ holds if g holds at some state in *all* possible futures (*ie.*, along all possible computation paths), while $\exists\mathbf{F}g$ holds if g holds at some state in *some* possible future. Also, if g is a formula, then $\mathbf{G}g$ is true if g holds Globally in the future, *ie.*, in all future states. Path quantifiers also apply to the $\mathbf{G}$ operator.

The specifications for the Gigamax model break down into three categories: data consistency, absence of deadlock, and diagnostic correctness. If the Gigamax guaranteed strong consistency, a reasonable consistency specification would be

$$\forall p_n, p_m : \forall\mathbf{G}((p_n.\mathit{valid} \wedge p_m.\mathit{valid}) \Rightarrow (p_n.\mathit{data} = p_m.\mathit{data}))$$

That is, in all states along all paths, if two processor caches are in the valid state, then they hold the same data. Since the Gigamax guarantees a weak form of consistency, however, we use a weaker specification:

$$\forall p_n, p_m : \forall\mathbf{G}\forall\mathbf{F}(((p_n.\mathit{valid} \wedge p_m.\mathit{valid}) \Rightarrow (p_n.\mathit{data} = p_m.\mathit{data})) \vee \exists p_l : p_l.\mathit{write})$$

That is, if no processor writes (to the observed address) then eventually all copies become consistent. This specification is used because invali-

```
case
 ...
  Owned: case
    Stall | Idle : next(Owned);
    !mycyc : case
      WrInv & !RC : next(Xmem1);
      EchoRespPv & !RC : next(Owned);
      WrRespPv & RC : next(Owned);
      RdResp & RC: next(Owned);
      WrRespPbAlt & RC : next(Owned);
      WrMod & RC : next(Owned);
      CNack : next(Owned);
      RdPb : next(Xown1 & !FlPvPend);
      RdPv : next(Xown1 & FlPvPend);
      else: next(errstate);
      esac;
    else : case
      WrMod & !RC : next(Invalid);
      WrRespPbAlt & !RC : next(Shared);
      else : next(errstate);
      esac;
    esac;
  ...
esac
```

Figure 5.4
Fragment of Gigamax model text

date messages take some time to reach their destinations, hence some caches may hold out of date copies for a bounded length of time.

By absence of deadlock we mean in this case that the system cannot reach a state from which some "liveness" condition can never occur. Thus it is intended to include the absence of deterministic livelock conditions as well. In this case, the liveness conditions are readability and writability of the observed cache line at each processor cache:

$$\forall p_n : ((\forall \mathbf{G} \exists \mathbf{F} p_n.\mathit{shared}) \wedge (\forall \mathbf{G} \exists \mathbf{F} p_n.\mathit{owned}))$$

That is, in every reachable state, there must be a path to a state in which a given cache is in the *shared* state and a path to a state in which the cache is in the *owned* state.

Finally, the diagnostic correctness specification states that the diagnostic system never flags and error during normal operation of the system. This is simply stated in CTL as

$$\forall p_n : \forall \mathbf{G} \neg p_n.\mathit{error}$$

These three specifications are not intended to be a comprehensive list of the properties which the system should have. They represent instead a minimal set of properties which a designer would like to be certain of in order to be reasonably confident that the design is correct. There are certainly other properties which one might want to check. For example, the Gigamax makes weak guarantees of the sequentiality of writes to different addresses as seen by other caches. Obviously, a model with more than one cache line would be needed to check this property. Ideally, we would also like to show that all requests are eventually served. Unfortunately, because of the nature of the Gigamax bus protocols, this property only holds in a probabilistic sense. In fact, the system has watchdog timers to signal an interrupt in the very rare case when one processor is locked out for an extended period of time. Since we have no formal machinery for proving probabilistic properties of finite state systems, we concentrated on proving that no processor is ever deterministically locked out.

Another important question to consider is whether the refinement from abstract models back to detailed models actually preserves the properties expressed in the specification. In fact, this is the case for the consistency and diagnostic correctness specifications, since these include only universal path quantifiers, and computation paths are preserved in the abstraction. The absence of deadlock specification is a different case, however. Because this property relies on the *existence* of computation paths, it isn't necessarily preserved by refinement. For example, since our abstract model of the Gigamax has no state information relating to the scheduling of the bus, or the precise response times of certain components, certain potential livelock conditions may be ignored. From a practical point of view, though, the abstract model allowed us to find two significant deadlocks in the protocol (one of which was not found in simulation, and is described in the next section). Subsequent simulation revealed additional deterministic livelocks using a detailed model of the communications links.

5.3 The verification process

A model checker is a program which determines the truth value of logical formulas with respect to a specific model. A typical model checking program for CTL first constructs a complete state graph of the system. It then uses efficient algorithms for graph reachability and strongly connected components to label the vertices in this graph which satisfy each subformula of the specification, following the parse tree of the formula from inner to outer subformulas. Examples of finite state systems which have been verified, or partially verified, using this type of CTL model checker can be found in [8, 10, 11].

A very simple model checking algorithm for CTL is based on finding the fixed points of certain monotonic functions on sets of states. A function f is said to be monotonic with respect to the relation $\subseteq$ if $a \subseteq b \Rightarrow f(a) \subseteq f(b)$. A fixed point of f is any a such that $f(a) = a$. The least fixed point of a monotonic function is found by starting with the empty set, and iteratively applying f until a constant value is reached. That is,

$$\text{l.f.p.}f = \lim_{n \to \infty} f^n(\emptyset)$$

A finite state machine is represented by a directed graph $G = \langle V, E \rangle$, where V is the set of vertices (states) and E is the set of edges (transitions). If we let $Sat(g)$ stand for the set of vertices satisfying a formula g, then the set of states satisfying the formula $\exists\mathbf{F}g$ is the least fixed point of the function

$$f(R) = \{v | v \in Sat(g) \vee \exists w : (vEw \wedge w \in R)\} \tag{5.1}$$

In other words, $f(R)$ is the set of all vertices which either satisfy g or which have a successor w which is in R. It is not difficult to see that iterating this function (starting from the empty set) yields the set of all vertices which are on a path to $Sat(g)$.

For example, consider the following graph.

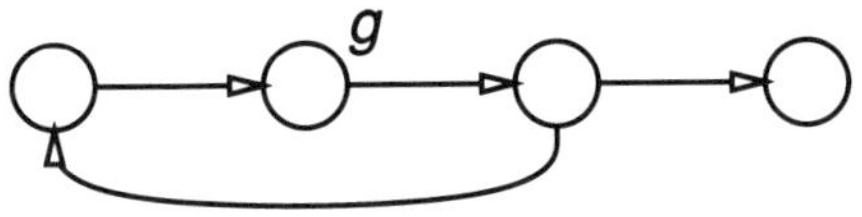

The first iteration, $f^1(\emptyset)$ gives us

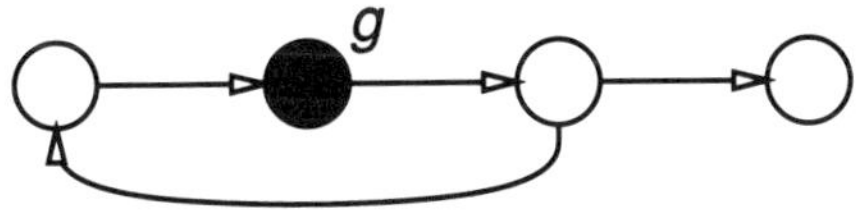

that is, exactly the states satisfying g. The second iteration, $f^2(\emptyset)$ yields

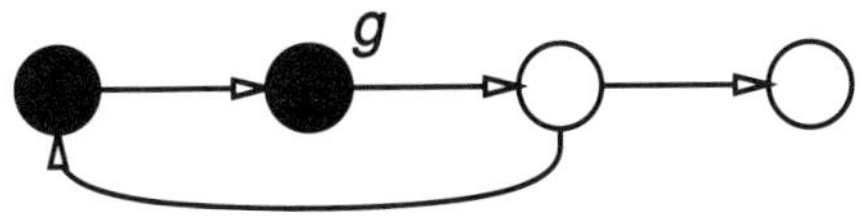

which is the set of states satisfying g plus those with a successor in $f^1(\emptyset)$. Finally, the third iteration, $f^3(\emptyset)$ gives

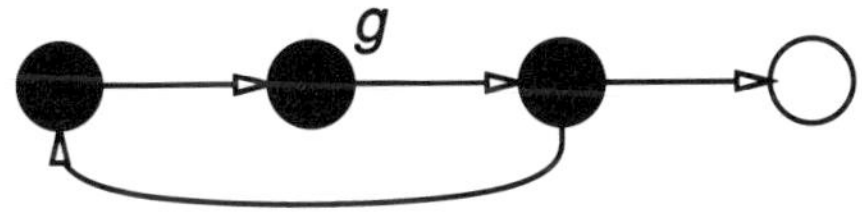

which is the least fixed point of f, since any further application of f yields the same result. Notice that we have labeled exactly the set of vertices on a path to $Sat(g)$. Notice also that this algorithm corresponds to a backward chaining breadth first search of the graph.

The remaining operators of CTL can also be characterized in terms of fixed points. For example the set of vertices satisfying $\exists \mathbf{G} g$ is the *greatest* fixed point of the function

$$f(R) = \{v | v \in Sat(g) \wedge \exists w : (vEw \wedge w \in R)\}$$

This algorithm is effective so long as the number of vertices in the graph G is small enough to store the graph in memory. However, a finite state machine with n binary storage devices can have as many as 2^n reachable vertices in its state graph. Even in the abstracted model of the Gigamax protocol, n is on the order of 100. Thus, it seems unlikely that a model checking algorithm which enumerates the state graph would be effective in this case. There are a number of methods for dealing with this explosion of states, however. One, which has already been mentioned, is abstraction – replacing a complex model with a simpler one which preserves the properties of interest. Another class of methods can be grouped under the heading of compositional reasoning, where one proves properties of small pieces of the system, and then combines these results in some way to prove something about the system as a whole. A third way, which we discuss here, is to use a symbolic representation for large sets and graphs, rather than an explicit one.

For example, one can represent a set by its characteristic function. If a finite state machine has n storage elements, then its state is a Boolean vector of length n, *ie.*, $V = \{0,1\}^n$. A set of states $S \subseteq V$ has a characteristic function

$$\chi_S : \{0,1\}^n \to \{0,1\}$$

which yields one if its argument is in the set, and zero otherwise. Likewise, a binary relation $R \subseteq V \times V$ has a characteristic function

$$\chi_R : \{0,1\}^{2n} \to \{0,1\}$$

which yields one if and only if its argument is a *pair* of vertices in the relation. In this way both $Sat(g)$, the set of states satisfying g, and E, the edge relation of a graph, can be represented by boolean functions. A boolean function, in turn, can be represented by a Boolean Decision Diagram [6]. This is a very useful canonical form which is derived from ordered decision trees. An example of an ordered decision tree representing the function $f(a,b,c,d) = a \cdot b + c \cdot d$ is shown in figure 5.5. The result of the function is obtained by tracing the tree from the root to a leaf, branching at each vertex based on the binary value of the variable labeling that vertex. In an ordered decision tree, the variables appear in the same order along any path in the tree. Two facts are significant about this tree. First, the subtrees rooted at the vertices labeled (*) are

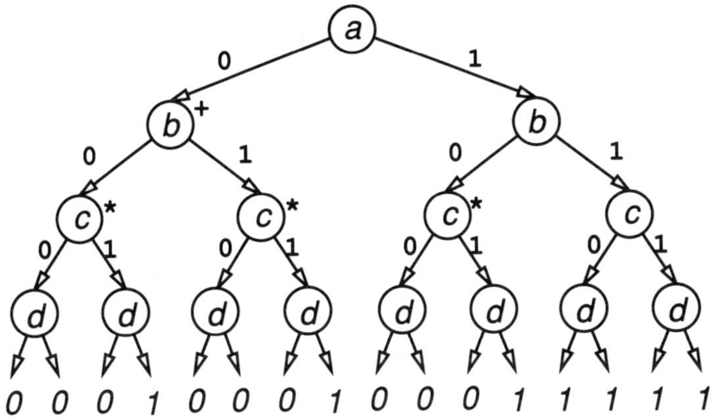

Figure 5.5
Ordered Decision Tree

all isomorphic. Thus, we could save storage by combining these three subtrees. Second, the vertex labeled (+) is redundant, since branching in either direction from this vertex reaches the same subtree.

A Boolean Decision Diagram (BDD) is obtained from an ordered decision tree by combining all isomorphic subtrees, and eliminating all vertices with isomorphic children. The result of this process for the ordered decision diagram discussed above is show in figure 5.6. Note the dramatic reduction in the number of vertices. In general the amount of reduction can depend critically on the ordering of variables chosen for the ordered decision tree. Given this ordering, the BDD representation of a Boolean function is unique up to isomorphism.

BDD's for complex functions can be built from the BDD's for simpler functions using logical operations. For example, the logical negation of a BDD is obtained by simply negating the values of all of the leaves. The logical conjunction and disjunction of two BDD's can be obtained by an algorithm which is linear in the sizes of both BDD's (see [6]). There is also an efficient procedure for quantification of a BDD with respect to a Boolean variable. For example, $\exists a : f \equiv f|_{\bar{a}} \vee f|_{a}$.

These operations are sufficient to implement the fixed point algorithms for CTL model checking, using BDD's to represent the characteristic functions of the function parameter R and the edge relation E. For example, let's say that a finite state machine has two storage elements a

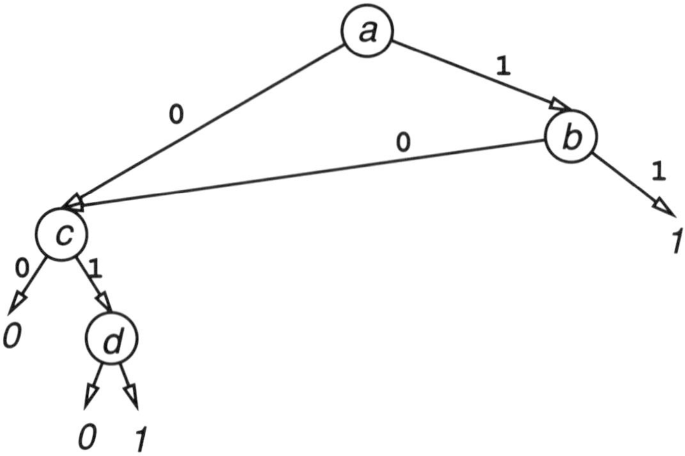

Figure 5.6
Boolean Decision Diagram

and b. The set R can be represented by a Boolean function $R(a,b)$, while the edges of the state graph can be represented by a Boolean function $E(a,b,a',b')$. If $g(a,b)$ represents the set of states satisfying formula g, the the set of states satisfying $\exists\mathbf{F}g$ is (represented by) the least fixed point of

$$f(R(a,b)) = g(a,b) \vee \exists a', b' : (E(a,b,a',b') \wedge R(a',b'))$$

(see equation 5.1). This function can be computed using BDD's to represent the Boolean functions, since we have BDD algorithms for the $\wedge$, $\vee$, and $\exists$ operations. The least fixed point is obtained by iterating this function starting with the characteristic function of the empty set (false). Convergence of this iteration is simple to detect, since BDD's are a canonical form. In this way, we can evaluate CTL formulas without actually constructing the state graph G.

To do this, of course, we must construct the BDD representing the edge relation E, without building the graph. This can also be done using the BDD operations. The edge relation E is the conjunction of the edge relations of the components. For example, consider a state machine with n state bits, denoted $v_1 \ldots v_n$, and m inputs, denoted $w_1 \ldots w_m$, where the next value of each state bit v_i is determined by a function $f_i(\bar{v}, \bar{w})$.

The edge relation of the system is

$$E(\bar{v}, \bar{v}') = \exists \bar{w} : \bigwedge_{i=1}^{n} (v_i' \Leftrightarrow f(\bar{v}, \bar{w}))$$

5.3.1 Applying the model checking algorithm

Using the symbolic model checking algorithm, we can verify that the abstract Gigamax model satisfies the formal specifications in CTL. If the model fails the specification, the model checker outputs an execution sequence which is a counterexample to the formula (to the extent such a counterexample exists). A number of interesting counterexamples were produced by the model checker for failures of the absence of deadlock specification. The following is a summary of a counterexample which was obtained using the unbalanced abstraction (see figure 5.3). It begins with a processor in cluster 2 holding an *owned* copy of an address checked out from the main memory of cluster 1.

1. A processor in cluster 1 encounters a read miss, and issues a *read public* command. The UIC in cluster 1 intervenes in this request and sends a *flush public* command (implemented by *read public*) to the global bus, which stores the command in a queue. The processor in cluster 1 sets its interlock.
2. A processor in cluster 3 encounters a read miss, and issues a *read public* command. This command reaches the global bus, where the global UIC for cluster 2 intervenes (since cluster 2 holds an owned copy), and a *flush public* is sent to cluster 2. The global bus UIC for cluster 3 sets an interlock.
3. The response from cluster 2 (a *write response public* command) is transmitted via the global bus to cluster 3. This results in the global UIC bus watchers for both clusters being in the shared state, and the interlock being released. Since main memory is now implicit owner, a *write response public* command, with null destination, is sent to cluster 1 by the global UIC for cluster 1.
4. The *write response public* message reaches cluster 1, and the data are deposited in main memory. This does not supply data to the waiting processor in cluster 1, however, since the command has a null destination field.
5. The processor in cluster 2 invalidates its copy by cache replacement, then encounters a read miss and issues a *read public* command, which is

forwarded to the global bus. Since no global UIC is in the *owned* state, the command is routed normally to cluster 1 and enqueued there. The global bus UIC for cluster 2 sets its interlock.
6. The original *read public* command from step 1 is issued on the global bus, but is blocked by the interlock held by cluster 2. Likewise the *read public* from step 5 is issued on the cluster 1 bus, and is blocked by the interlock set in step 1. Since neither interlock can be released until the request that switched it on is satisfied, a deadlock occurs at this point.

This is an example of the classic deadlock situation which occurs when two processes attempt to obtain locks on two resources in different orders. Nonetheless, the sequence of events that lead to this situation were sufficiently complex that the designers were unable to predict that the situation might occur. In fact, the deadlock situation was found at a search depth of thirteen transitions. At each step in this sequence, there were several alternatives that might have averted the deadlock. Thus it is unlikely that this deadlock would be found by a random simulation run, or a simulation run based on address traces, and in fact, it was not found in behavioral level simulations.[3]

The fact the the model checker was able to print out automatically an example of this deadlock highlights an important practical aspect of the technique. These counterexamples are of perhaps even greater value than a proof that the system is correct, since such a proof is useful only to the level of detail at which the system is modeled, and only if the original specification was correct and complete. A counterexample, however, provides an important clue as to where a bug in the system lies, and how it might be corrected.

Checking the diagnostic correctness specification also proved to be a particularly useful application of the model checker which turned up numerous bugs in the design, since predicting by hand which bus events might be seen by a bus watcher in any given state turned out to be an extremely error prone process. In fact, it would have been possible

[3] In fact, the number of possible transitions from a given state ranges from 6 to 12. The probability of a random simulation run executing this trace is therefore in the range $6^{-13} = 7.7 \times 10^{-11}$ to $12^{-13} = 9.3 \times 10^{-15}$. The expected time for a random simulation to exhibit this behavior would be somewhere between 2.4 years and 29 millenia, assuming the simulation could be carried out at 10,000 steps per second.

run	$\|E\|$	$max(\|f^n(\emptyset)\|)$	$\|V\|$	iterations
1	11146	1429	2.99×10^9	15
2	44100	898	1.04×10^{13}	5
3	8823	2550	3.30×10^9	20

Table 5.1
Performance of symbolic model checker for three different models.

for the model checker to compute the conditions for signaling errors, although we had no tools for directly translating this into the design.

All three specifications were eventually proved on a corrected design, although as stated previously, there are certain caveats regarding the absence of deadlock specification.

5.3.2 Performance of the model checker

We now examine the performance of the symbolic model checking algorithm in verifying the Gigamax model with respect to our specifications. Table 5.1 summarizes three separate runs of the model checker. The first run was to check the absence of deadlock property on a model with the data part completed abstracted. The second run checked the consistency property, and failed at a search depth of 5. The third run used a later model, without the unbalanced abstraction, and checking only the diagnostic correctness specification. The number of states here is comparable to that in the first run because of a simplification of the model of the message queues. The table gives the number of BDD nodes needed to represent the edge relation ($|E|$), the largest number of nodes needed to represent an iteration of the fixed point algorithm ($max(|f^n(\emptyset)|)$), the number of vertices in the state graph ($|V|$), and the greatest number of iterations needed for convergence of the fixed point algorithm. A comparison of the number of reached states with the size of the BDD's is of some interest, since traditional model checking algorithms must store the entire global state graph. With state spaces as large as 10^{13} states, it is clear that the models could not have been handled directly using traditional model checking methods. None of these three runs required more than a few minutes, however, using a symbolic model checker running on a Sun3/60.

We now examine some reasons why the BDD representation is more compact than an explicit storage of the state graph. Roughly speaking, the reason that the edges of such a large graph can be represented is related to the fact that a bounded amount of communication occurs over a bus in a single cycle. This results in a property of the set of edges which we will refer to as "loose coupling". This property is shared by the sets of states obtained in the fixed point iterations, owing to the nature of the protocol. In short, knowing the state of one part of the system entails only weak knowledge of the state of the remainder of the system. This informal notion can be quantified, and is directly related to the number of nodes in the BDD representation. Consider, for example, a horizontal slice through the decision tree from our earlier example, as depicted in figure 5.7. If the value of the variables above the slice is known, this identifies a particular subtree below the slice as representing the set of possible values of the remaining variables. The number of unique such subtrees, which we will refer to as the "coupling factor", is a measure of the mutual information between the two sets of variables, and is also the width of the BDD when cut at this particular level. In the figure, the coupling factor is two. Note that the coupling factor is robust in the sense that it does not change if the variables on either side of the slice are re-ordered, or if the the two sides are exchanged. In the case of a snooping cache protocol, the coupling factor through any slice is likely to be bounded by a small number, as knowledge of the state of some caches allows one to know whether other caches may be in certain states, but not which caches are in particular states. Thus we expect the BDD representing the reachable states to be small, in fact, linear in the number of caches. The BDD representing the edge relation of a bus based system is also expected to be linear in the number of bus clients, as there are a finite number of messages which can be passed on the bus, and the number of distinct subtrees below any given slice is bounded by the number of possible messages on the bus (provided that slice does not separate state variables of any client.)

5.4 Future Plans and Conclusions

There are a number of limitations to the current work, which we will attempt to address in the future. One obvious area of extension is in refining the model to include more detail of the protocol implementation.

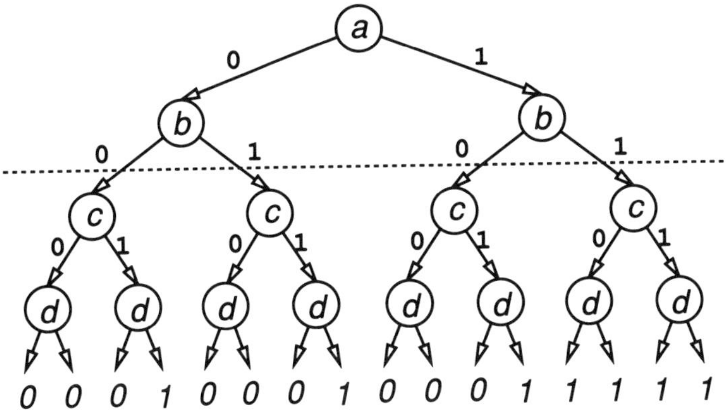

Figure 5.7
Horizontal slice through a decision tree.

A refined model, for example, could reveal deterministic livelocks which are not apparent in the high level model. Although verification at the architectural level has been useful, this has not prevented significant problems from developing in aspects of the design below this level of detail. Once the high level protocol is verified, it is important to verify that the individual components of the system are implemented correctly. Perhaps a more important problem is that the current model considers only one memory address in the system. By including information about two or more memory locations that may replace each other in the caches, more information may be obtained about deadlocks relating to cache replacement. (Recall that in the model, replacement may occur at any time. In actuality, replacement will only occur when all associates are full. This more restricted behavior may not lead to any consistency violations not present in the more abstract model, but may lead, for example, to livelocks which would not otherwise occur). Also, there are other properties of the model that should be verified if more than one memory location is modeled. For example, the system guarantees write sequentiality under certain circumstances, and this should be formally verified.

Another possible area of extension is proving that the system specifications are satisfied for models with an arbitrary rather than a fixed number of bus clients. This can in theory be accomplished using the induction method described in [12]. An example of this process can already be seen in the abstract UIC/cluster model. If this model can be shown to be a formal abstraction of a UIC model connected to a cluster bus which in turn is a collection of UIC/cluster models, then an inductive argument will show that it is an abstraction of a hierarchy of any depth. The UIC/cluster model serves in this case as a *process invariant.* Finding such invariants is the key to doing inductive proofs about processes. To show that the system specification holds for a cluster bus with an arbitrary number of clients, it is sufficient to find a process invariant which is an abstraction of itself with one added bus client, and which itself satisfies the specification. This method is practical if such an invariant can be constructed for realistically complex models, such as the present one. At present, only simple, fairly theoretical problems have been solved using this method, and it will be interesting to see how well it transfers to practice.

What conclusions can we draw from this experience? It seems to support the notion that formal modeling can be a valuable tool in the early phases of design of a complex protocol, and can save a great deal of wasted effort in the detailed design of systems which are flawed at the architectural level. The techniques presented here are limited to systems which can be represented with finite state models. This would seem to cover a fairly broad range of protocols implemented in both hardware and software, however. Another apparent conclusion is that the number of states of a system is not a very good measure of the complexity of verifying the system automatically, and that other measures based on the structure of the state space may be more appropriate. Using techniques of abstraction and compact symbolic representations, such as BDD's, we can automatically prove properties of extremely complex systems. Perhaps more importantly, automatic verification systems can produce examples of behavior which contradicts the specification. Thus instead of asking the question "What happens when this input sequence is applied", we ask the question "What input sequence causes this system to fail".

Acknowledgments

K. L. McMillan is supported by an AT&T Bell Laboratories Ph.D. scholarship. The Gigamax research at is sponsored by the Defense Advanced Research Agency (DoD) ARPA Order No. 5875 monitored by Space and Naval Warfare Systems Command under Contract No. N00039-86-C-0158.

References

[1] J. Archibald and J. L. Baer. Cache coherence protocols: Evaluation using a multiprocessor simulation model. *ACM Transactions on Computer Systems*, 4(4):273–298, 1986.

[2] J. R. Burch, E. M. Clarke, K. L. McMillan, D. L. Dill, and J. Hwang. Symbolic model checking: 10^{20} states and beyond. In *Proceedings of the Fifth Annual Symposium on Logic in Computer Science*, June 1990.

[3] J. R. Burch, E. M. Clarke, K. L. McMillan, and D. L. Dill. Sequential circuit verification using symbolic model checking. In *ACM/IEEE Design Automation Conference*, June 1990.

[4] S. Bose and A. Fisher. Verifying pipelined hardware using symbolic logic simulation. In *IEEE International Conference on Computer Design*, 1989.

[5] Soumitra Bose and Allan L. Fisher. Automatic verification of synchronous circuits using symbolic logic simulation and temporal logic. In Luc Claesen, editor, *Proceedings of the IMEC-IFIP International Workshop on Applied Formal Methods For Correct VLSI Design*, pages 759–764, November 1989.

[6] R. E. Bryant. Graph-based algorithms for boolean function manipulation. *IEEE Transactions on Computers*, C-35(8), 1986.

[7] Randal E. Bryant. Verifying a static ram design by logic simulation. In Jonathan Allen and F. Thomson Leighton, editors, *Advanced Research in VLSI: Proceedings of the Fifth MIT Conference*, pages 335–349. MIT Press, 1988.

[8] E. M. Clarke, S. Bose, M. C. Browne, and O. Grumberg. The design and verification of finite state hardware controllers. Technical Report 87-145, Carnegie Mellon University, 1987.

[9] Olivier Coudert, Christian Berthet, and Jean Christophe Madre. Verification of synchronous sequential machines based on symbolic execution. In Joseph Sifakis, editor, *Automatic Verification Methods for Finite State Systems, International Workshop, Grenoble, France*, volume 407 of *Lecture Notes in Computer Science*. Springer-Verlag, June 1989.

[10] E. M. Clarke, E. A. Emerson, and A. P. Sistla. Automatic verification of finite-state concurrent systems using temporal logic specifications. *ACM Transactions on Programming Languages and Systems*, 8(2):244–263, 1986.

[11] E. M. Clarke, D. E. Long, and K. L. McMillan. A language for compositional specification and verification of finite state hardware controllers. In *9th International Symposium on Hardware Description Languages and their Applications*, 1989.

[12] R. Kurshan and K. L. McMillan. A structural induction theorem for processes. In *ACM Symposium on Principles of Distributed Computing*, Edmonton, Alberta, 1989.

[13] R. P. Kurshan. Testing containment of ω-regular languages. Technical Report 1121-861010-33-TM, Bell Laboratories, 1986.

6 An Evaluation of Cache Coherence Protocols for Multiprocessors

Sandra Johnson Baylor, Kevin P. McAuliffe, and Bharat D. Rathi

This paper presents the results of a study conducted to evaluate the performance of three cache coherence protocols for multistage interconnection network (MIN) based multiprocessors. Two hardware protocols (both directory-based) and one software protocol are evaluated in this study. Both hardware protocols implement the same coherence protocol; however, the *hardware* scheme implements this protocol on *all* data references and the *hybrid* scheme implements this protocol *only* on shared data. The *software* protocol only caches private data and does not cache shared data. Engineering/scientific application traces are used to drive the simulator. The results show that with an average of 5% of all references shared, the false sharing effects degrade the performance of the hardware and hybrid protocols to the extent that the software protocol is competitive.

6.1 Introduction

The use of private caches in a shared-memory multiprocessor may result in the well-known cache coherence problem. Numerous solutions have been proposed to solve this problem [1]. These solutions may generally be classified into two distinct types; hardware and software. Hardware coherence protocols typically incorporate all consistency maintenance in the hardware and have the advantage of user-transparency. Software protocols require the user and/or a compiler to explicitly declare data as either shared or private. Consistency is then maintained by not caching shared data or by caching shared data only during certain phases of program execution, *i.e.*, epochs [2].

Hardware protocols may be divided into three types; snoopy-based [3], hierarchical bus [4] and directory-based [5, 6, 7]. Directory-based protocols have been proposed for multiprocessors with a multistage interconnection network (MIN). These protocols are generally broadcast or multicast invalidation-based or some combination of the two. A global or distributed directory is associated with main memory or the cache. Software protocols may be divided into two types, static and dynamic. In the static protocol, all shared data is non-cachable. The dynamic protocol allows shared data to be cached during certain phases of program execution [8].

This paper presents the results of a study conducted to evaluate the performance of two variations of a directory-based hardware cache coherence protocol and a conservative (static) software protocol. One of the hardware protocols, denoted *hardware*, uses a directory-based coherence protocol for *all* data accesses. The second directory-based protocol, denoted *hybrid*, uses the same coherence protocol but *only* on shared data references (as explicitly declared by the user and/or compiler). The *software* protocol evaluated allows caching of private data, but prohibits the caching of shared data. These three protocols have the potential to scale well beyond the limits of snoopy-based protocols because the MINs are not communication bandwidth limited relative to the shared bus.

The results presented contribute to the correct execution of the applications by guaranteeing sequential consistency as described by Lamport [9]. However, other consistency models, *i.e.*, weak consistency [10], may be used with the hybrid and software protocols. We did not use the weak consistency model because our traces used did not explicitly specify synchronization addresses.

The next section (Section II) discusses the motivations for this work. Section III presents the system organization assumed in this study as well as a state diagram of the directory-based protocol evaluated. Section IV briefly discusses the simulation methodology and presents the performance analysis. Section V presents some conclusions and suggestions for future work. Finally, Appendix A discusses the engineering/scientific applications used.

6.2 Motivation

This work was motivated by three issues that have not been extensively evaluated in the literature. First, it is not currently clear what type of coherence protocol (hardware, software or some combination of the two) will provide the best overall performance for multiprocessors with multistage interconnection networks (MINs). Therefore, we wanted to develop a mechanism for evaluating various cache coherence protocols for MIN-based systems. Secondly, while numerous distributed-directory protocols have been proposed, we are not aware of any detailed study that quantitatively considers the impact of combined multicast/broadcast invalidation-based distributed directory design features on the performance of these systems. Third, we wanted to determine the limits of scalability for the coherence protocols evaluated.

There have been extensive studies on snoopy-based protocols and some work on hierarchical bus and directory-based protocols. Agarwal, *et. al.*, evaluated the performance of directory-based and snoopy-based protocols for a 4 processor multiprocessor. Owicki and Agarwal [11] compared the performance of two software protocols and one snoopy-based protocol. Min and Baer [12] conducted a performance comparison of Censier and Feautrier's [13] directory-based hardware protocol and their timestamp-based software protocol for MIN-based multiprocessors with private data caches. Finally, Chaiken, *et. al* [14], compared the performance of several non-broadcast protocols. Our work concentrates on the study of combined multicast/broadcast invalidation-based protocols.

6.3 System Organization and Cache Coherence Protocol

6.3.1 System Organization

The organization assumed is illustrated in Figure 6.1. It consists of P processors with private data and instruction caches, a packet-switched multistage interconnection network (MIN) and M memory modules. The MIN actually consists of two networks: a request network, which routes requests from the processors to the memory modules; and a response network, which routes requests from the memory modules to the processors. Associated with each memory module is the *distributed global directory* (DGD) used in enforcing cache coherence for the hardware and hybrid protocols. It is assumed that a processor issues a request at each cycle provided its associated cache can accept the request. Otherwise, the request is held until the cache is free. In reality, data requested by the processor may be stored in a processor register, eliminating the need to submit a request to the cache. Therefore, this absence of a processor model results in a lower bound on the performance results obtained. All instruction references in the traces used in this study are non-self-modifying and do not contribute to the performance degradations caused by cache inconsistencies. Therefore, only the data caches implement the coherence protocols. Furthermore, the instruction caches are assumed to be infinite and are not modelled in this study.

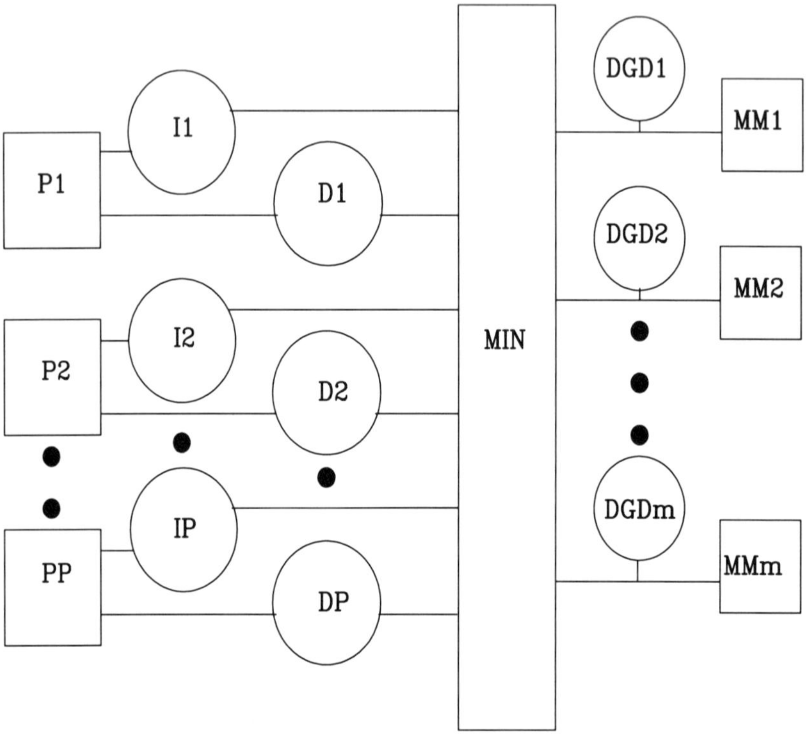

Figure 6.1
Multiprocessor Architecture. P-Processors, I-Instruction Cache, D-Data Cache, DGD-Distributed Global Directory, MM-Memory Module.

A virtual address data cache is used in the model. One of the disadvantages of using virtual address caches is the fact that several virtual addresses may be mapped to the same physical address (the *synonym* problem). This problem (as well as others) and its solution is discussed in [15]. In this study, it is assumed that all processes sharing data also share the same virtual address space and two virtual pages within the same virtual address space do not map to the same physical page.

Figure 6.2 presents a functional diagram of the data cache used in this study. It consists of a modified version of Goodman's virtual cache organization [15] and implements a write-back strategy. The cache consists of two directories, one virtual and one real, a pending store buffer (PSB) and a store-back buffer (SBB). The virtual tag store functions as a typical cache directory (servicing processor requests) whereas the real tag store functions as a snooping controller, servicing coherence requests from the distributed global directory. It is accessed using real addresses supplied by the network.

Both the virtual and real tag stores contain the traditional cache directory information as well as additional coherence state information used in implementing the cache coherence protocol. Details on this state information are presented in Section III.B. The store-back buffer (SBB) is used to hold words to be written back to main memory. Each entry in the SBB contains an address/word/pointer combination. The word contains the modified data for the given address, while the pointer indicates the SBB location of another word, within the same line, that has been modified. The modified words of a line are transferred together, whenever free request network cycles are encountered.

The pending store buffer (PSB) is used to hold write hits to shared data until the DGD grants permission to apply the modified data to the cache data store. This buffer is used to avoid the write-back of this data if an invalidation signal is received before the permission-to-modify signal (Section II.B describes this signal). Each entry in the PSB contains a word/pointer combination as well as information indicating the cache data store location where this data is to be placed. Once the permission-to-modify signal is received from the DGD, the data is placed in the data store. Write misses are applied directly to the data store. Read hits are serviced immediately whereas read misses require a line transfer from a memory module. In the latter case, space is allocated for the line and a filling bit is set in the cache directory (indicating the

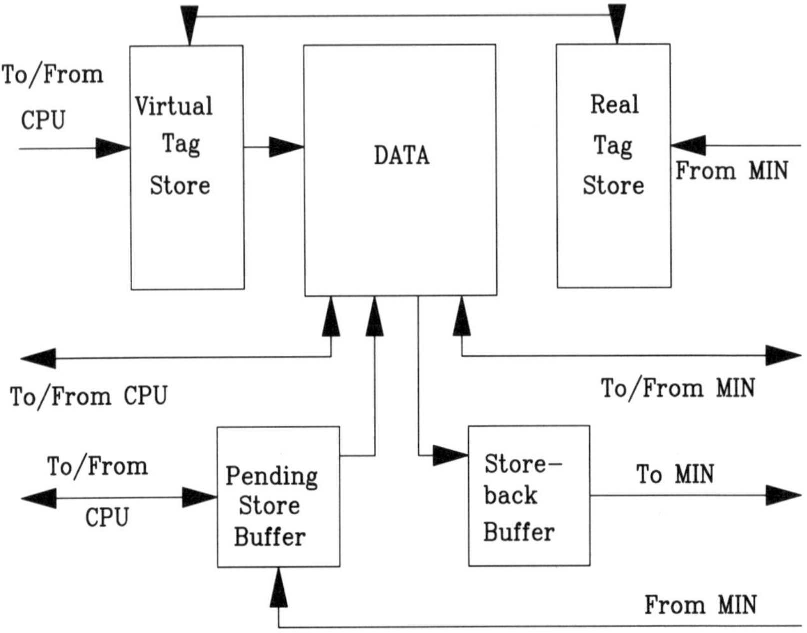

Figure 6.2
Functional Diagram of Private Data Cache.

line has been requested from a memory module). It is assumed that a cache hit is serviced in one cycle.

The request and response networks used in this study are modified omega networks [16] as illustrated in Figure 6.3 for eight inputs and outputs. Both the request and response networks consist of log_2P stages of $P/2$ 2x2 switches. A traditional omega network routing scheme is assumed in this study, *i.e.*, the low-order bits of the real address are used to determine the routing of messages through the network. A message crossing either of the networks consists of a variable number of one word (32-bit) packets, dependent upon the type of request. all packets of a message are transferred sequentially. Also, the order of messages submitted to the network by a processor is preserved. Furthermore, it is assumed that the response network supports broadcast routing.

Each memory module has a six cycle access time. However, decoding of network requests and data access are assumed to be pipelined. Consecutive cache lines are interleaved across the memory modules in order to reduce contention. Requests to the memory module originate from the processors, the private caches and/or the distributed global directory.

The implementation of the global control information required to maintain consistency is a design issue, *i.e.*, it may be located in a designated portion of the memory module, it may be implemented as a linked list in software (whose entries are composed of the actual shared lines) or some other alternative. In this study, a segment of memory, denoted the coherence control directory (CCD), is used to hold this global control information. The majority of the cache protocol accesses to this CCD are attributed to requests that do not directly require the data located in the module, *i.e.*, invalidation acknowledgements and non-modified line replacement notification. Therefore, to reduce the time required to process these non-data cache protocol requests, a DGD associated with every memory module is added to serve as a cache for the CCD. A coherence request originating from the network is directed to the DGD. If the entry is not present, the DGD will select an entry to be replaced. Next, the DGD will send a request to the CCD to obtain the entry and then write-back the replaced entry.

The DGD contains 0 to P processor identifiers (PIDs). These PIDs indicate the processors having a copy of the line. If $i, i < P$, PIDs are included in the design, then when line invalidations are required they

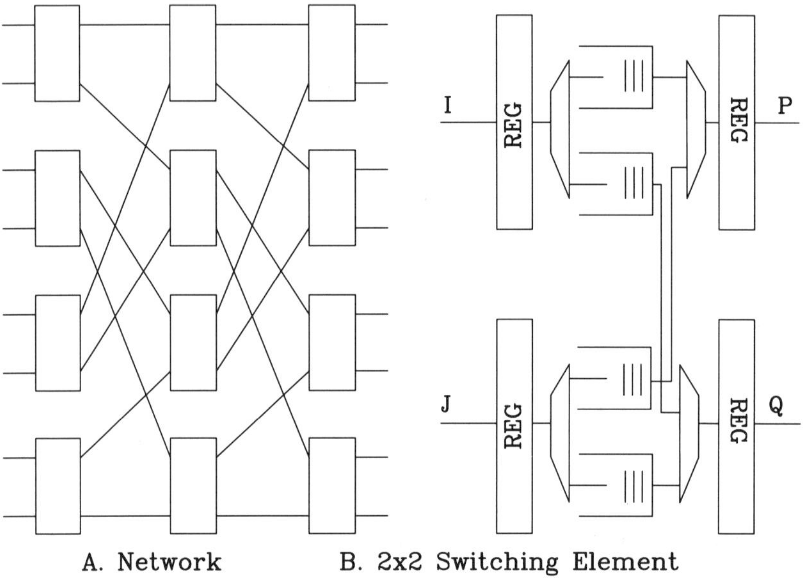

Figure 6.3
Interconnection Network and Switch.

are only sent to the caches having a copy of the line (as specified by the PIDs), if *i.e.*, or fewer processors actually share the line. Otherwise, broadcast invalidations are required. This is the increased hardware complexity. This is the DIR_iB scheme described in [5]. Additionally, when broadcast invalidations are required, one of the PIDs holds a count of the number of processors having a copy of the line. As a result, only the caches having a copy of the line will send invalidation acknowledgements (IACKS) to the DGD. This count indicates the number of IACKS the DGD needs to receive. This increases performance over non-count based designs because all unnecessary IACKS are eliminated (this may be substantial for a large number of processors).

6.3.2 Cache Coherence Protocol

The cache coherence protocol used is an extension of the directory-based protocol proposed in [20]. The extensions are made to accommodate outstanding cache misses (either reads or writes) and write hit requests. Coherence state information is located in the private caches (local information) and the DGD/CCD. Presented in Figure 6.4 is the state diagram of the coherence protocol used in the private caches. Each cache line may be in one of four non-transient or three transient states. The non-transient states are outlined below:

- **Exclusive (EX)** - the line is present in only one cache and it has not been modified.
- **Read-only (RO)** the line may be in two or more caches and it has not been modified.
- **Exclusive Read-Write (RW)** - the line is present in only one cache and it has been modified.
- **Invalid (INV)** - space has been allocated in the cache for the line but the data is not valid.

The three transient states are outlined below:

- **Exclusive Filling (EXF)** - a read miss has occurred and the cache is awaiting data (line transfer)
- **Exclusive Read-Write Filling (RWF)** - a write miss has occurred and the cache is awaiting data (line transfer)

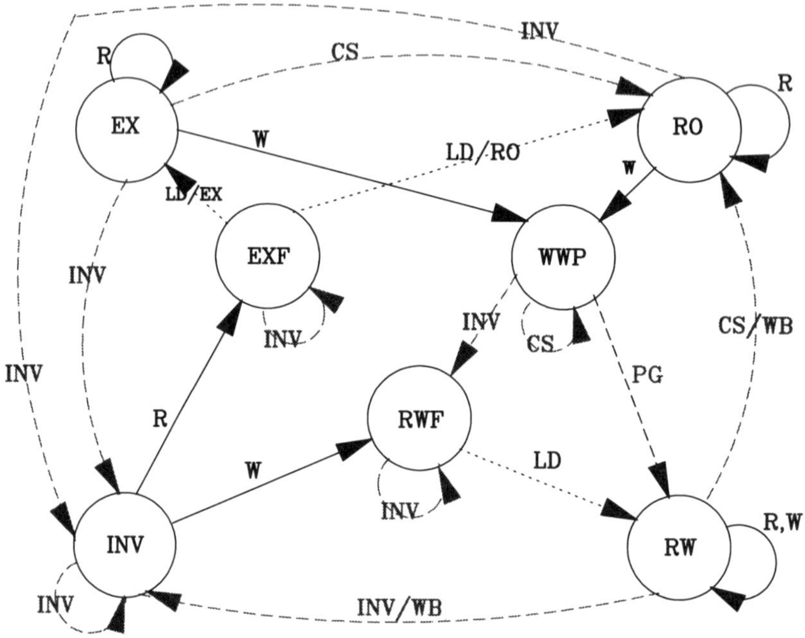

R – Read
W – Write
CS – Change State of Line
PG – Write Permission Granted
INV – Invalidate
WB – Write–back
LD–Load

Figure 6.4
State Diagram of Private Cache Coherence Protocol.

- **Waiting for Write Permission (WWP)** - awaiting permission to modify a line

State transitions are initiated either by processor requests (R and W), data returning from a read or write miss (LD) or protocol requests issued from the DGD (PG, INV, WB and CS).

Illustrated in Figure 6.5 is the state diagram of the coherence protocol used in the DGDs. An entry in the DGD may be in one of four non-transient states as outlined below:

- **Global Exclusive (GEX)** - the line is present in only one cache and it has not been modified
- **Global Read-only (GRO)** - the line may be present in more than one cache and it has not been modified
- **Global Exclusive Read-Write (GRW)** - the line is present in only one cache and it has been modified, resulting in a private cache-main memory inconsistency
- **Not Present (NP)** - the line is not present in any cache

Initially, the global state of all lines in the CCD is NP and the DGD is empty.

Three cache events signal the operation of the local cache coherence protocol. They are a read miss, a write miss and a write hit. When a read miss occurs the local state is set to EXF and the DGD is consulted to determine the global state of the line. If this global state is NP it is changed to GEX and a pointer is updated to indicate the processor holding the exclusive copy. The line is then transferred to the appropriate cache. If the global state is GEX it is changed to GRO. If an invalid pointer is available then it is validated by recording the processor requesting the line. Otherwise, the pointer that has the dual function as a counter is incremented. The line is then transferred to the cache. If the global state is GRW then a change-state signal is sent to the private cache possessing the exclusive modified copy of the line. When the private cache receives the change-state signal, it sets the local state of the line to RO and writes-back the modified datum. The DGD pointer or counter is then updated as previously discussed. The line is

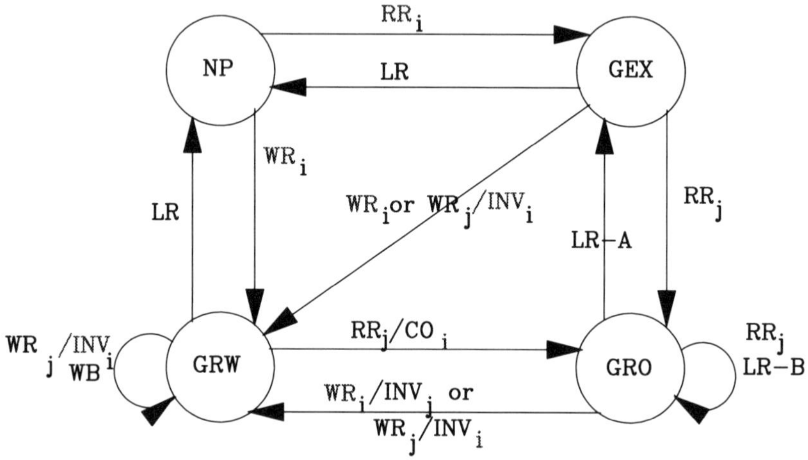

Figure 6.5
Distributed Global Directory Protocol. Initial Request is From Processor i and Subsequent Requests are from Processors i and j, $i \neq j$. LR-Line Replaced, RR-Read Reference, WR-Write Reference, INV-Invalidate, WB-Write-back, CO-change state of line and WB, LR-A-line present in only two caches and one of them has replaced line, LR-B-line present in more than two caches and one of them has replaced line.

then transferred to the cache processing the miss and its local state is set to RO. The global state of the line is set to GRO in the DGD.

When a write miss occurs the local state of the line is set to RWF and the DGD is queried to determine the global state of the line. If the global state is NP it is changed to GRW, the pointer is updated to indicate the appropriate processor and the line is transferred to the cache. If the state is GEX or GRW then an invalidation signal is sent to the cache having the exclusive copy. This cache then invalidates its copy by setting the local state of the line to INV. A write-back of modified data occurs if the local state is RW (*i.e.*, the global state is GRW). Conversely, if the local state is RO (*i.e.*, the global state is GEX) then an invalidation acknowledgement signal is sent to the DGD. Once the write-back or invalidation acknowledgement occurs, all pointers are invalidated except one which is updated to indicate the processor initiating the request. The line is then transferred to the cache processing the miss and the local state in that cache is changed from RWF to RW. The global state in the DGD is set to GRW.

If the global state of the line is GRO then a multicast or broadcast invalidation occurs depending on the number of processor pointers included in the DGD. If the number of processors sharing the line is less than or equal the number of pointers, then a multicast occurs and the DGD waits for the invalidation acknowledgements from the processors indicated by the pointers. If the number of processors sharing the line is greater than the number of pointers then one of the pointers is used as a counter to indicate the actual number of processors sharing the line (although in this case, it is not known which processors have a copy of the line). A broadcast invalidation occurs and the DGD waits for the number of invalidation acknowledgements indicated by this counter. When all invalidation acknowledgements are received the line is then transferred to the cache processing the miss, all pointers are invalidated except one which is modified to indicate the appropriate cache and the local state of the line is changed from RWF to RW.

If a write hit occurs then a modify request is sent to the DGD if the local state is EX or RO. No DGD action is necessary if the local state is RW. The modify request is necessary for the EX state to alleviate possible race conditions between the DGD and the local cache. For example, assume two processors P_1 and P_2 access line L. Initially, P_1 obtains exclusive read-only access to this line (global state is GEX, local state is EX). Next, P_1 issues a write request to line L and P_2 issues a read request. If P_1 sends a modification *update* to the DGD (instead of a modification *request*), then P_2 may receive stale data if the read request from P_2 is processed before the modification update from P_1. Therefore, a modification request signal is sent to the DGD from P_1. When a modify request is sent to the DGD the local cache state is set to WWP. If the global state of the line is GEX it is changed to GRW and a permission-to-modify signal is sent to the private cache. When the private cache receives this signal, the local state is changed to RW.

If the global state is GRO then a multicast or broadcast invalidation is initiated as previously discussed. However, one of the pointers (multicast) or processors counted in the counter (broadcast) is the processor who initiated the modify request. In this case, an additional unneeded invalidation acknowledgement will be received by the DGD. To eliminate this unnecessary invalidation, a processor identifier is included with every invalidation (multicast and broadcast) to indicate the processor initiating the request. Therefore, when a cache receives an invalidation signal it compares its PID with the PID associated with the invalidation. If there is a match then the request is discarded. Furthermore, if the global state is GRO then the DGD will wait for C-1 invalidation acknowledgements in the case of a broadcast (C is the number of processors sharing the line as indicated by the counter) and one minus the number of valid pointers in the case of a multicast. When all invalidation acknowledgements have been received then the global state is set to GRW and one of the pointers is updated the indicate the cache having the exclusive copy (all other pointers are invalidated). A permission-to-modify signal is then transferred to this cache and the local state of the line is set to RW.

Figure 6.6 presents the contents of each DGD entry. It includes the tag which consists of a variable number of bits, the global state of the line, N processor identifiers ($0 \leq N \leq P$), the waiting status of the line (*i.e.*, is the directory waiting for a line to be written back to main memory) and the event that caused the directory to wait for a line write-back or invalidation acknowledgement. There are $log_2 P$ bits used to identify the processor for each PID. Also, one bit is used to determine whether or not the processor is waiting for a write-back or invalidation acknowledgement and two bits are used to determine the type of request that initiated the write-back request (RQEVNT).

Distributed Directory Entry

dtag (v)	gstate (2)	PID_1 ($\log_2 P$)	...	PID_N ($\log_2 P$)	WTEVNT (1)	RQEVNT (2)

Figure 6.6
DGD Entry. Parentheses Indicate Number of Bits. dtag-Directory Tag, gstate-Global State, PID-Processor Identifier, WTEVNT-Waiting for Write-back, RQEVNT-Requested Event that Caused Write-back, V-Variable.

6.4 Simulation Methodology and Results

The trace-driven simulator explicitly models each functional block of the system shown in Figure 6.1 with two exceptions. For reasons previously discussed, the processor and the instruction cache are not modelled (see section III.A). A discussion of the applications is included in Appendix A. The trace collection methodology is discussed in [17]. The same traces were used for all protocols evaluated, resulting in the same number of references issued for each of the three protocols studied. A processor cycle is simulated by utilizing the period of time during which one reference, if any, is issued by each processor in the system, *i.e.*, the time in which each processor services the next element in its reference stream. Infinite buffers are associated with each functional block simulated. Furthermore, it is assumed that all processors access the same global memory. Table 6.1 lists the various simulation parameters for each subsystem and their associated values. As a result of memory limitations during simulations, the 16 byte line was not evaluated for the 32 processor system. Also, since the matrix size for the 4 processor CT FFT application is small, it was not simulated and simulation execution time constraints prohibited the simulation of the 32 processor CT FFT.

Two cache coherence events have the potential to cause the greatest performance degradation: invalidations and change-states. The number

Table 6.1
Simulation Parameters.

SUBSYSTEM	PARAMETER	VALUE
Processor	number	4 - 32
Cache	size	64 Kbytes
	linesize	16-64 bytes
	placement policy	2-way set-associative
	update policy	write-back
	access time	1 processor cycle
Network	switch size	2x2
	header/packet size	32 bits
	message size	variable
	data path	32 bits
	switch cycle time	1 processor cycle
Distributed Global Directory (DGD)	size	2K - 16K bytes
	placement policy	direct-mapped
	number of PIDs	1
	access time	1 processor cycle
Memory Module / Coherence Control Directory (CCD)	access time	6 processor cycles

of change-states occurring in the algorithms evaluated is minimal and their results are not presented. However, to measure the severity of the degradation, the invalidation ratio and other related parameters are evaluated. All of the parameters are defined from the viewpoint of the DGD. Table 6.2 summarizes the parameters measured in this study. Finally, as a result of limited resources, only one PID is simulated in this study.

6.4.1 Results

Many of the results obtained follow the same general trend. Therefore, we only present a few results. We do, however, present results that vary significantly from the generally observed behavior. Presented in Table 6.3 is the total number of references made for all processor configurations and for all four applications evaluated (see Appendix A). These numbers ranged from an average of 1.35 million for the hydrodynamics

Table 6.2
Simulation Results Evaluated.

RESULT	DEFINITION
Execution Time	time required to process trace
Invalidation Ratio	fraction of writes received by the DGD requiring invalidations
Invalidation Write-back Ratio	fraction of invalidations issued by the DGD requiring write-backs
Invalidation - Write-back processing time	time required by DGD to send an invalidation and receive a write-back
Invalidation - IACK processing time	time required by DGD to send an invalidation and receive all acknowledgements
Invalidation Sharing Statistics	number of processors sharing a line when an invalidation is required

application to over 38 million for the 32 processor CT FFT application. Observe that the number of references increase as the number of processors increase. This is largely the result of the replicate sections within the applications. Illustrated in Table 6.4 is the memory reference statics for the targeted applications. The percentage of total references that are shared ranges from 4-9% with an average of 5%. The percentage of data references that are shared ranges from 9 to 23% with an average of 12%. Since shared data references, in particular shared read-write data references, contribute to the performance degradation that occurs as a result of cache coherence, the smaller these percentages, the better the system performance.

Presented in Figure 6.7 is the execution time versus the number of processors and linesize for the SORT application. The execution time decreases as the number of processors increase. The rate at which this execution time decreases also decreases as the number of processors increase. Moreover, for the hybrid and hardware protocols (64 byte line size), this execution time increases as the number of processors increase from 16 to 32. This is a direct result of the *false sharing*, particularly the false sharing of read-write data [18], that occurs for this application.

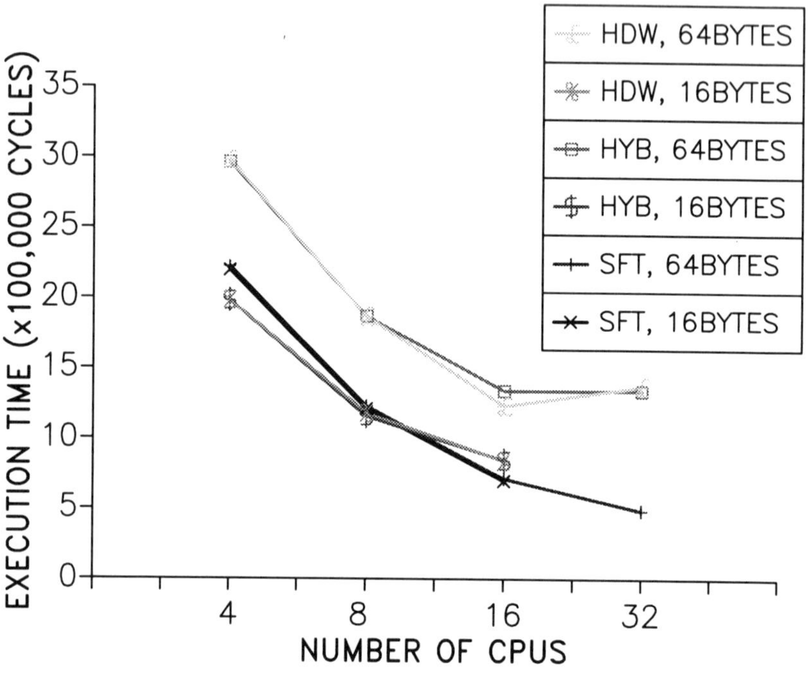

Figure 6.7
Execution Time versus the Number of Processors and Linesize. SORT, 64Kbyte Cache, 16Kbyte DGD.

Table 6.3
Total Number of Memory References.

CODE	TOTAL NUMBER OF PROCESSORS			
	Number of Processors			
	4	8	16	32
MVS FFT	2,382,065	2,398,713	2,432,009	2,498,601
CT FFT	-	1,777,816	8,257,648	38,448,896
SORT	5,795,195	5,920,495	6,171,095	6,672,295
HYDRO	1,338,062	1,356,774	1,394,198	1,469,046

Table 6.4
Memory References Statistics. I-Instructions, D-Data, P-Private, S-Shared, R-Read, W-Write.

CODE	REFS		REFS		D-REFS		S-DATA	
	%I	%D	%P	%S	%P	%S	%R	%W
MVS FFT	59	41	91	9	77	23	68	32
CT FFT	53	47	96	4	93	7	60	40
SORT	64	36	97	3	92	8	65	35
HYDRO	57	43	96	4	91	9	65	35

False sharing occurs when two or more processors access different data elements within the same cache line; however, it is dependent upon the application's chunk size (the number of consecutive iterations assigned to a single processor) and access patterns. In this study, most applications were executed with a chunk size of four. With matrix/vector sizes greater than or equal to 64, a chunk size of four produces more false sharing than a chunk size of N/P where N is the number of iterations. The smaller chunk sizes were used to facilitate the comparison of the various number of processors used in the system. If the access pattern of the application is such that consecutive elements of a vector or matrix are accessed during consecutive iterations within a parallel loop, then the combined effect of the access patterns and small chunk sizes produce false sharing.

The additional number of invalidations required to maintain coherence as the number of processors increase from 16 to 32 is such that the SORT application runs faster on the 16 processor system. This behavior is also evident for the hydrodynamics application; however, the execution time continues to decrease for the MVS FFT application as the number of processors increase from 16 to 32.

Three counterintuitive results are also exhibited in Figure 6.7. First, the execution time is generally independent of the hybrid and hardware protocols. Since shared data accesses constitute only 3% of the total references for SORT, intuition dictates that the hybrid protocol should run faster because less coherence protocol overhead is needed. However, private data exhibits better locality than shared data. In fact, most of the misses processed by the hardware protocol are shared misses. As a result, only a few private data requests are processed by the DGD. Therefore, the execution times of the hardware and hybrid protocols are competitive.

Second, the execution time increases as the cache line size increases from 16 to 64 bytes for the hybrid and hardware protocols. This is in direct opposition to the abundance of empirical data illustrating a decrease in execution time as the line size increases (for traditional uniprocessor caches). The results presented are attributed to the fact that a considerable amount of false sharing occurs in this application. This false sharing increases as the line size increases, resulting in an effective amount of cache invalidations to occur. This in turn increases the performance degradation and therefore the execution time.

Thirdly, the software protocol is generally competitive with the hybrid and hardware protocols. In fact, for 16 and 32 processors the SORT application runs fastest when using the software protocol. Again, this behavior is attributed to false sharing. As you increase the number of processors, the penalties resulting from the increase in the number of invalidations become costly for the hybrid and hardware protocols. Observe that the execution time is independent of the line size for the software protocol. This shows that in spite of the fact that only 3% of the total references are shared, the penalty due to the accessing of memory on every shared data reference dominates any potential locality gains for private references as the line size varies.

Presented in Table 6.5 is the invalidation ratio (IR) versus the number of processors and linesize for the hybrid and hardware protocols for all applications evaluated. Generally, the IR increases as the linesize increases for a given number of processors. The variances are more substantial for the hydrodynamics and CT FFT applications. Also, this ratio is relatively independent of the number of processors in the

Table 6.5
Invalidation Ratio versus the Number of Processors and Linesize. LS-Linesize, B-Hybrid, H-Hardware.

CODE	LS	Number of Processors							
		4		8		16		32	
		B	H	B	H	B	H	B	H
MVS FFT	16	.95	.94	.94	.96	.93	.92	-	-
	32	.98	.97	.97	.98	.98	.95	.98	.93
	64	.99	.98	.98	.99	.99	.97	.99	.96
SORT	16	.96	.95	.97	.95	.98	.94	-	-
	32	.99	.98	.99	.99	.99	.98	.98	.96
	64	.99	.99	.99	.99	.99	.99	.99	.98
HYDRO	16	.75	.68	.75	.62	.75	.53	-	-
	32	.92	.88	.93	.86	.94	.73	.94	.75
	64	.97	.94	.97	.93	.97	.90	.98	.85
CT FFT	16	-	-	.97	.66	.99	.89	-	-
	32	-	-	.97	.72	.99	.91	-	-
	64	-	-	.97	.84	.98	.94	-	-

system for a given linesize. This table also shows that in most cases, more than 94% of all write misses and modify requests processed by the DGDs require an invalidation before they can be serviced. Again, this is because a substantial amount of false read-write sharing occurs in these applications, particularly for the MVS FFT and sort applications. Also, the hybrid IRs are slightly larger than the hardware IRs. This is attributed to the additional private write requests that are included when calculating the hardware IRs. Since the number of invalidation events processed by the DGD for both protocols are relatively equal, a smaller hardware IR results. This also partially quantifies the fact that only a small number of private requests are processed by the DGD for the hardware protocol.

The invalidation write-back ratio (IWBR), invalidation write-back processing time (IWB-PT) and invalidation acknowledgement processing time (IACK-PT) are presented in Table 6.6 versus the number of processors and the linesize for the hybrid protocol and all applications. The IWBR varies widely from 0.02 to 0.85; however, with the exception of the hydrodynamics application, less than half of all invalidations

Table 6.6
Invalidation Write-back Ratio (IWBR), Invalidation Write-back Processing Time (IWB-PT, in cycles) and Invalidation Acknowledgement Processing Time(IACK-PT, in cycles) versus the Number of Processors (P) and Linesize, Hybrid Protocol.

Code	P	IWBR			IWB-PT			IACK-PT		
		Linesize (bytes)								
		16	32	64	16	32	64	16	32	64
MVS FFT	4	0.10	0.02	0.07	15.8	16.8	19.5	14.2	15.4	18.8
	8	0.29	0.10	0.07	20.9	24.2	27.3	21.1	22.7	26.0
	16	0.28	0.35	0.20	24.9	26.9	30.5	29.5	30.2	35.0
	32	-	0.48	0.37	-	35.0	36.1	-	43.5	47.3
SORT	4	0.04	0.10	0.19	19.5	19.3	24.3	13.7	15.1	20.5
	8	0.05	0.15	0.25	14.9	23.8	30.4	18.9	20.8	27.8
	16	0.06	0.19	0.29	8.9	28.5	38.4	25.1	27.5	35.3
	32	-	0.23	0.31	-	32.6	39.2	-	37.2	45.2
HYDRO	4	0.49	0.80	0.83	16.1	19.2	29.0	14.7	18.6	31.3
	8	0.47	0.80	0.84	20.5	24.0	37.5	20.3	25.2	40.7
	16	0.46	0.81	0.84	25.0	29.0	44.3	27.4	31.7	49.6
	32	-	0.81	0.85	-	33.4	49.7	-	41.2	58.1
CT FFT	8	0.44	0.50	0.49	21.6	24.5	32.2	20.7	22.3	35.5
	16	0.42	0.54	0.56	25.3	28.7	35.3	26.6	28.8	36.4

result in a write-back. This is because the read/write sharing patterns consist of many reads and few writes by the various processors. For hydrodynamics, the IWBR increases to over 80% for line sizes greater than 16 bytes. This results from the read/write sharing patterns consisting of several writes from different processors. The IWBR generally increases as the number of processors increase for a given linesize. It also increases as the linesize increases for a given number of processors (the MVS FFT application is the exception). Again, this is attributed to the effects of false sharing. Similar results were obtained for the hardware protocol.

The IWB-PT and IACK-PT exhibit similar behavior. They increase as the linesize increases for a given number of processors. They also increase as the number of processors increase for a given linesize. This is primarily the result of the increased contention in the request and response networks as the linesize and the number of processors increase, respectively. The processing times range from 16 to 50 cycles for the IWB-PT and from 14 to 58 cycles for the IACK-PT. Also, observe that the IACK-PT is smaller than the IWB-PT for the smaller processor configurations and then increase to the point where they are generally larger for the larger processor configurations. This is primarily due to false sharing and the fact that the penalty for broadcast invalidations increases as the number of processors increase.

Illustrated in Figure 6.8 is the percentage of invalidation events that result in up to P invalidations (P is the total number of processors) for the MVS FFT application and the 32 byte linesize. The figure shows that for four processors, 28% of all invalidation events result in invalidations sent to two caches. The remainder is evenly distributed between one, three and four processors. As the number of processors increase, the percentage of invalidation events that do not produce two invalidations remains uniformly distributed, however, they do decrease substantially. Conversely, the percentage for the two-invalidation case generally increases as the number of processors increase. These results show that a DGD with two PIDs can account for 52%, 32%, 44% and 50% of all invalidations for the 4, 8, 16 and 32 processors, respectively. The incremental increases in the invalidation percentages that occur as you increase the number of PIDs have a declining effect as you increase the number of processors. The majority of the read-write sharing occurs between two processors. Similar results are obtained for all other linesizes examined.

Illustrated in Figures 6.9 and 6.10 is the total execution time versus the DGD size for the hydrodynamics and MVS FFT applications (respectively), for the hybrid and hardware protocols, for 16 processors and for the 32 byte linesize. While the execution times are competitive for all three applications, the hybrid protocol generally exhibits slightly faster execution times, particularly for the hydrodynamics application. Also, the execution time is generally non-increasing as the DGD size increases. This trend holds for both line sizes shown. In the case where the execution time decreases as the DGD size increases, the entire coherence working set of the application is not contained in the DGDs for the smaller DGD sizes. As a result, increasing the DGD size increases the number of working set lines in the DGD, improving performance. In the case were the execution time is independent of the DGD size, the entire coherence working set may be contained in the DGD. The figure shows that a small DGD size (4K bytes) is adequate for acceptable system performance.

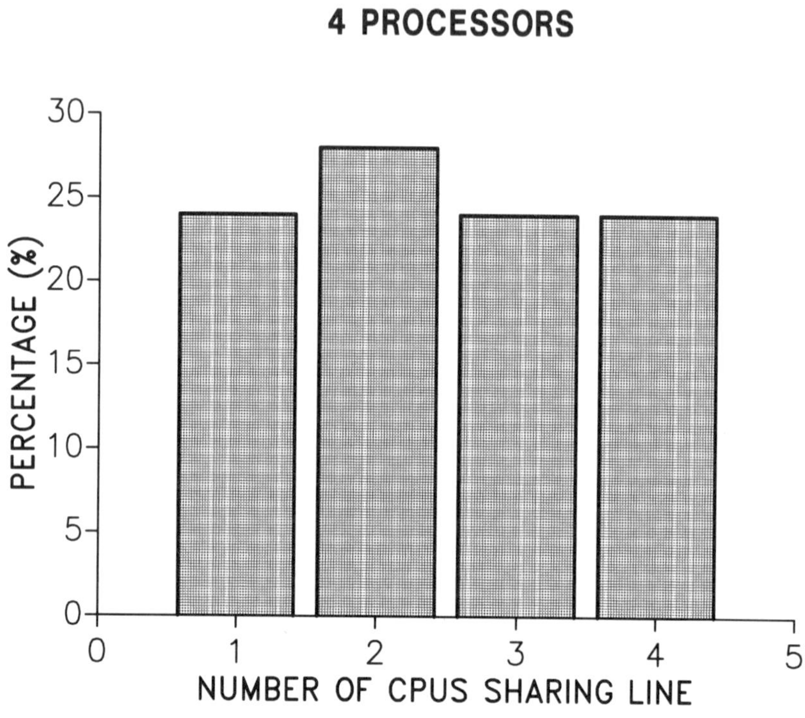

Figure 6.8
Invalidation Sharing, MVS FFT, Hybrid Protocol, 32 Byte Linesize.

For the hydrodynamics application, as the DGD size increases, the differences between the hybrid and hardware protocol decrease. These differences, however, are small, irrespective of the DGD size. The execution times for the hybrid protocol are independent of the DGD size for the sort application (not shown). This is because the working set is contained in the DGD for all DGD sizes evaluated. Also, the execution times are slightly higher for the hardware protocol and the 32 byte line size. This is because in spite of the fact that the entire working set may be contained in the DGDs for the hybrid protocol, a high degree of contention occurs for these lines, resulting in relatively longer processing times for this protocol. For the MVS FFT application, the hybrid protocol is generally faster, although the differences in execution times are small.

6.5 Conclusions

Presented in this paper are three coherence protocols (a software protocol, a hardware protocol and a hybrid protocol) and a comparison of their performance using trace-driven simulation. Comparisons are made for various system parameters. The results show that an average of 5% of the total number of references are shared and an average of 12% of all data references are shared. Also, the hybrid and hardware protocols exhibit similar performance with large DGD sizes *i.e.*, 16Kbytes. Smaller DGD sizes result in somewhat faster executions for the hybrid protocol; however, these smaller DGD sizes produce slower application execution times.

While the software protocol is competitive with the hybrid and hardware protocols, it is conservative with respect to caching shared data. This suggests that the more aggressive software coherence protocols may be integrated with the hybrid and hardware protocols to produce a system exhibiting better performance. For example, software techniques may be used to improve the performance of both protocols by reducing the amount of false sharing during algorithm execution. Additionally, it has been shown that a large fraction of the shared data is read-only shared during the entire execution of the algorithms evaluated [19]. Therefore, software techniques may be used to further improve the hybrid protocol, relative to the hardware protocol, by treating these read-only lines as private lines. More research is needed in this area.

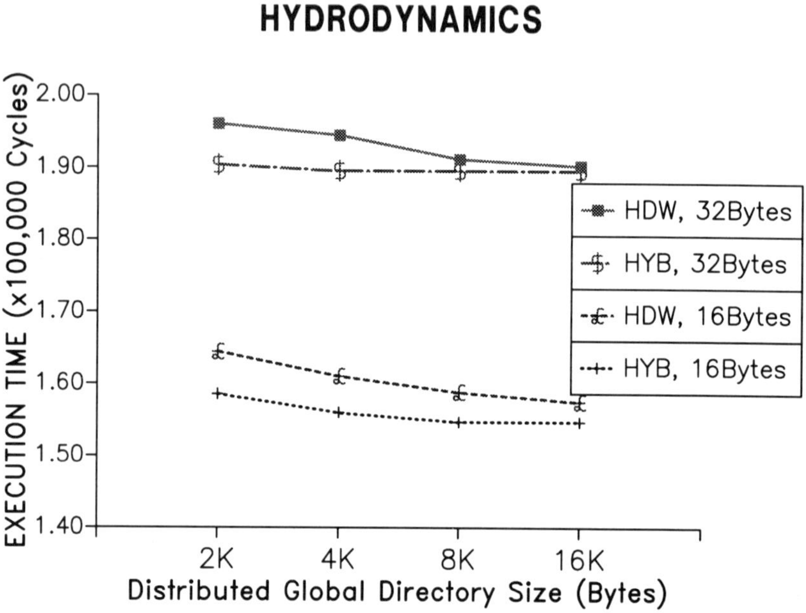

Figure 6.9
Total Execution Time versus DGD Size, 16 Processors, 16 and 32 Byte Linesizes, Hydrodynamics.

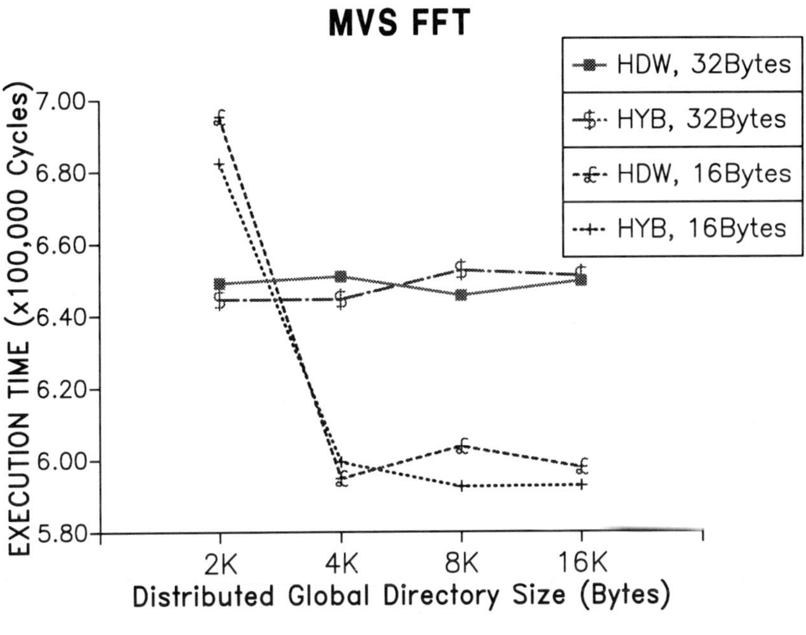

Figure 6.10
Total Execution Time versus DGD Size, 16 Processors, 16 and 32 Byte Linesizes, MVS FFT.

Moreover, more than 94% of all write requests processed by the DGDs result in some type of invalidation event. These events exhibit processing times ranging from 16 to 58 cycles. This is primarily the result of network contention. The high invalidation ratios are attributed to the extensive false sharing evident in the applications. In many instances, only two processors share a line when an invalidation is needed. This, in cooperation with that fact that additional PIDs result in minimal performance improvement for a large number of processors, suggests that the additional hardware requirements for more than two PIDs in a DGD entry may not be necessary. More work is needed to quantify this assessment.

The effects of network contention is apparent in the large processing times for invalidation events; however, more work is needed to determine the effects of network cycle times and memory module access times on system performance. Also, limited resources and relatively small traces prohibited the the evaluation of larger numbers of processors, (*i.e.*, > 32) and cache sizes. We plan to study these factors in future work. Finally, while non-broadcast invalidation-based directory protocols were not the subject of this research, they do have several advantages. Further study comparing the performances of broadcast, combination broadcast/multicast and non-broadcast invalidation protocols for MIN-based systems is needed.

6.6 Appendix. Parallel Applications

The four parallel engineering/scientific applications used in this study are all coded in FORTRAN. They include an MVS FFT application which is a parallelized version of a sequential application. Another FFT application is also evaluated, Cooley-Tukey; however, this application was explicitly written for parallel processors. The remaining applications included a explicitly parallelized uniprocessor hydrodynamics application, and a binary sorting application written for a parallel processor.

The MVS FFT application performs the FFT computation on a 64x64 element matrix in two phases. In the first phase, the FFT for each element composing a row of the matrix is computed. The last phase computes the FFT for each column element. The chunk size for this computation is one; therefore, the trace scheduler assigns a single processor to execute the FFT computation of each element. The Cooley-Tukey application is a 1-dimensional FFT computation of variable length, depending upon the number of processors used in the system. It was designed to maximize performance by performing the FFT computation on a pre-determined subset of vector elements. This subset, as well as the chunk size, is a function of the number of processors and the vector size.

A serial hydrodynamics application was obtained from the Los Alamos National Laboratory. This program was then parallelized using EPEX for a 1000 element vector. The algorithm is a Reiman problem solver with two shock approximation and artificial shock viscosity approximation. The sorting application performs a binary sort on 1000 numbers. A chunk size of 4 was used for both the hydrodynamics and sorting applications. The full traces of all of these applications are used in this study.

Acknowledgments

We would like to thank Alan Norton, Frederica Darema and Shing-Chong Chang for supplying us with their application codes, Caroline Benveniste for supplying us with her trace scheduling program, and Yarsun Hsu for supplying us with his MIN network simulator. We also thank Tony Bolmarach for his helpful EPEX insights.

References

[1] P. Stenstrom, "A Survey of Cache Coherence Schemes for Multiprocessors," *Computer*, vol. 23, no. 6, pp. 12-24, 1990.

[2] R. L. Lee, P. Yew, and D. H. Lawrie, "Multiprocessor Cache Design Considerations," *Proceedings of the 14th Annual International Symposium on Computer Architecture*, pp. 253-262, June 1987.

[3] J. Archibald and J. L. Baer, "Cache Coherence Protocols: Evaluation Using a Multiprocessor Simulation Model," *ACM Transactions on Computer Systems*, vol. 4, no. 4, pp. 273-298, November 1986.

[4] M. K. Vernon, R. Jog, and G. S. Sohi, "Performance Analysis of Hierarchical Cache-Consistent Multiprocessors," *Performance Evaluation*, vol. 9, pp. 287-302, 1989.

[5] A. Agarwal, R. Simoni, J. Hennessy and M. Horowitz, "An Evaluation of Directory Schemes for Cache Coherence," *Proceedings of the 15th Annual International Symposium on Computer Architecture*, pp. 280-289, 1988.

[6] P. Stenstrom, "A Cache Consistency Protocol for Multiprocessors with Multistage Networks," *Proceedings of the 16th Annual International Symposium on Computer Architecture*, pp. 407-415, 1989.

[7] D. Lenoski, J. Laudon, J. Gharachorloo, A. Gputa and J. Hennessy, "The Directory-Based Cache Coherence Protocol for the DASH Multiprocessor," *Proceedings of the 17th Annual International Symposium on Computer Architecture*, pp. 148-159, 1990.

[8] H. Cheong and A. V. Veidenbaum, "Compiler-Directed Cache Management in Multiprocessors," *Computer*, vol. 23, no. 6, pp. 39-47, 1990.

[9] L. Lamport, "How to Make A Multiprocessor Computer that Correctly Executes Multiprocess Programs," *IEEE Transactions on Computers*, vol. C-28 no. 9, pp. 241-248, September 1979.

[10] M. Dubois, C. Scheurich and F. A. Briggs, "Memory Access Buffering in Multiprocessors," *Proceedings of the 13th Annual International Symposium on Computer Architecture*, pp. 434-442, 1986.

[11] S. Owicki and A. Agarwal, "Evaluating the Performance of Software Cache Coherence," *ASPLOS III*, pp. 230-242, April 1989.

[12] S. L. Min and J. L. Baer, "A Performance Comparison of Directory-Based and Timestamp-Based Cache Coherence Schemes," *Proceedings of the 1990 International Conference on Parallel Processing*, vol. 1, pp. 10-20, August 1990.

[13] L. M. Censier and P. Feautrier, "A New Solution to Coherence Problems in Multicache Systems," *IEEE Transactions on Computers*, vol. C-27, no. 12, pp. 1112-1118, December 1978.

[14] D. Chaiken, C. Fields, K. Kurihara and A. Agarwal, "Directory-Based Cache Coherence in Large-Scale Multiprocessors," *Computer*, vol. 23, no. 6, pp. 48-58, June 1990.

[15] J. R. Goodman, "Coherence for Multiprocessor Virtual Address Caches," *ASPLOS II*, pp. 72-81, 1987.

[16] D. H. Lawrie, "Access and Alignment of Data in an Array Processor," *IEEE Transactions on Computers*, vol. C-24, pp. 1145-1155, December 1975.

[17] S. J. Baylor, K. P. McAuliffe and D. B. Rathi, "An Evaluation of Cache Coherence Protocols for MIN-Based Multiprocessors," *IBM Research Report RC 15220*, September 1990.

[18] S. J. Eggers and R. H. Katz, "The Effect of Sharing on the Cache and Bus Performance of Parallel Programs," *ASPLOS III*, pp. 257-270, April 1989.

[19] S. J. Baylor and B. D. Rathi, "An Evaluation of the Memory Reference Behavior of Engineering/Scientific Applications in Parallel Systems," *International Journal of High Speed Computing*, vol. 1, no. 4, pp.603-641, 1989.

[20] W. C. Yen, D. W. L. Yen and K. S. Fu, "Data Coherence Problem in a Multicache System," *IEEE Transactions on Computers*, pp. 56-65, January, 1985.

7 KRPP: The Kyushu University Reconfigurable Parallel Processor: Cache Architecture and Cache Coherence Schemes

Kazuaki Murakami, Shin-ichiro Mori, Eiji Iwata, Akira Fukuda, and Shinji Tomita

The *Kyushu University Reconfigurable Parallel Processor (KRPP)* system is an MIMD-type multiprocessor which consists of *128 processing elements (PEs)* interconnected by a *full (128 × 128) crossbar network*. KRPP employs *reconfigurable memory architecture*, a kind of *local/remote memory architectures* or *NUMA (Non-Uniform Memory Access) architectures*, and encompasses a shared-memory TCMP (tightly coupled multiprocessor) and a message-passing LCMP (loosely coupled multiprocessor).

When KRPP is configured as a shared-memory TCMP, memory contentions will be obstacles to the performance. To relieve the detrimental effects, KRPP provides each PE with a private unified cache. Each PE may have the cached copy of shared data in its cache whether it accesses to local or remote memory, and therefore the multicache consistency, or *inter-cache coherence*, problem arises.

The cache is a virtual-address, direct-mapped cache to meet the requirements for the cache-hit time and the cache size. The virtual-address cache implementation causes the other cache consistency problem, the *synonym* problem, which we call *intra-cache coherence* problem.

This paper presents the following cache coherence schemes that we have chosen for resolving these cache coherence problems: i) *cacheability marking* scheme, ii) *fast selective invalidation* scheme, iii) *distributed limited-directory* scheme, and iv) *dual-directory cache* scheme. Cache coherence protocols and their tradeoffs between several design aspects are also discussed.

7.1 Introduction

The *Kyushu University Reconfigurable Parallel Processor (KRPP)* system is an MIMD-type multiprocessor which consists of 128 processing elements (PEs) interconnected by a *full (128 × 128) crossbar network* [25]. Figure 7.1 shows the block diagram of KRPP.

The goals of KRPP are: i) to construct a high-performance, multiple-purpose multiprocessor system which can be tailored to a broad range of applications, and ii) to offer an experimental environment, or testbed, which encourages many researchers in the studies of highly parallel processing [23].

To satisfy these goals, KRPP employs *reconfigurable network architecture*, which provides dynamic flexible interconnection topologies to fill the gap between intercommunication topologies inherent in parallel

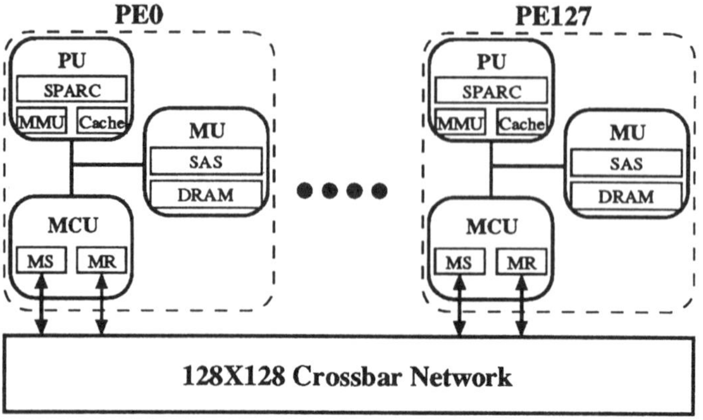

MCU	: Message Communication Unit	MU	: Memory Unit
MMU	: Memory Management Unit	PE	: Processing Element
MR	: Message Receiver	PU	: Processor Unit
MS	: Message Sender	SAS	: SMW-Access Server

Figure 7.1
Block Diagram of KRPP

algorithms and those of the system. KRPP also employs *reconfigurable memory architecture*, a kind of *local/remote memory architectures* or *NUMA (Non-Uniform Memory Access) architectures.* Although the it is built in the form of distributed memory organization without global memory, KRPP can be reconfigured as either a *shared-memory TCMP (tightly coupled multiprocessor)* or a *message-passing LCMP (loosely coupled multiprocessor)* [24].

When KRPP is configured as a shared-memory TCMP, memory contentions will be obstacles to the performance. To relieve their detrimental effects, KRPP provides each PE with a private unified cache. Each PE may have the cached copy of shared data in its cache whether it accesses to local or remote memory, and therefore the multicache consistency, or *inter-cache coherence*, problem occurs.

The cache is a virtual-address, direct-mapped cache to offer the cache-access time of one clock cycle and the large cache size of 128K bytes. The virtual-address cache implementation causes the other cache consistency problem, the *synonym* problem, which we call *intra-cache coherence* problem.

This paper presents the cache coherence schemes that we have chosen for resolving these cache coherence problems. From the standpoint of a testbed, KRPP provides the various schemes below:

- *Cacheability marking* scheme to enforce inter-cache coherence,
- *Fast selective invalidation* scheme to enforce inter-cache coherence,
- *Distributed limited-directory* scheme to enforce inter-cache coherence, and
- *Dual-directory cache* scheme to enforce both intra-cache and inter-cache coherence.

The next section overviews the PE configuration and the local/remote memory architecture. Section 7.3 discusses several cache aspects that we have taken into consideration on designing the cache. Section 7.4 introduces the cache coherence schemes above. In Section 7.5, we develop the inter-cache coherence protocols and examine two issues: *write policies* and *memory consistency*. In Section 7.6, we develop the intra-cache coherence protocols and analyze the *collision* problem caused by the dual-directory cache scheme. The final section offers a few concluding remarks.

7.2 Overview

7.2.1 Processing Element

Each PE comprises the following main units.

- *PU (Processor Unit)*: PU consists of a Fujitsu SPARC[1] MB86901 (S-20) and a WEITEK[2] Abacus 3170. The MB86901 is a RISC microprocessor which performs at roughly 10 VAX MIPS when operating at 16.67 MHz clock frequency. The Abacus 3170 is a floating-point coprocessor, which achieves 1.6 single-precision LINPACK MFLOPS and 1.1 double-precision LINPACK MFLOPS at 16.67 MHz clock frequency.
- *MMU (Memory Management Unit)*: MMU is a subunit of the PU and provides zero-wait-state address translation and instruction/data caching for the processor. It contains a TLB (translation-lookaside buffer) and a virtual-address cache of 128K bytes. Most of the MMU

[1] SPARC is a trademark of Sun Microsystems, Inc.
[2] WEITEK is a registered trademark of WEITEK Corp.

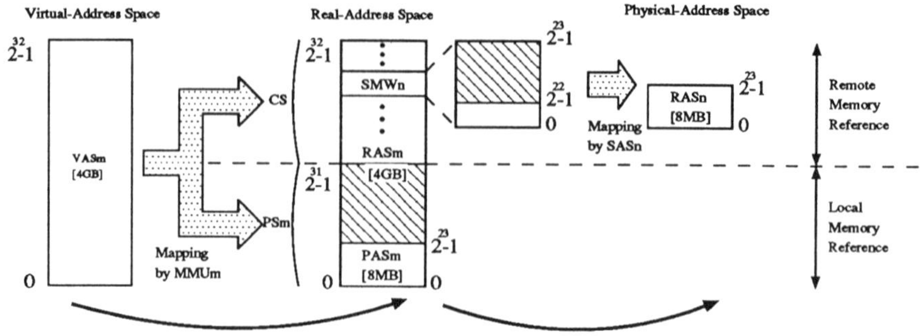

(a) Mapping VASm to RASm **(b) Mapping SMWn to PASn**

CS	: Common Space
MMU_m	: Memory-Management Unit of PE_m
PAS_m	: Physical-Address Space for PE_m
PAS_n	: Physical-Address Space for PE_n
PS_m	: Private Space for PE_m
RAS_m	: Real-Address Space for PE_m
SAS_n	: SMW-Access Server of PE_n
SMW_n	: Shared-Memory Window of PE_n
VAS_m	: Virtual-Address Space for PE_m

Figure 7.2
Addressing Scheme

facilities, except for the RAM array of cache, are implemented in a single-chip semicustom LSI.

- *MCU (Message Communication Unit)*: MCU provides the network interface and serves remote memory references which are forwarded to/from other PEs.
- *MU (Memory Unit)*: MU has 8M bytes of local memory. It includes a *SAS (Shared-memory-window Access Server)* which realizes remote memory references from other PEs and maintains multicache consistency.

7.2.2 Local/Remote Memory Architecture

As shown in Figure 7.1, KRPP employs a distributed memory organization and thus provides no global memory. To exploit the memory reconfigurability, however, KRPP allows more than one processor to share a local memory. A processor of each PE can directly access the local memories of other PEs, which memories are called *remote memories*, via the crossbar network. The memory architecture is referred to as *local/remote architecture* or *NUMA (Non-Uniform Memory Access)*. As the result, KRPP encompasses a shared-memory TCMP and a message-passing LCMP.

Local/remote architectures are employed by some multiprocessor systems such as the *CMU Cm** [30], the *IBM RP3* [4], and the *BBN Butterfly*[3] [26]. Those local/memory architectures, including ours, differ in their addressing schemes.

Figure 7.2 schematically depicts the addressing scheme of KRPP. The scheme is achieved by two-level address translation. Because of the two-level address translation, three address representations are required: *virtual*, *real*, and *physical*. The two-level address translation is performed as follows.

1. **Mapping VAS to RAS (First-level address translation):**
For $\boldsymbol{PE_m}$, a *virtual-address space* ($\boldsymbol{VAS_m}$) of 4G bytes is mapped to the *real-address space* ($\boldsymbol{RAS_m}$) of 4G bytes, as shown in Figure 7.2–a. The *memory-management unit* ($\boldsymbol{MMU_m}$) translates a 32-bit *virtual address* ($\boldsymbol{VA_m}$) generated by a SPARC microprocessor into a 32-bit *real address* ($\boldsymbol{RA_m}$) with a conventional two-level paging. The page size is 4K bytes.
2. **Partitioning RAS into CS and PS:**
Each $\boldsymbol{RAS}$ is partitioned into the following two spaces.

- *Private Space (PS)*: For $\boldsymbol{PE_m}$, a low-order 2G-byte space (i.e., MSB of real address is 0) is its *private space* ($\boldsymbol{PS_m}$), which is identical to its *physical-address space* ($\boldsymbol{PAS_m}$). Thus a *private-space real-address* ($\boldsymbol{PSRA_m}$), excluding its MSB, is directly used as a *physical address* ($\boldsymbol{PA_m}$).
- *Common Space (CS)*: A high-order 2G-byte space (i.e., MSB of real address is 1) is common to all PEs. The common space comprises 128 *SMWs (Shared-Memory Windows)*, each of which is 16M bytes in size and segmented into 4K SMW-pages. An SMW is assigned to a PE, and is indexed by the PE number.

3. **Mapping SMW to PAS (Second-level address translation):**
If an $\boldsymbol{SMW_n}$ is a target of remote memory reference by a $\boldsymbol{PE_m}$, an SMW-access request is forwarded from the $\boldsymbol{PE_m}$ to the $\boldsymbol{PE_n}$ via the

[3] Butterfly is a registered trademark of Bolt Beranek and Newman, Inc.

crossbar network in message form. On the $\boldsymbol{PE_n}$, the target $\boldsymbol{SMW_n}$ is mapped to its *physical-address space* ($\boldsymbol{PAS_n}$), as shown in Figure 7.2–b. That is, the *SMW-access server* ($\boldsymbol{SAS_n}$) translates the received *common-space real-address* (**CSRA**), excluding a portion of SMW index, into a *physical address* ($\boldsymbol{PA_n}$) with a conventional one-level paging.

From the viewpoints of a processor and a local memory, the addressing scheme makes no difference between local and remote memory references in the sense that both references can equally perform memory reads/writes for all the data sizes (i.e., byte, halfword, word, and doubleword). The only difference is the local/remote memory access time ratio, and therefore the scheme falls under *NUMA (Non-Uniform Memory Access) architectures.* Rough estimates of local/remote memory access time ratio are given in [21, 24]. The effects on cache-miss penalty is shown in Table 7.1.

7.3 Cache Design

7.3.1 Design Considerations

To provide zero-wait-state instruction/data caching for a SPARC microprocessor at 16.67 MHz clock frequency, each PE should have a private cache. On implementing a particular cache, we must consider the various aspects of cache design [27]. Figure 7.3 and Table 7.1 respectively show the block diagram and the specifications of the cache we have designed.

The cache design parameters we take into consideration here are *cache-access (cache-lookup) address* and *associativity.* Here we do not address the questions of *block sizes* and *write policies.* We can select either 32-byte block or 64-byte block appropriately. There are two write policies: *write through* and *write back*; we have chosen the write-through policy for the reason given in Section 7.5.2.

There are two options on the addresses used to access the cache: *virtual-address cache* and *real-address cache* [27]. In the 2-level address translation scheme there is an additional option, *physical-address cache*; but we neglect it since it is obviously impractical. For real-address caches, there are three additional options on the ordering cache lookup and address translation: *pre lookup*, *parallel lookup*, and *post lookup* [17]. There are at least two options on associativity or mapping: *direct-*

Table 7.1
Specifications of Dual-Directory Cache

CACHE	Access Address		Virtual Address	
	Associativity		Direct Mapped	
	Replacement Policy		—	
	Write Policy		Write Through	
	Write-Miss Option		No-Write-Allocate	
	Unified or Split		Unified	
	Block Size	Address Block (Line)	32 bytes	64 bytes
		Transfer Block	32 bytes	64 bytes
		Coherence Block	32 bytes	64 bytes
	Cache Size		64K bytes	128K bytes
	Number of Sets		2048	
	Cache Hit Time		1 clock cycle	
	Miss Penalty	Local Memory	17 clock cycles	25 clock cycles
		Remote Memory	64 clock cycles	96 clock cycles
RTB	Access Address		Real Address	
	Associativity		4-Way Set Associative	
	Replacement Policy		LRU	
	Number of Sets		512	

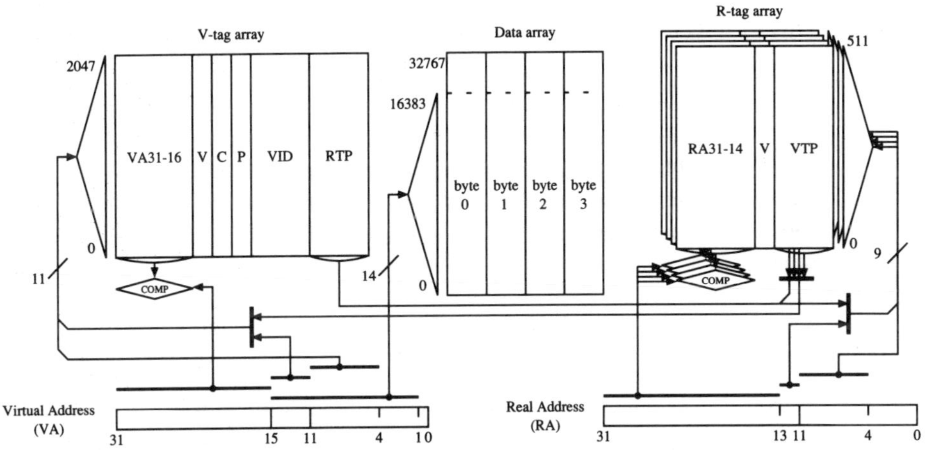

C : Change bit
COMP : COMPare
P : Protection bits
RA : Real Address
RTP : R-Tag Pointer
V : Valid bit
VA : Virtual Address
VID : Virtual-address-space IDentifier
VTP : V-Tag Pointer

Figure 7.3
Block Diagram of Dual-Directory Cache

mapped cache and *set-associative cache* [27, 13]. As a result, the following eight design alternatives are possible with respect to the cache-access address and the associativity:

- *Virtual-address, direct-mapped cache,*
- *Virtual-address, set-associative cache,*
- *Real-address, pre-lookup, direct-mapped cache,*
- *Real-address, pre-lookup, set-associative cache,*
- *Real-address, parallel-lookup, direct-mapped cache,*
- *Real-address, parallel-lookup, set-associative cache,*
- *Real-address, post-lookup, direct-mapped cache,* and
- *Real-address, post-lookup, set-associative cache.*

Table 7.2 summarizes their impact on cache-access time (or cache-hit time), cache size, and hardware cost. We assume that the critical timing path for the cache access is dominated by the tag-access time and the tag-compare time rather than by the data-read time.

We have chosen the *virtual-address, direct-mapped cache* organization, because: i) the cache-access time is the smallest, ii) the hardware cost is the lowest, and iii) the cache size can get larger only by increasing the number of sets (or lines) without any additional costs.

On the other hand, with respect to miss ratio, there are arguments against direct-mapped caches. The most important one is that direct-mapped caches have worse miss ratios than set-associative caches of the same size. In fact, however, the miss ratio differences between direct-mapped caches and set-associative caches diminish as the caches get larger [13].

7.3.2 Homonym and Synonym Problems of Virtual Address Cache

There are also arguments against virtual-address cache with regard to consistency inside a single cache. These consistency problems are called *homonym* and *synonym* problems. We have given the problems the following additional considerations in designing the virtual-address cache.

7.3.2.1 Support to multiple virtual-address spaces Virtual address caches incur the problem of homonym between two or more virtual-address spaces. All addresses must be tagged with the identifier of the virtual-address space with which they are associated, or else the cache

Table 7.2
Cache Design Alternatives

Access Address	*Order w.r.t. Address Translation*	*Associativity*		
			Time	*Cache-Access Time*
			Size	*Cache Size*
			Cost	*Hardware Cost*
Virtual Address	—	Direct Mapped	**Time**	$T_{tag} + T_{comp}$
			Size	$L \times S$
			Cost	H_{way}
		Set Associative	**Time**	$T_{tag} + T_{comp} + T_{sel}$
			Size	$L \times S \times W$
			Cost	$H_{way} \times W + H_{sel}(W)$
Real Address	Pre Lookup	Direct Mapped	**Time**	$\max(T_{tag}, T_{TLB}) + T_{comp}$
			Size	$L \times S(\leq P)$
			Cost	$H_{TLB} + H_{way}$
		Set Associative	**Time**	$\max(T_{tag}, T_{TLB}) + T_{comp} + T_{sel}$
			Size	$L \times S \times W(\leq P \times W)$
			Cost	$H_{TLB} + H_{way} \times W + H_{sel}(W)$
	Parallel Lookup	Direct Mapped	**Time**	$\max(T_{tag}, T_{TLB}) + T_{mpx} + T_{comp}$
			Size	$L \times S(= P \times SS)$
			Cost	$H_{TLB} + H_{way} + H_{mpx}(SS)$
		Set Associative	**Time**	$\max(T_{tag}, T_{TLB}) + T_{mpx} + T_{comp} + T_{sel}$
			Size	$L \times S \times W(= P \times SS \times W)$
			Cost	$H_{TLB} + (H_{way} + H_{mpx}) \times W + H_{sel}(W)$
	Post Lookup	Direct Mapped	**Time**	$T_{TLB} + T_{tag} + T_{comp}$
			Size	$L \times S$
			Cost	$H_{TLB} + H_{way}$
		Set Associative	**Time**	$T_{TLB} + T_{tag} + T_{comp} + T_{sel}$
			Size	$L \times S \times W$
			Cost	$H_{TLB} + H_{way} \times W + H_{sel}(W)$

Time Components:

T_{comp} : Tag-Compare Time
T_{mpx} : Tag-Multiplex Time
T_{sel} : Way-Select Time
T_{tag} : Tag-Access Time
T_{TLB} : TLB-Lookup Time

Size Components:

L : Line Size
P : Page Size
S : Number of Sets
SS : Number of Sets per Superset
W : Number of Ways

Cost Components:

$H_{mpx}(SS)$: Hardware Cost for Multiplexing Sets
$H_{sel}(W)$: Hardware Cost for Selecting Ways
H_{TLB} : Hardware Cost for TLB
H_{way} : Hardware Cost per Way

must be purged every time a virtual-address space is switched [27]. We have chosen the *tagging* scheme.

As shown in Figure 7.3, the cache, along with the TLB not shown in Figure 7.3, supports up to 256 virtual-address spaces with 8-bit VID (Virtual-address space IDentifier). An operating system need not flush the the cache or the TLB on switching virtual-address spaces unless the number of the active spaces exceeds 256.

7.3.2.2 Combined solution to both the synonym problem and the multicache consistency problem Virtual address caches also incur the serious problem of synonym when two or more different virtual addresses map to the same real address. There are a number of possible ways to deal with the synonym problem [11]. Among them, we have chosen the *dual-directory cache* scheme proposed in [11].

The dual-directory cache scheme exploits the similarity of the synonym problem to the multicache consistency problem, and therefore gives a combined solution to both problems. Since both problems can be resolved in an integrated way to enforce cache coherence, we sometimes call them *cache coherence problems* in the general. Otherwise, we particularly call the synonym problem *intra-cache coherence problem*, and call the multicache consistency problem *inter-cache coherence problem*.

As shown in Figure 7.3, one of the two directories is called *V-tag array*, which is normally accessed by a SPARC microprocessor with virtual addresses; the other is called *R-tag array*, which is normally accessed by the cache coherence logic in an MMU using real addresses.

7.4 Cache Coherence Schemes

The cache we have designed has two kinds of cache coherence to enforce: *intra-cache coherence* and *inter-cache coherence*. From the standpoint of a testbed, KRPP provides the various schemes of cache coherence as follows:

- *Cacheability marking* scheme to enforce inter-cache coherence [4],
- *Fast selective invalidation* scheme to enforce inter-cache coherence [6],
- *Distributed limited-directory* scheme to enforce inter-cache coherence [2, 5], and

- *Dual-directory cache* scheme to enforce both intra-cache and inter-cache coherence [11].

7.4.1 Cacheability Marking Scheme

The inter-cache coherence problem can be solved easily if shared data, or writable shared data strictly, are not cached.

An attribute bit, called *cacheable* bit, is provided in each page-table entry to specify whether data in the associated virtual page are cacheable or not. An operating system, with the help of a compiler, *marks* only virtual pages, which are mapped to either private space or read-only common space, as cacheable pages.

When a cache miss occurs on accessing a line of a noncacheable page, an MMU does not load the line into the cache. While the page is marked noncacheable, all accesses to the page are always performed in either local or remote memory.

Although the scheme is easy to implement, the performance will suffer because shared-data accesses account for a large portion of common-space accesses.

7.4.2 Fast Selective Invalidation Scheme

In recent years, several compiler-directed cache coherence schemes have been proposed [7]. Among those schemes, we have chosen the *fast selective invalidation* scheme proposed in [6]. And, we have modified the scheme slightly to tailor it to KRPP, as follows [16].

1. In addition to a valid bit, a status bit called *change* bit is introduced and associated with each cache line as shown in Figure 7.3. Although the original scheme assumes a line size of one word [6], KRPP cache has a different line size. As pointed out in [7], it is not a problem. The change bit is set when a line is loaded into the cache, and reset by a cache-control instruction.
2. The original scheme uses two types of cache-control instructions [6]:

- `Clear-Cache` instruction to reset all the valid bits, and
- `Invalidate` instruction to reset all the change bits.

Although these functions are easy to implement, the SPARC instruction set cannot be augmented. We therefore have implemented them as user I/O commands to the MMU.

3. The original scheme uses two types of load instructions [6]: one is marked **cache_read** and the other is marked **memory_read**. Since the load instruction marked **cache_read** is a normal load instruction, it is not a problem. On the other hand, the load instruction marked **memory_read** is not included in the SPARC instruction set. The load instruction marked **memory_read** is defined below.

- If the change bit of the line accessed is reset, it causes a miss to occur, and therefore the data are loaded from memory.
- Otherwise, it is the same as a normal load instruction.

We cannot implement the load instruction marked **memory_read** straightforward. Instead we have introduced the following two user I/O commands to the MMU.

- `memory_read-on`: This command causes the cache to treat all load operations as accesses marked **memory_read**. The cache hereafter checks the change bit of the line accessed.
- `memory_read-off`: This command causes the cache to treat all load operations as accesses marked **cache_read**. The cache hereafter neglects the change bit.

Thus a load instruction marked **memory_read** will be replaced by a 3-tuple of {`memory_read-on`, `load`, `memory_read-off`}. Since the execution of two extra I/O commands introduces overhead, a compiler will be required to reduce the number of commands. One approach might be an *instruction reordering* technique which schedules two or more load instructions marked **memory_read** near each other.

7.4.3 Distributed Limited-Directory Scheme

A number of hardware-based cache coherence schemes have been proposed [29]. Most of them are *bus-based* schemes which use the bus as a broadcast medium to ensure cache coherence [3]. Each cache *snoops* on the bus for broadcasted coherence commands to maintain coherence information in the cache. Most of these snoopy cache protocols can ensure *sequential consistency* [8]. In other interconnection networks (such as the crossbar network of KRPP), however, the network traffic caused by broadcast is unacceptable. Neither are the snoopy cache protocols scalable to a large number of processors (such as 128 PEs in KRPP).

Others are *directory-based* schemes which do not broadcast but (multi)-cast coherence commands exactly to those caches having a copy of the memory block. The schemes use a *directory*, either centralized or distributed, to track all cached copies of each memory block. A directory entry for each memory block maintains pointers to identify the caches having a copy of the block. The directory protocols are classified into three categories: *full-map directory*, *limited directory*, and *chained directory* [2, 5]. Advantages and disadvantages of these protocols are reported in [5].

We have chosen the *limited-directory* scheme to alleviate the directory-size problem of full-map-directory protocols and the complexity of chained-directory protocols. The directory is distributed over all the PEs, as is the memory.

Each directory is placed at a SAS (SMW-Access Server) in each MU (Memory Unit). We refer to it as *coherence directory (CD)*. The coherence directory is indexed using real addresses assuming that all shared data are allocated in the common space of real-address spaces. Each directory entry contains one pointer and two attribute and status bits: *CC (Coherence Check)* bit and *CA (CacheAble/CAched)* bit. The pointer, called *PE pointer*, specifies the PE having the cached copy of the memory block in its cache. This scheme is classified as Dir_1NB [2]. Since the number of simultaneously cached copies is restricted to only one, the *thrashing* or *ping-pong effect* problem will occur if too many PEs share the block. The attribute bit, CC bit, is introduced to alleviate the problem.

For each directory entry, the CC and CA bits are reset and set by user I/O commands to the SAS. The CC and CA bits represent four states of the corresponding memory block, as follows. Figure 7.4 shows the state transition diagram.

- *Noncacheable* State [$CC = 0$ and $CA = 0$]: The memory block is noncacheable.
- *Multiple-copy* State [$CC = 0$ and $CA = 1$]: The memory block is cacheable but not subject to cache coherence enforcement. As a result, more than one cached copy of the block are allowed to be present simultaneously.

- *Zero-copy* State [$CC = 1$ and $CA = 0$]: The block is cacheable and subject to cache coherence enforcement. A cached copy of the block is absent.
- *Single-copy* State [$CC = 1$ and $CA = 1$]: The block is cacheable and subject to cache coherence enforcement. A cached copy of the block is present in the cache of the PE specified by the PE pointer.

The inter-cache coherence protocol based on the distributed limited-directory scheme is detailed in Section 7.5.1.

7.4.4 Dual-Directory Cache Scheme

Dual-directory cache scheme ensures both inter-cache and intra-cache coherence. The inter-cache coherence protocol using this scheme and the distributed limited-directory scheme is described in Section 7.5. The intra-cache coherence protocol with this scheme is described in Section 7.6. Here we give some background information on the dual-directory cache organization.

The dual-directory cache organization is based on that proposed in [11], but it is tailored to our cache design [15]. Both directories contain a tag for each line in the data array. We assume that the page size is 4K bytes and that the block (line) size is 32 bytes.

One of two directories, *V-tag array*, is a direct-mapped tag memory of 2048 sets. It is normally indexed using 11 bits of virtual addresses (**VA15-5**). The index includes the least significant 4 bits of the virtual-page number (**VA15-12**). Each V-tag entry contains the following fields that are used for enforcing cache coherence (see Figure 7.3).

- *Virtual-address tag*: This field contains the most significant 16 bits of the virtual address (**VA31-16**).
- *Status bits*: These are a valid bit and a change bit (see Section 7.4.2.
- *R-tag pointer (RTP)*: This field points to the corresponding R-tag entry. The 4-bit pointer includes the least significant 2 bits of the real-page-frame number (**RA13-12**) that identify the set in the R-tag array, and two bits that specify the way within the set.

The other directory, *R-tag array*, is a 4-way set-associative tag memory of 512 sets. It is normally indexed using 9 bits of real addresses (**RA13-5**). The index includes the least significant 2 bits of the real-page-frame number (*RA13-12*). Each R-tag entry contains the following fields, all of which are related to cache coherence enforcement (see Figure 7.3).

• *Real-address tag*: This field contains the most significant 18 bits of the real address (**RA31-14**).
• *Valid bit.*
• *V-tag pointer (VTP)*: This field points to the corresponding V-tag entry and the corresponding line in the data array. The 4-bit pointer is the least significant 4 bits of the virtual-page number (**VA15-12**) that identify the set in the V-tag array.

As implied by the description above, a pair of V-tag and R-tag must be *doubly-linked* using RTP and VTP, if the corresponding line in the data array is valid.

Although the V-tag array and the R-tag array have the same number of entries, they differ in the associativity: direct-mapped for the V-tag array and 4-way set-associative for the R-tag array. The reason is given in Section 7.6.2.

7.5 Hardware-Based Inter-Cache Coherence Enforcement

7.5.1 Inter-Cache Coherence Protocols

The inter-cache coherence protocol is based on the *distributed limited-directory* scheme and the *dual-directory cache* scheme. Recall that a memory block is subject to cache coherence enforcement only when the *CC* bit in the corresponding coherence-directory entry is set. Thus we assume that the *CC* bit is set in the description below. Inter-cache coherence is maintained in the following way (see Figure 7.4).

7.5.1.1 On read miss When a read miss occurs in the cache of $\boldsymbol{PE}_j$, $\boldsymbol{PE}_j$ sends a line-fetch message to the memory of $\boldsymbol{PE}_k$. On receiving the line-fetch message, $\boldsymbol{PE}_k$ looks up the *CA* bit and the PE pointer in the coherence-directory entry corresponding to the requested memory block. There are three cases according to the states.

1. *Zero-copy* state [$CA = 0$]: A cached copy of the memory block is absent. $\boldsymbol{PE}_k$ sets the *CA* bit (i.e., the state is changed to *single-copy*)

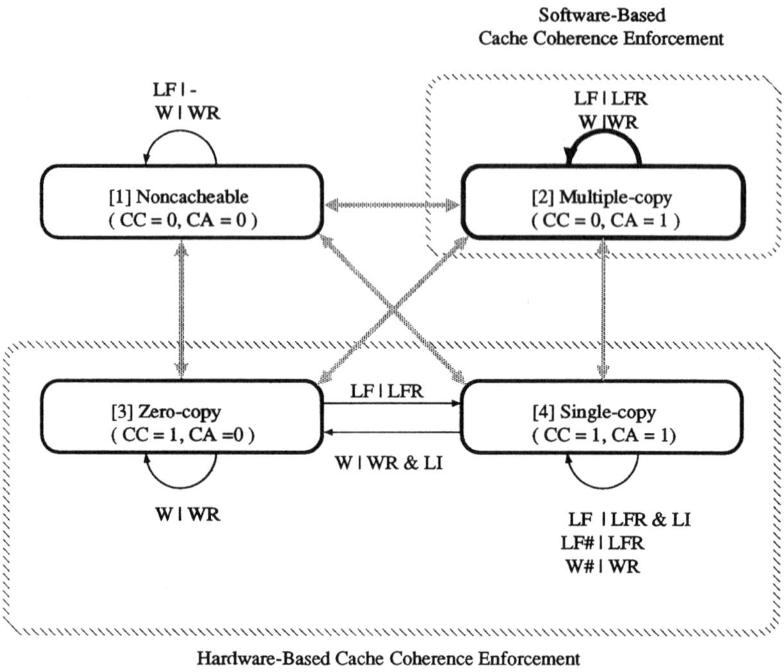

$\Longleftrightarrow$: State transition with no response, caused by software with setting CC and/or CA bits
$\longrightarrow$: State transition with responses, caused by hardware

Command | Responses

Commands:

- LF : Line-Fetch message from other PE than the PE specified by the PE pointer
- LF# : Line-Fetch message from the PE specified by the PE pointer
- W : Write message from other PE than the PE specified by the PE pointer
- W# : Write message from the PE specified by the PE pointer

Responses:

- LFR : Line-Fetch-Reply message to the PE requesting the line-fetch
- LI : Line-Invalidate message to the PE having the line
- WR : Write-Reply message to the PE requesting the write

Figure 7.4
State Transition Diagram

and causes the PE pointer to specify $\boldsymbol{PE}_j$. $\boldsymbol{PE}_k$ returns the requested data as a line-fetch-reply message to $\boldsymbol{PE}_j$. When the reply is received at $\boldsymbol{PE}_j$, the data are copied into the cache of $\boldsymbol{PE}_j$. In this case, a read miss results in two messages.

2. *Single-copy* state $[CA = 1]$ and the PE pointer specifies $\boldsymbol{PE}_j$: The latest owner of the memory block is $\boldsymbol{PE}_j$, but a cached copy of the block may not be in the cache of $\boldsymbol{PE}_j$. $\boldsymbol{PE}_k$ just returns the requested data as a line-fetch-reply message to $\boldsymbol{PE}_j$. When the reply is received at $\boldsymbol{PE}_j$, the data are copied into the cache of $\boldsymbol{PE}_j$. In this case, a read miss results in two messages.

3. *Single-copy* state $[CA = 1]$ and the PE pointer specifies $\boldsymbol{PE}_i$ (see Figure 7.5–a): A cached copy of the memory block is present in the cache of $\boldsymbol{PE}_i$. $\boldsymbol{PE}_k$ sends the real address of the block as a line-invalidate message to the cache of $\boldsymbol{PE}_i$ ([2] in Figure 7.5–a). $\boldsymbol{PE}_k$ makes the pointer to specify $\boldsymbol{PE}_j$ and returns the requested data as a line-fetch-reply message to $\boldsymbol{PE}_j$ ([3] in Figure 7.5–a). When the reply is received at $\boldsymbol{PE}_j$, the data are copied into the cache of $\boldsymbol{PE}_j$. In this case, a read miss results in three messages.

In the case 3, $\boldsymbol{PE}_i$ invalidates its cached copy on receiving the line-invalidate message, as described later.

7.5.1.2 On write miss We assume the *write-through* policy here. When a write miss occurs in the cache of $\boldsymbol{PE}_j$, $\boldsymbol{PE}_j$ sends a write message to the memory of $\boldsymbol{PE}_k$. Since no write buffer is provided in hardware, $\boldsymbol{PE}_j$ stalls until a write-reply message is returned from $\boldsymbol{PE}_k$. On receiving the write message, $\boldsymbol{PE}_k$ looks up the CA bit and the PE pointer in the coherence-directory entry corresponding to the requested memory block. There are three cases according to the states.

1. *Zero-copy* state $[CA = 0]$: A cached copy of the block is absent. $\boldsymbol{PE}_k$ just returns a write-reply message. When the reply is received at $\boldsymbol{PE}_j$, $\boldsymbol{PE}_j$ resumes. In this case, a write miss results in two messages.

2. *Single-copy* state $[CA = 1]$ and the PE pointer specifies $\boldsymbol{PE}_j$: The latest owner of the memory block is $\boldsymbol{PE}_j$, and a cached copy of the block may or may not be in the cache of $\boldsymbol{PE}_j$. The CA bit remains set. $\boldsymbol{PE}_k$ just returns a write-reply message. When the reply is received at $\boldsymbol{PE}_j$, $\boldsymbol{PE}_j$ resumes. In this case, a write miss results in two messages.

3. *Single-copy* state $[CA = 1]$ and the PE pointer specifies $\boldsymbol{PE_i}$: A cached copy of the memory block is present in the cache of $\boldsymbol{PE_i}$. There are two policies for maintaining inter-cache coherence: *write-invalidate* and *write-update*; we have chosen the *write-invalidate* policy for its simplicity. $\boldsymbol{PE_k}$ sends the real address of the block as a line-invalidate message to the cache of $\boldsymbol{PE_i}$. $\boldsymbol{PE_k}$ resets the CA bit and returns a write-reply message. When the reply is received at $\boldsymbol{PE_j}$, $\boldsymbol{PE_j}$ resumes. In this case, a write miss results in three messages.

In the case 3, $\boldsymbol{PE_i}$ invalidates its cached copy on receiving the line-invalidate message, as described below.

7.5.1.3 Line invalidation When a line-invalidate message is received at $\boldsymbol{PE_i}$, $\boldsymbol{PE_i}$ looks up the R-tag array using the real address in the message. If a matching is found, then $\boldsymbol{PE_i}$ accesses the V-tag array using the VTP and resets the valid bit of the V-tag entry corresponding to the line to invalidate. Line-invalidate messages are allowed to be buffered, provided $\boldsymbol{PE_i}$ processes buffered messages before handling a cache miss.

7.5.2 Write-Policy Issues

In Section 7.5.1, we assumed the write-through policy. Consider the write-back policy for the case 3 of the read miss above. In this case, the cached copy may have been updated by $\boldsymbol{PE_i}$ and, if so, the status for the copy is dirty. Since the data of the memory block in $\boldsymbol{PE_k}$ may be stale, $\boldsymbol{PE_k}$ cannot simply return the data to $\boldsymbol{PE_j}$. Instead, $\boldsymbol{PE_k}$ causes $\boldsymbol{PE_i}$ to forward the dirty copy to $\boldsymbol{PE_j}$. The following three schemes are possible for the dirty-copy forwarding.

1. *Direct-forwarding scheme with four massages* (see Figure 7.5–b): This scheme corresponds to the read-miss case of the *SCI (Scalable Coherent Interface)* coherence protocol [18]. $\boldsymbol{PE_k}$ sends the pointer specifying $\boldsymbol{PE_i}$, instead of the requested data, as a line-fetch-fault message to $\boldsymbol{PE_j}$ ([2] in Figure 7.5–b) and makes the pointer to specify $\boldsymbol{PE_j}$. When the pointer is received at $\boldsymbol{PE_j}$, $\boldsymbol{PE_j}$ sends a line-transfer message to $\boldsymbol{PE_i}$ ([3] in Figure 7.5–b). On receiving the massage, $\boldsymbol{PE_i}$ returns the requested data as a line-transfer-reply message to $\boldsymbol{PE_j}$ ([4] in Figure 7.5–b) and resets the valid bit. When the reply is received at $\boldsymbol{PE_j}$, the data are copied into the cache of $\boldsymbol{PE_j}$. In this scheme, a read miss results in four messages.

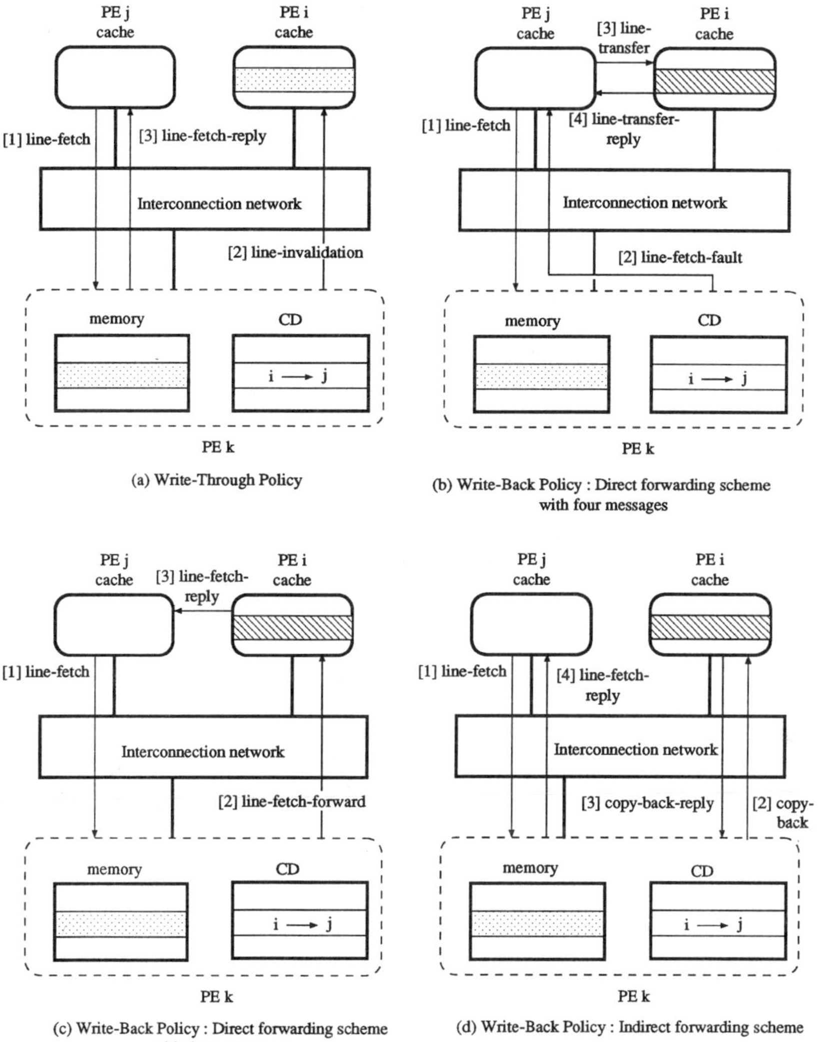

(a) Write-Through Policy

(b) Write-Back Policy : Direct forwarding scheme with four messages

(c) Write-Back Policy : Direct forwarding scheme with three messages

(d) Write-Back Policy : Indirect forwarding scheme

CD : Coherence Directory

Figure 7.5
Inter-Cache Coherence Protocols

2. *Direct forwarding scheme with three massages* (see Figure 7.5–c): This scheme corresponds to the read-miss case of the *SDD (Stanford Distributed-Directory)* coherence protocol [31]. $\boldsymbol{PE}_k$ makes the pointer to specify $\boldsymbol{PE}_j$ and sends the pointer as a line-fetch-forward message to $\boldsymbol{PE}_i$ ([2] in Figure 7.5–c). On receiving the massage, $\boldsymbol{PE}_i$ returns the requested data as a line-fetch-reply message to $\boldsymbol{PE}_j$ ([3] in Figure 7.5–c) and resets the valid bit. When the reply is received at $\boldsymbol{PE}_j$, the data are copied into the cache of $\boldsymbol{PE}_j$. In this scheme, a read miss results in three messages.
3. *Indirect forwarding scheme* (see Figure 7.5–d): $\boldsymbol{PE}_k$ continues to intervene between $\boldsymbol{PE}_i$ and $\boldsymbol{PE}_j$ until the dirty-copy forwarding is complete. $\boldsymbol{PE}_k$ sends the real address of the block as a copy-back message to $\boldsymbol{PE}_i$ ([2] in Figure 7.5–d). On receiving the massage, $\boldsymbol{PE}_i$ returns the requested data as a copy-back-reply message to $\boldsymbol{PE}_k$ ([3] in Figure 7.5–d) and resets the valid bit. When the reply is received at $\boldsymbol{PE}_k$, the data are written into the memory of $\boldsymbol{PE}_k$. $\boldsymbol{PE}_k$ makes the pointer to specify $\boldsymbol{PE}_j$ and returns the requested data as a line-fetch-reply message to $\boldsymbol{PE}_j$ ([4] in Figure 7.5–d). On receiving the reply, the data are copied into the cache of $\boldsymbol{PE}_j$. In this scheme, a read miss results in four messages.

The first and third schemes require four messages instead of three as in the case of the scheme based on the write-through policy. Although the second scheme requires only three messages, it would create potential deadlock dependences, as would the third scheme.

7.5.3 Memory Consistency

The correctness of the inter-cache coherence protocols is a function of the *memory consistency model* adopted by the system. There is a spectrum of memory consistency models proposed in the literature: the strictest *sequential consistency* model [19], *processor consistency* model [9, 12], *weak consistency* model proposed by Dubois, Scheurich and Briggs [8], less strict *weak consistency* model proposed by Adve and Hill [1], and the least strict *release consistency* model [9].

KRPP provides a conservative implementation of the weak consistency model proposed by Dubois, Scheurich and Briggs [8], and imposes an additional constraint on programming models. As stated in Section 7.5.1, KRPP supports no write buffering; a processor that issued a write message stalls until it receives a write-reply message. Write accesses may be buffered in a sense, however, since a write-reply message does not ensure that the corresponding line-invalidate message has been sent out. A processor that issued a write can proceed after receiving a write-reply message even while the corresponding line-invalidate message is on its way to the other processor having a line to invalidate, i.e., even while the write access is not performed.

To ensure weak consistency in KRPP, we need a mechanism for delaying a synchronization access until all previous write accesses have been performed. One of such mechanisms is a *fence* [9] that delays the issue of synchronization accesses. To implement a fence, an acknowledge message must be returned to a processor that issued a write message in response to the corresponding line-invalidate message, and the originating processor must provide a counter for keeping track of outstanding write accesses. The counter is incremented when a write access is issued, and is decremented when the acknowledge message is received. The fence mechanism requires an additional message for a write access.

Instead of making a processor delay the issue of a synchronization access with a fence, KRPP makes a memory module delay a synchronization access from being performed with respect to any other processor. No additional message is required. This is realized by prohibiting a memory module from performing a synchronization access for some memory location in the module until all previous writes to the module are performed, i.e., until all the corresponding line-invalidate messages have been sent out from the memory module. This conservative implementation, however, introduces a constraint into programming models; all shared writable data within a critical section should be allocated in the same memory module.

7.6 Intra-Cache Coherence Enforcement

7.6.1 Intra-Cache Coherence Protocols

The intra-cache coherence protocol is based on the *dual-directory cache* scheme. Intra-cache coherence must be preserved on every cache miss, both read and write misses, in the following way.

7.6.1.1 On read miss For a read miss, the protocol is defined as a part of the line replacement procedure as follows.

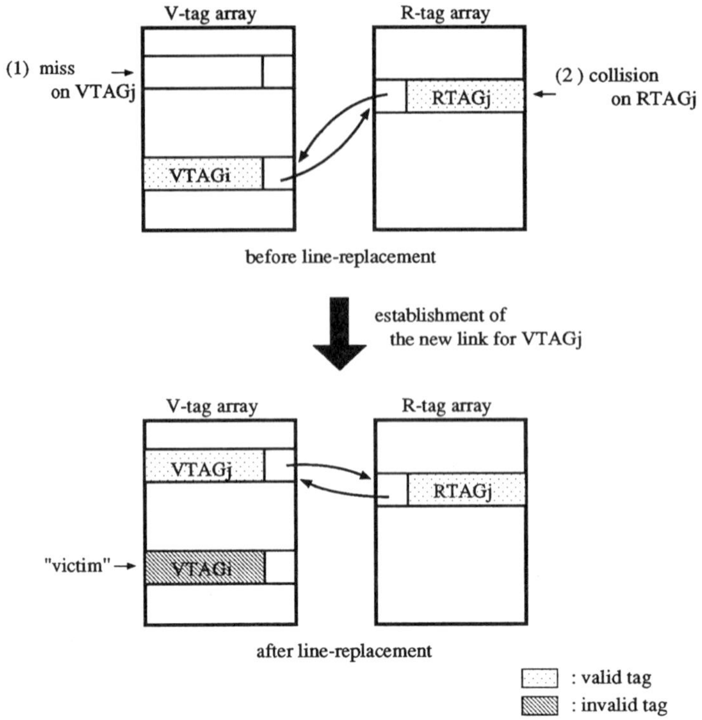

Figure 7.6
Collision Problem

1. The virtual address causing the miss is translated into a real address through the TLB lookup. Once the real address is obtained, the intra-cache coherence enforcement proceeds in parallel with the line-fetch transaction.
2. The R-tag array is examined using the real address. If a hit occurs, the matching R-tag entry remains the entry for the new line, and skip the step 3. In this case, the virtual address corresponding to the real address might be a synonym.
3. Otherwise, an R-tag entry is selected for the new line. Recall that the R-tag array is 4-way set-associative; thus there are four candidates for a replacement *victim*. The choice of a victim is done by comparing all the VTPs (V-tag pointers) of the four R-tag entries with the virtual address (VA15-12) causing the miss. If a matching is found, the matching R-tag entry will be a (false) victim. Otherwise, any R-tag entry will fall a (true) victim to *collision* (see Figure 7.6).
4. The valid bit of a V-tag entry doubly-linked to the selected R-tag entry is reset. Thus an old double-link is broken, and the corresponding line is removed.

5. When the new line is fetched, the valid bit of the corresponding V-tag entry is set. Its RTP (R-tag pointer) is also made to point to the R-tag entry selected in the step 3; similarly, the VTP (V-tag pointer) of the R-tag entry is caused to point to the V-tag entry. Thus a new double-link is created.

7.6.1.2 On write miss Although the write-through policy usually regards every write as miss, we below assume a write miss for an absent line.

1. The virtual address causing the miss is translated into a real address through the TLB lookup. Once the real address is obtained, the intra-cache coherence enforcement proceeds in parallel with the write transaction.
2. The R-tag array is examined using the real address. If a miss occurs, the protocol is complete.
3. Otherwise, the valid bit of a V-tag entry doubly-linked to the R-tag entry is reset. Thus a double-link is broken, and the corresponding line is removed.

7.6.2 Collision Problem

In the step 3 of the protocol for read miss, a replacement victim must be selected from a set of the R-tag array. Line replacement normally causes another victim to be selected from a set of the V-tag array. If there is at least one line belonging to exactly the same pair of sets as the new line, the single line is enough to be purged from the data array. Thus the R-tag entry selected results in a *false* victim. Otherwise, two lines must be purged from the data array: one is replaced because its tag is purged from the V-tag array (see the step 5), and the other is replaced because its tag is purged from the R-tag array (see the step 4). The latter is called a *true* victim, because it falls the victim to an avoidable *collision* situation.

Intuitively, no collision occurs when the R-tag array is fully associative. If the R-tag array is set-associative, a collision is caused by the difference between the *superset* size and the set size of the R-tag array. A superset is a collection of all lines attainable by specifying only those bits that are common to both the virtual and real addresses [11]. The number of lines within a superset (i.e., superset size) is determined by the number of bits of virtual-page number used to index the V-tag array. In KRPP, the least-significant four bits of virtual-page number is used as an index, and therefore the superset size is 16 lines. On the other hand, the set size of the R-tag array is 4 lines; there is the difference between both the sizes. Even for set-associative, if the R-tag is 16-way set-associative, a collision never occurs.

The effect of collisions appears to depend on the associativity of the R-tag array assuming that the superset size is fixed. Obviously a direct-mapped implementation of the R-tag array will suffer the most detrimental effect. We have examined the relationship between the associativity and the effect of collisions using two methods: one is a probabilistic analysis using a Markov Chain based on the proposal in [14], and the other is a trace-driven simulation. We have shown the methodology and their preliminary results in Appendixes A and B of [22].

Finally, taking the hardware cost into consideration, we have chosen four as the associativity [17].

7.7 Concluding Remarks

In this paper we have described the KRPP cache architecture and discussed the inter-cache and intra-cache coherence problems involved in KRPP. To ensure cache coherence and to measure the effectiveness of individual coherence schemes, KRPP provides the various schemes: i) *cacheability marking* scheme, ii) *fast selective invalidation* scheme, iii) *distributed limited-directory* scheme, and iv) *dual-directory cache* scheme.

Both the cacheability marking scheme and the first selective invalidation scheme are compiler-directed inter-cache coherence schemes and their effectiveness relies heavily on the ability of a parallelizing compiler. IPC (Integrated Parallelizing Compiler) system [16] being built at Kyushu University is a promising compiler for this end.

On the other hand, the distributed limited-directory (Dir_1NB) with the dual-directory cache scheme offers hardware-based inter-cache coherence protocols. The write-through policy we have chosen facilitates the protocols as compared with the write-back policy. The correctness of the protocols depends on the memory consistency model adopted by the system. KRPP provides a conservative implementation of the weak consistency model [8], and imposes an additional constraint on programming models.

The dual-directory cache scheme gives a solution to the intra-cache coherence problem, but it might suffer the collision problem if the R-tag array does not have sufficient associativity. We have analyzed the relationship between the associativity and the effect of collisions [22], and have chosen four as the associativity.

An interesting issue on inter-cache coherence is how we combine the software-based approach with the hardware-based approach or how we cause both approaches to share the burden of coherence enforcement. KRPP provides a method for enabling to make the tradeoffs between software and hardware approaches; a *CC* (Coherence Control) bit of each limited-directory entry for a memory block. A quantitative performance analysis will give us a promising direction on the software and hardware synergy to inter-cache coherence.

Acknowledgments

We would like to thank Prof. T. Sueyoshi of Kyushu Institute of Technology and the following students who have contributed or are now contributing to the KRPP project: H. Akaboshi, Y. Fukuzawa, K. Hamaguchi, Y. Hirotani, N. Imamura, J. Ishida, K. Kai, T. Kamachi, K. Kusano, M. Kuwayama, T. Onoue, K. Sugiyama, K. Tanaka, N. Tokunaga, K. Tsunedomi, T. Ueno, K. Yasaka, and N. Yasutomi. We would like to acknowledge the considerable contributions from Asia Electronics Inc., Bussan Electronics Systems Technology Inc., Fujitsu Ltd., Kyocera Corp., Nishimu Electronics Industries Co. Ltd., and Toshiba Corp. We also wish to thank Prof. Mark D. Hill of University of Wisconsin for his comment to the collision problem.

References

[1] Adve, S. V. and Hill, M. D., "Weak Ordering – A New Definition," *Proc. 17th Int'l. Symp. on Computer Architecture*, pp.2–14, May 1990.

[2] Agarwal, A., Simoni, R., Hennessy, J., and Horowitz, M., "An Evaluation of Directory Schemes for Cache Coherence," *Proc. 15th Int'l. Symp. on Computer Architecture*, pp.280–289, June 1988.

[3] Archibald, J. and Baer, J. -L., "Cache Coherence Protocols: Evaluation Using a Multiprocessor Simulation Model," *ACM Trans. Computer Systems*, vol.4, no.4, pp.273–298, Nov. 1986.

[4] Brantley, W. C., McAuliffe, K. P., and Weiss, J., "RP3 Processor-Memory Element," *Proc. 1985 Int'l. Conf. Parallel Processing*, pp.782–789, Aug. 1985.

[5] Chaiken, D., Fields, C., Kurihara, K., and Agarwal, A., "Directory-Based Cache Coherence in Large-Scale Multiprocessors," *IEEE Computer*, vol.23, no.6, pp.49–58, June 1990.

[6] Cheong, H. and Veidenbaum, V., "A Cache Coherence Scheme with Fast Selective Invalidation," *Proc. 15th Int'l. Symp. Computer Architecture*, pp. 299–307, May 1988.

[7] Cheong, H. and Veidenbaum, A. V., "Compiler-Directed Cache Management in Multiprocessors," *IEEE Computer*, vol.23, no.6, pp.39–47, June 1990.

[8] Dubois, M., Scheurich, C., and Briggs, F., "Memory Access Buffering in Multiprocessors," *Proc. 13th Int'l. Symp. Computer Architecture*, pp. 434–442, June 1986.

[9] Gharachorloo, K., Lenoski, D., Laudon, J., Gibbons, P., Gupta, A., and Hennessy, J., "Memory Consistency and Event Ordering in Scalable Shared-Memory Multiprocessors," *Proc. 17th Int'l. Symp. Computer Architecture*, pp.15–26, May 1990.

[10] Gharachorloo, K., Gupta, A., and Hennessy, J., "Performance Evaluation of Memory Consistency Models for Shared-Memory Multiprocessors," *Proc. ASPLOS-IV*, pp.245–257, Apr. 1991.

[11] Goodman, J. R., "Coherency for Multiprocessor Virtual Address Caches," *Proc. ASPLOS-II*, pp.72–81, Oct. 1987.

[12] Goodman, J. R., *Cache Consistency and Sequential Consistency*, Technical Report no.61, SCI Committee, Mar. 1989.

[13] Hill, M. D., "A Case for Direct-Mapped Caches," *IEEE Computer*, vol.21, no.12, pp.25–40, Dec. 1988.

[14] Hill, M. D., *Private Communication*, 13 Sept. 1989.

[15] Iwata, E., Mori, S., Murakami, K., Fukuda, A., and Tomita, S., "Cache System of the Kyushu University Reconfigurable Parallel Processor (in Japanese)," *IPS Japan WGARC report*, no.79–3, Nov. 1989.

[16] Iwata, E., Mori, S., Murakami, K., Fukuda, A., and Tomita, S., "Integrated Parallelizing Compiler System — Compiler-Assisted Cache Coherence Scheme — (in Japanese)," *IPS Japan WGARC report*, no.83–21, July 1990.

[17] Iwata, E., Mori, S., Murakami, K., Fukuda, A., and Tomita, S., "Cache Architecture of the Kyushu University Reconfigurable Parallel Processor — Cache Design and Intra-cache Coherence Protocol — (in Japanese)," *Trans. IPS Japan*, vol.32, no.6, pp.777–789, June 1991.

[18] James, D. V., Laundrie, A. T., Gjessing, S., and Sohi, G. S., "Scalable Coherent Interface," *IEEE Computer*, vol.23, no.6, pp.74–77, June 1990.

[19] Lamport, L., "How to Make a Multiprocessor Computer that Correctly Executes Multiprocess Programs," *IEEE Trans. Computers*, vol.C-28, no.9, pp.241–248, Sept. 1979.

[20] Lenoski, D., Laudon, J., Gharachorloo, K., Gupta, A., and Hennessy, J., "The Directory-Based Cache Coherence Protocol for the DASH Multiprocessor," *Proc. 17th Int'l. Symp. Computer Architecture*, pp.148–159, May 1990.

[21] Mori, S., Kamachi, T., Hamaguchi, K., Murakami, K., Fukuda, A., Sueyoshi, T., and Tomita, S., "Inter-PE Communication Subsystem of the Kyushu University Reconfigurable Parallel Processor (in Japanese)," *Trans. IPS Japan*, vol.30, no.12, pp.1593–1602, Dec. 1989.

[22] Mori, S., Murakami, K., Iwata, E., Fukuda, A., and Tomita, S., "The Kyushu University Reconfigurable Parallel Processor — Cache Architecture and Cache Coherence Schemes —," *Proc. Int'l. Symp. Shared Memory Multiprocessing*, pp.218–229, June 1991.

[23] Murakami, K., Fukuda, A., Sueyoshi, T., and Tomita, S., "An Overview of the Kyushu University Reconfigurable Parallel Processor," *ACM SIGARCH Computer Architecture News*, vol.16, no.4, pp.130–137, Sept. 1988.

[24] Murakami, K., Mori, S., Fukuda, A., Sueyoshi, T., and Tomita, S., "The Kyushu University Reconfigurable Parallel Processor — Design of Memory and Intercommunication Architectures —," *Proc. 1989 ACM SIGARCH Int'l. Conf. Supercomputing*, pp.351–360, June 1989.

[25] Murakami, K., Mori, S., Fukuda, A., Sueyoshi, T., and Tomita, S., "The Kyushu University Reconfigurable Parallel Processor — Design Philosophy and Architecture —," *Proc. IFIP 11th World Computer Congress*, pp.995–1000, Aug. 1989.

[26] Rettberg, R. and Thomas, R., "Contention is no Obstacle to Shared-Memory Multiprocessing," *Commun. ACM*, vol.29, no.12, pp.1202–1212, Dec. 1986.

[27] Smith, A. J., "Cache Memories," *ACM Computing Surveys*, vol.14, no.3, pp.473–530, Sept. 1982.

[28] Stenström, P., "Reducing Contention in Shared-Memory Multiprocessors," *IEEE Computer*, vol.21, no.11, pp.26–37, Nov. 1988.

[29] Stenström, P., "A Survey of Cache Coherence Schemes for Multiprocessors," *IEEE Computer*, vol.23, no.6, pp.12–24, June 1990.

[30] Swan, R. J., Fuller, S. H., and Siewiorek, D. P., "Cm* — A Modular, multi-microprocessor," *Proc. National Computer Conf.*, vol.46, pp.637–644, 1977.

[31] Thapar, M. and Delagi, B., "Stanford Distributed-Directory Protocol," *IEEE Computer*, vol.23, no.6, pp.78–80, June 1990.

III SOFTWARE SYSTEM

8 MUSTARD: A Multiprocessor UNIX for Embedded Real-Time Systems

Shuichi Hiroya, Takeshi Momoi, and Katsutoshi Nihei

MUSTARD is a portable multiprocessor UNIX[1] for microprocessor embedded real-time systems. This UNIX is a two-layered OS consisting of a real-time kernel and UNIX kernel. It is operated on a tightly coupled multiprocessor without a dedicated kernel processor. In addition, to simplify the structure of the fault-tolerant system, MUSTARD supports the addition/separation of a processor during system operation. This paper presents the features, implementation, some performance measurements, hardware construction to evaluate MUSTARD, and user programming tools for MUSTARD.

8.1 Introduction

In embedded systems, a guarantee for real-time response has been in strong demand. In addition, the improvement of throughput using the present software resources and the fault-tolerant support in the switching systems and communication systems are recently in strong demand. To satisfy these requirements, the authors developed real-time UNIX MUSTARD [1, 2, 3] which is operated on a tightly coupled multiprocessor by reconstructing a single processor version real-time UNIX RX-UX832 [4, 5] for NEC's 32-bit microprocessor V60/V70 [6, 7].

Some UNIXs for multiprocessors, such as CMU Mach [8] and UCB Sprite [10, 9], have already been developed. The configuration of operating systems for tightly coupled multiprocessors and performance scalability for increasing processors are relatively well-known. However, there are few reports that describe the response time, a practical method of mutual exclusion [11], and the actual scheduling costs. In this paper, we will discuss some of these items from our experience.

On the other hand, there are few real-time UNIXs for tightly coupled multiprocessors. One of them is D-NIX [12] that is shipped from DYNATECH COMPUTER SYSTEMS. D-NIX's response time is relatively short by fixed priority process scheduling and short time slices, but UNIX processes still have heavy contexts. We will introduce another operating system structure to guarantee a short response time by using light-weight contexts.

This paper describes the features and implementation of MUSTARD where a two-layered OS consisting of a real-time kernel and a UNIX

---

[1] UNIX is a registered trade mark of UNIX System Laboratories, Inc.

kernel are structured with multiprocessors. This paper then presents the hardware, MUSTARD-POT, where up to eight V70 microprocessors for evaluating OS can be mounted. The paper then describes user programming tools.

8.2 Two-Layered OS for Multiprocessors

8.2.1 Configuration of the Single Processor Version Two-Layered OS RX-UX832

Before the explanation of MUSTARD, We will discuss about a structure of a real-time UNIX that is independent of multiprocessors.

Generally, a real-time UNIX has the following features:

1. Fixed-priority task scheduling
2. Preemptive task scheduling
3. Preemptive UNIX kernel
4. Resident in memory
5. Contiguous block file

Several real-time UNIXs are available, and most of them are type (a) shown in Fig.8.1 They are basically UNIX, but they are modified to implement the above real-time facilities. In these UNIXs, the time period from the interrupt to the startup of the corresponding task ranges from several milliseconds to several tens of milliseconds, for example, 5 milliseconds (MC68030) in D-NIX. On the other hand, RX-UX832 and MUSTARD are arranged as shown in Fig. 8.1 (b). To guarantee a short response time, it is possible to chose the light-weight real-time task and the light-weight interrupt handler using a real-time kernel that have also the above real-time facilities. In MUSTARD, the response time from the interrupt to the startup of the corresponding task is less than 350 microseconds (V70, 4 processors, kernel running ratio 20%), which is more than 10 times faster than D-NIX. In general, the response time of type (b) is superior to that of type (a). Also, the low-layer real-time kernel portion can be used independently. Thus, it is suitable for a small embedded system.

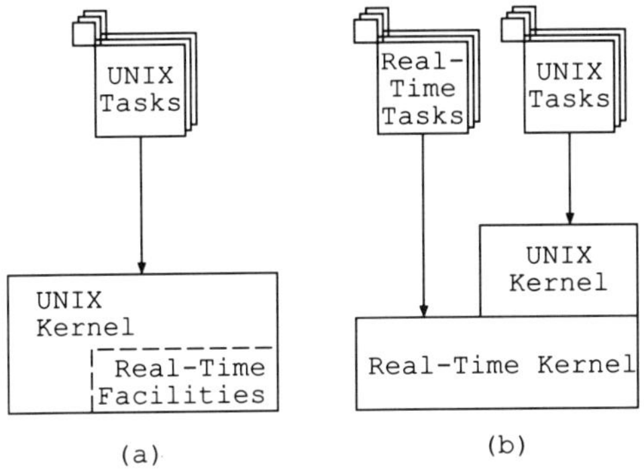

Figure 8.1
Configuration of Real-Time UNIX

8.2.2 Design Objectives for the Multiprocessor System

To design a multiprocessor UNIX MUSTARD, the authors used the following design objectives.

1. To accomplish a performance scalability for up to 8 processors by using real-time tasks
2. To prevent the response time from degradation by modifications to RX-UX832.
3. To support the fault-tolerant facilities for processor faults
4 To keep the programming model provided by RX-UX832 and allow system calls to be upwardly compatible.

In MUSTARD, UNIX kernel is mainly used for creating a user interface and an environment for developing software, Therefore, the authors don't implement a thread mechanism. The results obtained by using a thread programming model can also obtained by using light-weight tasks and shared-memory that can be used by real-time tasks.

8.2.3 Configuration of the Multiprocessor Version Two-Layered OS MUSTARD

The multiprocessor version two-layered OS MUSTARD is designed so that the real-time kernel and the UNIX kernel are able to run on a multiprocessor. Also each kernel can be processed by any processor in the system (floating kernel).

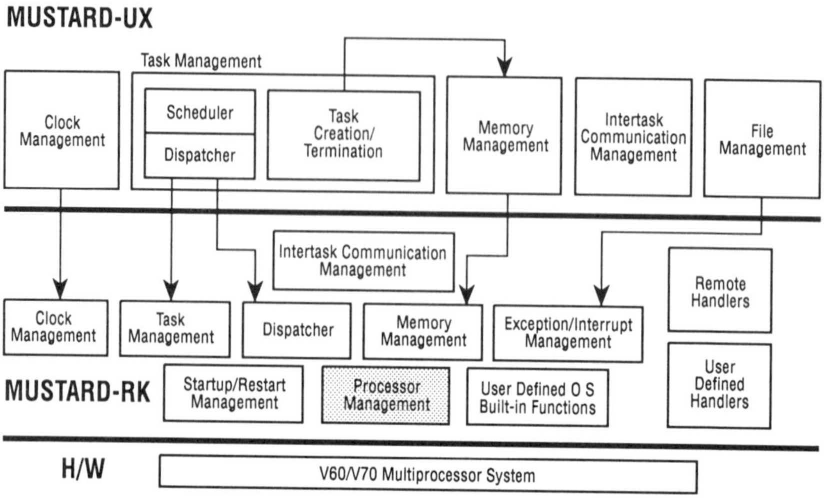

Figure 8.2
Overall Configuration of MUSTARD

To reduce the modifications to UNIX, it was considered that only real-time tasks are run in parallel and the UNIX tasks are processed by only one processor. However, this method was found to increase the overhead of the scheduler/dispatcher in the real-time kernel, and so it was not used.

8.3 Real-Time Kernel MUSTARD-RK

MUSTARD-RK is a portable kernel which is upwardly compatible with ITRON [13] and which is applicable for embedded systems. MUSTARD consists of real-time kernel MUSTARD-RK and UNIX kernel MUSTARD-UX, where the basic functions relating to the multiprocessor, such as processor management and interprocessor communication, are processed by MUSTARD-RK and the results are used by MUSTARD-UX. Fig. 8.2 shows the overall configuration of MUSTARD.

```
INIT:    lock = FREE;
LOCK:    if (TestAndSet(lock) == LOCKED) {
            do {
               while (lock == LOCKED);
            } while (TestAndSet(lock) == LOCKED);
         }
UNLOCK: lock = FREE;

      (a) Spin on Read

INIT:    served = arrival = 0;
LOCK:    mynum = AtomicIncrement(arrival);
         while (mynum != served);
UNLOCK: served++;

      (b) First Come First Served
```

Figure 8.3
Mutual Exclusion Method of Real-Time Kernel

8.3.1 Mutual Exclusion of Real-Time Kernel

In MUSTARD-RK, most of the kernel is arranged as a critical section. However, sections such as the interrupt handler which must be strictly real-time are exclusively controlled by locking each kernel partial resource. There are problems in the tightly coupled multiprocessor, namely bus neck in hardware and kernel mutual exclusion neck in software. Therefore, the authors verified the appropriateness of mutual exclusion control through a simulation based on the real system.

There are main two kernel mutual exclusion methods, spin lock and dispatching. In addition, these are two spin lock methods. Fig. 8.3 shows the two spin lock methods that were actually tried for the kernel entry. Now, MUSTARD uses the FCFS (First Come First Served) method, The authors verified the appropriateness of this selection by the following method.

The representative system call processing time of MUSTARD is about 80 microseconds. In this condition, the authors attempted to simulate the spin lock of the system call entry to check the mean/maximum spin lock time and the speed-up ratio with a single-thread real-time kernel. Fig. 8.4 shows the result of simulation for the various kernel running ratios and numbers of processors. There is no difference between the spin on read and the FCFS in (a) and (b). A difference was only found in (c). It is known that the UNIX kernel running ratio is half of the applications in the software development environment, but the real-time kernel running ratio is generally very low. Even in switching systems that are known to use the kernel heavily, the real-time kernel ratio is about 20%.

The result of Fig. 8.4 (b) indicates that it is better to select the spin lock method for up to 4 processors. This is because the MUSTARD dispatching time is 44 microseconds (V70, 20MHz). There is no difference in mean spin lock time between the spin on read and the FCFS. However, there are two other main differences, the mutual exclusion cost and the maximum spin lock time. The mutual exclusion cost of the spin read is 4.3 microseconds and that of the FCFS is 7.8 microseconds. Fig. 8.4 (c) shows that the spin on read cannot guarantee the maximum spin lock time.

8.3.2 Task Scheduling and Response Time

In MUSTARD-RK, the highest priority tasks are usually assigned in the range of the number of active processors. However, it is impossible to strictly assure such a rule due to delays in interprocessor communication. When this rule is assured, the overhead becomes large. In present MUSTARD-RK, one of the following scheduling policies can be selected when the system is generated.

Exact This scheduling policy which is most faithful to the rule and which provides system level preemption. In this policy, the priority of a target task is compared with that of all other running tasks. When the number of processors is large, the overhead becomes large.

Moderate Like "exact", this policy provides system level preemption. However, unlike "exact", when a task having lower priority than the target task is found, the comparison is stopped.

Rough This policy provides preemption which is local to a processor. It improves the utilization factor of processors rather than providing a strict priority scheduling. The worst case for the priority inversion time

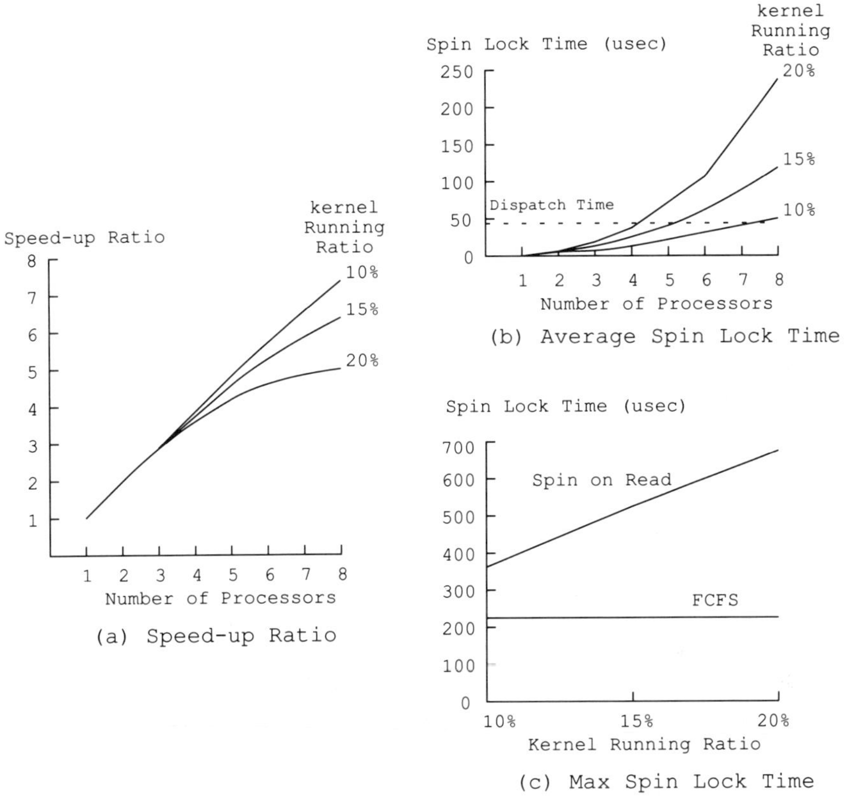

Figure 8.4
Speed-up Ratio and Spin Lock Time

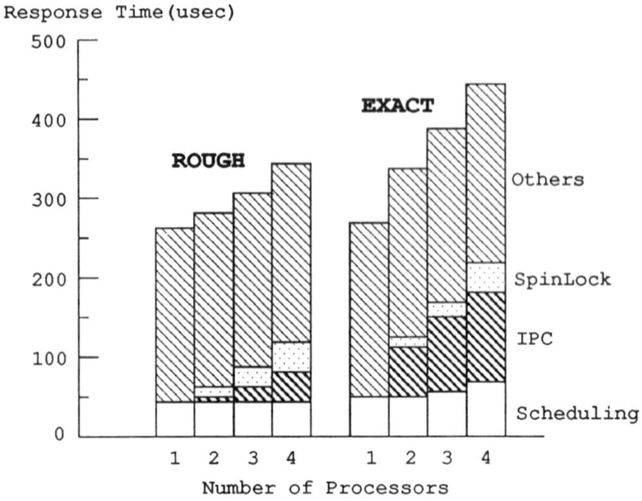

Figure 8.5
Response Time of the Highest Priority Tasks

is up to one time slice. However, tasks having the highest priority are always scheduled.

The exact and moderate scheduling policy improves the response time for tasks having relatively higher priorities compared with rough scheduling policy. However, the overhead degrades the response time of the tasks having the highest priority. This problem is discussed with our some measurement data. The mean response time for tasks having the highest priority is defined as the total time of the interrupt delay time, the interrupt handling time, the kernel waiting time, the wake-up system call processing time, the scheduling time, the IPC (InterProcessor Communication) time, and the dispatching time. Fig. 8.5 shows this mean response time for the rough and exact scheduling policy. The figure shows that the mean response time of tasks having the highest priority is mainly depends on the IPC overhead, while the effect of the scheduling overhead is small. Therefore, the support of the rough and exact scheduling policy is meaningful, but the moderate scheduling policy is meaningless in the present MUSTARD.

8.3.3 Fault-Tolerant Facilities and Processor Management

MUSTARD has three fault-tolerant facilities. It supports mirrored file system, duplex system of tightly coupled multiprocessors, and functional redundancy monitoring of processor. In this section, we will introduce the processor management that is the base of processor fault-tolerance and the dynamic processor power improving.

In MUSTARD-RK, the processor management section is in the lowest layer of MUSTARD-RK, and all actions concerned with processor resources are managed through Processor Control Block (ProcB). ProcB contains the physical/logical processor ID, processor active/inactive state, pointer to TCB (Task Control Block) of a task allocated to a processor, interprocessor communication request flag, and so forth. To check the state of the self processor and a request to the self processor, first, the physical processor ID is obtained by checking a hardware level ID, and next, the physical processor ID is converted to the logical processor ID and last, contents of ProcB are referenced. This method enables it to control the increase/decrease in the number of processors, and to localize an interprocessor communication.

Fig. 8.6 shows the state transition diagram of the processor. When the system is initialized, the kernel passes a logical processor ID starting with 0 to the total number of the processors which starts up in the particular time period so as to set the processor state to ALIVE. When a processor starts up with a delay, the kernel sets the processor state to DEAD and logically stops the processor in the system until mnt_prc() system call described later is issued. In this initialization, even if there is a processor which cannot operate due to a problem, it is possible to start up the system only with a normal processor.

In MUSTARD-RK, mnt_prc()/umt_prc() system calls for supporting live-insertion/withdrawal of a processor are provided for the following purpose.

1. To improve the processor power
2. To disconnect a processor which becomes frequently defective
3. To replace a processor board for maintenance

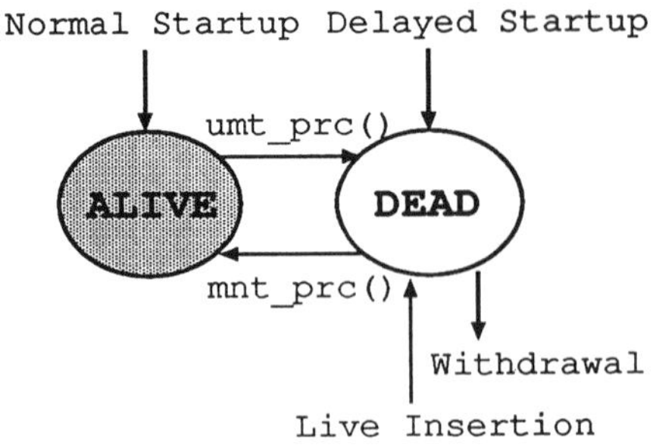

Figure 8.6
Transition of Logical Processor State

8.4 UNIX Kernel MUSTARD-UX

Although several multiprocessor UNIXs have been developed, the authors encountered the following problems in addition to the conventional problems in parallelizing the UNIX kernel.

1. Problem related to the real-time response guarantee
2. Problem related to the increase/decrease of the number of processors
3. Problem related to a two-layered structure

8.4.1 Mutual Exclusion of UNIX Kernel

In MUSTARD-UX, most of the UNIX kernel, excluding the device drivers and few small kernel resources, is exclusively controlled by the dispatching mechanism. As was described in Section 3, MUSTARD-UX uses several resources in MUSTARD-RK, such as the dispatcher, when a UNIX task issues a system call for using a MUSTARD-RK resource. Therefore, it is necessary to gain both the UNIX kernel and the real-time kernel. In the modification of the UNIX kernel for multiprocessors, it was found that the time that the UNIX kernel occupies the real-time kernel is less than the average time that the real-time task occupies the real-time kernel. Table 8.1 shows the major locks in MUSTARD-UX.

In MUSTARD-UX, the floating kernel method is used. Therefore, the kernel and device driver cannot be exclusively executed by the interrupt-

Table 8.1
Major Locks in MUSTARD-UX

Name	Type	Object
UNIXmaster	Dispatch	UNIX System Call Body, Pager
SYS_LOCK	Spin	Real-Time Kernel Resources
L_KEY	Spin	TTY Drivers
L_SDD	Spin	Block Devices
L_CALLOUT	Spin	Callout Table
L_HSQUE	Spin	UNIX Sleep Queue

controller masking method local to the processors that is used in the conventional UNIX. Like TOP-1 [14], when the kernel processor is assumed and interrupts are issued only to this processor, exclusive control is available with the conventional mutual exclusion method.

In MUSTARD-UX, the kernel and the device driver are exclusively controlled using an interrupt-controller masking method and explicit spin lock functions for each shared resources. In the first stage of developing the MUSTARD, it was designed that all the device drivers are exclusively controlled by an exclusive control flag for each common resources. However, in the practical implementation, such a method was used only for character devices. For block devices, the UNIXmaster lock was used to exclusively control the entire UNIX kernel.

When conducting a page-out operation in a multiprocessor environment, there is a problem where cache data of an old PTE (Page Table Entries) reside in another processor's TLBs (Translation Lookaside Buffers). To solve this problem, Shootdown [15] using communication among processors has been used. In MUSTARD-UX, the Shootdown method is extended so that it is applicable when the increase/decrease in the number of processors and switching to the standby system occur at the same time.

8.4.2 UNIX Task Scheduling

In MUSTARD-UX, scheduling uses two queues, the UNIX user level queue and the UNIX kernel level queue. The former queue is used for UNIX tasks to gain the processor and the latter queue is used to gain the UNIX kernel. Fig. 8.7 shows that these queues are assigned to two levels of the real-time kernel's ready queue. In UNIX, the priority of tasks is

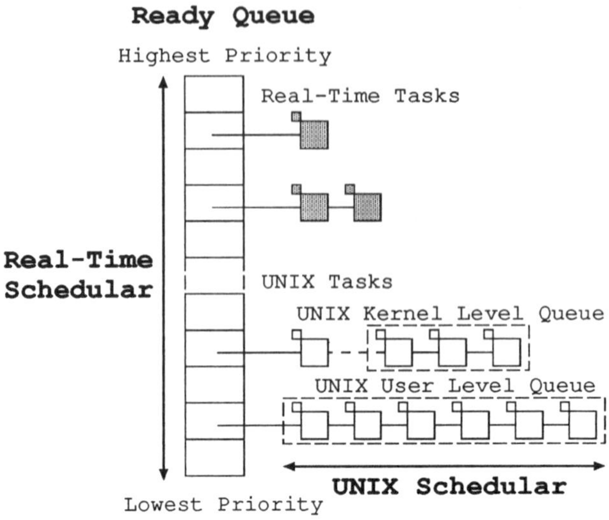

Figure 8.7
Two Level Scheduling

recalculated once per second. This UNIX priority scheduling is independent from the real-time kernel scheduling. Tasks in the UNIX user wait queue and UNIX tasks currently running are recalculated. UNIX tasks currently running are temporarily stopped by communication between processors, and are then scheduled.

8.5 Hardware MUSTARD-POT

To evaluate the performance of MUSTARD and its application programs, and to debug them, a tightly coupled multiprocessor system MUSTARD-POT has been developed. This system can accommodate up to eight 32-bit microprocessors. (See Fig. 8.8.)

8.5.1 Basic Hardware

There were four design objectives for the bus MUSTARD-POT, as follows:

1. Easiness of debugging and evaluating
2. A data transfer rate applicable for four to eight processors

3. Controlling equivalent priority for all bus masters
4. Connectability of standard bus for using a commercially available I/O board
5. Compact system design

For the CPU and floating point co-processor, a 32-bit microprocessor V70 (20 MHz) and μPD72691 were used. For the cache controller, a μPD71641 was used. For the VMEbus control circuit and SMB (Shared Memory Bus) control circuit, gate arrays were used. Thus, a compact multiprocessor board could be developed. Since the memory cycle is completed at 2 machine clocks when hit in the cache, V70 can run at the highest speed.

This design has a 4-way set associative cache, and its capacity of 32 KB, and 16 bytes/block. Since μPD71641 is a write through cache, a single-stage write buffer was added to suppress bus contention caused by write operations.

As shown in Fig. 8.8, in MUSTARD-POT, a write operation takes place from two buses, SMB and VMEbus, to the shared memory. It is therefore necessary to monitor these two buses. Actually, when the shared memory is accessed from the two buses at the same time, one bus access operation waits and the shared memory is accessed by the same address. Therefore, a monitor address selection circuit is provided on the processor board so as to monitor both the buses.

The authors measured the performance of MUSTARD-POT using the 10-queen program that is described by real-time kernel tasks. The result was that the speed-up ratio of MUSTARD-POT is 3.9 using 4 processors.

For interprocessor communication, interprocessor interrupt and the tracer control mechanism for other processors are provided. They are controlled by a processor communication control register. Interprocessor communication can be conducted by the unicast method and broadcast method. Either a maskable or non-maskable interrupt can be selected. Also, either start or stop tracer control can be selected.

8.5.2 Large Capacity Tracer Board

Since operations in the multiprocessor environment are complex, it is effective to obtain a dynamic execution history for debugging/evaluating them. This trace operation can be conducted by using an external logic analyzer or an in-circuit emulator in usual. However, to conduct this

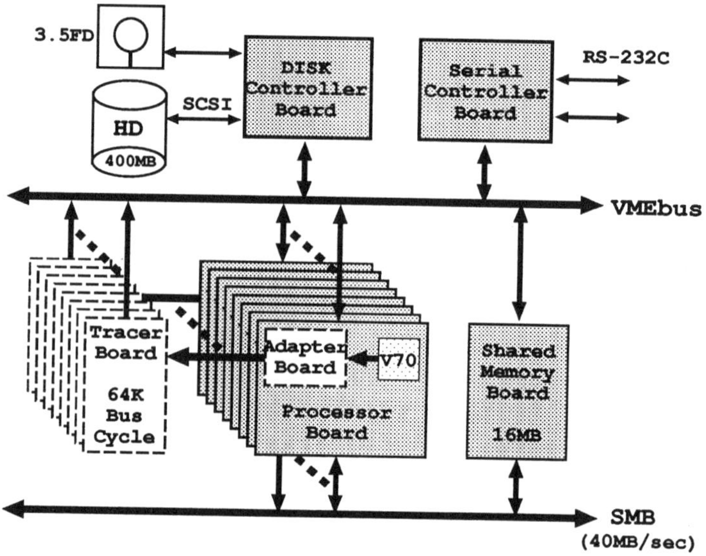

Figure 8.8
Overall Configuration of MUSTARD-POT

trace operation in the multiprocessor environment, such instruments are required according to the number of processors. Thus, the trace operation becomes complicated. To solve this problem, a large-capacity tracer for storing 64K bus-cycle trace data was added to each processor. With the tracers, trace results of approx. 20,000 instructions for 6 milliseconds or more can be collected. When the cycle is 6 milliseconds, an event which is longer than the interval time of clock interrupts can be obtained. The trace data can be used for the counter for time measurement and the sampling of external signals besides address/data/status/interrupt of the processors. The trace data is read from the VMEbus.

When the large-capacity tracer board is mounted, an adapter board is inserted between the tracer board and the processor board. Although the adapter board is mainly used to buffer signals, it is provided with a local memory of 256KB for running a debug monitor and a program for diagnosing hardware.

8.6 User Programming Tools

To extract a fine-grain parallelism from a application program on a tightly coupled multiprocessor effectively, it is necessary to provide a light-weight mutual exclusion method. In MUSTARD, low-level spin lock libraries, such as lock, unlock, and critical_add, are provided. However, if a careless program is written by these libraries, a dead-lock is occurred easily. To prevent this problem, the authors introduce the extended C language that generate the spin lock functions to the place where the critical_region statements are described. (see Fig. 8.9). The extended C language is provided as a preprocessor, and portions where a dead-lock easily occurs, a warning is issued. Also, this language is modified to include Ada's randezvous syntax for accomplishing safe intertask communication with high software productivity.

8.7 Conclusion

The authors developed MUSTARD-RK, MUSTARD-UX, and MUSTARD-POT to prepare an environment for real-time control and UNIX evaluation/experiment in a tightly coupled multiprocessor. The authors will evaluate the performance using an application program over and

```
SPINLOCK         rsrc1 = FREE;
SPINLOCK         rsrc2 = FREE;
atomic_op_with_res1_and_res2()
{
   critical_region(&rsrc1) {    /*  lock(&rsrc1)   */
      critical_region(&rsrc2) { /*  lock(&rsrc2)   */
           op_with_both_rsrcs();
      }                         /* unlock(&rsrc2) */
   }                            /* unlock(&rsrc1) */
}
```

Figure 8.9
Extended C Language for Multiprocessor

then measure the overhead in detail and tune the kernel. In addition, the author will evaluate the influence of the scheduling policy on the response time and throughput by using more practical application programs.

Acknowledgments

The authors would like to express their thanks to members of the MUSTARD project. Limited space does not allow us to acknowledge all of them, but we would like to give special thanks to Dr. T.Miyachi in C&C Common Software Laboratory for their valuable advice.

References

[1] S.Hiroya, T.Momoi, and T.Miyachi, "Multiprocessor Real-Time UNIX MUSTARD and its Software Development Environment," in Proc. JSPP'90, Japan, May 1990, pp.241-248.

[2] T.Momoi, M.Seki, and S.Hiroya, "A Method for UNIX Kernel on the Multiprocessor Operating System MUSTARD," 40th Conf. of Information Processing Soc., Japan, 1990.

[3] K.Nihei, S.Hiroya, and H.Kawaguchi, "Memory Management of Multiprocessor UNIX MUSTARD," IPSJ SIG Reports 90-ARC-83-27, 1990, pp.157-162.

[4] Y.Mizuhashi, and M.Teramoto, "Real-Time UNIX Operating System: RX-UX832," Euromicro'89, 1989, pp.533-538. 1989.

[5] T.Shimojima, and M.Teramoto, "V60 Real-Time Operating System," Euromicro'87, 1987, pp.197-204.

[6] Y.Yano, Y.Koumoto, and Y.Sato, "V60/V70 Microprocessor and its Systems Support Functions," COMPCON'88, 1988, pp.36-42.

[7] S.Kimura, Y.Komoto, and Y.Yano, "Implementation of the V60/V70 and its FRM Function," IEEE MICRO, 1988, pp.22-36.

[8] R.Rashid, A.Tevanian,Jr., M.Young, D.Golub, R.Baron, D.Black, W.J.Bolosky, and J.Chew, "Machine-Independent Virtual Memory Management for Paged Uniprocessor and Multiprocessor Architectures," IEEE Trans. Computers, Vol.37, No.8, Aug. 1988, pp.896-908.

[9] J.H. Hartman, and J.K.Ousterhout, "Performance Measurements of a Multiprocessor Sprite Kernel," in Proc. USENIX Summer Conf., Jun. 1990, pp.279-287.

[10] J.K.Ousterhout, A.R.Cherenson, F.Douglis, M.N.Nelson, and B.B.Welch, "The Sprite Network Operating System," IEEE Computer, Feb. 1988, pp.23-36.

[11] T.E.Anderson, "The Performance of Spin Lock Alternatives for Shared-Memory Multiprocessors," IEEE Trans. Parallel and Distributed Systems, Vol.1, No.1, Jan. 1990, pp.6-16.

[12] "D-NIX Operating System," DYNATECH COMPUTER SYSTEMS, 1989.

[13] H. Monden, "Introduction to ITRON, the Industry-Oriented Operating System," IEEE Micro, 1987, pp.45-52.

[14] H. Monden, M.Hozumi et al., "TOP-1 Operating System (1) Basic Direction", 39th Conf. of Information Processing Soc., Japan, 1989.

[15] D.L.Black, R.F.Rashid, D.B.Golub, C.R.Hill, and V.Baron, "Translation Lookaside Buffer Consistency: A Software Approach," Proceedings of the Third International Conference on Architectural Support for Programming Languages and Operating Systems, ACM, 1989, pp.113-122.

9 An Empirical Investigation of the Effectiveness and Limitations of Automatic Parallelization

Jaswinder Pal Singh and John L. Hennessy

Automatic recognition and exploitation of parallelism in scientific code has been proposed as a major method for employing parallel processors. A compiler based approach also yields machine-independence, a property notably lacking in many parallel programs. This paper investigates the limitations of a compiler-driven approach in parallelizing three scientific applications. The investigation examines a wide range of factors that prevent effective parallelization. Some of these factors are "simple" shortcomings in compiler technology. Overcoming these—together with extending the scope of analysis beyond a single loop nest—allows the compiler to concurrentize most of the loops in the programs studied. However, the loop nests that consume most of the execution time are often complex and require much more sophisticated analysis and data restructuring. The compiler parallelizes the wrong loops in these nests, leading to insignificant speedups on the program. Finally, sometimes algorithm implementations, or even the algorithms themselves, have to be significantly altered for parallelism, transformations that are beyond the scope of compilers as we know them today. All three applications studied show substantial speedups as the type and scope of transformations are enlarged. Based on these case studies, recommendations for further development of automatic parallelization technology are given.

9.1 Introduction

Shared memory multiprocessors are interesting because of the familiar programming model they provide and the ease of building them (at least on a small scale). Especially for small-scale machines, however, their success as parallel processors may depend significantly on the ability of compilers to automatically extract parallelism from sequential programs and implement it efficiently. Three factors appear most important:

1. How well can a compiler find the appropriate parallelism in real applications?
2. What overheads are encountered in implementing this parallelism, and how do these translate to reduced speedups?
3. How significant are other interactions between parallelization and architecture, such as the data locality and sharing traffic?

The regular structure of scientific (numeric) applications makes them popular candidates for automatic parallelization. Since the data-parallelism they afford is typically embodied in loops that iterate over array elements, and since loops are easily identifiable constructs, the approach of compilers so far has been to attempt to parallelize individual loops or loop nests. Much sophistication has been developed in dependence analysis and in the types of loop transformations performed, but the complexity of dependence analysis has restricted the techniques to a localized approach.

This paper examines the effectiveness of automatic parallelization — as we know it today—on real, complete scientific programs, and tries to understand some of the limitations of this approach in obtaining efficient parallel performance on shared-memory multiprocessors. We focus mostly on the first two factors listed above, using a machine environment that deemphasizes the performance impact of the third. Some questions of interest are: What characteristics of fully or partially parallelizable loops found in real programs make a "good" compiler fail to parallelize them? If compiler technology were sufficiently advanced to succeed in parallelizing all such loops, would this be enough to obtain effective parallel performance on real applications, even on a small-scale multiprocessor? If not, what kinds of program transformations are actually needed, what is the nature and scope of the knowledge they require, and can such transformations be automated? Finally, what role must a user play in this process, and how should the interaction between user and system be structured? We explore some of these questions in the context of three scientific applications, hoping that the insights drawn will have wider applicability and that understanding the failings of current automatic parallelization technology will be useful in the future design of parallelizing tools, parallel programming environments, and multiprocessors.

9.2 Methodology

Given a sequential program as a starting point, we can identify four types or levels of approach to its parallelization:

1. **Loop Parallelization**: the approach taken by current parallelizing compilers. Data dependences are analyzed among statements within a loop, and the parallelizability of every loop determined. The single thread executing the program is joined by others when a parallelizable loop is encountered. No high-level program restructuring or knowledge of the application is required.

2. **Algorithm Parallelization**: parallelizing an algorithm used by the sequential program, without modifying the basic algorithm. Scientific algorithms are very often implemented by loops. We therefore reserve the name algorithm parallelization for those situations that require a restructuring of control beyond the parallelization of existing loops. Note that the program module implementing the algorithm may be a code segment within a subroutine, an entire subroutine, or a set of subroutines.

3. **Global Parallelization**: finding and implementing parallelism across these modules by global dependence analysis. This often involves high-level restructuring of the program.

4. **Problem Parallelization**: reexamining the physical or mathematical problem to discover other methods—more amenable to parallelization—that can be used to solve it. This is the only level of parallelization for which the information required is not available in the sequential program.

Besides implementation overhead and hardware interactions, then, the inability of an automatic parallelizer to obtain adequate speedup can arise from three sources: not being sophisticated enough to find parallelism that actually exists even within the scope of its analysis, not looking for or finding parallelism at the right level in the sequential program, and lacking the problem domain knowledge required to change algorithms when necessary. An often used measure of the quality of a parallelizing compiler is its percentage success (ability to parallelize) rate on a test suite of commonly occurring or specially designed loops (see, for example, the study of vectorizing compilers in [1]). We do not feel this is adequate, however, since real applications often require concurrentization[1] at higher levels than represented in these suites, and are written with programming quirks that might not be represented therein; also, the number of loops parallelized or references determined to be independent does not tell us much about performance.

Our first step is to run the sequential program through a commercial parallelizing compiler, without any user assistance, and measure speedups (see Section 9.5). Next, we use the summaries of paralleliza-

[1] We use the words *concurrentization* and *parallelization* interchangeably in this paper. Vectorization is not included in these.

tion activity produced by the compiler to understand why it failed on fully or partially parallelizable loops (Section 9.6). Based on this understanding, we introduce hints and directives at various levels (Section 9.7) into the code, to overcome limitations in the dependence analysis of the particular compiler used. Depending on how sophisticated one considers a "state of the art" compiler to be, some of these instances of user assistance might be unnecessary in such a compiler. More significant (in scope and programmer effort) local program transformations and data restructuring are also introduced, bringing us to the limits of what we would call automatic loop parallelization. For each application and each type of user assistance, we measure improvements in the static number of loops optimized, the dynamic performance of those loops, and the performance of the whole application.

Owing to the nature of the applications used here, the importance of global parallelization becomes visible only with significantly larger numbers of processors than are available on the multiprocessor we use. Algorithm parallelization, however, is found to be very useful, and we evaluate the additional performance gains it yields by explicitly parallelizing the applications on the same multiprocessor (Section 9.8). Finally, one of our applications requires changing an algorithm (problem parallelization) for efficient parallel performance, and we present the results obtained by that transformation in Section 9.9. Section 9.10 summarizes our findings and their implications for the future development of automatic parallelization technology.

9.3 The Multiprocessor and Compiler

Our experiments were performed on an Alliant FX/8, an eight-processor bus-based shared memory machine. The processors are MC68000 compatible with vector capability, and all share a 128 KB cache. The absence of per-processor caches and distributed memory is useful to our study since it removes the effects of per-processor data locality from the performance measurements, allowing us to focus on effectiveness in finding parallelism. We use the FX/FORTRAN parallelizing compiler [2], found in [1] to be one of the best performing commercially available compilers for vectorization. Note that the methodology described above ensures that limitations of the particular compiler used do not significantly constrain our findings except in the first set of results, which describe performance without any user assistance. Briefly, this compiler offers three major types of optimization, which may be used in any combination: concurrentization, vectorization, and scalar optimizations. To aid the first two, the programmer may provide the compiler with assertions and directives of various types (see Section 9.7). The compiler also provides for the partial concurrentization of a loop to the extent possible, inserting synchronization to order potentially data-dependent accesses. Since we are interested only in concurrency, we turn vectorization off for all the results we present.

9.4 The Applications Used

One of the three applications we use in this work is the benchmark called MDG or LWS in the `PERFECT CLUB` suite [3]. The program performs an N-body molecular dynamics simulation—specifically, that of water molecules in liquid state in a cubical box—over a series of time-steps, using a predictor-corrector method to solve the equations of motion at every time-step. We call this application **water**. Another application (called **ocean**) studies the role of eddy currents in influencing large-scale ocean movements. Here, a system of partial differential equations is set up and solved on two-dimensional grids over a series of time-steps, using a block cyclic reduction method for the solution. More complete descriptions of these two applications can be found in [4] and [5], respectively. The third application is significantly smaller in source code size (only about 150 lines, compared with a few thousand each in the other cases): This is the SPEC benchmark **tomcatv**, a mesh generation program written with vectorization in mind [6].

9.5 Results Without User Assistance

In this section, we present performance results obtained by simply running the raw sequential programs through the parallelizing compiler, with no user assistance. Scalar optimization is enabled in all cases, and associative transformations (for dot-product like operations) as well in concurrentization. We present *normalized* or *true* speedups; that is, the ratio of the execution time of the original sequential program (compiled without concurrentization) on a single processor of the Alliant FX/8 to the time using p processors on the program compiled with concurrentization.

In measuring execution times, we omit process creation, the one-time input/output and the cold-start cache misses during initialization. This omission is especially valid because we are simulating only a small number of time-steps, so that the impact of process creation and initialization is far greater in our simulations than in the actual use of the applications (where it is measured to be negligible).

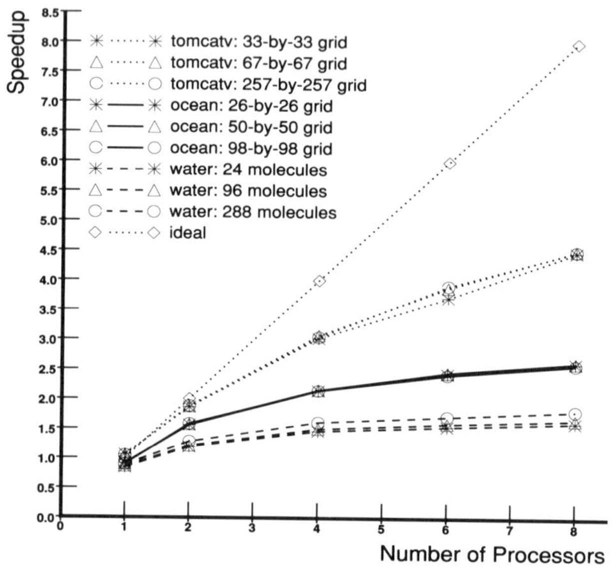

Figure 9.1
Normalized Speedup using the Compiler without User Assistance.

Figure 9.1 shows the results for all three applications, using three problem sizes in every case. Note that the speedups on this machine do not vary significantly across the problem sizes used. We also measured performance with vectorization enabled in all cases; now, almost no additional speedups were obtained by concurrentization. Interestingly enough, the concurrency yielded by the compiler is much more encouraging for the small benchmark tomcatv—where the parallelism is all within simple consecutive loops, fitting the parallelizing compiler model—than for the large applications. In the latter case, it clearly does not buy us much performance. Let us now try to understand why, looking first at limitations in finding parallelism within the scope of loop parallelization.

9.6 Why the Compiler Failed to Parallelize Loops

In this section, we present some example loops in these applications that the compiler tried to concurrentize but failed on (either partially or completely). In each case, we discuss the reasons for the failure and identify features that would have enabled the compiler to succeed. Some of these features might exist in more sophisticated compilers; others do not so far but evidently ought to if their cost can be kept reasonable.

In determining which loop to concurrentize in a nest, the compiler proceeds from outer to inner, usually stopping at the outermost loop that it is able to concurrentize. Sometimes, this turns out to be the wrong thing to do. Consider the following initialization of two grids, stored together as a three-dimensional array, in the ocean code.

```
do K = 1,2
  do J = 1,JMAX
    do I = 1,IMAX
      A[I,J,K] = 0.0
    end do
  end do
end do
```

All three loops are fully parallelizable, so the compiler concurrentizes the outermost. This, however, can only keep two processors busy; the preferred loop to concurrentize is the middle (J) loop, since its bound is proportional to the dimension of the grid. For the compiler to choose an inner loop over a concurrentizable outer one (and perhaps interchange them), it must know the number of iterations in at least the former. In almost all the loop nests in these applications, however, the preferred loop to concurrentize has a symbolic bound equal or proportional to the problem size, which is a run-time input. This bound is passed down through subroutine arguments, and it is its *interprocedural symbolic propagation* and intraprocedural *forward substitution*—as well as knowing the role (or at least typical values) of that input—that allow us to urge the compiler to select the correct loop first. The incorporation of profile information—and/or a mechanism that allows the user to specify which program inputs represent desirable degrees of parallelism, combined with the above analyses—is perhaps the best approach here.

Symbolic loop bounds, and particularly loop increments, often complicate dependence analysis as well. It is sometimes the case, particularly when routines written for software libraries are used, that the variables used as loop increments or bounds are passed as arguments from the main, user-written program, in which they are assigned constant values at the beginning and never modified thereafter. Interprocedural constant propagation can be very useful in these cases. While the analysis required for interprocedural constant and symbol propagation can be very expensive in general, we found it sufficient to limit such propagation to only those subroutine arguments or common block variables that are used as, or can be intraprocedurally forward substituted to, loop increments or bounds.

The prediction phase of the predictor-corrector method used in the water code is represented by the following (simplified) loop nest:

```
IK = 1
do I=1,6
  do K = 1,NATM03
    IKL = IK + NATM03
    do L = I,6
      IKL = IKL + NATM03
      S = S + V(IKL)
    end do
    V(IK) = V(IK) + S
    IK = IK + 1
  end do
end do
```

The preferred loop to parallelize in this case is the middle (K) loop, whose bound is proportional to the number of molecules. However, the compiler sees dependences among accesses—V(IKL) and V(IK)—to the V array. Left to itself, it partially concurrentizes only the innermost loop. When directed to examine the middle loop first, it partially concurrentizes that loop, with accesses to V unnecessarily synchronized. This loop is, in fact, fully parallel. If the array subscripts are expressed explicitly in terms of the loop indices, V(IKL) can be written as V(K + L*NATM03) while V(IK) becomes V(K + (I-1)*NATM03). For a given value of I, one reason these references don't collide is that L goes from I to 6 (that is, the loop structure is triangular) and is therefore always greater than (I-1); another is that the symbolic index offset, NATMO3, is the same as the loop bound. Note that the expanded subscripts are nonlinear in this case (since both L and NATMO3 are variables in L*NATMO3, for example), and that the dependence analysis of most compilers gives up in nonlinear situations. The fact that the same variable, NATMO3, is involved in both cases of nonlinearity makes it possible to get away with inexpensive special-case analysis here again, although delinearizing subscripts would be a better general solution. To do the delinearization and successfully concurrentize this loop, the compiler would have to perform the following analyses: the fairly sophisticated *induction variable analysis* described above, and *symbolic analysis incorporating relationships among multi-level loop bounds and symbolic offsets.* While many other loops in these applications require induction variable analysis, none is quite so sophisticated as this. Loop bound analysis (particularly symbolic) of multi-level loops was also found to be needed very often. Simple forms of this analysis are likely to be present in a state-of-the-art compiler, and its absence is best thought of as a limitation of this particular compiler.

It is worth noting here that most of the need for sophisticated symbolic analysis owes itself primarily to the inappropriate (from the dependence analysis point of view) data structure design and programming style in the water code. The main data structure in this program (the V array above) is a one-dimensional array divided into several sections. Every section represents a different physical quantity and has entries for all molecules, atoms and spatial dimensions. In the loop nest just discussed, for example, the I loop iterates over six sections, the J loop over all the atoms and spatial dimensions, and the K loop over all sections that follow the current one in the I loop. The computation in the prediction and correction phases is indeed easier to express in a sequential program if some of these sections are part of the same data structure, but there is no reason to not have the sections be separate dimensions of a two (or more) dimensional array. This would not only simplify the symbolic analysis involving induction variables, index offsets and multi-level loop bounds, but would also remove the nonlinearities in the expanded subscripts. Even with this linearized array, however, it is often possible to code the loops in a way that simplifies the task of dependence analysis, rather than in a sectioned manner that results from following the physical meaning of the computation, as is the wont of scientists. Finally, there are many instances of disjoint sections of the original linearized array being passed to the same subroutine. They are passed using a permutation array to index the beginning of every section, which further complicates the compiler's analysis by making it have to worry about aliasing.

A programming style inappropriate for automatic parallelization inhibits the compiler in the tomcatv program as well, this time in the treatment of boundary values . Consider the following example:

```
do I = 1,N
  Y(I,N) = Y(1,N) + Y(N,N)
end do
```

`Y(1,N)` is written in the first iteration and read in all subsequent ones, inhibiting concurrentization with a true dependence. Similarly, `Y(N,1)` is read in the first `(N-1)` iterations and written in the last, causing an anti-dependence. If boundary values are treated outside the main loop by *unrolling* the first and last iterations, the loop is left with iterations between `I=2,N-1` that are fully concurrent. Section 9.8.2 describes other ways in which the inappropriateness of sequential programming styles interacts with the limitations of the compiler to exacerbate the problem of automatic parallelization.

The ocean code has some simple loops in which symbolic relationships between subscript increments and loop bounds are defined outside the loop but within the subroutine:

```
ID2 = M
ID3 = ID2+M

do I=1,M
  W(I) = S1
  J = ID2+I
  W(J) = S2
  J = ID3+I
  W(J) = S3
end do
```

The compiler sees a dependence between W(I) and the second reference to W(J) (not the first, since its increment is defined more simply in terms of the loop bound). More advanced *forward substitution* and symbolic analysis would have concurrentized this loop.

Accumulating a running sum (or finding a maximum) from all iterations of a loop nest was found to be a fairly common calculation. In this situation, the compiler inserts synchronization to enforce ordered access to the running sum. There are two ways to speed up such a calculation. If the code is simple enough to recognize as a reduction, the compiler can have every process compute a private running sum independently (*scalar privatization*) and accumulate it into the global sum once at the end. (Note that while this does alter the order of accumulations, causing rounding discrepancies from the sequential program, in no case did we find the order used in the sequential program to be of any special significance to the application. A compiler would be well advised to take hints from the user about such associative situations, since they allow the enforcement of a specific ordering to be replaced by mutual exclusion.) In more complex situations, *scalar expansion* can be used to compute partial results independently in every iteration, and perform the reduction in a different loop at the end. This is particularly useful in the water code, where a running sum is accumulated into several times in each iteration of the loop nest that computes intermolecular forces.

In some cases, subroutine calls within a loop inhibit its parallelization. The FX/FORTRAN compiler does not perform interprocedural analysis; however, it does provide directives to inline or concurrentize subroutine calls under certain conditions. We found calls to only three subroutines—two in the ocean code and one in the water code—within loops that we wanted to concurrentize; all these routines are short and without nested calls, and can be inlined without code explosion. In all our cases, however, simple inlining or concurrent calls do not suffice. The subroutines modify arrays that are passed to them as arguments, and these arrays are reused in subsequent loop iterations. Even interprocedural dependence analysis, by itself, rightly finds references to these arrays to collide across loop iterations. Dataflow analysis, however, reveals that the use of these arrays is essentially as temporary storage: The values written into them in one iteration are used only in that iteration, not in any other. In addition to *interprocedural analysis*, then, parallelizing the calls to these routines requires *array expansion* (adding another dimension to give every loop iteration its own array, just as in scalar expansion) or—to save storage and improve memory referencing patterns—*array privatization* (giving every process its own array).

Both the loops that require concurrentizing subroutine calls are very large and complex (the compiler chooses to concurrentize simpler loops within these, as well as within the subroutines, where possible). A loop computing intermolecular interactions in the water program, for example, has the following structure:

```
do I = 1, NMOL-1
  do J = I+1, NMOL
    call a subroutine and compute some
        local arrays
    compute X-direction forces
    compute Y-direction forces
    compute Z-direction forces
  end do
end do
```

Each of the force computation sections comprises several conditionally executed, non-nested loops that access different parts of the same data structures. Each also updates the force locations for each molecule in the (I,J) pair under consideration. While the array expansion required to concurrentize the subroutine calls is not difficult to recognize here, several other parts of the loop require array and *scalar privatization/expansion* as well, and synchronization is required in the updates to the force locations. Even after all the data structure expansion is done, the sheer complexity of the outer loop nest and the number of dependences in its different parts cause the compiler to give up. It takes *loop-splitting*—into four separate J loops—to coerce the compiler to concurrentize each J loop with the appropriate synchronization[2]. In the ocean code, the need for concurrentizing subroutine calls is encountered in an equation-solving software package. The routines to be called in parallel have complicated control flow and dependence structures within and across them, and the analysis required to discover concurrentization through privatization is somewhat beyond the sort of compiler technology we are dealing with here. We leave further discussion of this to Section 9.8.

[2] Note that we were unable to coax the compiler to concurrentize the I loop. However, explicit parallelization reveals that the performance the compiler would have been able to yield (without much more control over partitioning and scheduling) is not much better.

Finally, it is worth noting that the available directives were sometimes found to be restrictive or incapable of expressing the exact information we wished to convey to the compiler. For example, the smallest entity for which we can tell the compiler not to check for dependences is an entire loop, which includes all references to all data structures in that loop. Often, multiple arrays are referenced in the same loop, accesses to only some of which we know to be independent. If the loop we want parallelized is complex enough, the compiler might run out of storage when checking dependences on all array accesses; however, its task would be greatly simplified if we could control dependence checking at the array-within-loop, rather than simply loop, level: turning if off for those arrays to which we know the references are independent. We also observed a need for the compiler to convey the reasons for its failures more precisely to the user. Ideally, this would be done in an interactive environment, with successive attempts to parallelize a loop punctuated by progressively more refined exchanges of information between compiler and user.

9.7 With User Assistance

Having understood the limitations of the compiler in parallelizing loops, our next step is to overcome these where possible by providing some user assistance. The kinds of assistance provided by the user can vary a lot in their power and in the amount of user analysis and program knowledge they require. For example, a user may tell the compiler to inline a certain subroutine, to select a certain loop first for an optimization, that two arrays aren't equivalenced, or that there are no dependences across the iterations of a loop. Some of these can easily be viewed as hints to the compiler; it is unclear, however, whether the last can be termed thus or whether it is more appropriately thought of as loop-level hand-parallelization (since all the analysis is done by the user) that leaves only the lowest-level implementation of the parallel loop to the compiler. For want of a more accurate nomenclature, we somewhat subjectively divide user assistance into three categories: *hints*, *directives*, and *restructuring*. For each category, we summarize (from Section 9.6) desirable compiler features that would have obviated the need for that category of assistance in concurrentizing the loops of our applications.

9.7.1 Hints

Hints either give the compiler some additional information that can be gleaned *simply* and *locally* from the code, or tell it which loop in a nest to attempt first (or not at all), but require it to analyze dependences itself. The additional information might be the specification of locally determined relationships between control or induction variable increments, information about equivalencing, etc. This type of hint is rarely found to be useful in itself in these applications, but can sometimes help to reduce the amount of synchronization inserted by the compiler in complex loops. Hints with greater effects are those that tell the compiler to attempt a particular loop first for concurrentization, rather than the one it originally chose in that nest. This almost always results in the selected loop being partially concurrentized, with the appropriate synchronization inserted where the compiler sees potential dependences (an exception is the first example in Section 9.6, in which the loop is perfectly concurrentized). Desirable compiler features that could replace these hints are:

- incorporation of profile information, or a facility for specifying which variables represent desirable degrees of parallelism.
- interprocedural symbolic propagation of those subroutine arguments or common block variables that are used as, or can be intraprocedurally forward substituted to, loop bounds or increments.

9.7.2 Directives

Directives tell the compiler not to check for dependences in specified code segments, since the user has already done the dependence analysis. They could be rendered unnecessary by the following compiler features:

- symbolic analysis incorporating relationships among subscript increments and multi-level loop bounds.
- more sophisticated induction variable analysis, capable of handling triangular loops.
- more sophisticated intraprocedural forward substitution, to account for symbolic relationships defined outside the loop.
- dependence analysis with nonlinear subscripts, and/or a delinearization pass in the compiler.

These two categories of assistance limit themselves to aiding dependence analysis. They do not include any manual restructuring of code or data.

9.7.3 Restructuring

As discussed in section 9.6, some of the more complicated loops cannot be successfully concurrentized by hints or directives alone. The require manually restructuring the code and expanding/privatizing data structures, through dataflow and often interprocedural analysis. Since we do not have control over the assignment of iterations to processes by the compiler, we implement expansion instead of privatization by adding another dimension to the relevant data structures. One set of results we present is for *directives with scalar expansion*, manually expanding an accumulated scalar where the compiler fails to do so automatically, and introducing a separate loop to accumulate it at the end. Array expansion is required in the intermolecular interactions loop nest in the water code, in conjunction with interprocedural analysis (to concurrentize subroutine calls) and loop splitting, to yield partial concurrentization; these transformations are therefore grouped together in measuring their effect on performance, and the version of the (water) code they yield is called *directives with restructuring*. A scalar variable is also accumulated into several times per iteration of the interactions loop. The restructured code that expands this variable and accumulates it in a separate loop is called *final restructuring*. It leaves the interactions loop nest almost fully concurrent, with the necessary synchronization around force updates. Note that restructuring is also applicable to the equation solver in the ocean code, but results for this are not presented since the parallelism it leads to is ultimately realized only by explicit algorithm parallelization. Tomcatv requires two fairly light forms of assistance that we include under restructuring only because we had to actually modify the code ourselves: *unrolling* the boundary iterations of a loop, and *scalar expansion* along one dimension in a two-level loop (see Section 9.7.4).

We now present two types of results obtained with the different levels of user assistance: Static, describing the number of loops concurrentized with and without the assistance, and dynamic — showing the resulting performance improvements.

9.7.4 Static Results

Omitting the control structure of the equation solver, which we submit to algorithm parallelization, the ocean code has 70 parallelizable loops and loop nests. Of these, the compiler is able to concurrentize 64 perfectly without any user assistance, two more with hints to select the right level of nesting, and another two with directives. The remaining 2 loops are only partially concurrentized due to an accumulation. There are two loops in this code that are serialized by a recurrence and are not part of a loop nest parallelized at any level.

The water code has eight major loop nests. Hints are useful in partially concurrentizing two of these. Directives allow the compiler to fully concurrentize these two as well as two others. Three loop nests have the preferred loop partially concurrentized due to an accumulation. Two of these are manually scalar expanded to be fully concurrent, with accumulation in a separate loop. What remains is the intermolecular interactions loop nest, which requires various types of restructuring for the outer loop structure to be partially concurrentized.

Tomcatv has twelve loop nests. Nine of these are fully concurrentized without any assistance. Another two are concurrentized by unrolling the boundary iterations. The remaining, doubly-nested loop finds the largest entry of a matrix and also records the indices of that entry. The maximum and one index are scalar-expanded in one dimension, yielding a fully concurrent loop that finds the maximum of every column, followed by a serial loop that finds the maximum of these maxima. Hints and directives are not employed at all.

9.7.5 Dynamic Results

We measure the impact of every type of assistance in two ways: the speedup it provides on the loops it is used in, and its performance impact on the whole application. For the latter purpose, each of the larger applications is divided into two parts because of the widely different characteristics of each part: The ocean code is split up into the software package that solves the elliptic equations and the rest of the application; the water code into the intermolecular interactions and the rest. Note that successive levels of assistance include all previous ones in the results we present; that is, results for directives are for the code that includes hints and directives, etc.

Figures 9.2 and 9.3 show the results obtained with the compiler. Normalized speedups are presented for a representative problem size of each application: 288 water molecules[3], and a 96-by-96 ocean grid. For clarity of presentation, the y-axis is drawn to a different scale in (a) and (b) than in (c) and (d). The results for loops (in (d)) are averages over all loops in the application to which the user assistance under consideration was applied with some effect. Every loop is executed five hundred times, and speedups are normalized to the execution of the raw sequential loop (with no user assistance) on a single processor. Note that the intermolecular interactions loop nest is omitted in the loop measurements for the water code; its results are displayed separately in Figure 9.2(b).

For the loops that hints are applied to in the water code, they speed up one-processor execution of the parallel loops by about 25 percent, by reducing the number of synchronization instructions inserted by the compiler. However, in one of the two loop nests that they are employed in, partially concurrentizing the "preferred" loop turns out to be the wrong thing to do from the speedup point of view, since the fully concurrent inner loop has enough iterations to keep the small number of processors we use busy. The net result is that hints have little effect on loop performance (Figure 9.2(d)). Directives concurrentize both the above "hint loop" nests perfectly, and dramatically improve the parallel performance of these as well as the "directive loops". This translates to good speedups on most of the static program: all but the intermolecular interactions (Figure 9.2(c)). However, the impact on the whole program is negligible, since the intermolecular interactions dominate execution time (constituting over 95 percent of it) and are unaffected by hints or directives (Figure 9.2(b)). The transformations that constitute restructuring (see Section 9.7.3) are critical to helping the performance of the interactions loop nest by partially concurrentizing it. However, the multiple synchronized scalar updates per iteration still greatly impede its performance as the number of processors increases, and it takes "final restructuring" to have a significant impact on the automatic parallel performance of the water program (Figure 9.2(a)). It is worth noting that the less efficient reuse of storage caused by array expansion diminishes the one-processor performance of the parallel program by about 8 percent.

[3] the Perfect Club provides input data for a maximum of 343.

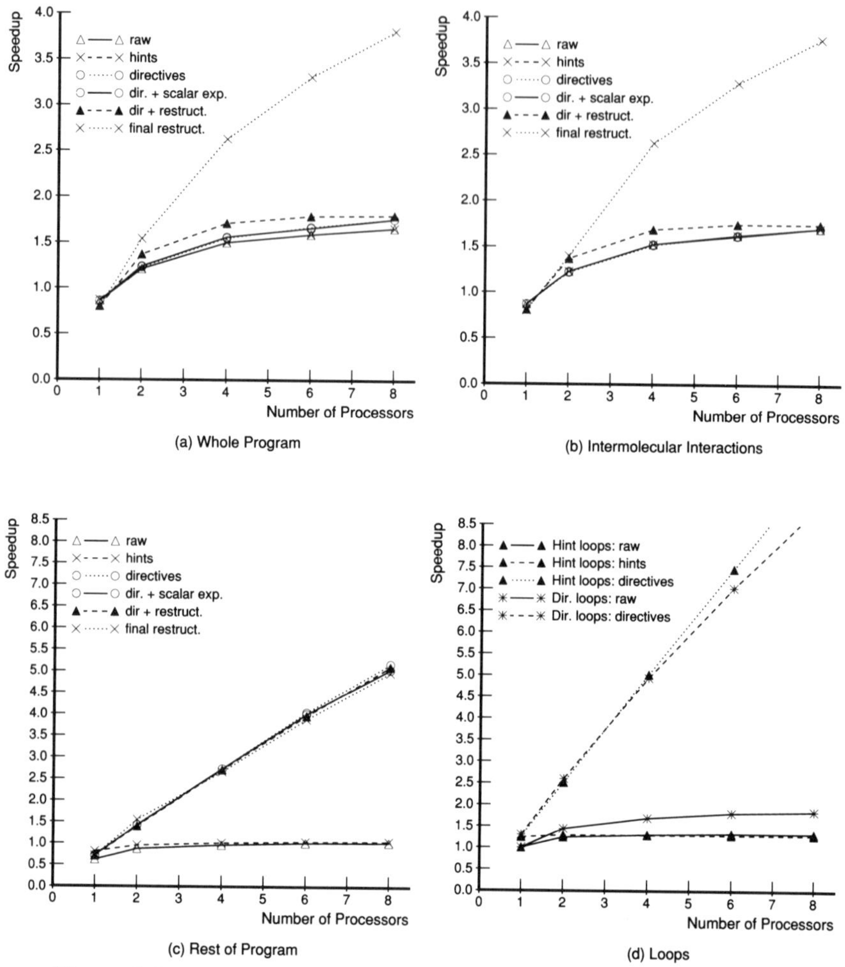

Figure 9.2
Normalized Speedup using the Compiler on the Water Code.

Using hints to choose the correct fully parallel loop on the two ocean code loop nests described at the beginning of Section 9.6 speeds these loop nests significantly (Figure 9.3(d)). This has an impact (albeit small) on the the part of the ocean code other than the equation solver (Figure 9.3(c)). Directives are similarly effective on two loops in the equation

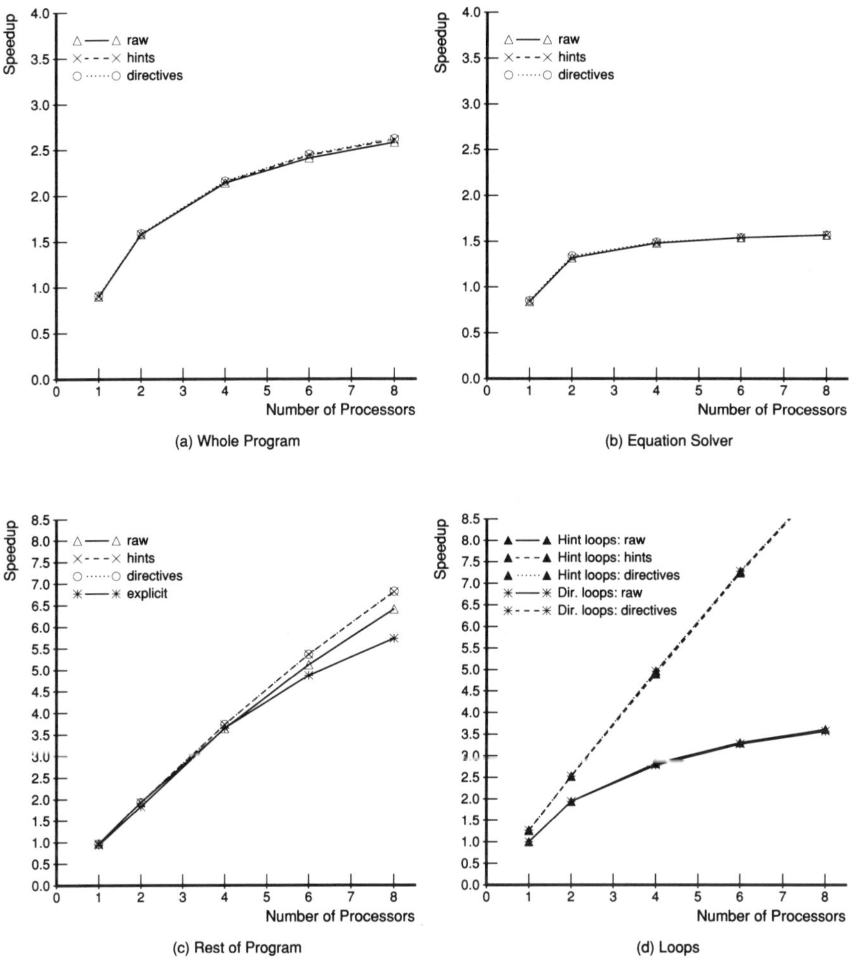

Figure 9.3
Normalized Speedup using the Compiler on the Ocean Code.

solver, but have a negligible effect on the performance of the solver itself. The result is an almost unnoticeable impact of hints and directives on the whole program.

Figure 9.4 presents the results for tomcatv. Only the results for loops and the whole application are shown. Of the two loops to which it is

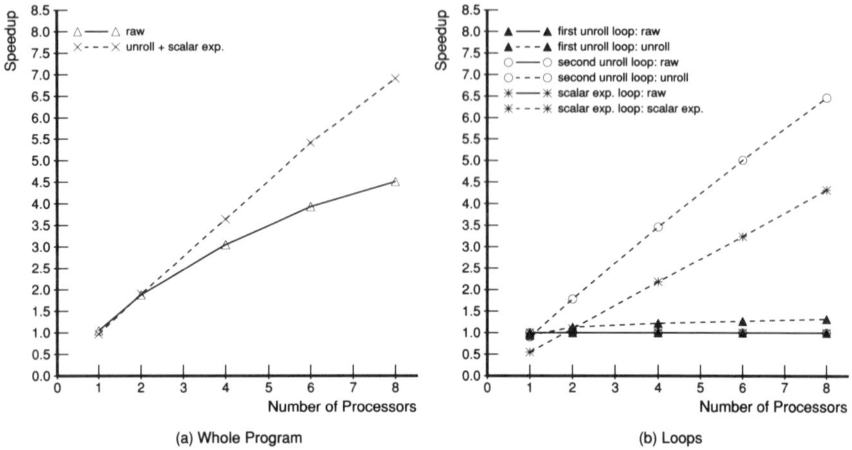

Figure 9.4
Normalized Speedup using the Compiler on Tomcatv.

applied, unrolling boundary iterations helps the smaller a lot and the other a little. However, these loops are only executed once, not every time-step, so the effect on the whole program is negligible. Scalar expansion improves the self-relative speedup of the maximum-finding loop nest dramatically, but the normalized speedup less so because it reduces the performance of the one-processor execution by almost a factor of two. Still, the normalized speedup of the loop rises from none to a factor of 4.3 with eight processors, and the parallel performance of the whole application is improved by a factor of two (Figure 9.4(a)). Tomcatv provides another example of a transformation that appears useful not working well, this time owing to architectural interactions. Two of the nine loop nests we described as being fully concurrentized without user assistance (see Section 9.7.4) are doubly nested with a recurrence in one level. Since tomcatv is written for vectorization, the recurrence is in the outer loop, and the compiler fully concurrentizes the inner one. We experimented with loop interchange to concurrentize the outer loop instead. While this improved the self-relative speedups of these loops somewhat, the deleterious effect on uniprocessor performance of keeping the recurrence in the row-order traversed inner loop made normalized speedups worse. Loop interchange was therefore not retained in the program.

It is worth noting that all our applications confirm the inadequacy of static parallelization results for predicting performance, since the fraction of time spent in different loop nests is a critical factor ignored in such evaluation. Most of the code in our applications yields good parallel performance with the analyses that constitute hints and directives (tomcatv, with no assistance at all). The most complex analyses and transformations are required in only a very small number of loops, but these turn out to be very important in all cases. It is also interesting that each of our larger applications has one section of code (one algorithm) that cannot be made to yield good speedups through automatic parallelization, despite all the user assistance described above: the intermolecular interactions in the water code, and the equation solver in the ocean code. Since these algorithms take up large fractions of their applications' execution times (96 and 40 percent, respectively, for these problem sizes), the failure to obtain good speedups on them makes automatic parallelization quite ineffective in rendering acceptable parallel performance on our larger applications. Fortunately, further parallelism is available in both cases. Finding it, however, requires an understanding of the algorithm beyond simple dependence analysis or data restructuring, and takes us into the realm of algorithm parallelization.

9.8 Algorithm Parallelization

We implement algorithm parallelization in explicitly parallel Fortran programs, augmented with `parmacs` macros [7]. Let us look at the two cases individually.

9.8.1 Intermolecular Interactions in the Water Code

To compute intermolecular forces, all pairs of molecules are examined and the forces they exert on each other computed if they are separated by less than a fixed cutoff radius. The outermost control structure is implemented with a doubly-nested loop:

```
do I = 1, NMOL-1
  do J = I+1, NMOL
    complicated code, including loops,
     to compute intermolecular forces
  end do
end do
```

Maintaining this loop structure allows us, after all the transformations discussed in Section 9.6, to concurrentize either the inner (J) loop or the outer (I) loop[4]. Neither option, however, yields load-balanced partitions. A good solution is to view the computation as a pool of $\frac{NMOL^2}{2}$ potentially concurrent interactions, and share these equally among processors. This can be done by restructuring the control (roughly) as follows, and concurrentizing the outer loop:

```
do I = 1, NMOL
  do J = I+1, (I + NMOL/2) mod NMOL
    complicated code, including loops,
     to compute intermolecular forces
  end do
end do
```

The speedups obtained are shown in Figure 9.5. Although compiler generated parallelization is more efficiently supported by the Alliant FX/8 than the constructs generated by the **parmacs** macros (see Figure 9.3(c) for an example of this), explicit algorithm parallelization is clearly a winner in the water code, and is in fact able to obtain good speedups.

9.8.2 Solving the Equations in the Ocean Code

Here, the sequential algorithm solves a block tridiagonal system of equations using a variant of block cyclic odd-even reduction [8]. The algorithm can be divided into three phases: reduction to a single unknown (in successive steps), solution for that unknown, and back substitution. Within every step in the reduction phase, for example, an outer loop iterates over the matrix columns (unknowns) to be worked on (written) in that step, the number of these being halved in successive steps. The last column in a reduction step is left out of this outer loop; it is treated by different code sections depending on whether the number of columns

[4] Recall that this compiler was finally able to concurrentize only the J loop.

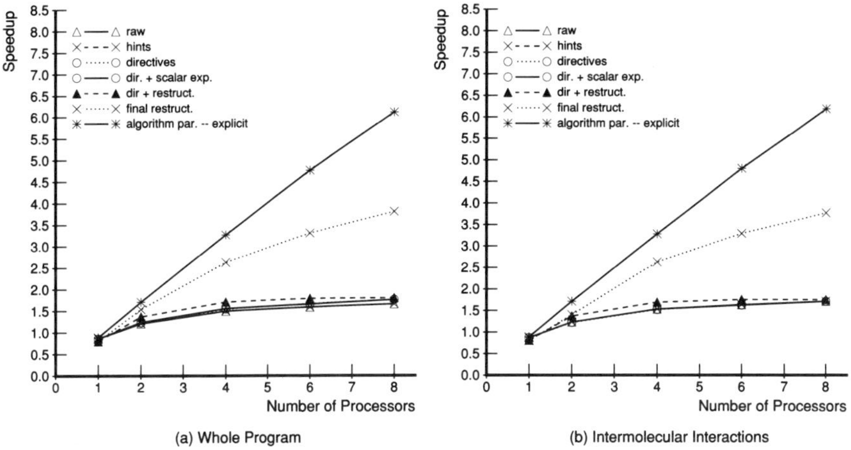

Figure 9.5
Normalized Speedup for the Water Code.

worked on in that step is even or odd, and is incorporated in the control flow using `GOTO` statements. Although the outer loop in every step is concurrentizable, the (interprocedural) analysis needed to discover this and the expansions and data manipulations required to implement it are far more sophisticated than in even the intermolecular interactions loop of the water code. There are several reasons for this:

- The loop increment and both loop bounds are variables. These variables, as well as their relationships with subscript offsets used to index the columns to be read, are redefined outside the loop in every step.
- Modifications to some scalar variables, used to determine control flow within the loop, statically appear to rely on the sequential semantics. However, it turns out that these modifications are made within conditionals that are satisfied only in the last iteration of the loop, for use in the next step. A conceptual understanding of the algorithm, run-time conditional resolution, and/or *extremely* sophisticated symbolic analysis are therefore required to determine parallelizability.
- The sequential program allocates a large one-dimensional array for temporary storage, portions of which are passed as subroutine arguments to the cyclic reduction routine. Since these subarrays cannot be

expanded in place, the array expansion required to concurrentize subroutine calls translates to allocating completely new local arrays within the cyclic reduction routine.

The work done for every column (i.e. every iteration of the above loop) itself involves several loops, both within and without the subroutines it calls, and it is these that the compiler ends up concurrentizing wherever possible. Parallelizing across columns is left to an explicitly parallel program, in which even the last column in a reduction step is included in the set of parallel columns.

Simple parallelization across columns within a step is clearly not efficient. There are steps — for example, the last few in the reduction phase, the single step in the solution phase, and the first few in the back substitution phase — in which the processes may outnumber or not exactly divide the columns to be worked on, causing a severe load-imbalance. Having processes share the leftover columns requires greater analysis (especially in determining which data and control variables to make private and which shared), but was found to provide little performance improvement since there is an inherently serial section within the work done on a column.

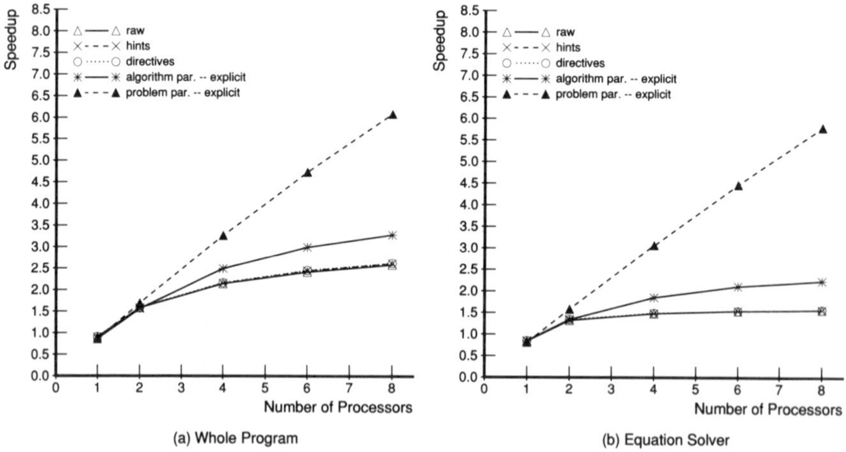

Figure 9.6
Normalized Speedup for the Ocean Code.

Normalized speedups obtained with algorithm parallelization are juxtaposed with those obtained from the compiler in Figure 9.6. Figure 9.6(b) shows that while algorithm parallelization helps the equation solver significantly, the speedups obtained from it are still very limited. The performance impact on the whole application can be seen in Figure 9.6(a).

9.9 Problem Parallelization

The block cyclic reduction algorithm used in the ocean code is one of the most efficient direct sequential methods for solving elliptic equations. As we saw in the previous section, however, there are significant limitations on its parallel performance. To obtain efficient parallel performance, we had to return to the problem at hand (solving a system of partial differential equations) and move to a completely different, iterative algorithm for solving it. The algorithm we chose is Successively Over-Relaxed Gauss-Seidel Iteration (SOR) [9]. Partitioning is done in chunks of adjacent columns, and while every process follows the Gauss-Seidel ordering within its partition, this ordering is violated at inter-partition boundaries by allowing all processes to begin an iteration simultaneously.

Figure 9.6 shows that problem parallelization is able to obtain effective parallel performance on the ocean code (even though we choose a tolerance that makes the uniprocessor execution of the iterative algorithm about 5 percent slower than that of the original direct algorithm for this problem size).

9.10 Summary and Directions for Tools

Automatic Parallelization Our results show that it often takes a much higher level of analysis and transformation to obtain an effective parallel program than current compiler technology provides. Parallelizing loops through standard dependence analysis has its place, and a wish list of compiler features needed for this can be constructed. While some of these features (mostly involving symbolic analysis) can be very expensive in general, such generality is not necessary and cheaper analyses can usually be employed to handle cases that commonly occur in practice. At least on small-scale machines, this level of parallelization can yield fairly successful performance on small programs such as tomcatv that are often used as evaluative benchmarks (particularly if we include the scalar expansion described in the paper), and is also very successful on most of the code in our larger applications. However, a very small number of very time-consuming loop nests in the latter applications are large and complex, consisting of several smaller loops and subroutine calls. Concurrentizing them requires dataflow and interprocedural analyses, as well as the privatization/expansion of data structures that these lead to, and it is these transformations that have the greatest effect on automatic parallel performance. Standard dependence analysis is at best able to concurrentize the wrong loops in these nests. Inclusion of these sophisticated analyses, at least designed to handle cases that programmers commonly generate, is therefore recommended. However, even this very aggressive automatic parallelization is unable to provide acceptable speedups on either of our larger applications, since it fails on one important section in each.

Explicit Parallelization Programs written without parallelization in mind often have quirks—in their control structure or in the way they allocate and reference storage—that are perhaps reasonable for sequential programming but significantly complicate the task of automatic parallelization by requiring more sophisticated analyses. In some cases, the inappropriateness of the programming style and the complexity of analysis required make it quite unreasonable to expect a fully automatic tool to find the most appropriate parallelism. Effective parallelization in these situations requires the user to understand the computational structure as well as the data structure usage patterns, and restructure them for load-balanced execution. Our experience with these codes suggests that this understanding might be greatly facilitated by a tool that allows the user to visualize the access patterns to active data structures, as well as the changing values of certain control variables, in slow motion while simultaneously viewing the code. The regularity of scientific computations is particularly useful here, since it affords the potential for such understanding to be extrapolated from very small problem sizes. The explicit algorithm parallelization that results from such restructuring is sufficient for the water code. While it also helps the section of the ocean code that automatic parallelization fails on, effective parallel performance on this code requires moving to a completely different algorithm for that section, a transformation clearly beyond the realm of the sort of compiler technology we are discussing here.

Global Parallelization and Scalability All the results we have presented are for the small number of processors available on the Alliant FX/8. Scaling the performance efficiently to larger numbers of processors might require increasing granularity (and eliminating unnecessarily restrictive synchronization) by exploiting parallelism across the modules that implement particular algorithms (global parallelization). Such high-level parallelization might also allow the division of processors among independent modules/tasks that each have only limited parallelism within them (for example, the two equation solves per time-step in the ocean code). Discovering parallelism at this level has three requirements: identifying the boundaries of the appropriate program modules, summarizing the data structure use-modification information for every module, and interprocedural dependence analysis of the summarized information. Global parallelization is discussed in more detail in the context of the ocean code in [5]. The usefulness of dependence analysis at a hierarchy of levels—with the three-step process above being performed at every level—is also discussed there. We only mention here that the modules we wish to identify, and the parallelism across them, do not correspond well to the conventions governing modularity in sequential programming styles: another negative interaction between the latter and automatic parallelization. Finally, the incorporation of data locality —which has been ignored in this paper—is a critical factor in obtaining scalable parallelism, a factor which can be aided by effective run-time scheduling, by the visualization tool referred to above, and by global parallelization.

We found in Section 9.7.5 that sometimes transformations which increase the degree of parallelism or its granularity can have a negative impact on the performance of loops, particularly when sufficient parallelism is already available or when architectural interactions hurt uniprocessor performance substantially. This fact, the need for intelligent and progressive communication between the compiler and user, the usefulness of profiling and perhaps visualization in uncovering parallelism, the process of higher-level dependence analysis, and the importance of incorporating data locality all point to the near-term desirability of multifaceted interactive parallelization environments.

Acknowledgements

This work was supported by DARPA under Contract No. N00014-87-K-0828.

References

[1] D. Callahan, J. Dongarra and D. Levine, "Vectorizing Compilers: A Test Suite and Results," *Proc. Supercomputing Conference*, November 1988.

[2] *FX/FORTRAN Programmer's Handbook*, Alliant Computer Systems Corporation, July 1988.

[3] M. Berry et. al., "The Perfect Club Benchmarks: Effective Performance Evaluation of Supercomputers," *CSRD Report No. 827*, Center for Supercomputing Research and Development, Urbana, Illinois, May 1989.

[4] J.P. Singh and J.L. Hennessy, "Automatic and Explicit Parallelization of an N-body Simulation," Tech. Report No. CSL-TR-91-462, Stanford University, March 1991..

[5] J.P. Singh and J.L. Hennessy, "Finding and Exploiting Parallelism in an Ocean Simulation Program: Experience, Results and Implications," to apperar in *Journal of Parallel and Distributed Computing*, 1991. Also available as "Parallelizing the Simulation of Ocean Eddy Currents," Tech. Report No. CSL-TR-89-388, Stanford University, August 1989.

[6] "SPEC Benchmark Suite Release 1.0," October, 1989.

[7] E.L. Lusk and R.A. Overbeek, "Use of Monitors in FORTRAN: A Tutorial on the Barrier, Self-scheduling DO-Loop, and Askfor Monitors," Tech. Report No. ANL-84-51, Rev. 1, Argonne National Laboratory, June 1987.

[8] R. Sweet, "A Cyclic Reduction Method for the Solution of Block Tridiagonal Systems of Equations," *SIAM Journal of Numerical Analysis*, Vol. 14, No. 4, pp. 706-720, September 1977.

[9] G.H. Golub and C.F. Van Loan, *Matrix Computations*, Second Edition, Chap. 10, The Johns Hopkins University Press, 1989.

10 Fine-Grain Loop Scheduling for MIMD Machines

Carrie J. Brownhill, Ki-chang Kim, and Alexandru Nicolau

Previous algorithms for parallelizing loops on MIMD machines have been based on assigning one or more loop iterations to each processor, introducing synchronization as required. These methods exploit iteration level parallelism, but ignore lower level parallelism.
In order to exploit parallelism both within and across iterations, our algorithm analyzes and schedules the loop at the statement level. The loop schedule reflects the expected communication and synchronization costs of the target machine. We provide test results that show that this algorithm can produce good speedup of loops on an MIMD machine.

10.1 Introduction

Loop scheduling is the process of mapping the operations inside a loop to the available processing units at compile time. When the loop executes, each processor will execute only the operations assigned to it, but may need to communicate or synchronize with the other processors, if they share data. The scheduling algorithm should minimize the amount of idle time caused by this communication and synchronization.

To schedule the work to the available processing units, a loop may be partitioned along operation boundaries, so that some or all executions of a particular operation are done by one processor. This mode of execution can be very efficient, as is the case for vector machines [4]. Unfortunately, many real-life loops contain dependencies that make them hard to vectorize.

Another way to divide a loop is along iteration boundaries. In this case, one or more iterations are assigned to each processor [8], with synchronization added as necessary to handle loop-carried dependencies, e.g., Doall, Dopipe, and Doacross loop scheduling [5, 7]. This method of loop scheduling has been extensively used on MIMD machines. It exploits coarse grain (iteration level) parallelism, but ignores any parallelism that may exist at a lower level of granularity.

The algorithm we discuss in this paper uses fine-grain (statement level) loop parallelization techniques in an attempt to fully exploit the parallelism available in a loop. While not all of the fine-grain parallelism exposed by these techniques can be utilized on machines with relatively high communication and synchronization costs, we have found that the extra parallelism is often useful in speeding up the execution time of loops by masking the latency of communication and synchronization delays.

In principle, the parallelization technique we use is able to expose *all* of the parallelism available in a loop, subject only to the data dependencies [1, 2]. However, in order to map a loop effectively to an MIMD machine, the communication and synchronization costs of the machine need to be taken into account. These costs may vary dynamically even on the same architecture. Nevertheless, a good *estimate* of the typical cost can usually be obtained. Adapting a loop schedule according to expected communication and synchronization costs can improve the execution time of the loop, while minimizing run-time overhead.

10.2 Algorithm

Perfect Pipelining (PP) [1, 2] is a fine-grain parallelization technique that has been developed for use on VLIW (Very Large Instruction Word) machines, with synchronous processors and no communication costs. On this type of machine, with sufficient resources, PP produces an optimal loop schedule. The same schedule will be optimal for an MIMD machine with sufficient resources, if communication and synchronization costs are negligible. For MIMD machines with measurable communication and/or synchronization costs, the schedule must be adapted to allow for these costs.

This paper decribes the technique for adapting the PP schedule for use on MIMD machines. The algorithm presented will 'trade-off' communication and synchronization costs for extra parallelism. It will only schedule a statement on a separate processor if that assignment is expected to improve the execution time of the loop. Thus, the granularity of the parallelism is automatically adapted to the operating parameters of the machine.

10.2.1 Loop Model

To begin, we describe our model of a loop using a dependence graph representation. In the graph of a sequential loop, each node represents a statement, and each arc represents a data dependence. See Figure 10.1. For simplification of our examples, we will assume that the dependence distances in the graph are all either zero or one. That is, all dependencies

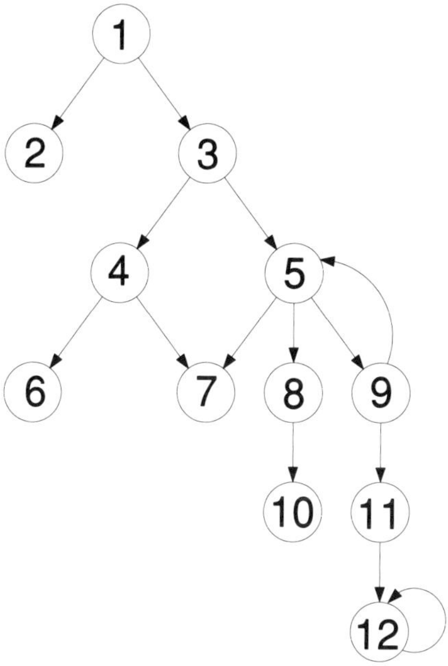

Figure 10.1
Example dependence graph

are within the same iteration, or between adjacent iterations. Loops with larger dependence distances can be handled by unwinding the loop as required [6]. In addition, any branch tests present in the loop must be if-converted, as described in [3].[1]

For our purposes, it is useful to partition the statements of the loop into three disjoint sets. The set of *flow-in* statements includes all statements which either have no predecessors in the data dependence graph, or which only have predecessors which are themselves in the flow-in set. Similarly, the set of *flow-out* statements includes all statements which are not flow-in and which have no successors, or which have only successors which are themselves in the flow-out set. The set of *cyclic* statements

[1] While PP can exploit fine-grain parallelism beyond conditional branches without if-conversions, the use of such parallelism does not seem efficient when communication costs are high. Therefore, for the purposes of this paper, we assume that conditionals are if-converted.

includes all statements which are neither flow-in nor flow-out. In Figure 10.1, statements 1, 2 3, 4, and 6 are flow-in. Nodes 8, 9, and 11 are flow-out. The rest are cyclic.

Separating the loop into these three sets is a key part of the algorithm. Essentially, the cyclic statements are those statements on the 'critical path' of the loop. They are involved in both producing and consuming values. By scheduling the cyclic statements first, the expected execution time of the loop can be estimated. The flow-in and flow-out statements can then be allocated sufficient processors to insure that they finish at about the same time as the cyclic statements.

10.2.2 Partitioning the Statements

The first step in the algorithm is to divide the statements in the loop into the cyclic, flow-in and flow-out subsets. The following algorithm is used.

1. All statements without predecessors are marked 'flow-in'.
2. The set of non-marked statements is searched for statements with only predecessors marked 'flow-in'. These are also marked 'flow-in'. This step is repeated until one iteration is completed without finding any new flow-in statements.
3. All non-marked statements which have no successors are marked 'flow-out'.
4. The set of non-marked statements is searched for statements with only successors marked 'flow-out'. These are marked 'flow-out'. This step is repeated until one iteration is completed without finding any new flow-out statements.
5. All remaining non-marked statements are cyclic.

10.2.3 Scheduling Cyclic Statements

Intuitively, Perfect Pipelining (PP) schedules on an 'as soon as possible (ASAP)' basis, as restricted by data and control flow dependencies. Each operation in the loop is scheduled to be executed as soon as the operations it is dependent on finish execution. The scheduling process continues across iteration boundaries, with the loop being incrementally unwound. On VLIW machines, the exact execution time of each operation is known, so that the loop schedule consists of sets of operations which will be executed in parallel at each cycle. As an example, the

Table 10.1
Schedule for four iterations of Perfect Pipelining example.

Time	Scheduled Operations (Iteration)			
0	1(1)			
1	2(1) 3(1)			
2	4(1)	1(2)		
3	6(1)	2(2) 3(2)		
4	5(1)	4(2)	1(3)	
5	7(1) 8(1) 9(1)	6(2)	2(3) 3(3)	
6	10(1) 11(1)	5(2)	4(3)	1(4)
7	12(1)	7(2) 8(2) 9(2)	6(3)	2(4) 3(4)
8		10(2) 11(2)	5(3)	4(4)
9		12(2)	7(3) 8(3) 9(3)	6(4)
10			10(3) 11(3)	5(4)
11			12(3)	7(4) 8(4) 9(4)
12				10(4) 11(4)
13				12(4)

Table 10.2
Pattern for Perfect Pipelining example.

Time	Operation (Iteration)
0	1(4) 4(3) 5(2) 10(1) 11(1)
1	2(4) 3(4) 6(3) 7(2) 8(2) 9(2) 12(1)

schedule of four iterations of the example loop represented in Figure 10.1 is shown in Table 10.1. In the table, the first number corresponds to the operation, and the number in parentheses is the iteration number.

Eventually, the sets of scheduled operations form a repeating pattern. Once this pattern is recognized, the loop does not need to be unwound any further. The pattern itself can be substituted for the body of the loop. [2] The pattern for the example loop is outlined in Table 10.1 and shown in Table 10.2.

In this algorithm, the PP technique is used to find the loop pattern for the cyclic, flow-in, and flow-out subsets of statements. The optimal pattern found, is then adjusted to take communication and synchronization costs into account.

[2] For the majority of loops encountered in practice, the above description is accurate. However, there are some loops for which a pattern does not emerge naturally. To provide for these loops, restrictions can be placed on the scheduling transformation. Namely, a limit is put on the distance that operations from the same iteration can stretch from each other in the schedule. This guarantees detection of the pattern, while leaving the optimality virtually unaffected. For proofs, see [2, 1].

10.2.4 Adapting the Ideal Pattern

Once the cyclic statements are identified, they can be scheduled. The PP algorithm is used to find the loop pattern of these statements. This pattern is an optimal schedule for this loop subset, if there are no communication costs. To produce a schedule which reflects communication costs, the algorithm is as follows.

1. Allocate P_c processors, where P_c is equal to the maximum number of statements scheduled in parallel in the optimal pattern. (If resources are limited, the number of allocated processors can be decreased as described in the next section. However, this may increase execution time.)

2. Taking each statement in order according to the pattern, schedule it on the processor which allows it to begin execution soonest, taking into account any synchronization and communication costs. To do this, the following things are determined for each possible processor assignment.

   (a) Set S_p, the earliest possible start time, to initially be the value of the next free time slot on this processor.

   (b) Iterate over the set of statements in the loop on which this statement is dependent.

      i. Statements which are scheduled on the current processor can be ignored. There is no synchronization necessary. Statements that are scheduled on other processors, or not yet scheduled, are counted. (We include statements not yet scheduled to produce a conservative count.) This gives us R, the number of receives that will be necessary.

      ii. For those statements that are already scheduled on another processor, record the latest start time of a send. This time, LS, is equal to the scheduled start time of the sending statement plus its estimated execution time.

   (c) The earliest start time of the statement on this processor, S_p, is therefore equal to the following:

   $S_p = \max(S_p, LS + T_s + T_c) + (R * T_r)$

   where:

   LS = Latest expected send time

   T_s = Execution time of one send

T_c = Expected communication delay between processors

R = Number of receives required

T_r = Execution time of one receive

3. Schedule the statement on the processor that has the earliest S_p, and update the next free cycle time for that processor.

4. Record the longest expected execution time (including communication time) of these processors. This number, E_c, is used when allocating processors to the flow-in and flow-out statements.

10.2.5 Allocating Processors for Cyclic Statements

The number of processors allocated to the cyclic statements is ideally equal to the maximum number of statements scheduled in parallel in the pattern. As each cyclic statement is scheduled, it is assigned to the processor on which it has the earliest expected execution time.

Unless there is no communication and synchronization cost, there is an advantage to scheduling a statement on the same processor as statements on which it is dependent, thereby making synchronization unnecessary. However, if there are intervening statements already scheduled on that processor, then the statement may execute sooner on another, available processor, rather than having to wait for the intervening statements to finish execution. Therefore, there is a trade-off between the parallelism, and the communication and synchronization costs. If these costs are high, the scheduler may actually assign all of the statements to some subset of the allocated processors, because of the reduced amount of synchronization. Processors which are not actually assigned any cyclic statements can easily be reclaimed for use by the flow-in and flow-out statements.

If there are limited resources, the number of processors allocated to the cyclic statements can be reduced to fit the target machine. A good heuristic is to make the number of cyclic processors, P_c = min (maximum parallelism, expected execution time of the cyclic statements / expected execution time of (flow-in + flow-out statements)). Once P_c has been determined, the scheduler considers those processors to be the only ones available to execute cyclic statements. Therefore, the schedule is adjusted automatically.

10.2.6 Allocating Processors for Flow-in and Flow-out Statements

The scheduler attempts to allocate enough processors to the flow-in and flow-out statements to ensure that they finish at approximately the same time as the cyclic statements. To do this, it must calculate the expected execution time, E_f, of one iteration of the loop subset (flow-in/flow-out). The execution time of the cyclic statements, E_c, is equal to the longest expected execution time of all the cyclic processors. (This number was stored as described in Section 10.2.4.) The number of processors allocated is then $\lceil E_c/E_f \rceil$.

Again, if there are a limited number of processors, then the number of processors allocated to the flow-in and flow-out statements can be reduced heuristically, at the cost of increasing the execution time of the loop. As in the case of the cyclic statements, the processors are allocated in the same ratio as the expected execution time of the loop subsets.

10.2.7 Scheduling Flow-in and Flow-out Statements

The flow-in and flow-out statement sets are scheduled separately, but the algorithm for both is the same, so it is described only once. First, the pattern for each subset is generated, and the following method followed.

1. P_f is defined as the number of processors allocated to this set of statements. Give each processor a unique number p, ranging from zero to $(P_f - 1)$.
2. For each statement in the set, schedule it on all processors. However, each processor, p, only executes iterations i, where $(i \bmod P_f) = p$.

The flow-in and flow-out statements are rearranged according to the pattern found using the PP technique to reduce the delay caused by loop carried dependencies. Given enough resources, the flow-in and flow-out processors should not dominate the execution time of the loop, because all of the dependencies in these subsets go forward.

10.2.8 Generating the Schedule

Once the schedule has been determined, the program must generate the final schedule for each process. Any loop prologue or epilogue necessary must be included in the final schedule. In addition, the program must generate all the necessary synchronizations.

If a statement requires a synchronization with a flow-in or flow-out statement which is scheduled on multiple processors, the processor identity will depend on the iteration number. The correct processor can be calculated at run-time according to the iteration number in the synchronization. Otherwise, the loop can be unrolled by the scheduler, so that the synchronization can be explicit.

10.3 Examples

Our algorithm was implemented on a Sequent Symmetry with eight processors. The Sequent is a shared memory MIMD machine. Processors share direct access to memory, governed by synchronization inserted to preserve the original execution semantics.

The program takes as input the dependence graph of the loop and the expected execution time (latency) of each statement. The communication and synchronization costs are specified with three numbers: The estimated time for a send (or synchronization), the estimated time for a receive (or synchronization), and the communication delay. The number of processors available is also specified. The scheduler outputs the loop schedule for each processor. The cost of synchronization was timed as described in the following section, and used as input into the scheduler.

10.3.1 Synchronization cost

To implement the required synchronization, mailboxes (storage spots) are allocated. Each pair of communicating statements gets a mailbox. The 'sending' statement waits until the mailbox is available, stores the data and then sets the mailbox. The 'receiving' statement waits until it sees the signal, reads the data, and then resets the mailbox. Because only one processor does a 'send' and only one processor does a 'receive' to each mailbox, no race conditions exist, and therefore no locking is necessary. This makes the synchronization fairly efficient, even on the Sequent.

The execution of the synchronization primitives was timed, so that this information could be used when scheduling loops. In addition, the execution times of operations on data of type double were also measured, in order to estimate the execution time of the loop statements. The results are in Table 10.3. The average execution times were calculated

Table 10.3
Execution times on the Sequent.

Operation	Average Time
Synchronization	1
Load & Store	1
2 Loads, Add & Store	2

by taking the total execution time of 360 iterations, subtracting the loop overhead time, and dividing the result by 360.

The execution times were used to estimate the cost of synchronization and the execution times of loop statements on the Sequent. Although the actual excution times could be used, the variance on a multi-processing machine like the Sequent do not warrant such precision; we chose to approximate the synchronization cost as one unit. Each statement in the loop was estimated to take an execution time in units equal to the number of data loads.

10.3.2 The Effect of Communication Costs on Schedules

By using parallelism to mask synchronization latency, our performance improves over previous techniques, since more parallelism is available for this purpose. Of course, if communication cost is disproportionately large, relative to instruction execution time, the most efficient way of executing the code may be sequential, and neither our approach, or any other, will be able to speedup execution.

The possible effect of the communication and synchronization costs on the loop schedule can be seen in an example taken from [5]. The sequential code for this loop is shown in Figure 10.2 and the dependence graph is shown in Figure 10.3. In this example, there are six cyclic statements (1, 2, 3, 4, 6, and 7) and eleven flow-in statements. There are no flow-out statements.

If the communication costs are input as zero, the schedule produced for the cyclic statements is that shown in Figures 10.4 and 10.6. However, if the synchronization costs are specified as being one unit for a send and one unit for a receive (as was timed on the Sequent), the schedule for the cyclic statements changes to that shown in Figures 10.5 and 10.7. (The schedule for the flow-in statements does not change and therefore is not shown.) Notice that there is less synchronization required in the second schedule, but there are more statements scheduled on one

```
for (i = 1; i <= N; i++)
{
    A[0][i] = B[i];
    A[1][i] = A[7][i-1];
    A[2][i] = A[4][i-1];
    A[3][i] = A[2][i] + A[6][i-1];
    A[4][i] = A[1][i];
    A[5][i] = A[0][i] + A[12][i-1];
    A[6][i] = A[3][i];
    A[7][i] = A[3][i] + A[4][i] + A[16][i-1];
    A[8][i] = A[0][i];
    A[9][i] = A[8][i] + A[14][i-1];
    A[10][i] = A[8][i];
    A[11][i] = A[8][i];
    A[12][i] = A[11][i];
    A[13][i] = A[12][i];
    A[14][i] = A[13][i];
    A[15][i] = A[13][i];
    A[16][i] = A[13][i];
}
```

Figure 10.2
Sequential loop example from [5].

Table 10.4
Execution times and speedup on the Sequent.

	Time	Speedup
Sequential	4067 μs	
Assuming No Communication Cost	25772 μs	24 %
Assuming Communication Cost	22571 μs	38 %
Doacross	68037 μs	-100 %

processor than on the other, which would appear to be less efficient, if the communication delay was not taken into account.

These two schedules were run on the Sequent. As a comparison, the loop was also scheduled and run using a Doacross scheduling algorithm, with redundant synchronizations removed. The same synchronization method was used for all the loops. The total execution times were measured and are shown in Table 10.4. Speedup is also shown and was calculated using the standard formula, speedup = (sequential time - parallel time) / sequential time. These numbers illustrate that adapting the schedule to the expected communication costs can produce a better speedup.

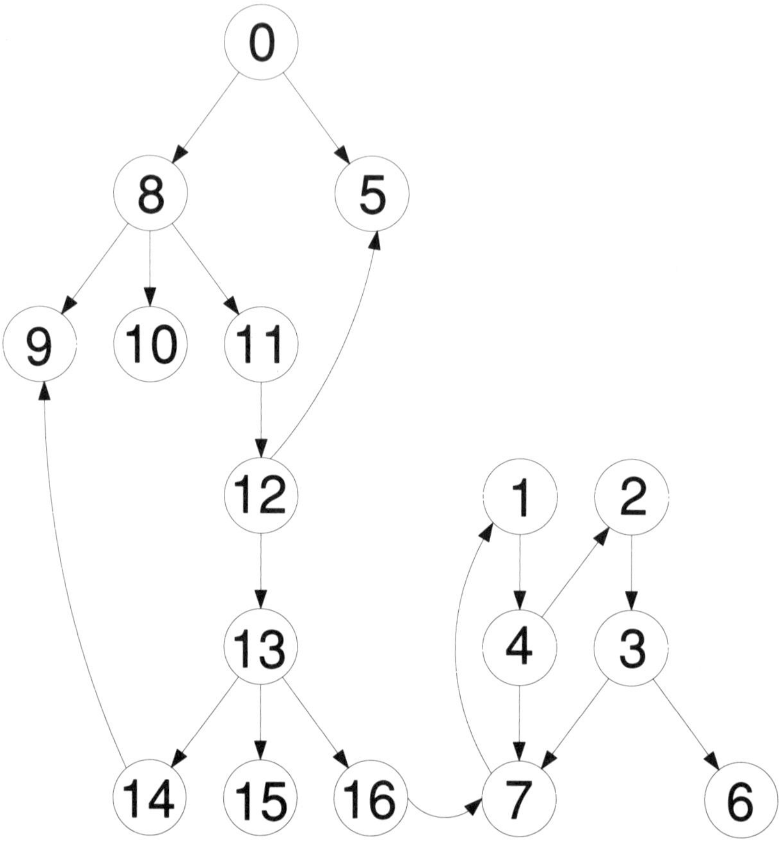

Figure 10.3
Dependence graph

```
for (i = 1; i <= N - 1; i++)
{
    A[2][i] = A[4][i-1];
    RECEIVE_FROM_S6;
    A[3][i] = A[2][i] + A[6][i-1];
    SEND_TO_S6;
    SEND_TO_S7;
    RECEIVE_FROM_S7;
    A[1][i] = A[7][i-1];
    A[4][i] = A[1][i];
    SEND_TO_S;
}
```

Figure 10.4
Schedule for P_0, no communication costs.

```
for (i = 1; i <= N - 1; i++)
{
   RECEIVE_FROM_S4;
   A[2][i] = A[4][i-1];
   A[3][i] = A[2][i] + A[6][i-1];
   SEND_TO_S7;
   A[6][i] = A[3][i];
}
```

Figure 10.5
Schedule for P_0, with communication costs.

```
/* Loop prologue */
RECEIVE_FROM_S3;
A[6][i] = A[3][i];
SEND_TO_S3;

for (i = 1; i <= N - 1; i++)
{
    RECEIVE_FROM_S16;
    RECEIVE_FROM_S3;
    RECEIVE_FROM_S4;
    A[7][i] = A[3][i] + A[4][i] + A[16][i-1];
    SEND_TO_S1;
    RECEIVE_FROM_S3;
    A[6][i+1] = A[3][i+1];
    SEND_TO_S3;
}

/* Loop epilogue */
RECEIVE_FROM_S16;
RECEIVE_FROM_S3;
RECEIVE_FROM_S4;
A[7][i] = A[3][i] + A[4][i] + A[16][i-1];
SEND_TO_S1;
```

Figure 10.6
Schedule for P_1, no communication costs.

```
/* Loop prologue */

A[1][i] = A[7][i-1];
A[4][i] = A[1][i];
SEND_TO_S2;

for (i = 1; i <= N - 1; i++)
{
   RECEIVE_FROM_S16;
   RECEIVE_FROM_S3;
   A[7][i] = A[3][i] + A[4][i] + A[16][i-1];
   A[1][i+1] = A[7][i];
   A[4][i+1] = A[1][i+1];
   SEND_TO_S2;
}
/* Loop epilogue */

RECEIVE_FROM_S16;
RECEIVE_FROM_S3;
A[7][i] = A[3][i] + A[4][i] + A[16][i-1];
```

Figure 10.7
Schedule for P_1, with communication costs.

Table 10.5
Percentage of loop statements of various sizes [9].

RHS Operands	Real Programs	Test Loops
1	80	77
2	15	16
3	3	5
4	2	2

10.3.3 Test Results

To test the scheduling algorithm, a random loop generator was implemented. The loop generator takes four inputs: the number of statements in the loop, the total number of in-loop dependencies, the total number of loop carried dependencies, and the maximum number of dependencies for each statement. The loop generator uses a standard random number generator with a timestamp seed and outputs the loop dependencies.

By varying the parameters to the loop generator, loops with a variety of characteristics can be obtained. The question is, how to create loops which are similar to loops found in real programs. According to [9], loops in real programs can be characterized by the number of operands on the right hand side of assignment statements. The percentage of statements of each size found in loops in real programs is shown in Table 10.5. We chose our test parameters to create loops with similar characteristics. These are also shown in Table 10.5. The test loop parameters were permutations of the following: 20 and 25 statements, 10 and 15 in-loop dependencies, and 5 and 10 loop carried dependencies, with a maximum of 4 dependencies for each statement. Each combination of parameters was used to generate 4 different loops, for a total of 32 loops. Of the 32 loops, 10 had cyclic statements. Therefore, at least 22 of the loops were vectorizable.

A code generator was used to translate the dependencies into actual statements. The statements were created so that the dependencies specified by the loop generator actually existed in the statements. This was done by putting the appropriate data values on the right hand side of an assignment statement. For example, if statement 5 was specified as having a loop-carried dependence on statement 7, and an in-loop dependence on statement 3, then the code generator would output statement

Table 10.6
Test loop parameters, execution times in μs and percent speedup.

#	Size	In-Loop	Lcds	Serial	PP	Doacross	PP	Doacross
0	20	10	5	39,674	14,117	62,420	64%	-57%
1	20	10	5	39,244	14,019	60,458	64%	-54%
2	20	10	5	38,622	14,071	36,716	64%	5%
3	20	10	5	37,536	12,422	24,900	67%	34%
4	20	10	10	41,634	16,630	59,599	60%	-43%
5	20	10	10	42,760	16,081	57,887	62%	-35%
6	20	10	10	44,420	17,641	51,978	60%	-17%
7	20	10	10	41,674	16,820	37,521	60%	10%
8	20	15	5	41,591	13,282	53,635	68%	-29%
9	20	15	5	46,381	14,883	51,584	68%	-11%
10	20	15	5	41,492	14,116	13,268	66%	68%
11	20	15	5	38,531	13,344	17,418	65%	55%
12	20	15	10	40,437	16,709	69,969	59%	-73%
13	20	15	10	42,626	47,630	72,954	-12%	-71%
14	20	15	10	50,530	31,266	76,702	38%	-52%
15	20	15	10	46,192	30,720	67,412	33%	-46%
16	25	10	5	39,635	14,998	50,319	62%	-27%
17	25	10	5	41,754	16,649	60,277	60%	-44%
18	25	10	5	42,759	19,397	41,664	55%	3%
19	25	10	5	45,579	15,699	52,873	66%	-16%
20	25	10	10	44,969	23,759	73,034	47%	-62%
21	25	10	10	46,354	19,168	56,848	59%	-23%
22	25	10	10	47,932	19,472	73,137	59%	-53%
23	25	10	10	46,790	18,205	27,232	61%	42%
24	25	15	5	47,393	15,914	16,187	66%	66%
25	25	15	5	45,819	27,918	58,697	39%	-28%
26	25	15	5	46,458	15,476	53,670	67%	-16%
27	25	15	5	48,915	16,269	37,620	67%	23%
28	25	15	10	53,843	29,842	81,972	45%	-52%
29	25	15	10	50,557	22,483	41,506	56%	18%
30	25	15	10	56,750	24,258	62,066	57%	-9%
31	25	15	10	56,697	20,972	76,251	63%	-34%

5 as, A[5][i] = A[7][i - 1] + A[3][i]. Statements which were allocated no dependencies by the loop generator were assumed to read constants. For example, statement 3 might have the form, A[3][i] = B[i]. The code generator was used in conjuction with the scheduler to automatically produce, schedule, and run various test loops.

For each loop, the sequential loop, the schedule produced by our algorithm, and one produced by a Doacross schedule were run for 360 iterations and timed. The total execution time and percent speedup are shown in Table 10.6 and graphed in Figure 10.8.

Although negative speedups were recorded for some of the loops scheduled using Doacross, in practice, expected speedup can be checked at compile time. Those loops estimated to have a negative speedup would

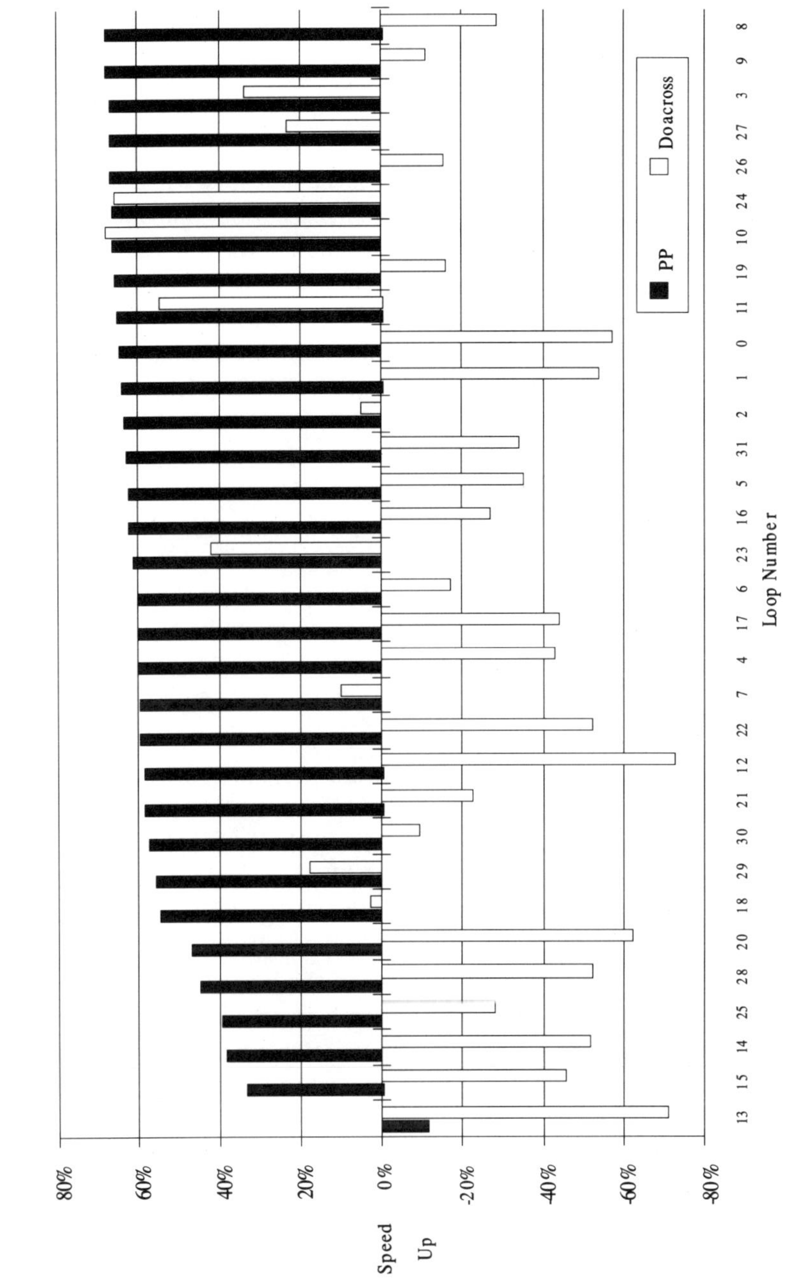

Figure 10.8
Test loop speedup in percent, PP versus Doacross.

instead be run sequentially. (Negative speedup results when communication costs are greater than the decrease in execution time due to parallel execution.) By averaging the speedup over all of the test loops (weighted according to number of statements), we can estimate what the overall speedup would be for a real program. Even assuming that loops with negative speedup are instead run sequentially, the overall speedup for a program containing these 32 loops would be 57.2% with our technique, as opposed to 10.1% with Doacross.

In order to see the effect of limited resources on the loop execution time, we ran the same 32 loops on 5, 6, and 7 processors. The results are graphed in Figure 10.9. Most loops showed a steady incremental decrease in execution time as processors were increased. The exceptions were those loops whose ideal schedule already used less than 8 processors, which were therefore not affected by the processor limit.

10.4 Conclusions

In the past, loop scheduling on MIMD machines has consisted primarily of assigning one or more loop iterations to each available processor, with synchronization added if necessary. This technique exploits any coarse grain (iteration level) parallelism available, but ignores any parallelism that may exist at a lower level. The scheduling algorithm presented in this paper uses fine-grain (statement level) parallelism techniques to try to exploit all of the parallelism present in the loop.

In addition, the algorithm adjusts the loop schedule according to the expected communication and synchronization costs of the target machine. Extra parallelism is exploited only when it is expected to improve the loop execution time.

A heuristic approach to rearranging statements *within* iterations to maximize Doacross overlap was presented in [6]. While interesting, this approach does not take into account communication costs, and is therefore not directly comparable with our technique. In the absence of communication costs, Perfect Pipelining is provably superior in exposing parallelism, and is therefore a better starting point when scheduling for MIMD machines.

We tested the algorithm on a synthetic benchmark of 32 loops. The loops were run on a Sequent, a shared memory MIMD machine, with 8 processors. The overall speedup of the loops was 57.2%. In addition,

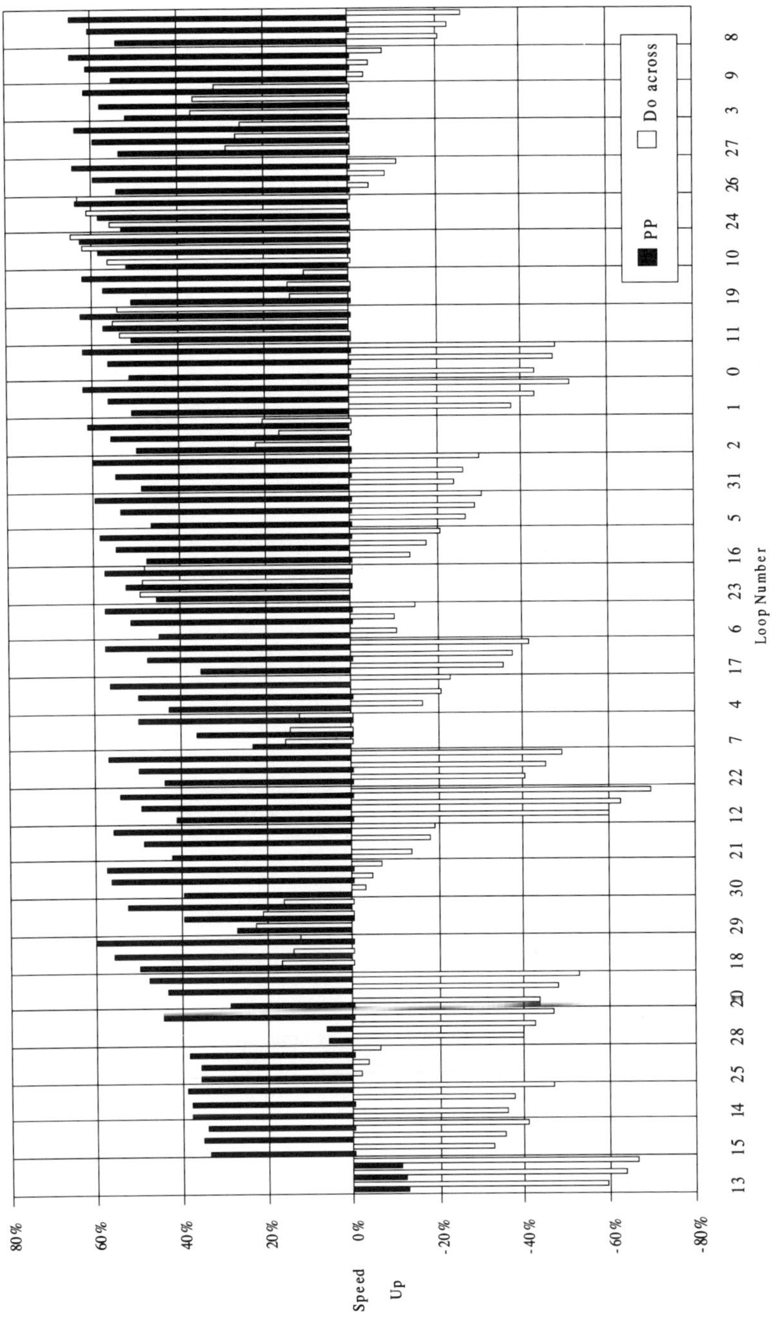

Figure 10.9
Test loop speedup in percent, versus Doacross with 5, 6, and 7 processors.

we ran the loops with resources restricted to 5, 6, and 7 processors, and found that the speedup tended to increase incrementally as the number of processors increased.

References

[1] Alexander Aiken and Alexandru Nicolau. Optimal loop parallelization. In *Proceedings of the 1988 ACM SIGPLAN Conference on Programming Language Design and Implementation*, June 1988.

[2] Alexander Aiken and Alexandru Nicolau. Perfect pipelining: A new loop parallelization technique. In *Proceedings of the 1988 European Symposium on Programming*. Springer Verlag Lecture Notes in Computer Science no. 300, March 1988.

[3] J.R. Allen, K. Kennedy, C. Porterfield, and J. Warren. Conversion of control dependence to data dependence. In *Proceedings of the 1983 Symposium on Principles of Programming Languages*, pages 177–189, January 1983.

[4] R. Allen and K. Kennedy. Automatic translation of FORTRAN programs to vector form. *ACM Transactions on Programming Languages and Systems*, 9(4), October 1987.

[5] R. G. Cytron. Doacross: Beyond vectorization for multiprocessors. In *Proceedings of the 1986 International Conference on Parallel Processing*, pages 836–844, August 1986.

[6] A.A. Munshi and B. Simons. Scheduling sequential loops on parallel processors. In *Proceedings of the 1987 ACM International Conference on Supercomputing*. Association for Computing Machinery, Springer Verlag Lecture Notes in Computer Science no. 298, May 1987.

[7] D.A. Padua. *Multiprocessors: Discussion of some theoretical and practical problems*. PhD, University of Illinois at Urbana-Champaign, 1979.

[8] C.D. Polychronopoulos and D.J. Kuck. Guided self-scheduling: A practical scheduling scheme for parallel supercomputers. *IEEE Transactions on Computers*, C-36(12), December 1987.

[9] Andrew S. Tanenbaum. *Structured Computer Organization*. Prentice-Hall, Inc., Englewood Cliffs, NJ 07632, 3 edition, 1990.

11 Restructuring a Parallel Simulator to Improve Cache Behavior

David R. Cheriton, Hendrik A. Goosen, and Philip Machanick

The cache behavior of a parallel program is a critical factor in the performance of the program on a shared-memory multiprocessor. In particular, cache misses and contention between caches must be minimized for good performance, especially for large-scale systems. This will become more important as processor performance improves relative to the speed of memory and large-scale interconnects. In previous work on shared-memory multiprocessor machines, we hypothesized that cache architecture sensitive parallel application restructuring (CASPAR) could significantly improve the cache behavior of parallel programs, particularly for machines that use large cache blocks. We present the results of an initial investigation in which we measured the impact of CASPAR on the caching behavior of MP3D, a parallel particle simulator for rarefied flow. We achieved an order of magnitude improvement in the cache miss ratio of shared data by restructuring the program. Measurements on four multiprocessor machines showed a substantial performance improvement for the restructured program. Although a single effort is an inadequate basis for general conclusions, this favorable experience suggests that further efforts to generalize our strategies will be worthwile.

11.1 Introduction

Structuring a parallel program to take advantage of the available processors is just one aspect of the design of efficient parallel programs. On a shared-memory multiprocessor, the program must also be structured to have a high degree of locality within each per-processor cache and a low degree of contention for access to data shared between processors. On machines with multilevel caches, misses caused by contention should be minimized since they always incur the high cost of handling a second level cache miss. E.g., in the MIPS RC6280 system (a uniprocessor based on a high-performance microprocessor), a second level cache miss costs 65 processor cycles [16]. As processor speed increases, the relative cost of a cache miss (measured in processor clock cycles) in the second level cache is expected to increase to hundreds of cycles [12].

With the large caches feasible in these architectures, most second level cache misses are caused by contention. For example, a previous study [4] showed that contention-induced misses account for over 90% of the misses on realistic parallel programs. Eggers [7] found that contention-induced misses were responsible for between 30% and 90% of misses in the programs studied. A good optimizing compiler further increases the fraction of shared references by keeping private data in the processor registers [20].

Although some level of contention is intrinsic and necessary for synchronization and communication in any shared-memory parallel program, the amount can vary significantly depending on program structure. As an extreme example, a parallel simulation program that counts the total number of events it handles would have very high contention if it used a single counter that was incremented by each processor every time it handled an event—compared to the alternative program design in which each processor has its own event counter, with the program summing the per-processor counters at the end of the simulation. While the programmer does not need to explicitly define structures as being in "local" memory (caching takes care of this automatically), some sensitivity to the architecture is useful to avoid such extreme cases.

The level of contention caused by a poorly-structured program can increase dramatically if the cache block size is large. For example, if a program places two independently accessed and frequently write-shared variables within the same cache block, it can result in a high degree of *false sharing.* False sharing occurs when two processors access the same cache block (consistency unit) because two independent writeable variables are in that block. This can raise the level of cache misses significantly. With small cache blocks, false sharing is reduced, if not eliminated altogether.

However, large cache blocks are particularly attractive for systems using high performance RISC microprocessors, because of the high cost of a cache miss in relation to the number of clock cycles per instruction. Many high-performance uniprocessor systems therefore use much larger block sizes than the 4 to 16 bytes usually considered optimal for multiprocessors [13]. For example, both the IBM RS/6000 [1] and the MIPS RC6280 [16] have a cache line size of 128 bytes, and this is expected to increase even further [12].

If a parallel program is structured carefully, large cache blocks can be used to hold significant collections of related data, such as the state of an object. In this case, multiple co-referenced data items can be brought in on a single cache miss, avoiding the multiple cache misses that would be required with small cache blocks. Similarly, only one invalidation is required when the data is used by another processor.

If relatively low cost multiprocessor computers are to be built from off-the-shelf components, potentially conflicting requirements must be reconciled. The advantages of a large cache block size in a uniprocessor and the undesirable property of increased false sharing in a multiprocessor is an example of such a conflict.

The VMP project [5, 4, 2] and its follow-on effort ParaDiGM [3] have explored the merits of using a relatively large cache block size, ranging from 32 bytes up to 512 bytes, in a shared-memory multiprocessor. This work was based in part on the hypothesis that program (re)structuring could significantly improve the cache behavior over structures that are independent of caching characteristics. We are now testing this hypothesis as part of our on-going work on scalable shared-memory multiprocessor architectures. We refer to this (re)structuring as cache architecture sensitive parallel application restructuring (CASPAR).

In this paper, we describe some initial experiences and measurements from the restructuring of a parallel direct particle simulator for rarefied hypersonic flow (MP3D) as an exercise in developing CASPAR techniques and to gather initial measurements to evaluate the merits of proceeding further. While this one effort is inadequate to draw general conclusions about the merits of CASPAR, our experience has been favorable and it has resulted in some general strategies that appear promising well beyond the individual program under consideration.

The next section describes the general strategies and techniques of CASPAR and briefly sketches the tools that we hope will eventually implement these techniques with minimal effort from the application programmer. Section 11.3 describes the MP3D program in its original form. Section 11.4 describes the specifics of the restructuring experience. Section 11.5 presents measurements of the cache behavior and the system performance of the restructured program, comparing it with the original program. Section 11.6 compares our work to other relevant projects. We close with a summary of our results, identification of the significant open issues, and our plans for the future.

11.2 Strategies, Techniques, and Tools for Restructuring

Unless generally applicable strategies, techniques and tools can be developed, CASPAR will be of interest only to the most dedicated parallel application programmers. Ideally, CASPAR should be handled entirely by the compiler, linker and supporting program development tools. More realistically, these tools can provide significant assistance in combination with programming techniques and standard libraries that support CASPAR for a significant class of programs.

11.2.1 Strategies

A key strategy is to increase the *processor affinity* of objects by using suitable data structures and work allocation techniques. For example, an object should be repeatedly processed by the same processor in the course of a computation, rather than move between processors. Similarly, the processing of one object frequently leads to the processing of other, related objects. Such groups of related objects should preferably be associated with the same processor.

As an example of such a strategy, simulation of physical systems frequently involves objects interacting in three-dimensional space (this can be generalized to k dimensions). Such objects interact predominantly with – resulting in contention with – objects that are nearby (we recognize that there are some models of gravity for which this claim is not quite true). Contention is reduced if all the objects in such a bounded region of the space (which we call a *precinct*) are asigned to the same processor. Contention can be further reduced by modifying the shape of precincts to minimize the probability that objects will cross precinct boundaries, and by allocating precincts to processors so as to minimize the probability of objects moving between precincts allocated to different processors. These points will be elaborated on when the original implementation of MP3D is described in Section 11.3.

The internal processing increases significantly faster than the boundary region as the size of the precinct is increased, provided that the internal processing per precinct is proportional to its volume. The relative level of contention can therefore be reduced by picking a suitably large precinct for the problem. Thus, the strategy is to structure the program so that the activity in each cache statistically corresponds to a portion of the three-dimensional space and inter-cache traffic corresponds to interactions between these portions of the space. In MP3D, for example, processors are allocated portions of the space with the assignment to simulate all particles in that portion of the space.

A second strategy is to minimize false sharing by *separation*—forcing certain data to occupy separate cache blocks (this was also suggested in [7]). First, read-only shared data should be separated from writeable data. Otherwise, a write could invalidate a cache block containing read-only data, which may cause an unnecessary cache miss when the read-only data is read. Second, write-shared data should be separated from private writeable data, for a similar reason. Third, independently write-shared data should be separated so no two such data are on the same cache block.

A third strategy is to enhance the effect of automatic pre-fetching by *co-location*—that is placing data that will be accessed within a short time frame and with compatible read/write behavior on the same cache block. This reduces the number of misses and bus transactions that are required to get the data on access, and reduces the number of invalidations on contention.

In addition to these approaches, we recognize the merits of more established strategies such as minimizing locking and using relatively fine-grain locks to minimize interference on access to locks.

11.2.2 Techniques

For three-dimensional simulations, the processor affinity of objects can be increased by mapping the spatial structure of the physical process to a collection of objects that interact with each other within a subspace or precinct. This is supported using a *space directory* to record the state and object population of the precincts. Each processor updates the set of objects contained in the precincts allocated to it. A processor can also move objects between precincts as a result of the object interactions.

Separation and alignment can be achieved by allocating data structures so that they start on cache block boundaries, and by padding out the data structures so that components with conflicting access patterns are not stored in the same cache block. This could be done either at compile/link time, or at run-time, as discussed in the next section.

Co-residency can be achieved by placing the variables to be co-resident in the same data structure or object, and relying on the above techniques to make them co-resident to a cache block (assuming that the data fits into one cache block).

A potential concern is that the program structuring could end up being too architecture specific, or at least specific to particular cache block sizes. However, we can reasonably assume cache blocks to be multiples of 32 bytes and adapt according to the actual value at run-time, handling the architectures of interest. Similarly, there can be different versions of the space directory for different architectures, all defining the same interface so applications need only be linked with the appropriate library version to be ported to another architecture.

11.2.3 Tools

An important insight we have used is the value of exploiting the inherent spatial and temporal locality of the physics of a particle simulation in the design of the program, to achieve the locality required by a caching architecture. The high-level design resulting from this insight led naturally to considering object-oriented programming as appropriate to the task.

The ease of CASPAR at a more detailed level is dependent on proper tools. Sophisticated compilers could recognize data access and sharing patterns for data and use this information to select the layout of the data in memory. For example, the fields of an object descriptor might be rearranged and padded from that specified so that read-only data is separated from modified data. Similarly, the linker could be modified to provide alignment to cache block boundaries.

Object-oriented programming languages such as C++ provide a number of additional features that facilitate CASPAR. First, the co-location of fields of an object descriptor provide a high degree of locality for operations on an object and separation for operations on different objects. For example, a typical FORTRAN simulation uses an array per object attribute so the attribute values of several objects are contained in a single cache block, leading to false sharing. In contrast, an array of objects, each aligned on cache block boundaries, eliminates this false sharing. However, the array organization is suited to vectorization [9].

Second, C++ (and some other object-oriented languages) allows the programmer to define object-specific allocation routines, allowing the objects to be placed in memory to minimize cache overhead. For example, if it is possible to dynamically determine the cache block size, allocation aligned to cache blocks may be performed using suitably designed allocators.

In this vein, an allocator that uses part of the allocated memory chunk for its own data structures should be avoided, since scanning and updating the allocator data structures will force unnecessary cache misses when a cache block contains both allocator data structures and program data. Instead, out-of-line allocation techniques such as those used with operating system page frame allocators should be used.

Finally, object-oriented programming languages clearly separate the interface of a module from its implementation, allowing the same interface to have different implementations on different architectures, if needed, without modifying the application.

Support for CASPAR is still in an early stage. We foresee the development of compiler and language support and the availability of standard libraries supporting CASPAR, following a better understanding of CASPAR and its benefits. This better understanding was our objective in restructuring a particular application, implementing the above techniques largely "by hand".

11.3 MP3D

MP3D is a three-dimensional particle simulator for rarefied hypersonic flow, originally developed for a vector architecture (the CRAY-2) by Jeff McDonald [15], and subsequently ported to an Encore multiprocessor by using the ANL macro package [14]. MP3D is a real application and is used at the NASA-AMES Research Center.

Figure 11.1 shows the output of the Encore version of MP3D, simulating a wind tunnel containing a flat plate perpendicular to the direction of air flow, at a speed of mach 10. The figure shows the particle density (corresponding to air pressure) for a two-dimensional slice through the wind tunnel, with the obstacle occupying the low-density region at the bottom corner. The horizontal axes are the spatial dimensions, while the vertical axis is particle density. The resulting shock wave is clearly visible. The output of the program was compared with that from other implementations, as a validation. If the program were to be put to "real" use, more thorough validation would be required; our emphasis was on ensuring that each version of the program had a realistic memory reference pattern.

Briefly, the program moves the particles through space constrained by boundaries (such as the wind tunnel walls), and adjusts the velocities of the particles based on collisions with the boundaries and other particles.

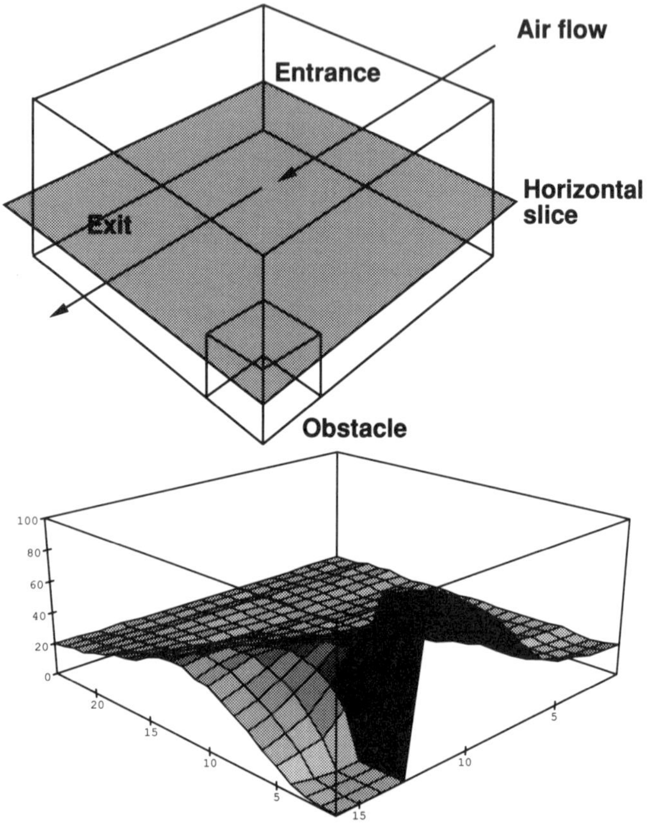

Figure 11.1
MP3D output from Encore version of MP3D (normalized particle density in one plane)

In the original structure of the program, there is an array for each physical attribute of a particle, such as its x, y and z coordinates, and velocity components along these coordinates. There is no relation between the array index of a particle and its spatial co-ordinates.

Each simulated time step consists of a *move* phase and a *collide* phase for each particle. In the move phase, each processor gets an index into the particle attribute arrays. It moves the particle by calculating a new position from the current position and velocity, also taking into account boundary interactions. In the collide phase, each processor determines whether the particle it just moved will collide with another particle. If a collision occurs, the velocities of both particles are modified.

The significance of the original MP3D algorithm is that it reduces the n^2 problem of finding collision partners to order n. The wind tunnel is divided into discrete *cells*. A *Cell Array* (indexed by spatial cell coordinates) stores a pointer to the last particle that arrived in each particular cell. A new particle arriving in a given cell is eligible for collision with the last particle that arrived in that cell. If such a pair of particles is found, a probabilistic test determines whether the collision will occur [15].

It is essential for the correct statistical behavior of the program that collision partners are selected randomly. This is ensured by the method of allocating particles to processors, and the random distribution of particles in the arrays.

There are several reasons why the original structure exhibits a high degree of contention [2], especially on an architecture with large cache blocks such as the VMP. When a processor updates the position of a particle, it writes to three separate cache blocks that also contain values for other particles, resulting in significant contention caused by false sharing. The false sharing is due to the array representation of particles. Second, the program structure does not result in any processor affinity—particles can be processed by a different processor on each time step (or even within a time step), resulting in significant inter-cache traffic. Finally, a processor has to perform a global lock when it gets a particle from the global particle arrays, resulting in considerable contention. This is exacerbated by the additional traffic generated by the memory-based lock.

We view MP3D as an attractive program to restructure because it represented an important and cycle-intensive class of applications, it behaved particularly poorly on architectures of interest to us, and the program source was available to us. We preferred to use an existing application rather than to write our own, to give a basis of comparison and to ensure the resulting program was not simply a toy. MP3D has further been implemented on a variety of architectures, including vector processors [15] and the Connection Machine [6], which potentially supplies opportunities for comparing our results and for validating output. In addition, the implementation of the program on a variety of architectures will supply a basis for comparison when we do more detailed performance modeling.

11.4 The Restructuring of MP3D

In essence, we aimed to preserve the desirable properties of the original MP3D (low cost of collision pairing), while eliminating the most problematic aspects for the target architecture: high contention and poor caching performance.

As a first step, the MP3D program was converted from C to C++ by adding function prototypes and cleaning up a few type coercion problems. There was no measurable performance cost. This baseline version is called MP3D-0.

Although we believe that *processor affinity* is the key strategy for improving the cache behavior of MP3D, it is important to quantify the benefits of simpler and more obvious optimizations. Two restructured versions of MP3D were therefore developed: in MP3D-1 only the data structures in the baseline program were restructured to reduce false sharing, while MP3D-2 implemented our notion of space-based work allocation and data structuring.

In MP3D-1, a particle was described as a class in C++ and the global arrays of particle attributes were replaced by an array of instances of the *Particle* class, aligned to cache block boundaries. We also restructured other data structures in a similar way (for example, the *Cell Array* mentioned in Section 11.3). Except for cache block sizing and alignment, this program structure is far more natural for object-oriented programming than the original program design. Although MP3D-1 performs better than MP3D-0, it shows that the mere elimination of false sharing does not guarantee good performance on high-speed multiprocessors, as discussed in Section 11.5.

In MP3D-2, we incorporated the notion of a space directory and restructured the handling of processor task allocation around portions of the space, rather than around particles. The space directory serves three major purposes. First, it records the particles in each cell of the space so that each processor can efficiently locate the particles that it has to move. Second, it helps in selecting pairs of particles for possible collision after they have been moved. Finally, it records aspects of the space such as boundaries and obstacles.

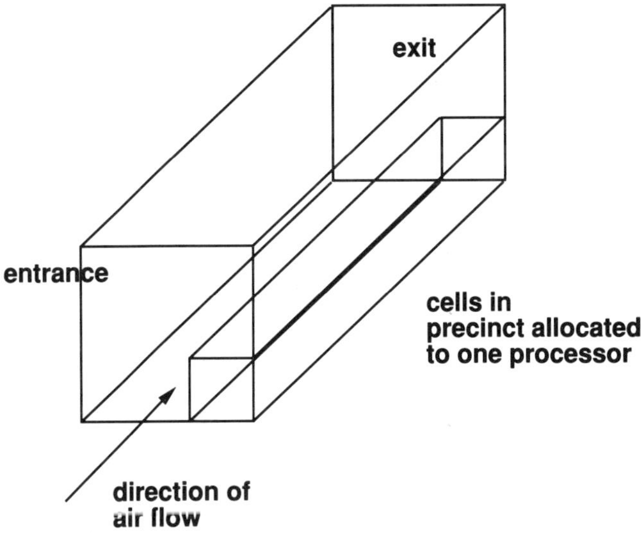

Figure 11.2
Precinct Allocation in MP3D to Minimize Interprocessor Activity

Compared to particle-based work allocation, the space-based work allocation sharply reduces the amount of inter-processor communication, provided that precincts are large enough. Because of the cell size dictated by the physics of the process, the number of inter-cell movements per time step is large (roughly 1/3 of the particles move inter-cell on each time step), making the cell an unsuitable unit of space to assign to a processor. Instead, cells in a contiguous portion of space are grouped together in a precinct.

Precincts can be shaped so that the probability of objects moving between precincts of different processors is minimized. In this case, each precinct consists of cells corresponding to a straight path through the wind tunnel, so that only those particles that are deflected from this straight path end up switching processors. Our measurements of MP3D show that air flow dominates the random thermal motion of the particles. This organization is illustrated in Figure 11.2.

In the examples we studied, only about 5% of the particles actually move between precincts during a time step, i.e., 5% of the particle moves resulted in interprocessor traffic. This is the case because all the cell data structures in a precinct are assigned to one processor (subject to dynamic load balancing constraints), and therefore most moves do not require access to data structures that are shared between processors. The effect of this relatively low movement of data between processors is to minimize cache contention, without moving away from a simple shared-memory model, in which all processors share the same address space.

The amount of processing was further reduced by two optimizations. First, we recognize when a particle is moving to a cell under the control of the same processor and move the particle without any form of locking or synchronization. Since this represents 95% of all moves, this is a significant optimization. As a second optimization, all particles moving to a cell belonging to another processor are transferred as a block only once per time step. Consequently, the lock and data contention on that processor's data structures are incurred at most once per time step, rather than every time the particle is processed.

We also added an explicit randomization of collision partners, as we could no longer rely on the random dispersion of particles and the random allocation of particles to processors. After all particles for a specific cell have been moved, they are assigned random positions in an array. The array is then scanned sequentially, and adjacent particles are collision candidates. This should be compared with other implementations of MP3D on multiprocessor architectures, where particles have generally been sorted to randomize them [6], and with MP3D-0, in which randomization was obtained at the expense of very high contention for a global lock (as well as poor caching performance).

Our experience with the space directory and space-based task allocation in MP3D-2 suggests that it may be of general applicability. We plan to develop general library support for space-based task allocation, although MP3D-2 has not evolved its space directory to the desired level of generality.

Several issues remain outstanding. First, there may be a need for automatic load balancing by reallocation of cells to processors if work is not sufficiently uniformly distributed across the cells of the space. There are a number of possible approaches and the implementation does not appear inordinately difficult. The challenge is largely to balance the load without incurring excessive contention both to perform the load redistribution (query and update of data structures) and as a result of the load redistribution.

Second, we did not optimize aspects of the program that do not affect the cache behavior significantly. For example, we performed only rudimentary static load balancing, and could do more to make locking more efficient (though we have considerably reduced it compared with the original program). However, we do not believe the potential for performance improvement or optimization in these areas is as significant as it was in the caching behavior of the program.

The work to date has taken about six man-months of fairly intensive effort, but this includes startup time to become familiar with the details of the original program. The resulting program is about twice the size of the original source, but much of this increase is due to extra comments, instrumentation and the redundancy required for defining classes in C++. A more realistic measure of the overhead of introducing the space directory is an increase of about 25% in the object (compiled code) size. We expect that inheritance will pay off in reducing the increase in size when adding extra features (for example, a more physically complete simulation, modeling chemical reactions and multiple species gases).

11.5 Evaluation

After the various restructuring steps, the modified versions of MP3D were run both to verify the accuracy of the output relative to the original version, and to measure the performance. Measurements were obtained by using trace-driven simulation and by executing the programs on two different multiprocessor architectures: the DEC Firefly and the Silicon Graphics Iris (SGI). The simulation results give insight into the effect of the restructuring on the behavior of shared data, while the measurement of real program execution shows the impact the restructuring has on the system performance.

11.5.1 Simulation Results

Since we argued earlier that the performance of large-scale multiprocessors will be dominated by the behavior of shared data, and since much longer and therefore more realistic program executions are possible when only shared data behavior is monitored, our simulation effort concentrated on shared data. The cache miss and contention behavior of the original and the restructured programs were measured using a trace-driven memory system simulator. Multiprocessor traces of references to *shared data only* were obtained using the Tango multiprocessor simulator [10] to simulate a 16-processor machine with MIPS R2000 processors. All the versions of MP3D code were produced using the MIPS compiler with -O2 level optimization. The memory system simulator models infinite caches, which is appropriate for this study of large second-level caches, in which we are interested in the effects of contention on shared data.

The system was initialized with 8000 particles and run for 1000 time steps to reach steady state (when particle densities in the wind tunnel have stabilized). Tracing of shared data references was done for a further three time steps. The total simulation corresponds to the execution of approximately 500 million simulated instructions per processor, of which the final 1.5 million instructions per processor are traced. The resulting trace file is about 40 Mbytes, corresponding to 3.3 million shared references (for all 16 processors).

The example is realistic, although a "real" simulation would use a much larger data set (typically on the order of 10^7 particles for a CRAY-2 run, requiring 320 Mbytes to store the particle data). It was necessary to choose a scaled down problem to obtain traces in a reasonable amount of time. For the given data set, obtaining a trace took from 20 minutes to 2 hours, depending on the version of the program. A Cray-2 would take about 10 seconds to run the same problem. Aside from the reduced size of the data set, however, our program was typical of this class of simulator. With present technology and prices, it is feasible to have second level caches of 10 Mbytes or more, costing $500 per processor at present prices. A 100-processor machine will therefore have 1 Gbyte of second-level cache, easily accomodating the particle data for a "real" run without excessive cache interference misses.

The directly measured miss ratios were adjusted by ignoring cold-start references, which were defined as the first reference by each processor to each block, until a write occurs to the block. This approach was validated by comparing the resulting adjusted miss ratios to miss ratios measured from much longer traces (fifty time steps, at which time cold-start effects are negligible). It was found that the adjusted miss ratios accurately reflect the contention traffic generated on accesses to shared data. For completeness, the measured raw miss ratios and the adjusted figures are presented in Table 11.1. The adjustment has more of an effect on MP3D-2 since it suffers less from contention-induced misses, and therefore has a higher fraction of cold-start misses, than the other versions of the program.

The relative improvements of MP3D-1 and MP3D-2 over MP3D-0 are illustrated in Figure 11.3. MP3D-1 had a lower cache miss rate than MP3D-0, as expected. Depending on the cache block size, the improvement varied from a factor of 1.5 (4-byte blocks) to 6.7 (32-byte blocks). We also investigated the effect of padding; it made little difference, probably because the main particle structures were coincidentally already 32 bytes in size (we did all our padding to 32-byte boundaries).

MP3D-2 reduced the cache miss ratios even further. With objects padded and aligned to 32-byte boundaries, the miss ratios were lower than those for MP3D-0 by a factor ranging from 11 (128-byte blocks) to 21 (32-byte blocks).

In general, MP3D-1 represented a five-fold reduction in miss ratios, while MP3D-2 reduced miss ratios by at least an order of magnitude, compared with MP3D-0. The fact that MP3D-1 has a relatively poor miss ratio for small cache block sizes suggests that the program benefits from the prefetch effect of larger cache blocks, up to 32 bytes, beyond which size false sharing becomes significant, and the miss ratio increases again due to contention. MP3D-2 does not exhibit this behavior for smaller blocks, probably because a larger percentage of invalidations is caused by small data structures (e.g., maintaining state information) which were not padded and aligned. This view is supported by the fact that the unaligned unpadded version of MP3D-2 achieves its lowest miss ratio for a block size of 4 bytes.

Padding and alignment significantly reduced the miss ratios for MP3D-2, though the miss ratios are much lower than for either MP3D-0 or MP3D-1 for all block sizes considered, even without this improvement. The effect of padding and alignment can be seen in Figure 11.4.

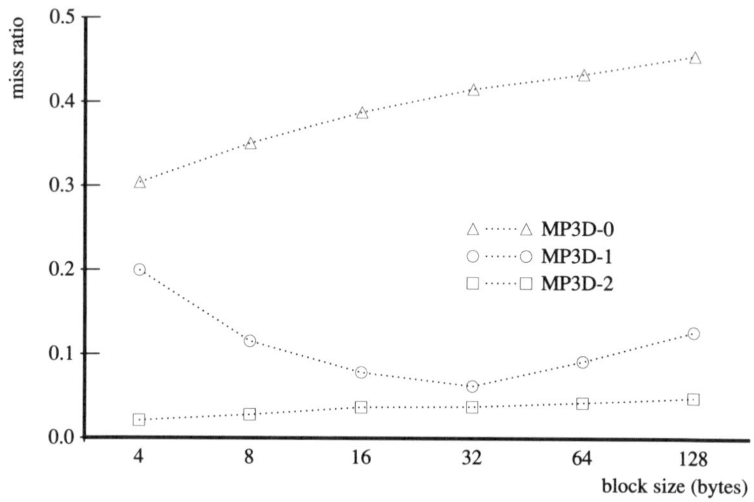

Figure 11.3
Shared Data Miss Ratios for Variations on MP3D

MP3D-0 had its lowest miss ratio with the smallest block size measured (4 bytes), whereas the padded and aligned object-oriented programs had their lowest miss ratios for a 32-byte block size. The padded and aligned version of MP3D-2 has a small variation in miss ratio for all block sizes up to 32 bytes (a difference of only 12% between best and worst), whereas for MP3D-1 it is relatively large (200%). MP3D-2 therefore seems to be less dependent on specific details of the architecture.

The high shared data miss ratios suggest that both MP3D-0 and MP3D-1 will have serious performance problems as the number of processors are increased, since our measurements show that in MP3D there is approximately one reference to shared data for every 6 instructions executed. The performance impact will be more severe for machines with faster processors relative to the memory and bus speed.

11.5.2 Program Execution Results

We report here the execution time of the three versions of MP3D on four different machines: two versions of the DEC Firefly running the V distributed operating system, and two versions of the Silicon Graphics Iris (SGI) Multiprocessor family running Unix. The machines are:

1. The DEC *MicroVAX* Firefly, using 5 MicroVAX II CPUs [19]. One CPU is dedicated to I/O, so, for our purposes, this is a 4-processor machine. The I/O processor is on a conventional VAX QBus, while the other CPUs are on a special-purpose bus, known as the MBus. The MBus is relatively slow (10 Mbytes per second). Because of the slow processors, the penalty for a cache miss is relatively low (less than the number of cycles for a typical instruction). Each processor has a 16 Kbyte cache with a block size of 4 bytes.
2. The DEC *CVAX* Firefly. The 4 processors on which user programs run are replaced by CVAX CPUs, that are about 3 times as fast as the MicroVAX II CPUs. The cache is increased to 64 Kbytes (the block size remains at 4 bytes), and the penalty for a miss is doubled because of the faster clock.
3. The Silicon Graphics 4D/240S, with four 25MHz MIPS R3000 processors. Each processors has 64 Kbytes of instruction and 64 Kbytes of data cache. The processors are similar to those used to obtain our simulation results.
4. The Silicon Graphics 4D/380S, with eight 33MHz MIPS R3000 processors (i.e., about 24% faster than the CPUs in the 4D/240S). The caches are the same sime as in the 4D/240, and the memory and bus speed is unchanged.

We did not try to account for differences in compiler strategy, instruction sets, etc., which could explain differences in the relative performance of the programs on each machine (e.g., the reason a specific version is the slowest on one machine but not on another). Our focus here is on scalability.

On all of the machines, we ran all three versions of MP3D on 1, 2 and 4 processors, as well as on 8 processors on the SGI 4D/380. In all cases, we used unloaded systems. We ran each variation (version of program, number of processors) 3 times. In most cases, the variation from the mean is under 1%. The largest variation is under 5%.

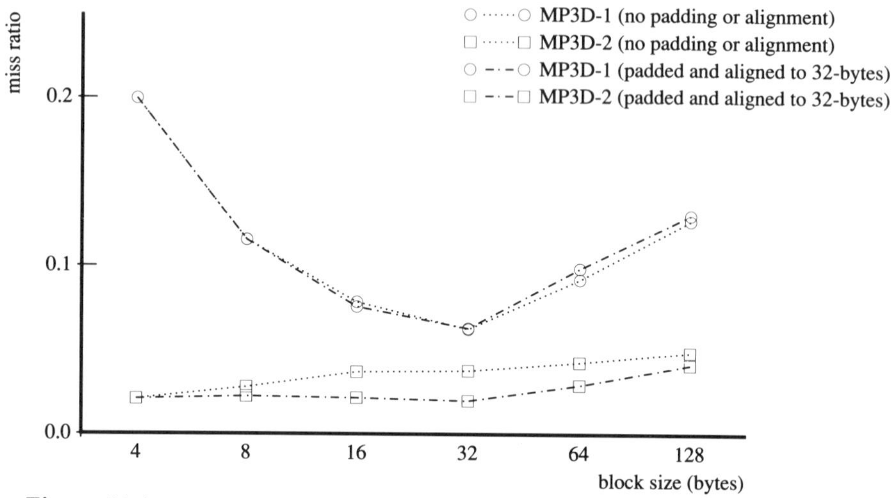

Figure 11.4
The Effect of Padding and Alignment of Shared Data for MP3D-1 and MP3D-2

Block size (bytes)		△ MP3D-0	○ MP3D-1	□ MP3D-2
4	raw	0.3688	0.2503 (0.2503)	0.0829 (0.0829)
	adjusted	0.3039	0.1995 (0.1995)	0.0208 (0.0208)
8	raw	0.3992	0.1411 (0.1410)	0.0654 (0.0568)
	adjusted	0.3505	0.1155 (0.1154)	0.0278 (0.0223)
16	raw	0.4249	0.0970 (0.0944)	0.0581 (0.0446)
	adjusted	0.3880	0.0785 (0.0757)	0.0368 (0.0214)
32	raw	0.4450	0.0693 (0.0700)	0.0498 (0.0342)
	adjusted	0.4157	0.0625 (0.0630)	0.0376 (0.0198)
64	raw	0.4529	0.0975 (0.1043)	0.0491 (0.0375)
	adjusted	0.4334	0.0919 (0.0985)	0.0426 (0.0291)
128	raw	0.4655	0.1319 (0.1355)	0.0520 (0.0454)
	adjusted	0.4554	0.1269 (0.1304)	0.0487 (0.0412)

Table 11.1
Shared data miss ratio (padded to 32 bytes in parentheses): 8000 particles traced for 3 steps

As in the simulations, each run is with 8000 particles initially in the system, and the time measured is for 1000 initial steps to eliminate transients, followed by 500 steps to obtain an averaged result (for a total of 1500 time steps). The execution times are shown in Figure 11.5 (for the SGI) and in Figure 11.6 (for the Firefly). The measurements are summarized in Table 11.2. The table also shows the speedup for each version of the program relative to itself on one processor.

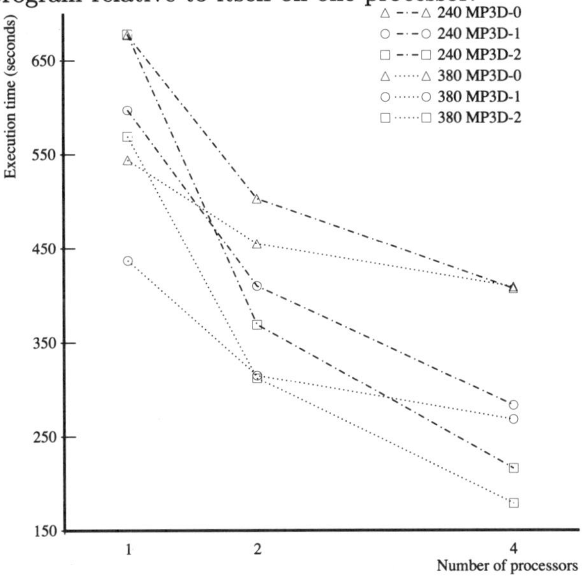

Figure 11.5
Measured execution times for MP3D on the SGI

Our simulation results lead us to expect that MP3D-2 should be the least dependent on specifics of the architecture. The speedup figures confirm this, with only a small variation between the four machines measured. The difference between MP3D-0 and MP3D-1 is mainly that MP3D-1 should suffer less from false sharing than MP3D-0, due to improved data layout in MP3D-1. On the Silicon Graphics machines, where the cache block size is big enough for false sharing to be a factor, MP3D-1 indeed outperforms MP3D-0 on more than one processor. On the other hand, MP3D-0 and MP3D-1 have very similar performance on both Firefly models, where false sharing does not occur due to the one-word cache blocks.

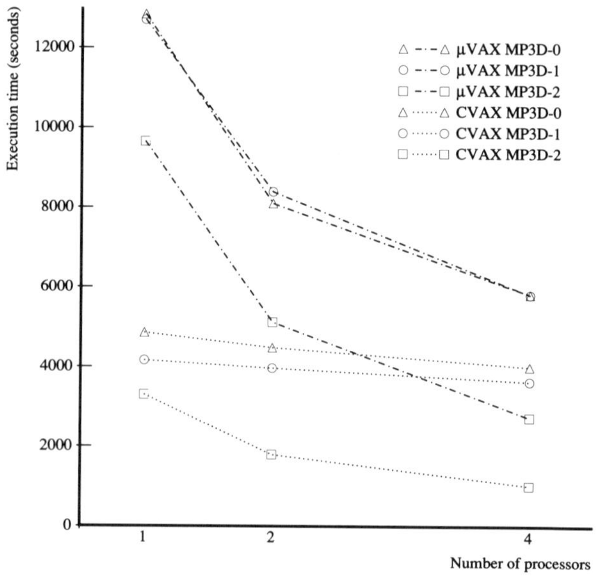

Figure 11.6
Measured execution times for MP3D on the Firefly

	no. processors	△ MP3D-0		○ MP3D-1		□ MP3D-2	
SGI 4D/240S	1	677		597		678	
	2	503	(1.3)	410	(1.5)	369	(1.8)
	4	407	(1.7)	283	(2.1)	216	(3.1)
SGI 4D/380S	1	544		437		569	
	2	455	(1.2)	315	(1.4)	312	(1.8)
	4	409	(1.3)	268	(1.6)	179	(3.2)
	8	431	(1.3)	265	(1.6)	141	(4.0)
MicroVAX Firefly	1	12839		12700		9657	
	2	8096	(1.6)	8389	(1.5)	5116	(1.9)
	4	5818	(2.2)	5810	(2.2)	2732	(3.5)
CVAX Firefly	1	4854		4161		3303	
	2	4478	(1.1)	3964	(1.0)	1790	(1.8)
	4	4002	(1.2)	3632	(1.1)	1014	(3.3)

Table 11.2
Run time in seconds (speedup in parentheses)

The measurements allow a comparison between program execution time on two versions of the same architecture, where clock speed is the only difference. Designers of the CVAX Firefly expect it to be 2.5 times faster than the MicroVAX version, while one would expect the SGI 4D/380 to be approximately 24% faster per processor than the SGI 4D/240. On a four-processor Firefly, MP3D-2 is indeed 2.8 times faster on the CVAX version than on the MicroVAX version, while MP3D-1 and MP3D-0 are only about 1.5 times faster. Similarly, on the four-processor SGI, MP3D-2 is 17% faster on the 4D/380 than on the 4D/240, while MP3D-1 is only 5% faster and MP3D-0 does not improve at all.

The results show that MP3D-2 makes much better use of faster processors (where memory speed is kept constant) than the other versions, supporting our view that as the ratio between processor and memory speed increases, more attention will have to be paid to the memory reference behavior of programs.

A potential concern is that, on large data sets, the restructured program will perform poorly because the per-processor caches will be continuously flushed of particle data. However, experiments show that this does not have a substantial effect on program performance relative to performance on small data sets.

For this experiment, a large example consisting of a cylindrical geometry in a 131 × 131 × 7 wind tunnel was simulated using over 1 million particles. The wind tunnel contains more than 120,000 cells, and the total data structure size exceeds 60 MB. In comparison, the total L2 cache size on the 8-processor 4D/380 used for this run is 2 MB. The machine has 256 MB of main memory, and paging is therefore not a problem.

The performance, measured as the time it takes to process one particle for one timestep, *improved* slightly compared to the 8000 particle case, from 8 to 6 microseconds per particle per timestep, using the same machine. The speedup also improved slightly to 5.3 for an 8-processor machine. There are two reasons for these improvements. First, the large wind tunnel means it is easier to balance the load, since finer adjustments can be made to the size of the precinct assigned to each processor. Second, the overhead associated with precinct management can be spread over more particles, cutting down on the per-particle overhead.

The reason why replacement traffic does not kill the performance is that the space-based restructuring also reduces the number of replacements in the cache. During each timestep, the particles are moved and collided on a per-cell basis. This results in repeated accesses to the cell and particle data structures in that cell, thus amortizing the cost of bringing in the data.

11.6 Related Work

This work has some analogy to work of the mid 70's on program restructuring for good paging performance [8, 11, 17, 18]. However, that work was concerned primarily with replacement-induced misses, whereas we assume caches are large enough (at least beyond the first level cache) so that replacement-induced misses are insignificant. Also, the cache miss cost is significantly less in terms of processor cycle times than a virtual memory page fault.

Our direction of providing support to applications to reduce the performance penalties for caching and contention is the same motivation that led to memory-based locking support in the ParaDiGM [3]. In the ParaDiGM locking scheme, locks are part of the cache directory. This prevents thrashing on large cache blocks to check a lock when data in that cache block is locked and being updated by another processor. This mechanism nicely complements the approach being investigated in the work reported here, and is expected to lead to even better execution in large cache block architectures.

The object-oriented structuring of a particle simulation was also reported by Forslund et al. [9]. However, their main concern is the development of an object-oriented version of the simulation and an assessment of the performance costs of object-oriented programming, in particular using C++. They consider the performance impact of poor vectorization of C++ code rather than parallelism and cache performance. They point out a significant loss in vectorization since object-oriented programming tends to hide the underlying vectors in the data. Our preference is to focus on the potential of general-purpose shared-memory multiprocessors rather than accommodations for vector processing.

Finally, increasing attention is being paid to application-level control and management for efficient parallel execution. For example, Tucker and Gupta [21] describe the benefits of a run-time scheduling environment that adapts to a varying degree of parallel processing.

Overall, there is considerable attention being paid to the performance improvement of parallel applications. Our work represents "glue technology" between the technologies being used to realize multiprocessor machines, such as caching, and the application-specific techniques in algorithms and detailed program structuring.

11.7 Concluding Remarks

Cache and contention-sensitive program structuring (CASPAR) shows promise in providing significantly improved performance of parallel programs on shared-memory multiprocessors, especially as these systems are scaled to a large number of processors.

There are structuring techniques for CASPAR that appear applicable to a general class of programs. We have described several such general strategies and provided some preliminary measurements of their benefits for one example program, namely the MP3D particle simulator. It is significant that the largest improvement was a result of these general restructuring techniques, which are not as architecture-specific as, for example, cache block alignment, which may require special tools. It is encouraging that object-oriented programming, representing a strong direction in improved program structuring, seems both consistent with, and highly supportive of, CASPAR.

It appears feasible to provide some programming tool support for CASPAR to minimize the burden on the programmer and to allow programs to be matched to the characteristics of particular machines. In particular, the compiler can handle alignment and some adjustments for cache block size.

Although our experience has been favorable, there are significant limitations to this preliminary work that preclude drawing general conclusions. First, we have only restructured and measured one program, so we lack the data to claim general benefits to restructuring. However, we have argued that the key characteristics of MP3D define a large and important class of cycle-intensive programs. We also argue that the caching shared-memory multiprocessor architecture will become the dominant parallel machine in the future. The application of our experience and the CASPAR techniques to additional programs is part of our on-going research.

Second, we have yet to develop programming tools that implement CASPAR automatically. We hope to report on progress in the area over the next few years.

Some additional areas that we intend to explore are the validity of the infinite cache assumption for programs of this class, and the effect of sharing caches between groups of processors (a key aspect of the ParaDiGM design).

Acknowledgments

Jeff McDonald of NASA-AMES generously helped us to understand the physics of the simulation and the details of the algorithm, and assisted with validation of our output by running the same data sets on his version of the program. Also, Anoop Gupta made an SGI 4D/240S available to us, and James Winget at Silicon Graphics assisted us by running the program on their 4D/380. Helen Davis and Steve Goldschmidt developed the Tango simulator and made it available to us. This paper has also benefited from comments and criticisms by members of the Distributed Systems Group at Stanford. This work was sponsored in large part by the Defense Advanced Research Projects Agency under Contract N00014-88-K-0619. Philip Machanick (on leave from the Department of

Computer Science, University of the Witwatersrand, Johannesburg) received additional support from the Anderson-Capelli fund and the Mellon Foundation. Hendrik Goosen is supported by an IBM Graduate Fellowship.

References

[1] H.B. Bakoglu, G.F. Grohoski, and R.K. Montoye. The IBM RISC System/6000 processor: Hardware overview. *IBM J. Res. Develop.*, 36(1):12–22, January 1990.

[2] D.R. Cheriton, H.A. Goosen, and P.D. Boyle. Multi-level shared caching techniques for scalability in VMP-MC. In *Proc. 16th Int. Symp. on Computer Architecture*, pages 16–24, May 1989.

[3] D.R. Cheriton, H.A. Goosen, and P.D. Boyle. ParaDiGM: a highly scalable shared memory multi-computer architecture. *IEEE Computer*, 24(2):33–46, February 1991.

[4] D.R. Cheriton, A. Gupta, P.D. Boyle, and H.A. Goosen. The VMP multiprocessor: Initial experience, refinements and performance evaluation. In *Proc. 15th Int. Symp. on Computer Architecture*, pages 410–421. ACM SIGARCH, IEEE Computer Society, June 1988.

[5] D.R. Cheriton, G. Slavenburg, and P. Boyle. Software-controlled caches in the VMP multiprocessor. In *13th Int. Symp. on Computer Architecture*, pages 366–374. ACM SIGARCH, IEEE Computer Society, June 1986.

[6] L. Dagum. A fast sorting algorithm for a hypersonic rarefied flow particle simulation on the connection machine. Technical Report RIACS 89.44, NASA Ames Research Center, 1989.

[7] S.J. Eggers and R.H. Katz. The effect of sharing on the cache and bus performance of parallel programs. In *3nd Int. Conference on Architectural Support for Programming Languages and Operating Systems*, pages 257–270. ACM, April 1989.

[8] D. Ferrari. Tailoring programs to models of program behavior. *IBM Journal of Research and Development*, 19(3):244–251, May 1975.

[9] D.W. Forslund et al. Experiences in writing a distributed particle simulation code in C++. In *Usenix C++ Conference Proceedings*, pages 177–190. Usenix, Berkeley, CA, 1990.

[10] S.R. Goldschmidt and H. Davis. Tango introduction and tutorial. Technical Report CSL-TR-90-410, Computer Systems Laboratory, Stanford University, 1990.

[11] D. Hatfield and J. Gerald. Program restructuring for virtual memory. *IBM Systems Journal*, 10:168–192, 1971.

[12] N.P. Jouppi. Improving direct-mapped cache performance by the addition of a small fully-associative cache and prefetch buffers. In *Proc. 17th Int. Symp. on Computer Architecture*, pages 364–373. ACM SIGARCH, IEEE Computer Society, June 1990.

[13] R.L. Lee, P.-C. Yew, and D.H. Lawrie. Multiprocessor cache design considerations. In *Proc. 14th Int. Symp. on Computer Architecture*, pages 253–262. ACM SIGARCH, IEEE Computer Society, June 1987.

[14] E. Lusk, R. Overbeek, et al. *Portable Programs for Parallel Processors*. Holt, Rinehart and Winston, Inc., 1987.

[15] J.D. McDonald and D. Baganoff. Vectorization of a particle simulation method for hypersonic rarefied flow. In *AIAA Thermophysics, Plasmadynamics and Lasers Conference Proceedings*, June 1988.

[16] MicroDesign Resources Inc. Mips chip set implements full ECL CPU. *Microprocessor Report*, 2(12), December 1989.

[17] R. Snyder. On a priori program restructuring for virtual memory systems. In *Proc. 2nd Int. Colloq. on Operating Systems*. INRIA, October 1978.

[18] J.R. Spirn. *Program Behavior: Models and Measurement*. Elsevier/North-Holland, 1977.

[19] C.P. Thacker, L.C. Stewart, and Satterthwaite. Firefly: A Multiprocessor Workstation. *IEEE Transactions on Computers*, 37(8):909–920, August 1988.

[20] J. Torellas, M.S. Lam, and J.L. Hennessy. Measurement, analysis, and improvement of the cache behavior of shared data in cache coherent multiprocessors. In *Workshop on Scalable Shared-Memory Architectures*. Seattle, May 1990.

[21] A. Tucker and A. Gupta. Process control and scheduling issues for multiprogrammed shared-memory multiprocessors. In *Proc. 12th ACM Symp. on Operating Systems Principles*, pages 159–166, December 1989.

12 A Replay Mechanism for Mostly Functional Parallel Programs

Robert H. Halstead, Jr., and David A. Kranz

Performance measurement and debugging of parallel programs can both be aided by a *replay* mechanism that can reproduce prior, *traced* program executions by reading log information collected during tracing. The primary design goals of a replay mechanism should be to (1) produce correct results for any program and (2) keep the overhead of tracing small, so it does not seriously distort program execution. This is an extremely challenging pair of goals that no extant system meets completely.

This paper introduces a novel tracing and replay scheme—the *side-effect touch protocol*—that always meets goal (1), and also meets goal (2) for programs that are *mostly functional* (have few side effects). This scheme has been implemented in MULTVISION, a system for visualizing the execution of parallel Multilisp programs. MULTVISION imposes no tracing overhead on reads from memory (even from shared variables) and adds only a small amount of tracing overhead to Multilisp's touch operation. Greater overhead is added to side-effect operations, since they are presumed to be rare.

Measurements on MULTVISION show that the overhead added for tracing is generally less than the overhead already incurred for task management and touch operations. While currently limited to program executions lasting seconds or less and creating at most tens of thousands of tasks, MULTVISION is already useful for an interesting class of programs.

12.1 Introduction

Performance measurement and debugging of parallel programs are both challenging. Aggregate performance statistics such as total run time give little information about the efficiency of individual parts of a program or the location of bottlenecks. Debugging is often complicated by the presence of (possibly unintended) nondeterminism, making it difficult to reproduce an erroneous execution for investigation.

Both performance measurement and debugging can be aided by a visualization tool that helps a programmer understand what happens during a specific execution of a program. A programmer using such a tool first runs a program in *trace mode.* Trace-mode execution yields whatever output the program produces when executed in *production* (untraced) mode, but also yields as a by-product a *trace file*, or *log*, which records the history of the traced computation. A visualization interface (the *debug monitor*) offers a way to browse through the log and extract information about the traced execution.

MULTVISION is a visualization tool for programs written in Multilisp [9, 10, 11, 12], which is the Lisp dialect Scheme [1, 23] extended with the `future` construct [3] for concurrency. Multilisp's computational model is essentially that of a shared-memory multiprocessor in which tasks interact through shared objects.

Determining what information to log is a difficult design decision in systems for visualizing parallel executions. Minimizing the trace-mode cost of generating the log is important to strengthen the correspondence between the timing details of trace-mode and production-mode execution, enhancing the system's usefulness for performance visualization. It also reduces the risk that tracing will change the program's qualitative behavior in a significant way (e.g., cause a pesky bug to disappear). On the other hand, the purpose of generating a log is to "freeze" a particular program execution and preserve it for detailed study: enough information must be logged to answer a wide range of questions from the user. An alternative to explicitly logging all information of interest is to log only enough information to characterize the nondeterministic choices made during the traced execution. A *replay engine* can then be guided by the log to follow the same path as the traced execution and regenerate the states through which the traced execution passed. Typically, a *partial replay* is performed to regenerate a state of interest, which can then be examined interactively. P-sequences [4], Instant Replay [18, 19], and PPD [20] all use this approach.

However, the opportunities for nondeterministic choices are so numerous in shared-memory parallel processing that developing a cheap tracing strategy allowing faithful replay of arbitrary programs has been difficult, and existing systems make compromises. PPD's logging strategy depends on compile-time identification of variables shared between tasks. Constructs, such as pointers or arrays, that preclude identification of a small number of shared variables will cause PPD's logs to become hopelessly enormous. PPD's strategy is thus unattractive for Multilisp programs, which use pointers heavily.

P-sequences and Instant Replay, by contrast, instrument synchronization objects (semaphores in the case of P-sequences, arbitrary linearizable objects in the case of Instant Replay) to record necessary log information. These systems assume that all nondeterminism in programs comes from the order in which operations are performed on these objects. If a program, perhaps inadvertently, accesses shared variables outside the control of such synchronization objects, replay may be inaccurate.

Most existing Multilisp applications are mostly (or wholly) functional: they have few *true side effects* (writes to previously existing data structures that are—or may be—shared between tasks).[1] These applications are mostly functional not just because Multilisp and `future` support this style well, but because it is far easier to write a correct, highly parallel program this way.

MULTVISION capitalizes on the mostly functional nature of typical Multilisp applications to make a different performance tradeoff than other systems. It adds a significant overhead burden to performing side effects[2] and to using values they store (both rare operations in mostly functional programs), but in return, MULTVISION guarantees correct replay for *all* Multilisp programs, not just those written using a certain style.

The essence of MULTVISION's approach is that side-effect operations in trace mode are modified to (1) log a *side-effect event* and (2) store a distinctive *side-effect value* encapsulating the actual value stored by the side-effect operation. No overhead is added to trace-mode memory read operations, but every touch operation[3] executed in trace mode checks to see if its operand is a side-effect value and, if so, logs a *side-effect touch event* and returns the value encapsulated within the side-effect value. (This check adds little cost because every touch operation already has to check its operand's type code, to see if it is a future.) The resulting log contains enough information to provide a completely faithful replay. Since only side effects and touches of the values they store are subjected to trace-mode overhead, tracing of mostly functional programs is efficient; in particular, *no* overhead is added to ordinary memory reads in trace mode, even if the location read is a shared variable on which side effects could be performed. (It is interesting that starting from a mostly functional base may enable construction of a debugging environment that provides services that could never be provided efficiently on a C or FORTRAN base that emphasizes side effects.)

---

[1] Allocation and initialization of a new data object, although it involves writing to memory, does not involve true side effects, since the data object does not become accessible to other tasks until its initialization is complete, and hence no nondeterminism can result from these writes.

[2] In this paper, we informally use "side effect" to mean "true side effect."

[3] See Section 12.2.

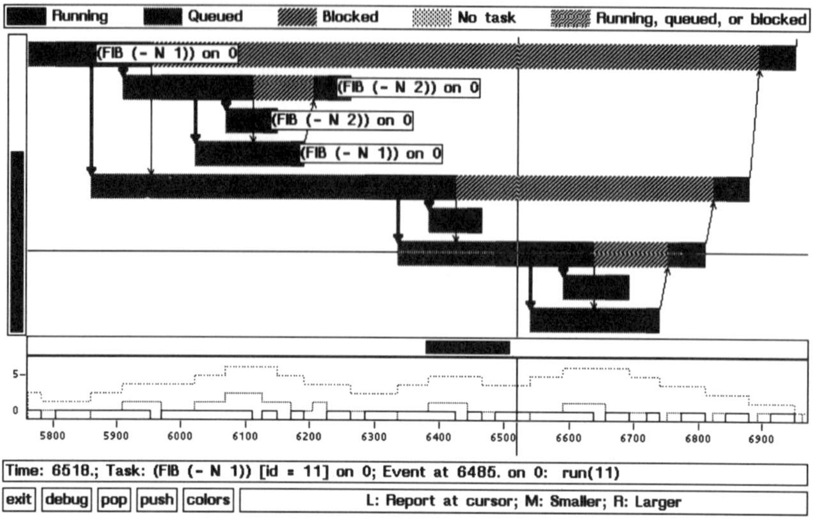

Figure 12.1
The MULTVISION debug monitor's display.

12.1.1 Organization of MULTVISION

The visualization component of MULTVISION has two parts: the *debug monitor* and the *replay engine*. Both parts read the log produced by a trace-mode execution of a program, which contains events recording every instance when a task was created, terminated, began to execute on a processor, or became blocked, in addition to the side-effect and side-effect touch events discussed above. The debug monitor graphically displays the execution of the traced computation and allows the programmer to examine parts of that execution. (See Figure 12.1.) Every logged event contains a *timestamp* derived by reading a real-time microsecond timer, used by the debug monitor to display events in their true temporal sequence.

The replay engine is built into the Mul-T system [14] on which MULTVISION is built and allows any data value generated during the traced execution to be regenerated for inspection. Such inspection is obviously useful when debugging, but can also help in performance visualization by identifying the inputs of specific computations shown in the debug monitor's display.

12.1.2 Overview of the Paper

Section 12.2 introduces relevant Multilisp concepts and Sections 12.3 and 12.4 explain our definition of "replay." Sections 12.5–12.9 explain MULTVISION's log protocol and its implementation. Section 12.10 gives preliminary performance figures, Section 12.11 reviews related work, and Sections 12.12 and 12.13 offer some perspective on the material presented in this paper.

12.2 Multilisp, Futures, and Mul-T

By default, execution of Multilisp programs is sequential (and follows the semantic rules of Scheme [1, 23]). Concurrency is introduced using the `future` construct: if X is a Multilisp expression, (`future` X) is an expression that evaluates X in a separate *task*. Without waiting for that evaluation of X to terminate, the expression (`future` X) returns a *future*—a placeholder that stands for the value that X's evaluation will eventually yield. When evaluation of X yields a value, the future *resolves* to that value, essentially losing its identity as a future and becoming the value of X.

Non-strict operations such as passing a parameter to a procedure, returning a result from a procedure, initializing a data-structure element, or storing into a memory location can use an unresolved future as an operand. However, *strict* operations such as addition and comparison (or any operation that requires information about its operand), if applied to an unresolved future, must block and wait for the future to resolve. (If applied to a resolved future, strict operations simply use the value to which the future resolved.) Hence, a strict operation must check each of its operands to see if it is an unresolved future, and if so the operation must block pending the resolution of the future. This check and possible suspension of execution is known as *touching* the operand. Note that resolving a future does not count as a side effect: a future can only resolve once, and any task requiring the future's value will block until the value is ready, so no nondeterminism can result.

Mul-T [14] is an implementation of Multilisp that was built by extending the Yale T system [22] with an implementation of the `future` construct. In Mul-T, futures are distinguished from all other types of data by giving them a special type tag. All strict built-in operations include code to touch their operands.

Mul-T's optimizing compiler Orbit [15, 16] generates in-line code for many simple built-in operations. The type checks for the associated touch operations are also generated in-line, but if a touched operand is found to be a future, then control is transferred to an out-of-line subroutine to check further whether the future is resolved, and either suspend the current task or return the value to which the future resolved, as appropriate [14].

12.3 Replay

What does it mean to replay an execution of a program? Intuitively, it means to re-execute every operation performed during the original execution, with the same operands. The meaning of "same" here is subtle, however, since objects may have been created and then discarded during the original execution. Such objects must be "re-created" during the replay. These re-created objects should be indistinguishable, for all practical purposes, from the corresponding objects created during the original execution, but they are not identically the same objects.

It is only important to replay the programmer-visible aspects of a computation. In other words, if a traced computation built and manipulated a collection of interreferencing objects, the replay must build and manipulate a corresponding collection of objects, isomorphic to the original, and manipulate them in a corresponding way. But the replay need *not* reproduce the exact structure of task queues and other objects hidden within the implementation, except as required to perform corresponding operations at the programmer-visible level.

A satisfactory formal definition of the correspondence we desire between a traced execution and its replay would not fit in this paper, so we define the correspondence informally here. A correct replay E' of a traced execution E must *correspond to* E by containing a unique operation that is the image of, or *corresponds to*, every (programmer-visible) operation in E. A similar correspondence must exist between the data objects manipulated by E and E'. Corresponding objects must be observationally equivalent (e.g., if one is a number, the other must be the same number) even though, as discussed above, they will not always be the same object. Finally, if a replayed operation I' in E' corresponds to the operation I in E, then the objects on which I' operates must correspond in the obvious way to the operands of I. In this paper, we say "replaying the operation I" to mean, "during replay, performing the operation I' that corresponds to the operation I performed during the traced execution."

12.4 Nondeterminism

No special mechanism is required to replay a deterministic program; it suffices just to execute the program again, stopping at the point where inspection of run-time data values is desired. Thus, a log is needed only for replay of nondeterministic programs. But what does "deterministic" mean in this context? Informally, "deterministic" means that a program always performs the same computation: the meaning of "deterministic" thus turns on what we look at when deciding whether two computations are the "same."

We define "same" in terms of those aspects of the computation classified in Section 12.3 as "programmer-visible." Values of variables and data-structure slots, for example, are considered visible; the numerical value of the free-storage allocation pointer, the contents of physical processor task queues, and timing details not forced by precedence constraints among operations are examples of items that we choose to consider as invisible. We use the term *visible nondeterminism* to refer to nondeterminism in a visible aspect of a computation. A computation without visible nondeterminism might still have "invisible" nondeterminism, for example, in the assignment of tasks to processors for execution, but such nondeterminism is of no consequence to us, since reproducing all visible nondeterministic choices will, by definition, reproduce the programmer-visible aspects of the computation state during replay.

We can now clarify what is "true" about "true side effects": they are writes to memory that have the potential for causing visible nondeterminism. The trace file must record enough information about a traced execution that all visible nondeterministic choices made during the traced execution are made in the same way during replay. Visible nondeterminism can have several sources:

- Write-write conflicts, wherein the value found in a memory location at some point during program execution represents a nondeterministic choice between the values written by several write operations to that location.

- Read-write conflicts, wherein the value obtained by reading a memory location represents a nondeterministic choice between several values written to that location during program execution and possibly a preexisting initial value in that location.
- Input and output conflicts, where input or output operations can be interleaved nondeterministically. These conflicts can be viewed as read-write conflicts on pointers that point to the current positions in input or output streams.

Some inputs result from real-time interaction, where the result of a program operation depends on the time at which it is executed, relative to events in the external world. Examples of this kind of operation include reading a real-time clock and inquiring as to the availability of input on an interactive input stream. MULTVISION does not currently support real-time input operations, but logging the results of such operations would be a natural extension of our approach.

The programs we have focused on while developing MULTVISION are primarily computational, rather than input/output-intensive. Neither input nor output conflicts are significant in these programs, so we have concentrated on write-write and read-write conflicts as the important sources of nondeterminism to log. However, since input and output operations are normally less frequent than side effects, and (usually) are already considerably more expensive than side effects, tracing these operations should not introduce excessive overhead, compared with the overhead of tracing side effects. They could be traced either by viewing them as side effects on a stream pointer, as suggested above, or by other means, such as recording explicitly the data returned by an input operation.

12.5 Log Protocols for MULTVISION

Our major assumptions about our domain of mostly functional programs are

- True side effects are rare.
- Reads from potentially side-effectable locations are frequent, but reads from locations that have actually had true side effects performed

on them are rare. For example, any pair object can have a side effect performed on it using the `set-car!` or `set-cdr!` operations, but typically, few pairs are side-effected in this way. Thus, while `car` and `cdr` operations to read the contents of pairs are usually frequent, few of those operations actually read a value stored as the result of a true side effect.

From these assumptions, and our desire to minimize the overhead introduced while executing in trace mode, we conclude that it is tolerable to write an event to the log every time a true side effect is performed, but it is highly undesirable to have to log an event every time a read is performed. On the other hand, we must log events recording the result of reading locations that have been side-effected, because these read operations may participate in read-write conflicts.

How can we tell whether a side effect has been performed on a location that is being read? We answer this question by giving an example log protocol, the *side-effect read protocol*, that has some of the properties we desire but is not actually the protocol used by MULTVISION. Then we explain the more intricate *side-effect touch protocol*, which is the protocol actually used.

12.6 The Side-Effect Read Protocol

Consider a side-effect operation S that writes a value V into a location L. In trace mode, S writes into L a *side-effect value* that contains V and also contains a unique *version ID* identifying which *version* of L this value is. S also logs a *side-effect event* recording this version ID. Every read operation performed in trace mode checks whether the value read is a side-effect value. If so, a *side-effect read event* is logged, recording the version ID found in this side-effect value.

Every time we replay a side-effect operation S, we must locate the side-effect event that was logged by S. Suppose S wrote a value V into a location L and logged a side-effect event carrying the version ID U. If, during replay, the corresponding side-effect operation S' writes a value V' into a location L', we can infer that V' corresponds to V (and L' also corresponds to L). Furthermore, suppose a logged side-effect read event with the same version ID U was produced by a read operation R that read V from L; the corresponding replayed read operation R' should be a read of L' that yields V'.

Interestingly, it is not necessary to write the actual value V to the log when logging the side-effect event: as long as the replay is carried out faithfully, when the corresponding replayed side-effect operation is executed, its operand V' is guaranteed to correspond to V. Since the same version ID U appears in every event that references V, simply associating V' with U during replay will provide a means to find V' whenever it is needed, without any representation of the value V ever having been written to the log! This association can be recorded in a *version database*, to which information is added every time a side effect is replayed, and which is consulted every time a read operation that logged a side-effect read event is replayed.[4]

The fact that values do not have to be included in logged events has two useful consequences. First, there is a time savings, since Multilisp programs often work with complex, structured values that would be expensive to dump. Second, since the log does not contain actual memory addresses in any form, replay need not use the same heap size or memory configuration as the traced execution.

Thus far, we have glossed over the question of how we decide which logged event (if any) corresponds to a given operation executed during replay. If every instruction in a program were executed at most once, establishing this correspondence would be easy: just include the instruction's address in the logged event, and when replaying an instruction, search for the logged event with the matching address.[5] However, real programs contain structures such as loops and procedure calls, so an instruction may be executed many times with (possibly) different operands. We need to match up the corresponding *instances* of executing each instruction. This can be done by maintaining an *instruction counter* and including its current value in each logged event that is used by the replay engine. The instruction counter need not be incremented for every instruction executed; it need only be incremented frequently

[4] Other replay algorithms for the side-effect read protocol are possible. For example, instead of using a version database, reads and writes to a given location could be forced to occur in timestamp order, using a strategy similar to that of Instant Replay [18, 19]. This approach would be simpler and use less space, possibly at the cost of increased execution time. But since MULTVISION does not actually use the side-effect read protocol, these issues are moot: replay using a version database is introduced here to pave the way for explaining the side-effect touch protocol that MULTVISION actually uses.

[5] This strategy would require that the instruction's address not change between the traced execution and the replay—not necessarily true in MULTVISION.

enough so that no two events logged by the same task can have the same instruction count.

Tasks may execute concurrently and asynchronously. It thus makes sense for each task to have its own instruction counter, initialized at 0 when the task is created. Each logged event then includes a task ID as well as an instruction count, and together they uniquely identify the instruction instance that logged the event. For easy lookup in the log, however, tasks during replay must carry the same ID's as their corresponding tasks did during the traced execution. This means that *task creation events* must also be logged. Each such event indicates the ID given to a newly created task, and every task creation operation during replay must find the matching task creation event in the log and take the new task's ID from that event.

It is worth noting that if every instruction deterministically either generates or does not generate a log entry, then an instruction counter is not needed: each replayed instruction that should match an event can simply take the next logged event. Thus, the fact that a replayed read operation cannot tell (except by consulting the log) whether or not there should be a matching logged event is what makes the instruction counter necessary.

12.7 The Side-Effect Touch Protocol

The side-effect read protocol has the desired property that only true side effects and references to the values that they wrote create log entries. (Task creation also generates log entries, but the MULTVISION debug monitor needs task creation events anyhow, to generate its display.) Thus, a functional program, completely free of side effects, will log no extra events for replay. However, the potential logging of side-effect read events still burdens read operations during trace mode with checking for side-effect values, even if no side-effect read events are actually logged. An alternative, used in MULTVISION, is to defer checking for side-effect values until touch operations. Read operations in trace mode then work exactly as in production mode, but every touch operation has an extra duty: if it finds a side-effect value W as its operand, it logs a *side-effect touch event* recording the version ID found in W, and then returns the data value encapsulated within W. Touch operations that encounter futures still perform the same operations as in production mode.

The informal justification of the side-effect touch protocol is as follows. Visible nondeterminism can arise out of a read operation only when there is a read-write or write-write conflict and one of several values might be returned by the read. However, the only way that a nondeterministically chosen value can cause nondeterminism in the execution of a program is if the program contains an operation that acts differently according to what the value is. Any such operation is strict and hence touches its operands before using them. Therefore, knowing the nondeterministic outcome of the read operation at the time the value is touched is as good (for replay purposes) as knowing it when the value is read.

During tracing, it is possible to have a future that resolves to a side-effect value, a side-effect value that contains a future, or, in fact, an arbitrary chain of futures and side-effect values. A touch operation on such a chain must follow the chain until it finds a value that is neither a future nor a side-effect value. Since such a chain may have more than one side-effect value in it, a single touch operation may generate more than one side-effect touch event. During replay, we need to match logged side-effect touch events correctly with the steps along the touching chain to which they correspond. Therefore, during tracing the instruction counter is incremented once before every touch operation and once for each step down the touched chain: for every time that a touch finds that its operand is a future or a side-effect value and recursively begins another touch, the instruction count is incremented again.

Checking for side-effect values during touch operations rather than read operations is desirable because of the way Mul-T implements side-effect values and touch operations. Side-effect values in Mul-T carry the same basic type tag as futures, but are distinguished from futures by a subsidiary type tag. Thus, when the touched operand is neither a future nor a side-effect value, touch operations in trace mode are no more expensive than in production mode (except for incrementing the instruction counter). When the touched operand is a future, there is the extra cost of distinguishing it from a side-effect value before dispatching to the appropriate handler, but touches of futures happen far less often than reads from memory, making our approach cheaper than generating side-effect read events. Moreover, by the time a touch operation sees that it is handling a future (or side-effect value), control has already been transferred to out-of-line code, while any checking during read operations would either have to be coded in-line (greatly expanding code size) or introduce an out-of-line call for every read operation (seriously reducing performance in trace mode).

12.7.1 Read Values

During replay using the side-effect touch protocol, a read operation needs to return a value that, when touched, will trigger a check for a matching side-effect touch event in the log. We handle this requirement by using *read values*, which (like side-effect values) are "future-like." A touch operation on a read value traps to a special handler that performs the appropriate check in the log. If no matching event is found, then the initial value of the read location (its value at the beginning of the traced execution or when the object containing the location is initially created) should be returned. Consequently, every read value holds this initial value encapsulated within it.

When a location is read, there is no simple way to tell whether the location is ever side-effected. Therefore, every read operation during replay returns a read value, and every readable location conceptually contains the read value that will be returned when that location is read. MULTVISION's way to create the appearance that every readable location contains a read value is to lazily coerce the contents of any location that is read, to make it contain a read value if it doesn't already. A read operation then works as follows: if the read location contains a read value, just return it; otherwise, construct a read value containing the read location's current value, store that read value in the location, and also return it. During replay, new objects are created with read values already in the objects' slots (on the assumption that most slots will eventually be read) but lazy coercion is used to create the needed read values for pre-existing locations.

12.7.2 The Replay Algorithm

A MULTVISION replay begins by creating a version database from the events recorded in the log. Events are first classified by task ID and for each task ID a collection of *version-database entries*, each corresponding to an event logged by that task, is created. Each version-database entry includes the event's instruction count, timestamp, and a pointer to a *version object* that is shared by all version-database entries whose event had the same version ID. Each version object contains

- a *value* field to hold the actual value associated with this version;
- a *location* field to hold the read value found in the location where this version is written; and
- a queue of touchers waiting for this version's value.

These fields are all initially empty.

Every time a touch operation in replay mode finds a read value as an operand, it looks for a version-database entry that matches its task ID and instruction count. If such an entry is found, the touch operation returns the value field of the associated version object; if the value field is empty, the touch operation is suspended and enqueued, awaiting this version's value. If no matching version-database entry is found, the touch operation simply returns the initial value encapsulated in the read value. (When a read value is touched and no matching log entry is found, the instruction count is *not* incremented, since this read-value touch does not correspond to a side-effect-value touch during the traced execution.)

Every replay-mode side-effect operation locates the version-database entry that matches its task ID and instruction count. The value to be written by that side effect is then stored into the associated version object (along with the read value found in the side-effected location) and any touchers awaiting this value are awakened. Interestingly, the side-effected location is not written when operating in replay mode, since any touches of side-effected versions of the location's value are recorded explicitly in the log! Also interesting is the fact that side-effect operations during replay are not required to occur in the same order as during the traced execution. (This reordering of side effects is permissible because each use of a value stored by a side effect indicates explicitly which version is used.) In fact, the ordering constraints on replay are so loose that it need not even use the same number of processors as were used in tracing. This fact can be exploited either to speed replay by using more processors or to reduce replay's impact on other system users by using fewer processors.

Side-effect events in the log do not identify the side-effected locations, yet accurate replay is still possible because the task ID and instruction count that are recorded establish the correspondence between the side-effect operations performed in trace mode and those performed in replay mode. However, it is convenient, while debugging, to be able to inquire about the current value of a location after a partial replay. For this purpose, it is useful to be able to identify the side-effect event, for a given location, having the largest timestamp less than the time of interest. Since a side-effect event in the log does not identify the side-effected location, the identity of that location must be recorded when the side-effect operation is replayed. This is done by having each side-effect operation fill the location field of its associated version with a pointer to the read value (lazily created if necessary) found in the side-effected location. Then the side-effect events pertaining to a location L can be found by searching the version database for entries that point to a version whose location field matches the read value found in L. When read values are used in this way, it is important to create only one read value for each location, so that the read values in two version objects are equal if and only if they are versions of the same location. (This imposes some synchronization constraints on the operation of lazily coercing a location's contents to a read value during replay.)

12.8 Partial Replay

MulTVision has two procedures for performing a partial replay. `(replay-to-time` *time*`)` replays a prefix of the traced execution containing all events whose timestamp field is less than *time* and no events whose timestamp field is greater or equal. Thus, every task that finished executing before *time* will be replayed in its entirety; every other task will be replayed up to the instruction that matches the first event logged by that task with a timestamp greater than *time*. Conceptually, every replay begins at the initial state of the computation; however, if a replay has just been performed to a time T and a replay to a time $T' > T$ is then desired, `(continue-replay` T'`)` will start with the already available state at time T and only replay the portion of the computation from T to T'.

The intent of `replay-to-time` is to reproduce the situation as it existed at the time specified. Creating that situation exactly will not be possible, since some tasks will have no event at *time* and such tasks will have progressed all the way to their next logged event, but `replay-to-time` does ensure that all side effects occurring before *time*, and only those side effects, will be replayed.

`replay-to-time` is useful for determining the state of mutable data structures at a particular time. It can also be used to examine the state of any task at the point where an event was logged: just replay up to that event's timestamp and then use the Mul-T debugger to look around. However, it is sometimes useful to step through a task's history in more detail, so we also plan to provide `(replay-to-instruction` *taskID icount*`)`, which allows a particular task to be replayed to the precisely defined point where its instruction count was incremented to *icount*, allowing inspection of the task's local, immutable variables (e.g., stack frames) that might be deallocated before the next event logged by the task.

One approach to implementing `(replay-to-instruction` *taskID icount*`)` first estimates a time T by interpolating between the timestamps of the two events in *taskID* that bracket *icount*. Then, a minor variant of `(replay-to-time` T`)` is performed, in which all tasks other than *taskID* are replayed to time T, but *taskID* itself is replayed only up to its last event preceding T. Then *taskID* is stepped carefully until its instruction count reaches *icount*. (This will require some modification of the replay-mode code sequence for incrementing the instruction count.)

When examining a computation state generated by a partial replay, determining the correct value to attribute to read values is a major problem. If a read value R is found in a heap memory location, the version database must be searched for versions that have R in their location field. The value to attribute to R is the value found in the version created by the side-effect event with the most recent timestamp. A read value found elsewhere—for example, in a register, stack frame, or even in the value field of a version-database version—presents more of a problem. Such a read value represents a value that has been read but not yet touched. If the location in which the read value originated is in fact subject to side effects, we cannot tell which version of the location's value this read value represents until the read value is touched and we can see the associated side-effect touch event.

If after a replay to time T the version database contains no versions referencing a given read value R, then it is safe to assume that the location from which R came has not been side-effected before time T. It is then safe to assume that R stands for its own initial value anywhere it is found. This observation will help in some situations; a more aggressive solution would be to implement a "protocol converter" replay mode that reads a side-effect touch log and yields a side-effect read log, which could then be replayed without the problems of interpreting read values. We have been waiting until we can assess the magnitude of these problems in a practical setting before exploring this option, but it is clear that such a protocol converter could be implemented.

12.9 Structure of Compiled Code

The Mul-T compiler was modified to produce three different versions of object code for production-, trace-, and replay-mode execution. These versions differ, as described above, in the code sequences generated for a side effect, a touch, or a read from a potentially side-effectable location. The task creation code also has three different versions—in trace mode, the task ID of the created task is written to the log; during replay, this task ID is looked up and used as the task ID of the created task. For an operation (such as a touch) that has little to do in some cases but much to do in others, the generated code checks for the simple case and handles it in-line, but calls an out-of-line subroutine if a complex case is detected. Operations such as trace-mode or replay-mode side effects, whose handling is always complex, are coded simply as a call to an out-of-line subroutine.

Precompiled library procedures such as `length` and `print` present an interesting code management problem. Most such procedures perform touches, memory reads, or even side effects and thus need to be compiled differently for trace- and replay-mode execution. Whenever a program calls a library procedure, it must call the version compiled for the program's current execution mode.

We solve this problem using the *locale* feature [22] of the T system on which Mul-T is built. We create three locales, one for each execution mode. Each compiled version of a program is loaded into the locale corresponding to its execution mode. The library procedures compiled for each execution mode are bound to their names in the corresponding locale and thus are called only when that execution mode is active.

12.10 Performance

Since the initial implementation of MULTVISION's replay engine has only recently become functional, performance figures presented here are necessarily preliminary. MULTVISION's value as a debugging and tuning tool will not be clear until it has been used on some real Multilisp application programs, and correctable deficiencies in MULTVISION exposed by that experience have been corrected. Nevertheless, some basic data about MULTVISION's performance when executing primitive Multilisp operations are presented in Table 12.1. For each of four simple expressions, this table gives the execution time in production mode ("Prod. exec."), trace mode ("Trace exec."), and replay mode ("Replay exec."), and finally the number of log bytes generated by the expression ("Log bytes"). All times were measured on our Encore Multimax[6] multiprocessor, with 30 MHz NS32532 processors. (All times are averages over several executions.)

The first expression in Table 12.1 is `(touch (future 0))`, which serves as a basic benchmark of task management performance: it requires one task creation, one touch operation, one task suspension, one resolution of a future, and one reawakening of a suspended task. The 78 bytes of log data for this expression include one task creation event and several other events used by the debug monitor but not by the replay engine. The expression `(set-car! x 0)`, where `x` is bound to a pair, is a benchmark of side-effect performance. The cost of side-effect touches is gauged by evaluating the expression `(touch (car x))` for the case where the `car` of the pair bound to `x` has been side-effected and for the case where it has not.

We can see from line 1 of Table 12.1 that the tracing overhead for creating a future is less than a factor of 2. (It is lower still in the common case where the future resolves before being touched.) A touch operation that does not discover a side effect also suffers tracing overhead (for incrementing the instruction counter) of about a factor of 2, so the total tracing overhead for a side-effect-free program will be at most about a factor of 2—less, to the extent that the program emphasizes operations other than task creation and touches. The tracing overhead for side effects is a factor of about 100, so a program densely populated with side effects will slow down dramatically when traced, but a program that averages one side effect or less per future (a reasonable standard for what it means to be mostly functional) will incur a tracing overhead for side effects that is a small fraction of the overhead already present for task

[6] Multimax is a trademark of Encore Computer Corporation.

Expression	Prod. exec.	Trace exec.	Replay exec.	Log bytes
1. `(touch (future 0))`	100	170	146	78
2. `(set-car! x 0)`	0.27	22	26	18
3. `(touch (car x))`, side effect	1.0	15	18	18
4. `(touch (car x))`, no side eff.	1.0	2.3	9	0

Table 12.1
Preliminary MULTVISION performance measurements (times in microseconds)

Benchmark	Tasks created	Side effects	Side-eff. touches
1. `(ffib 18)`	4180	0	0
2. `(ffib! 18)`	4180	12,540	8360
3. `(queens 8)`	2056	0	0
4. `(seq-union 50)`	1	0	0
5. `(par-union 50)`	51	0	0

Table 12.2
Characteristics of MULTVISION benchmark programs

Bench-mark	Proc-essors	Prod. exec.	Trace		Replay		Log bytes
			exec.	dump	load	exec.	
1.	1	0.50	0.79	0.66	13.1	0.69	326,123
2.	1	0.56	1.27	1.48	29.6	1.45	702,324
3.	1	0.55	0.72	0.50	6.4	1.41	160,562
	8	0.07	0.10	0.53	6.4	0.19	159,000
4.	1	2.68	2.79	0.10	0.04	4.63	251
	8	2.70	2.75	0.16	0.04	4.78	279
5.	1	2.70	2.77	0.15	0.23	4.63	4151
	8	0.42	0.43	0.14	0.16	0.70	3001

Table 12.3
Preliminary MULTVISION performance measurements (times in seconds)

creation. Finally, replay execution time is generally longer than trace-mode execution time, but the difference in most cases is not dramatic.

The times to dump a log to disk, and to read in a log and build a version database, are greater than the trace-mode and replay-mode execution times, but are difficult to measure precisely. The time to dump a log is governed by file-system bandwidth, which in our experience varied over a range of 100–500 kilobytes per second. Fortunately, although the time to dump the log is considerably larger than the tracing overhead itself, it does not distort the timing of the traced execution. In the current MulTVision implementation, the time to read a log is even longer and is dominated by the computing time used to build the version database; however, no attention has yet been paid to optimizing this process and we expect that major performance improvements are possible here. In any case, since the events logged for each task are sorted into a list in order of their timestamps, the time to read and process an individual logged event depends on the number of other events arising from the same task. Happily, the log need not be reloaded before each replay—a given execution may be replayed over and over again without reloading the log.

MulTVision's performance for some actual programs is shown in Tables 12.2 and 12.3. Table 12.2 gives some characteristics of the test programs used. ("Tasks created" counts the number of tasks created. "Side effects" and "Side-eff. touches" count the number of side-effect and side-effect touch events, respectively.) Table 12.3 contains some new column labels not seen in Table 12.1: "Trace dump" and "Replay load" give the times to dump the log file to disk, and read the log to build a version database, respectively. These columns give some idea of the log dumping and loading costs in practice.

`ffib` is the familiar doubly-recursive program for computing Fibonacci numbers, written to create one task for each pair of recursive calls. It is given here as an example of a program that creates tasks of very fine granularity. `ffib!` is a version of `ffib` modified to use side effects in storing temporary results. The performance of `ffib!` shows the effect of incorporating modest numbers of side effects into a program. `queens` solves the familiar 8-queens problem. It creates and discards list structure actively, and thus illustrates the performance of a program that emphasizes heap-allocation and use of data structures in a functional style. `seq-union` and `par-union` are sequential and parallel versions, respectively, of a set-union program, written to have a very large task granularity. These programs do relatively little allocation from the heap, but access heap-allocated data structures quite intensively. Their performance during replay thus illustrates the cost of using and managing read values.

For benchmarks 3–5, the performance of both 1- and 8-processor executions is shown. We see that neither tracing nor replay reduces the ratio between 1-processor and 8-processor execution times. Moreover, measurements not reported in Table 12.3 show that if a program has usable parallelism, its replay can be speeded up by using many processors even if the original traced execution used fewer: for example, even the trace generated by running `(queens 8)` on one processor still takes only 0.19 seconds to replay on eight processors.

Statistics such as those in Table 12.3 can never "prove" anything. However, we are encouraged that for all of these programs, the trace-mode and replay-mode execution times are less than 3 times the production-mode execution time.

12.11 Related Work

Both MULTVISION's trace-file format and its debug monitor evolved from the ParVis system [2]. ParVis did not have a replay engine (though the idea of incorporating one is mentioned in [2]), but other researchers have developed systems for replay of parallel programs. These other replay projects can be classified first by the type of interprocess communication they were designed for: either message-passing or shared-memory.

BugNet [5], Radar [17], and Schiffenbauer's debugger [24] are three systems for replay in message-passing environments. All work by logging interprocess messages and can replay a process by feeding it its logged input messages. Groups of processes can be replayed in a similar manner. In this approach, the log contains the actual data values communicated between processes, so its size is proportional to the actual volume of information communicated.

MULTVISION belongs in the shared-memory category. Previous work on replay of shared-memory parallel programs includes P-sequences [4], Instant Replay [18, 19], and PPD [20]. PPD divides programs into *E-blocks* and writes *prelogs* and *postlogs* containing the values of selected variables when entering and exiting E-blocks. Compile-time analysis selects the variables to include in prelogs and postlogs and identifies shared variables that require more frequent logging. Thus PPD, like BugNet and Radar, records actual data values in a log. Since shared-memory architectures enable quite high rates of communication between processors, PPD's logs can quickly get quite large. On the other hand, the mass of information recorded in the prelogs and postlogs makes it possible to answer most questions without performing a full replay from the beginning of the log, an advantage for interactive use. Any use of pointers that expands the set of variables that may be accessed in an E-block will cause major problems for PPD's approach.

P-sequences and Instant Replay share MULTVISION's approach of logging ordering information rather than actual data values. For Instant Replay, a program is viewed as operating on a set of objects whose history can be viewed as a sequence of *versions*. Every version is created by a *write* operation on an object; *read* operations retrieve data that is version-dependent, but do not change the object they are applied to. The Instant Replay log indicates the sequence of accesses to, and creation of, object versions. Replay is guided by this log so that each object's versions are created in the same order, and each read operation reads the same version, as in the original execution. The implementor of the basic object operations (who may also be the application programmer) is responsible for ensuring that they are implemented correctly (they must be linearizable) and that they handle the log entries properly; otherwise, replay may be performed incorrectly. P-sequences are essentially a specialization of this approach to the case where all synchronization is performed using semaphores.

By logging only ordering information, rather than actual data values, P-sequences and Instant Replay achieve significant reductions in log size and concomitant reductions in the cost of writing and then reading the log. The price of this optimization is that answering questions about a computation's intermediate data values requires replaying the computation from the beginning. Recap [21] is a system that takes periodic checkpoints and also records a log: a replay to reach a given state can start from the most recent checkpoint instead of from the beginning, and hence can take less time. (Other systems that use checkpoints to optimize replay, but don't focus on parallel computing, include [25] and [26].)

MultVision's approach is closest to that of P-sequences and Instant Replay, but MultVision differs from them in that it does not require programs to adhere to special disciplines to ensure accurate replay.

12.12 Discussion

While the soundness of MultVision's replay algorithm is clear, the biggest unanswered questions concern the size of the program executions to which MultVision can be applied effectively. Three factors may limit this size:

- Version-database size. Currently, the entire version database is built before replay begins, consuming storage proportional to the total number of task-creation, side-effect, and side-effect touch events in the log. This storage remains allocated for the entire duration of the replay; if it exceeds 10–20 megabytes in size, it will begin to seriously strain physical memory resources. If version-database size proves to be a bottleneck, we will need to explore strategies for incrementally creating the version database as replay progresses and already-used portions of the version database can be deallocated and recycled.
- Trace-file size. A mostly functional 16-processor execution that takes 20 seconds in production mode and has moderate task granularity might create 1,000,000 tasks and generate 100 megabytes of trace data. Since file systems are usually larger than physical memory, trace-file size looks like a weaker constraint than version-database size, but it clearly imposes a limit—finding a file system with room for a 100-megabyte trace file is often difficult!
- Debug-monitor performance. While this paper is not about the debug monitor, it is currently far more expensive for the debug monitor to load a trace file for display than it is for the replay engine to build its version database from the same trace file. There is little point in worrying about the replay engine's performance on a trace that is too expensive to use with the debug monitor; thus, the debug monitor will probably be the first target of optimization efforts.

While the limitations listed above are significant, MultVision is already valuable, even at the current performance level. Not all computations of interest can be performed on the scale of thousands of tasks to which the current MultVision implementation is generally limited, but quite elaborate computations can be performed on that scale—more than elaborate enough to benefit from the detailed investigation that MULTVISION allows. Moreover, many computations that take much longer than that can be scaled down to smaller problem instances with analogous properties. Investigation of these smaller problem instances using MULTVISION can yield useful insights about the behavior of the larger computations. From our past experiences with Multilisp, we have questions about several problems of this kind that MULTVISION is already a powerful enough tool to answer.

To expand MULTVISION's range further, we can take the following steps:

- Careful performance measurement and tuning of the MULTVISION implementation.
- Preprocessing of the log to produce checkpoints or other useful information to accelerate replay, such as a side-effect read log or preformatted version database.
- Improving the debug monitor's record-keeping. If the debug monitor carefully records all interaction with the replay engine, the user may be able to answer a question about a previously visited state without performing another replay to revisit it: the answer may be found in the record of previous interaction with that state.

It would also be desirable to expand the set of programs that we can classify as mostly functional and apply MULTVISION to. A significant gap in the current paradigm affects programs that use arrays. Typically, Mul-T programs allocate arrays in an uninitialized state. Array initialization is then performed using side effects, generating a large number of side-effect events even if the array is used in a completely deterministic way (e.g., no other task sees it until initialization is complete). One solution to this problem is to introduce explicitly functional language constructs, such as the *array comprehensions* of Haskell [13], to use when creating arrays in a functional way. A more ambitious alternative is to develop compile-time analysis techniques that can identify these kinds of side effects as not being true side effects and therefore not requiring special treatment during tracing or replay.

A final question concerns ensuring that a replay starts with the same initial conditions as a traced execution. If the initial conditions are different, the replay obviously risks being inaccurate. This problem is exacerbated by the interactive nature of Lisp programming environments: a C program, for example, always begins execution with its data memory in a given state, but Lisp programs execute in a "workspace" where variable bindings may have been created or changed interactively before a traced execution. Automatically reproducing such interactive inputs before replay looks infeasible in the general case, but simple tricks may help a lot in real life. For example, when a side effect is performed during tracing and the value overwritten is not a side-effect value, the value overwritten could be recorded somewhere in memory; if a replay is then performed during the same Mul-T invocation, the recorded initial value can be used. However, if replays are performed days later, there is no obvious option other than warning the programmer about the dangers of using the wrong initial conditions and advising either the taking of careful notes or specification of all relevant initial state in the Multilisp program source file where it is unlikely to be forgotten.

12.13 Conclusion

Our basic objective was to develop a replay mechanism for Multilisp programs that would produce correct results for *any* program and would add minimal tracing overhead to mostly functional programs. Both the side-effect read and side-effect touch protocols satisfy the correctness requirement, provided only that the user establishes the proper initial state before attempting a replay. Notably, neither protocol requires programs to observe any stylistic restrictions or be amenable to compile-time analysis to enable accurate replay. The side-effect touch protocol also satisfies the trace-mode performance requirement by adding no overhead to reads and little overhead to touches, the two most common operations in mostly functional programs. This protocol and a replay algorithm for it have both been implemented in the MULTVISION system and their performance for simple applications has been measured. This performance is good enough to be immediately useful, although (as with all replay schemes) better performance would add significant further value.

Plans for further development of MULTVISION must strike a balance between two goals: (1) efficiently handling larger and more varied program executions and (2) improving the visualization tools that can be applied to the program executions that are already handled efficiently. Most of the ideas in Section 12.12 are aimed at the former goal, but now we must accumulate enough experience with MULTVISION and substantial Multilisp programs to see whether ease of visualization or speed of tracing and replay is the most important next area for improvement.

Acknowledgments

We are grateful to Patrick Sobalvarro for his help in building the debug monitor and to Rick Mohr for helpful comments on this manuscript. Support for this research project was provided by Digital Equipment Corporation and by DARPA under contract number N00014-87-K-0825.

References

[1] Abelson, H., and G.J. Sussman with J. Sussman, *Structure and Interpretation of Computer Programs*, MIT Press, Cambridge, 1985.

[2] Bagnall, L., *ParVis: A Program Visualization Tool for Multilisp*, S.M. thesis, MIT E.E.C.S. Dept., Cambridge, Mass., Feb. 1989.

[3] Baker, H., and C. Hewitt, "The Incremental Garbage Collection of Processes," M.I.T. Artificial Intelligence Laboratory Memo 454, Cambridge, Mass., Dec. 1977.

[4] Carver, R., and K.-C. Tai, "Reproducible Testing of Concurrent Programs Based on Shared Variables," *6th Int'l. Conf. on Distributed Computing Systems*, May 1986, pp. 428–433.

[5] Curtis, R., and L. Wittie, "BugNet: A Debugging System for Parallel Programming Environments," *3rd Int'l. Conf. on Distributed Computing Systems*, Oct. 1982, pp. 394–399.

[6] Gabriel, R.P., and J. McCarthy, "Queue-based Multi-processing Lisp," *1984 ACM Symp. on Lisp and Functional Programming*, Austin, Tex., Aug. 1984, pp. 25–44.

[7] Goldman, R., and R.P. Gabriel, "Preliminary Results with the Initial Implementation of Qlisp," *1988 ACM Symp. on Lisp and Functional Programming*, Snowbird, Utah, July 1988, pp. 143–152.

[8] Goldman, R., R. Gabriel, and C. Sexton, "Qlisp: An Interim Report," *Parallel Lisp: Languages and Systems (Lecture Notes in Computer Science 441)*, (Proc. US/Japan Workshop on Parallel Lisp), Springer-Verlag, Berlin, 1990, pp. 161–181.

[9] Halstead, R., "Multilisp: A Language for Concurrent Symbolic Computation," *ACM Trans. on Prog. Languages and Systems 7:4*, October 1985, pp. 501–538.

[10] Halstead, R., "Parallel Symbolic Computing," *IEEE Computer 19:8*, August 1986, pp. 35–43.

[11] Halstead, R., "An Assessment of Multilisp: Lessons from Experience," *Int'l. J. of Parallel Programming 15:6*, Dec. 1986, pp. 459–501.

[12] Halstead, R., "New Ideas in Parallel Lisp: Language Design, Implementation, and Programming Tools," *Parallel Lisp: Languages and Systems (Lecture Notes in Computer Science 441)*, (Proc. US/Japan Workshop on Parallel Lisp), Springer-Verlag, Berlin, 1990, pp. 2–57.

[13] Hudak, P., P. Wadler, et al., *Report on the Programming Language Haskell*, version 1.0, April 1990.

[14] Kranz, D., R. Halstead, and E. Mohr, "Mul-T, A High-Performance Parallel Lisp", *ACM SIGPLAN '89 Conf. on Programming Language Design and Implementation*, Portland, OR, June 1989, pp. 81–90.

[15] Kranz, D., R. Kelsey, J. Rees, P. Hudak, J. Philbin, and N. Adams, "Orbit: An Optimizing Compiler for Scheme," *Proc. SIGPLAN '86 Symp. on Compiler Construction*, June 1986, pp. 219–233.

[16] Kranz, D., *ORBIT: An Optimizing Compiler for Scheme*, Yale University Technical Report YALEU/DCS/RR-632, February 1988.

[17] LeBlanc, R., and A. Robbins, "Event-Driven Monitoring of Distributed Programs," *5th Int'l. Conf. on Distributed Computing Systems*, May 1985, pp. 515–522.

[18] LeBlanc, T., and J. Mellor-Crummey, "Debugging Parallel Programs with Instant Replay," *IEEE Trans. Computers C-36:4*, April 1987, pp. 471–482.

[19] Mellor-Crummey, J., *Debugging and Analysis of Large-Scale Parallel Programs*, Technical Report 312, University of Rochester Computer Science Dept., Sept. 1989.

[20] Miller, B., and J.-D. Choi, "A Mechanism for Efficient Debugging of Parallel Programs," *ACM SIGPLAN '88 Conf. on Programming Language Design and Implementation*, Atlanta, June 1988, pp. 135–144.

[21] Pan, D., and M. Linton, "Supporting Reverse Execution for Parallel Programs," *Workshop on Parallel and Distributed Debugging (SIGPLAN Notices 24:1, January 1989)*, May 1988, pp. 124–129.

[22] Rees, J., N. Adams, and J. Meehan, *The T Manual*, fifth edition (pre-beta draft), Yale University Computer Science Department, October 1988.

[23] Rees, J., and W. Clinger, eds., "Revised^3 Report on the Algorithmic Language Scheme," *ACM SIGPLAN Notices 21:12*, Dec. 1986, pp. 37–79.

[24] Schiffenbauer, R., *Interactive Debugging in a Distributed Computational Environment*, M.I.T. Laboratory for Computer Science Technical Report TR-264, Cambridge, Mass., Sept. 1981.

[25] Tolmach, A., and A. Appel, "Debugging Standard ML Without Reverse Engineering," *1990 ACM Symp. on Lisp and Functional Programming*, Nice, France, June 1990, pp. 1–12.

[26] Wilson, P., and T. Moher, "Demonic Memory for Process Histories," *ACM SIGPLAN '89 Conf. on Programming Language Design and Implementation*, Portland, OR, June 1989, pp. 330–343.

13 Abstracting Data-Representation and Partitioning-Scheduling in Parallel Programs

Gail A. Alverson and David Notkin

Efficient parallel programs must make appropriate data-representation and partitioning-scheduling decisions. Many programs intertwine these decisions with the code that describes the program's basic algorithm. Abstracting these decisions separates them from the basic algorithm and makes them easier to change. The separation makes it easier to experiment with other, potentially more efficient, decisions. In addition, the separation makes it easier to port programs while retaining efficiency. In this paper, we show how to abstract data-representation and partitioning-scheduling decisions with little or no performance penalty. Our domain is UMA and NUMA shared memory multiprocessors, with a focus on explicitly parallel interval and dynamic tree algorithms. Our prototype system and applications are written in C++.

13.1 Introduction

Efficient parallel programs must use representations of data structures that limit memory contention and minimize the cost of memory references. They must also use partitioning-scheduling policies for parallel work that balance load while limiting overhead costs. Because overhead costs can include the cost of memory latency, ideal partitioning-scheduling policies and data representations are not independent.

Many explicitly parallel programs intertwine statements concerning data-representation and partitioning-scheduling with statements implementing the program's basic algorithm. An example of this interleaving is shown in Figure 13.1. In general, the intertwined approach makes it difficult to determine if a source statement is part of the basic algorithm, the data-representation, or the partitioning-scheduling scheme. In other words, the approach can obscure a program's true function.

Lack of clarity leads to three related problems. First, even basic maintenance (and understanding) of the program becomes more difficult, because it is hard to change (or understand) a single aspect in isolation. Second, it is hard to improve performance on a given architecture, because this typically requires experimentation with data-representation and partitioning-scheduling schemes, and these aspects may be confusingly interleaved. Third, porting programs to other architectures often causes either a significant loss of efficiency or a significant added development cost, because different data-representation and partitioning-

This function, for use on a Butterfly multiprocessor, is called in parallel to execute the inner loop of a matrix multiply algorithm. a and c are global, distributed matrices whose elements are stored in row major order. b is a global, distributed matrix whose elements are stored in column major order. Given row and column identifiers, the function computes c[row,column] by calculating the dot product of a[row,*] and b[column,*]. btransfer is a high speed block copy operation supported by the Butterfly hardware.

```
int * * a, * * b, * * c;
int rows_a, cols_a, rows_b, cols_b;

void multiply(int row, int col)
{
  int i, sum, *rra, *rrb;
  int transa, transb;

  // ensure data is in local (fast) memory
  if (Where_Is(a[row]) != Proc_Node){
    rra = (int *) malloc (cols_a * sizeof(int));
    btransfer(a[row], rra, cols_a*sizeof(int));
    transa=1; }
  else {
    rra = a[row];
    transa=0; }
  if(Where_Is(b[col]) != Proc_Node){
    rrb = (int *) malloc (cols_b * sizeof(int));
    btransfer(b[col], rrb, cols_b*sizeof(int));
    transb=1; }
  else {
    rrb = b[col];
    transb=0; }

  // multiply
  for (i=0; i<cols_b; i++)
    sum += rra[i] * rrb[i];
  c[row][col] = sum;

  // release temporary storage if necessary
  if (transb) free(rrb);
  if (transa) free(rra);
}
```

The intertwining of data-representation and partitioning-scheduling decisions is visible in the statements that cache the topic row and column in local memory (knowledge of data-representation) and the operation of the function on a single row and column (knowledge of partitioning size).

Figure 13.1
Inner Loop of a Matrix Multiply Program

scheduling schemes may be necessary for high performance on different architectures.

Thus, to ease maintenance, experimentation, and porting of parallel programs, it is important to find abstractions for data-representation and partitioning-scheduling that isolate these decisions from the basic algorithms. The challenge, however, is to ensure that the performance of programs written using these abstractions is not significantly compromised. Our work addresses this challenge in the context of explicitly parallel shared memory programs that execute on the class of uniform memory and non-uniform memory access time (UMA and NUMA) shared memory multiprocessors.[1] In addition, we have to date limited ourselves to two large classes of algorithms: interval algorithms, which are frequently used by the scientific community to solve numerical problems and which employ iterative and array-based techniques; and tree algorithms, such as branch-and-bound, $\alpha\beta$ search, and divide-and-conquer algorithms that occur frequently in nonnumeric computing. This architectural and algorithmic domain is diverse yet allows results to be practically as well as theoretically realized.

Section 13.2 introduces our view of data-representation and partitioning-scheduling, including their effects on performance. Section 13.3 describes how we abstract these two operations in our programming model. Section 13.4 concretely illustrates the strengths of the abstractions. Section 13.5 puts our work in perspective with other work in the area. Section 13.6 draws several overall conclusions from the research.

13.2 The Basic Activities

Data-Representation. Layout and distribution characterize the data-representation (d-r) of a data structure. Both can significantly affect a parallel program's performance.

Layout specifies how the elements in a data structure correspond to their positions in memory. For example, a matrix can be laid out in row or column major form, or even in blocks or diagonals. To best exploit cache prefetching, software caching, and compiler address optimizations,

[1] In Section 13.5 we discuss our choice of context, comparing it to other approaches such as the implicitly parallel programming style of parallelizing compilers.

the layout of a data structure should match the application's access pattern of the structure.

Distribution specifies how a data structures' elements are allocated amongst the memory modules of a multiprocessor. For example, a structure can be spread across several modules, it can be replicated in each module, or it can be stored entirely in one memory module. Distribution is critical for machines with distributed shared memory, since the cost of accessing a certain memory module can vary significantly among processors. Distribution in these machines generally affects the contention for, and the cost of remote accesses to, data.

Figure 13.2 shows a sample of the effects of data-representation on performance [6]. The experiment repeatedly timed a matrix multiply program (ab=c) on a Sequent Symmetry 81 and on a BBN Butterfly GP1000, modifying only the code managing the data-representations. In the program, processors multiplied a sequence of rows by a single column, in parallel. The programs were applied to dense matrices of size (200 x 400) and (400 x 300). The Sequent, a UMA machine, is configured with 20 Intel 80386 processors. Each processor has a 64 Kbyte cache; the write strategy is copy-back. All processors access a 32 Mbyte memory through a shared bus. The Butterfly, a NUMA machine, is configured with 32 processing nodes connected by an omega interconnection network. Each Butterfly node contains a MC68020 processor, 4 Mbytes of shared memory, and a node controller.

Our experiences with d-r are not isolated. Scientific programmers, for example, often transpose their matrices to better match access patterns and layout. Many languages and systems for nonshared memory multiprocessors include support for distributed structures [3, 5, 7, 12]. Other empirical studies, by comparing the performance of programs whose data structures have different implementations, have also demonstrated the importance of locality of reference and of reduction of memory contention on performance [8, 13].

Dynamic Partitioning-Scheduling. Partitioning-scheduling (p-s) is best described in terms of our program execution model. A program consists of a set of tasks, where a parallel task is composed of units that can be processed in parallel. When a task is to be executed it is placed in a work pool. Each processor runs a single process called a worker. Workers repeatedly select and execute tasks from the pool.

Butterfly (using 25 processors)

a layout/ distribution	b layout/ distribution	c layout/ distribution	cache row (col) ptrs	cache topic row (col) data	speedup
row/contig	row/contig	row/contig	–	–	2
row/distr	row/distr	row/distr	a,b,c	–	8
row/distr	row/distr	row/distr	a,b,c	a	12.5
row/distr	col/distr	row/distr	a,b,c	a,b	14.5

Sequent (using 16 processors)

a layout	b layout	c layout	speedup
row	row	row	15.5
row	col	row	16.3

On the Butterfly, program data was stored only in the memory modules of participating processors. Speedups were calculated as the elapsed time of a sequential matrix multiply program divided by the elapsed time of the parallel program. The column "cache row ptrs" refers to a scheme in which a copy of the pointer array to the rows of a matrix was stored in local memory of each processor. The copies reduced contention for the contiguous pointer array. The superlinear speedup on the Sequent was due a high cache hit rate, assisted by the layout decisions.

Figure 13.2
The Effect of Data-Representation on the Performance of a Matrix Multiply Program

Several workers may simultaneously operate on a given parallel task. A worker coordinates its activities with other workers by invoking a task's self-directing p-s policy. The policy guides the worker in choosing the size and identity of the task unit to execute next. For simplicity, we often call a worker executing a p-s policy a partitioning-scheduler.

One facet of p-s is the dynamic partitioning of parallel tasks, where the granularity at which a task is executed can be determined by the run-time environment. By granularity, we mean the time a worker spends executing work before synchronizing for more work. If granularity is too fine, a worker's synchronization overhead can dominate execution time. If granularity is too coarse, load balancing can be compromised: several workers may be idle while others operate on large final task units. Moreover, if granularity is fixed for the entire execution of a task or program, the execution cannot be responsive to changes in the number of active workers and the amount of pending work — which may harm performance.

The other facet of p-s is dynamic work choice. A worker can minimize its execution time by selecting a task or task unit wisely. For example, to increase the amount of work available and minimize starvation, units generating more work can be processed before terminating units.

There is a natural connection between the partitioning and scheduling activities. We demonstrate this by example in the next section.

Interaction between d-r and p-s. The d-r and p-s activities are often related, especially on distributed shared memory multiprocessors. Two common approaches, data-directed scheduling and software caching, are employed to alleviate the cost of a processor accessing remote data.

Using data-directed scheduling, whenever possible a worker chooses task units whose data are locally resident. Because local data are faster to access, the worker can complete these units more quickly than it can complete units whose data are remote. Knowledge of the data associated with each task, along with the location of that data (the data-representation), is necessary to determine which workers prefer which task units.

When the data of a task are located in several memory modules, or when no pending task has data local to the worker, data-directed scheduling is not sufficient for reducing all remote memory reference costs. To augment data-directed scheduling, a worker can, under certain conditions, use software caching techniques to make a local copy of the remote data on which it operates. Specifically, software caching must be safe and worthwhile.

Caching is safe if making a copy of the data does not jeopardize the correctness of the program. For example, data that are only read are always safe to cache.

Caching is worthwhile if it would provide overall performance improvement. In other words, the cost of copying and accessing the cached data must be compared to the cost of accessing the data remotely. On the Butterfly, for example, it is often more efficient to copy remote data into local memory and then access it there. Because the block transfer operation of the Butterfly is fast, time savings can result even when the data are accessed only once.

As Figure 13.1 illustrated, code for software caching is often interleaved in the algorithmic code of the program. We want abstractions that allow us to remove these tailoring details from the main program, leaving the logical function of the program clear. Encapsulating the caching statements in the p-s achieves this goal. Additionally, the encapsulation: enables the granularity of caching to be influenced by the semantics of the p-s policy; enables the data-directed schedule to influence the presence or absence of caching; and collects performance related functions—functions whose most efficient implementation may differ between targets—together. To determine whether caching is useful, and how to make a local copy of a structure, the p-s routine must have knowledge of the location and structure (the representation) of the data it will potentially cache.

13.3 Abstracting the Activities

Our programming model, Chameleon, defines how the activities of data-representation and partitioning-scheduling can be abstracted from a program while sacrificing little or no performance. In general, an abstraction is defined by an interface, which is a set of functions through which the abstraction can be accessed. An implementation is the realization of an interface. Our approach heavily exploits the ability of one interface to be independently realized by multiple implementations. At a high level, then, a program in our model consists of a source component and a library component that interact through a set of abstract interfaces.

The source component references abstract entities—in particular, data structures and ps-policies—while the library component references concrete entities—specific data representations and partitioning-scheduling implementations. The rest of this section outlines our model, using the interval algorithm domain for clarity.

We have defined four categories of abstractions. Tasks and chores abstract the basic parallel computation of a program, while data structures and ps-policies abstract activities critical to parallel performance. Since our prototype is written in C++, our descriptions of the abstractions have an object-oriented flavor.

Data Structures. A Chameleon program must allocate and access each of its data structures through a fixed interface to that structure. The interface separates the logical data structure from its physical representation in memory. Consequently, a program interacts with a logical entity that is less complex than its tuned physical representation, and the physical representation can change without affecting the rest of the program.

There are a variety of ways in which a representation can be chosen for, or bound to, an abstract data structure. One approach is for the programmer to state a binding in the source program. The advantage of the static choice is that the choice is explicit in the program text, and the programmer can consciously experiment with different representations. The disadvantage is that the program must be recompiled and relinked when the binding is changed. Another approach is for every data abstraction to include a routine to select a representation. Run-time values, such as the size of the structure, can then influence the representation chosen. As an example of the latter, on a distributed memory machine a replicated representation could be chosen for a small read-only array, yet a distributed representation chosen for a large read-only array. The advantage of the dynamic choice is that there is added flexibility at run-time. The disadvantage is the run-time cost of selecting the representation.

We use the dynamic approach but without precluding a variant of the static approach. To permit different representations for different abstract arrays of a program, and to permit the dynamic selection of a representation, two objects are used to represent an array: an interface object and a representation object. When a source program creates an array through a call to an abstract array constructor, an object representing an interface to that array is created.

If the constructor is passed a representation identifier, it then binds a representation object of that type. Although our current prototype does not support it because of limitations of the compiler, these statically selected bindings could occur at compile-time. Logically, this option is equivalent to the static approach above.

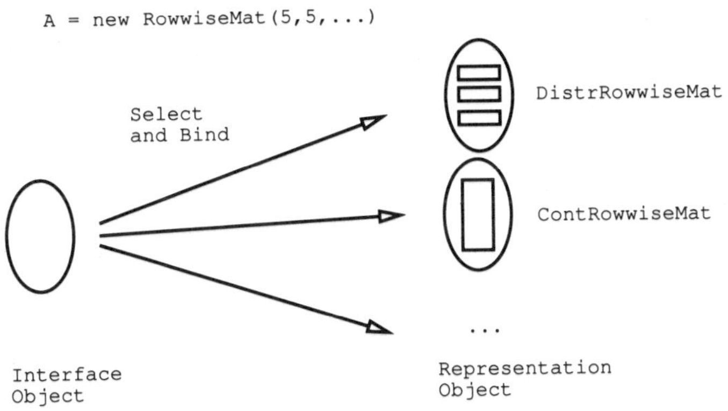

Figure 13.3
Data Interface – Representation Binding Process

If the constructor is to dynamically select a representation, it then invokes the select method provided by the array abstraction. This method selects and binds a representation object [Figure 13.3] using information provided to the abstract array constructor, as well as information about the memory hierarchy of the target machine. Information provided to the constructor includes the size, frequency, and access type of the array.

With both static and dynamic selections, subsequent calls made by the program to the methods of the interface object are handled as calls to the methods of the representation object. The critical point is that the source program interacts with the array only through the interface object. Thus, the representation object can change without affecting the source.

All together then, an abstract array has a constructor that binds a representation object either directly or by invoking a select method, a destructor that releases the memory first of the bound representation and then of itself, and access operators that reference the associated access operators of the representation object. A representation has a constructor that allocates the array's memory in a particular layout and distribution, a destructor that releases this memory, and access operators (associated with those of the abstract array) that access the memory structure.

Chores. Encapsulating the partitioning-scheduling activity requires several abstractions. To allow the ps-policy to control the program's granularity, parallel work must be dynamically decomposable. The chore is the Chameleon abstraction that describes a dynamically sizable unit of computation. The task, as we will soon detail, specifies the bounds over which a particular chore is to be applied; thus, a task specifies a decomposable composite of parallel work.

The principal component of a chore is its work procedure, which defines a sequence of instructions to be executed sequentially. A work procedure has parameters that control its length of execution. Hence, by calling the work procedure with different actual parameters, partitioning-schedulers (workers executing ps-policies) can vary the granularity at which the program is run. A work procedure, for example, might contain a loop and be parameterized by the bounds of the loop.

Because of the interaction between work procedures and ps-policies, the parameter list of a work procedure must conform to a signature known to the ps-policy. The signature of this simple loop example, for instance, could be

```
(Vector* vec, int start, int stop, int globalstart),
```

where start and stop indicate the interval of vec to be operated on by the procedure. The globalstart integer denotes the global name of the start index. This value is necessary since, as we will soon explain, the start and stop indices may refer to a cached object, yet the name of the original section is needed by the computation.

Tasks. A Chameleon task describes parallel work. Specifically, it is a decomposable composite of work that can be executed in parallel at various granularities and according to a preferred schedule of execution.

When a task is created it binds to itself a ps-policy object instantiated with task-specific information. This information includes a chore (the task work descriptor) and the bounds over which the chore is to operate (the task scope). On activation of the task, each cooperating worker independently executes the partition routine of the ps-policy object. This routine directs workers in the partitioning and scheduling of the task's parallel work.

A task contains a constructor, an activate method, and a synchronize method.

The constructor creates a task, creates an associated ps-policy object, and associates the ps-policy object with the task. When the ps-policy object is predefined, the constructor need only create the task and bind the provided ps-policy. As an example, a task describing an interval algorithm is constructed by passing the constructor either: (1) a chore, the endpoints of the interval(s) to be partitioned, data objects corresponding to the partitioning intervals, and a partitioning-scheduling keyword used to identify the ps-policy of choice; or (2) a ps-policy object instantiated with this information. To change the ps-policy used to execute a task in the former case, the keyword is modified; to make the change in the latter case, a new ps-policy object is supplied.

The activate method of the task starts its asynchronous execution. The method places the task in the system workpool for workers to find and execute. For synchronous execution of a task, the activate call can be immediately followed by a call to synchronize. synchronize completes when the work of the task is complete.

PS-Policy. The function of a ps-policy is to guide workers in their parallel execution of a task. A ps-policy provides several key methods.

The constructor of a ps-policy object instantiates the object with its task-specific information. For interval algorithms, this information includes a chore, the endpoints of the interval(s) to be partitioned, and the data objects corresponding to the partitioning intervals.

The partition method is called by workers to self-direct their scheduling and partitioning of the work composite. Specifically, it defines the parameters with which the workers invoke the chore work procedure. Because the workers synchronize on the common synchronization data included in the ps-policy object, workers do not interfere with the work that another has claimed. The outermost loop of the partition method is shown in Figure 13.4.

To manage the granularity of a task's execution, the ps-policy includes a method determinechunk that identifies a partition size. When a task is

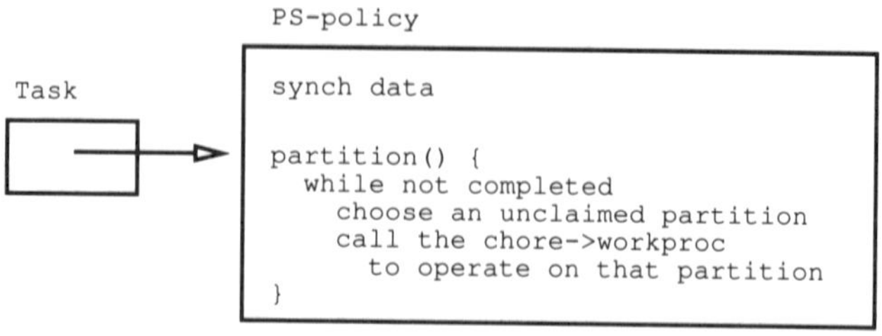

Figure 13.4
Task and PS-Policy Objects

to be executed with fixed granularity, this method is called in the partition routine only once. For variable granularity, it is called each time a worker synchronizes. To make its granularity decision, determinechunk can refer to values such as the size of the initial interval, the amount of pending work, the number of active workers, and the overheads of the target. Consequently, the granularity at which a program is executed can be easily modified by changing the determinechunk method for a given policy.

Interacting Aspects of the Implementations. To assist with data-directed scheduling on NUMA machines, the ps-policy includes a preferred method. The method identifies, for each worker, a set of work that will maximize its local and minimize its remote memory references. The work sets are disjoint and include all possible work of the task. Together, they serve as a list of pending work that is updated by workers as they execute. Because workers can prefer to take large portions of preferred work but small portions of nonpreferred work, the partitioning and scheduling activities are connected.

Since a source program interacts with the ps-policy only through its constructor, it is straightforward to change the ps-policy used to execute a task.

Data-directed scheduling requires knowledge of how the data structures of a task are represented in memory. Each abstract data structure thus includes a method, mirrored in each representation object, that returns a description of its location. When a ps-policy object is created, its preferred method is executed to develop the worker preference

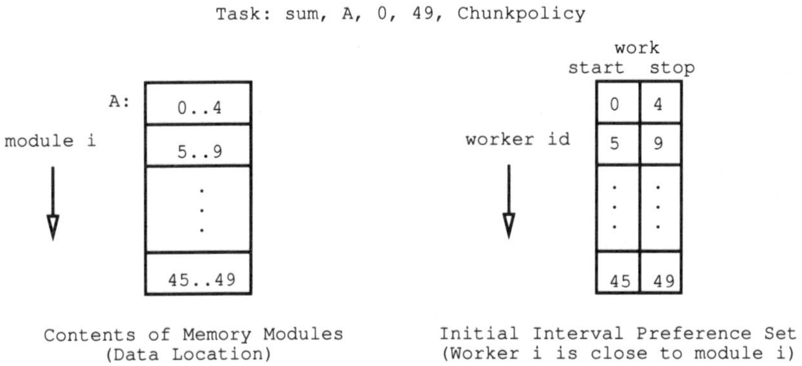

The task is to sum the elements of an array A of 50 integers. The target is a distributed memory machine where memory module i is local (closest to) worker i.
Let A have a distributed representation as illustrated by the left side of the figure. On the basis of this representation (discovered by querying a method of the array), the preferred routine of ps-policy ChunkPolicy creates the preferred work sets shown on the right side of the figure. A worker will be guided to operate first on the interval defined in its preferred set. In this simple case, the interval directly corresponds to the data segment local to the worker.

Figure 13.5
Sample Construction of Preferred Work Sets

sets. The method queries the tasks' data structures about their location and uses this information in its development. The preferred method must, of course, execute quickly. Consequently, the preference methods we have developed refer only to the distribution information associated with those data structures passed in the task/ps-policy constructor—those objects that correspond to a partitioning interval. Figure 13.5 outlines the construction of the preferred sets for a simple interval task.

Notably, although the operation of data-directed scheduling requires that the implementations of the d-r and p-s abstractions cooperate, the abstractions themselves are independent (from the point of view of the source program).

Software caching of the work procedure parameters can also be encapsulated in the ps-policy. Consider the general signature of a interval work procedure operating on one interval:

(Object* array, int start, int stop, int glstart).

Essentially, the partitioning-scheduler first operates on its preferred (local) work, passing pointers to the uncached object as an argument. It then operates on non-preferred (remote) work. The partitioning-scheduler caches the remote data and passes a pointer to the cached object as an argument. Note that the work procedure, the code of the source program, need not be aware of whether its formal parameters are original or cached objects [Figure 13.6].

To foster independence between the d-r and p-s decisions, each abstract data structure (and the associated representation) includes a method to clone a full or partial copy of itself in the local memory of the caller. This method can be used by partitioning-schedulers to construct the cached object. The method is defined to succeed only if caching is safe and worthwhile. If the method fails, the original object is used by the partitioning-scheduler.

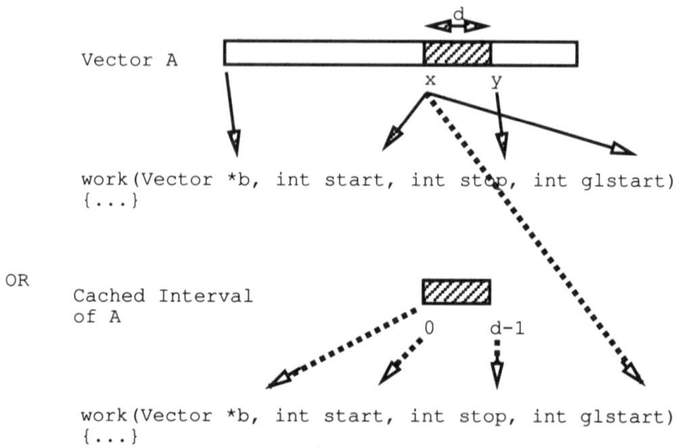

The upper diagram illustrates an invocation of the chore work procedure with an actual data object. The lower diagram illustrates an invocation with a cached object. Because caching statements are encapsulated in, and directed by, the ps-policy, the source program is unaware as to whether it is operating on an actual or cached object. Moreover, the function of the program is unobscured by these tailoring details.

Figure 13.6
Possible Work Procedure Parameter Bindings

13.4 Strengths of the Model

This section outlines the strengths of the Chameleon model. Specifically, we demonstrate how Chameleon programs foster lower development costs, experimentation, and efficient, as well as portable, performance.

```
void
multiply(RowwiseMatrix *mata, int rstart, int rend, int glrs,
        ColwiseMatrix *matb, int cstart, int cend, int glcs)
{
  int row, col, grow, gcol, i, sum, rowsb;

  rowsb = matb→rows();
  for (row=rstart, grow=glrs; row≤rend; row++, grow++)
    for (col=cstart, gcol=glcs; col≤cend; col++, gcol++){
      sum=0;
      for (i=0; i<rowsb; i++)
        sum += mata→ref(row,i) * matb→ref(i,col);
      c→ref(grow,gcol)=sum;
    }
}
```

The method `ref(int i, int j)` references the element in logical row `i` and column `j` of the matrix.

Figure 13.7
Inner Loop of a Chameleon Matrix Multiply Program

Maintenance. Collecting the tailored partitioning-scheduling and data-representation statements in the library component of a program clarifies the function of the source component. Consequently, the maintenance programmer can more easily determine the purpose of the program (readability is eased), debug the algorithmic operation of the program (correctness debugging is eased), and modify the capabilities of the program (evolution is eased).

Figure 13.7 displays the work procedure of a matrix multiply program written in the Chameleon model for execution on the Sequent, Butterfly, and potentially other shared memory multiprocessors. In contrast to

Figure 13.1, the d-r and p-s dependent statements are abstracted from the source and are collected in the program's library component. Although the function of the code is more complex than Figure 13.1—this procedure is parameterized for variable grain execution—the purpose of the code is clearer.

Software Reuse. Reuse decreases development costs by reducing the amount of new software that must be written. Because similar functions are often performed in distinct applications, as well as within a single application, the potential for reuse appears in practice.

Due to the encapsulation of the d-r and p-s activities, sets of data structure and ps-policy abstractions can be built and structured as hierarchical libraries. The hierarchies aid in both the organization and extension of the set of available activities, which in turn increases reuse. Figures 13.8 and 13.9 display segments of our prototype libraries.

Because library ps-policy routines are general and have no knowledge of the chore work procedures on which they are to operate, characteristics of the procedure must be expressly specified and accessible. For this purpose, a chore can include several values characterizing its procedure. A chore's unit cost, for example, estimates how large a work procedure's partition must be for its execution time to exceed its overhead. Consequently through the chore's interface (and not its work procedure implementation) all ps-policies have access to information about the chore's work. This information can be used to execute the program more efficiently.

Experimentation. The abstractions isolate performance critical decisions. The identification of these decisions, together with their independence from the rest of the code, eases both performance debugging and experimentation.

Performance debugging, locating and recoding bottlenecks, is eased because the abstractions identify two critical activities that affect performance. Isolation of these implementations enables the functions to be directly tailored and easily monitored. Moreover, specific methods used to determine grain size, preference sets, and to select data distribution, further ease performance tuning.

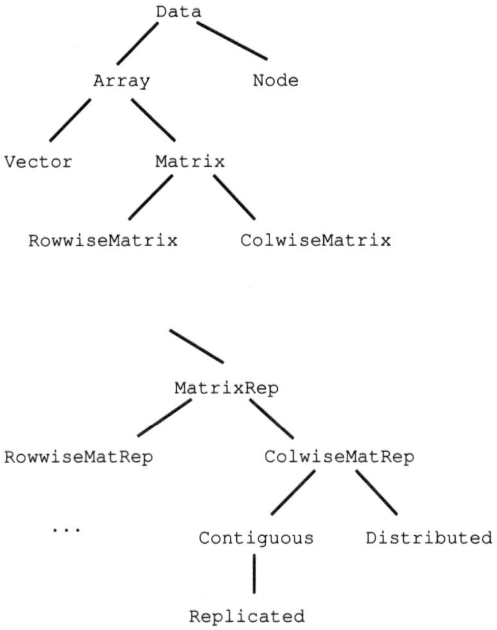

Figure 13.8
Partial Hierarchies of Data Interfaces (upper) and Representations (lower)

Experimentation is enhanced because the source program, being written in terms of interfaces, is unaffected by changes in implementations.

Performance. We developed a set of interval and tree applications in the Chameleon model. To take advantage of software reuse and to fully test our isolation of the implementations from the source, we built, and our programs used, libraries of data and ps-policy representations. Figure 13.10 displays the performance of four of these applications on the Sequent.

Three applications are interval algorithms. The first, matrix multiply, computes the product C of two matrixes A and B. We applied the programs to dense matrices of size (200 x 400) and (400 x 300). This straightforward computation is interesting because it is a component of many numerical applications and has the potential to speed up linearly in the number of processors. The second application takes two n x n matrices, A and Q, and computes the congruence transformation C of A, which is defined as $C=QAQ^T$. This computation is often a component of larger numerical applications and can be executed in two phases: one, calculate $B=QA^T$; two, calculate $C=QB^T$. The programs were applied to two (500 x 500) dense matrices. The third application, Gaussian elimination, is a technique for solving a set of linear equations. To solve Ax=b using Gaussian elimination without pivoting, A is put in upper triangular form with b reflecting the reduction operations. x is found by backsubstitution. The Gaussian elimination programs were applied to a set of 500 linear equations, and the triangulization phase was timed.

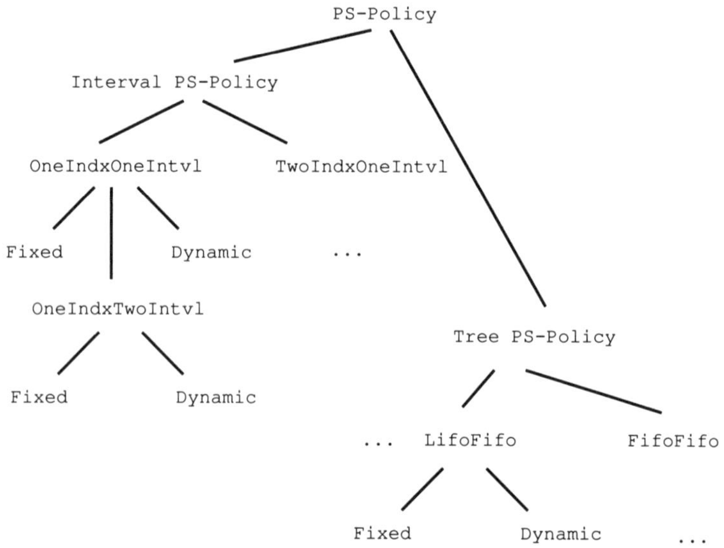

As these hierarchies illustrate, different ps-policies can be most suitable for different algorithms and algorithm classes. Tree algorithms, for example, can be executed according to fixed or dynamic height or depth cutoff (partitioning). They can be explored in a breadth or depth first manner (scheduling). Similarly, interval algorithms can operate on one or more objects of different dimensions (index ranges). The dimensions can be partitioned in different ways and using different policies.

Figure 13.9
Partial Hierarchy of Interval PS-Policy Interfaces

Application	Version	Sequential (msec)	1	2	4	8	16
Matrix	Chameleon	108000	1	1.99	4.00	8.10	16.21
Multiply	Fine-Tuned	110000	1.0	1.99	3.98	8.17	16.34
Congruence	Chameleon	1273792	1.0	2.01	4.01	8.03	16.01
Transformation	Fine-Tuned	1282324	1.0	2.0	4.0	8.02	16.02
Gaussian	Chameleon	169901	0.99	1.97	3.91	7.64	14.44
Elimination	Fine-Tuned	169721	1.0	1.99	3.99	7.94	14.64
Adaptive	Chameleon	30600	0.89	1.7	3.33	6.49	11.5
Quadrature	Fine-Tuned	30599	0.92	1.76	3.45	6.67	11.7

To limit the effect of any operating system/hardware changes between the timings of each program, the sequential program was timed with each timing run.

Figure 13.10
Speedups on the Sequent

The fourth application is a tree algorithm that approximates the integral of a function using the adaptive quadrature method with Simpson's rule.[2] Nodes represent regions to integrate. If the approximation of a region is outside a specified tolerance, the region is divided into two smaller regions (child nodes) for future approximation. If the approximation is within the tolerance, the approximation is posted, possibly recursively, in the parent node. The programs were invoked to approximate the integral of a trigonometric function.

The results of the application set reminded us that abstraction, particularly at a fine grain, is not free. To limit the amount of indirection induced by the abstract array interfaces, in several cases a method of an array was called to return a reference to one of its rows/columns. The reference was then used to index the rest of the elements in that row/column. Until compiler technology can minimize the cost, the impact of abstracting small frequently called operations, such as array ref-

[2] As an aside, the parameter list signature of a tree work procedure has the general form: `(Node* topnode, Task* envelop, int depth)`. The depth parameter controls the procedure's length of execution. Essentially, a partitioning-scheduler invokes the procedure with a node, a task, and a depth value. The invocation expands the node to a tree of the given depth, and returns any remaining nodes to the enveloping task. The ps-policies of the prototype are based on per-worker work lists of pending nodes. A worker first processes nodes of its own list before processing nodes of others. Returned nodes are placed on the worker's own list.

erences, cannot be ignored. The source code must unfortunately reflect this limitation to some degree.

We evaluated performance by comparing speedups of Chameleon programs on the Sequent to speedups of unabstracted (fine-tuned) Sequent programs. The fine-tuned programs were written in C++ and call the Sequent parallel programming library[10] for their parallel functions.[3] Summarizing the results of Figure 13.10, programs of the Chameleon model performed within 1% of fine-tuned programs, in the worst case. Performance was minimally, if at all, compromised.

Effective Portability. Another advantage of abstracting the d-r and p-s activities is that it makes it easier to port a program to another multiprocessor without significant loss of efficiency. We call this effective portability [1]. The most efficient implementation of a d-s or p-s policy on one multiprocessor may not be the most efficient on another. By writing the source program in terms of interfaces to these activities, the source program can port with no or minimal modification between machines. By changing the implementations of abstractions used in the program to those most effective for the current target, high performance on each target can be achieved.

Figure 13.11 illustrates the performance of our sample set of programs on the Butterfly. The "Chameleon" entry refers to the same Chameleon source programs that were used on the Sequent, where the interfaces are now matched with most effective Butterfly implementations. The "Ported (Sqnt)" program illustrates the Chameleon source programs with the Sequent implementations. Clearly, selecting the more appropriate implementations for the d-r and p-s activities significantly aids performance. The "Fine-tuned" entry provides an upper bound on performance. These unabstracted programs were written in C++ and call the Uniform System [16] for their parallel functions.

Overall, the Chameleon programs perform, in the worst case, within 10% of the fine-tuned Butterfly programs.

[3] Because we wrote both Chameleon and fine-tuned codes, tailoring statements in the programs could contain common information. The performance difference shows in the least, however, the overhead of the Chameleon abstractions.

Application	Version	Sqtl (msec)	1	2	4	8	14	20
Matrix Multiply	Ported (Sqnt)	118000	1	0.78	0.93	1.02	0.10	.83
	Chameleon	118000	1	1.16	2.72	5.72	11.22	14.42
	Fine-Tuned	127000	1	1.42	3.29	6.85	13.32	15.99
Congruence Transform	Ported (Sqnt)	1232863	1.0	0.90	0.93	0.95	0.87	0.75
	Chameleon	1232744	1.0	1.16	2.73	6.08	12.14	17.43
	Fine-Tuned	1336611	1.0	2.0	4.0	7.85	13.41	18.85
Gaussian Elimination	Ported (Sqnt)	224041	0.98	0.74	0.93	0.87	0.80	0.74
	Chameleon	224049	0.95	1.51	2.73	4.90	7.93	10.54
	Fine-Tuned	223897	0.98	1.54	2.79	5.01	8.16	10.93
Adaptive Quadrature	Ported (Sqnt)	152567	0.55	0.64	0.96	1.58	2.70	3.55
	Chameleon	152629	0.55	1.07	2.1	4.15	7.12	9.74
	Fine-Tuned	152731	0.57	1.11	2.18	4.32	7.42	10.19

To limit the effect of any operating system or hardware changes between the timings of each program, the sequential program was timed with each timing run. These times are shown in the "Sqtl" column. The sequential adaptive quadrature program performs so much faster than the parallel version on one processor because of the Butterfly memory allocators. Private memory (sequential version) is faster to dynamically allocate than shared memory (parallel versions).

Figure 13.11
Speedups on the Butterfly

13.5 Related Work

Parallelizing compilers [3, 11, 14, 17] typically restructure sequential programs into parallel form, offering some of the same advantages as Chameleon. They are responsible for identifying, partitioning, and scheduling the parallel tasks of a program. Maintenance is fostered because the source program, a sequential program, is clear of parallel and tailoring activities. Efficiency is achieved if the compiler can adequately detect and manage the parallelism implicit in the program. (Current compilers are fairly successful on regular, loop structured numerical algorithms.) Effective portability, in addition, requires the compiler to adapt its management to the current multiprocessor target. Because d-r and p-s policies are generally encoded in the compiler, it may be difficult for a programmer to experiment with different policies as easily as in Chameleon. Also in contrast to parallelizing compilers, our focus is on supporting explicitly parallel parallel programs. Explicit parallelism can force the programmer to think of parallel solutions that sometimes can be qualitatively better than their parallelized sequential counterparts [2, 15]. Certain classes of algorithms, including the tree algorithms in which we are interested, currently appear to be more successfully parallelized by hand.

Parallel languages for shared memory parallel programming are related to a system built using the Chameleon structure. Both provide abstractions to express and execute explicitly parallel programs. The Argonne tools [9], for example, are a set of constructs (macros) for portable parallel programming. The constructs hide operating system specific functions, such as locks, process creation, and monitors, from the source program. Unlike Chameleon, the tools do not include abstractions for data structures. System implementations of the constructs also tend not to address the memory hierarchy of the target. Another parallel language example is Linda [4], a system developed at Yale. To some degree, data-representation is abstracted in Linda through its virtual shared memory, the tuple space. To foster effective portability, the system represents its tuple space differently on different targets. The implementation can cause elements of the space to be distributed and/or replicated. The tuple space can support more general memory management, such as data migration, than can Chameleon. However, unlike

Chameleon, the granularity of data distribution is based on tuple size and thus controlled by the source program.

There is a large body of other work in parallel systems, much of which touches on some aspect of our work. However, our goals of clarity in the source program, along with the resulting benefits, are generally distinct.

13.6 Conclusion

In this work we have not developed new data-representation or partitioning-scheduling schemes. Rather, we have generalized from existing schemes to identify abstractions that allow us to increase the flexibility with which we can manipulate and use parallel programs. In our context—UMA machines (specifically, the Sequent) and NUMA machines (specifically, the Butterfly), and interval and tree algorithms—we have met two challenges. First, we have discovered and designed appropriate abstractions that can be realized by existing data-representation and partitioning-scheduling schemes. Second, we have designed these abstractions so that little performance is sacrificed. A more detailed presentation of this work is available separately [1].

Acknowledgements. The authors would like to thank Robert Alverson and the ISSMM reviewers for their useful comments on earlier drafts of this paper. The research was supported in part by a Natural Sciences and Engineering Research Council of Canada scholarship, in part by NSF grants CCR-8619663 and CCR-8858804, and in part by the Advanced Systems Lab, Boeing Computer Services.

References

[1] G. Alverson. *Abstractions for Effectively Portable Parallel Programs.* PhD dissertation, Department of Computer Science and Engineering, University of Washington, 1990.

[2] R. Anderson. An experimental study of parallel merge sort. Technical report, Department of Computer Science, University of Washington, December 1988.

[3] D. Callahan and K. Kennedy. Compiling programs for distributed-memory multiprocessors. *The Journal of Supercomputing*, October, 1988.

[4] D. Gelernter. Generative communication in Linda. *ACM Transactions on Programming Languages and Systems,* January, 1985.

[5] W. Griswold, G. Harrison (Alverson), D. Notkin, and L. Snyder. Scalable abstractions for parallel programming. In *Proceedings of the 5th Distributed Memory Computing Conference*, Charleston, South Carolina, April, 1990.

[6] G. Harrison (Alverson) and D. Notkin. Effective parallel portability. Technical Report 89-09-08, Department of Computer Science and Engineering, University of Washington, 1989.

[7] C. Koelbel, P. Mehrotra, J. VanRosendale. Supporting shared data structures on distributed memory architectures. In *Proceedings of the ACM/SIGPLAN Symposium on Principles and Practice of Parallel Programming*, Seattle, Washington, March, 1990.

[8] T. LeBlanc, M. Scott, and C. Brown. Large-scale parallel programming: Experience with the BBN Butterfly parallel processor. In *Proceedings of PPEALS, ACM Symposium on Parallel Programming*, New Haven, Connecticut, July, 1988.

[9] E. Lusk, J. Boyle, R. Butler, T. Disz, B. Glickfeld, R. Overbeek, J. Patterson, and R. Stevens. *Portable Programs for Parallel Processors.* Rinehart and Winston, Inc., New York, NY, 1987.

[10] A. Osterhaug. *Guide to Parallel Programming.* Sequent Computer Systems, Inc., Beaverton, Oregon, second edition, 1987.

[11] C. Polychronopoulos. *Parallel Programming and Compilers.* Kluwer Academic Publishers, Norwell, Massachusetts, 1988.

[12] M. Rosin, R. Schnabel, and R. Weaver. Dino: Summary and examples. Technical Report CU-CS-386-88, University of Colorado, March, 1988.

[13] J. Saltz, V. Naik, and D. Nicol. Reduction of the effects of the communication delays in scientific algorithms on message passing MIMD architectures. In *SIAM Journal Sci. Statist. Computing*, January, 1987.

[14] V. Sarkar. PTRAN — the IBM parallel translation system. Technical Report RC-70566, IBM Research Division, T.J. Watson Research Center, May, 1990.

[15] L. Snyder. Type architectures, shared memory, and the corollary of modest potential. In *Annual Review of Computer Science*, 1986.

[16] R. Thomas, and W. Crowther. The uniform system: An approach to runtime support for large scale shared memory parallel processors. In *Proceedings of the International Conference on Parallel Processing*, St. Charles, Illinois, August, 1988.

[17] M. Wolfe. *Optimizing Supercompilers for Supercomputers.* Pitman Publishing, 1989.

IV SCALABLE SHARED MEMORY MULTIPROCESSOR

14 Latency Tolerance through Multithreading in Large-Scale Multiprocessors

Kiyoshi Kurihara, David Chaiken, and Anant Agarwal

In large-scale distributed-memory multiprocessors, remote memory accesses suffer significant latencies. Caches help alleviate the memory latency problem by maintaining local copies of frequently used data. However, they cannot eliminate the latency caused by first-time references and invalidations needed to enforce cache coherence. Multithreaded processors tolerate such latencies by rapidly switching between threads when they encounter cache misses. This paper evaluates the effectiveness of multithreading in Alewife, a scalable multiprocessor that is being developed at MIT. For the applications used in this study, multithreading results in a modest 20% improvement in execution time on a 64-processor machine. The impact of multithreading is expected to be far more significant in larger machines, when remote memory latency becomes a dominant term in the performance equation.

14.1 Introduction

Long communication latencies impose limits on the performance attainable by large-scale multiprocessors. As Figure 14.1 illustrates, processor utilization diminishes when the time a processor spends waiting for responses to remote memory requests is wasted. Idling on remote memory requests wastes not only processor resources but also the bandwidth of the processor interconnection network. When processors remain idle for large periods of time, they do not sustain request rates that fully utilize the available network capacity. Unfortunately, the proportion of time wasted by processors not only increases as machines get larger, but also grows as advances in technology increase the mismatch between the speeds of processors and the speeds of memory and communications components.

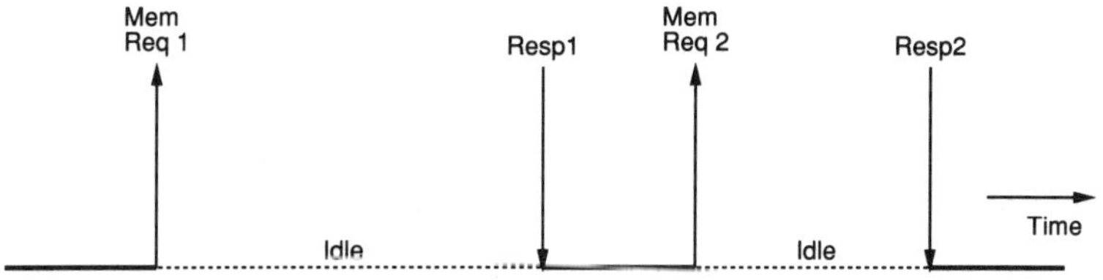

Figure 14.1
The Long Latency Problem.

Processor utilization can be improved if a processor that would otherwise have to wait for a pending memory or synchronization request can rapidly switch between threads of control, thereby performing useful computation. This strategy attempts to hide the latency of interprocessor communication by allowing multiple outstanding transactions per processor. While previous architectures have implemented multithreading with cycle-by-cycle interleaving of instructions from different processes [11, 12, 16, 21] (termed *fine* multithreading), we use the same name for systems that interleave blocks of instructions from different processes as well [3, 23] (termed *coarse* or *block* multithreading).

Block multithreaded processors do not force a context switch every cycle and can achieve high single-thread performance. They switch between threads only on long-latency memory requests or synchronization attempts. We are using such a block multithreaded processor architecture [3] in the Alewife design. Alewife is a large-scale multiprocessor being implemented at MIT; it is described in more detail in the next section. Sparcle, the initial implementation of Alewife's processor, supports multithreading by providing four register sets that hold the state of four threads of control.

Multithreading has several negative side-effects, including increased cache miss rates and higher network contention. In addition, multithreading requires the applications running on a system to provide enough parallelism to sustain several contexts per processor. Performance gains due to hiding communication latency must be traded off against the requirements of a multithreaded system. Our evaluation methodology includes these negative effects while measuring the performance of block-multithreaded processors.

Using multiprocessor simulations, we compare the performance of a system with multithreaded processors to the performance of a system with standard processors. In terms of the speed-up over a single processor system, we find that a 64-processor multithreaded system performs about 20% better than a system with no mechanisms for tolerating communication latency. By presenting an analysis of the cost of various types of memory transactions, we show that the benefits of block multithreading outweigh the negative side-effects of the technique. We conclude that multithreading will provide even higher performance gains in larger systems that suffer from higher interprocessor communication latencies.

The rest of this paper is organized as follows. Section 14.2 describes the features of Alewife that are relevant to the study of latency tolerance. Section 14.3 analyzes the problem of communication latency in large-scale multiprocessors and discusses how multithreading can be used to solve the problem. Section 14.4 presents our simulation methodology, and Section 14.5 evaluates the simulated performance of Alewife's multithreaded architecture. Section 14.6 draws conclusions from our simulations and analysis.

14.2 The Alewife Architecture

The Alewife group at MIT is designing and implementing a large-scale multiprocessor that uses multiple contexts for latency tolerance. The machine, as depicted in Figure 14.2, is designed to be physically scalable. The system consists of a set of processing nodes that are connected by a two-dimensional mesh network. This type of network is scalable, because the network bandwidth grows with the number of processors and because the interconnection wire lengths do not depend on the number of nodes in the system. Each node consists of a network router, a Sparcle processor, a floating-point unit, a cache, a cache-memory controller, and a portion of globally-shared memory. The shared memory is distributed to the processing nodes so that the system does not suffer from the bandwidth bottleneck of a single, monolithic memory.

Alewife's cache controllers synthesize a globally shared memory address space. It uses a directory-based cache coherence scheme called the LimitLESS protocol [7], which realizes the performance of full-map directory protocols [5, 22], with the memory overhead of a limited directory protocol [4]. The directory used by the cache coherence protocol is also distributed to the processing nodes.

Latency tolerance in Alewife is part of a layered approach to automatic management of multiprocessor communication locality. Several components in the Alewife system cooperate in automatic minimization of latency. Hardware-managed distributed caches significantly reduce the frequency of remote communications by automatically copying frequently used data locally. The software run-time system allows process and data partitioning, placement, and migration for improving locality. When the system can not avoid a remote memory request and is forced to incur the latency of the interprocessor communication net-

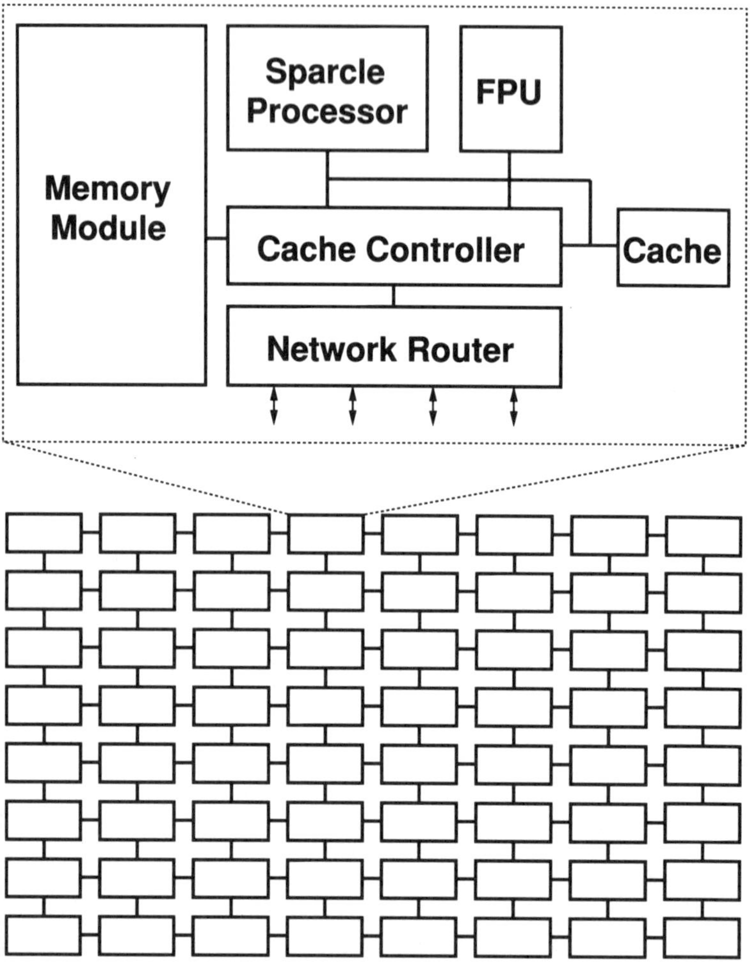

Figure 14.2
The Structure of the Alewife System.

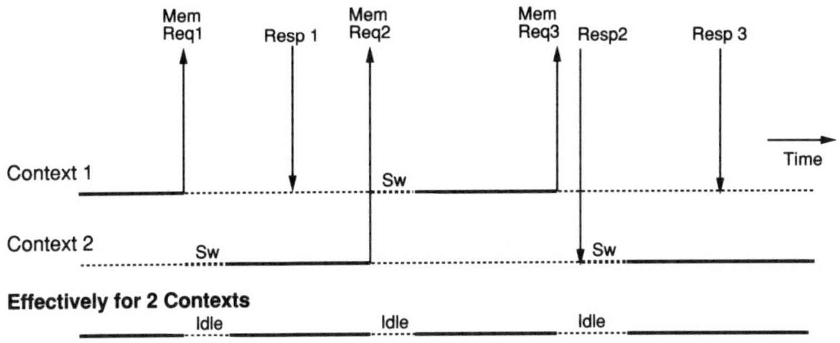

Figure 14.3
Multithreaded Timeline.

work, the Alewife processors attempt to tolerate this latency through the technique of block multithreading. The next section details the role of multithreading and its implementation.

14.3 Using Multithreading to Tolerate Latency

While caching data reduces the average memory access latency by minimizing the frequency of remote memory accesses, a fraction of memory transactions still require service from remote memory modules. When transactions cause the cache coherence protocol to issue invalidation messages in order to ensure sequential consistency [14], the remote memory access latency is especially high. Transactions that require any invalidations do not complete until all the invalidations are complete. When the resulting remote memory access latency is much longer than the time between memory accesses, processors spend most of their time waiting for memory transactions to be serviced.

This problem, caused by an imbalance between local and remote communication latency, is similar in principle to the problem caused by the imbalance between main memory and i/o device speeds in uniprocessors. The memory versus i/o speed imbalance has been solved by using multi-programming. By time-sharing a processor and multiplexing the communication path between the processor and its i/o devices, their speed differences are efficiently hidden.

Although the absolute communication costs in the uniprocessor system differ from the analogous costs in a multiprocessor, the same type of solution can be applied to solve the problem caused by the imbalance between local and remote memory access speeds in multiprocessors. By allowing each processor to have multiple outstanding memory requests, it is possible for a processor to switch between threads of control in order to mask the latency of remote memory accesses. This solution may be implemented efficiently by designing a processor that can rapidly switch between a number of hardware contexts and allocating one thread of control to each context.

As shown in Figure 14.3, this technique can increase processor utilization considerably. In the figure, solid lines represent the portion time that a processor executes application code, and dotted lines represent the time that a processor remains idle. The vertical lines designate the requests to remote memory modules, and the corresponding responses. Time flows from left to right. At the beginning of the scenario, Context 1 is active, but becomes idle when it issues Memory Request 1. After a short context switch period (marked with the Sw label), Context 2 becomes active, and runs until it issues Memory Request 2. Again, the processor switches contexts. Since Memory Request 1 was satisfied by Response 1, Context 1 is ready to continue executing. Figure 14.3 shows one more context switch, which happens when Context 1 issues Memory Request 3. At this point, Context 2 is not yet ready to run, because Memory Request 2 has not yet completed. This illustrates the important point that in order to mask long communication latencies, threads must maximize the time between remote memory accesses.

The type of system depicted in Figure 14.3 is referred to as a *multithreaded architecture.* The idea of multithreading in multiprocessor systems is not new. The prototypical multithreaded architecture is the HEP [17]. Eight threads reside in each of the HEP's processors, and each thread uses its own dedicated register set. In order to hide long memory access latency and achieve high processor utilization, the system schedules the threads in round-robin fashion. Multithreading is also used in data flow machines [15], and some Lisp-oriented architectures [11].

These multithreaded architectures switch contexts after every instruction execution. Although this switching policy offers the potential of high processor utilization, it results in relatively poor scalar performance observed by any single thread. When there is not enough parallelism to fill all of the hardware contexts, the system performance degrades significantly. For example, in HEP, if there are exactly eight threads, the processor utilization reaches 100%. Otherwise, the processor cycles executed by the idle contexts are wasted. Context switching on a cycle-by-cycle basis reduces system performance on inherently sequential portions of an application.

It is possible to provide reasonable performance on sequential code while still enjoying the merits of multithreading for highly parallel sections of applications. In Alewife's processor architecture, APRIL [3], context switches occur only when a thread executes a memory request that must be serviced by a remote node in the multiprocessor. As long as a context's memory requests hit in the cache or can be serviced by a local memory module, the context continues to execute. This context switching policy allows a single thread to benefit from the maximum performance of the processor.

Sparcle, the initial APRIL implementation, uses the register windows of the SPARC processor [19] to implement multithreading. With a small number of hardware modifications, the register window mechanism can be used to implement both the hardware contexts and the rapid context switch needed for multithreading. Sparcle dedicates one register window to each thread. When a cache miss occurs and a context issues a memory access request that must be serviced remotely, the cache controller traps the processor. The trap routine saves the Program Counter (PC) and Processor Status Register (PSR), switches register sets by setting the Frame Pointer (FP) register, flushes the pipeline, and switches to the next context by setting the Frame Pointer (FP) register to point to a new register window. [3] shows that even with a low-cost implementation, a context switch can be done in about 11 cycles. By maintaining a separate PC and PSR for each context, a custom processor could switch contexts faster than our current implementation. However, Section 14.5 shows that even with 11 cycles of context switch overhead, multithreading significantly improves the system performance.

Sparcle's context switching mechanism can also be used to reduce synchronization overhead by switching contexts when a thread encounters a delay due to a synchronization variable access. This feature is not evaluated in this paper.

A multithreaded architecture is not free in terms of either its hardware or software requirements. The implementation of such an architecture requires multiple register sets or some other mechanism to allow fast context switches, additional network bandwidth, support logic in the cache controller, and extra complexity in the thread scheduling mechanism. Other methods for allowing multiple outstanding requests, such as weak ordering [1, 8, 10], incur similar implementation complexities in the cache controller. In Alewife, since the same context-switching mechanism is used for fast traps and for masking synchronization latencies, we feel the extra complexity in the processor is justified. See [2] for a detailed analysis of the interaction of multithreading with cache interference, network contention, context-switching overhead, and data-sharing effects.

14.4 The Simulation System

We use ASIM, the Alewife machine simulator, to estimate the extent to which multiple contexts can overlap communication latency. ASIM is a cycle-by-cycle simulator of the entire machine, including processors, caches, and interconnection network. ASIM can use two sources of stimulus. First, programs written in a high-level language can be compiled, linked with a run-time system, and executed on the Alewife machine. Second, address traces of parallel programs containing embedded synchronization information can be used to drive the simulations. This paper uses the latter source.

ASIM uses a *coupled* trace-driven simulation method. In a coupled scheme, memory requests obey the synchronization constraints on the parallel program and respond to feedback from the interconnection network. This type of simulation models a correct ordering of memory requests. The coupled simulation system is depicted in Figure 14.4. An address trace of a single-processor execution of the parallel program drives the simulation system. The post-mortem scheduler generates a parallel trace, obeying the synchronization constraints specified in the uniprocessor trace. The scheduler sends address requests to the cache and network simulator, which responds to the requests from the scheduler and accumulates statistics that measure memory latency and other parameters.

The single processor trace is derived from a uniprocessor execution of an application parallelized using the single-processor-multiple-data (SPMD) computational model. Single processor traces are gathered using PSIMUL [18], a system for tracing parallel applications on IBM S/370 machines. In the SPMD model, each code section (task) in the

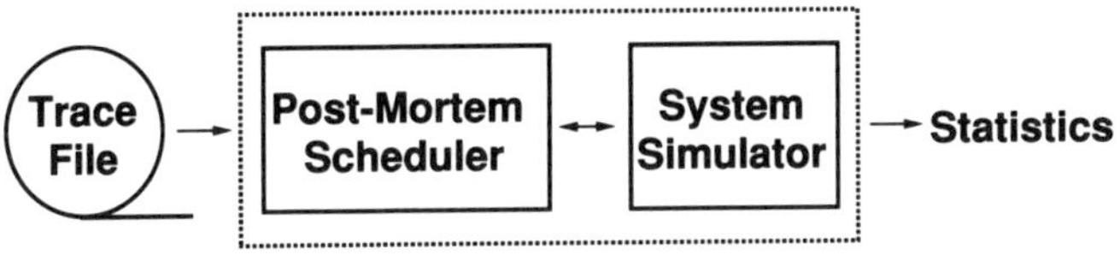

Figure 14.4
Coupled Trace-Driven Simulation.

system ends with a synchronization event, typically a barrier. The single processor trace describes the memory reference behavior of all the tasks and annotates the points where synchronizations must occur.

The dynamic post-mortem scheduler produces a parallel trace by simulating processors executing the task segments in the trace. Figure 14.5 illustrates its structure. Comparable simulators have been developed by other researchers [13]. The scheduler first makes a pass through the uniprocessor trace and constructs a task trace from the synchronization markers. It then simulates the processors executing these tasks in a round-robin fashion with each processor making one reference each cycle from its task. The scheduler simulates the synchronization behavior of the processor and synthesizes synchronization references according to prespecified waiting algorithms. The implementation in this study uses software combining trees for barrier synchronizations [6].

In general, a processor issues a memory request from its task only after its previous network request is satisfied. However, the simulator can also choose to switch to a different thread after a network request to model a multithreaded processor. When simulating multithreaded processors, each processor maintains multiple control blocks corresponding to the state of multiple processor contexts.

The cache and network simulators model the memory system of the Alewife machine. Each processor has its own combined instruction and data cache. Each processing node also contains a portion of globally-shared memory. We assume that all instructions are replicated in each processor's local memory. Shared data is interleaved at a cache block size across all the processing nodes. We simulate several cache coherence protocols including full-map directories, LimitLESS directories, and chained directories. Since the effects of multithreading are uniform for all of the coherence protocols that we studied, we report results only for the LimitLESS protocol. The network is a two dimensional mesh.

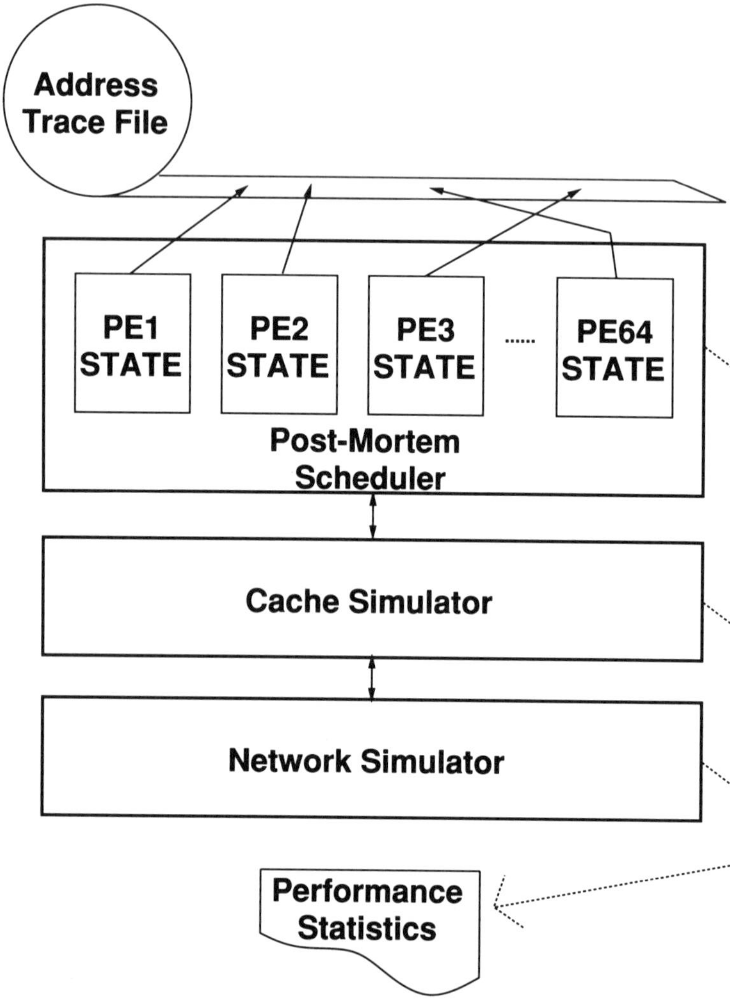

Figure 14.5
Coupled Post-mortem Scheduler.

Table 14.1
Application Characteristics.

	SIMPLE	Weather
Total Memory Accesses	24.0M	26.7M
Instruction Fetch	42.1%	40.1%
Shared Read	15.1%	7.6%
Shared Write	1.9%	1.8%
Private Read	26.7%	42.8%
Private Write	14.2%	7.7%
CRCW PRAM Speed-up	105	108

14.5 Simulation Results

This section analyzes the performance of two FORTRAN applications when running on simulations of a 64 processor machine. After describing the parameters of the simulations, we compare the behavior of a multithreaded architecture to a standard configuration. We then analyze how multithreading affects the contribution of synchronization, local memory access latency, and remote memory access latency to the time that it takes to run each application. Finally, we compare multithreading with weak ordering, another method for masking remote memory access latency.

14.5.1 Simulation Parameters

Our simulations use two application programs to evaluate Alewife's multithreaded architecture. The SIMPLE application simulates the hydrodynamic and thermal behavior of a fluids in two dimensions, and the Weather application forecasts the state of the atmosphere given an initial state. Both SIMPLE and Weather are written in EPEX/FORTRAN [9, 20], a version of FORTRAN that has been extended with parallel constructs at IBM.

Table 14.1 summarizes the characteristics of these programs. The total number of memory references for each trace is the number of memory transactions that are issued in a uniprocessor execution of the trace. The table gives the percentage of each of five types of memory references in the trace. In a multiprocessor simulation, a processor's local memory module satisfies all cache misses on private data. Since the simulator interleaves shared data addresses over all of the memory modules in the system, cache misses on shared data are usually serviced by a remote memory module. The interleaved memory mapping policy differs from Alewife's memory system, which allocates a consecutive block of addresses to each processor's memory module. Interleaving is used for the simulations reported in this paper, because the post-mortem scheduler makes no attempt to address the problem of data allocation in a system with non-uniform memory access latencies.

We approximate the available parallelism of each application by simulating it on a 128 processor concurrent-read, concurrent-write parallel random access machine (CRCW PRAM). This model assumes that any memory transaction takes exactly one cycle to complete. The parallelism reported in Table 14.1 is the speed-up of each application on a CRCW PRAM.

Our metric for evaluating the performance of a multiprocessor is speed-up, the ratio between the execution time of an application on a uniprocessor, and the execution time on a multiprocessor. The uniprocessor execution time does not include any of the overhead inherent in multiprocessing, including synchronization and communication delay. Thus, the speed-up metric encapsulates all of the factors that contribute to a multiprocessor's execution time, including network latency, network contention, synchronization delay, cache coherence overhead, and load imbalance among processors.

In addition to determining the execution time of an application, the multiprocessor simulator generates raw statistics that measure an application's memory access patterns and the utilization of various system resources. We will use these statistics to explain the performance of the multithreaded architecture. The simulations reported in the following sections use the parameters listed in Table 14.2.

14.5.2 Effect of Multithreading

Figure 14.6 shows the simulated performance for the Weather and SIMPLE applications using one and two threads per processor. The vertical axis shows the speed-up of the application with 64 processors, relative to a uniprocessor execution of the same application without synchronization overhead. Both of the applications realize about a 20% performance increase from multithreading. Since neither of the application problem sets are large enough to sustain more than 128 contexts, no performance gain results from increasing the number of contexts from

Table 14.2
Default Simulation Parameters.

Processing Elements	64
Coherence Protocol	LimitLESS_4
Cache Size	64KB (4096 lines)
Cache Block Size	16 bytes
Network Topology	2 Dim. Mesh (8×8)
Channel Width	16 bits
Network Speed	$2 \times$ processor speed
Memory Latency	5 processor cycles
Context Switch	11 processor cycles

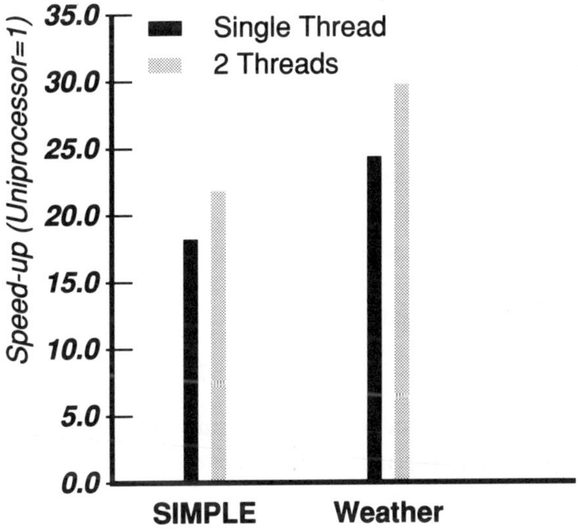

Figure 14.6
Effect of Multithreading.

two to three per processor. This behavior is not surprising, given the fact that both applications' CRCW PRAM parallelism is less than 128. The simulations of several cache coherence protocols (including limited, full-map, and LimitLESS) show that the 20% performance increase is largely independent of the coherence mechanism. The performance of the single-link chain coherence protocol improved slightly more than the other protocols, due to the greater latency of requests to write shared data.

The simulations reveal the increase in the demand for network bandwidth due to multithreading. Table 14.3 shows the effect of multithreading on the average network channel utilization and the average packet transit latency. The higher bandwidth demands, evident from the increased channel utilizations, cause larger packet communication latencies. However, the speed-up results validate the prediction in [2]: as long as the network does not approach saturation, the benefits of tolerating remote access latency outweigh the increase in packet communication latency. Since the multithreaded architecture is designed to tolerate remote access latency, its higher network utilization indicates that it uses the system resources more efficiently than the standard (one thread) configuration. The efficient use of network and processor resources allows the multithreaded architecture to realize increased speed-up when running the two applications.

The simulations performed during the Alewife design process will reveal the effects of multithreading on other applications. Some preliminary results are currently available from full system simulations run with compiled programs instead of trace-driven input. Applications that exhibit good communication locality did not perform better with multithreading, as expected. Other applications with poor locality, such as matrix transpose, exhibit 20% improvement with 2 contexts per processor and 25% with 4 contexts.

14.5.3 Cost Analysis

An analysis of the costs of memory transactions confirms the intuition that a multithreaded architecture yields better performance by reducing the effect of interprocessor communication latency. Our multiprocessor simulation system collects information about the distribution and the latency of various types of memory transactions. We have refined the statistics into a summary of the costs of four basic types of transactions.

1. *Application transactions* are the memory requests issued by the program running on the system. These transactions are the transactions in the original unscheduled trace.
2. *Synchronization transactions* are memory requests that implement the barrier executed at the end of a parallel segment of the application.

Table 14.3
Network Statistics.

Application	Threads	Channel Utilization	Packet Latency
SIMPLE	1	21.0%	9.8
	2	25.7%	12.3
Weather	1	14.7%	8.4
	2	18.8%	9.3

3. *Local cache miss transactions* occur when an application or synchronization transaction misses in the cache, but can be serviced in the local memory module.
4. *Remote transactions* occur when an application or synchronization transaction misses in the cache or requires a coherence action, resulting in a network transmission to a remote memory module. Multithreading is designed to alleviate the latency caused by this type of transaction.

The contribution of each type of transaction to the time needed to run an application is equal to the number of transactions multiplied by the average latency of the transaction. We assume that the latency of application and synchronization transactions is equal to 1 cycle, while the simulator collects statistics that determine the average latency of the cache miss transactions. Table 14.4 shows the cost of each transaction type, normalized to the number of application transactions. For example, in the simulation of SIMPLE with one context per processor, the memory system spends an average of 3.98 cycles servicing remote transactions for every cycle it spends servicing an application data access.

The statistics in Table 14.4 are calculated directly from the raw statistics generated by the multiprocessor simulator using the parameters in Table 14.2, except for the cost of remote transactions in the multithreaded environment. A multithreaded architecture can overlap some of the cycles spent servicing remote transactions with useful work performed by switching to an active thread. We approximate the number of cycles that are overlapped from the average remote transaction latency, the context switch overhead, and the number of remote transactions. The number of overlapped cycles is subtracted from the latency of re-

Table 14.4
Memory access costs, normalized to application transactions.

	SIMPLE		Weather	
Transaction Type	1 Thread	2 Threads	1 Thread	2 Threads
Application	1.00	1.00	1.00	1.00
Synchronization	1.17	1.08	0.76	0.45
Local Cache Miss	0.41	0.36	0.34	0.36
Remote	3.98	2.83	1.25	0.94
Total	6.56	5.27	3.35	2.75

mote transactions in order to adjust the cost of remote transactions. For all of the simulations summarized in the table, the total cost multiplied by the number of application cycles is within 5% of the actual number of cycles needed to execute the application.

The analysis shows that remote transactions contribute a large percentage of the cost of running an application. This conclusion agrees with the premise that communication between processors significantly affects the speed of a multiprocessor. The multithreaded architecture realizes higher speed-up than the standard configuration, because it reduces the cost of remote transactions. Because communication latency grows with the number of processors in a system, the relative cost of remote transactions increases. This trend indicates that the effect of multithreading becomes more significant as system size increases.

14.5.4 Comparison to Weak Ordering

In order to evaluate the contribution of multithreading, we compare the performance of our multithreaded system to the performance of a system with weak ordering [1, 8, 10]. Weak ordering is an alternate method of tolerating remote memory access latency by allowing multiple outstanding transactions per processor. When using a weakly ordered memory system, if a programmer obeys certain synchronization semantics, then the system will appear to enforce sequential consistency, a convenient model of shared memory. In return, the memory system permits individual threads to overlap the latency of certain types of remote transactions with useful computation. In contrast, Alewife's memory system guarantees sequential consistency without placing restrictions on the synchronization semantics of programs, and overlaps remote transaction latency with multiple threads of computation.

Table 14.5
Speed-up achieved by tolerating latency.

	Sequentially Consistent		Weak
Application	1 Thread	2 Threads	Ordering
SIMPLE	18.2	21.8	20.4
Weather	24.4	29.8	28.6

To compare these two methods for masking remote memory latency, we instrumented the simulator to estimate the performance of a system with weak ordering. The simulator collects statistics about a weakly ordered memory system while simulating a single-context processor with a memory system that provides sequential consistency. For the purposes of our analysis, we modeled a weakly ordered system that allows all write transactions to be overlapped with computation, until the program encounters a synchronization point. At synchronization points, the system must wait for all write transactions to complete.

The approximation method records the latency of the memory transactions that may be overlapped with execution, namely write misses and attempts to write to read-only cache blocks. At any point in the simulation, the algorithm can determine the latest time that overlapped transactions will be completed for each processor. When a thread that is running on a processor performs a synchronization, the system knows how long to stall the processor to ensure that all of the outstanding memory transactions are complete. The simulator calculates the performance of weak ordering for each processor by subtracting overlapped cycles from the normal execution time and adding the extra wait time at synchronization points. The performance of weak ordering for the entire system is calculated by averaging the execution time over all processors.

Our simulations indicate that multithreaded architectures with two contexts compare favorably with weakly ordered systems. Table 14.5 shows the speed-up values that are measured for one thread (conventional), two thread, and weakly ordered systems. With the addition of a single extra thread, the multithreaded system achieves approximately the same speed up as the weakly ordered system. Both multithreading and weak ordering increase hardware and software complexity in order to provide latency tolerance. Both techniques use a similar approach to the latency problem, and both strategies result in comparable performance gains for our two applications.

14.6 Conclusions

This paper evaluated the potential for using a multithreaded architecture to tolerate remote memory access latencies in a shared memory multiprocessor. Simulations of a 64 processor system demonstrate performance gains with two contexts per processor and an 11 cycle context switch overhead. The higher performance of the multithreaded system indicates that the benefit of overlapping useful computation with communication latency outweighs the overhead of implementing multiple contexts per processor. For the applications that we studied, multithreaded processors realize a 20% performance increase over single-thread processors on a 64 processor Alewife machine.

Simulations of the Alewife system show that multithreading mitigates the negative impact of communication latency in multiprocessors. Because communication latency grows with the number of processors in a system, we expect the effect of multithreading to become even more significant as system size increases. Like any other technique that allows multiple outstanding memory requests, multithreading provides performance gains as long as the interconnection network has spare bandwidth.

Multithreading, a technique for tolerating remote access latency, should be viewed within the context of a layered approach to automatic management of communication locality in scalable multiprocessors. In a complete system, processor caches and compiler techniques decrease the proportion of memory accesses that require interprocessor communication. Run-time software can also attempt to minimize the average latency of remote accesses by efficiently allocating threads to the grid of processors. Multithreading provides the last line of defense when all of the attempts to exploit communication locality fail. The fundamental challenge in our research lies in understanding the interaction between the various mechanisms for implementing an efficient shared-memory system.

Acknowledgments

We are grateful the the other members of the Alewife development team, who have participated at every stage of the research reported in this paper. In particular, John Kubiatowicz is responsible for the design of the Alewife processing node, Beng-Hong Lim implemented the bulk of the run-time system that manages multithreading, and Gino Maa wrote the network simulator.

The serial version of the SIMPLE application was originally from Lawrence Livermore Laboratory. It was parallelized by Boris D. Lubachevsky while at NYU to run under WASHCLOTH, an instruction-level simulator of the NYU Ultracomputer, written by Allan Gottlieb. Pat Teller modified Lubachevsky's code to run under EPEX/FORTRAN at NYU. Weather was originally developed at the NASA Space Flight Center. David Korn and Norman Rushfield parallelized the code to run under WASHCLOTH, and Pat Teller modified the code to run under EPEX/FORTRAN. Pat Teller and Allan Gottleib provided the sources for the programs. Harold Stone and Kimming So helped us obtain the traces from IBM. The static post-mortem scheduling process was developed by Mathews Cherian and Kimming So at IBM.

Machines used for simulations were donated by Sun Microsystems, Digital Equipment Corporation, and Encore Computer Corporation. The Sparcle implementation effort is a collaboration with LSI Logic Corporation and Sun Microsystems. The research reported in this paper is funded by DARPA contract # N00014-87-K-0825, and by grants from the Sloan Foundation and IBM.

References

[1] Sarita V. Adve and Mark D. Hill. Weak Ordering - A New Definition. In *Proceedings 17th Annual International Symposium on Computer Architecture*, June 1990.

[2] Anant Agarwal. Performance Tradeoffs in Multithreaded Processors. *IEEE Transactions on Parallel and Distributed Systems*, 1991. To appear.

[3] Anant Agarwal, Beng-Hong Lim, David A. Kranz, and John Kubiatowicz. APRIL: A Processor Architecture for Multiprocessing. In *Proceedings 17th Annual International Symposium on Computer Architecture*, pages 104–114, June 1990.

[4] Anant Agarwal, Richard Simoni, John Hennessy, and Mark Horowitz. An Evaluation of Directory Schemes for Cache Coherence. In *Proceedings of the 15th International Symposium on Computer Architecture*, IEEE, New York, June 1988.

[5] Lucien M. Censier and Paul Feautrier. A New Solution to Coherence Problems in Multicache Systems. *IEEE Transactions on Computers*, C-27(12):1112–1118, December 1978.

[6] David Chaiken, Craig Fields, Kiyoshi Kurihara, and Anant Agarwal. Directory-Based Cache-Coherence in Large-Scale Multiprocessors. *IEEE Computer*, June 1990.

[7] David Chaiken, John Kubiatowicz, and Anant Agarwal. LimitLESS Directories: A Scalable Cache Coherence Scheme. In *Fourth International Conference on Architectural Support for Programming Languages and Operating Systems (ASPLOS IV)*, ACM, April 1991. To appear.

[8] Michel Dubois, Christoph Scheurich, and Faye A. Briggs. Synchronization, coherence, and event ordering in multiprocessors. *IEEE Computer*, 9–21, February 1988.

[9] D. A. George. *EPEX - Environment for Parallel Execution.* Technical Report RC 13158 (58851), IBM T. J. Watson Research Center, Yorktown Heights, September 1987.

[10] K. Gharachorloo, D. Lenoski, J. Laudon, P. Gibbons, A. Gupta, and J. Hennessy. Memory Consistency and Event Ordering in Scalable Shared-Memory Multiprocessors. In *Proceedings 17th Annual International Symposium on Computer Architecture*, June 1990.

[11] R.H. Halstead and T. Fujita. MASA: A Multithreaded Processor Architecture for Parallel Symbolic Computing. In *Proceedings of the 15th Annual International Symposium on Computer Architecture*, pages 443–451, IEEE, New York, June 1988.

[12] W. J. Kaminsky and E. S. Davidson. Developing a Multiple-Instruction-Stream Single-Chip Processor. *IEEE Computer*, 66–78, December 1979.

[13] Manoj Kumar and Kimming So. Trace Driven Simulation for Studying MIMD Parallel Computers. In *International Conference on Parallel Computing*, pages I–68 – I–72, 1989.

[14] Leslie Lamport. How to Make a Multiprocessor Computer That Correctly Executes Multiprocess Programs. *IEEE Transactions on Computers*, C-28(9), September 1979.

[15] G. M. Papadopoulos and D.E. Culler. Monsoon: An Explicit Token-Store Architecture. In *Proceedings 17th Annual International Symposium on Computer Architecture*, June 1990.

[16] B.J. Smith. A Pipelined, Shared Resource MIMD Computer. In *Proceedings of the 1978 International Conference on Parallel Processing*, pages 6–8, 1978.

[17] B.J. Smith. Architecture and Applications of the HEP Multiprocessor Computer System. *SPIE*, 298:241–248, 1981.

[18] K. So, F. Darema-Rogers, D. A. George, V. A. Norton, and G. F. Pfister. *PSIMUL - A System for Parallel Simulation of Parallel Systems.* Technical Report RC 11674 (58502), IBM T. J. Watson Research Center, Yorktown Heights, November 1987.

[19] SPARC Architecture Manual. 1988. SUN Microsystems, Mountain View, California.

[20] J.M. Stone, F. Darema-Rogers, V.A. Norton, and G.F. Pfister. *Introduction to the VM/EPEX FORTRAN Preprocessor.* Technical Report RC 11407 (#51329), IBM T. J. Watson Research Center, Yorktown Height, NY, September 1985.

[21] H. Sullivan and T. R. Bashkow. A Large Scale, Homogeneous, Fully Distributed Parallel Machine. In *Proceedings of the 4th Annual Symposium on Computer Architecture*, pages 105–117, March 1977.

[22] C. K. Tang. Cache Design in the Tightly Coupled Multiprocessor System. In *AFIPS Conference Proceedings, National Computer Conference, NY, NY*, pages 749–753, June 1976.

[23] Wolf-Dietrich Weber and Anoop Gupta. Exploring the Benefits of Multiple Hardware Contexts in a Multiprocessor Architecture: Preliminary Results. In *Proceedings 16th Annual International Symposium on Computer Architecture*, IEEE, New York, June 1989.

15 Cenju: A Multiprocessor System with a Distributed Shared Memory Scheme for Modular Circuit Simulation

Toshiyuki Nakata, Norio Tanabe, Nobuki Kajihara, Satoshi Matsushita, Hiromi Onozuka, Yoshihiro Asano, and Nobuhiko Koike

Cenju is an experimental multiprocessor system with a distributed shared memory scheme developed mainly for circuit simulation. The system is composed of 64 PEs which are divided into 8 clusters. In each cluster, 8 PEs are connected by a cluster bus. The cluster buses are in turn connected by a multi-stage network to form the whole system. Each PE consists of MC68020 (20MHZ), MC68882 (20MHZ), 4MB of RAM and a floating point processor WTL1167(20MHZ). In this system, a distributed shared memory scheme in which each PE contains a part of the whole global memory is adopted. The simulation algorithm used is hierarchical modular simulation in which the circuit to be simulated is divided into subcircuits connected by an interconnection network. For the 64 processor system, a speed up of 14.7 and 15.8 was attained for two DRAM circuits. Furthermore, by parallelizing the serial bottleneck, a speedup of 25.8 could be realized. In this article, we describe the simulation algorithm and the architecture of the system. We also give some preliminary evaluation of the memory scheme.

15.1 Introduction

Circuit simulation, with detailed device models such as SPICE[1], simulates circuits by solving a set of differential equations describing the properties of the circuit using backward differential formulae and Newton-Raphson techniques. Thus, circuit simulation can be categorized as a numerical solution problem and is very computation intensive using double precision floating point numbers.

Circuit simulation is heavily used in such areas as memory chip design, because it is the only approach that allows chip designers to decide the circuit's performance including the effects of the technological variations such as channel length and oxide thickness of MOS transistors. However, device scaling for higher density and improving chip performance increases design complexity in both device behavioral and electrical sense, spirally increasing the cost for circuit simulation because of the need for enhanced accuracy and of the larger network to be solved.

Various approaches have been reported in the past to dissolve the simulation cost and to provide the desired throughput for the designers.

Vector processors do provide some speedup, but the speed enhancement is determined mainly by the degree of detail in the device model and the network structure. As the device model becomes more detailed, the vectorization rate decreases, since the precise device characteristic is often modeled by the parts of the locally operating modes which dissect the vector length. Likewise the many feedback loops in the circuit may shorten the vector operation during sparse LU factorization due to fill-in.

Parallel processors provide another answer to the problem. In this case, the choice of the algorithm, together with the correct architecture is the key in providing a powerful tool, which can be used regardless of technologies and design methods.

So, we decided to develop a modular circuit simulator based on the direct method and to develop a 64 multiprocessor system dedicated to circuit simulation named *Cenju.*[1].

Due to the interprocessor communication characteristics of the simulation algorithm, we decided to adopt a distributed share memory scheme in which each PE's local memory is mapped on to a global address space.

As the architecture of the system is closely determined by the circuit simulation algorithm, we first explain the simulation algorithm in detail. We then describe the architecture and the system software of the Cenju in detail, and also show some preliminary evaluation.

15.2 Choice of the Algorithm

In an MIMD system, the following three factors affect the overall performance of the system.

1. The ratio of time spent in the sequential phase.
2. Load balance among the processors.
3. Amount of communication/synchronization overhead.

Because of its mathematical formulation, a high degree of parallelism exists in circuit simulation, namely in device model evaluation, predic-

[1] *Cenju* is named after a Buddhist goddess *Cenju-Kan'non* which has one thousand arms.

Table 15.1
Distribution of CPU Time

Processing	Ratio of CPU Time
Model Evaluation	83%
Matrix Computation	9%
Time Discretization	6%
Others	2%

tion of solution, truncation error computation for timestep control and convergence check.

Table 15.1 shows the distribution of the CPU time for the transient simulation of a MOS static RAM having about 500 transistors executed on a single processor. The CPU time for model evaluation which includes matrix setup takes more than 80% of the total CPU time, while 9% of the time is spent in matrix computation and 6% is spent in time discretization respectively. These figures show that if we are to attain a speedup of 60 to 100, then we would have to parallelize not only model evaluation but also, matrix computation and the time discretization phase.

The following three methods are the candidates for parallelizing circuit simulation.

- Direct parallelization of the direct method
- Relaxation algorithm
- Parallel simulation based on modular circuit simulation

In modular circuit simulation algorithm, the entire circuit is partitioned into subcircuits connected by an interconnection network. The solution of the subcircuit and the interconnection network is repeatedly calculated until the solutions converge.

This algorithm allocates subcircuits to processors making it possible to let the processors share the various tasks, namely, device model evaluation, prediction of solution, truncation error computation for timestep control and convergence check.

Furthermore, if we adopt a *distributed shared memory scheme,* this algorithm naturally dissolves the memory update conflicts during the matrix setup phase. Also it makes it possible to break through the serial tasks inherent in the matrix computation of the entire circuit. The only serial task left is the solution of the matrix for the inter-connection network. This scheme makes it possible to apply coarse grained parallelism using up to 100 processor elements.

Thus, we decided to adopt modular circuit simulation as the bases for our system. For decomposition strategy, we adopted tearing decomposition at the linear equation level[2] because the simulation reliability is promised just as for conventional tools.

15.3 Simulation Algorithm

15.3.1 Actual Algorithm

The circuit to be simulated is hierarchically divided into a set of subcircuits which are connected by an interconnection network (See Fig. 15.1).

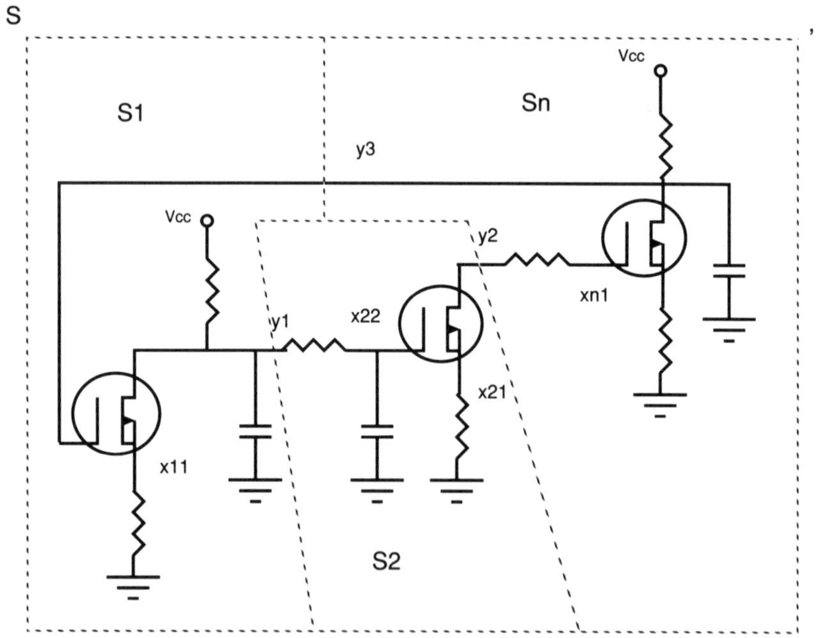

Figure 15.1
Model of Parallel Circuit Simulation

Each of these subcircuits and the network is statically allocated to a process. And the processes are statically allocated to the processors. So the whole system can be viewed as a tree of processes. The process at the root of the tree corresponds to the interconnection network of the modules at the highest level, the processes at the intermediate nodes correspond to sub-interconnection of modules, while the processes at the leaves correspond to subcircuits.

The core of the simulation algorithm in the Newton Raphson algorithm is recursively composed of the next three phases.

Parallel Phase 1
Each processor derives the approximate solution for the internal nodes of the subcircuit allocated to it by evaluating the models, then sends the Norton equivalent to the processor corresponding to the interconnection network.

Serial Phase
The processor corresponding to the interconnection network solves the linear equation using LU factorization and sends the solution of the interface variables to the processors corresponding to the subcircuit

Parallel Phase 2
Each processor derives the actual solution of the internal nodes by solving a linear equation using the values of the interface variables sent from the interconnection network.

For simplicity's sake, we present in Figure 15.2 the transient simulation algorithm for a single-level hierarchy model, in which a master processor executes the process for the interconnection network, which connects the subcircuits executed by the processes in the slave processors.

In order to parallelize the simulation, we had to inevitably introduce some overhead unnecessary in the conventional approaches. These extra works include, for the subcircuit processes, generation of Norton equivalent and recomputation of internal variables, and for the interconnection network, matrix computation itself.

Although the system can simulate circuits having an arbitrarily hierarchical structure, our major concern is currently with the single level partitioning approach.

	Master	Slave
1)	Let $t_{n+1} = t_n + dt$, compute the coefficients of the backward differentiation integration formula (BDF). Predict the solution vector and compute the given charge currents using the BDF and their coefficients.	
2)	Load the independent source values into the solution vector.	
3)	Synchronize Master and the Slaves.	
4)	Send the values of the interconnection network variables to the Slaves.	
		Load the values of the port variables sent by the Master into the solution vector.
5)	Synchronize Master and the Slaves.	
6)	Evaluate models and setup matrices.	
		Solve the internal variables and generate the Norton equivalent, then send it to the Master.
	Merge the Norton equivalents sent from the slaves with its own matrix, then solve the variables for the interconnection network and send the solution to the Slaves.	
	Check convergence.	Load the values of the port variables sent from the Master into the solution vector, then correct the solution of the internal variables. Check convergence.
7)	Synchronize Master and the Slaves.	
8)	If the entire circuit is not converged yet then goto 5) else continue	
9)	Synchronize Master and the Slaves.	
10)	Update BDF and compute the truncation error.	
11)	Find the maximum truncation error of the entire circuit, then determine the new time step and integration order. Send them to the Slaves.	
12)	Continue 1) until TSTOP.	

Figure 15.2
Algorithm for the Transient Simulation

15.4 The Architecture of a Multiprocessor System for Circuit Simulation

15.4.1 Interprocessor Communication Scheme

In designing a multiprocessor system, the interprocessor communication scheme is one of the key factors that characterizes the system.

- *Tightly Coupled Shared Memory Scheme* which is used in systems such as Sequent's Symmetry and IBM's TOP-1 [3] are bus based systems in which a shared memory is placed on the bus. In order to avoid the bus-access from becoming a bottleneck, these systems utilize elaborate snooping caches. The main advantage of the tightly coupled shared memory processors are,

  - Supporting dynamic load balancing is relatively simple.
  - If a single address scheme such as light weight processes or threads are used, the inter-processor communication becomes transparent to the programmer. Thus, it is relatively easy to program or to convert sequential programs to parallel code.

  The disadvantages of the tightly coupled shared memory processors are

  - In the end, the bus becomes the bottleneck. – Usually it is not feasible to connect more than 16-20 PEs on a single bus.
  - It is not possible to support broadcasting mechanism for data which all the processors need to access, such as elements of the pivot rows in LU factorization.

- *Distributed Shared Memory Scheme* which is used in systems such as BBN Butterfly, and IBM's RP-3 are systems in which each PE contains a part of the global memory. Using packet switching, it is possible to write remote processor's data. By using circuit switching, it becomes to possible to read/write remote processor's data. The main advantage of the distributed shared memory processors are,

  - It is possible to build larger systems.
  - If the inter-processor communication is explicitly specified then it becomes possible to support broadcast by hardware/software.

- As in the tightly coupled shared memory schemes, it is relatively easy to program or to convert sequential programs to parallel code.

The disadvantages of the distributed shared memory processors are

- It is not easy to support a coherent caching scheme. although the issues are currently being investigated in systems such as PLUS.

  So, accessing remote data (especially reading remote processor's data) is slow. When one tries to optimize parallel code, it becomes necessary to explicitly specify data transfer (copying).
- It is difficult to support dynamic load balancing.

• *Message Based Scheme* which is used in systems such as NCUBE and Intel IPSC are systems in which each PE has its own memory space. In order to communicate with other PEs, it is necessary to explicitly send/receive messages. The main advantage of the distributed shared memory processors are,

- It is possible to build larger systems.
- It is possible to support broadcast by hardware/software.
- Caching local data becomes simple.

The disadvantages of the message based systems are

- Since interprocessor communication has to be explicitly specified, it becomes more difficult to convert sequential programs to parallel code.
- When many processors are sending data to one processor, the receiver may become a bottleneck.

15.4.2 Interprocessor Communication Scheme for Circuit Simulation

In circuit simulation, the characteristics of interprocessor communication is as follows.

• In the simulation algorithm, there are two places where interprocessor communication takes place, namely,

Comm.1

At the end of *Parallel Phase-1* where each of the processor corresponding to the subcircuit sends the Norton equivalent to the processor corresponding to the interconnection.

Comm.2

At the end of *Serial Phase* where the processor corresponding to the interconnection sends the solution of the interface variables.

It should also be noted that since in **Comm1.** the matrix coefficients as well as the values for the right hand side are transferred, the amount of data transferred in **Comm1.** is much larger than the amount of data transferred in **Comm2**.

Especially, in the single level model which is used often, the former interprocessor communication is realized as data transfer from n processors to 1 processor, and the latter is realized as data transfer from 1 processor to n processors. (Where n is the number of processors in the whole system.)

- Communication among processes takes place only between the parent process and the child process. (That is to say, no communication takes place among the children processes.) So management of critical sections can be simplified.

- In order to make the most use of parallelism, the time spent at the root of the tree must be minimized.

So, the following are the key conditions for attaining a high-performance circuit simulation system.

1. Systems with high-throughput interconnection such as the bus-structure are more suited than systems with arbitrary connection with low throughput such as hypercubes.
2. In order to prevent the processor corresponding to the interconnection network from becoming a bottleneck in *Comm.1*, interprocessor communication based on shared memory schemes, where each of the processor can directly write the data to the recipient's memory, is more suited than interprocessor communication based on message communication scheme where the two processors must synchronize.
3. On the other hand, if we adopt a tightly coupled shared memory scheme, the shared memory will become a bottleneck in the *Parallel*

Phase 1 and *Parallel Phase 2*. So a local memory scheme would be preferable.

15.4.3 Architecture of Cenju

In designing Cenju, we took the following architectural features into consideration, which were mainly derived from the discussions in the last section and from the experience we gained in a 4 PE prototype system [4].

Employment of 60 to a 100 Processors
In order to attain practical simulation speed for realistic circuits, we wanted to employ as many processors as possible. However, having more than 100 PEs would make the granularity of each process small, so that efficient usage of the devices would not be realized. [4]

Adoption of a Distributed Shared Memory Scheme
For the efficient interprocessor communication, we adopted a shared memory scheme. Furthermore we implement them in a *distributed* manner by assigning a unique *global* address to all the local memory in each processors. In order to suppress global bus traffic, we attach a separate *local* bus to all the processors. Each processor can access its own memory via this local bus without worrying about bus contention.

Utilization of a Hierarchical Bus Structure
Experience gained in the prototype showed that inter-processor communication will take place sporadically. So we felt that a common bus scheme with a wide-data transfer rate would be suitable. However, connecting more than ten processors on a bus is not realistic. So, some kind of a *hierarchical bus structure* would be necessary.

15.5 Hardware Organization of Cenju

The system is composed of 64 simulation processor elements which are divided into 8 clusters. In each cluster, 8 processor elements are connected by a cluster bus.[5] The cluster buses are in turn connected by a multi-stage network to form the whole system. (See Figure 15.3.)

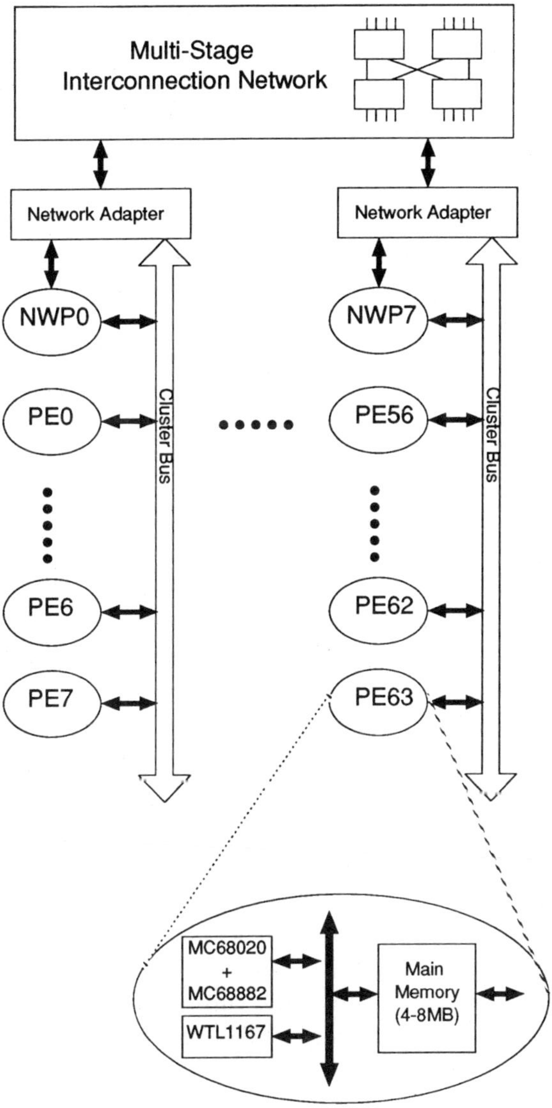

Figure 15.3
System Configuration

Table 15.2
Memory Map for Global Access of Cenju

Processor Number	Global Address
0	0x80000000-0x803fffff
1	0x80800000-0x80bfffff
2	0x81000000-0x813fffff
...	...
7	0x83800000-0x83bfffff
8	0x88000000-0x883fffff
...	...
56	0xb8000000-0xb83fffff
...	...
63	0xbb800000-0xbb3fffff

15.5.1 Processor Element

Each Processor element consists of MC68020 (20MHz), MC68882 (20MHz) and a fast floating point processor WTL1167(20MHz). The dedicated floating point processor (WTL1167) makes it possible to speed up the simulation by 1.5 to 2 compared with the MC68882. In order to realize an efficient distributed shared memory scheme, we made all the memory dual ported. Each CPU is connected to its own local memory (4 MB) via a local bus (This access is called *local memory access*), so the cluster bus is only used when the CPU accesses the data in the other processors' memory. (This access is called *global memory access.*) Address space for local memory access for all the processor elements are mapped from 0x0 to 0x3fffff. The address space of each processor element for the global is allocated as shown in Table 15.2. As can be seen, the memory space allows for expansion from the current configuration of 64 processor elements with 4MB of memory to 256 processor elements with 8 MB of memory.

15.5.2 Inter-Cluster Communication

In order to realize a global-distributed memory scheme, considering the trade-off between hardware cost and system efficiency, we decided to implement the inter-cluster *write* access by hardware, and the inter-cluster *read* access by a combination of hardware and software. For

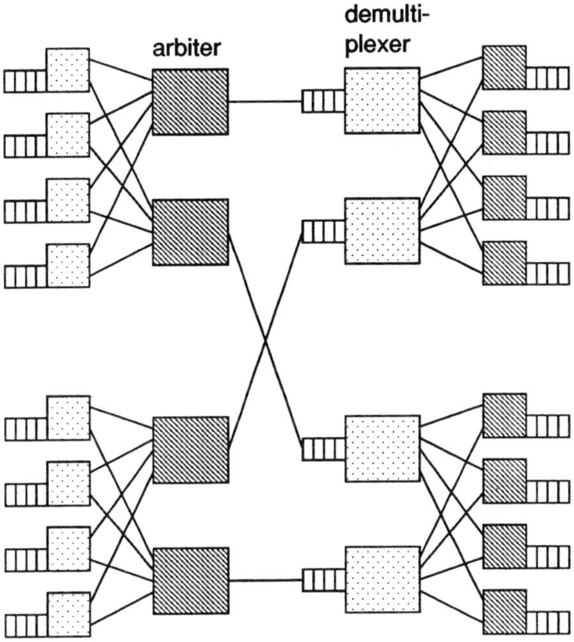

Figure 15.4
Organization of the Inter-cluster Network.

this purpose, we attached a network adapter (NADA for short), and a network processor (NWP for short) to each cluster.

Figure 15.4 shows the configuration of the inter-cluster network. The network is composed of a 4-in-2-out switch and a 2-in-4-out switch connected by FIFO (first in first out) queue buffers. The arbiters in each switch works in a round-robin fashion, so that there is no possibility of a deadlock. Table 15.3 shows the function of each packet. Note that the only packet recognized and processed by hardware is the *write* packet. The rest of the packets are handled by software on the network processor.

Figure 15.5 shows the configuration of the network adapter(NADA). The essential functions of NADA are to

- Detect an inter-cluster write access on the cluster bus, take in the address and the data to form a *write* packet and send the resultant packet to the network.

Table 15.3
Function of a Packet

Kind	Function	Parameters
01	Write Packet	Address, Data
02	Read Request	Address, Requester
03	Semaphore (P-op)	Address, Requester
04	Semaphore (V-op)	Address, Requester
05	Reset NWP	Requester Mode
1x	Message Packet	Requester, Destination, Vec number, args

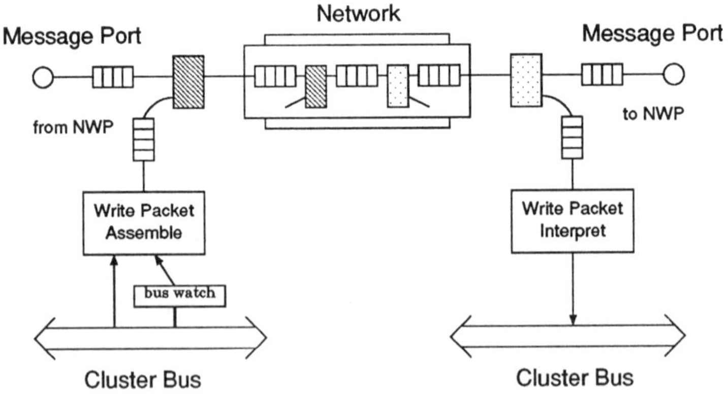

Figure 15.5
Organization of the Network Adapter

- Detect an inter-cluster read access on the cluster bus and signal a bus error.
- Receive a data sent from the NWP in form of a packet and send it to the network.
- Receive the packet sent from the network.
  - If it is a write data packet then decompose it and write the data to the destination address.
  - If it is not a write data packet, then send the packet to the NWP.

The hardware organization of the network processor (NWP) is same as the configuration of the simulation processors, except for having a dedicated port to NADA.

This configuration made it possible to make the inter-cluster access completely transparent to the user's programs. However, the inter-cluster read access is *very slow*. This is due to overhead in bus-error stack frame generation, timeout control to prevent hangouts, mutual exclusion control in message queueing and message handling in NWP.

We alleviated this problem in the circuit simulation by utilizing, whenever possible, a *producer-consumer* model in which, the producer of the data writes the data to the consumer of the data.

Besides this interprocessor communication scheme, Cenju is equipped with an interprocessor interrupt mechanism in which a processor can send an interrupt to any other processor by accessing a certain address.

15.6 System Software

15.6.1 Kernel Software

Based upon the interprocessor memory access scheme and the interprocessor interrupt scheme described in the previous section, we built a hierarchy of system software as shown in Figure 15.6[6].

At the lowest of the hierarchy, in order to manage the asynchronous events among the processors, we use a vectored remote procedure call (RPC) scheme. In vectored RPC, the address of the procedures to be called are registered on the system vector table. The procedures are

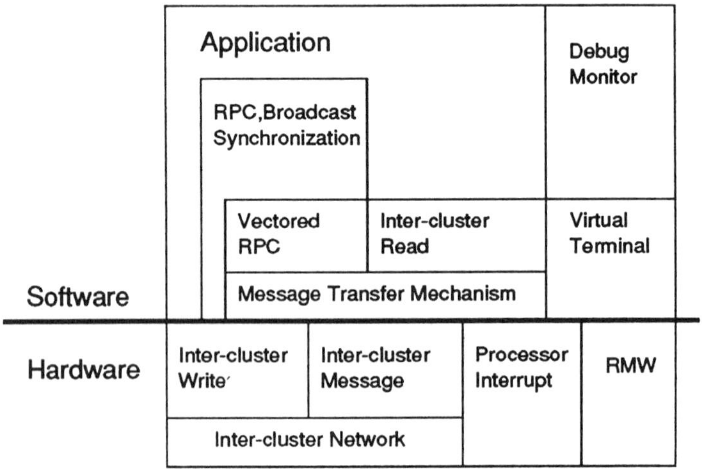

Figure 15.6
System Software Hierarchy

called via interrupts with the number of the entry of the routine to be called.

The procedures can be called *atomically*, thus essentially implementing Hoare's monitor [7] by introducing a lock-queue mechanism. In this case, the requests will not interrupt the processor, but will wait in a queue until the processor has finished servicing the current request. Furthermore, in order to deal with emergency processing such as aborts, we implemented a high-priority RPC. The priority of the RPCs are also determined by the vector entry number. Using this vectored RPC, we implemented the following functions.

- Process invocation.
- Process termination.
- User-level RPC routine (described below).
- Inter-processor data communication.

15.6.2 User-level RPCs

In Cenju, we implemented two kinds of user-level remote procedure calls, namely

Blocking RPC
The caller's process waits until the result is sent back from the called procedure.

Non-Blocking RPC
The caller's process does not wait for the result to be sent back from the called procedure, but continues execution and synchronizes later using a *wait* primitive.

15.7 Performance Evaluation

15.7.1 Speedup Gained in Cenju

Table 15.4 shows the size of the circuits we used for the evaluation on Cenju. Both of the circuits are part of the control circuit for dynamic RAMs.

Circuit-1 is rather small and we expected that we would not get much speedup beyond 16 processors. On the other hand, **Circuit-2** is a

Table 15.4
Size of Circuit Used for Evaluation

Circuit Name	**Circuit-1**	**Circuit-2**
Number of Transistors	1688	6974
Number of Subcircuits	64	191

Table 15.5
Execution Time and Speedup

PE Number	**Circuit-1**	**Circuit-2**
1	13 hr 44min (1.0)	...
2	7 hr 36min (1.81)	...
4	4 hr 07min (3.33)	...
8	2 hr 19min (5.93)	10hr 35min (6.25)
16	1 hr 26min (9.58)	6hr 35min (9.94)
32	1 hr 26min (10.56)	4hr 47min (13.82)
64	0 hr 56min (14.7)	4hr 11min (15.81)

circuit with the size we had set up as target for Cenju. Unfortunately, as we still do not have a good decomposer, we had to rely upon the hierarchical design of the designer in order to decompose the circuit. This has resulted in a great many more number of subcircuits –191– than would have been ideal. On the other hand, when there are more subcircuits than there are processors, then the system allocates subcircuits so as to balance the load as much as possible. This results in reducing overhead due to load-balancing.

Table 15.5 shows the simulation time and the relative speed up we could get for the two circuits. (Unfortunately, the size of **Circuit-2** had been to large to fit into 1-4 processors. We rather pessimistically estimated the speedup for 8 processors as being 6.25.) Please note that we did not change the number of subcircuits as we varied the number of processors.

The speedup for **Circuit-1**– 14.7 for 64 processors – was as we had expected. The surprising thing was that even for the **Circuit-2**, the speedup was only 15.8. (We had hoped for a speedup of somewhere around 30.) However, this is the highest speedup that has been attained in circuit simulation so far. The reason that we could not get enough speedup is that due to the following factors, the time spent in the serial phase had become larger than we had expected.

1. The large number of subcircuits –191– (nearly three times the number of processors) had resulted in a larger matrix to be solved at the serial phase.
2. Due to the characteristics of the DRAM model, the ratio of non-zero elements in the matrix were about 20%. Which is much larger than we had expected.

We estimate the ratio of time spent in the serial phase when executed on 1 processor to be a little less than 4%.

15.8 Speeding Up the Serial Phase

15.8.1 Parallelizing LU Factorization

In the last section, we showed that as the number of subcircuits goes up, the time spent in the serial phase becomes a serious bottleneck, as was noted by the Amdahl's law [8]. So, in this section, we try to determine whether it would not be possible to speed up the serial phase by parallelizing some of its parts which we had not parallelized before.

The largest task that is executed in the serial phase is the solution of the matrix for the interconnection variables, using the Norton Equivalents sent from the subcircuits. In solving the system we use LU factorization for the matrix solution. The matrix is sparse, but the structure of the matrix is predetermined at link time, so that the space for the resulting matrices is preallocated.

Parallelizing LU factorization (or Gaussian Elimination in some cases) has already been reported (for example see the reference [9]), but they have not been widely used due to the following reasons.

1. Even in dense matrices, the maximum speed one can get is usually less than 10 due to the overhead in broadcasting the elements of the pivot row and overhead in synchronization.
2. In sparse matrices, one has also to take into account the load imbalance among the processors.

Row 1 → PE 0
Row 2 → PE 1
Row 3 → PE 2
...
Row n → PE n-1
Row n+1 → PE 0
Row n+2 → PE 1
...
Row m → PE k

Figure 15.7
Processor Allocation in LU Factorization

However, we decided to tackle this problem for the following reasons:

1. The matrix for the interconnection variables is rather dense (20% or so, compared to 2 or 3 % for the subcircuits).
2. This part had been left as a serial part. Even if there is only a speed gain of 50% or so, the actual speed-gain for the whole system is large.

15.8.2 Parallel Algorithm for LU Factorization

Parallel LU factorization is based upon allocating each row to the processors as shown in Figure 15.7 and decomposing each row in parallel using LU Factorization algorithm of the outer-product form[10].

For simplicity's sake, we present the algorithm for parallel LU factorization for a dense matrix A whose elements are denoted as a_{ik}. Figure 15.8 shows the serial algorithm for row-wise LU factorization [10]. By substituting (3) and (4), and merging (1) and (4), we get the parallel version of LU factorization as shown in Figure 15.9.

(a) in Figure 15.9 corresponds to broadcasting the elements of the pivot row to all the PEs. Note that for rows in which a_{ik} is zero, the computations in (2) and (5) should not be executed for sparse matrices.

The potential bottlenecks in parallel processing are:

- Overhead due to pivot row broadcasting in (a).
- Overhead due to load imbalance among the processors because of the case where $a_{ik} = 0$ in (b).

```
for k:= 1 to n do
  for i:= k+1 to n do ...(1)
    a_ik := a_ik/a_kk ...(2)
  end.
  for j:= k+1 to n do ...(3)
    for i:= k+1 to n do ...(4)
      a_ij := a_ij - a_ik * a_kj ...(5)
    end
  end
end.
```

Figure 15.8
Algorithm for LU Factorization

```
for k:= 1 to n do
  if(PeContainsPivotRow){
    Broadcast a_kj (j=k to n)    (a)
  }
  Barrier(); /*Synchronize all the PEs*/
  for All i in k+1 to n which concerns this PE do
    ...(1),(4)...(b)
    a_ik := a_ik/a_kk ...(2)
    for j:= k+1 to n do ...(3)
      a_ij := a_ij - a_ik * a_kj ...(5)
    end
  end
  Barrier(); /*Synchronize all the PEs*/
end.
```

Figure 15.9
Algorithm for Parallel LU Factorization

- As the granularity of parallel processing is finer (so called medium-grained parallelism), overhead due to processor synchronization might stand out as well.

15.8.3 Improving the Algorithm

In order to reduce the overhead described in the last section, we made the following improvements.

1. Use Multiple PEs in a tree-like manner to broad cast the pivot value.
2. Absorb the load imbalance and eliminate explicit synchronization by adding a "ready bit" to each row.

In implementing the scheme, we noted that the most suitable number of processors for LU factorization might not coincide with the most suitable number of processors for the other part of circuit simulation. So we made it possible to have different number of processors to be used for LU factorization from the rest of circuit simulation. Thus, we might have 64 processors for the whole simulation and use only 8 of them for LU factorization.

15.8.4 Effect of Parallelizing LU Factorization

Figure 15.10 shows the speedup that we could get by using parallel LU-Factorization for Circuit-2. We had been able to attain a speed up of 25.8. Note that in order to simplify programming, the the processors corresponding to the subcircuits (SubPEs) sent the Norton Equivalent to the processor corresponding to the network (NetPE), which distributed the matrix to each of the processors in a row by row fashion. If the SubPEs had directly sent the rows to each of the processors, the speedup would be greater.

15.9 Effect of the Distributed Shared Memory Scheme

In order to evaluate the distributed shared memory model, we decided to compare the model used on Cenju with other memory schemes. Since, evaluating the "Ease in programming" is difficult, we concentrate on the performance issues.

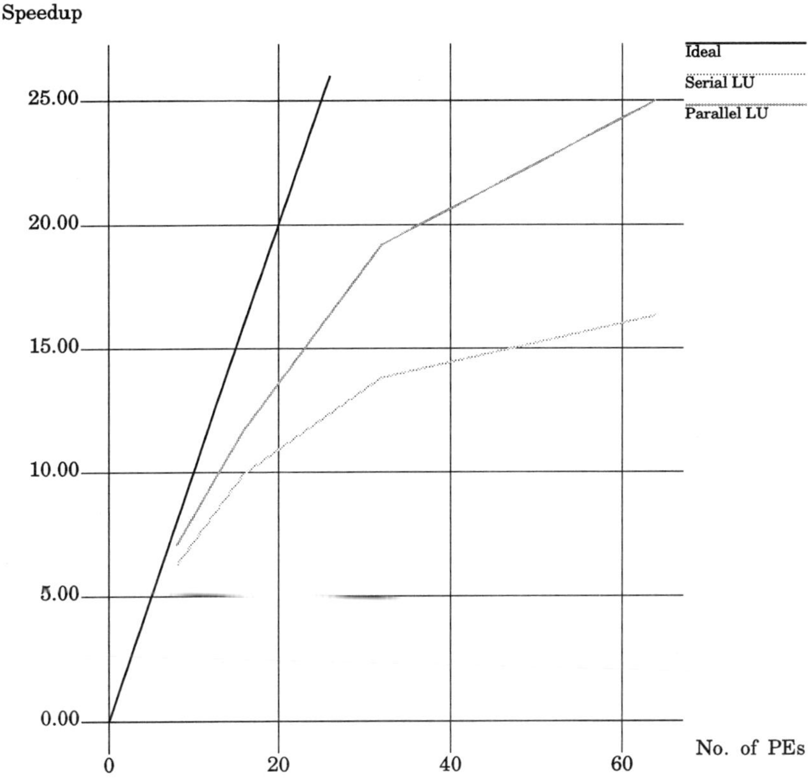

Figure 15.10
Effect of Parallel LU Factorization

Scheme	Simulation Time
Distributed Shared Memory	2,520
Message Based (Short Message)	3,143
Message Based (Long Message)	2,547

Table 15.6
Comparison with the Message Based Scheme

15.9.1 Comparison with the Message Based Scheme

In order to compare with the message based model, we simulate the message based model in **Comm1.** by

1. Writing the data to a system buffer on the processor corresponding to the network.
2. Invoking a remote procedure call to the processor corresponding to the network to copy the data from the system buffer to the designated area.

This corresponds to having a DMA controller which copies the messages sent to the processor to a system buffer ad then interrupting the processor to process the message. The performance of the model depends on the length of the message allowed. Table 15.6 shows the result for the cases when

1. Each row of the matrix and the right hand side values were sent as separate messages, and
2. When all the coefficient matrix variables and the right hand side value of a subcircuit were connected to form a long message. (Sometimes with the length of more than 4Kbytes).

In the latter case, each processor sends 3messages on an average then synchronize.[2]

In the latter case, a pipelining effect in which when the NetPE is copying the data from the buffer, another SubPE is writing to the system buffer, resulted in a surprisingly little difference. (about 1%)

[2] In order to shorten the evaluation time, we chose different time from the values shown in the last section.

Scheme	Simulation Time
Distributed Shared Memory	2,520
Tightly Coupled Shared Memory	2,725

Table 15.7
Comparison with Tightly Coupled Shared Memory Scheme

15.9.2 Comparison with the Tightly Coupled Shared Memory Model

Putting aside the fact that it is rather difficult to build a tightly coupled shared memory system with 64 PEs, the effects that may degrade system performance on a tightly coupled shared memory scheme are

1. When there are a large number of cache miss hits and the bus becomes congested.
2. In parallel LU factorization, where it is not possible to broadcast data in a tree-like fashion.

Assuming the ideal case for the tightly coupled shared memory scheme, in which former factor can be ignored, we modified the LU factorization so that the processor which contains the pivot row sequentially writes the data to the other processors. (This corresponds to the tightly coupled shared memory model, in which the processor containing the pivot row writes the data to the shared memory, and then each of the other processors read the data from the memory.)[3]

It might be thought that, in multiprocessors with update snoop protocols such as TOP-1 [3], the broadcast mechanism would be automatically realized if the data in the pivot row resides in the cache. However this will not hold as the processors will try to read the data in the pivot row *after* they are written by the processor containing the pivot row. Thus, the cache will always miss.

The results are shown in Table 15.7. Distributed shared memory scheme proved to be about 10% more efficient.

[3] Note that this model assumes that the whole pivot row will reside in the cache after being read. This will probably hold true.

15.10 Conclusion

We have described the algorithm and the architecture of a multiprocessor system for modular circuit simulation named Cenju. By using the modular circuit simulation algorithm based on tearing decomposition, it became possible to minimize the time spent in LU factorization. Preliminary evaluation showed that for the simulation of a D-RAM circuit composed of 7,000 transistors, a speedup of 16 was attained for a 64 Processor system. Furthermore, we had been able to attain a speedup of 25.8 by using parallel LU factorization.

We also showed that the distributed shared memory scheme is best suited to modular circuit simulation.

Cenju is currently used as a dedicated simulation machine for the actual development of MOS memory chips.

Although we had originally built Cenju as a special purpose machine for modular circuit simulation, it turned out that Cenju could be applied to a wide range of coarse-grained parallel applications, as long as the *Producer-Consumer* model is adhered to. Besides circuit simulation, we are considering various applications, such as concurrent fault simulation, Monte-Carlo simulations, and finite element analysis.

Acknowledgments

The authors would like to thank Vice President Tatsuo Ishiguro of Research and Development Group, NEC Corporation, Director Shizuo Itoh of VLSI CAD Engineering Division NEC Corporation, Director Masahiro Yamamoto of C &C Systems Research Laboratories, NEC Corporation, Vice-Director Tohru Sasaki of VLSI CAD Engineering Division, NEC Corporation, and Vice-Director Satoshi Goto of C &C Systems Research Laboratories, NEC Corporation for their constant encouragement and interest in the Cenju Project.

References

[1] L. W. Nagel. SPICE2 A Computer Program to Simulate Semiconductor Circuits. Technical Report ERL-M520, University of California, Berkeley, May 1975.

[2] P. Yang. Practical Consideration for the VLSI Circuit Simulator - SLATE. In *Proceedings of IEEE ICCC*, pages 184–188, 1982.

[3] T. Shimizu, N. Ohba, J. Moriwaki, T. Nakata, and A. Ohara. High-Performance Multiprocessor Workstation TOP-1. In *Proceedings of Joint Symposium on Parallel Processing 89*, pages 155–162, Feb. 1989. (In Japanese).

[4] T. Nakata, N. Tanabe, H. Onozuka, T. Kurobe, and N. Koike. A Multiprocessor System for Modular Circuit Simulation. In *Proceedings of ICCAD 87*, pages 364–367, Nov. 1987.

[5] T. Nakata, N. Tanabe, N. Kajihara, S. Matsushita, H. Onozuka, Y. Asano, and N. Koike. Cenju: A Multiprocessor System for Modular Circuit Simulation. *Journal of IPS Japan*, 31(5):593–601, May. 1990. (In Japanese).

[6] S. Matsushita, T. Nakata, N. Kajihara, Y. Asano, and N. Koike. Parallel Simulation Machine. In *Proceedings of the 37th Annual Convention of IPS Japan (6C-8)*, pages 97–98, Sep. 1988. (In Japanese).

[7] C. A. R. Hoare. Monitors: An Operating System Structuring Concept. *Communications of ACM*, 17(10):549–557, Oct. 1974.

[8] G. M. Amdahl. Validity of the Single-Processor Approach to Achieving Large Scale Computing Capabilities. In *Proceeding of Spring Joint Computer Conference*, volume 30, Apr. 1967.

[9] T. Hoshino. *PAX Computer*. Ohm-Sha, 1985. (In Japanese).

[10] T. Tsuda. *Numerical Programming*, volume 9 of *The Iwanami Software Science Series*. Iwanami-Shoten, 1988. (In Japanese).

16 Overview and Status of the Stanford DASH Multiprocessor

Daniel Lenoski, James Laudon, Kourosh Gharachorloo, Wolf-Dietrich Weber, Anoop Gupta, and John Hennessy

The Stanford DASH project represents an experiment in understanding the scalability issues for shared-memory multiprocessors. As in message-passing machines, the main memory in DASH is distributed among the processing nodes and a scalable interconnection network is used to connect the nodes together. Unlike message-passing machines, however, the processing nodes share a single global address space, and have caches that are kept coherent using a distributed directory-based coherence protocol. Additional mechanisms to hide the latency of remote accesses (e.g., prefetching) are also provided. The DASH architecture thus combines the scalability of message-passing machines with the ease of programming associated with single address space machines. We are currently building a DASH prototype. The prototype will consist of 16-64 MIPS R3000/R3010 processors delivering up to 1600 MIPS and 300 scalar MFLOPS. The interconnection network consists of a pair of meshes, each with 16-bit wide channels. There will also be considerable support for performance monitoring. A 16 processor version of the prototype has been built and is currently being debugged.

16.1 Introduction

In this paper we present an overview of a scalable multiprocessor being built at Stanford's Computer Systems Laboratory. The goal of this research is to provide a general purpose machine that is easy to program and is scalable to support a large number of high-performance processors. To satisfy this goal, DASH (Directory Architecture for SHared-memory) supports shared-memory with hardware-supported cache coherence and provides special mechanisms for dealing with memory latency and synchronization.

Current shared-memory machines have one of two drawbacks: either they are not scalable, or if they scale well, they do not support coherent caches. The fundamental premise in DASH is that it is possible to build a *scalable* shared-memory machine with hardware-supported coherent caches by using a distributed directory-based cache coherence protocol. The high-level organization of the DASH machine is shown in Figure 16.1. The architecture consists of a number of processing nodes connected through a low-latency scalable interconnection network. Physical memory is distributed among the nodes. Each processing node, or *cluster*, consists of a small number of high-performance processors with their individual caches and a portion of the shared memory connected by a snooping bus. The cluster interfaces to the interconnection network through the directory controller. The directory controller includes directory memory that tracks the remote caching state of the memory within the cluster. A bus-based snoopy scheme keeps caches coherent within a cluster while inter-cluster coherence is maintained using a distributed directory-based protocol.

The idea of directory-based coherence was first proposed by Tang [8]. DASH extends it in several ways to make it suitable for scalable shared-memory multiprocessors [1, 6]. Each processing node has a directory memory corresponding to its portion of the shared physical memory. For each memory line (aligned memory block that has the same size as a cache line), the directory memory stores identities of all remote nodes caching that line. Thus, using the directory, it is possible for a node writing a location to send point-to-point messages to invalidate remote copies of the corresponding cache line. This is in contrast to the invalidating broadcast usually required by the snoopy protocols. The scalability of DASH is greatly enhanced by this ability to avoid broadcasts, coupled with the key observation that most of the time a memory location is cached by only a *small* number of processing nodes [9]. Another important attribute of the directory-based protocols is that they do not depend on any specific interconnection network topology. Therefore, any scalable network, such as meshes, hypercubes or multi-stage networks, can be used to connect the processing nodes.

The key to scalability of any multiprocessor lies in the ability to scale the memory bandwidth available to each processor. DASH provides scalable bandwidth for private and shared data in local memory by distributing the physical memory among the processing nodes. For shared data accesses that must be serviced remotely, DASH uses a scalable interconnection network. The amount of global traffic on the network is reduced by providing coherent caches for shared data. Although the network bandwidth still needs to scale linearly, caching shared data reduces access latency, and allows a better match between local processing speed and the achievable bandwidth of the global interconnect.

The rest of the paper is organized as follows. Section 16.2 describes the DASH architecture and then discusses how our design addresses some of the important problems faced by scalable shared-memory multiprocessors. Section 16.3 briefly describes the implementation of the prototype

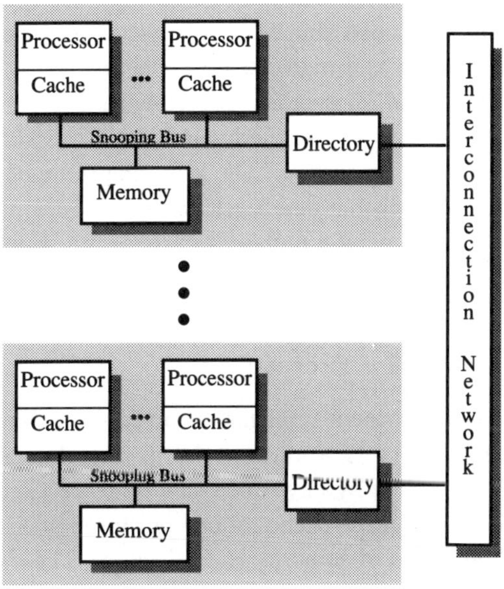

Figure 16.1
The DASH architecture.

and Section 16.4 provides preliminary performance measurement of the architecture and hardware.

16.2 The DASH Architecture

The DASH architecture has a two-level structure. At the top level, the architecture consists of a set of processing nodes (clusters) connected through a mesh interconnection network. In turn, each processing node is a bus-based multiprocessor. Intra-cluster cache coherence is implemented using a snoopy bus-based protocol, while inter-cluster coherence is maintained through a distributed directory-based protocol.

The cluster functions as a high-performance processing node. A bus-based cache protocol is chosen for implementing small-scale shared-memory multiprocessors because the bus bandwidth is sufficient to support a small number of processors. The grouping of multiple processors on a bus within each cluster amortizes the cost of the directory logic and network interface among a number of processors. Furthermore, this grouping reduces the directory memory requirements by keeping track of cached lines at a cluster as opposed to processor level.

16.2.1 The Coherence Protocol

The directory-based protocol implements an invalidation-based coherence scheme. A memory location may be in one of three states: *uncached*, that is not cached by any processing node at all; *shared*, that is in an unmodified state in the caches of one or more nodes; or *dirty*, that is modified in the cache of some individual node. The directory keeps the summary information for each memory line, specifying the clusters that are caching it.

The DASH memory system can be logically broken into four levels of hierarchy. The level closest to the processor is the processor cache and is designed to match the speed of the processor. A request that cannot be serviced by the processor cache is sent to the second level in the hierarchy, the *local cluster* level. This level consists of other processors' caches within the requesting processor's cluster. If the data is locally cached, the request can be serviced within the cluster, otherwise the request is sent to the *directory home* level. The home level consists of the cluster that contains the directory and physical memory for a given memory address. For some addresses, the local and home cluster are the same and the second and third level access occur simultaneously. In general, however, the request will travel through the interconnect to the home cluster. The home cluster can usually satisfy a request; if the directory is in the dirty state, or in the shared state when the requesting processor requires exclusive access, the fourth, *remote cluster* level, must be accessed. The remote cluster level responds directly to the local cluster level while also updating the directory level.

To illustrate the directory protocol, we first consider how a processor read traverses the memory hierarchy. If the location is present in the processor's cache, the cache simply supplies the data. Otherwise, the request goes to the cluster level. If the local cluster fails to satisfy the request, the request is sent to the home cluster. The home cluster examines the state of that memory location. If the location is uncached or shared, then the home cluster supplies the data and updates the directory to show sharing by the requester. If the location is dirty remote, the request is forwarded to the remote cluster. The remote cluster sends the data to the requester, and writes back the data to the home cluster, which in turn updates main memory and the directory state appropriately.

We now consider the sequence of operations that occurs when a location is written. If the location is dirty in the writing processor's cache, the write succeeds immediately. If not, then the processor needs to obtain exclusive ownership for the cache line corresponding to the written location. If the data is already dirty in one of the caches in the cluster, then the ownership and data request can be serviced at the local cluster level. Otherwise, the ownership request needs to be sent to the home cluster. The home cluster can immediately satisfy the ownership request if the memory location is not cached by any remote clusters. If the cache line is in shared state, all copies of the data must be invalidated. The contents of the directory memory indicate the processing nodes that need to be invalidated. Invalidation requests are sent to all such clusters. If the cache line is in dirty remote state, the write request is forwarded to the remote cluster. The remote cluster sends the data and ownership to the requesting cluster and a directory update message to the home directory. For a more detailed discussion of the protocol, see [6].

When the writing processor receives all the invalidation acknowledgments, or the acknowledgment from the home directory that the state has been changed, it is guaranteed that the directory state is current and all copies of the old data have been purged from the the system. If the processor delays completing the write until all acknowledgments are back, then the new value will become available to all processors at the same time. However, invalidations may involve round trip messages to multiple caches through the network, resulting in a long wait for the acknowledgment messages. The next subsection describes how the constraints on memory request ordering are relaxed to allow the processor to proceed with the write while acknowledgments are pending.

16.2.2 Memory Consistency

The level of memory consistency required by an architecture directly affects the amount of buffering and pipelining that can take place among memory requests. In addition, it has a direct effect on the complexity of the programming model presented to the user. Our goal in DASH is to provide maximum freedom in the ordering among memory requests, while still providing a reasonable programming model to the user.

At one end of the consistency spectrum is the *sequential consistency* model [5], which requires the execution of the parallel program to appear as some interleaving of the execution of the parallel processes on a sequential machine. Sequential consistency, while conceptually appealing, imposes a large performance penalty since memory accesses can not be overlapped. A weaker consistency model can be derived by relating memory request ordering to synchronization points in the program. The consistency can be relaxed by only requiring all previous operations to complete before a synchronization operation is observed. We call this model of consistency *release consistency* [4].

DASH supports the release consistency model in hardware. Such a scheme has two advantages. First, it provides the user with a reasonable programming model, since the programmer is ensured that when the critical section is exited, all other processors will have a consistent view of the modified data structure. Second, it permits for the latency of writes to be hidden by allowing overlap among accesses within a critical section, thus resulting in lower latencies for writes and higher overall performance. The disadvantage of the model is that all synchronization accesses must be identified by the programmer or the compiler. Detailed simulation studies of the weaker models have shown a 10% to 40% increase in performance over sequential consistency [3].

16.2.3 Memory Access Optimizations

The use of release consistency allows for an effective way of hiding the latency of remote write operations. However, since read operations are blocking, remote read operations stall the processor for the entire duration of access. In addition, no pipelining occurs on read requests initiated by the same processor. The DASH architecture uses three different mechanisms for dealing with the latency of read requests.

A *prefetch* operation is an explicit non-blocking request to fetch the data before the actual memory operation is issued. Hopefully, by the time the process needs that data value, the data has already been brought into its cache, thus hiding the latency of the regular blocking fetch. The prefetch operation in DASH brings the data into the remote access cache. A subsequent memory access will then be serviced by this cache. The prefetched data is kept consistent like any other data. If another processor happens to write into the cache line before the data is accessed, the data will simply be invalidated. Although the prefetch is rendered ineffective, the program will execute correctly. This makes the programming and compilation task easier as prefetching a location that may be touched by another processor will not result in incorrect execution. Detailed simulation studies of scientific applications with prefetching have shown improvements of two to three times due to hiding the latency of accesses [7], though there are some applications whereby prefetching fails to significantly improve the performance (e.g., applications that traverse link lists, etc.). Research on compiler optimizations to prefetch data is currently under way.

Prefetching can sometimes be ineffective due to the consumer process not being able to prefetch data early enough. Therefore, DASH provides two operations that allow the producer to send the data directly to the consumers: the update-write and deliver operations. The *update-write* operation updates the value of all existing copies of a data word. Using this primitive, data is directly written into the home memory and all caches that are caching the line containing the update word. Update semantics are particularly useful for event synchronization, such as the release event from a barrier where an update-write can be used to release all waiting processors. The *deliver* operation explicitly specifies the destination clusters of the transfer. In this scheme, the producer first writes out the data to the cache line using regular write operations. At that time, any other cached copies are invalidated. The producer then issues a deliver instruction, explicitly giving the destinations in a bit vector. The data is sent to all the specified clusters, and the directory is updated with the fact that the data is now shared between the various clusters.

16.2.4 Support for Synchronization

The access patterns to locations used for synchronization are often different from those for other shared data [9]. For example, whenever a highly contended lock is released, a large number of waiting nodes rush to grab the lock. Such phenomena often cause hot spots in the memory system and can degrade the performance of large multiprocessors. Consequently, synchronization variables usually warrant special treatment.

DASH provides two extensions to the cache coherence protocol to support synchronization primitives: queue-based locks, and fetch-and-increment. The queue-based locks in DASH work by keeping a list in directory memory of the nodes spinning in their cache for the lock. Caching a locked lock minimizes network traffic while a processor is spinning. When the lock is released, if there are any waiting nodes in the directory, one node is chosen at random and is granted the lock. Informing only one processor about the release eliminates unnecessary traffic and reduces the latency that would be incurred if all waiting nodes were allowed to contend. The *fetch-and-increment* primitives [2] provide atomic increment and decrement operations at the memory site. These operations have low latency and serialization and are useful for implementing several synchronization primitives such as barriers, distributed loops, and work queues. The serialization of these operations is small because they are done directly at the memory site.

We are also exploring software techniques that will help reduce latency, traffic, and hot spots. For example, for primitives such as barriers, it is possible to distribute the load by gathering and releasing through a tree, thus eliminating heavily contended locations. Using trees also reduces the latency for the gather and release stages. We are currently studying such trade-offs for other synchronization primitives.

16.3 The DASH Implementation

A prototype implementation of DASH is being developed to verify the feasibility of the architecture and to provide a platform for studying real applications running on a large ensemble of processors. To manage the size of the prototype design effort, the processing node is based on a commercially available bus-based multiprocessor. The prototype system uses the Silicon Graphics POWER Station 4D/340 as the base processing node. The 4D/340 system consists of four MIPS R3000 processors and R3010 floating-point coprocessors running at 33 MHz. Each R3000/R3010 combination is nominally rated at 25 VAX MIPS and 5 LINPACK MFLOPS. Each CPU contains a 64 Kbyte instruction cache and a 64 Kbyte write-through data cache. The 64 Kbyte data cache interfaces to a 256 Kbyte second-level write-back cache. The interface consists of a read buffer and a 4 word deep write-buffer. Both the first and second level caches are direct-mapped and support 16 byte lines. The first level caches run synchronous to the 33 MHz processors while the second level cache runs synchronous to the 16.67 MHz memory bus.

The memory bus (MPBUS) of the 4D/340 is a synchronous bus and consists of a 32-bit address bus and a 64-bit data bus. The MPBUS is pipelined and supports memory-to-cache and cache-to-cache transfers of 16 bytes every 4 bus clocks with a latency of 6 bus clocks. This results in a maximum bandwidth of 67 Mbytes/sec. While the MPBUS is pipelined, it is not a split transaction bus. To use the 4D/340 in DASH, we have had to make minor modifications to the existing system boards and design a pair of new boards to support the directory memory and inter-cluster interface. The main modification to the existing boards is to add a bus retry signal that is used when a request requires service from a remote cluster. The central bus arbiter has also been modified to accept a mask from the directory boards which holds off the processor's retry until the remote request has been serviced. This effectively creates a split transaction bus protocol for remote requests. The new directory boards contain the directory memory, remote access cache, intercluster coherence state machines, and a local section of the global interconnection network. The interconnection network is a pair of wormhole routed meshes, each with 16-bit wide channels. One mesh is dedicated to the request messages while the other handles replies. A block diagram of

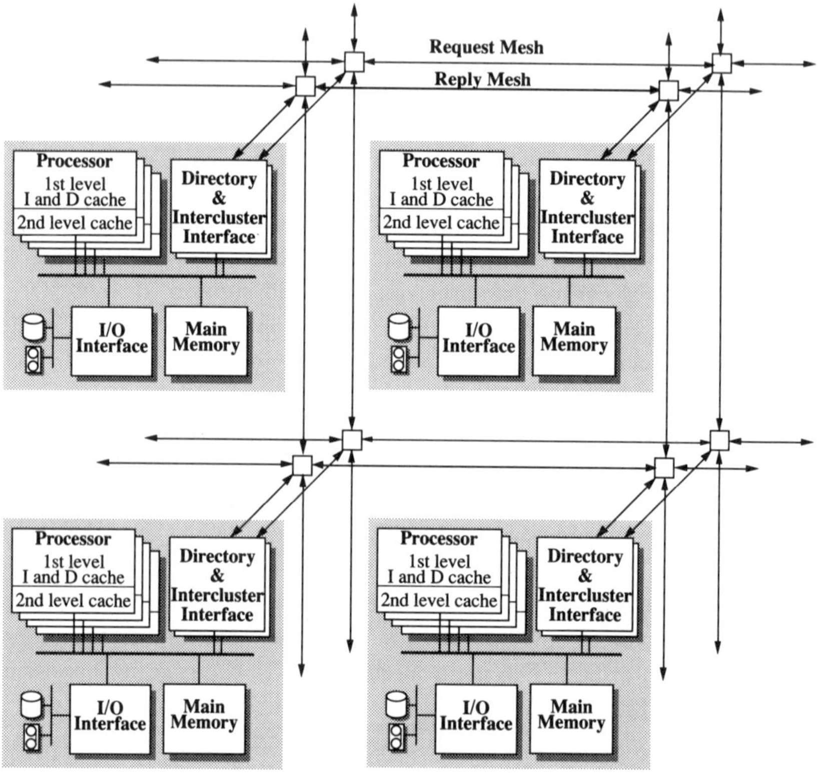

Figure 16.2
Block diagram of a 2 x 2 DASH system.

four clusters interconnected to form a 2 x 2 DASH system is shown in Figure 16.2.

The directory logic is divided between two logic boards roughly between the logic used to generate outbound messages and that to handle inbound messages. The DC board handles outbound messages and is composed of three major subsystems. The first section is the *directory controller* (DC) itself, which includes the directory memory associated with the cachable main memory contained within the cluster. The DC logic also controls processor retry and initiates outbound network requests and replies. The second section is a performance monitor which can count and trace a variety of intra- and inter-cluster events. The third section is the request and reply outbound network logic together with the horizontal dimension of the network itself. The second board is the RC board which is also composed of three major sections. The first section is the *reply controller* (RC) which tracks outstanding requests made by the local processors and receives and buffers replies from remote clusters using the *remote access cache* (RAC). The second section is the *pseudo-CPU* (PCPU) which is responsible for buffering incoming requests and issuing such requests onto the cluster bus. The PCPU mimics a CPU on this bus on behalf of remote processors except that responses from the bus are sent out by the directory controller. The final section is the inbound network logic and the vertical dimension of the mesh routing networks.

16.4 Experimental Results

We are currently debugging a two cluster version of the prototype hardware. Debug has proceeded reasonably well. Along with the normal set of fabrication problems, we have uncovered approximately fifteen logic bugs. Most of these have occured in logic that we were unable to simulate, or are attributable to a misunderstanding of the base SGI hardware. Our biggest problems have come from electrical issues within the mesh networks. At present, we can consistently boot UNIX and use the system, but the system is not stable due to the network problems. We hope to work around these network problems in the near future and complete our initial four cluster prototype.

The performance of the prototype is dictated by a combination of the DASH architecture and the constraints of our implementation. Shown in Figure 16.3 are the latencies of cache fill operations satisfied in the local cluster, the home cluster or a third, dirty cluster. The first two cases were measured on an unloaded two cluster prototype, while the third case is extrapolated based on the two cluster delays. Larger configurations would increase unloaded network latencies by 50 ns per hop in the mesh. Latencies for read-exclusive requests issued by the processor's write-buffer are similar. The penalty for a read miss to the local cluster is 29 processor clocks (dictated by the SGI hardware). A remote miss takes roughly 3.5 times as long. The delays arise primarily from the relatively slow bus in the 3D/340, and our conservative implementation technology and packaging. Simulation studies have shown that queuing adds, on average, an additional 20-120% to these delays. While these latencies are not minimum in absolute terms, when measured in processor clocks, we believe they are similar to what would be observed in a fully integrated system. Given the increasing clock rates of single chip processors and the inherent latencies of a large system, access to remote memory will inevitably be costly.

Applications for large multiprocessors must utilize locality in order to realize good cache hit rates, minimize remote accesses and achieve high processor utilization. Figure 16.4 shows the speed-up for three applications on simulated DASH systems consisting of 1 to 64 processors (1 to 16 clusters). The numbers in parentheses indicate the relative speed-up compared with the previous data point on the curve. The three applications simulated are WATER, MINCUT and MP3D. The WATER code performs molecular dynamics calculations to compute the energy levels of a system of water molecules, while MINCUT uses parallel simulated annealing to solve a graph partitioning problem. MP3D models a wind tunnel using discrete particle-based simulation. The applications were simulated using a combination of the Tango multiprocessor simulator and a detailed memory simulator for the DASH prototype. The tight coupling between Tango and the memory simulator, together with calibration of the memory simulator to the prototype hardware, produces an accurate simulation of the application running on the real hardware.

The simulations show that WATER and MINCUT achieve reasonable speed-ups up to 64 processors. For WATER, the reason is that the application exhibits good locality. Miss rates are fairly constant, and the fraction of misses handled by the local cluster decreases only from 69% to 64% as the number of clusters increases from 2 to 16. Thus, cache

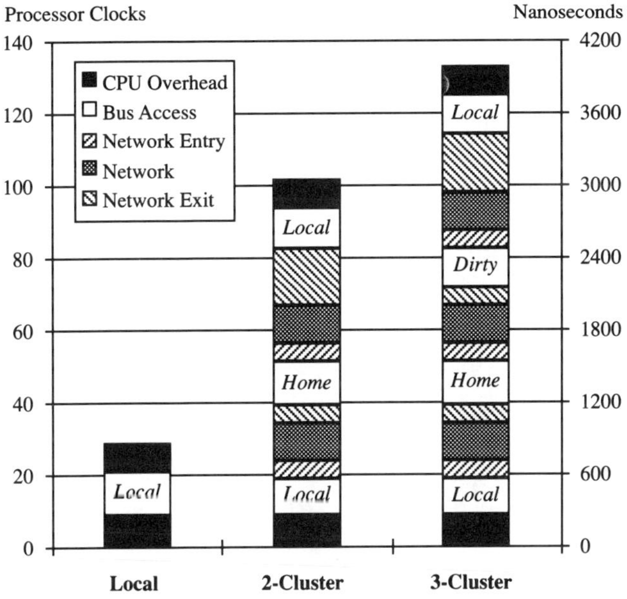

Figure 16.3
Latency of read requests measured on the two cluster DASH prototype without contention.

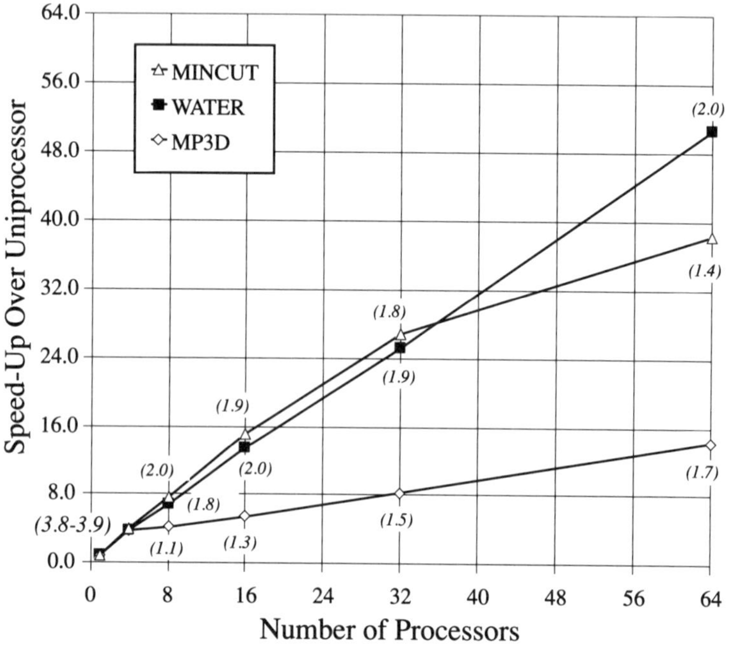

Figure 16.4
Speed-up of the three parallel application on simulation of the DASH prototype.

miss penalties increase slowly with system size, and do not adversely affect processor utilizations. For MINCUT, good speed-up results from very good cache hit rates (> 98% hit rate for shared references). The roll-off in MINCUT with 64 processors is due to contention for locks within the application itself. MP3D obviously does not exhibit good speed-up on DASH. This is due to MP3D's acute sensitivity to memory latency. On average, about 4% of the instructions executed in MP3D generate a read miss for a shared data item, and these misses exhibit very little locality. Thus, when a second cluster is added the average miss latency doubles and cancels the potential gain from the added processors. Likewise, when four clusters are used, the full benefit is not realized because most misses now become 3-hop misses satisfied by remote dirty clusters. Reasonable speed-up is finally achieved when going beyond 16 processors (relative speed-up of 1.5 and 1.7), but overall speed-up is still limited to 14.2. Even for MP3D, however, caching is beneficial. A 64 processor system with the timing of DASH, but without the caching for shared data, achieves only a 4.1 speed-up over the cached uniprocessor.

16.5 Concluding Remarks

In this paper we have described DASH, a large scale single-address space multiprocessor with coherent caches being designed at Stanford. The key concepts in achieving scalability are the use of a distributed directory-based cache coherence protocol, distributed memories and directories, and a scalable interconnection network. The design optimizes along the dimensions of scaling the memory bandwidth and reducing the latency of remote memory accesses. We have also discussed several other performance enhancements for DASH. These include mechanisms for reducing and tolerating latency such as prefetch, the release consistency model and synchronization primitives such as queue-based locks. Based on the preliminary performance evaluation here, it is clear that exploiting locality and these features will be important to achieve good speed-up on a wide range of applications.

We are proceeding with our work on the DASH prototype hardware. We hope to confirm the simulation results presented here on the hardware in the near future. We also plan to increase the size of the prototype hardware, and study in detail how the system performs with the operating system and applications working on large data sets.

16.6 Acknowledgments

This research was supported by DARPA contract N00014-87-K-0828. In addition, Daniel Lenoski is supported by Tandem Computers, James Laudon and Wolf-Dietrich Weber are supported by IBM, and Kourosh Gharachorloo is supported by Texas Instruments. Anoop Gupta is partly supported by a NSF Presidential Young Investigator Award.

References

[1] Anant Agarwal, Richard Simoni, John Hennessy, and Mark Horowitz. An evaluation of directory schemes for cache coherence. In *Proceedings of the 15th Annual International Symposium on Computer Architecture*, pages 280–289, June 1988.

[2] J. Elder, A. Gottlieb, C. K. Kruskal, K. P. McAuliffe, L. Rudolph, M. Snir, P. Teller, and J. Wilson. Issues related to MIMD, shared-memory computers: The NYU Ultracomputer approach. In *Proceedings of the 12th Annual International Symposium on Computer Architecture*, pages 126–135, June 1985.

[3] Kourosh Gharachorloo, Anoop Gupta, and John Hennessy. Performance evaluation of memory consistency models for shared-memory multiprocessors. In *Fourth International Conference on Architectural Support for Programming Languages and Operating Systems*, April 1991.

[4] Kourosh Gharachorloo, Daniel Lenoski, James Laudon, Phillip Gibbons, Anoop Gupta, and John Hennessy. Memory consistency and event ordering in scalable shared-memory multiprocessors. In *Proceedings of the 17th Annual International Symposium on Computer Architecture*, pages 15–26, May 1990.

[5] Leslie Lamport. How to make a multiprocessor computer that correctly executes multiprocess programs. *IEEE Transactions on Computers*, C-28(9):241–248, September 1979.

[6] Daniel Lenoski, James Laudon, Kourosh Gharachorloo, Anoop Gupta, and John Hennessy. The directory-based cache coherence protocol for the DASH multiprocessor. In *Proceedings of the 17th Annual International Symposium on Computer Architecture*, May 1990.

[7] Todd Mowry and Anoop Gupta. Tolerating latency through software-controlled prefetching in shared-memory multiprocessors. In *To appear in Journal of Parallel and Distributed Computing*, June 1991.

[8] C. K. Tang. Cache design in the tightly coupled multiprocessor system. In *AFIPS Conference Proceedings, National Computer Conference, NY, NY*, pages 749–753, June 1976.

[9] Wolf-Dietrich Weber and Anoop Gupta. Analysis of cache invalidation patterns in multiprocessors. In *Proceedings of the Third International Conference on Architectural Support for Programming Languages and Operating Systems*, pages 243–256, April 1989.

17 An Analysis of Shared-Memory Synchronization Mechanisms

Philip J. Woest and James R. Goodman

17.1 Introduction

Parallel computing is not an end in itself. It is necessary in order to achieve the high level of performance required to solve the biggest problems, and even to provide cost-effective solutions to moderately large problems. The advent of ever-faster processors at moderate costs focuses the drive for high performance on parallel computing. Thus parallel computing is confronted with the need to coordinate increasing numbers of processors, while at the same time the individual processors are becoming more powerful.

One might hope that arbitrarily powerful systems could be built simply by connecting together a sufficiently large number of processors, limited only by cost. Experience has shown that this is not the case. Any parallel algorithm requires processors to communicate periodically, that is, to synchronize and to share data. While some algorithms allow large amounts of computation between points of communication, many others do not, or at least complete more rapidly if communication is more frequent.

Conceptually, one might add processors incrementally, thereby reducing the granularity of the computation between points of communication. But because communication also involves some delay, the benefit of adding more processors is diminished until, when most of the time is spent on communication, little further improvement can be achieved. In fact, as the number of processors grows, the communication time will almost certainly increase as the interconnection network and memory system becomes more complicated. Thus, there is an optimal number of processors beyond which the performance actually declines.

Intuitively, a balanced system is attained when approximately equal time is spent in computation and communication. Adding more (or faster) processors does not provide major speedups—infinitely fast processors would only speed up the application by a factor of two. Neither does increasing the granularity of the computation—the application will only run a factor of two faster if communication time is reduce to zero. At such a point, significant additional speedup can be achieved only by increasing computational power *and* reducing communication delays.

While increasing computational power is straightforward, if not easy, reducing communication time is neither. Communication delays are fundamentally limited by speed-of-light delays, and it is probably not reasonable to expect a significant reduction in physical size for large systems. Thus the absolute time for communicating information is not likely to be reduced greatly.[1]

The above discussion indicates that in order to achieve higher performance, hardware and software techniques must be used to reduce communication delays. This paper explores the performance of such mechanisms in the context of large-scale shared-memory multiprocessors. Section 2 describes hardware and software for synchronization. Section 3 discusses the reduction of communication latency in systems that employs directory-based cache coherence. A number of synchronization algorithms are described and evaluated using simulation and simple analytical techniques in Section 4. Conclusions are presented in Section 5.

17.2 Hardware and Software for Synchronization

In parallel processing, process communication can be thought of as having two distinct goals: process synchronization and data sharing. The send and receive primitives of non-shared memory multiprocessors implement both of these functions simultaneously. However, in shared-memory systems these functions are generally carried out by separate mechanisms. Read and write operations are used to move data around a system—in accordance with a coherence protocol if cache consistency is maintained by the hardware—while special read-modify-write primitives are generally provided for process synchronization. We take a brief look at some synchronization mechanisms below and address the problem of reducing latency for both synchronization and data sharing in the next section.

A number of hardware primitives have been proposed as a basis for process synchronization in shared-memory multiprocessors. These in-

[1] There is, of course, the opportunity to select algorithms that exhibit geographical locality and to exploit this property to minimize the average communication distance. This does not improve the worst-case delay, and places an additional burden on the programmer to select algorithms that can exploit such locality. It is, nevertheless, part of the solution.

clude traditional Test&Set and Unset, Test&Test&Set [19], the full/empty bits of the HEP multiprocessor [20], and Fetch&Add [11], as well as generalizations, known collectively as Fetch&Φ operations [12, 4, 23]. Unfortunately, most synchronization algorithms which rely on these primitives require spinning over the interconnect or, as in the case of using Test&Test&Set to acquire a lock, cause excessive bus traffic.

The QOLB[2] primitive, was proposed [8] to alleviate these problems, as well as to provide additional benefits by reducing memory latency. It is a shared-memory operation that adds a processor to a hardware queue of waiters for a line. QOLB allows a process to spin on a locally-cached *shadow* copy of a line. When the actual line is released by the process at the head of the queue it is automatically transferred to the cache where the next waiting process resides. The software algorithm for maintaining QOLB queues is discussed in the section on performance.

The QOLB mechanism allows for efficient process synchronization by providing a direct implementation of binary semaphores. As a non-blocking operation, QOLB can prefetch (*i.e.* make local) a line of data while a process performs useful work. Combining these two operations along with a simple software convention, QOLB becomes a *synchronizing prefetch* operation. That is, QOLB can be used to prefetch a line of data, allowing local tests to determine when the data has become available. If a line is prefetched sufficiently in advance, a process could synchronize on and obtain (make local) the shared data without experiencing interconnect delay.

The QOLB primitive was proposed independently of any architecture, and is feasible for any shared-memory multiprocessor, including ones that do not provide caches at all, and those that provide caches but do not include hardware cache coherence. QOLB is largely independent of the communication medium; however, a natural way to implement it efficiently is to extend a cache coherence protocol. QOLB provides its greatest advantages in a network that allows multiple outstanding requests and has a high latency/bandwidth product. It is currently being investigated in two contexts: (1) the Multicube topology [10] employing a broadcast-based cache coherence protocol, and (2) the Scalable Coherent Interface (SCI) [1], a proposed IEEE standard multiproces-

[2] QOLB (Queue On Lock Bit) is pronounced "Colby". It was originally was called QOSB in [8] but was changed to be more precise.

sor interface supporting point-to-point links and a non-broadcast-based cache coherence protocol.

Two software algorithms inspired by QOLB have been developed. Each of these implements queues as software-maintained data structures. Anderson [3] presents a scheme to implement a queue using Fetch&Add an array of flags, and a counter. Mellor-Crummey and Scott [16] present a second algorithm that implements a software queue using Compare&Swap and pointers. Although these algorithms provide queues for locks in software, they introduce substantial synchronization and data acquisition delays. Discussion and analysis of these algorithms are postponed until the section on performance.

As a final note, Fetch&Φ primitives may be implemented in a shared memory environment in two different ways. First, they may be implemented as cache operations, performed locally by locking the appropriate cache word to insure that the read-modify-write operation is performed atomically. In this case the primitive is treated as a write operation by the underlying cache coherence protocol, which responds by supplying an exclusive copy of the line containing the desired word to the local cache. Second, Fetch&Φ primitives may be implemented as remote memory operations, performed on the desired word by the controller at the appropriate memory. The first implementation will be denoted as "coherent" operations and the second as "at-memory" operations. QOLB is always treated as a coherent operation.

17.3 Reducing Communication Latency

A shared-memory programming model provides a powerful, yet conceptually simple framework for constructing parallel applications. In addition, shared-memory hardware, such as a cache coherence protocol, typically provides a finer granularity of sharing than that of message-based systems. The finer the granularity the more processors that can be applied to a problem. Thus, shared-memory systems would seem to have a performance advantage over message-based systems as well.

Unfortunately, higher performance is difficult to achieve with shared-memory multiprocessors due to the overhead of synchronization and sharing. For example, cache coherence constraints typically require three or four traversals of the interconnect, each followed by an access to some type of memory, in order to acquire write access to shared data.

Synchronization operations usually must follow the same protocol, with additional constraints to insure that data accesses occur in a sequentially consistent manner.

As an example, suppose that process B executes a simple critical section that is guarded by a lock currently held by process A. A typical "efficient" method of synchronization in a shared-memory system requires process B to spin locally on a cached copy of the lock. For reasons of efficiency it is assumed that the line containing the lock is an exclusive copy. To release mutual exclusion on the critical section, process A writes the lock. This write operation requires a minimum of three traversals of the interconnect: (1) to interrogate the directory, (2) to forward the request from the directory to the cache with the exclusive copy of the lock, and (3) to forward the line containing the lock to the process performing the write. Process B, upon losing its cached copy of the lock attempts to reacquire it by performing a write operation (*i.e.* a Test&Set on the lock. Again three traversals of the interconnect are required. Because process B is spinning on the lock, the operation from that process to interrogate the cache is issued while the lock is being forwarded to process A. This permits the accesses of process A and process B to overlap slightly, resulting in a total synchronization latency of as little as five traversals of the interconnect.

Once the lock has changed hands, process B typically attempts to acquire the shared data necessary to execute the code in the critical section. Assuming that this data fits into a single cache line, another three traversals of the interconnect are needed. Process B then completes the critical section by performing the desired computation.

This situation is depicted in the first time line of Figure 17.1. Each short segment is a traversal of the interconnect, and is labelled as either A or B, depending on which process issued the request which that traversal is part of. The latency for executing a critical section is divided into three parts: (1) the delay due to synchronization (acquiring the lock), (2) the delay due to accessing shared data, and (3) the time to perform the desired computation. Note that any delay waiting for the previous process to finish its critical section is not included. Eliminating or reducing such a delay can only be handled by the programmer, not the synchronization hardware.

From the above discussion it is not difficult to see why message-based systems may hold a performance advantage over shared-memory sys-

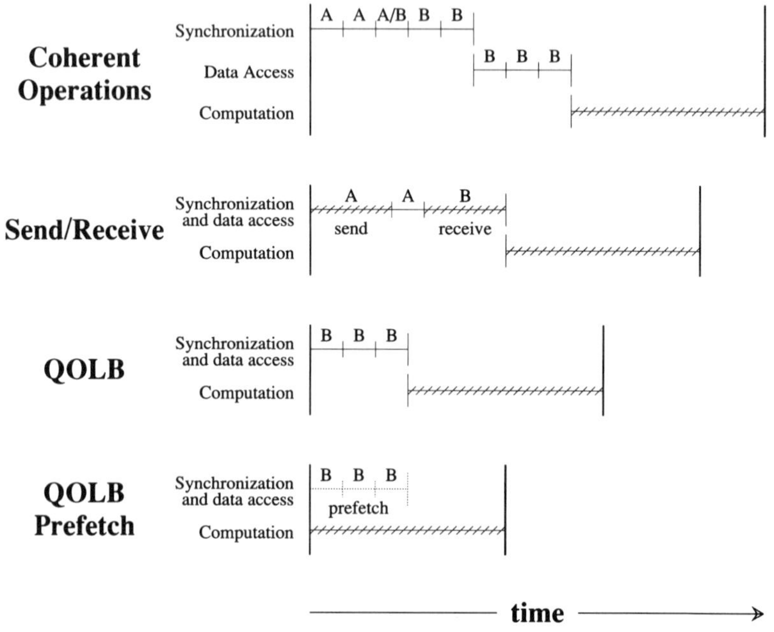

Figure 17.1
Access Times for Critical Sections. Shown is the time to access a critical section for different synchronization models and levels of support. Each time line is broken down into the times for synchronization (excluding waiting for the data to become available), access to shared data, and computation. Interconnect delays are shown as simple straight lines, while computational delays are depicted as lines with cross slashes.

tems. First, the send/receive mechanism overlaps synchronization with the acquisition of shared data. Intuitively, the send primitive supplies data as soon as it becomes available to the process that will request it next (assuming the identity of that process is known). Thus, the combined synchronization and data latency is made up of three parts: (1) the execution of the send primitive, (2) a single interconnect traversal to supply the data, and (3) the execution of the receive primitive. This section execution profile is shown as the second time line in Figure 17.1. Note that the middle portion of the synchronization and data access latency, the interconnect latency, could potentially be overlapped with useful computation, further improving the efficiency of message-based multiprocessors.

Unfortunately, implementations of send and receive result in primitives that require a significant amount of processor time to execute, although they can be sped up by the use of special hardware [18]. This situation is exacerbated if the operating system is invoked, which requires context switches. Thus message passing systems experience substantial latencies for process communication, much longer than those of a typical shared-memory operation.

What is needed is a mechanism with the latency of a shared-memory primitive that can acquire shared data as soon as it becomes available. Such a primitive is QOLB. QOLB overlaps synchronization (*i.e.* the acquisition of a lock) with a request for exclusive access to the data, actually eliminating the interconnect latency of following reads and writes by allowing them to occur locally once the lock is transferred to the waiting process. This overlap occurs explicitly because the shared data and the lock guarding that data can be placed in the same line when QOLB is used along with Test&Set. Thus, the total latency is that for a single remote access, namely, three interconnect traversals. This situation is depicted by the third time line of Figure 17.1.

Because QOLB is a non-blocking synchronizing operation, it can be used to prefetch a line containing a lock and shared data. A line may be prefetched as soon as a process knows what data it needs, and that the lock guarding the data has been acquired by the process producing the needed data. If prefetching is performed sufficiently in advance then the latency of the first two traversals used to locate the data may be avoided. If the data itself becomes available soon enough, then the entire communication latency, both synchronization and data acquisition, may be overlapped with useful computation. This situation is shown as the last time line of Figure 17.1.

The relative performance of QOLB to send/receive depends primarily on two factors. First, the type and efficiency of support that a message-passing system provides can have a dramatic effect on the time required by a processor to execute the send and receive primitives. Second, the structure of the application must allow prefetch QOLB operations to be performed early enough to overlap the computation of earlier critical sections.

Figure 17.1 is useful for a final observation. If the granularity of the critical section computations was sufficiently coarse to allow a balance of latencies for the case of typical cache coherent synchronization, then obviously using QOLB and prefetching will support a finer granularity to achieve that same balance. Thus, the time to complete a unit of work may be substantially reduced by increasing the number of processors. A finer granularity can be used to split the work of the critical section into a number of smaller critical sections which can then be distributed among the processors.

17.4 Performance

In evaluating hardware memory primitives for large-scale shared-memory multiprocessors one must consider those scenarios that require efficient synchronization and data sharing among large numbers of processes. The synchronization scenarios chosen for this study consist of locks (especially for pairwise sharing), counters, barriers, and global event notification. These scenarios are the same as those proposed by Goodman, Vernon, and Woest [8] with one exception. The work queue scenario has been replaced by incrementing a counter. The provision of fast counters represents the crux of the problem of implementing highly parallel queues, and is much more general. We believe the above scenarios represent, or are typical of, the most critical problems in providing efficient support for parallel applications.

First analytical and simulation methods used to perform the evaluations are discussed. Then the synchronization scenarios are presented, each followed by the description of several algorithms either constructed by the authors or chosen from previous studies, and a discussion of their performance.

17.4.1 Performance Methods

Both analytical techniques and simulation were used to provide performance results for the chosen synchronization scenarios. Specifically, simple counting techniques were used for evaluating lock algorithms, and verified using a simulator. Simulation was used to analyze counter and barrier methods. The advantage of using simulation for these scenarios are two-fold. First, a simulator can be used to test the correctness of algorithms, as well as assist in pointing out where algorithms may be modified to improve performance. It is especially important to realize that synchronization algorithms contain complex interactions that may be overlooked when attempting to estimate performance using analytical techniques. Second, an appropriate simulator can evaluate arbitrary synchronization algorithms without major modifications.

Simulation results were obtained using a simulator that models the execution of a single synchronization algorithm by a set of processors. An algorithm is represented by a stored program consisting of simple arithmetic operations, program control, and memory operations. The primary requirements of the simulator are that it is capable (1) of evaluating arbitrary synchronization algorithms and (2) of accurately modeling the delays associated with accesses to shared variables.

To assist in the analysis, a model of a shared-memory cache-coherent multiprocessor was constructed. This model is very similar to the the Multicube topology [10], especially in its implementation of the interconnect, with a directory-based cache coherence protocol. The model consists of a multidimensional grid of buses (the global interconnect), with processing nodes located at the intersections. A node consists of a processor, a two-level cache hierarchy, and a portion of main memory. For purposes of this study each processor executes a single process. It should be made clear that the term "cache" in the context of this paper refers to the second-level cache. Processors are allowed multiple outstanding requests, but only the software combining counter algorithm actually makes use of this feature. The lock, barrier, and other counter algorithms do not require such a capability. For this study, the processors must wait for acknowledgements for write operations before proceeding.[3]

[3] The QOLB primitive is complete in the sense that no other hardware support is needed to assure correct synchronization, *i.e.*, even fences [4] are unnecessary.

A number of simplifying assumptions were made in the model in order to allow the analysis of competing algorithms to focus on shared variable latency issues. These assumptions are that (1) caches are infinite in size, (2) processors are infinitely fast, and (3) message queues are "large".

Infinite caches ensure that misses will occur only for shared data that has been invalidated due to a request from another cache.[4] However, since none of the synchronization algorithms require much data, either private or shared, this should cause little perturbation in the results. Likewise, infinitely fast processors (and infinitely fast first-level caches) need have little effect on the results, since processors can be arbitrarily delayed at any point in there execution of an algorithm. In addition the second level cache will only allow non-local memory requests to be issued, or replies to be received, at a specifiable rate. Finally, the most significant impact of large queues is likely to be the reduction of hot-spot effects by mitigating tree saturation effects.[5] Fortunately, few algorithms in this study exhibit hot spots, and the ones mostly likely to benefit from large queues are those that already perform poorly in comparison to other algorithms.

At-memory requests always bypass the cache and are performed on a single word at the appropriate memory. Coherent line requests are routed to the appropriate memory and either obtain the line from the memory or are forwarded to the cache that currently has the exclusive copy of the line. At-memory and coherent line operations are never performed on the same cache line. In fact, they are generally not used in the same algorithm, except for some of the lock examples where the choice of synchronization method involves at-memory primitives and the shared data is exchanged using coherent line read and write operations.

The service times for the system we envision are based on an assumption of approximately 10 ns per cycle, but some scaling of these numbers either direction is appropriate. The following specific timings were used. A memory read requires 5 cycles, although updating the directory or the line itself (usually the case) requires 10 cycles. Directory and cache memory have the same characteristics as those of main memory.

Sequential consistency [15] deals with the correct observable ordering of memory accesses. Several models of "weaker" forms of consistency have been developed, for example [6, 9, 2, 7]. Relaxing the restrictions on sequential consistency using QOLB is the subject of a separate study [21].

[4] Cold start misses are also ignored.

[5] See [17] for a discussion of hot-spot contention and tree saturation.

Bus arbitration and synchronization requires 4 cycles. Requests may be address only (2 cycles), address plus a line of data (8 cycles), or address plus a word for at-memory operations (generally 3 cycles). These are in addition to the initial 4 cycles for arbitration. A request can be forwarded as soon as the address portion is transmitted (6 cycles total). Reliability constraints dictate that an entire request be received and error correction performed (2 additional cycles) before service can be completed. Buses service requests in a round robin fashion.

17.4.2 Locks (Critical Sections)

Locks are used to restrict access to shared data to a single process at a time, so that reading and writing of the data may occur without interference from competing accesses. This type of synchronization is called a critical section. If the critical section is empty, then the lock is basically being used as a timing mechanism. Such a situation may exist, for example, in barrier synchronization where one process may wish to let another know that it has completed its appointed computation.

Two situations are common. These correspond to the two states which a lock may be found in, namely, idle or busy. Idle locks are typical of situations where locks are precautionary, that is, where contention is possible but infrequent. Busy locks are commonly found in many situations, especially those involving pairwise sharing, whenever one process is waiting for data being written by another. However, if a lock is released before it is requested then the lock is considered to be idle.

It should be pointed out that serialized access to data implies that, in a large-scale shared-memory multiprocessor, high contention for a lock will cause a severe bottleneck. In addition, with high contention, starvation of some processes may be much more likely, depending on the specific mechanism used for granting the lock. While parallel applications may use locks which change hands frequently, these algorithms are unlikely to scale as the number of contending processes increases. Thus, the behavior of locking mechanisms under conditions of high contention does not appear to be a good indicator of performance. In addition, since most of the mechanisms analyzed are "contentionless", a simple analysis of the time required for a (busy) lock to change hands is likely to provide at least a lower bound on a situation where there is high contention.

Results are provided for three algorithms: spinlocks, QOLB locks, and a software queue-based locking mechanism (MCS locks [16]). Both idle

```
while(test&set(lock))
     /* wait */

critical work
unset(lock)
```

Figure 17.2
Spinlocks.

and busy lock performance are studied. Locks are compared for two types of computation, the first where the critical section is empty, and the second where the critical section performs some simple function, for example, incrementing a counter. The null critical section provides an estimate of the overhead incurred by the lock mechanism itself. The counter critical section is more indicative of true performance since, realistically, a critical section will generally contain at least one read and one write to shared data. For the non-null critical section, coherent line primitives are always used to read and write the line.

Critical sections requiring access to multiple lines of data are not specifically considered. Given a system which supports a model of consistency that allows multiple outstanding requests from a single processor, techniques are possible which allow the acquisition of multiple lines of data to be overlapped with the latency for acquiring the first line. Details concerning appropriate hardware and software (*e.g.* lockup free caches) is considered beyond the scope of this study.

17.4.2.1 Lock Algorithms The first lock algorithm is a simple spinlock using Test&Set and Unset. For coherent line primitives, on each lock access the corresponding line is first transferred to the cache of the requesting process before being accessed. For at-memory primitives, these operations are performed at the memory where the word normally resides. A simple spinlock is shown as Figure 17.2.

QOLB locks are very similar to Test&Set spinlocks with the exception that a QOLB lock is issued before the spin loop. The QOLB operation allocates a hardware queue entry in the local cache which allows the process to spin locally using Test&Set. Through the hardware queuing mechanism the desired line is eventually written into the cache when the

```
procedure acquire(lock)
begin
     QOLB(lock)
     while(test&set(lock))
          QOLB(lock)
end

acquire(lock)

critical work
unset(lock)
```

Figure 17.3
QOLB Locks.

lock is free and the process is at the head of the queue. After the line becomes local the next Test&Set operation will succeed.

Since a QOLB request is for an entire line, transfer of the first line of data is overlapped with the acquisition of the lock. Also, since QOLB is non-blocking, multiple locks can be acquired simultaneously and/or computation can be performed before the process actually attempts to set the lock. Both of these possibilities point to the use of QOLB as a synchronizing prefetch operation. The acquisition of locks, as well as shared data, can be overlapped with useful work. Thus, it is possible to reduce the latency of a critical section to the processor time for executing the critical section code. The QOLB lock scheme is shown as Figure 17.3. An extended discussion is given elsewhere [8].

The MCS algorithm [16] implements queue-based locks in software, rather than in hardware, as QOLB does. It improves on Anderson's lock algorithm [3] by forcing all spinning to be performed locally. An atomic Swap operation and an atomic Compare&Swap operation are provided, along with both Fetch and Store, as at-memory primitives. The Compare&Swap operation is not strictly required, however replacing it by other at-memory operations would only serve to increase the latency of the algorithm. The MCS lock scheme is described briefly below and is shown as Figure 17.4.

In the MCS algorithm a process adds itself to a queue of waiting processes, where each queue entry contains a pointer to another queue

```
struct entry                  /* queue entry   */
     integer next             /* next process */
     boolean locked           /* local flag    */
end

shared integer lockid         /* queue tail    */
shared entry lock[nprocs]     /* lock entries */
integer pred                  /* predecessor   */
integer succ                  /* successor     */
integer myid                  /* my process id*/

  /* allocate lock[x] local to process x */

lock[myid].next = NIL
pred = swap(lockid,myid)
if (pred != NIL)
     lock[myid].locked = 1
     lock[pred].next = myid
     while (lock[myid].locked)
          /* wait */


critical work

if (lock[myid].next == NIL)
     if (!compare&swap(lockid,myid,NIL))
          while (lock[myid].next == NIL)
               /* wait */
          succ = lock[myid].next
          lock[succ].locked = 0
else
     succ = lock[myid].next
     lock[succ].locked = 0
```

Figure 17.4
MCS Locks.

Table 17.1
Idealized Critical Section Times for Locks Mechanisms. Given is the latency in bus cycles of various lock mechanisms (spinlocks, MCS locks, QOLB locks) for two types of critical sections (null, counter) and two types of memory primitives (coherent, at-memory).

Lock Algorithm	Type of Primitive	Critical Section	Latency (Cycles) Idle	Busy
Spinlock	coherent	null	59	103
		counter	118	162
Spinlock	at-memory	null	62	48
		counter	121	107
MCS lock	at-memory	null	79	57
		counter	138	116
QOLB lock	coherent	null/counter	59	25
		prefetched	0	25

entry and a boolean flag. This is accomplished by swapping a pointer to the process's locally allocated queue entry with the tail pointer of the queue. The value returned from the Swap operation is a pointer to the queue entry of the process's predecessor in the queue. If there is no predecessor the process has acquired the lock. Otherwise, the process writes a pointer to itself into the predecessor's queue entry and waits on its own local flag. The write informs the predecessor as to which process to unblock when it releases the lock.

The release operation simply requires that a process unblock its successor by writing the successor's local flag. If there is no known successor the process performs a Compare&Swap operation to guarantee that the queue is empty. If another process (successor) has recently joined the queue then the process holding the lock must wait until the pointer in its queue entry is written with the identity of its successor in order to perform the unblock operation.

17.4.2.2 Lock Performance Table 17.1 summarizes the performance of the various lock algorithms for a two-dimensional, unloaded system. A coherent line operation requires 59 cycles in which to to interrogate the directory, find the exclusive copy of the line, and move that copy to the requesting processor's cache. Since three interconnect traversals and three memory access are involved, this indicates that about 20 cycles are required per traversal/memory access pair.

A spinlock requires exactly one coherent operation (*i.e.* a Test&Set operation) to acquire an idle lock, and two such operations if a line of data is needed as well. If the lock is busy then additional time is required to release the lock which, according to Figure 17.1, is about 5 traversals total, or 100 cycles. This agrees very well with the analytical results.

Spinlocks can be made more efficient for acquiring busy locks by using at-memory operations instead of coherent operations to synchronize. At-memory operations require only about 15 cycles per traversal, since a line of data need not be transferred, and do not cause a ping-pong effect when a lock is released. Thus a spinlock using at-memory primitives requires two traversals to set an idle lock and two to release it (about 60 cycles total). Likewise it can be shown that on average about three traversals are needed if the lock is busy (about 45 cycles), although the timing is more complicated. The exact numbers, verified by the simulator, agree well with these estimates. Again, requiring a line of data using a coherent write operation adds another 59 cycles to the latency.

The latency of the MCS lock algorithm is just slightly longer than that for spinlocks, which is unexpected given that it requires more memory accesses. The key is that many of these accesses are to variables allocated in local main memory (not cache). While MCS locks have slightly higher latency, it must be remembered that they cause no spinning over the interconnect. In a real system this translates into less bandwidth consumption and the elimination of the synchronization hot spot that spinlocks cause when more than a single process waits on the same lock. Thus, MCS locks can be used when spinlocks are inappropriate.

The fastest mechanism, however, is the QOLB algorithm. For busy locks, that is for cases where the QOLB queue is set up while the critical section is in use, only a single traversal of the interconnect is necessary to transfer the lock to the next process in the queue once the lock is released. This is the same efficiency as send/receive, which also requires only a single traversal. However, QOLB still has lower latency, since shared-memory operations do not require as much processing. The result is a factor of four speedup over other shared-memory algorithms, for a non-null critical section.

For idle locks QOLB requires a single coherent operation. This results in a factor of two speedup over any of the other schemes. However, if the lock can be prefetched, that is, if the process knows in advance that the lock is needed, the QOLB operation can completely overlap useful computation, and perform the critical section with zero synchronization and data sharing overhead. With prefetching of a busy lock QOLB still requires a single traversal of the interconnect. It is exactly in these prefetching situations where QOLB can improve performance the most.

17.4.3 Counters

Unlike general locks, incrementing a counter is an example of a critical section where high contention must be handled efficiently. Counters have a number of uses, from obtaining a unique number, to determining which loop iteration to perform, to obtaining an index into a work queue. Algorithms for barriers generally are not appropriate for counters. Although a barrier essentially counts the arrival of processes, counter applications do not necessarily assume that all processes will participate, or at least not necessarily within a reasonable time frame.

There are four major classes of hardware/software support for counters: (1) serial, (2) pipelined (serial only at memory), (3) software combining, and (4) hardware combining. Assuming that the interconnect involves $O(\log n)$ latency for a request to traverse it, the time required for n processes to acquire a unique number can be computed for each class. For serial techniques $O(n \log n)$ time is required since each request requires a traversal of the interconnect. For pipelined techniques, memory may complete an increment operation every t cycles for a total latency of $O(n)$. Using software combining, a tree requires $O(\log n)$ operations, each requiring a memory request for a total latency of $O(\log^2 n)$. Finally, hardware combining requires time proportional to a single request over the interconnect. Thus, its time is $O(\log n)$. Below, examples of each of the first three classes of counters are examined. The performance of hardware combining is represented by the most ideal situation, which for this model is the completion of an increment operation for every process every 32 cycles.

Of all of the serial algorithms studied in the lock section, QOLB locks performed the best. The fastest pipelined algorithm is a Fetch&Increment operation performed at memory. The choice of a software combining method is that developed in a previous work [8]. Since the QOLB algorithm has already been described, and the lock algorithm is a simple Fetch&Increment instruction, we will turn to the software combining algorithm.

The software combining algorithm, simplified to use a binary tree, is shown as Figure 17.5. The algorithm consists of four parts. In part one a process proceeds up the tree acquiring nodes, marking them as visited, and unlocking them. The process stops when it either reaches the root or finds a node already visited. In part two the process reacquires the nodes it has visited, combining any results from other processes participating in incrementing the counter. These nodes are then left locked so further combining is prohibited. In part three, the process performs the increment if it has reached the root. Otherwise, the process places its combined increment in the topmost node it has reached, unlocks that node so that it may be combined in higher stages of the tree, and waits for a result. In part four, the process distributes the result to all nodes that it had performed the combining for. New combining is now allowed to continue in a following wave. The interested reader is directed elsewhere [8] for a more detailed description.

Figure 17.6 shows the latency of the counter algorithms, for a fixed size system, as the number of participating processes increase. In this graph the curve for hardware combining is indistinguishable from the baseline. The performance for the algorithms is as one would predict. To obtain a better view of the relative performance of the algorithms for fewer numbers of processes, the latency may be divided by the number of competing processes to yield the time per between increment operations. From this second graph some additional performance details become clear. Even with a small constant for the pipelined Fetch&Increment operation and a rather large constant for software combining, the crossover point between the two schemes is at only 64 processes. However, there are two factors that may decrease the performance of software combining. First the degree of combining is artificially high in that all processes are participating all of the time. Second, no computational delays were included in the simulation which, although small in comparison to memory and interconnect latencies, may slow down the algorithm a bit. These factors would tend to move the curve for software combining farther to the right in the second graph.

17.4.4 Barrier Synchronization

Barrier synchronization is a mechanism which guarantees that all processes have reached a specific point in their execution before any are allowed to proceed. It is used to synchronize the exchange of shared

```
/* PART 1: Mark free nodes going up tree */

     value = 1
     i = leaf(pid)
     loop
          acquire(tree[i].lock)
          while (tree[i].state == RESULT)  /* wait */
               unlock(tree[i].lock)
               acquire(tree[i].lock)
          if (tree[i].state != FREE)
               break
          tree[i].state = MARKED
          unset(tree[i].lock)
          i = up(pid,i)
     end
     highest = i

/* PART 2: Reacquire nodes and combine increments */

     i = leaf(pid)
     while (i != highest)      /* prefetch first */
          qolb(tree[i].lock)
          i = up(pid,i)
     i = leaf(pid)
     while (i != highest)
          acquire(tree[i].lock)
          if (tree[i].state == COMBINE)
               value = value + tree[i].value
               tree[i] = value - tree[i].value
          i = up(pid,i)

/* PART 3: Enter increment and wait for result */

     if (tree[i].state == ROOT)
          tree[i].value = tree[i].value + value
          v = tree[i].value - value
     else
          tree[i].value = value
          while (tree[i].state == COMBINE) /* wait */
               unset(tree[i].lock)
               acquire(tree[i].lock)
          value = tree[i].value
          tree[i].state = FREE
     unset(tree[i].lock)

/* PART 4: Distribute results back down tree */

     while (i != leaf(pid))
          i = down(pid,i)
          if (tree[i].state == COMBINE)
               tree[i].state = RESULT
               tree[i].value = tree[i].value + value
          else
               tree[i].state = FREE
          unset(tree[i].lock)
```

Figure 17.5
Software Combining of Increment Operations.

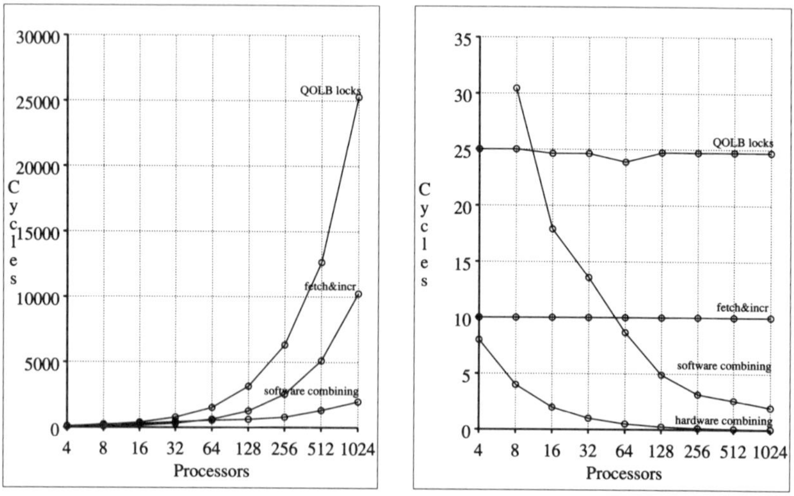

Figure 17.6
Time per Increment Operation: System and Process Views. Shown on the left is the average latency for an increment operation to complete. On the right is the same information, but with latency divided by the number of competing processors. This yields the time between increment operations, as seen by the system, and gives a better view of the relative performance of the algorithms for fewer numbers of processes. The system size is 1024 processors, with the actual number of competing processors given by the x-axis.

data so that updates to that data have completed before the next phase of computation. A typical case is synchronizing between iterations of a loop.

A barrier consists of two functions: (1) insuring that all processes have reached the barrier and (2) notifying all of the processes once that point is reached. Since barriers need to handle large numbers of processes efficiently, tree-based combining algorithms have been proposed to allow processes to declare themselves as having arrived. Such an algorithm, employing Fetch&Increment and a tree of counters, was analyzed by Yew, Tzeng, and Lawrie [22].

The second part, notifying processes that the barrier has been reached, is a useful technique in any instance requiring notification of a global event, such as in majority (or k out of n) decisions, or for indicating the successful termination of a parallel search. Three methods of notification are studied: (1) a simple write to a global flag, (2) a broadcast write to a global flag, and (3) a tree-based method of distributing the notification. The difference between a simple write and a broadcast write is that the former causes an invalidation with subsequent traffic to re-read the flag, while the latter does not.

In this section, the performance of several barrier algorithms are analyzed in terms of latency for large numbers of processes. The relative performance of the three notification schemes are also analyzed. Finally, estimates of the advantage of locality optimizations are presented.

17.4.4.1 Barrier Algorithms The first algorithm is a combination of the fastest serial counter, Fetch&Increment, with the fastest method of notification, NOTIFY. The last process to increment the shared counter performs a broadcast write allowing all processes to proceed past the barrier. The sense of the the notification flag is reversed each iteration in order to speed up execution. This algorithm is shown as Figure 17.7.

While it is natural to separate the two functions of counting arrivals and global notification, it is also possible to combine them, as in the case of the butterfly barrier [5]. This algorithm requires a process to perform $\log n$ pairwise synchronizations, the pairs being chosen in such a way that a process can complete all of the synchronizations only when all processes have reached the barrier. An improved algorithm, the dissemination barrier, has also been developed and studied [13]. This algorithm reduces the cost of synchronizations by making them one-way and employing

```
if (fetch&incr(count) == n)
     count = 1
     NOTIFY(flag,sense)
else
     while (flag != sense)
          /* wait */
sense = ! sense
```

Figure 17.7
Serial Barrier Using Fetch&Increment.

```
i = 0
while (i < log(n))
     p = partner(i,pid)
     flag[set,i,p] = sense
     while (flag[set,i,pid] != sense)
          /* wait */
     i = i + 1
set = 1 - set
if (set == 0)
     sense = ! sense
```

Figure 17.8
Dissemination (Butterfly) Barrier.

a different pattern of processor-to-memory writes. Two copies of the synchronization variables are used to ensure that there is no interference between consecutively executed barriers. The dissemination barrier is given in Figure 17.8.

Restricting the number of processors per bus to a power of two, an appropriate partner function for this study is given by $partner(i, k) = i \oplus 2^k$. If processes are assigned to processors in a consecutive manner then each synchronization traverses only a single stage of the interconnect, independent of the number of stages, potentially reducing the latency of the barrier by a significant factor.

Hensgen, Finkel, and Manber propose a second algorithm called a tournament barrier [13]. In this scheme processes race up a binary tree. Since the winner is statically determined at each level, the loser simply

```
if (level(pid) != LEAF)
     while (tree[pid] != sense)
          /* wait */

if (level(pid) != ROOT)
     p = parent(pid)
     tree[p] = sense

p = right_child(pid)
if (p != nil)
     flag[p] = sense
p = left_child(pid)
if (p != nil)
     flag[p] = sense

sense = ! sense
```

Figure 17.9
Tournament Barrier with Tree Wakeup.

writes a flag to let the winner know that it has reached the barrier. The winner at the root node initiates the notification process, which is passed down the tree until it reaches the leaves.

The tournament algorithm presented here is very similar. Each process waits on a single shared variable that is initialized to the total number of winning rounds for that process. Losing processes simply decrement the appropriate variable by one, allowing a winner to stop spinning when its shared variable becomes zero. The reason for the different algorithm is in the choice of an appropriate parent function which is given by $parent(i) = i - 2^{\log n - k - 1}$. If processes are assigned to processors in a consecutive manner then each synchronization traverses only a single stage of the interconnect. Wakeup may be performed using any of the notification schemes described earlier. The tournament barrier using a separate tree of flags to perform the wakeup operation is shown as Figure 17.9. This algorithm can be easily modified to use a broadcast NOTIFY operation along the lines of the Fetch&Increment algorithm.

Performance results for a tournament barrier modified to use QOLB and NOTIFY are also given. This algorithm is quite naive, employing no prefetching techniques. The purpose of its inclusion is simply to show barrier performance for an algorithm using coherent line primitives. Prefetching may be added to any of the Fetch&Φ based algorithms by using multiple copies of the barrier structure and appropriately locking and prefetching synchronization variables in advance. In the case of tournament and dissemination barriers, QOLB requires the *same* traversal of the interconnect for each variable as does the Fetch&Φ based algorithms. Thus, it should be clear that QOLB prefetching will yield essentially the same level of performance. QOLB has no significant advantage in performance since no data is associated with the lock.

17.4.4.2 Barrier Performance Figure 17.10 shows the average time to complete a barrier for each of the various algorithms. The 8 processor case uses a single bus, while each 8-fold increase in the number of processes requires an additional stage in the interconnect. Each process is delayed 180 to 220 cycles between barriers according to a uniform distribution. This delay randomizes the arrival of processes to the barrier. In addition, processes are assigned randomly to processors. Although a process is allowed to spin locally on a wakeup flag, nonlocal accesses to synchronization variables require, on average, latency proportional to the number of stages in the interconnect.

The first graph demonstrates that using schemes that create hot-spots, such as Fetch&Increment yields performance which is unacceptable beyond a small number of processors. The second graph gives a more detailed view of the performance of the lower latency barrier algorithms. All of the plots in Figure 17.10 curve upwards since the latency of a barrier is at least $O(\log^2 n)$, one factor of $\log n$ for the number of synchronization levels in the barrier, and the other for the latency of the interconnect. The tournament barrier, using a binary arrival tree and NOTIFY, has the lowest latency, closely followed by the dissemination barrier. The difference is due to the larger number of synchronizations required by the dissemination barrier as compared to the the tournament barrier. The tournament barrier using tree notification and the QOLB barrier using NOTIFY have roughly twice the expected latency of the other two schemes.

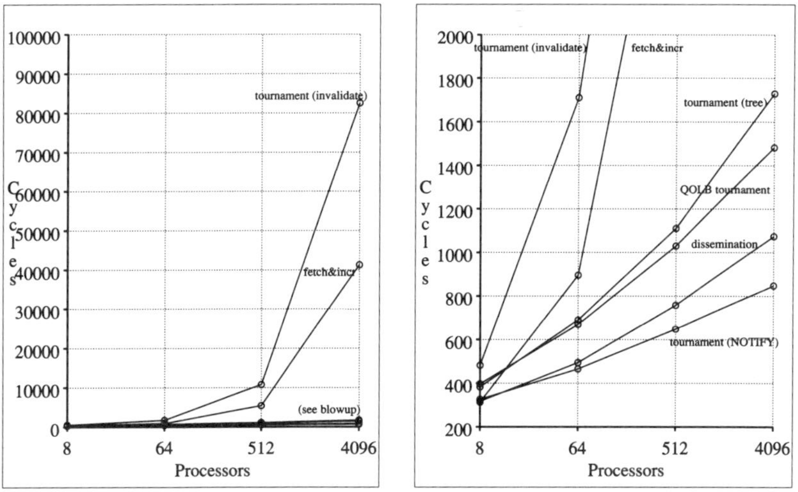

Figure 17.10
Performance of Barrier Algorithms. Shown is the average time to complete a barrier. Each process is delayed 180 to 220 cycles between barriers according to a uniform distribution. The 8 processor case uses a single bus, with another stage (dimension) added to the interconnect for each 8-fold increase in the number of processors. The graph on the right is a blowup of that on the left detailing the performance of the lower latency algorithms. Processes are assigned randomly to processors.

These performance results have several implications for global event notification. First, read-sharing[6] generally causes unacceptable performance, such as in the case of a write invalidation of a globally shared wakeup flag. Furthermore, the use of the NOTIFY primitive is only acceptable if the initial traffic to read the shared notification variable is amortized over a large number of iterations of the barrier. This number is on the order of 1000 cycles for 4K processors. An alternative is to provide hardware support for combining read-sharing traffic. Thus, notification through a tree of shared variables may perform better over a wide range of situations, even though its latency is approximately twice as long. The best alternative may be to use a dissemination barrier, which provides almost the speed of a tournament barrier using NOTIFY, but does not incur the read-sharing overhead.

[6] Read-sharing refers to the situation where a large number of processors simultaneously attempt to read a shared variable [14].

Barrier performance can generally be improved if processes are assigned to processors in a specific order and there is sufficient symmetry in the interconnect. For the Multicube architecture and the previously described *partner* and *parent* functions of the dissemination and tournament barriers, the latency of the interconnect is substantially reduced. Synchronization operations are required to traverse only a single stage of the interconnect, independent of the number of stages. This results in $O(\log n)$ latency for the two barrier algorithms, as demonstrated by the straight curves for the optimized algorithms in Figure 17.11. The locality optimizations are more important for the dissemination barrier, which requires $O(\log n)$ times the traffic of the tournament barrier, and thus experiences more queuing delays in the interconnect. The savings due to the locality optimizations are approximately 36 and 26 percent for the dissemination and tournament barriers, respectively, for 4K processors.

17.5 Conclusions and Future Work

The QOLB hardware provides a very efficient mechanism for both process synchronization and data sharing. First, QOLB directly implements the queuing mechanism of binary semaphores, making a single non-local operation sufficient to acquire a lock, independent of whether the critical section is idle or busy. Second, by placing locks with data, both can be acquired in a single access. This technique effectively cuts in half the latency required to enter a critical section and acquire the first line of data. Specifically, from Table 17.1 it is clear that QOLB reduces the latency to enter a critical section and start computation by a factor of four over software schemes when a lock (*i.e.* critical section) is busy. For idle locks the improvement due to using QOLB is only a factor of two, which is due to the additional latency of software algorithms to acquire shared data.

However, QOLB has an additional advantage in the case of idle locks. Since QOLB is both synchronizing and non-blocking, it can be used to prefetch shared data. Thus communication latency can effectively be reduced to zero if the shared data is prefetched sufficiently in advance to allow the latency of the QOLB operation to overlap useful computation. Through smaller communication latency, finer grained parallelism can be supported and, thus, applications can effectively use more pro-

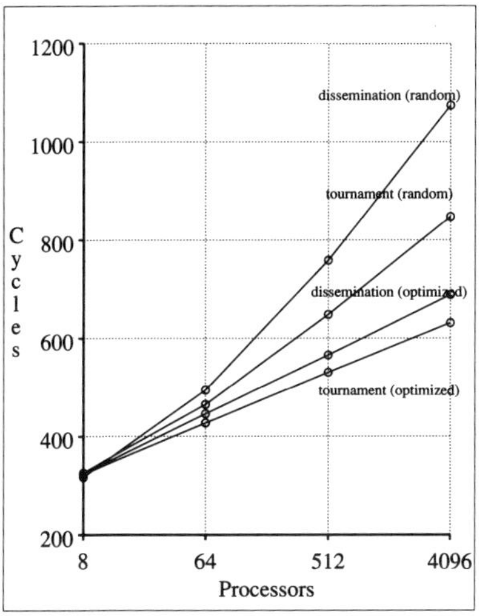

Figure 17.11
Effect of Random Placement of Processes on Barrier Performance. Shown is the average time to complete tournament and dissemination barriers for both optimized and random assignments of processes to processors. For both sets of curves spinning is performed locally. Parameters are the same as in the previous figure.

cessors than otherwise possible. Even if Fetch&Φ primitives could be issued as non-blocking operations, it would be much more difficult to structure the computation of an application to issue the multiple steps of an appropriate prefetching algorithm correctly.

The study of counter algorithms demonstrates the effectiveness of the software combining algorithm presented elsewhere [8]. Even with only 64 participating processes software combining performs as well as a pipelined Fetch&Increment operation. Thus, it holds much promise for implementing efficient counters without resorting to hardware combining.

The barrier synchronization study demonstrates that software algorithms can be constructed that experience a logarithmic number of interconnect latencies. With sufficient interconnect symmetry it is even possible to make the traversal time of the interconnect relatively independent of the size of the system. Overall, the dissemination barrier seems to perform the best over a wide range of assumptions. QOLB does not show a performance improvement over software algorithms since at-memory Fetch&Φ operations are particularly efficient for the dataless, pairwise synchronizations of barriers. In general, at-memory operations seem to be more effective than their cache coherent counterparts for all types synchronization.

The barrier studies also yield insight into methods for performing global event notification. It is clear that efficient (*i.e.* combinable) read sharing is a necessity for broadcast invalidation protocols. Even algorithms employing a broadcast write operation like NOTIFY may suffer from hot-spot contention when the line is initially distributed to all of the participating processes. Thus, tree algorithms may be necessary. For cases other than barriers, event notification of an arbitrary subset of processes requires software combining, such as that demonstrated for counters.

QOLB's performance advantage extends to systems that enforce weaker forms of consistency. These machines allow the issue of multiple outstanding memory operations from a single processor. However, synchronization operations are still required to enforce various logical constraints on the order of operations, and shared data cannot be fetched before such constraints are satisfied. Thus, QOLB can be used to reduce these communication latencies where other memory operations cannot.

The benefit of relaxed consistency constraints is that, once synchronization is performed, multiple accesses to shared data can be handled concurrently. This is true of systems using QOLB as well. However, the QOLB hardware can be augmented to provides a framework for enforcing an even weaker form of consistency, *QOLB consistency*, where the consistency is restricted only to the variables for which there is a data race. It is expected that implementations of QOLB consistency, if not faster than other forms of weak consistency, will at least be easier to implement. This work is part of an on-going study.

Acknowledgments

We wish to acknowledge Mary Vernon and Guri Sohi, as well as the referees, for their comments on an earlier version of this paper. This work was supported by NSF grant CCR-892766.

References

[1] Aboulenein, N. M., S. Gjessing, J. R. Goodman, and P. J. Woest, "Hardware Support for Synchronization in the Scalable Coherent Interface (SCI)," University of Wisconsin-Madison, Computer Science Technical Report #984, December 1990.

[2] Adve, S. V., and M. D. Hill, "Weak Ordering—A New Definition," *Proceedings of the 17th Annual International Symposium on Computer Architecture*, May 1990, pp. 2-14.

[3] Anderson, T. E., "The Performance of Spin Lock Alternatives for Shared-Memory Multiprocessors," *IEEE Transactions on Parallel and Distributed Systems*, January 1990, pp. 6-16.

[4] Brantley, W. C., K. P. McAuliffe, and J. Weiss, "RP3 Processor-Memory Element," *Proceedings of the 1985 International Conference on Parallel Processing*, August 1985, pp. 782-789.

[5] Brooks, E. D., "The Butterfly Barrier," *International Journal of Parallel Programming*, August 1986, pp. 295-307.

[6] Dubois, M., C. Scheurich, and F. Briggs, "Memory Access Buffering in Multiprocessor," *Proceedings of the 13th Annual International Symposium on Computer Architecture*, June 1986, pp. 434-442.

[7] Gharachorloo, K., D. Lenoski, J. Laudon, P. Gibbons, A. Gupta, and J. Hennessy, "Memory Consistency and Event Ordering in Scalable Shared-Memory Multiprocessors," *Proceedings of the 17th Annual International Symposium on Computer Architecture*, May 1990, pp. 15-26.

[8] Goodman, J. R., M. K. Vernon, and P. J. Woest, "A Set of Efficient Synchronization Primitives for a Large-Scale Shared-Memory Multiprocessor," *Proceedings of the Third International Conference on Architectural Support for Programming Languages and Operating Systems (ASPLOS III)*, April 1989, pp. 64-75.

[9] Goodman, J. R., "Cache Consistency and Sequential Consistency," Scalable Coherent Interface (SCI), IEEE P1596 Standards Group, Technical Report #61, March 1989.

[10] Goodman, J. R., and P. J. Woest, "The Wisconsin Multicube: A New Large-Scale Cache-Coherent Multiprocessor," *Proceedings of the 15th Annual International Symposium on Computer Architecture*, June 1988, pp. 422-431.

[11] Gottlieb, A., B. D. Lubachevsky, and L. Rudolph, "Basic Techniques for the Efficient Coordination of Very Large Numbers of Cooperating Sequential Processors," *ACM Transactions on Programming Languages and Systems*, April 1983, pp. 164-189.

[12] Gottlieb, A., R. Grishman, C. P. Kruskal, K. P. McAuliffe, L. Rudolph, And M. Snir, "The NYU Ultracomputer—Designing an MIMD, Shared Memory Parallel Machine," *IEEE Transactions on Computers*, February 1983, pp. 175-189.

[13] Hensgen, D., R. Finkel, and U. Manber, "Two Algorithms for Barrier Synchronization," *International Journal of Parallel Programming*, 1988, pp. 1-17.

[14] Karlin, A. R., M. S. Manasse, L. Rudolph, and D. D. Sleator, "Competitive Snoopy Caching," *Algorithmica*, **3**, 1988, pp. 79-119.

[15] Lamport, L., "How to Make a Multiprocessor Computer that Correctly Executes Multiprocess Programs," *IEEE Transactions on Computers*, September 1979, pp. 690-691.

[16] Mellor-Crummey, J. M., and M. L. Scott, "Algorithms for Scalable Synchronization on Shared-Memory Multiprocessors," University of Rochester, Computer Science Technical Report #342, April 1990.

[17] Pfister, G. A., and V. A. Norton, "Hot Spot Contention and Combining in Multistage Interconnection Networks," *Proceedings of the 1985 International Conference on Parallel Processing*, August 1985, pp. 790-797.

[18] Ramachandran, U., M. Solomon, and M. K. Vernon, "Hardware Support for Interprocess Communication," *IEEE Transactions on Parallel and Distributed Systems*, June 1990, pp. 318-329.

[19] Rudolph, L., and Z. Segall, "Dynamic Decentralized Cache Schemes for MIMD Parallel Processors," *Proceedings of the 11th Annual International Symposium on Computer Architecture*, June 1984, pp. 340-347.

[20] Smith, B. J., "Architecture and Applications of the HEP Multiprocessor Computer System", *SPIE Vol. 298 Real-Time Signal Processing IV (1981)* pp. 241-248. Also appears in *Supercomputers: Design and Applications*, IEEE Catalog Number EHO219-6.

[21] Woest, P. J., and J. R. Goodman, "QOLB Consistency," *in preparation.*

[22] Yew, P. C., N. F. Tzeng, and D. H. Lawrie, "Distributing Hot-Spot Addressing in Large-Scale Multiprocessors," *IEEE Transactions on Computers*, April 1987, pp. 388-395.

[23] Zhu, C. Q., and P. C. Yew, "A Scheme to Enforce Data Dependence on Large Multiprocessor Systems," *IEEE Transactions on Software Engineering*, June 1987, pp. 726-739.

18 A Cache Coherence Mechanism for Scalable, Shared-Memory Multiprocessors

Steven Scott

In order to build very-large-scale multiprocessors while retaining high processor efficiencies, a *scalable* design must be used. While intuitively clear, there is no consensus on the exact meaning of scalability. We provide a useful, working definition of scalability that lends insight into the suitability of a design for implementation with a very large number of processors. We then propose a topology (the k-ary n-cube) and a cache coherence mechanism (*pruning cache* directories) for use in large scale systems. Using scalability arguments, we demonstrate that a system based on the k-ary n-cube topology and pruning caches, will scale properly to very large numbers of processors.

18.1 Introduction

Very-large-scale multiprocessors offer the possibility of enormous computing power. However, the straight forward extension of existing system configurations to large numbers of processors can lead to significant per-processor performance degradation. Intuitively, these systems need to be *scalable*, in order to be efficient with large numbers of processors. Scalability, however, is not a well defined property. Though the term is widely used, there is no consensus as to its meaning. We claim that while a precise (but useful) definition of scalable may not be possible, a useful working definition can be given. We find that scalable is generally used to mean suitable for very large systems . This requires that the system avoid bottlenecks that preclude implementations with large numbers of processors.

Scalability is not an end goal, in itself. For a given implementation, cost and performance are the primary concerns. However, as system size increases, a scalable design will eventually provide higher performance than a non-scalable design. For example, a ring interconnect may provide higher performance than a 3-dimensional mesh for small system sizes, due to smaller switching delays. However, the traffic over a link in the ring (assuming uniform communication) is proportional to the system size, while the traffic over a link in the mesh is proportional to the cube root of the system size. A 3-dimensional mesh, therefore, will perform better than a ring for sufficiently large systems. Even a

---

Steven Scott was supported by a fellowship from the Fannie and John Hertz Foundation.

3-dimensional mesh will saturate eventually, however. We are interested in designs that can be efficiently implemented with thousands, or tens of thousands, of processors. How a design scales can lend valuable intuition as to its behavior for such large system sizes.

This paper focuses on shared-memory multiprocessors with hardware-maintained cache coherence. It is widely agreed that these machines present a convenient abstraction to the programmer, and, while not the only choice, they are at least an important class of multiprocessors. The bottlenecks in such systems can be due to software, hardware (communication topology) or the communication protocol (including the cache coherence mechanism). As a minimum, the software must have a parallel component that can be grown while keeping the serial component fixed [14]. However, the three components cannot always be considered in isolation, as their interaction can significantly affect scalability. This will be addressed more fully in later sections of the paper.

In this paper, we suggest a topology and coherence mechanism that we believe is appropriate for very large systems. The notion of scalability is developed in order to gain insight into how this and other systems will behave as system sizes increase. In section 18.2, we present a working definition of scalability, complete with several caveats concerning its meaning and application. In section 18.3, we examine the scalability of multiprocessor topologies, and choose a topology (the k-ary n-cube) for use as a framework for discussing cache coherence mechanisms. In section 18.4, we examine the scalability of various cache coherence mechanisms. We propose a novel mechanism (*pruning caches*) for maintaining hierarchically-distributed directories that has excellent scaling properties. Finally, concluding remarks are given in section 18.5.

18.2 Scalability

As was mentioned in the introduction, there is no consensus on a precise definition for scalability. Amdahl [5] originally pointed out that the efficiency of a parallel computer will decrease as more processors are used to solve a fixed-size problem. This is due to the (reasonable) assumption of a fixed serial portion of the algorithm. As the number of processors executing the parallel portion of the algorithm increases, the relative time spent doing the serial computation increases. This eventually dooms attempts to speed up the execution of a program by using more processors. Gustafson [14] suggested that instead of increasing the number of processors used to solve a fixed-size problem, the execution time should be held constant and the parallel portion of the problem should be increased with the number of processors. We agree that this is a necessary condition to maintain high processor efficiency as system size increases.

There have been several suggestions as to what scalability means. Patton [21] stated that a scalable design can be adjusted up or down in size without loss of functionality to scale effects . Goodman, et al [12], define a scalable *algorithm* as one whose serial portion does not grow with problem size and whose parallel portion contains parallelism at least proportional to the algorithm's complexity. They define a scalable *system* according to the speed at which it executes a scalable algorithm. Johnson [17] presents a rigorous set of definitions for scalable hardware which is independent of the workload. Using asymptotic behavior, he defines 11 classes of scalability, including *uniformly, architecturally* and *implementationally scalable.* Hill [16], on the other hand, questions whether scalability can be usefully defined at all. He challenges the technical community to either define the term rigorously, or stop using it altogether. Still others [20, 8, 15] use the term without accompanying definition.

We believe that a rigorous definition of scalability may be of little use, but that we *can* arrive at a useful working definition. Several qualifications need to be offered at the start, however. First, scalability is not a simple binary property. Certain designs may be more or less scalable than others, however that does not preclude some designs from being clearly not scalable. Second, scalability, in and of itself, says nothing about the cost or performance of a given, fixed-size system. It is useful primarily for providing insight into the behavior of a system as the number of processors grows very large. Third, even though we are interested in the performance for very large systems, asymptotic behavior of a system may not be of any interest. The state of the art is pushing thousands of processors. The behavior of systems with billions of processors is simply not relevant for the foreseeable future.

18.2.1 A Working Definition of Scalability

We define scalability in terms of three metrics: cost, latency, and bandwidth. Each of these can be approximated as growing by some order of N, the number of processors in the system.

Cost: The cost of the system is measured in terms of the required hardware. A full crossbar interconnect, for instance, requires $O(N^2)$ switching elements. An Omega network requires $O(N \log N)$ switching elements. A ring requires only $O(N)$ switching elements. Another effect on the cost metric is the size of memory needed to store directory information. If a directory scheme requires that every line of memory be accompanied by a tag that is proportional to N in size, then the tag memory must grow as $O(N^2)$ (we assume that the size of main memory grows linearly with N). Some costs should be ignored, as they are practically constant for all but truly asymptotic behavior. For instance, the number of bits used to specify a processor grows as $O(\log N)$. But if a single word (32 bits) is used, this effect is not seen until the number of processors exceeds $2^{3}2$. This sort of behavior can be ignored for scalability considerations. For a system to be considered scalable at all, we require that the cost be less than $O(N^2)$. By this measure, a full crossbar is not considered scalable. Beyond that, a system may scale better or worse than another regarding cost. For example, a 2-dimensional mesh scales better in cost ($O(N)$) than an Omega network ($O(N \log N)$).

Latency: The latency metric is the *average* latency of a memory request. This is affected by the topology of the system, and can also be affected by the communication protocol and the workload. Ideally, we would like the average latency to remain $O(1)$ as system size increases. Realistically, this is not possible for more than incremental growth of the system. Several interconnection networks (such as the Omega network) provide $O(\log N)$ latency upon first approximation. Eventually, however, wire lengths grow, and latency must increase at least as $O(N^{1/3})$, due to propagation of signals in 3-dimensional space. A three dimensional cube topology, which can be implemented with constant length wires, provides latency of $O(N^{1/3})$.

We argue, however, that asymptotically, the latency of any system must increase as at least $O(N^{1/2})$. Consider an idealized sphere of processors with radius r. The sphere contains $O(r^3)$ processors. The communication distance between any two processors is $O(r)$. The bisection area of the sphere is $O(r^2)$. The traffic across the bisection (assuming uniform communication) is proportional to the number of processors, or $O(r^3)$. Thus the traffic density across the bisection increases as r. This cannot be supported asymptotically. If the traffic density is kept constant, then the sphere may only be packed with $O(r^2)$ processors. The communication latency is then $O(N^{1/2})$. As an example of this phenomenon, the Tera Computer System populates a 3-dimensional mesh of size r^3 with only r^2 processors [4].

Considering this, the tightest absolute requirement that we can impose is that latency cannot grow faster than $O(N^{1/2})$. Even for very large systems, however, we may be able to ignore the asymptotic latency of a design, so certain topologies may scale better than others ($O(N^{1/3})$ versus $O(N^{1/2})$, for instance). Recall, also, that for a given size (even a very large one) a specific system may perform better than another, even if the other has better scaling properties.

Bandwidth: The bandwidth metric is the maximum of the average traffic over each wire and through each node resulting from every processor issuing a single memory request. The traffic can be caused by the requests themselves, by associated data, or by extra traffic generated by the cache coherence mechanism (to retrieve data from another processor or to invalidate lines after a write, for instance). For limited scalability, a system may be able to handle $O(N^{1/2})$ or $O(N^{1/3})$ traffic, but eventually this will saturate the available bandwidth. Thus, we require the traffic to be $O(\log N)$ or less in order for the system to be considered scalable.

18.2.2 The Effect of Software on Scalability

The three scalability metrics are affected by a combination of hardware, software and the communication protocol. The default assumption about software is the *uniform workload* model. The processors make a uniform distribution of requests to different memory modules. In addition, the percentage of accesses that are writes to shared variables remains fixed as system size increases. This means that the number of invalidations per request per processor remains roughly constant. If the scalability of a topology is discussed without mention of the software, it is the uniform workload model that is being assumed.

Under a *hot-spot workload*, processors make a higher than average fraction of their requests to a particular memory location or module.

This will prevent a system from scaling unless the hardware or communication protocol takes explicit steps to handle it. Concurrent *read* requests are expected to occur frequently, such as after a barrier synchronization or after a widely read variable is invalidated. Concurrent write requests are not expected to occur often.

In contrast to the hot-spot workload, a *conspirator workload* can make a multiprocessor scalable that otherwise would not be scalable. For example, if the workload has high geographic locality of communication that matches the physical layout of the system, and the communication protocol allows for localized communication, then the average message will traverse only a fraction of the distance across the system, and an otherwise non-scalable system may scale. Another example of a conspirator workload is one whose fraction of writes to shared variables decreases with system size. This makes the rate of invalidations per request per processor decrease as system size grows larger. This sort of workload occurs, for instance, when shared variables are read by all processors between successive writes.

18.3 A Scalable Topology

Using our definition, it is easy to identify certain topologies as non-scalable. A ring will not scale (for all but extreme conspirator workloads) because both the traffic across each link and the average communication latency increase as $O(N)$. A single shared bus will not scale, because the traffic on the bus increases as $O(N)$. In addition, though it may not be immediately apparent, the latency of shared bus accesses increases with N (apart from the queueing delay). This is because the physical length of the bus, as well as its capacitance, increases with N. This suggests an important point: a ring of point-to-point links can be used to simulate a bus. Both have the same scaling properties, but point-to-point links can be clocked at a higher rate (independent of N), leading to higher performance. A broadcast operation is simulated by passing a message completely around the circle. This does not provide global event ordering, however, so modifications are necessary for snooping protocols that depend on this.

One topology that has been widely studied [25, 26, 23, 6] for large numbers of processors is the bus hierarchy (see Figure 18.1). This topology will not scale, however, for uniform workloads. Each time a line is

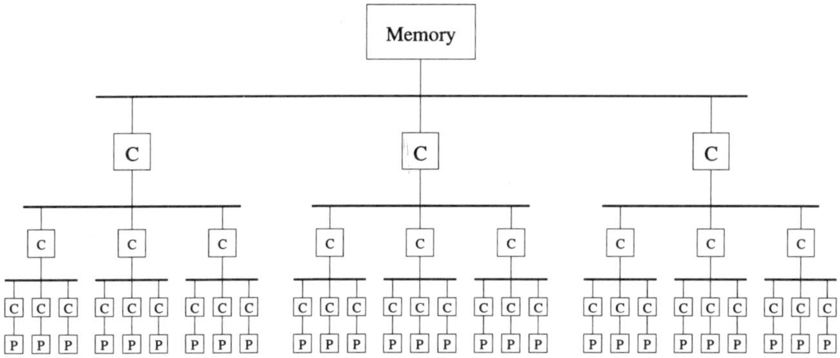

Figure 18.1
A Hierarchical Bus-based Multiprocessor

written, if a copy exists in any of the other primary subtrees of the hierarchy, an invalidate or other message will have to travel over the root bus. Thus the traffic over this bus is O(N), and the system does not scale. For a conspirator workload, where the fraction of writes to shared variables decreases with N, the traffic over the root bus can remain O(1). A recent analysis of hierarchical bus-based multiprocessors [23] concluded that the systems scale well only if the average fraction of processors that read a shared line between writes, f_{RI}, remains large as system size increases. This can only be accomplished with the conspirator workload mentioned above. If the fraction of writes to shared variables, f_{WS}, remains constant, then the average number of processors that read a shared line between writes is limited to $\frac{1-f_{WS}}{f_{WS}}$. Thus, f_{RI} is limited to $\frac{1-f_{WS}}{Nf_{WS}}$, which decreases with system size (the paper accidentally used a workload where both f_{WS} and f_{RI} remained fixed as system size increased). Their analysis showed that when f_{RI} is small, the system is extremely inefficient for large numbers of processors (due to contention for the root bus).

Another widely advocated topology is the k-ary n-cube. Rings, 2-dimensional toruses, 3-dimensional toruses and hypercubes are all subclasses of this topology. The k-ary n-cube has n dimensions, with k processors in each dimension, for a total of $N = k^n$ processors. For example, a 2-dimensional torus with 64 processors is a 8-ary 2-cube. While a torus implies point to point links, an k-ary n-cube can also be implemented with buses (with k processors per bus and n buses per processor). Figure 18.2 shows a 4-ary 3-cube, implemented with buses. The buses may either be actual buses or logical buses implemented with rings of point-to-point links. The k-ary n-cube is scalable, according to our definition, if it is grown in the proper way. The cost of the system is $O(Nn)$, where $n = \log_k N$. There are N processors and $\frac{Nn}{k}$ buses (Nn links). The average distance between two processors is $O(n)$ bus hops ($O(nk)$ link hops). Thus, assuming uniform traffic, the latency of a communication request is $O(nk)$, and the traffic over a bus or link is $O(k)$. The cost and latency metrics do not preclude scaling, by our definition, regardless of how the system is grown. The bandwidth requirement, however, can only be met by increasing the dimensionality (n). Thus a fixed dimension network (a 2-dimensional torus, for instance), is not scalable, due to increasing link traffic.

Dally [9] concludes that for optimum performance, both k and n must be increased as system size increases (in fact, he increases k primarily). His work assumes, however, that the network is being implemented on a single VLSI chip, and is thus limited by wiring density. He constrains the bisection width of the network to be held constant for a given system size as the dimensionality of the network is chosen. The constant bisection constraint causes the width of the links to be substantially reduced as the dimensionality increases for a given system size. For a multiple-board-level multiprocessor, however, a constant pinout per processor constraint may be more realistic. Agarwal [2] studies k-ary n-cubes with the constant pinout per processor constraint, and also models processing overhead in the switching elements, which Dally's work did not. He does not specifically address how a system should be grown, but finds that higher dimensional systems should be chosen under the constant pinout per node constraint than under the constant bisection constraint. He further finds that heavier traffic calls for higher dimensionality. This agrees with our observation that the traffic over a link is $O(k)$ and supports the claim that the systems should be grown by increasing n.

18.4 A Scalable Directory For Cache Coherence

The basic function of a cache coherence mechanism is to make sure that after a memory location is modified, subsequent reads of that location return the new (modified) value. Unfortunately, in a multiprocessor

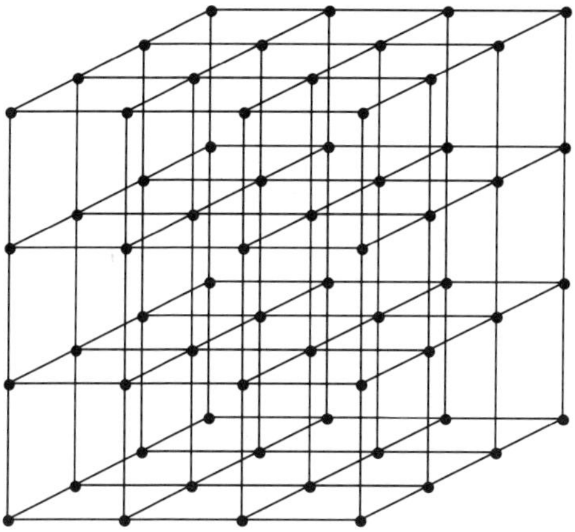

(a) The complete 3-cube

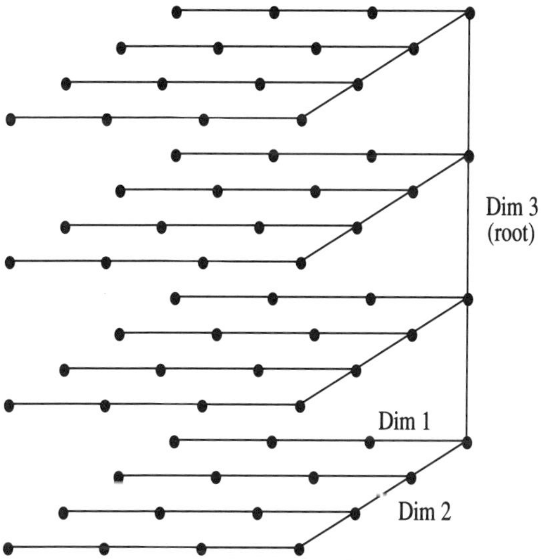

(b) One of 16 distinct trees

Figure 18.2
A 4-ary 3-cube Multiprocessor ($N = 64$, $k = 4$, $n = 3$)

Each processor is connected to n buses, and each bus is connected to k processors (if implemented with point-to-point links, each processor would have $2n$ links, one incoming and one outgoing in each dimension, and each bus would be a ring of k processors). Each processor is accompanied by a portion of main memory and one or more levels of cache. Memory is *interleaved* by cache lines amongst the memory modules. For any given memory module, a tree of busses is formed as shown in 2(b). This tree is equivalent to the one shown in Figure 18.1, given that each parent node (those in the right-most plane of Figure 18.2(b)) is allowed to be one of its children. This allows communication protocols based on a hierarchical topology to be implemented.

system, it is difficult to specify the exact time of a write; because of nondeterministic delays to access memory, requests to different locations and from different processors may complete in a different order than that in which they were issued. In addition, as system sizes increase, so does the interval of time between when an event occurs, and when that event can be observed in other parts of the system. The cache coherence mechanism need only make the following two guarantees. First, writes to a given memory location by a given processor, cannot be observed by any processor to occur out of program order. Second, there must exist some global ordering of writes to a given memory location, such that no processor observes any other order.

In addition to cache coherence, a multiprocessor may guarantee some level of *sequential consistency*, which makes some guarantee about the global ordering of writes to *different* memory locations [19, 10, 1]. Providing sequential consistency can significantly impact the cache coherence mechanism. In order to make any assertions concerning a global ordering of writes, the system must be able to determine when all processors have seen the new value of a write (or at least can no longer see the old value). This paper does not address the issue of sequential consistency other than by placing this constraint upon the cache coherence mechanism.

We assume that coherence is maintained over cache lines, and that each line of memory has an associated state (such as *modified, shared* or *private*) in each processor cache where it resides and possibly in main memory as well. When a line is written, all shared copies must be either updated or invalidated. The choice of whether a *write update* or *write invalidate* protocol should be used has been analyzed by Eggers and Katz for single-shared-bus multis [11]. They concluded that write invalidate protocols were preferable for the workloads they analyzed. We further argue that write invalidate protocols become more appropriate as system size increases. As systems grow beyond a single bus, the bandwidth used to broadcast a modified block to all processors (or all processors that previously read the block) becomes increasingly larger relative to the bandwidth used by a read request. Thus, in situations where write updates must be *broadcast* (or where only a small fraction of processors that currently have a copy of the line will by reading the new data) it is potentially far more economical to broadcast (or multicast) the smaller invalidation message. For these reasons, we will assume the use of invalidates rather than write updates.

18.4.1 Broadcast Invalidate

One simple coherence mechanism is to broadcast an invalidate to all processors whenever a shared line is written. This is the approach used for single bus multiprocessors, where a broadcast requires only a single bus transaction. We can immediately see, however, that this approach does not satisfy our notion of uniform scalability. As the system size increases, each processor will receive invalidations at a rate proportional to N. This will saturate the network or the processors at some point, regardless of topology, and therefore this mechanism is not appropriate for very large systems.

Formally, if the fraction of requests that are writes to shared variables remains fixed (the uniform workload assumption), then $O(N)$ invalidations are generated on each request, each of which must be sent to every processor. From a latency viewpoint, queueing of messages in the network implies that the average latency of a request will grow as $O(N)$, clearly violating the requirement for scalability. From a bandwidth viewpoint, since the number of input lines to any processor can grow by at most $O(\log N)$ (the cost requirement for scalability), and the number of incoming invalidation messages per request is $O(N)$, the traffic per line per request grows as at least $O(N/\log N)$, again, clearly violating the requirement for scalability.

It should be noted that for a conspirator workload in which the fraction of writes to shared variables decreases as $O(1/N)$, a broadcast invalidate protocol can scale. In addition, for sufficiently small implementations, a broadcast invalidate protocol may be quite feasible and relatively simple to implement.

18.4.2 Global Directory

Another possible coherence mechanism is to keep track of all shared copies of a line in a global directory. The directory can be distributed along with the memory of the system (as opposed to a centralized directory, which would create a bottleneck in the system). Censier and Feautrier [7] proposed keeping a bit vector of size N for each line, with the corresponding bit set for every processor that has a copy of the line. When the line is invalidated, individual messages are sent to each processor whose bit is set. This does not violate the bandwidth requirement for scalability, assuming that general read traffic scales, because the number of invalidation messages is directly proportional to the number of original read requests that caused the directory bits to be set. However, it clearly violates the cost requirement. The amount of memory storage needed to implement this directory is $O(N^2)$ (we assume the size of the memory is $O(N)$). In addition, the latency of such an invalidate grows linearly with the number of shared copies, which precludes scalability for workloads with heavy read sharing.

Another way to maintain a global directory is to have a fixed number, i, of processor pointers in each directory entry. Either the number of shared copies of a line must be limited to i, or when the number exceeds i, this fact must be recorded and a broadcast invalidate must be issued when the line is modified. Agarwal, et al [3] suggested a label of Dir_iB or Dir_iNB to represent the versions of this protocol which do, and do not, use broadcast, respectively. We restrict our attention to Dir_iB, as Dir_iNB does not allow data to be globally shared.

In order to scale to very large systems, the number of processor pointers that are stored in each directory entry cannot be significantly increased (our cost requirement for scalable systems allows it to increase only as $\log N$). Therefore, the bandwidth and latency requirements will only be met if the number of shared copies of a line is well behaved for very large systems. This means that upon invalidation, the number of shared copies of a line must be less than or equal to i, or it must be on the order of N. If a fixed fraction of the invalidations require broadcasts when the number of shared lines is only slightly larger than i, then the bandwidth of the system will not scale, as discussed in section 18.4.1. Certain workloads may display the correct behavior for large systems, but it is not clear whether programs will behave correctly in general.

Weber and Gupta [24] analyzed five parallel traces and recorded the distribution of the number of shared copies that needed to be invalidated on a write, for 4, 8 and 16 processor systems. They found that the number of shared lines that needed invalidation on a write was typically low, but that the distribution *did* spread out as the system size increased. It is difficult to say what the distribution would look like with 100, 1000, or 64K processors.

Agarwal, et al [3], evaluated Dir_1NB and Dir_0B as well as two snooping protocols (Write-Through-With-Invalidate and Dragon) for three 4-

way-parallel traces and found Dir_0B to be competitive with the Dragon protocol. Unfortunately, their traces were of limited parallelism and the topology simulated was a single shared bus (where there is little difference between a point-to-point message and a broadcast), so it is difficult to draw conclusions from this work regarding the scalability of the directory protocols.

18.4.3 Hierarchical Directories

In systems with a hierarchical topology (such as cubes and trees) and a multicast capability, the directory can be partitioned hierarchically in order to fit the topology. As a framework for discussing such systems, we will use a n-dimensional cube topology, as discussed in section 18.3. We will assume the use of buses with k processors per bus, but, as was emphasized in section 18.3, the buses can easily be implemented as rings of point-to-point links. Recall that every address in our system has a home memory, and, for each address, there exists a n-deep tree with branching factor k, that is rooted at the home memory and includes all processors (Figure 18.2(b)).

At each level of the hierarchy, a directory entry consists of a *pruning vector* of length k. A bit in the vector is set if the corresponding subtree beneath the vector may contain one or more copies of the line. When a line is invalidated, the invalidate is placed on the root bus along with the top-level pruning vector, and it is propagated only to those subtrees that may contain a copy of the line. This process is repeated at lower levels by looking up pruning vectors in *sub-directories*. A total of $n-1$ levels of sub-directory accesses are needed (the lowest level is arguably not needed, as it only reduces traffic when a copy resides in the parent of a leaf node, but not in any of its children).

There are several advantages to such an approach for very large systems. First, invalidation bandwidth is reduced over a global (non-hierarchical) directory, because multiple invalidates share part or all of their path through the network (recall, however, that the bandwidth of a global directory still scaled). Second, invalidation latency is reduced by not serializing invalidation messages. Lastly, the hierarchical organization allows the directory to be maintained while concurrent read requests are combined in the network. With a global directory, each read request must be routed to the directory. This will not scale for workloads with concurrent read contention. The cube topology, however, allows requests to be combined on their way to memory. When a request reaches a node where there is currently an outstanding read request for the same line, the request may be dropped, and the result obtained when the first request completes. This is compatible with a hierarchical directory, as the second request would have been from the same subtree as the first request, and thus would not have affected any directory entries above the point at which combining took place.

The hierarchical directory, however, still does not scale in cost. It uses $O(N)$ bits ($[N-1]\frac{k}{k-1}$) distributed over several directory structures, for each directory entry. Thus, just as the global bit vector, this scheme requires $O(N^2)$ storage for the directories.

18.4.4 Multi Level Inclusion

A coherence mechanism that is similar to hierarchical directories in some ways is the *multi level inclusion* (MLI) property [18, 25, 6]. The MLI property requires that a cache in a hierarchy contain a superset of all lines residing beneath it it the hierarchy. When the line is invalidated, a parent only propagates the invalidate to its children if it has a copy of the line. This prunes a broadcast invalidate in much the same way as a hierarchical directory. In order to save space, the parent may be required only to have *directory* information about all lines beneath it in the subtree. This can be kept in *inclusion caches.* An inclusion cache simply contains tags for each cache line residing within the corresponding subtree. The logical *inclusion bit* for a line is considered to be set if there is an entry for that line in the inclusion cache, and cleared if there is no entry.

The VMP-MC system [8] enforces multi level inclusion within a VMP node, but uses directory entries similar to pruning vectors rather than inclusion bits. A pruning vector at a given node is simply the collection of its childrens' inclusion bits for the same line. The directory entries in VMP-MC are associated directly with memory and cache lines, so MLI is required for the actual data, as opposed to just the tags.

The directory overhead required to enforce MLI does not grow as $O(N^2)$, because inclusion information for a line is not maintained in subtrees that do not contain the line. Rather, the required directory space grows as $O(N \log N)$. Each of the $O(N)$ lines in the leaf caches requires inclusion information in at most $O(\log N)$ parent caches. This overhead is further reduced if data in the leaf caches is shared. Although the directory overhead for MLI scales, it can still be quite large. This will be addressed further in section 18.4.5.4.

18.4.5 Pruning Caches — A New, Scalable Solution

We now propose a variation of hierarchical directories that is similar in flavor to MLI. We implement hierarchical directories as described in section 18.4.3, but limit their size and manage them as caches (*pruning caches*) [12]. We no longer *require* a sub-directory to contain the pruning vector for a given line when it is accessed on an invalidate. If it does contain the entry, then we proceed as with the hierarchical directory. If it doesn't contain the entry, then we must make the conservative assumption that any subtree may contain a copy of the line (a pruning vector of all ones) and propagate the invalidate to all subtrees.

18.4.5.1 Pruning cache performance The performance of this mechanism depends upon the hit ratio, h, of the pruning caches. When $h = 1$, the pruning caches act identically to a full hierarchical directory. When $h = 0$, the top level pruning vector acts as a *coarse vector* [13]. The invalidation traffic in this case is less than with a broadcast scheme, but still does not scale. In order to demonstrate that a system with pruning caches will scale, we must demonstrate that the bandwidth and cost requirements are both met.

Recall that to provide sequential consistency, we must be able to know when an invalidate has been seen by all processors. This requires returning acknowledgements from all processors that received the invalidate. In a hierarchical system, acknowledgements from a broadcast invalidate can be combined at each level such that each parent propagates a single acknowledgement up, after receiving the acknowledgements from its children. Parents that propagate an invalidate down onto a leaf bus, may immediately propagate an acknowledgement up. When each of these acknowledgements is received by the next parent up, it will propagate an acknowledgement up to the next level. Except for the invalidate on the root bus, there is a one-to-one correspondence between invalidates and acknowledgements. However, because some parents and children are the same node in a cube-based hierarchy, $1/k^{th}$ of the acknowledgements will not actually have to be placed on a bus. The number of buses in a broadcast tree is $\frac{k^n-1}{k-1}$, so the bus load for a full broadcast invalidate is

$$B_{broad} = \left(\frac{k^n-1}{k-1}\right) + \left(\frac{k^n-1}{k-1} - 1\right)\left(\frac{k-1}{k}\right)$$
$$= \left(\frac{k^n-1}{k-1}\right) + k^{n-1} - 1 \tag{18.1}$$

Given the hit rate, h, we can compute the expected number of bus operations needed using pruning caches to invalidate m shared copies randomly distributed throughout the system. Label the buses as in Figure 18.2(b). A subtree at level i contains the k^i processors that come at or below the dimension i bus in the tree. The probability that at least one copy exists in a given level i subtree is

$$P_C(i,m) = 1 - \frac{b(k^n-k^i,m)}{b(k^n,m)} \tag{18.2}$$

where $b(x,y)$ is the binomial function. If we exclude the k^{i-1} processors in the level i subtree whose path to the root of the tree does not traverse the level i bus, then the probability that one of the m shared copies resides in the level i subtree is equivalent to the probability that an invalidate packet *must* traverse the level i bus on an invalidation, and is given by

$$P'_C(i,m) = 1 - \frac{b(k^n-k^i+k^{i-1},m)}{b(k^n,m)} \tag{18.3}$$

The expected load from an invalidate using pruning caches with a hit rate of h is

$$B_{PC}(m) = \sum_{i=1}^{n} k^{n-i}\, P_{inval}(i,m) + \sum_{i=1}^{n-1} k^{n-i}\, P_{inval}(i,m)\left(\frac{k-1}{k}\right) \tag{18.4}$$

where $P_{inval}(i,m)$ is the probability that an invalidate reaches a bus at level i, which is given by

$$
\begin{aligned}
P_{inval}(i,m) \;=\;& P'_C(i,m) + \\
& \sum_{j=i}^{n-2} \Big[(P'_C(j+1,m) - P_C(j,m))\,(1-h)^{j-i+2} + \\
& (P_C(j,m) - P'_C(j,m))\,(1-h)^{j-i+1} \Big] \\
& + \; [P_C(n-1,m) - P'_C(n-1,m)]\,(1-h)^{n-i} \quad (18.5)
\end{aligned}
$$

The first term of $P_{inval}(i,m)$ is the probability that an invalidate was *supposed* to traverse the bus at level i. The remaining terms account for the probability that an invalidate reaches the bus due to pruning cache misses. The first term inside the summation is due to invalidates that were supposed to traverse the level $j+1$ bus, but were not supposed to reach the level j subtree. The second term inside the summation is due to invalidates that were supposed to reach the the level j subtree, but not traverse the level j bus. The last term of $P_{inval}(i,m)$ is equal to the second term inside the summation for a value of $j = n-1$. For this value of j, the first term inside the summation does not exist because the top-level directory never misses.

If $h = 1$, then all traffic due to pruning cache misses goes away, and Equation (18.4) gives us the expected bus load used by a full hierarchical directory. Figure 18.3 plots the expected bus load of an invalidate versus m, for two example systems. The bus load is shown for a full broadcast (Equation 18.1) and for pruning cache systems with various values of h (Equation 18.4). Since pruning vectors for the root bus are kept in directories, a significant reduction in traffic is seen even when the pruning caches never hit.

The assumption of a random distribution gives somewhat conservative results, as shown in Figure 18.4. This figure plots the best-case, random, and worst-case bus load caused by a completely pruned invalidate versus the number of shared copies, m, in the system, for a 4096 processor system with $k = 8$ and $n = 4$. In the best-case distribution, shared copies are grouped along leaf buses as much as possible. This gives a bus load of

$$
B_{best\ case} = \sum_{i=1}^{n} \left\lceil \frac{m - k^{i-1}}{k^i} \right\rceil + \sum_{i=1}^{n-1} \left(\left\lceil \frac{m}{k^i} \right\rceil - \left\lceil \frac{m}{k^{i+1}} \right\rceil \right) \qquad (18.6)
$$

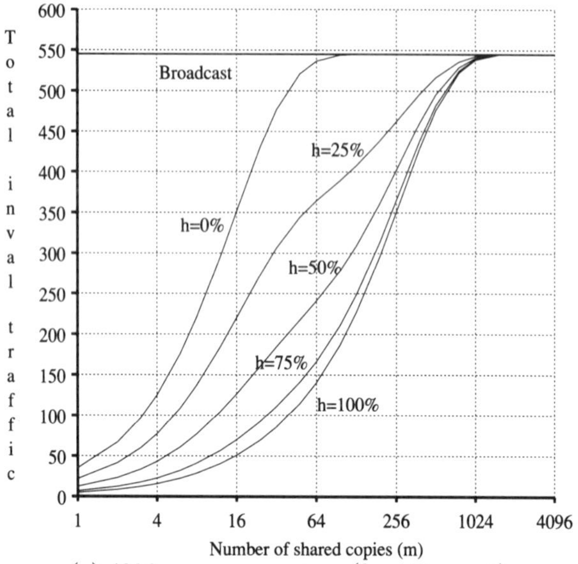

(a) 4096 processor system ($k = 16, n = 3$)

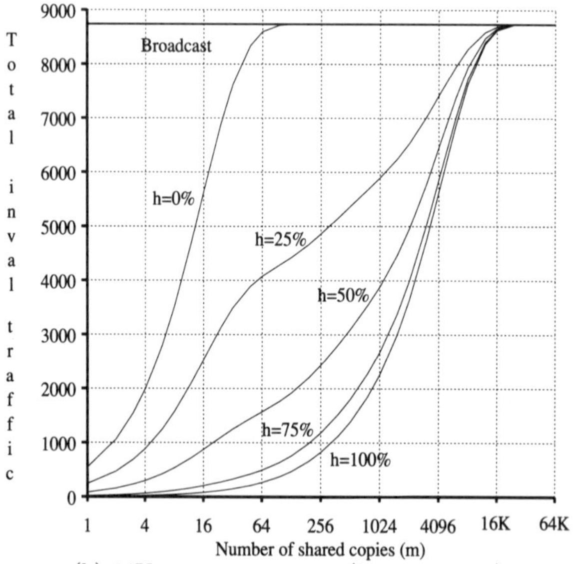

(b) 64K processor system ($k = 16, n = 4$)

Figure 18.3
Pruning Cache Performance

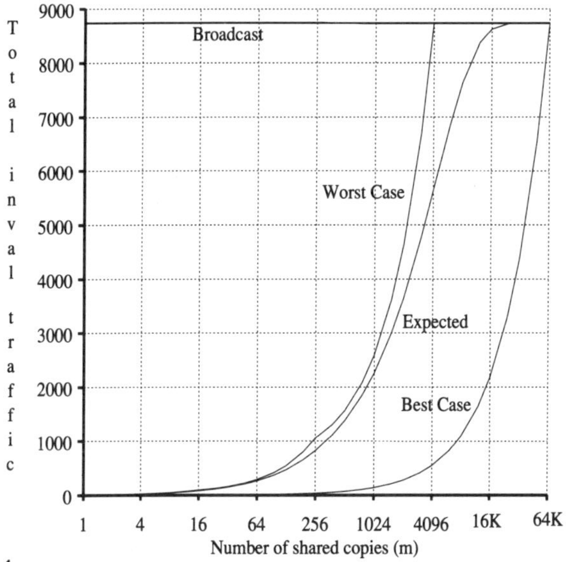

Figure 18.4
Distribution's Effect on the Bandwidth of Broadcasts ($N = 64K$, $k = 16$, $n = 4$, $h = 1$)

In the worst-case distribution, shared copies are spread out among leaf buses as much as possible. This gives a bus load of

$$B_{worst\ case} = \sum_{i=1}^{n} \min(k^{n-i}, m) + \sum_{i=1}^{n-1} \min(k^{n-i} - k^{n-i-1}, m) \quad (18.7)$$

The random distribution assumed in Figure 18.3 gives bus load estimates very close to the worse case, indicating that there is possibly much to gain by organizing sharing along leaf buses when possible. As an added incentive, sharing along leaf buses would increase the efficiency of pruning caches and read combining in the network. To meet the bandwidth requirement for scalability, the invalidation traffic over each bus caused by each processor making one request must be O(1). This implies that the traffic caused from a single invalidate, divided by the dimensionality of the system and the number of shared copies being invalidated, must also be O(1). For a system that uses a single message for each shared copy, an invalidation requires m messages, each of which requires $O(n)$ bus operations, so the bandwidth requirement is met.

Figure 18.5 shows the normalized invalidation traffic for broadcast and pruning cache-based systems, as system size increases. Part (a) shows the scaling behavior with a fixed, small number of shared copies. Part (b) shows the scaling behavior when the number of shared copies grows as the root of the system size. For the global directory scheme, the normalized traffic would be two, for all system sizes, regardless of m. We see that with a pruning cache hit rate of 100%, the normalized traffic appears almost constant as system size increases (this traffic *is* constant asymptotically). With even a modest hit rate of 75%, invalidation traffic increases very little with system size. With m fixed at 8, traffic increases by a factor of 10 as system size increases by a factor of 32K. By contrast, broadcast invalidation traffic increases by a factor of 10000. This indicates that, given high enough hit rates, pruning cache-based systems will scale to very large numbers of processors.

18.4.5.2 Pruning cache space overhead The question that remains to be addressed is whether the size of pruning caches can be kept to $O(logN)$, while maintaining the same level of performance. This can be answered with the following argument, which shows that the size of a pruning cache must grow as $O(n)$. The only entries that need be present in the pruning caches are those for actively shared lines. Entries for private, read-only and inactive shared lines may drop out of the pruning caches without harm (in fact, entries for private lines, if they can be identified, do not have to be placed in pruning caches at all). Assume that each processor cache contains a size-S set of actively shared data. Because memory is interleaved amongst the memory modules, we can assume that the home memory modules of the shared data are roughly spread out throughout the system. A given pruning cache, therefore, must contain approximately $\frac{S}{k}$ entries for each of the k caches along its level 1 bus (see Figure 18.2(b)), $\frac{S}{k^2}$ entries for each of the k^2 caches along its level 2 bus and below, ..., and $\frac{S}{k^{n-1}}$ entries for each of the k^{n-1} caches along its level $n-1$ bus and below. The total number of entries needed in a pruning cache is thus $(n-1)S$ and pruning caches should retain the same level of performance if they scale in size as $O(n)$.

18.4.5.3 Pruning cache maintenance Pruning caches are maintained as read results and invalidates propagate down through their respective trees. When a parent supplies a line to a child in response to a read request (the parent could have either had a copy of the line being

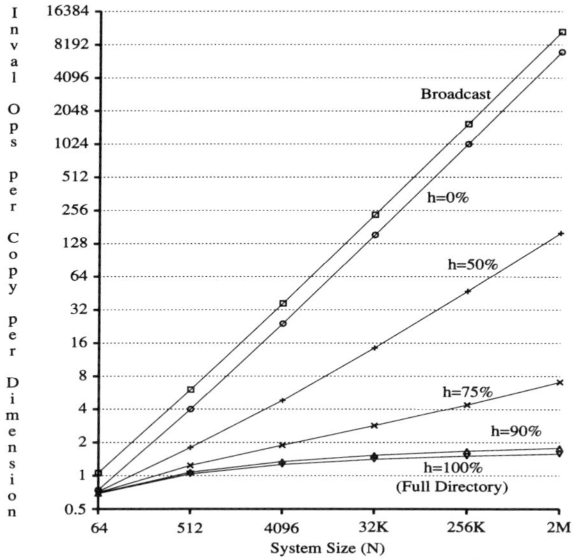

(a) Small number of shared copies ($m = 8$)

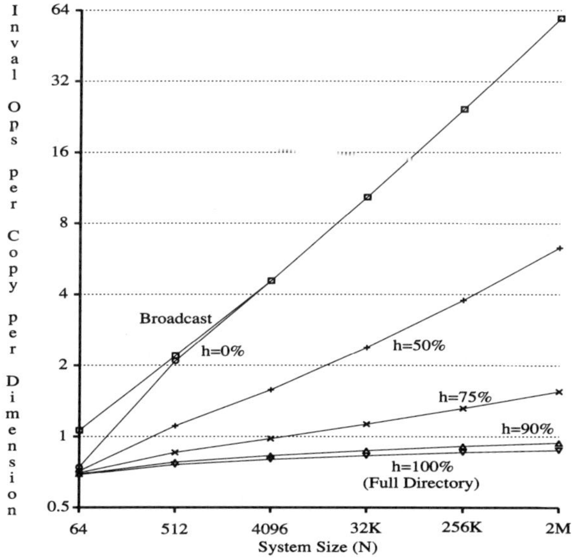

(b) Large number of shared copies ($m = sqrtN$)

Figure 18.5
Scalability of Broadcast and Pruning Caches ($k = 8$, $n = 2...7$)

requested, or have propagated the request up the tree and just received the result now) it must do two things. First, it looks up the corresponding pruning vector in its own pruning cache and includes it with the line (recall that if the cache misses, an all-ones vector is assumed). Second, if the pruning vector was in the cache, the bit corresponding to the child is set. When the child receives the line, if its bit in the supplied pruning vector is zero, then it knows that no cache in its subtree previously had a copy of the line, and it can create an all-zero pruning vector for the line in its pruning cache. If it in turn passes the line down to one of its children, then the appropriate bit in this newly created, all-zero vector would be set. The top-level pruning vector for a line is kept in the directory with main memory, and thus is always present.

On an invalidate, memory clears its pruning vector, as do all pruning caches that the invalidate passes through. An actual implementation may use the pruning cache entries to combine acknowledgements. In this case, a pruning cache entry would be locked into its cache when an invalidate for its line passed down. As acknowledgements propagated up, the corresponding bits would be cleared and an acknowledgement propagated up to the next level when the vector became zero.

An important issue relating to pruning caches is their replacement policy. Since the potential penalty for losing a pruning vector is greater the nearer the vector is to the root, a reasonable choice is to base replacements on dimension. Priority would be higher for higher-dimension vectors. An LRU policy would also be reasonable, as vectors for higher dimensions would tend to be accessed more frequently, and we want rarely used vectors to drop out of the cache.

18.4.5.4 Comparison to inclusion caches The key difference between inclusion caches and pruning caches, is that multi level inclusion *requires* an inclusion cache to contain entries for all lines beneath it. This means that either an inclusion cache must be built such that all lines that can possibly reside simultaneously in the subtree beneath it can also reside simultaneously in it [6], or when an inclusion cache has to throw out a line, it must invalidate that line in the subtree beneath it [25]. The first solution is only practical in a single tree system (such as that in Figure 18.1) where the number of caches decreases at each higher level. As was noted earlier, these systems do not provide scalable bandwidth. The second solution is feasible in a cube-based system, but provides inferior performance to a pruning cache-based system [22]. The penalty for purging an entry from an inclusion cache is that the line must be prematurely invalidated in the subtree beneath the cache. This may cause subsequent cache misses within the subtree. The penalty for purging an entry from a pruning cache is that a later invalidation of the line may have to be broadcast underneath the entry, increasing the bus traffic. The former penalty is greater.

The practical upshot of the differences between pruning and inclusion caches is that inclusion caches must be considerably larger than pruning caches to afford the same level of performance [22]. An inclusion cache must store information for *all* lines residing beneath it. A pruning cache need only store information for actively shared lines. Pruning vectors for lines that are not actively shared can fall out of their pruning caches while the data remains in the caches below.

18.5 Conclusions

We have provided a working definition of scalability and demonstrated its use on several topologies and cache coherence mechanisms. The basic notion is to keep the cost, communication latency and link traffic from growing too fast as system size increases. When used in the wrong way (considering scalability before performance, for instance), the concept of scalability can be abused, but when used correctly, scalability provides useful intuition about the behavior of very large systems. This intuition should prove valuable as efforts continue to build ever larger multiprocessors.

The k-ary n-cube is a promising topology for future, large-scale multiprocessors. When the dimensionality of cube networks is increased with size, the networks meet our criteria for scalability. They also provide a substitute for single-tree-based networks (which do not scale for uniform workloads) as a platform for hierarchical communication protocols. The equivalence of buses and rings, which came out of our definition for scalability, allows for cube networks to be implemented with either technology, and still employ the same basic protocols. It is likely that simulated buses, constructed from point-to-point links, will provide higher bandwidth than their conventional counterparts as logic speeds continue to outpace bus speeds.

The cache coherence mechanism used, greatly affects the scalability of a multiprocessor. A mechanism is needed that scales in both space, latency and bandwidth. The full hierarchical directory scales for latency and bandwidth. In addition, it allows for combing of concurrent read requests in the network, allowing for workloads with heavy read sharing to scale well. Unfortunately, it requires $O(N^2)$ space for the directory information. Pruning caches approach the performance of a full hierarchical directory, and yet require only $O(N \, logN)$ space. Space is additionally conserved because pruning caches need only contain entries for actively shared data. As such, they should scale well to very large systems.

Acknowledgments

I would like to thank Jim Goodman, Phil Woest and Mark Hill for ideas and discussion that assisted this work.

References

[1] S. V. Adve and M. D. Hill. Weak ordering - a new definition. In *Proc. 17th Annual International Symposium on Computer Architecture*, pages 2–14, May 1990.

[2] A. Agarwal. Limits on network performance. *IEEE Transactions on Parallel and Distributed Systems (to appear)*, 1991.

[3] A. Agarwal, R. Simoni, J. Hennessy, and M. Horowitz. An evaluation of directory schemes for cache coherence. In *Proc. 15th Annual International Symposium on Computer Architecture*, pages 280–289, June 1988.

[4] R. Alverson, D. Callahan, D. Cummings, B. Koblenz, A. Porterfield, and B. Smith. The tera computer system. In *Proc. 1990 International Conference on Supercomputing*, Amsterdam, The Netherlands, June 1990.

[5] G. M. Amdahl. Validity of the single processor approach to achieving large scale computing capabilities. In *Proc. AFIPS Conference*, pages 483–485, April 1967.

[6] J.-L Baer and W.-H. Wang. On the inclusion properties for multi-level cache hierarchies. In *Proc. 15th Annual International Symposium on Computer Architecture*, pages 73–80, Honolulu, HI, June 1988.

[7] L. M. Censier and P. Feautrier. A new solution to coherence problems in multicache systems. *IEEE Transactions on Computers*, C-27(12):1112–1118, December 1978.

[8] D. R. Cheriton, H. A. Goosen, and P. D. Boyle. Multi-level shared caching techniques for scalability in vmp-mc. In *Proc. 16th Annual International Symposium on Computer Architecture*, pages 16–24, May 1989.

[9] W. J. Dally. Performance analysis of k-ary n-cube interconnection networks. *IEEE Transactions on Computers*, 39(6):775–785, June 1990.

[10] M. Dubois, C. Scheurich, and F. Briggs. Memory access buffering in multiprocessors. In *Proc. 13th Annual International Symposium on Computer Architecture*, pages 434–442, June 1986.

[11] S. J. Eggers and R. Katz. The effect of sharing on the cache and bus performance of parallel programs. In *Proc. ASPLOS III*, pages 257–270, April 1989.

[12] J. R. Goodman, M. D. Hill, and P. J. Woest. Scalability and its application to multicube. Computer sciences technical report 835, University of Wisconsin-Madison, Madison, WI 53706, March 1989.

[13] A. Gupta, W. Weber, and T. Mowry. Reducing memory and traffic requirements for scalable directory-based cache coherence schemes. In *Proc. 1990 International Conference on Parallel Processing*, pages I312–I321, August 1990.

[14] J. L. Gustafson. Reevaluating amdahl's law. *Communications of the ACM*, 31(5):532–533, May 1988.

[15] E. Hagersten and Seif Haridi. The cache coherence protocol of the data diffusion machine. Sics research report r-89004, Swedish Institute of Computer Science, Kista, Sweden, May 1989.

[16] M. D. Hill. What is scalability? *Computer Architecture News*, pages 18–21, December 1990.

[17] R. E. Johnson. Scalable read-sharing in sci. Ph. d. preliminary exam, department of computer sciences, University of Wisconsin-Madison, Madison, WI, August 1990.

[18] C.-Y. Lam and S. E. Madnick. Properties of storage hierarchy systems with multiple page sizes and redundant data. *ACM Transactions on Database Systems*, 4(3):345–367, September 1979.

[19] L. Lamport. Time, clocks, and the ordering of events in a distributed system. *Communications of the ACM*, 21(7):558–565, July 1978.

[20] D. Lenoski, J. Laudon, K. Gharachorloo, A. Gupta, and J. Hennessy. The directory-based cache coherence protocol for the dash multiprocessor. In *Proc. 17th Annual International Symposium on Computer Architecture*, pages 148–158, May 1990.

[21] P. C. Patton. Multiprocessors: architecture and applications. *IEEE Computer*, 18(6):29–40, June 1985.

[22] S. L. Scott and J. R. Goodman. Performance of pruning-cache directories for large-scale multiprocessors. Computer sciences technical report 983, University of Wisconsin-Madison, Madison, WI 53706, December 1990.

[23] M. K. Vernon, R. Jog, and G. S. Sohi. Performance analysis of hierarchical cache-consistent multiprocessors. *Performance Evaluation*, 9:287–302, 1989.

[24] W. Weber and A. Gupta. Analysis of cache invalidation patterns in multiprocessors. In *Proc. ASPLOS III*, pages 243–256, April 1989.

[25] A. W. Wilson. Hierarchical cache/bus architecture for shared memory multiprocessors. In *Proc. 14th Annual International Symposium on Computer Architecture*, pages 244–252, Pittsburgh, PA, June 1987.

[26] D. C. Winsor and T. N. Mudge. Analysis of bus hierarchies for multiprocessors. In *Proc. 15th Annual International Symposium on Computer Architecture*, pages 100–107, June 1988.

19 Dynamic Pointer Allocation for Scalable Cache Coherence Directories

Richard Simoni and Mark Horowitz

The efficient implementation of cache consistency is one of the primary challenges in building shared memory multiprocessors with hundreds or thousands of processors. While directory-based coherency schemes are promising because they rely on point-to-point messages rather than a network broadcast mechanism, traditional directory organizations would use a prohibitive amount of memory in a large-scale machine. In this paper we introduce a *dynamic pointer allocation* directory that exploits reference behavior characteristics of large-scale parallel programs to reduce directory storage requirements to manageable levels while maintaining performance comparable to traditional directory organizations.
Rather than building a fixed number of pointers per entry into the hardware, this scheme allocates pointers as they are needed from a pool of available pointers. We highlight the differences in the resulting protocol relative to standard limited pointers directory organizations, including the steps taken in exceptional circumstances, such as running short of available pointers. We also focus on implementation issues by detailing one possible approach and examining some possible performance optimizations. Several extensions to the basic dynamic pointer allocation technique are examined and evaluated as well.

19.1 Introduction

One challenge facing designers of shared-memory multiprocessors today is building machines with a large number, hundreds or thousands, of processors. A major obstacle to reaching that goal is the design of an efficient cache coherence protocol. Directory-based protocols make up one class of coherence schemes that show promise in this regard, because they need not rely on frequent broadcast messages to all the caches in the system. Unfortunately, most of these strategies require a large amount of memory to implement the directory, and what's worse, the size of this memory often grows as $O(n^2)$, where n is the number of processors in the system. This memory growth makes many conventional directory-based schemes unfeasible in large scale machines.

In this paper we present a *dynamic pointer allocation* protocol that takes advantage of the fact that most data blocks are shared at any given time by only a few caches, while a few blocks may be widely shared. Like several previously proposed methods, this directory scheme uses *pointers* that contain the unique identities of those caches containing the data.

Unlike previous schemes, the number of pointers available in an entry is not fixed, but is rather allocated on-the-fly from a pool of available pointers. When a pointer is no longer needed, it is returned to the pool.

The remainder of the paper is organized as follows. In the next section we provide some background about directory-based cache consistency schemes. We present the dynamic pointer allocation directory in Section 19.3, highlighting protocol and implementation issues, and exploring possible enhancements to the basic schemes. The final section summarizes the paper and presents our conclusions.

19.2 Directories for Cache Coherence

Most of today's high-performance processors are designed to be paired with a cache memory to keep the average memory access time low. In a system where many processors all access the same shared data space, some means must be employed to solve the *cache consistency problem*, i.e., the problem of updating all cached copies of a datum when one processor modifies that datum. In small-scale multiprocessors where all of the processing nodes sit on a single bus, this problem is usually solved with a *snoopy cache* protocol [7, 11, 12] in which all writes to shared data are broadcast on the bus. The caches in the system *snoop* on the bus, checking to see if they have a cached copy of the written data. If a cache does have a copy, it either updates its copy with the new value (in a *update* protocol) or invalidates its now-stale copy of the data (in an *invalidation* protocol). When a miss to a block of data is transmitted on the bus, the caches also snoop to see if they have a dirty copy of the data that should be supplied to the requesting processor.

Though some have been proposed [8, 20], systems with large numbers of processors that rely on snoopy cache strategies to maintain cache consistency have severe interconnect design constraints due to their reliance on broadcast messages. From the standpoint of interconnect design, a more versatile class of protocols is *directory* protocols [1, 2, 3, 18]. In these schemes a separate directory memory is maintained that identifies the caches containing each cache-line-sized block of memory. When data is written, the directory information is used to direct invalidation or update messages (depending on the type of protocol) to only those caches that must receive them. Since messages are directed at particular processing nodes, these protocols are well suited to general point-to-

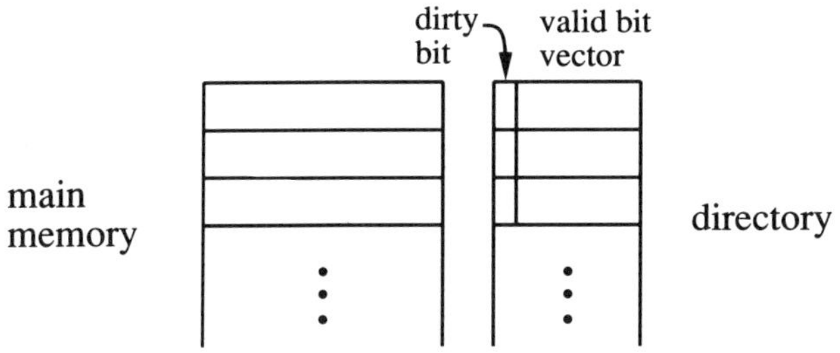

Figure 19.1
Conventional directory scheme.

point interconnection networks, and are therefore an attractive option for large-scale multiprocessors.

Perhaps the most straightforward directory scheme that maintains full information in the directory about the current state of cached data is an invalidation protocol[1] described by Censier and Feautrier [3]. The directory information for each block of memory data resides with that data at main memory, by adding some additional number of directory bits per memory block. Each of these directory entries contains (1) a dirty bit that is set if the block is modified in one of the caches, and (2) an n-bit vector of valid bits (where n is the number of caches in the system) identifying those caches with a copy of the data (see Figure 19.1). When a cache reads the block from memory, its valid bit in the bit vector is set. When a cache writes a shared block, it sends a message to main memory, which in turn uses the information stored in the corresponding directory entry to send invalidation messages to the other caches with copies of the data. If a cache miss results in a request for a block that is dirty in another cache, the directory information is used to retrieve the block from that cache.

The primary problem with this traditional scheme is that the storage required for the directory does not scale well as the number of processors increases. Assuming that the size of main memory grows linearly with the number of processors n, the *length* of the directory or the total number of directory entries is proportional to n. In addition, the *width*

[1] During the remainder of the paper we will discuss only invalidation protocols for brevity. Most coherence strategies proposed for large-scale machines are invalidation-based, and while the issue of updates vs. invalidates is an interesting one, it is orthogonal to the topic this paper addresses.

of the directory (i.e., the number of bits in each entry) is also roughly proportional to n, due to the vector of valid bits. These two factors result in a $O(n^2)$ relationship between the size of the directory storage and the number of processors. This explosion in the directory size renders this directory scheme impractical for large-scale multiprocessors. For example, the directory in a machine with 1024 CPUs and a 32-byte cache line size would occupy (1024 bits) / ($32 \cdot 8 + 1024$ bits) = 80% of main memory storage, an unacceptably high percentage.

Several modifications to this basic scheme have been suggested to support large numbers of processors while limiting the growth of the directory. One technique is to forgo the bit vector in each directory entry for a small number of *pointers*, thereby reducing the directory width [1]. The pointers in the entry contain the unique cache identifiers for those caches that have copies of the corresponding data block. These *limited pointers* protocols improve storage efficiency by exploiting the fact that most data blocks are actively shared by only a few processors at a given time. Of course, these schemes either impose a hard limit on the degree of simultaneous caching or lose full cache state information if that limit is exceeded.[2] Assuming the number of pointers per directory entry remains constant, the width of the directory grows only by $O(\log n)$ with the number of processors, since each pointer requires $\log_2 n$ bits.

There is also potential for cutting the storage space of directories by reducing their length. The key observation is that the number of directory entries that can be in use (i.e., non-empty) at any time in the system is limited by the number of data blocks that can be contained in the caches. For this reason, providing a directory entry for each block of main memory is inefficient from a storage standpoint. Perhaps the most promising solution in this regard uses a relatively small number of directory entries, each with a corresponding tag that stores the address of the block to which the entry applies [2, 9]. This organization is often called a *directory cache* since its addressing and tags are similar to traditional caches, though in fact no backing store is needed [9]. While the length of the directory still grows $O(n)$ with the number of processors in the system, the constant of proportionality is much smaller since it is related to the size of the caches instead of the size of main memory.

[2] Another option, proposed by the Alewife group at M.I.T. [4], is to interrupt the local processor when no pointers remain, allowing software to save additional pointers in main memory.

There are also decentralized approaches that do not maintain all information pertaining to a given data block in a directory at main memory. One such organization maintains a distributed linked list of pointers indicating the caches with copies of a given memory block [10]. The pointers on the list are stored with the data at the caches, while a field indicating the first node on the list is kept in a standard directory structure at main memory. The advantage of this organization is that sufficient pointers are always available for all cached data in the system, and the pointer storage scales linearly with the number of processors. The overhead at main memory is also reasonable; for example, a 65536-processor machine with a 16-byte line size uses only 11.1% of main memory for directory storage. However, because the directory is decentralized, operations on lists of pointers are not atomic, resulting in substantial additional protocol complexity. Furthermore, these operations require more network messages and incur greater latency than their centralized directory counterparts. In short, decentralized directories avoid the infrequent situations that may not be handled well by centralized schemes, but in doing so incur traffic and/or latency penalties on most directory operations.

19.3 Dynamic Pointer Allocation Directory

In several studies of small-scale multiprocessing (4 to 32 processors), simulation results indicate that most blocks written into are present in only a small number of other caches [1, 5, 19]. For instance, in the most common case exactly one invalidation is sent. The explanation is that most data is written frequently enough that it is not accessed by many processors before one of them performs a write. This reference behavior has led to the development of *limited pointers* directories [1] that store only a few *pointers* containing unique cache identifiers instead of the traditional valid bits for each cache in the system.

There is good reason to believe that even in future large-scale machines, only a small number of caches will typically contain a block of data at a given time. An analysis of the types of data found in shared memory applications shows several common data classes that naturally result in limited pointer usage. For instance, Weber and Gupta [19] identify applications with "migratory" data objects that are referenced in a stretch of time by only a single processor before they "migrate" to another. This class of data only results in a single invalidation at a time, since each of the processors accessing the data usually performs at least one write. We have also developed analytic models to predict the number of pointers required under different workload characteristics, and verified them against small-scale multiprocessing simulations [15]. Extending the model to large-scale machines produces results that support our contention that a small number of pointers will continue to be sufficient in most cases.

Even though limited pointers schemes take advantage of the common scenario in which only a few pointers are needed, they can still be somewhat inefficient in several ways. First, in order to attain a reasonable level of performance, they have to include enough pointers per entry so that running short of them is a relatively infrequent occurrence. Even if this is a fairly small number of pointers, most of these pointers will go unused since the most frequent case uses only one or two pointers. So the designer is forced to provide more pointers than are used in the typical case in order to prevent the less frequent (but not rare) cases from severely degrading machine performance. Thus, most entries are wider than we would really like them to be. Another inefficiency in many limited pointers schemes is that no measures are taken to decrease the length of the directory, so the (already excessive) width is repeated for each block of main memory. As mentioned in Section 19.2, only a fraction of these blocks will be cached in the system at any given time. Finally, there will be situations in which limited pointers schemes run short of available pointers in an entry, increasing the network traffic and/or cache miss rate. While the negative effects of this can be minimized through careful design [14], the protocols would be more robust if they included better support for these situations.

In this section we present a *dynamic pointer allocation* directory. Rather than building a fixed number of pointers per entry into the hardware, this scheme allocates pointers as they are needed from a pool of available pointers. This method has many of the same advantages as limited pointers organizations, but without the inefficiencies mentioned above. In fact, we can think of the new organization as an *un*limited pointers scheme, since the number of pointers that can be used by a directory entry is not fixed at a hard limit. It is similar in this sense to distributed linked-list protocols (see Section 19.2); however, the dynamic pointer allocation protocol is simpler and incurs lower latencies because it is centralized.

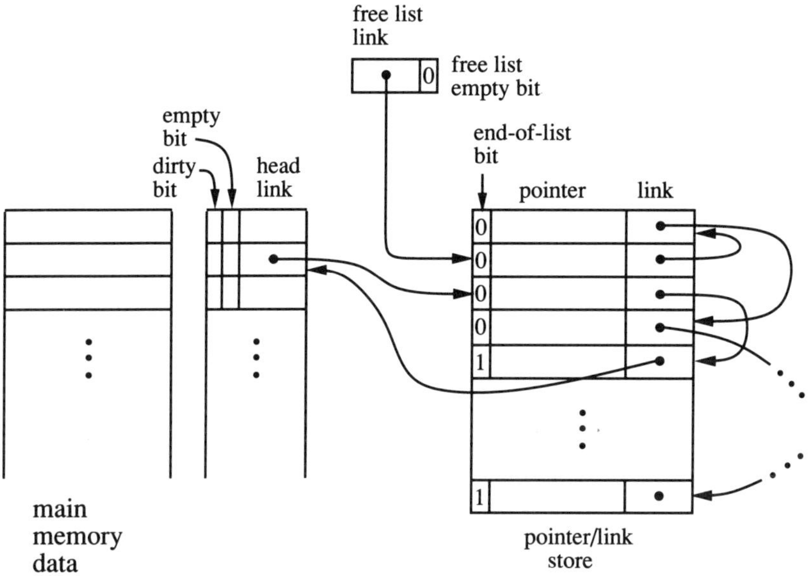

Figure 19.2
Basic dynamic pointer allocation scheme.

19.3.1 Directory Organization

The organization of the dynamic pointer allocation directory is shown in Figure 19.2. The primary structure is a memory containing a number of pointers, each paired with a *link*.[3] These pairs form the basic data structure that allows us to construct linked lists of cache pointers. In addition, each block of main memory has an associated dirty bit, a link to a list of pointers allocated to the block, and an *empty bit* that indicates whether or not the block's list of pointers is empty. When the list is not empty, the last pointer links back to the main memory block, forming a circular list. At system start-up, a single linked list consisting of all the pointers is built. A special register known as the *free list link* is set to contain the address of the first pointer/link pair; this register is a link to the head of the *free list*. On a cache miss, a pointer is removed from the free list and added to the head of the list for the desired memory

[3] Although the links operate as pointers to other locations in the memory, we will be careful to always refer to them as "links," to avoid confusing them with the cache pointers.

block. When permission to write a block is requested by a cache, the directory steps through the block's pointer list, sending invalidations to each cache on the list and returning the pointers to the head of the free list. The end of the list is reached when the *end-of-list bit* associated with each pointer/link pair is found to be set.

Notice that standard limited pointers schemes have a long and fairly wide directory. The dynamic pointer allocation organization, on the other hand, uses a long but narrow structure of head links at each block along with a relatively small pool of pointers. In this way, the amount of memory added to each data block is kept small, while allowing the effective width of each block's entry to adjust dynamically to the needs of the block. While the storage overhead of the links is not insignificant, the organization is still more efficient than a standard limited pointers scheme in which far more pointers are provided than are used at any given time.

The dynamic pointer allocation scheme, like the directory cache described in Section 19.2, relies on the caches in the system containing data that is reasonably distributed across the processing nodes in main memory. If the cached data's corresponding main memory blocks were perfectly distributed throughout the system, then we would only need to provide a number of pointers in a node equal to the number of blocks in a single cache. Similarly, a directory cache would only need a number of entries equal to the number of blocks in a single cache. Of course, the main memory blocks that are cached will not actually be perfectly distributed, so some additional pointers must be provided. When we discuss the implementation issues for the dynamic pointer allocation scheme (Section 19.3.3), we will examine the number of pointers that can be provided with a reasonably small number of parts.

Finally, we expect the dynamic pointer allocation organization to have very favorable scalability characteristics. In a given system, the number of pointers required on a node will depend on the size of the caches. We will see that a large number of pointers can be easily built using the same sized parts from which caches are typically constructed. The number of pointers that can be provided will therefore scale at the same rate as the size of cache memories.

19.3.2 Directory Protocol

The protocol for the dynamic pointer allocation directory is very similar to that of a straightforward Dir_n *NB* scheme[4] [13], so we will not repeat it here. The only difference in the protocol is due to a single exception case, running short of free pointers. This occurs if a pointer is to be allocated from the free list but the free list is found to be empty. The correct action to take in this situation is to use some means to select a pointer (or multiple pointers) and then free it by sending an invalidation to the cache identified by the pointer. It is probably reasonable to select the pointer on a pseudo-random basis using a free-cycling hardware register. Because the address of the block is needed to send an invalidation, the list beginning at the pointer indicated by the cycling register must be traversed until the last pointer on the list is found. At this point, because the list is circular, the link contains the address of the data block. This address and the pointer can be used to send an invalidation, thereby freeing the pointer/link pair.

An interesting effect occurs if caches are allowed to replace clean blocks without notifying the directory. *Stale* pointers indicating caches that no longer contain the data may accumulate in the pointer/link store. If they are not returned to the free list, these stale pointers could potentially occupy most of the pointers that would otherwise be free, perhaps causing the directory to run short of free pointers frequently. Therefore, while not required for correctness, we recommend enhancing the protocol by having caches send *replacement notifications* to the appropriate directory when a clean block is replaced.[5]

Of course, replacement notifications consume network bandwidth, and removing stale pointers consumes directory bandwidth. We can compute the increase in traffic by estimating the fraction of misses that cause replacement notifications and assigning appropriate costs. Replacement notifications are caused not by invalidation misses (where invalid cache data is replaced), but rather by other misses (where clean, valid data may be replaced). These misses are called *uniprocessor* misses by Eggers [6]. Assume each processor has a 64KB data cache with 32-byte blocks. Eggers reports 10% to 80% of the misses are uniprocessor misses for this

[4] Dir_n *NB* denotes a directory with as many pointers per entry as there are caches in the system [1].

[5] Separate notifications are not required when dirty blocks are replaced, since they must be written back to memory anyway.

cache organization, depending on workload. Furthermore, Smith [16] finds that roughly half of the data misses in his uniprocessor address traces cause a dirty line to be replaced. Let us assign costs in terms of network messages to each type of miss and to replacement notifications. Uniprocessor misses cost 2 messages (a request and reply), invalidation misses cost 4 messages (an invalidation/acknowledge pair and a subsequent miss request/reply), and replacement notifications cost 1 message (since no reply is necessary). The percentage increase in the number of network messages due to replacement notifications is therefore

$$\frac{(1)(.5)u}{(2)u + (4)(1-u)} \cdot 100,$$

where u is the fraction of all misses that are uniprocessor misses. For u in the range 0.1 to 0.8, the number of network messages increases 1% to 16.7%. These estimates are very conservative, for many reasons: (1) we have not counted invalidation messages that do not result in an invalidation miss, nor have we counted messages required to retrieve a dirty block from a cache in order to service a miss; (2) we assumed all uniprocessor misses were references to data subject to the 0.5 dirty replacement rate, but Eggers includes instruction misses in the uniprocessor miss count; (3) Eggers' traces show very little sharing, resulting in a relatively high ratio of uniprocessor to invalidation misses; (4) we assumed all replacement notifications require a separate message, when in fact some may be "piggybacked" on the cache miss request replacing the clean block. Additionally, we have not accounted for the differences in message size; since replacement notifications contain no data, they consume less bandwidth than other messages such as cache miss replies. Finally, we note that larger caches will exhibit fewer uniprocessor misses, further reducing the cost of replacement notifications.

We can also estimate the effect of consuming additional directory bandwidth to remove stale pointers. As before, assume a 64KB data cache with 32-byte blocks. For this cache, Smith [16, 17] suggests 2% as a fairly conservative miss rate. Further, let us assume 30% of the instructions issue a data reference, and the processors are 70% utilized. Finally, assume it takes 20 processor cycles on average at the directory to remove a stale pointer when a replacement notification arrives. We can now calculate the fraction of the directory bandwidth consumed by processing replacement notifications as follows:

0.7	instructions per cycle
× 0.3	data ref. per instruction
× 0.02	data ref. misses per data ref.
× 0.5	replacement notifications per data ref. miss
× 20	cycles per replacement notification
0.042	

While 4.2% is not insignificant, neither is it enough additional directory utilization to dramatically degrade machine performance. For this reason, and because the network traffic is not substantially increased, we believe replacement notifications to free stale pointers are a useful addition to the dynamic pointer allocation protocol.

One final concern about the dynamic pointer allocation scheme is the speed of the directory operations. After all, unlike limited pointers organizations, the pointers cannot be accessed concurrently; instead, the linked list must be serially traversed to reach all the pointers. But by examining each of the commonly occurring cases at the directory, we see that there is no inherent slowdown due to list traversal. Read misses (the most frequent directory operation) require accessing only the first pointer on the list. Write misses and write hits to clean blocks require traversing the list to send invalidation messages, but these messages would have to be queued for delivery serially anyway, so no time is lost. Write-backs imply that the block is dirty, i.e., the list contains only one pointer. We therefore conclude that there is no inherent speed limitation in the dynamic pointer allocation protocol caused by accessing multiple pointer/link pairs in a directory operation.

19.3.3 Implementation Issues

Perhaps the simplest approach for implementing the dynamic pointer allocation scheme is shown in Figure 19.3. The resources associated with the directory are placed on a single bus; a simple state machine (not shown) synchronously arranges the bus accesses required to perform a desired directory operation. The resources are as follows: the memory storing the head links associated with each data block, the store of pointer/link pairs and its address register, the register containing the free list link, and a temporary register. This register is used to hold the next pointer/link address as we step through a list sending invalidations

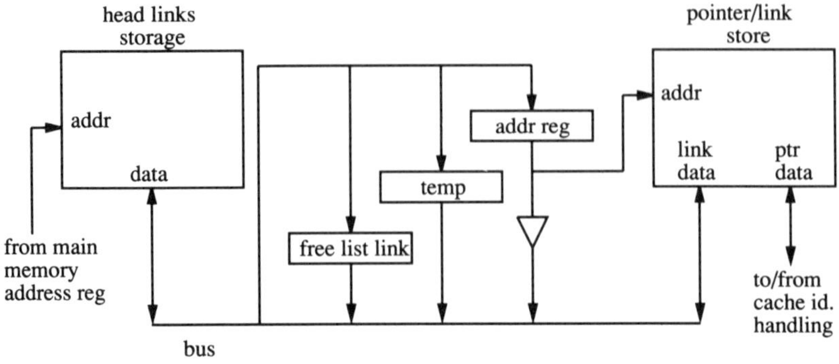

Figure 19.3
Dynamic pointer allocation scheme implementation.

to each pointer, so the current pointer/link can be returned to the the free list.

We can use pseudo-code at a register-transfer level to indicate the sequence of data transfers on the bus that must be coordinated by the directory controller to perform common directory operations. Figures 19.4 and 19.5 show the steps necessary to add a new cache identifier to a data block's list of pointers, and send invalidations to all of the caches on a block's list of pointers, respectively. As is made apparent by the pseudo-code, both of these operations take several cycles on the internal bus to complete. But there is opportunity for overlapping these steps in time, making the speed of the dynamic pointer allocation directory comparable to a standard limited pointers scheme. For instance, it is possible to hide the delay of looking up the next cache to invalidate by overlapping it with the time necessary to form and send the previous invalidation message. Further optimizations could overlap the steps for adding a new cache to a list of pointers (see Figure 19.4). Splitting the bus in Figure 19.3 would allow earlier initiation of the write into the slower head link memory, which could then proceed concurrently with the other steps. Also, adding a "next free pointer" register to the bus would enable a free pointer to be "pre-unlinked" from the free list during unused directory cycles before a new pointer is needed.

There are various options for implementing the directory resources and bus shown in Figure 19.3 and the associated controller. Obviously, a board-level implementation is possible, using discrete integrated cir-

```
begin
  if (free list empty)                        : are free pointers available?
     goto no_pointers                         : no, go handle this situation (not shown)
  addr reg ← free                             : address first free pointer/link
  if (end-of-list)                            : is this the last pointer/link on free list?
     free list empty ← 1                      : yes, set free list to be empty
  else
     free ← link data                         : no, remove pointer/link from free list
  ptr data ← new cache id.                    : set pointer to new cache
  if (not empty)                              : is this block's list of pointers empty?
     link data ← head link data; eol ← 0      : no, link to next pointer in block's list
  else
     link data ← mem block address; eol ← 1   : yes, link back to head of list
  head link data ← addr reg                   : make new pointer/link the first on list
end
```

Figure 19.4
Pseudo-code for adding a new cache to a data block's list of pointers. The abbreviation "eol" represents "end-of-list."

```
begin
  if (empty)                                  : is this block's list empty?
     goto done                                : yes; no invalidations to send, so we're done
  addr reg ← head link data                   : address first pointer/link on block's list
  while (true)                                : loop until we explicitly branch out of it
     send invalidation using pointer data     : send invalidation to cache id. in this pointer
     if (end-of-list)                         : more invalidations to send?
       goto final                             : no, go return last pointer/link to free list
     temp ← link data                         : save link to next pointer on list
     if (free list empty)                     : is free list empty?
       end-of-list ← 1                        : yes, freed pointer/link will end the free list
     else
       link data ← free; end-of-list ← 0      : no, freed pointer/link links to rest of free list
     free ← addr reg; free list empty ← 0     : insert freed pointer/link at head of free list
     addr reg ← temp                          : address next pointer/link on block's list
  endwhile
final:
  if (free list empty)                        : is free list empty?
     end-of-list ← 1                          : yes, freed pointer/link will be end of free list
  else
     link data ← free; end-of-list ← 0        : no, freed pointer/link links to rest of free list
  free ← addr reg; free list empty ← 0        : insert freed pointer/link at head of free list
  empty ← 1                                   : memory block is no longer cached
done:
end
```

Figure 19.5
Psuedo-code for sending invalidations to all of the caches on a block's list of pointers.

cuits or a register file part for the registers and a programmable logic array to build the controller. More compact options include conventional gate array or programmable gate array parts. A single part could easily accommodate the registers, the portion of the bus running between them, and the controller to generate the bus read/write signals for each resource. The I/O of the part would consist of the internal bus and the address bits for the pointer/link memory, as well as control signals for interfacing the directory with the rest of the processing node. The storage for the head links would of course be implemented using the same technology as main memory (dynamic RAM in most designs), while the pointer/link store would probably be built using conventional static RAM for speed.

Let us consider the pointer/link store in the context of the amount of memory and the parts count required to implement a given number of pointers. Although our goal is to provide cache coherency in large-scale machines of the future, we will consider typical cache sizes and RAM parts of today. As previously mentioned, we expect the ratio of the number of pointers to the cache size achievable with a certain number of parts to remain constant as circuit density increases, since caches and pointers are both built from the same storage technology. We will use the common 32K-by-8-bit static RAM chip as our basic building block, and then calculate the ratio of the number of pointers to the number of blocks in the cache. We will assume we want to use the same number of building block parts in the pointer/link store as in the cache. Since the memory for a cache typically occupies little board space, this is not an unreasonable design option.

The width of each link field depends on the number of addressable memory blocks on a node, since the field must contain the return links at the end of the lists. Assuming each node has 64MB of main memory and the cache line size is 16 bytes, the link field must be 22 bits wide. In addition, let us assume a very large-scale machine, say with 4096 processors. Each pointer field is therefore 12 bits. This results in a total pointer/link width of 34 bits, so the minimum number of eight-bit-wide parts we can use to implement the pointer/link store is five parts. For this cost we get 32,768 pointers. The same number of parts yields a 128KB cache, moderately large by today's standards. Since each cache is therefore comprised of 8192 lines, the ratio of pointers to cache lines is 4:1. Remember that with perfectly distributed node addresses for the data cached in the system, a 1:1 ratio would be sufficient (see Section 19.3.1). So using the same number of parts to implement the pointer/link store and the cache yields an "uneven distribution margin ratio" of 4. Of course, it is unknown what distribution will be exhibited by actual programs on large-scale machines. We should also note that the 4:1 ratio becomes an 8:1 ratio in a machine with a 32-byte line size.

Finally, we should comment that there is a ratio of pointers to cache lines beyond which it simply does not make sense to add more pointers to increase the ratio further. This is the point at which any multiprocessor execution that actually utilized all the pointers must be distributed so unevenly that machine performance is degrading due to network and/or memory module hot-spotting.

19.3.4 Possible Enhancements

Though the basic dynamic pointer allocation scheme is reasonable in the number of available pointers and the directory overhead at main memory, there are several enhancements possible to further improve these characteristics. In this section we examine two such enhancements.

19.3.4.1 Static/Dynamic Hybrid One potential criticism of the basic dynamic pointer allocation directory is that it does not make good use of the pointer memory. In the example from Section 19.3.3, 22 out of the 34 bits per pointer/link pair or 65% of the bits in the pointer/link store is overhead used to store the links. While we did end up with a respectable 4:1 ratio of pointers to cache blocks, perhaps we could achieve a better ratio with the same amount of memory if the links did not require so much space.

One approach for reducing the link overhead is to allocate a small fixed number of pointers at a time rather than just one at a time. The advantage is that there is now less than one link per pointer, allowing more pointers to fit into the same amount of memory. The down side is that some pointers will now be wasted since more may be allocated than are needed by a given data block. And because there are fewer links, the total number of distinct blocks that can be using pointers at a given time is reduced.

Because of increased protocol and implementation complexity, the hybrid scheme will have to be a strong win from a storage and performance standpoint to make it worthwhile. The primary impact on the protocol is that the fixed-size group of pointers at the head of a block's list must first be checked for an empty pointer before a new group is allocated. The implementation impact is that it will probably become necessary to store the fixed number of pointers and the corresponding link in successive memory words to keep the pointer/link store down to a reasonable width. This will undoubtedly result in more complicated control.

Unfortunately, the hybrid scheme is unlikely to offer significantly more usable pointers than the basic dynamic pointer allocation organization. This is because partitioning a small number of pointers per link (two, for instance) does not increase the number of pointers very much, so the additional complexity required to implement the hybrid scheme is not worthwhile in this case. And if we group more pointers with each link, potentially half or more of the pointers will go to waste since blocks often use no more than one pointer. This situation may leave us with fewer usable pointers than provided in the basic dynamic pointer allocation scheme.

It is the links that allow each pointer to have the widest possible flexibility in terms of being allocated to the data block where it is needed. Trading very flexible pointers for slightly more pointers with far less flexibility is a poor trade-off. For this reason we do not recommend hybrid static/dynamic directories.

19.3.4.2 Head Link Cache In Section 19.3.5 when we examine sample systems we will see that the fraction of main memory storage used by the directory bits of the dynamic pointer allocation scheme is within acceptable bounds. Yet, the amount of storage involved is nontrivial, and some designers may wish to spend extra logic to reduce the storage requirements further.

This enhancement is not substantially different than the directory cache described in Section 19.2. Rather than storing a separate directory entry (consisting of the dirty bit, empty bit, and pointer list head link) for each main memory data block, a small cache of entries is maintained with tags indicating the address of the corresponding block. In the event that a directory entry in the cache must be replaced to make room for a new entry, the old entry is purged by sending invalidations to each of the caches on the corresponding pointer list.

A bonus of using a cache to store the head links is the number of bits required by the link field in the pointer/link store is reduced, since the

Line Size	*Number of pointer/link pairs*		
	32K	128K	512K
16 bytes	11.7%	12.9%	14.1%
32 bytes	6.2%	6.9%	7.6%

Table 19.1
Dynamic pointer allocation main memory storage overhead.

return links need no longer address the main memory blocks on the node. Instead, the width of the link field becomes only enough bits needed to address the pointer/link store itself or the head link cache, whichever is longer.

19.3.5 Sample Systems

The dynamic pointer allocation scheme results in a pointer/link store that is reasonably small in size (see Section 19.3.3), and a long, relatively narrow head link memory. In this section we evaluate the storage requirements of this memory in various system configurations.

Each entry at main memory contains a dirty bit and an empty bit, as well as a link to the head of the data block's pointer list. The width of this head link field depends on the length of the pointer/link store, i.e., the number of pointer/link pairs. Since caches are growing larger with each new generation of systems, the length of the pointer/link store must grow as well. Therefore, the directory overhead will rise over time, due to increases in the width of the pointer list head link field. Table 19.1 shows the fraction of main memory storage devoted to the directory bits for various cache line sizes and pointer/link store lengths. The overhead ranges from 6.2% to 14.1%, and we can see that even increasing the size of the pointer/link store by a factor of 16 results in only a modest overhead increase for a given cache line size. The dynamic pointer allocation scheme therefore results in good storage efficiency even in the presence of large caches.

19.4 Summary and Conclusions

The efficient implementation of cache consistency is one of the primary challenges in building shared memory multiprocessors with hundreds or thousands of processors. While directory-based coherency schemes are promising because they rely on point-to-point messages rather than a network broadcast mechanism, traditional directory organizations would use a prohibitive amount of memory in a large-scale machine. In this paper we focus on a means of exploiting reference behavior characteristics of large-scale parallel programs to reduce directory storage requirements to manageable levels while maintaining performance comparable to traditional directory organizations.

Simulation studies of small-scale multiprocessors have shown that typically no more than a few processors access a data block between writes to the block [1, 19]. Modeling efforts [15] and reasoning about common data classes indicate that this will also be the case for large-scale machines. This reference behavior has motivated the development of *limited pointers* directories, which store a small number of cache identifiers in each directory entry. But these schemes often require large directories in which many pointers are wasted in both the length and width dimensions. We propose a *dynamic pointer allocation* technique that dynamically allocates pointers to blocks as they are needed, rather than supplying some fixed number of pointers for every block in the system. This scheme places no upper limit on the number of pointers that can be used by a block, while never using more pointers than necessary. There is a fixed directory storage overhead for each block of memory, but it is much smaller than that required by limited pointers directories.

We have focused on not only the storage efficiency of the dynamic pointer allocation scheme but also its hardware complexity. If the goal in directory design were to simply optimize storage efficiency, the result would almost certainly be a complicated, high-cost solution that switches between different techniques on-the-fly based on reference characteristics. The goal is rather to choose the simplest, cheapest directory mechanism that brings the performance of the directory within some chosen margin of the performance ideal, that being the impractical traditional directory with a full valid bit vector in each entry. The dynamic pointer allocation scheme is both simple and elegant, and has the potential for excellent performance in a large-scale multiprocessor.

Acknowledgments

We wish to thank Helen Davis, Kourosh Gharachorloo, and Wolf-Dietrich Weber for their comments about the paper, and Helen Davis in particular for helpful discussions. We also thank the referees for their useful suggestions. This research has been supported by DARPA/ONR under contract N00014-87-K-0828.

References

[1] Anant Agarwal, Richard Simoni, John Hennessy, and Mark Horowitz. An Evaluation of Directory Schemes for Cache Coherence. In *Proc. of the 15th Int. Sym. on Computer Architecture*, pages 280–289, May 1988.

[2] James K. Archibald. *The Cache Coherence Problem in Shared-Memory Multiprocessors.* PhD thesis, University of Washington, Department of Computer Science, 1987.

[3] Lucien M. Censier and Paul Feautrier. A New Solution to Coherence Problems in Multicache Systems. *IEEE Transactions on Computers*, C-27(12):1112–1118, December 1978.

[4] David Chaiken, John Kubiatowicz, and Anant Agarwal. LimitLESS Directories: A Scalable Cache Coherence Scheme. In *Proc. of the Fourth Int. Conf. on Architectural Support for Programming Languages and Operating Systems*, pages 224–234, April 1991.

[5] Susan J. Eggers and Randy H. Katz. A Characterization of Sharing in Parallel Programs and its Application to Coherency Protocol Evaluation. In *Proc. of the 15th Int. Sym. on Computer Architecture*, pages 373–382, May 1988.

[6] Susan J. Eggers and Randy H. Katz. The Effect of Sharing on the Cache and Bus Performance of Parallel Programs. In *Proc. of the Third Int. Conf. on Architectural Support for Programming Languages and Operating Systems*, pages 257–270, April 1989.

[7] James R. Goodman. Using Cache Memory to Reduce Processor-Memory Traffic. In *Proc. of the 10th Int. Sym. on Computer Architecture*, pages 124–130, May 1983.

[8] James R. Goodman and Philip J. Woest. The Wisconsin Multicube: A New Large-Scale Cache-Coherent Multiprocessor. In *Proc. of the 15th Int. Sym. on Computer Architecture*, pages 422–431, May 1988.

[9] Anoop Gupta, Wolf-Dietrich Weber, and Todd Mowry. Reducing Memory and Traffic Requirements for Scalable Directory-Based Cache Coherence Schemes. In *Proc. of the 1990 Int. Conf. on Parallel Processing*, pages I312–I321, August 1990.

[10] David V. James, Anthony T. Laundrie, Stein Gjessing, and Gurindar S. Sohi. Scalable Coherent Interface. *Computer*, 23(6):74–77, June 1990.

[11] R. H. Katz, S. J. Eggers, D. A. Wood, C. L. Perkins, and R. G. Sheldon. Implementing a Cache Consistency Protocol. In *Proc. of the 12th Int. Sym. on Computer Architecture*, pages 276–283, May 1985.

[12] Mark S. Papamarcos and Janak H. Patel. A Low-Overhead Coherence Solution for Multiprocessors with Private Cache Memories. In *Proc. of the 11th Int. Sym. on Computer Architecture*, pages 348–354, May 1984.

[13] Richard Simoni. Implementing a Directory-Based Cache Consistency Protocol. Technical Report CSL-TR-90-423, Stanford University, March 1990.

[14] Richard Simoni. *Cache Coherence Directories for Scalable Multiprocessors.* PhD thesis, Stanford University, 1991. In preparation.

[15] Richard Simoni and Mark Horowitz. Modeling the Performance of Limited Pointers Directories for Cache Coherence. In *Proc. of the 18th Int. Sym. on Computer Architecture*, pages 309–318, May 1991.

[16] Alan Jay Smith. Cache Evaluation and the Impact of Workload Choice. In *Proc. of the 12th Int. Sym. on Computer Architecture*, pages 64–73, June 1985.

[17] Alan Jay Smith. Line (Block) Size Choice for CPU Cache Memories. *IEEE Transactions on Computers*, C-36(9):1063–1075, September 1987.

[18] C. K. Tang. Cache Design in the Tightly Coupled Multiprocessor System. In *AFIPS Conference Proceedings, National Computer Conference, NY, NY*, pages 749–753, June 1976.

[19] Wolf-Dietrich Weber and Anoop Gupta. Analysis of Cache Invalidation Patterns in Multiprocessors. In *Proc. of the Third Int. Conf. on Architectural Support for Programming Languages and Operating Systems*, pages 243–256, April 1989.

[20] Andrew W. Wilson, Jr. Hierarchical Cache/Bus Architecture for Shared Memory Multiprocessors. In *Proc. of the 14th Int. Sym. on Computer Architecture*, pages 244–252, June 1987.

20 Fault-Tolerant Design for Multistage Routing Networks

André DeHon, Thomas Knight Jr., and Henry Minsky

As the size of digital systems increases, the average length of time between single component failures diminishes. To avoid component related failures, large computers must be fault-tolerant; that is, the computer must perform correctly even when some components fail. In this paper, we concentrate on providing fault tolerance in the interconnection network for massively parallel MIMD computers. Particularly, we focus on methods for achieving a high degree of fault tolerance in multistage routing networks. We describe a multipath scheme for providing end-to-end fault tolerance on large networks. The scheme improves routing performance while keeping network latency low. We also describe the novel routing component, RN1, which implements this scheme, showing how it can be the basic building block for fault-tolerant multistage routing networks.

20.1 Introduction

As we begin to design and construct larger computers, the issue of fault tolerance becomes increasingly important. The number of components increases with the size of the system. As the number of components increases, the length of time between single component failures necessarily decreases. If the system is incapable of operating correctly when components fail, the mean time to failures (MTTF) for the entire system decreases similarly. In the extreme case of very large systems, the MTTF becomes intolerably small. Even in moderately sized systems, this decrease in MTTF increases the frequency of downtime and the need for repair.

Any system which hopes to acheive some measure of scalability must be designed to offset the inevitable decrease of MTTF that accompanies increasing system size. While technology and processing improvements will have some affect on the achievable MTTF for single components, these improvements will not occur at a sufficient pace for us to rely on them to keep the system MTTF at an acceptable level. We are thus forced to seek other means to offset the impending increase in the failure rate of the system.

Given that the MTTF for any component is essentially constant, we wish to improve the system MTTF. This can effectively be done by designing the system so that it can operate when some of the components in the system are disfunctional. Multiple component failures must then

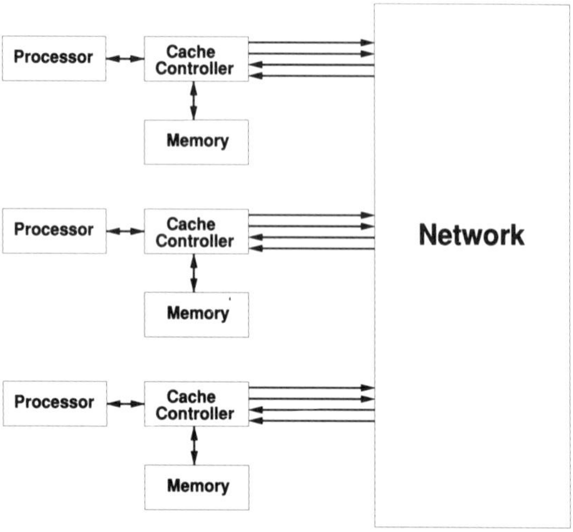

Figure 20.1
Network Processor Interface

accumulate in order for the system to be rendered inoperative. The more faulty components the system can tolerate simultaneously, the longer the MTTF.

Certainly, system failures are least tolerable when they are unanticipated. The effect of component failures can be further ameliorated when the system is capable of tolerating many faults and identifying the faults as they occur. Knowing which components have failed allows the failures to be repaired before the system is rendered inoperative. The downtime for component repair can be scheduled and will thus be less costly and inconvenient than are sudden and unexpected system failures.

In this paper, we describe a scheme for achieving a reasonable level of fault tolerance in the network of a massively parallel MIMD computer by providing multiple paths through the network between each pair of network endpoints. Connections are arranged so that any of several distinct routing components at each stage of routing can be used to route to the desired destination. We do not concern ourselves with fault tolerance issues outside of the network. The design presented is applicable across the wide range of networks constructed using multiple routing stages, including all kinds of banyan-like networks [10] and fat-tree networks [3, 6, 13].

20.2 Background

20.2.1 Network Processor Interface

In order for the network to be useful in the context of a large-scale parallel computer, it must interface coherently with the network endpoints. For a large parallel computer, each endpoint will consist of a processor and memory. A typical network processor interface suitable for a shared-memory multiprocessor is shown in Figure 20.1. Here each network endpoint is a processor with its own local memory and a cache-controller. The cache-controller is responsible for coordinating the interactions of the network, the processor, and the local memory as well as maintaining its local cache and keeping the cache coherent with the rest of the network. The exact details of the connection between the processor and the network are a separate architectural issue. In general, the processor has some number of inputs from and some number of outputs to the network. Multiple connections to and from the network are necessary in order to prevent any single routing component or wire in the network from being critical.

20.2.2 Critical Components

The term **critical** is used throughout this paper to refer to a component or wire when it must function properly in order for the system to operate correctly. A component is non-critical if the system can continue to operate correctly, perhaps with degraded performance, when the component fails.

In most current computer designs all components are critical. The most notable exception is the memory systems of many modern computer systems. Many computers use Error-Correcting Codes [5, 15] in their memory systems to tolerate faults in memory components. The Symbolics LISP Machine and Thinking Machine's Connection Machine are examples of computers that use ECC to protect their memory systems. The LISP Machine uses ECC on its main memory [17] while the Connection Machine uses ECC on its Data Vault disk memory [18].

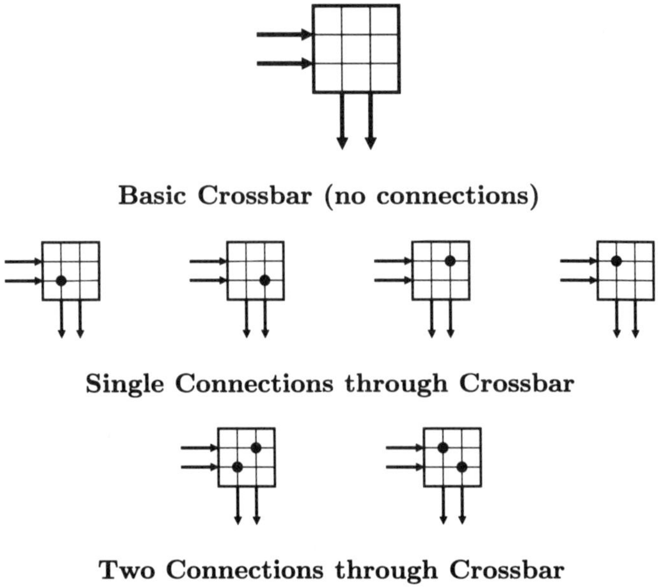

Figure 20.2
2×2 Crossbar Configurations

20.2.3 Multistage Networks

In multistage routing networks, each routing component is effectively a small crossbar. Traditional crossbars have i inputs and r outputs and can connect any of the i inputs to any of the r outputs with the restriction that only one input can be connected to each output at the same time. Each of the r outputs is logically distinct. That is, all of the outputs route in logically different directions. If more than one input wishes to connect to the same output direction, all but one of such inputs are blocked. The outputs in each logical direction each connect to exactly one routing component in the next routing stage; this connection is made over a single physical group of wires. The number of different routing directions a routing component distinguishes, r, is often referred to as the component's **radix**.

Figures 20.2 shows the simple 2×2 crossbar routing element and its possible configurations. The input wires and output wires are orthogonal to each other. Each input and output wire runs across the chip so

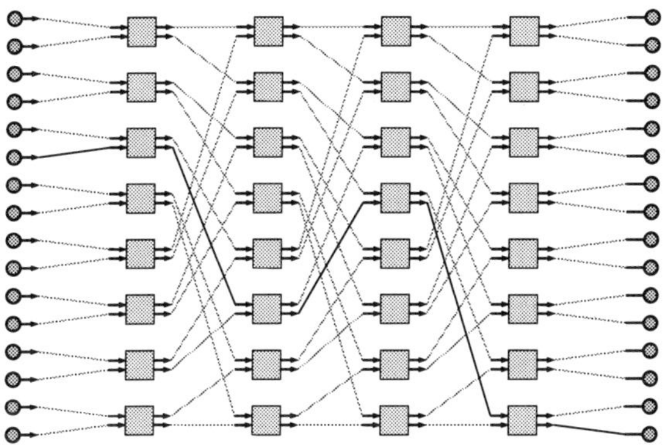

Figure 20.3
16 × 16 Square Multipath Network Constructed from 2 × 2 Crossbars

that any input can be connected to any output. Dots are used in Figure 20.2 to denote when two wires are connected to each other. Multiple inputs can be connected to outputs simultaneously as long as each input connects to a different output.

Figure 20.3 shows how a square network with 16 inputs and outputs can be constructed using the 2 × 2 crossbar routing elements shown in Figure 20.2. Input and output nodes are shown on separate sides of the network to keep the diagram simple; each pair of input and output nodes can represent a single component. The highlighted path through the network shows the path a connection would take from processor 6 to processor 16.

20.3 Network Inputs

Each network endpoint must have multiple input connections to the network in order to prevent any single wire or routing component in the first stage of routing from being critical. Network inputs from a single endpoint should connect through many different physical components to maximize fault tolerance. For banyan-style multistage networks, all inputs to the first routing stage are **logically equivalent**. That is, connections through all inputs to the first stage routers are capable of reaching the same destination with the same routing specification. Thus, inputs from the same endpoint can easily be spread across multiple routing components. In tree structures, such as fat-trees, only small sets of inputs are logically equivalent. In order to obtain maximal fault tolerance in tree topologies, there must be at least as many components composing each set of logically equivalent inputs as there are input connections for each endpoint.

With n inputs from each endpoint, n failures can isolate an endpoint from the network in the worst-case in which all faults concentrate around a single endpoint. More than n failures can be sustained as long as no more than $(n-1)$ failures are concentrated around a single endpoint. Whether or not the complete loss of an endpoint from the network is sufficient to cause the entire system to fail depends on the fault tolerance of the computational paradigm being used.

Additional wiring constraints can be utilized to minimize the effects of multiple component failures. Consider, for example, Figures 20.4 and 20.5. These two figures show the connection of processors to the first stage of routing components where each processor's inputs are attached to different physical routing components. In Figure 20.4, if the first two routing components in the first stage of routers fail, four processors are cut off from the network. However, in Figure 20.5, if the first two routing components fail, only one processor is isolated from the network. In fact with the configuration in Figure 20.5, any two component failures in the first stage of routing will isolate at most one processor from the network; similarly, any three component failures will isolate at most two processors from the network. For this simple case where each processor has two inputs to the network, the additional wiring constraint used to generate the wiring pattern in Figure 20.5 is: *no two processors sharing one first stage router should also share a second first stage router.* In a more general sense, the wiring in Figure 20.5 degrades more slowly than that of Figure 20.4 because the inputs have a greater fan-out or **expansion** into the network. A more formal characterization of expansion is provided in [12]. In contrast, it is possible to isolate one input in the expansive wiring (Figure 20.5) by any two faulty routers in the first stage; in the non-expansive wiring (Figure 20.4), two faulty routers in the first stage will only isolate an input when the routers fail as one of the four sets of pairs. In fact, it is possible to lose as many as half of the routing components in the Figure 20.4 without severing any endpoints

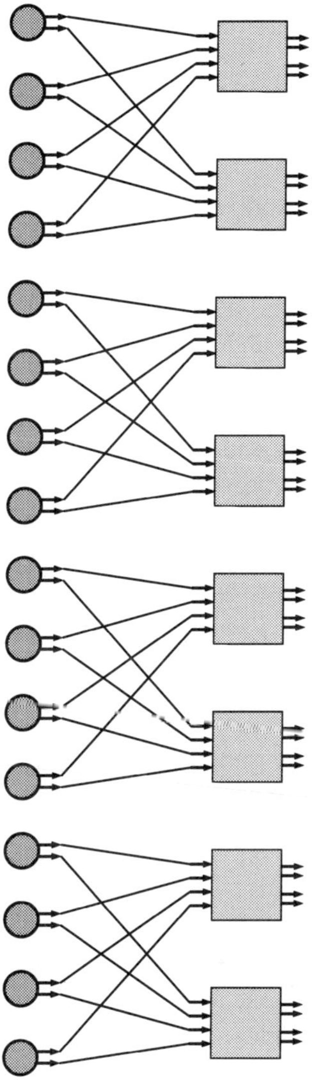

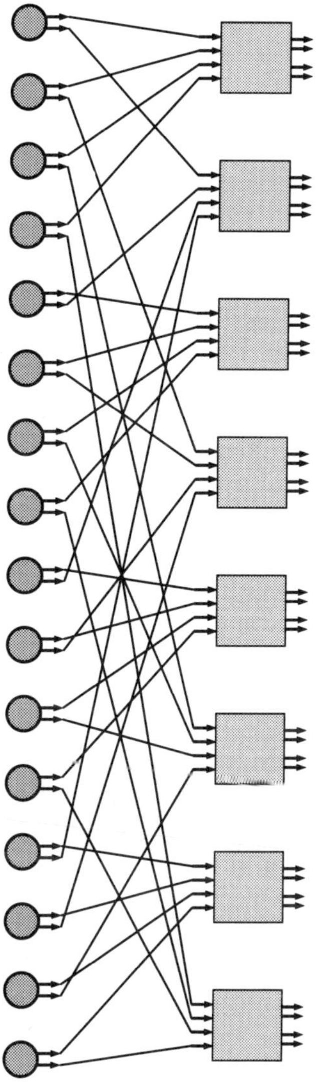

Figure 20.4
Left: Non-expansive Wiring of Processors to First Stage Routing Elements
Figure 20.5
Right: Expansive Wiring of Processors to First Stage Routing Elements

from the network. The non-expansive case degrades less gracefully, but is less likely to degrade in a manner that isolates endpoints.

20.4 Paths Inside the Network

Considering the traditional approach to multistage networks, we see that a single faulty component or wire in the network will prevent some inputs from reaching some outputs. That is, all the components and wires involved in routing between two network endpoints are critical to the functionality of the network. This can easily be seen by reviewing Figure 20.3. Each route between a given input and output can traverse exactly one path. If a single wire or component fails, some input will be isolated from some output.

To avoid making the internal network wires and routing components critical, we must redesigned the crossbar to provide redundant paths through the network. We can give each crossbar element multiple logically equivalent outputs in each logical direction. Two or more outputs are considered **logically equivalent**, when they can be reached with the same routing sequence and they connect to logically equivalent inputs. A router distinguishing r logically distinct destinations with d outputs in each logical direction will have a total of $r \cdot d$ outputs. The number of logically equivalent outputs in each logical direction from a routing component, d, is referred to as the **dilation** of the router. Outputs going in the same logical direction can be connected to distinct physical routing components. The number of possible paths through the network can, up to a point, expand at each routing stage. No single wire or routing component within the network remains critical.

If we consider that any connection entering the network can start through any of n routing components in the first stage and that the number of paths increases through the network, it is easy to see that the number of input connections provides a tighter bound on the worst-case number of tolerable failures than one would derive considering only internal routing component failures. The same kind of consideration can be applied to the number of outputs provided to each endpoint by the network. Section 20.6 expands this reasoning to provide a quantification of the number of paths through the network.

As mentioned for the network inputs, the redundant outputs from each routing component should be connected to as many distinct physi-

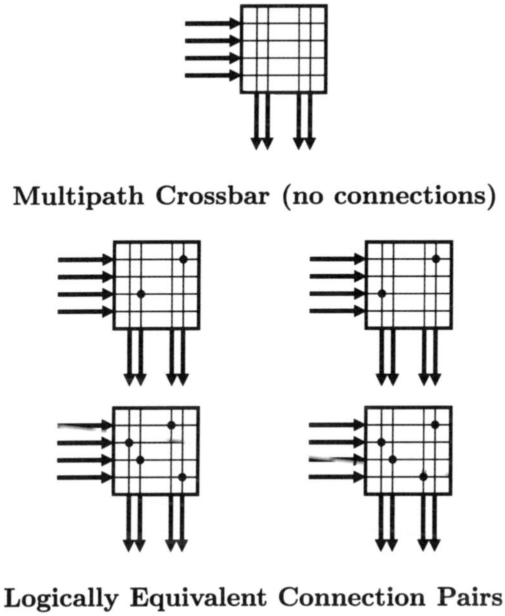

Figure 20.6
4 × 2 Crossbar with a dilation of 2

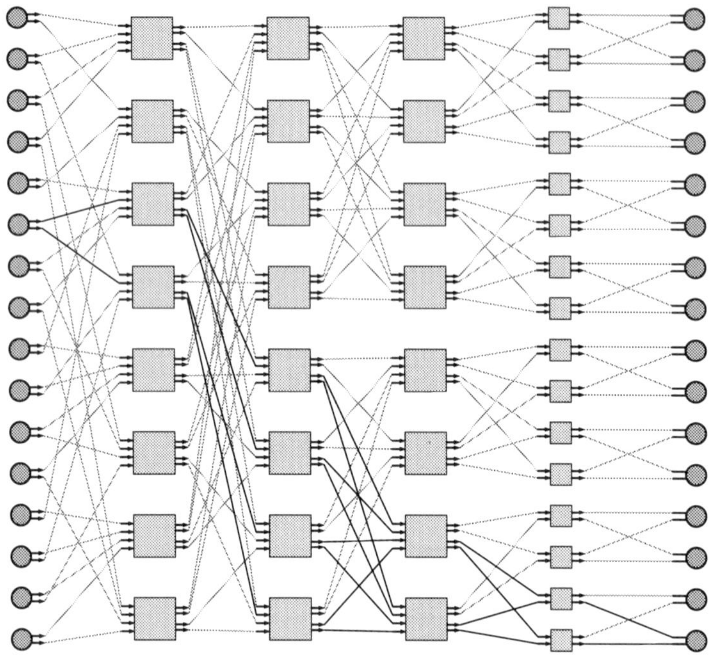

Figure 20.7
16 × 16 Square Multipath Network Constructed from 4 × 2 Crossbars with a Dilation of 2

cal routing components as possible to maximize fault tolerance. Expansion is just as important for connections between routers in subsequent routing stages within the network as it was for input connections. [12] characterizes this notion of expansion.

Figure 20.6 shows a 4 × 2 crossbar routing component with 2 outputs in each logical direction. Up to two inputs can be simultaneously routed in each logical output direction. Figure 20.7 shows a 16 × 16 multipath network constructed from the redundant output 4 × 2 crossbar routers shown in Figure 20.6. For comparison with Figure 20.3, all the wires which could be used to route a connection between processor 6 and processor 16 are highlighted. Figure 20.7 illustrates that there are always multiple links between routing stages which can make the connection; additionally, there are multiple routing components at each stage that could be used to make the connection.

Redundant paths through the network also improve network routing performance by reducing the probability that connections will block each other within the network. [7] shows the effects of these multiple paths on network routing statistics for a specific configuration. Knight and Sobalvarro describe tools for making more general performance comparisons in [8].

20.5 Network Outputs

As is the case with network inputs, there must be multiple output connections from the network to each endpoint. Multiple output connections prevent any single wire or routing component from being critical.

Using the crossbar routing component described in the previous section, each routing component would supply multiple outputs to each endpoint. From a fault tolerance perspective, this is non-optimal since this means a single component failure would sever multiple outputs to a single endpoint. If each endpoint had m output connections and a crossbar router with a dilation of d were used, an endpoint could be isolated from the network by only $\frac{m}{d}$ faults. To maximize the number of tolerable faults for a given number of output connections (m), the dilation (d) must be minimized. At the final routing stage, then, fault tolerance is maximized by using crossbar routing elements with a single output in each logical direction.

Using crossbar routers with a single output in each logical direction in the final stage of the routing network will give the network slightly inferior routing performance to a similar configuration in which crossbar routers with multiple outputs per logical direction are used in the final routing stage. However, the improvement in fault tolerance is considerable and generally worth the tradeoff.

Note that the last stage of the network in Figure 20.7 was constructed using standard crossbar routing components like the ones shown in Figure 20.2. Using these crossbars with a dilation of one, two separate routing components can provide an output to each endpoint. If the 4×2 crossbars with a dilation of 2 had been used in the final stage, then a single component would be providing outputs to each network endpoint; this single component would then be critical for the network to be fully operational.

20.6 Total Path Expansion

To quantify the fault-tolerant properties of these networks we can count the number of components in each routing stage which are available to route a connection between any pair of endpoints. In the previous sections five parameters have been used to characterize the multistage network: the number of input connections per endpoint (n), the number of outputs to each endpoint (m), the number of inputs to each crossbar router (i), the switch radix (r), and switch dilation (d). Assuming all the routing components are identical, we can roughly quantify the number of paths through the network. Let N be the number of routing stages in the network. The number of paths between a single source destination pair expands further away from the source into the network at the rate of dilation, d. Thus, we have $p_{in}(s)$, the number of paths to stage s given by Equation 20.1.

$$p_{in}(s) = n \times d^{[s-1]} \tag{20.1}$$

After a point in the network, the paths will have to diminish in order to connect to the proper destination. Looking backward from the destination node, we see that the paths must grow as the network radix, r. This constraint is expressed in Equation 20.2.

$$p_{out}(s) = m \times r^{[(N+1)-s]} \tag{20.2}$$

These two expansions must, of course, meet at some point inside the network. This occurs when p_{in} and p_{out} are equal. We may call this turning point stage s'. s' can be determined as follows:

$$\begin{aligned}
p_{out}(s') &= p_{in}(s') \\
n \times d^{[s'-1]} &= m \times r^{[(N+1)-s']} \\
s' &= \frac{(N+1)\cdot \ln(r) + \ln(m) + \ln(d) - \ln(n)}{\ln(r) + \ln(d)} \\
s' &= \frac{(N+1)\cdot \ln(r) + \ln\left(\frac{m \cdot d}{n}\right)}{\ln(r \cdot d)}
\end{aligned} \tag{20.3}$$

Once Equation 20.3 is solved for s', we can quantify the number of connections into each stage of the network by Equation 20.4.

$$p(s) = \begin{cases} n \times d^{[s-1]} & s < s' \\ \min(d^{[s-1]}, r^{[(N+1)-s]}) & s = s' \\ m \times r^{[(N+1)-s]} & s > s' \end{cases} \tag{20.4}$$

Table 20.1
Connections into Each Stage

s	1	2	3	4	5
$p(s)$	2	4	8	4	2

Note that Equation 20.4 expresses the maximum achievable number of paths between stages for a single source-destination pair. Not all wiring patterns will actually achieve this maximum between every pair of sources and destinations. In any case, Equation 20.4 provides a good first-order estimate of the number of paths available. The total number of distinct paths between each source and destination simply grows as Equation 20.1 and is thus given by Equation 20.5.

$$p_{total}(s) = n \times d^{[N-1]} \tag{20.5}$$

For the sake of example, consider the network in Figure 20.7 ($m = n = d = r = 2$, $i = 4$, $N = 4$). Solving Equation 20.3 for s', we find $s' = 3$. The number of connections into each stage can then be calculated as shown in Table 20.1. The total number of paths is simply $2 \times 2^3 = 16$. Noting Figure 20.7, we see it does achieve this maximum path expansion for the highlighted path; the paths between all other source and destination pairs in Figure 20.7 also achieve this path expansion.

20.7 Parameter Freedom

In the previous section we identified a number of parameters which characterize multistage networks (n, m, i, r, d). Additionally, the network is characterized by the number of endpoints it supports (N_p). While these parameters have been discussed separately, they are certainly not free to be specified completely independent of one another. The bandwidth into the network from the endpoints must match the bandwidth into the first stage of routing. The bandwidth between network stages must match. The bandwidth out of the network must match the output bandwidth to the endpoints. The number of processors is usually a power of the radix of the crossbar routers.

Square networks (*i.e.*, $n = m$) are often good configurations [10], especially when all endpoints are being treated equally. Square networks are usually constructed from square crossbar routing elements (*i.e.*, $i = r \times d$). Bandwidth matching is moderately easy in these cases. Rectangular networks with $n < m$ are often desirable because they offer less network congestion, since the number of inputs is less than the number of outputs. However, for a given network structure, the smaller the number of inputs to the network from each endpoint (n), the less fault-tolerant the network. A square network (*i.e.*, one in which the total number of inputs and outputs are equal) can gain the same advantages as the rectangular network, by only utilizing a fraction of the inputs at a given time. The network has the improved fault tolerance of the square network with the decreased congestion of a rectangular network.

20.8 Path Selection

Once we have constructed a network with redundant paths as described, there still remains the issue of how these paths are utilized. Standard multistage networks (*e.g.*, the network of Figures 20.3) have the general advantage that they are self-routing. That is, messages can be routed from source to destination using only a few bits of data from the message stream to perform routing at each stage in the network. Switching and arbitration to set up paths through the network can occur asynchronously at each routing element involved in a connection through the network without any global arbitration. It is not necessary to have global knowledge of the state of the network.

The distributed self-routing properties of multistage networks should be preserved when constructing networks with redundant paths. To achieve self-routing and fault tolerance in multipath networks, we use a circuit-switched, source-responsible, random-oblivious routing scheme.

20.8.1 Source-Responsible Protocol

Since the network can have faulty components while remaining functional, we must provide a mechanism for establishing when a connection succeeds in traversing the network. Likewise, when more connections need to be routed to a given logical output direction of a routing component than there are outputs in that logical direction, connections must be dropped due to the lack of available resources; this blocking case must also be detected. To deal with both these cases where a message can be *lost* in the network, we use a source-responsible protocol and provide a mechanism to obtain connection status. After a message has been sent, each routing component reports back to the source the outcome of its attempt to transmit the message. If all the routing components and the destination report that the connection was made as requested, the source knows that the complete connection through the network succeeded. When one of the routing components reports that it dropped the message or when a routing component fails to respond properly, the source knows that the connection failed and must be retried.

20.8.2 Random Oblivious Routing

At each switching stage, one of three things can happen. In the case in which there is exactly one output connection available in the desired logical output direction, the connection will obviously get routed through the available output. In the case where no outputs in the desired logical output direction are available, the connection must be dropped. When more than one output in the requested direction are available, the routing component *randomly* selects which output to use. Thus, all connections which can be made through a given component are made.

The routing component itself does not know the location of any faults in the network and so cannot route to avoid them; instead, the routing component routes obliviously to a logically correct output. If a connection through the network fails due to congestion or faulty components, the source will know of the failure and attempt to make the connection again. Since the choice of output ports is random at each routing stage, it is likely that subsequent connections through the network will take different paths. With this random routing, it is generally possible to get a complete connection through the network in a small number of attempts even when the network has multiple faults. Considering a network with two inputs from each endpoint, in the worst case one of the routing components in the first stage fails. On average, two attempts will be required to complete a connection through the network. Since the number of components available for a connection expands towards the middle of the network, it will generally require even less retries to avoid faulty components further inside the network.

20.9 Fault Identification

Fault localization in the network is facilitated by the connection status returned by each routing component. The data returned can include a checksum on the data sent through the routing component as well as an indication of which of the outputs, if any, was actually used in routing the connection. With a knowledge of the logical direction in which the connection was destined, the actual output port utilized at each stage of routing, and the point in the network where the connection was lost, the fault can be localized to the connection between exactly two components in the network. The fault can then lie in either component or in the wire connecting them. Information from additional failures can be used to further localize the fault as necessary.

Each endpoint only has connection information from its own network transactions. This necessarily means each endpoint has only a limited amount of information about faults in the network. A higher-level protocol should be used to monitor the global network state so that repairs can be scheduled as necessary.

20.10 Other Fault-Tolerant Multistage Networks

The approach predominantly used to achieve fault tolerance in multistage routing networks is to construct a network with more switching stages than are actually required to uniquely specify the destination [1, 2, 11, 16]. The set of destination specifications that reach the same physical destination defines a class of equivalent paths. Since any of several paths can reach the destination, it is possible to choose a path which avoids any single fault in the network. Most of these schemes require the processor to choose its own path through the network. These schemes almost exclusively assume each endpoint has a single input and a single output connection to the network. BBN's large Butterfly Plus computers actually implement this extra stage approach to fault tolerance.

An alternative approach for fault tolerance is to simply provide multiple redundant networks [4, 9]. The endpoint chooses a network over which to make the connection. The networks route the connections independently and reconverge at the destination endpoint. This approach does provide multiple input and output connections. Again, the endpoints are responsible for choosing fault-free paths.

Kruskal and Snir also propose a network with redundant paths using switches similar to ours in [9]. They, however, do not develop any of the details of the network. They suggest the redundant outputs from a routing element all go to the same physical component; this, of course, undermines many of the benefits of the dilated network.

Leighton and Maggs [12] suggest a related multipath network. Their theoretical work was influential to our design. In contrast to ours, their work details packet-switched routing of data presented synchronously into the network. They use a much more complicated routing scheme which requires approximately $4\log_r(N_p)$ (where r is the switch radix) steps in order to route a single connection and an intricate routing switch. Our network routes in $\log_r(N_p)$ steps, but does so using oblivious routing. With the additional arbitration in their network, Leighton and Maggs can guarantee that they can simultaneously route the maximum number of packets allowed by the network's physical topology. Our network simply relies on the probabilistic properties of the data and network in order to route a large portion of connections simultaneously.

20.11 Fault-Tolerant Crossbar Routing Component: RN1

RN1 is a custom CMOS routing component constructed to provide simple high-speed switching for fault-tolerant networks. RN1 has eight nine-bit wide input channels and eight nine-bit wide output channels. These nine-bit wide channels provide byte wide data transfer with the ninth bit serving as a signal for the beginning and end of transmissions. RN1 can be configured in either of two ways, as shown in Figure 20.8. The primary configuration is a 8×4 crossbar router with a dilation of two. In this configuration, all 8 input channels are logically equivalent. Alternately, the component can be configured as a pair of 4×4 crossbars, each with 4 logically equivalent inputs and a dilation of one.

Simple routing is performed by using the first two bits of a transmission to indicate the the desired output destination. If an output in the desired direction is available, the data transmission is routed to one such output. Otherwise, the data is ignored. In either case, when the transmission completes, the RN1 routing component informs the sender

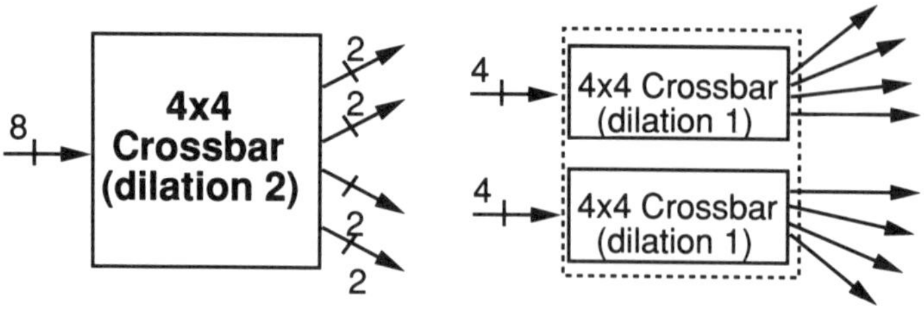

Figure 20.8
RN1 Logical Configurations

of the connection status so that the sender will know whether or not it is necessary to retry the transmission. When both outputs in the desired output direction are available, the component randomly chooses which port to use.

Figure 20.9 shows a 16 × 16 multipath network constructed from the RN1 routing component. A single physical RN1 routing component would implement two of the 4 × 4 crossbars in the second and final routing stage. To achieve the desired fault tolerance, each of the 4 × 4 crossbars in a single RN1 package should be connected to a different set of four network endpoints. As with Figures 20.3 and 20.7, the wires available for routing a connection from processor 6 to processor 16 are highlighted in Figure 20.9.

The RN1 routing component is described further in [7] and [14].

20.12 Conclusions

A high degree of fault tolerance is essential in order to build functional massively parallel computer systems. Fault tolerance can be achieved in the interconnection network by providing multiple paths through the network and multiple input and output connections to the network endpoints. Multiple paths can be realized utilizing crossbar routing components which provide multiple connections in each logical output direction. In the multipath scheme, paths through the network can be selected in a simple self-routing manner allowing cheap, low-latency interconnection. Multipath routing has the advantageous side-effect of improving the routing performance of the network. Fault recovery is

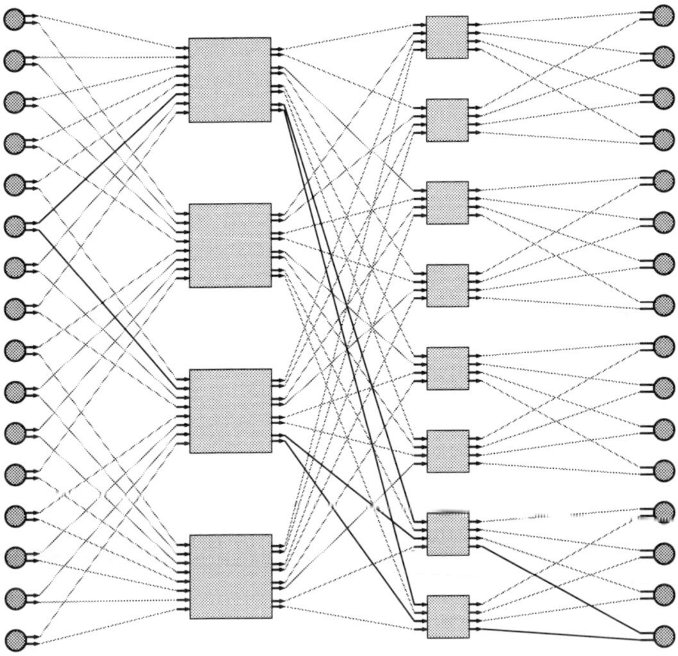

Figure 20.9
16 × 16 Square Multipath Network Constructed from RN1 Routing Components

facilitated by a simple source-responsible connection protocol utilizing connection status information from routing components in the network. Faults and blocking within the network can be handled in a uniform manner. The RN1 routing component implements this fault-tolerant scheme and forms the basis for fault-tolerant multistage networks.

Acknowledgments

Tom Leighton offered valuable suggestions which helped develop schemes for avoiding critical components at the network inputs and outputs. Thanks to Andy Berlin, Mike Bolotski, Max Hailperin, Pat Sobalvarro, and David Yu for reading and proofing drafts of this paper.

This research is supported in part by the Defense Advanced Research Projects Agency under contract N00014-87-K-0825.

References

[1] BBN Advanced Computers Inc., Cambridge, MA. *Inside the Butterfly Plus*, October 1987.

[2] Chin Chi-Yuan and Kai Hwang. Connection principles for multipath packet switching networks. In *10th Annual Symposium on Computer Architecture*, pages 99–108, 1984.

[3] André DeHon. Practical schemes for fat-tree network construction. In Carlo H. Séquin, editor, *Advanced Research in VLSI: International Conference 1991*. MIT Press, March 1991.

[4] Peter Franaszek and Christos Georgiou. Multipath hierarchies in interconnection networks. *Lecture Notes in Computer Science*, 297:112–123, December 1988.

[5] C. Clark Jr. George and J. B. Cain. *Error-Correction Coding for Digital Communications*. Plenum Press, New York, 1982.

[6] Ronald I. Greenberg and Charles E. Leiserson. Randomized routing on fat-trees. In *IEEE 26th Annual Symposium on the Foundations of Computer Science*. IEEE, November 1985.

[7] Thomas F. Knight Jr. Technologies for low-latency interconnection switches. In *Symposium on parallel architecures and algorithms*. ACM, June 1989.

[8] Thomas F. Knight Jr. and Patrick G. Sobalvarro. Routing statistics for unqueued banyan networks. AI memo 1101, MIT Artificial Intelligence Laboratory, 545 Technology Square, Cambridge MA 02139, September 1990.

[9] Clyde P. Kruskal and Marc Snir. The performance of multistage interconnection networks for multiprocessors. *IEEE transactions on Computers*, C-32(12):1091–1098, December 1983.

[10] Clyde P. Kruskal and Marc Snir. A unified theory of interconnection network structure. In *Theoretical Computer Science*, pages 75–94, 1986.

[11] Duncan Lawrie and Krishnan Padmanabhan. A class of redundant path multistage interconnection networks. *IEEE Tr. on Computers*, C-32(12):1099–1108, December 1983.

[12] Tom Leighton and Bruce Maggs. Expanders might be practical: fast algorithms for routing around faults on multibutterfiles. In *30th Annual Symposium on Foundations of Computer Science*. IEEE, 1989.

[13] Charles E. Leiserson. Fat-trees: Universal networks for hardware efficient supercomputing. *IEEE transactions on Computers*, C-34(10):892–901, October 1985.

[14] Henry Q. Minsky. A parallel crossbar routing chip for a shared memory multiprocessor. Master's thesis, MIT, 545 Technology Sq., Cambridge, MA 02139, January 1991.

[15] W. Wesley Peterson and E.J. Weldon Jr. *Error-Correcting Codes.* MIT Press, Cambridge, MA, 1972.

[16] Howard Siegel. *Interconnection Networks for Large-Scale Parallel Processing.* Lexington Books, Lexington, MA, 1985.

[17] Symbolics, Inc., Cambridge, MA. *Symbolics 3600 Technical Summary*, 1987.

[18] Thinking Machines Corporation, Cambridge, MA. *Data Vault Release Notes*, version 5.0 edition, September 1988.

List of Contributors

Anant Agarwal
Laboratory for Computer Science
Massachusetts Institute of Technology
Cambridge, MA

Gail A. Alverson
Department of Computer Science and Engineering
University of Washington
Seattle, WA

Yoshihiro Asano
NEC
Kanagawa, JAPAN

Sandra Johnson Baylor
IBM Thomas J. Watson Research Center
Yorktown Heights, NY

Carrie J. Brownhill
Department of Information and Computer Science
University of California, Irvine
Irvine, CA

David Chaiken
Laboratory for Computer Science
Massachusetts Institute of Technology
Cambridge, MA

David R. Cheriton
Computer Science Department
Stanford University
Stanford, CA

E. M. Clarke
School of Computer Science
Carnegie-Mellon University
Pittsburgh, PA

André DeHon
Laboratory for Computer Science
Massachusetts Institute of Technology
Cambridge, MA

Akira Fukuda
Interdisciplinary Graduate School of Engineering Sciences
Kyushu University
Fukuoka, JAPAN

Kourosh Gharachorloo
Computer Systems Laboratory
Stanford University
Stanford, CA

James R. Goodman
Computer Sciences Department
University of Wisconsin-Madison

Hendrik A. Goosen
Computer Science Department
Stanford University
Stanford, CA

Anoop Gupta
Computer Systems Laboratory
Stanford University
Stanford, CA

Robert H. Halstead, Jr.
DEC Cambridge Research Laboratory

Shuichi Hiroya
NEC
Kanagawa, JAPAN

John Hennessy
Computer Systems Laboratory
Stanford University
Stanford, CA

Mark Horowitz
Computer Systems Laboratory
Stanford University
Stanford, CA

Eiji Iwata
Interdisciplinary Graduate School of Engineering Sciences
Kyushu University
Fukuoka, JAPAN

Nobuki Kajihara
NEC
Kanagawa, JAPAN

Ki-chang Kim
Department of Information and Computer Science
University of California, Irvine
Irvine, CA

S. Kimura
Kobe University
Kobe, JAPAN

Thomas Knight, Jr.
Laboratory for Computer Science
Massachusetts Institute of Technology
Cambridge, MA

Nobuhiko Koike
NEC
Kanagawa, JAPAN

David A. Kranz
Laboratory for Computer Science
Massachusetts Institute of Technology
Cambridge, MA

Kiyoshi Kurihara
IBM Japan
Tokyo, JAPAN

James Laudon
Computer Systems Laboratory
Stanford University
Stanford, CA

Joonwon Lee
College of Computing
Georgia Institute of Technology

Daniel Lenoski
Computer Systems Laboratory
Stanford University
Stanford, CA

D. E. Long
School of Computer Science
Carnegie-Mellon University
Pittsburgh, PA

Philip Machanick
Computer Science Department
Stanford University
Stanford, CA

Satoshi Matsushita
NEC
Kanagawa, JAPAN

Kevin P. McAuliffe
IBM Thomas J. Watson Research Center
Yorktown Heights, NY

S. Michaylov
School of Computer Science
Carnegie-Mellon University
Pittsburgh, PA

Henry Minsky
Laboratory for Computer Science
Massachusetts Institute of Technology
Cambridge, MA

Kenneth McMillan
School of Computer Science
Carnegie-Mellon University
Pittsburgh, PA

Takeshi Momoi
NEC
Kanagawa, JAPAN

Shin-ichiro Mori
Interdisciplinary Graduate School of Engineering Sciences
Kyushu University
Fukuoka, JAPAN

Atsushi Moriwaki
IBM Tokyo Research Laboratory
Tokyo, JAPAN

Kazuaki Murakami
Interdisciplinary Graduate School of Engineering Sciences
Kyushu University
Fukuoka, JAPAN

Takeo Nakada
IBM Tokyo Research Laboratory
Tokyo, JAPAN

Toshiyuki Nakata
NEC
Kanagawa, JAPAN

Alexandru Nicolau
Department of Information and Computer Science
University of California, Irvine
Irvine, CA

Katsutoshi Nihei
NEC
Kanagawa, JAPAN

David Notkin
Department of Computer Science and Engineering
University of Washington
Seattle, WA

Nobuyuki Oba
IBM Tokyo Research Laboratory
Tokyo, JAPAN

Hiromi Onozuka
NEC
Kanagawa, JAPAN

Susan Owicki
DEC Systems Research Center
Palo Alto, CA

Umakishore Ramachandran
College of Computing
Georgia Institute of Technology

Bharat D. Rathi
IBM Thomas J. Watson Research Center
Yorktown Heights, NY

S. A. Schwab
School of Computer Science
Carnegie-Mellon University
Pittsburgh, PA

James Schwalbe
Encore Computer Corporation
Marlborough, MA

Steven Scott
Computer Sciences Department
University of Wisconsin-Madison

Gautam Shah
College of Computing
Georgia Institute of Technology

Shigenori Shimizu
IBM Tokyo Research Laboratory
Tokyo, JAPAN

Richard Simoni
Computer Systems Laboratory
Stanford University
Stanford, CA

Jaswinder Pal Singh
Computer Systems Laboratory
Stanford University
Stanford, CA

Anand Sivasubramaniam
College of Computing
Georgia Institute of Technology

Norio Tanabe
NEC
Kanagawa, JAPAN

Shinji Tomita
Interdisciplinary Graduate School of Engineering Sciences
Kyushu University
Fukuoka, JAPAN

H. Venkateswaran
College of Computing
Georgia Institute of Technology

J. P. Vidal
School of Computer Science
Carnegie-Mellon University
Pittsburgh, PA

Wolf-Dietrich Weber
Computer Systems Laboratory
Stanford University
Stanford, CA

Philip J. Woest
Computer Sciences Department
University of Wisconsin-Madison

The MIT Press, with Peter Denning as general consulting editor, publishes computer science books in the following series:

ACL-MIT Press Series in Natural Language Processing
Aravind K. Joshi, Karen Sparck Jones, and Mark Y. Liberman, editors

ACM Doctoral Dissertation Award and Distinguished Dissertation Series

Artificial Intelligence
Patrick Winston, founding editor
J. Michael Brady, Daniel G. Bobrow, and Randall Davis, editors

Charles Babbage Institute Reprint Series for the History of Computing
Martin Campbell-Kelly, editor

Computer Systems
Herb Schwetman, editor

Explorations with Logo
E. Paul Goldenberg, editor

Foundations of Computing
Michael Garey and Albert Meyer, editors

History of Computing
I. Bernard Cohen and William Aspray, editors

Logic Programming
Ehud Shapiro, editor; Fernando Pereira, Koichi Furukawa, Jean-Louis Lassez, and David H. D. Warren, associate editors

The MIT Press Electrical Engineering and Computer Science Series

Research Monographs in Parallel and Distributed Processing
Christopher Jesshope and David Klappholz, editors

Scientific and Engineering Computation
Janusz Kowalik, editor

Technical Communication and Information Systems
Edward Barrett, editor